P9-DTN-740

MANUFACTURING CONFUCIANISM

DUKE UNIVERSITY PRESS

Durham and London 1997

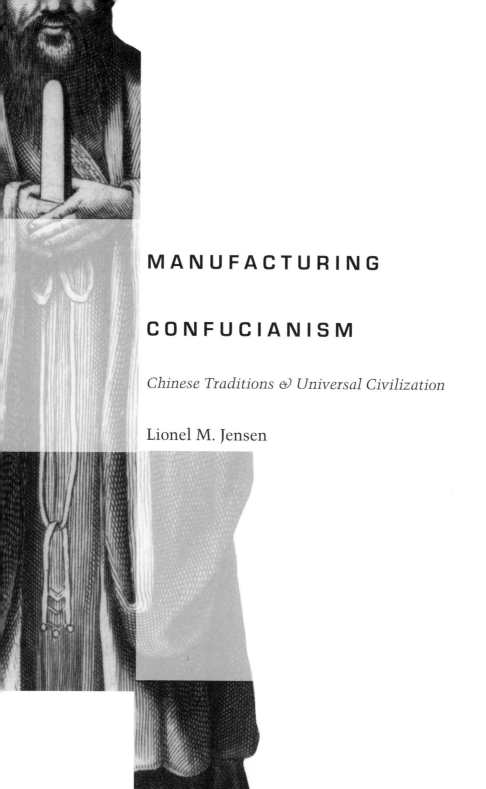

MANUFACTURING

CONFUCIANISM

Chinese Traditions & Universal Civilization

Lionel M. Jensen

© 1997 Duke University Press

All rights reserved

Printed in the United States of America

on acid-free paper ∞

Typeset in Trump Mediaeval by

Keystone Typesetting, Inc.

Library of Congress Cataloging-in-

Publication Data appear on the last

printed page of this book.

For my parents,

who lovingly gave me my life,

and for Susan, Hannah, and Elena,

who in giving me everything else,

taught me the joyful

meaning of it

CONTENTS

FIGURES

ACKNOWLEDGMENTS

Much of the work for this book began in the research and writing of my doctoral dissertation, submitted to the Department of History at the University of California at Berkeley in 1992. The criticisms and recommendations of my dissertation committee and early readers were invaluable. To that first audience, Robert Bellah, Don Price, David Keightley, and especially my patient dissertation director, Frederic Wakeman, I owe a great debt.

There are probably few endeavors as lonely as writing, but my enterprise has been made less solitary by the encouragement of a number of teachers and other scholars. Most notable have been Don Munro and Hoyt Tillman, who have been my most consistent supporters and intellectual inspiration, always providing the right proportion of encouragement and criticism. I hope that the present work will justify their loyalty and provide some evidence of the beneficial effects of their numerous years of guidance. For Don's indulgence, intellectual grace, and support I am deeply grateful.

David Mungello, who read part of this work, has far exceeded what a writer asks of an outside reader. For his detailed, incisive criticisms and his interest in my work as a historian and in my personal well-being, I express my gratitude.

My dear friend, Haun Saussy, graciously contributed to the book's final phases. Any strengths of the finished work are in part the legacy of his wise counsel.

I would also like to thank several of my graduate instructors at Berkeley: Marty Jay, Tu Wei-ming, Irwin Scheiner, Gene Irschick, and, above all, Gerard Caspary. My first graduate instructor and director of my master's thesis, George C. Hatch Jr., of Washington University, deserves the highest recognition. Under his aegis I learned the craft of sinology while absorbing everything I could about traditional Chinese intellectual history. It was George who disciplined and nurtured my zeal. For the many times that we discussed

Sima Qian, Kongzi, the Five Masters of the Northern Song, Su Shi, Zhu Xi, and Wang Yangming, until all hours of the night, I will constantly be repaying him. As a Chinese intellectual historian, George Hatch is without peer, yet he is no less the exemplar of graduate pedagogy and, unlike Cheng Yichuan, "ta you renqing." I wish him "wansui."

There have been many other people over the years whose critical reading of my work has been most welcome. I list here Tani Barlow, John Berthrong, Michael Bess (a constant source of inspiration, guidance, and levity), Peter Bol, E. Bruce Brooks, John Chaffee, Wing-tsit Chan, Susan Cherniack, Brad Clough, Ken DeWoskin, Pat Ebrey, Feng Youlan, Griff Foulk, Luís Gomez, John Henderson, Jim Hevia, Cappy Hurst, Keith Knapp, Livia Kohn, Vivienne Kouba, Matt Levey, Donald Lowe, John Lucy, Victor Mair, Masao Maruyama, Nancy Price, Lisa Raphals, Henry Rosemont, Hal Roth, Bob Sharf, Ed Shaughnessy, Jonathan Spence, Maryška Suda, Tang Xiaobing, Buzzy Teiser, Stephen Tobias, Jing Wang, Tom Wilson, Angela Zito, and especially Zhang Longxi.

I am indebted to a number of libraries and institutions in Asia, Europe, and the United States. I was especially well treated at the old quarters of the Zhongyang Tushuguan (National Central Library) in Taibei. The Yunnansheng Tushuguan (Yunnan Provincial Library) in Kunming, where I was granted unrestricted access to its holdings in ancient and medieval philosophy, proved a delightful site for research. Under the direction of associate professor and deputy director emeritus, Yang Wumei, the library's impressive classical archives were opened to me. Research was expertly facilitated by the directors of circulation of the Classical Collection, Wang Shuiqiao and Guo Jing, who searched for every item I needed, always bringing to my desk, with obvious enthusiasm, what they had found. The Bibliothèque Nationale in Paris permitted me to reproduce an illustration of "Le Système du monde au moment de la Naissance de Louis le Grand" from the Cabinet des Estampes.

In the United States, the Cleveland Public Library allowed me, under the direction of Alice Loranth, head of the Fine Arts and Special Collections, to examine and to photocopy Jesuit missionary texts from the John Griswold White Collection. The Bancroft Library of the University of California let me examine early works on China. Special thanks are due to the Department of Rare Books and Special Collections at the Harlan Hatcher Graduate Library of the University of Michigan for permission to photograph items in their collections. The East Asiatic Library of the University of California, the Asia Library of the University of Michigan, the Asian Library of the University of Colorado, the East Asian Library of Washington University, and the Van Pelt East Asia Library of the University of Pennsylvania were exceptionally resourceful. I particularly must thank Karl Kahler, Penn's East Asia bibliographer, for his interest in my work and for an untiring commitment to scholars of East Asia.

Various institutions provided support these last several years. The College of Arts and Sciences at Oklahoma State University provided summer funding to support my writing in 1989. The Institute of East Asian Studies and the Center for Chinese Studies at the University of California, Berkeley, provided office space and technical assistance. At the University of Colorado at Denver, the College of Liberal Arts and Sciences, under the aegis of Marvin D. Loflin, subsidized research and final revisions of the manuscript through summer grants and a junior faculty development award. The Office of the Vice Chancellor for Academic and Student Affairs, formerly headed by Georgia Lesh-Laurie, provided funds for travel to conferences.

I also thank the history department faculties at the Universities of Missouri, Colorado at Denver, and Florida, who offered opportunities to share my work with them. My colleagues in the Department of History at the University of Colorado at Denver, especially Frederick Allen, Michael Ducey, Mark Foster, Tom Noel, Myra Rich, and Jim Wolf, are the finest any historian could wish for, and I am privileged to have been favored by a professional life among them.

The Department of Asian and Middle Eastern Studies at the University of Pennsylvania provided a wonderful home for a scholar in the final year of revisions on this book—my colleagues, Victor Mair and Nancy Shatzman Steinhardt, gave me a vigorous department forum to present my ideas.

An invitation to deliver a paper before the Neo-Confucian Studies Seminar at Columbia University inspired me to develop the meditation on "traditionary invention" that figures in the book, and I thank my friends, Conrad Schirokauer and Anne Birdwhistell, the seminar's cochairs, and the seminar rapporteur, Ann Marie Satoh. For the discussion that followed, I am indebted to Conrad, Anne, Marie Guarino, Bob Hymes, Murray Rubinstein, Arthur Tiedeman, Jaret Weisfogel, and Ted de Bary.

Graduate students at the Universities of Colorado and Pennsylvania, Richard Burden and Robert Fisher, and Ari Levine, Sara Davis, Brian Ray, and Rosalind Bradford, offered regular and inspiring intellectual exchanges. It has been a delight to observe their professional and personal growth and to remember now how much they, especially Richard, have unselfconsciously contributed to the present work. Elisa Holland, the finest undergraduate student I have ever had, deserves immense credit for her indefatigable and endlessly inspired work in preparing a comprehensive index. In this demanding endeavor she was ably assisted by Richard Burden. I am—and the readers of the book surely will be—deeply grateful to them both.

The matter of personal debts is never settled by words. Nevertheless, I want to acknowledge publicly, however imperfectly, the family and friends who so generously contributed to this work.

Over the last four years, my editor, Ken Wissoker, has patiently and carefully stewarded the project to completion. His belief in this book has been undeviating, and I cannot convey the depth of my appreciation for his confidence in my scholarship and for his work in bringing it to the public. The book also owes much to two devoted readers and critics. I am especially grateful to Maura High, the copyeditor, whose insight and keen judgment have greatly improved the present work. Paula Dragosh's editorial supervision made the normally painstaking work of the copyediting and proofreading stages very pleasurable.

For camaraderie and animated scholarly exchange over the last sixteen years on the full breadth of the intellectual and social history of China, I wish to thank John Ewell and Ned Davis, who were always willing to read chapters and to offer advice, direction, and a needed sense of perspective. Their friendship and guidance have been a constant source of light for me.

I am greatly indebted to a number of friends, chief among them Stephen J. Clarke, who may be as thrilled as I am that this part of my *lebenswerk* has come to an end. Michael Krumholz continues to maintain a keen interest in my scholarly work and has proven a most sensitive listener. Hal and Risa Aqua have been an inspiration as parents, artists, and conversationalists of considerable moral seriousness. John and Rita Gasbarro have provided a second home for our daughters and a place where I could profitably discuss the lives of sixteenth-century Italian Jesuits and their texts. In this same context of friendship and intellectual interchange, the humor, advice, and loyal criticism of Timothy Ritter has kept me sane over the last four years.

I thank, too, my colleagues and friends at Oklahoma State University. Carol Moder and Brewster Fitz, godparents of our daughter Elena, have been a perpetual source of wit and repartee. Without their help at crucial times, this work would have taken much longer to complete.

Robert Mayer and Elizabeth Williams, colleagues and the godparents of our daughter Hannah, have been everything for me and my family during the last nine years: confessors, cheerleaders, advocates, baby-sitters, activists, critics, advisers. I cherish every moment of these years in which our families have grown together.

My friends and spiritual advisers Marc Fitzerman and Alice Blue have offered me moral sustenance that has enabled me always to remain focused on what matters. Lucien and Bonnie Miller have been soulmates in traversing the territory of southwest China, loving our children while raising queries of the heart, and always reminding me that life is an act of art played out in the wide space of creation for the benefit of a significant few.

It would require pages to properly recognize the contributions of Tami

Moore, who sorted out the bibliography and listened over and over to each of the book's different arguments and made many suggestions on their presentation. For her love of learning and her love of life, both of which she has shared with my family for many years, I thank her.

Lastly, I come to my family. It is hard to speak of something that is so much a part of you, and it feels strange to give credit to those who give so effortlessly of themselves. It is in the nature of family to give and not tally the debt. But let me thank first my wife's family, the Blums, for years of never-slackening encouragement and eternal optimism. In my immediate family, my sister, Anne Marie, has displayed an incomparable enthusiasm for my scholarly work. For the sixteen years of my graduate and early teaching career, it has been my parents, Gloria and Millard, who have consistently given the most. They have given their love and devotion to a cause that they have felt was their own. But most of all I thank them for giving me a life of love and for granting me the favor of following this path.

The greatest reward, the most rare, unexpected privilege, greater than life itself, I feel, has been the love of my wife, Susan Blum, and our daughters, Hannah Neora and Elena Oriana. Susan, an anthropologist of China, has given unreservedly of her time and energy for many years, for editing, proofreading, soul-searching, counseling, theorizing, cajoling, and, most of all, advising. It is accurate to say that Susan has "lived" this work with me through its numerous incarnations. She has shared her courage, vigilance, spirit, and strength—and always without complaint.

Our darlings Hannah and Elena, the center of their parents' world, have renewed and strengthened me often, instinctively offering a kiss, a hug, laughter, a gentle word. Indeed, their delight in living reminded me of the critical role joy plays in the making of a life. They, along with Susan, have been more transforming in their effects than the light of the sun. To write in this way is to attempt, perhaps awkwardly, to express a gratitude so profound that it defies expression. The gratitude and love that I feel can only be called a blessing. Thus, it is with full knowledge of this blessing that I dedicate this work to them, whose love gave me life and gave that life meaning.

NOTE

The pinyin transliteration system for Chinese is used throughout, except in certain instances of quoted text. Chinese authors' names and titles of works in which the Wade-Giles romanization system is used are unmodified in the text, but their pinyin equivalents are given in the bibliography. The sinographs (or characters) of the Chinese phrases and terms that occur frequently in their romanized form throughout the text are provided in the glossary and are explained. Most citations of traditional Chinese works that have been published as part of larger literary collections or series bear the notation *juan* or "volume," followed by the page number. In some cases where citation is of an older work that has been reprinted two pages to one in a sinological series, I have used ".1" and ".2" to designate the upper and lower portions of a single page of reproduction. All bibliographic information concerning standard editions and series may be found in the abbreviations section, which immediately precedes the notes. Years have been converted to the Gregorian calendar, using the designations B.C.E. and C.E. Unless noted otherwise, all translations are my own.

CHRONOLOGY

Historic Era and Approximate Dates

Xia (legendary), 1953–1576 B.C.E.
Shang, 1576–1046 B.C.E.
Zhou, 1046–771 B.C.E.
Springs and Autumns (Chunqiu), 771–479 B.C.E.
Warring States (Zhan'guo), 479–221 B.C.E.
Qin, 221–208 B.C.E.
Qin/Han Interregnum, 208–202 B.C.E.
Western Han, 202 B.C.E.–9 C.E.
Xin Interregnum, 9–23 C.E.
Eastern Han, 25–220 C.E.
Three Kingdoms, 220–280 C.E.
Western Jin, 265–316 C.E.
Northern and Southern Dynasties, 317–589 C.E.
Sui, 581–618 C.E.
Tang, 618–906 C.E.
Five Dynasties, 906–960 C.E.
Song, 960–1279 C.E.
N. Song, 960–1127 C.E.
S. Song, 1127–1279 C.E.
Jin, 1115–1234 C.E.
Yuan (Mongol), 1279–1368 C.E.
Ming, 1368–1644 C.E.
Qing (Manchu), 1644–1911 C.E.
Republic of China (mainland), 1912–1949 C.E.
People's Republic of China, 1949–

Italic indicates principal dynastic eras

MANUFACTURING CONFUCIANISM

INTRODUCTION:

CONFUCIUS, KONGZI, AND

THE MODERN IMAGINATION

Calderón likened glories to dreams, and had Segismundo ask where, in the end, truth finally lay. My response to that question has been to show that men who act for posterity can never be certain that their animating values will survive the historical future. Not only that; sometimes the acts themselves matter less than their images—however distorted—which are re-formed in the eyes of subsequent perceivers. This does not mean that historical myth is merely fiction, since events must have credibly occurred for the story to be effective. But it should warn any historical actor that "our virtues," as Shakespeare wrote in *Coriolanus*, "lie in th' interpretation of the time." Audiences are fickle, ideals labile, and glories fleeting. Conviction, after all, is the least—and noblest—of human certainties.—*Frederic Wakeman Jr.*

A little more than four centuries ago, a detachment of seamen in service to Philip II of Spain (r. 1556–1598) and a few missionaries of a new order of the Catholic Church, the Society of Jesus, sailed by Portuguese carrack to the south coast of China. We have lived the consequences of this passage ever since. Portuguese vessels, in particular, had been navigating this route for about three decades by the 1570s, calling twice a year at China's southern port of Guangzhou (Canton) for luxury items. Thus, there was nothing logistically unusual in the missionaries' arrival in 1579 on Chinese soil. The historical significance of their landing would not be apparent until several years later, when they would enter China as native priests (mendicant Buddhists, to be exact), and a conversation on indigenous ground was begun. From this dialogue of cultures at the far reaches of the known world, Christianity would assume a distinctive Chinese character and simultaneously a single Chinese teaching, and its founder would be translated through Latin into the language of contemporary moral science in Europe.

Before the European maritime expansion, China and Western Europe were isolated from each other. However, in the four centuries since the Jesuit contact, East and West have become bound by commerce and communication and joined, more importantly, in imagination. China and the West today are as near as they have ever been. Each is registered in the lexicon of the other: the Chinese are increasingly knowledgeable about the West, its culture as much as its technology, and Westerners are keenly aware of the politics, economy, and demography of China. The cultural vocabularies of both have been unselfconsciously enriched. For us in the West, the term "Confucianism" is richly familiar as an indigenous tradition translated by the Jesuits out of China. Indeed, China and the West have been bound in imagination by the concepts of Confucius and Confucianism since the late seventeenth century.

To any observer of the religions of China, it is evident that Confucianism holds a privileged place for us. Even to the casual browser of the local bookstore who finds works on Confucianism among the titles in "Eastern Religions" or "Eastern Thought/Mysticism" this is abundantly clear. In the West, Confucianism has long been considered the definitive ethos of the Chinese—their civil religion, their official cult, their intellectual tradition. Indeed, the term "Confucianism" has performed such varied service as a charter concept of Chinese culture for the West that it has become indistinguishable from what it signifies—China, especially the China of the ageless rhythms of family, field, and forebears.

In this particularity of reference also lies Confucianism's universality, for in its (Jesuit-created) role as the bearer of China's significance it was drawn into a seventeenth-century debate over truth, God, and representation that has continued to shape the cultural self-image of the West. Moreover, during the last century the linked history of Confucianism and Western thought has informed Chinese struggles to define culture, history, and identity by intellectuals who sought a conceptual vernacular that would unite the diverse cultural constituencies of a new nation.

As a native tradition it has also reached beyond the particularity of its local beginnings in that many of its followers and/or practitioners, known as *ru*, filled the ranks of an ever-expanding Chinese bureaucracy and served as advisers to the Supreme Lord (*huangdi*), or "Emperor." Their cult, also known as *ru*, constituted one of China's three teachings (*sanjiao*). Along with *dao* (Daoism) and *fo* (Buddhism), *ru* doctrine appears in the Western taxonomic pantheon of world religions in the nineteenth century as one of three teachings that were given specific names: "Boudhism" in 1801, "Tauism" in 1839, and "Confucianism" in 1862. Of the three, only Confucianism is fully Latinized, while the others are represented as hybrid Anglo-Romanizations of native terms. The linguistic distinction accorded Confucianism is a vestige of the seventeenth-century European banishment of Daoism and Buddhism and its embrace of Confucianism. Of the three, only Confucianism has been integrated into Western self-consciousness to any degree.

Whether one calls Confucianism a "religion," "philosophy," "social ethic," or "moral order," it clearly is something more than a native Chinese tradition; it is a way of life that reflects how Westerners understand, or wish to understand, themselves. For four centuries and through varied circumstances it has figured prominently in the cultural consciousness of the West, especially now, with the ascendance of New Age philosophy and Asia's growing role in the world market.

Confucianism, whether it is seen as a contemporary strategy for self-discovery or as a tool for understanding the Asian economic "miracle," is the consequence of centuries of relationship between China and the West. As such, it is a powerful and timely instrument for explaining how and why the early cultural intimacy of China and the West developed as it did.

The introduction of this book begins an extended meditation on Confucianism: how it was made, the Western and Chinese communities involved in its making, and the consequences of its invention. It begins with the premise that Confucianism is largely a Western invention, supposedly representing what is registered by the complex of terms *rujia* (*ru* family), *rujiao* (*ru* teaching), *ruxue* (*ru* learning), and *ruzhe* (the *ru*). Presuming that the ancient Chinese philosopher Confucius (known to the Chinese as Kongzi) is the source of this complex, it takes his figure as its focus.

I propose that we resist the reflex to treat these entities, Confucianism and *ru*, as equivalent and consider rather that what we know of Confucius is not what the ancient Chinese knew as Kongzi (Master Kong). I suggest instead that Confucius assumed his present familiar features as the result of a prolonged, deliberate process of manufacture in which European intellectuals took a leading role. Our Confucius is a product fashioned over several centuries by many hands, ecclesiastical and lay, Western and Chinese.

In this century in China, Confucius, the largely Western invention, inspired a re-creation of the native hero, Kongzi, who was then absorbed into Chinese intellectuals' font of mythological material and proved critical to their endeavor of making a new Chinese nation through historical construction. The joint quality of this invention is the main concern of this book: how the sixteenth-century Chinese supplied the raw material with storied forms of Kongzi that inspired the Western celebrity of Confucius and lent novel form to a contested European representation of science and theology; and how the imported nineteenth-century Western conceptual vernacular of nationalism, evolution, and ethos lent dimension to the nativist imaginings of twentieth-century Chinese, who reinvented Kongzi as a historicized religious figure.

The reader should not conclude that to establish a Western provenance for Confucius suggests some kind of fraud. This book is not mere iconoclasm, a simple act of demythologization, consonant with a contemporary, postmodern criticism that dismantles accepted ideas. Nor does it imply that there can be no native heroes, only foreign-made ones, or attack the hegemony of Western culture. My story of Confucius and Confucianism is a reverent account of an ecumenical impulse or spirit, definitive of a modern temper formed in the Renaissance, forgotten since the seventeenth century in the West, and recovered in the twentieth century in China. It is a tale of two different centuries of turmoil and of two eras of cultural reformation in which pious communities disposed to reasonableness and toleration recognized in their local circumstances the prophetic intimations of the absolute.

As the twentieth century draws to a close, images of Confucius (Kongzi, 551?–479? B.C.E.) and of the religion or philosophy inspired by his memory,

Figure 1. "Confucius at the Office." In this Far Side cartoon, Gary Larson illustrates the popular understanding of Confucius as wise man, bearer of platitudes. (Reproduced by permission of Chronicle Features, San Francisco, California, all rights reserved)

Confucianism, appear to grow in number and in salience. In the West, Confucius is seen, or rather represented, almost everywhere: in videotapes on conducting business with the cultures of the Far East; in software applications; in in-flight magazines; on T-shirts; in cartoons; in public television documentaries; on menus; in travel magazines; on yogurt containers; in recent efforts to portray Confucianism as a new world religion; on the World Wide Web; and in an increasing number of scholarly treatments of Chinese religion, Chinese thought, comparative philosophy, and the indigenous cultural roots of Asia's astonishing economic success. The number and variety of such images rival the array found in China in 136 B.C.E., when an imperial cult honoring Kongzi was purportedly inaugurated and when followers of his teaching in service to the emperor were too numerous to count.

Examples of Confucius's contemporary popularity range from the parody of "Confucius at the Office" (figure 1)—which shows the sage laboring to produce clichés—to the high regard in which Confucius is held by Freemasons. (A likeness of him, along with such other wise men of the East as Zoroaster and Mani, may be found on the interior walls of many Scottish Rites temples.) Other examples include the collection of witticisms "Cornfucius Say,"[1] or the self-help book *How Would Confucius Ask for a Raise?*[2] Confucius is part of the undigested mass of our modern cultural stock, one which has been accumulating since the seventeenth century, when European intellectuals appropriated the iconography of this figure and the native tradition identified with him and represented in the letterbooks, translations, and treatises of Jesuit missionaries stationed in southern China.

And it is with the work of this missionary community that the intertwined tales of Confucius the hero and Confucianism the religion begin, for it was from this community's mission among the Chinese that the man and the religion were made. Indeed, *he was made*, first fabricated in the late sixteenth century by a small, reverent band of "accommodationist"[3] Jesuit fathers living in the wilderness of southern China, who had been especially inspired by the example of a culture hero revered by the Chinese as Kongzi. Following their arrival in China in 1583, the fathers quickly produced a volume of testimony in Latin, Italian, Portuguese, and Chinese of the moral genius of their inspiration, Confucius, drawing on a thousand-year-long transmission of indigenous texts and tales about Kongzi.

Their Confucius was initially always paired with Kongzi. In fact, "Confucius" was invented as a Latinized equivalent for "Kong Fuzi," a rare, respectful title for the Chinese sage Kongzi that could only be found on the spirit tablets (*shenwei*) of certain regional temples devoted to worship of this hallowed figure and his extended apostolic lineage.[4] Thus for these sixteenth-century Jesuits, "Confucius"/"Kong Fuzi" was a dual symbol best likened to Janus, the Roman god whose two-headed face was identified with gates, doors, and beginnings.

This Jesuit-Chinese construct was formed at the beginning of what the Jesuits later termed "Christiana expeditio" (the Christian expedition) and served as a door through which the fathers passed into Chinese life, discarding in transit much of what defined them in their church's eyes as "soldiers of Christ." Moreover, "Confucius"/"Kong Fuzi" marked the humble beginning of something these missionaries could not have anticipated, but with which we are familiar—sinology. From this beginning, where the native Kongzi and the foreign Confucius were joined in the minds of the makers on local Chinese ground, "Confucius" quickly acquired a universal character. It is this newer, solitary Latin incarnation that was conveyed across the globe in the spirit of the Enlightenment and has reached us today through the polymorphous passion of commerce as the icon Confucius.

The Making of the Icon Confucius

Throughout the seventeenth century the fathers of the China Mission translated indigenous texts into Latin to demonstrate the inchoate monotheism of native Chinese faith. In the course of these labors, they provided their superiors and benefactors with encyclopedic documentation of Chinese habit and belief. Back home, an educated European laity excited by the intellectual passions of discovery—cartography, astronomy, mathematics, and linguistics—anxiously awaited the publication of the letterbooks and journals of the missionaries.[5] Among these observers, dilettantes, and scientists, the Jesuit "Confucius" found an especially hospitable ground, where his writings were welcomed as containing a wisdom remarkably compatible with Western morality.

At the dawn of what was then an empirical mapping of the world, geographically, linguistically, culturally, and, most important of all, religiously, the reification of Confucius by members of Europe's Royal Society—now without his alter ego, Kongzi—dissolved one-half of a bivalent symbol. The power of Confucius as a symbol derived from the European presumption that he was the iconic representation of Chinese native otherness. Consequently, as Jesuit letterbooks containing the missionaries' accounts of life in China were published in the last decade of the sixteenth century, his popularity spread along separate, contiguous fronts, ecclesiastical and lay.

The icon Confucius served two distinct European communities, for which it functioned differently: for the Jesuits, who knew him as Kongzi, he was dear to a small group of missionaries living among, and increasingly sympathetic to, the Chinese; for cultivated Europeans he was a symbol of either the nobility of the savage or of the inherent rationality of the "natural," known, as were most other admired intellectual figures of the day, by a Latin cognomen.

By the late eighteenth century, as Europe acquired an "Enlightened" cultural self-consciousness, Confucius was firmly entrenched in contemporary Western culture as a sage, and his Chinese followers were called "Confucians," a term that evoked a panoply of associations: deference, urbanity, wisdom, moral probity, reasoned and not slavish classicism, and a learned, paternal authoritarianism. These qualities, like the figure who embodied them, were the desiderata of Europeans doubtful of the institution of monarchy and despairing of religious war.

Confucius, and the China metonymically captured in this symbol, appeared in the writings of many Enlightenment figures: Voltaire, Rousseau, Montesquieu, Comte, Quesnay, Fontenelle, Diderot, Leibniz, Wolff, Malebranche, Bayle, even Defoe. Confucius's greatest moment came perhaps in 1758, when a French edition of Diogenes Laertius's work, *The Lives of the Philosophers*, published in Amsterdam, included a ninety-page exposition of his doctrines.[6] Confucius, as symbol of things Chinese, was critical to an emerging political, social, and theological criticism that yielded such works as Bayle's *Dictionnaire historique et critique* (1697–1702), Voltaire's *Essai sur les moeurs et l'esprit des nations* (1756) and *Dictionnaire philosophique* (1757), Montesquieu's *Lettres Persanes* (1721) and *De l'esprit des lois* (1748), and Quesnay's *Le Despotisme de la Chine* (1767).[7] At this moment of conflict between the *anciens* and the *modernes*, the image of the Chinese ancient helped shape the self-image of the modern, *our* modern.

The distribution of Confucius's name and image in Europe at this time may have been far-reaching because, like capital, his value was not bound by the conditions of his production. In this environment, Confucius simply existed as a finished product, a symbol of certain values, chief of which was otherness, and thus he could be appropriated by any person or group seeking to represent such values. For Voltaire, he could symbolize a genuine, non-European moral reason while for Montesquieu he represented despotism. This symbolic variability reflected contemporary European debates about self, society, and the sacred at the inception of the nation-state.

The wide popularity of Confucius was also coincident with global economic developments of the late sixteenth and early seventeenth centuries that brought Europe and China closer than ever before. At the end of the sixteenth century, a rudimentary global economy was in place that linked China economically with Europe, with the Americas and sites like the silver mines of Potosí in the New World. By the beginning of the seventeenth century nearly 50 percent of the precious metals mined throughout the world found their way to China. A conceptual market developed alongside the spice, metals, and luxury trade, bearing many icons of the Chinese that circulated widely in Europe, among them the icon Confucius.[8]

In the simultaneous circulation of ideas and material goods that linked China and Europe in the late sixteenth and early seventeenth centuries, Confucius was a significant, and salient, artifact. The frequency with which his name and image appeared in letters, memoirs, treatises, travel literature, and histories suggests that he was moved like New World specie in an expanding market of new ideas joining Rome with Paris, London, Berlin, Prague and then, in turn, with the missionary outposts at Goa, Canton, Macao, and Beijing. According to Paul Rule, the first engraved portrait of Confucius, which appeared in 1687, was "plagiarized by countless works of the late seventeenth and early eighteenth century," including a popular memoir by the French Jesuit and royal mathematician Louis le Comte (figure 2).[9] The chief intellectual consequence for us of this conceptual commerce was that the Confucius/Kongzi of the Jesuits of the Zhaoqing mission became, simply, Confucius: the person whom we know as teacher, moral exemplar, sage, political philosopher, and, above all, the patriarch of China's civil religion.

Scholars and the public alike often presume that these many different roles correspond to traits of the native Kongzi; all are sure they know who "Confucius" is. But despite the array of images that supposedly represent him, this Confucius, detached from his native ground, is a figment of the Western imagination. The Confucius and Confucianism to which we have granted a compelling authority are conceptual products of foreign origin, made to articulate indigenous qualities of Chinese culture. Of Kongzi himself, little is

Figure 2. "Confucius." Woodcut illustration from Father Louis le Comte's *Nouveaux mémoires sur l'état présent de la Chine*, vol. 1 (Paris, 1696). This image, used in hundreds of reproductions through the next century, was the most popular European representation of Confucius. (Photograph courtesy of the Bancroft Library, University of California, Berkeley)

known. It is this irony that accounts for the marvelous symbolic diversity of Confucius and of Kongzi.

Confucius, the celebrated etymon of *our* tradition, Confucianism, and Kongzi, the revered patriarch of the *ru* transmission, are tropes rather than persons. Confucius and Kongzi have, like all prophets, martyrs, and heroes, been granted an impressive collection of realia, vestiges of the many traditions made in the name of this hero. Indeed, in China and in the West, the making of such traditions displays an uncanny functional similarity, for in China for millennia Kongzi has been a popular focus of invention.

The Native Restoration of Kongzi:
Commerce and Fetishism

While the story of Confucius's popularity reveals much about the history of our culture, it also doubles back upon the Chinese today, where Kongzi, his native narrative substrate, has been restored to a prominence comparable to that of the Western invention. In present-day China, where tradition is again in (officially administered) vogue, Kongzi is quoted in public service advertisements warning of the perils of gambling; he is seen in television documentaries on such topics as *Han minzu wenhua* (the culture of the Han race) and as a symbol of the nobility of antique culture. For that matter, *wenming* (civilization) and *wenhua* (culture) are heard and seen everywhere—even on street signs (*wenming weisheng lu*, a civilized and sanitary street) and at work units (*wenming weisheng danwei*, a civilized and sanitary work unit). Both *wenming* and *wenhua* bear a single connotation—the proud superiority of Chinese tradition, of which Kongzi is increasingly the popular icon.

The Chinese, in the throes of hypergrowth and zealously promoted modernization, are borrowing from this indigenous ethos and have rediscovered their Kongzi—as Confucius. Characteristic of this national revaluation of Kongzi as a figure of international significance is a very recent work, titled *Ruxue yu dongfang wenhua* (Ruism and Eastern Culture), by Xu Yuanhe, who insists that East Asia's economic miracle is the epiphenomenon of what he calls *fuxing ruxue de daolu* (the moral road of revived Ruism).[10] Scholarly and popular works touting the resources of tradition and culture, in particular Confucianism, are increasingly numerous in China. At the same time, publishing houses, most notably the Guji Chubanshe (Classic Publishers) in Shanghai, have spawned a steady growth in reprints—in traditional rather than the officially sanctioned simplified characters—of the classical texts of Kongzi's era. And the current global popularity of the East Asian Development Model ensures that the interest in Confucianism will be sustained.

Kongzi and his teaching have enjoyed a steady resurgence since the late 1970s, when earlier campaigns to shape national moral fiber through criticism of Lin Biao (1907–1971) and Kongzi receded.[11] It is now politically correct to appreciate Kongzi, whereas from 1973 to 1978 the fervor of the country's socialist consciousness, its "redness" (hong), was displayed through the grandly choreographed public excoriation of this cultural patriarch. The winds of change in Chinese political culture blow furiously and always to extremes—as the fluctuations of reform and repression following the Tian'anmen Square demonstrations in the spring of 1989 demonstrate. But since the Department of History at Shandong University sponsored a reevaluation of Kongzi and *rujia sixiang* (ruist thought) in the fall of 1978, the political climate has favored Kongzi decidedly.

The annual observances of his birth, which many believe date back to the Han dynasty (202 B.C.E.–220 C.E.), have resumed with great pomp and circumstance—a celebration keyed to a new "great leap forward" in domestic and international tourism. In 1980 the Kongzi Research Center (Kongzi Yanjiu Zhongxin) was founded in Qufu (three years later it was renamed the Kongzi Research Institute, Kongzi Yanjiusuo). In the same period the Chinese government authorized publication of Cai Shangsi's *Kongzi sixiang de xitong* (The System of Kongzi's Thought [1982]) and Zhong Zhaopeng's *Kongzi yanjiu* (Research on Kongzi [1983]).[12]

The New World Press of Beijing followed this revival of Kongzi and in 1984 published an intriguingly titled memoir, *Kongfu neizhai yishi—Kongzi houyi de huiyi* (Anecdotes from the Women's Quarters of the Kong Residence—The Reminiscences of Kongzi's Descendant), written by Ke Lan and Kong Demao, a seventy-seventh-generation descendant of Kongzi. In the same year, the book appeared in English translation as *In the Mansion of Confucius' Descendants* and claimed to reveal "the legends, stories, ceremonies and intrigues connected with the mansion of the main branch of the Kong clan—the lineal posterity of Confucius."[13]

On September 22, 1984, when the 2,535th anniversary of Kongzi's putative birth was celebrated, three thousand selected Chinese and foreign guests presided over the ceremonies while the populace filled the temple grounds.[14] The statue of Kongzi, which had been demolished when Red Guards, on a mission to destroy all symbols of China's "old culture," ravaged Qufu during the high tide of the Cultural Revolution, was restored to mark the occasion. The most telling evidence of Kongzi's rehabilitation came in June 1985 with the establishment of another Kongzi Research Institute (Kongzi Yanjiusuo)—this one located in the former imperial temple to Kongzi, just southeast of the Forbidden City in Beijing.

Once an outcast, he is again the sage and has been received as would be any mythic hero returned home. At Qufu, in Shandong Province (Kongzi's disputed home,[15] the official locus of the ancient cult honoring him), shop owners proudly display bottles of San Kong Pijiu (Three Kongs Beer), "the number

Figure 3. The Little Red Books. The universally celebrated and maligned "Little Red Book" (*Quotations from Chairman Mao Zedong*) juxtaposed in this photograph with the 1984 "Little Red Book" of the *Lunyu* (Selected Sayings of Kongzi), which circulated for a brief period in Qufu and Beijing. The *Lunyu*'s appropriation of the format and color of Mao's book provoked officials to confiscate the former. (Photograph by author)

one beer in central Shandong," and in the center of the city stand three twenty-foot-tall mockups of the celebrated local brew.[16] Another beverage named for Kongzi has acquired an international following: the "Confucius Family Liquor" (Kong Fu Jia Jiu), made from sorghum, wheat, barley, and peas and produced by the Qufu Distillery, is now distributed in the United States by Conwell Import and Export, Inc., of South El Monte, California.[17]

On the streets of Beijing in 1984, the revered "Little Red Book" of Chairman Mao's selected quotations was not available, although several vendors proudly hawked Kongzi's *Selected Sayings* (*Lunyu*) in a handsomely bound vermilion-covered pocket book edition. A local publication of the Qufu Tanwenwu Guanli Weiyuanhui (Qufu Control Committee for Cultural Artifacts), the obviously imitative production contained all twenty chapters of the standard *Lunyu* printed in simplified characters (figure 3). Its resemblance to the first editions of Mao Zedong's quotations is startling—which may account for its sudden disappearance and replacement with a second, jade-colored edition. A restauranteur in Beijing has even opened the Confucius Restaurant (Kong Shangtang), justifying his choice of name with the rhetorical query, "Why not the best?" Kongzi is simply good business, a fact not lost on the nation's postal system, which in 1990 issued a commemorative stamp set bearing his likeness. One stamp was valued at 1 yuan 60—the exact amount needed to post a card to the West in 1990—and portrays Kongzi, riding high in a scroll-laden chariot, attended by four disciples on foot. In an interesting reflection of contemporary Chinese prosperity and the popular association of Kongzi with success, he is depicted as heavy, even corpulent.

More impressive than Chinese popular culture's reinvention of Kongzi has been the steady growth of Sino-Western scholarly interest in Confucius and the religiophilosophical complexes of Confucianism and Neo-Confucianism. While the Confucius of Gary Larson's cartoon and the Beijing restauranteur has attained universality at the expense of meaning, scholarship in Chinese intellectual history and philosophy has sought to confer global significance on Confucius and Confucianism on the basis of an uncanny relevance of the philosophy of the latter to contemporary problems, academic and social. These philosophical and religious claims to new universal status have been secured for Confucianism by East Asian scholars whose work reproduces in another form the interpretive predilections of the Jesuits while it reiterates the current commercial fetishization of Confucius.

Confucius, Confucianism, and the Politics of Scholarship

Asian politicians and scholars in the 1980s and 1990s have used images of Confucius and his teaching to counteract the spiritual and cultural consequences of rapid economic expansion. Engaging in an essentialist fetishization of Confucianism as a fundamental native value, such individuals, most prominently the former prime minister of Singapore, Lee Kuan Yew, have made Confucius the symbol of an Asia-specific religious ethos.[18]

Late in a century in which the integrity of the family—Western and Asian—is believed to be dissolving and in which alienation can no longer be assuaged with the balm of individualism, these scholars contend that the Confucian values of the home, moral self-discipline, reciprocity, mutual respect, and benevolence provide a way out of moral meaninglessness. They believe Confucianism to be both a defining ethos of Asian peoples and, not coincidentally, the spiritual force behind the Asian dominance of world economic markets. In this respect, Confucianism is less an intellectual or philosophical phenomenon and more a vital form of life, one reminiscent of the transformative impulses of Max Weber's Puritanism, though without Puritanism's otherworldly, transcendent yearnings.

East Asian scholars argue that there is a necessary generative relation between Asian "hypergrowth" and a fundamentalist Confucian culture.[19] They claim that the economic success of Hong Kong, Singapore, Taiwan, and South Korea (the "Four Little Dragons") is emblematic of an alternative development paradigm wherein the "ancient" cultural claims of family, respect for education, compliance with authority, and religious faith will counteract the deleterious effects of modernization so common in the West. Pace Weber, who had claimed that Confucianism sought accommodation with, not transformation of, the world, the Four Little Dragons display an aggressive entrepreneurial spirit and an indefatigable work ethic, thanks to Confucianism. Thus tradition yields modernity on its own terms, and Chineseness provides the model for a new "age of the Pacific Rim."

Tu Wei-ming is the principal spokesman for this creative reinvention of Confucianism as a form of religion. He claims that Confucianism is undergoing a "third wave" of rejuvenation. This contemporary incarnation of the tradition (which I call postmodern Confucianism) should, argues Tu Wei-ming, be recognized as a new world religion, on a par with Islam, Judaism, and Christianity, given to the same contemporary fundamentalist reactions:

> [This] position envisions Confucianism . . . as a tradition of religious philosophy. Confucianism so conceived is a way of life which demands an existential commitment on the part of Confucians no less intensive and comprehensive than that demanded of the followers of other spiritual traditions such as Judaism, Christianity, Islam, Buddhism, or Hinduism.[20]

Curiously, this universalist vision of postmodern Confucianism is grounded in the specific, parochial qualities definitive of the local tradition; both place especially strong emphasis on the family as a timeless ethical unit of labor. *Ru*, liberally reinterpreted as *xin ruxue* (new Confucian learning), is undergoing a revitalization that its advocates believe is continuous with a millennial cumulative tradition inaugurated with Kongzi. Claiming that their vision of a humane modernization requires a return to the fundamental virtues of Confucianism, these contemporary practitioners of Confucian religion are also involved in manufacturing a new moment of a tradition.[21]

The assertion that a Confucian resurgence in the form of the Asian family and work ethic is responsible for the preternatural economic growth of East Asia is more imaginative than empirical. Although quite different from American popular perceptions of Confucius, academic works such as these are no less manufactured and must be recognized as products of scholarly desire that mask their own status as fictions.

Within Western academic circles, another identifiable trend effected through the manufacture of Confucius and Confucianism is Neo-Confucianism, defined most fully by Wm. Theodore de Bary. The objective of this scholarly industry has been to establish incontrovertibly the vitality of the

Confucian tradition, now defined as a direct line of intellectual affinitive transmission from Kongzi through the Song period (970–1279 C.E.) *lixue* (learning of principle) and Ming (1368–1644 C.E.) *xinxue* (learning of the heart) fellowships to the present. From the twelfth through the eighteenth centuries, as de Bary tells it, Neo-Confucianism was the culturally hegemonic force produced from the union of Buddhism and the native Confucian tradition. As a cultural force it encapsulated the profound social, intellectual, technological, and political changes of these seven centuries and yet remained fundamentally consistent with the tradition of learning put forward by Confucius, who stressed *weiji* (learning for oneself) as the ideal.

De Bary construes the Neo-Confucian—read Zhu Xi (1130–1200 C.E.)—emphasis on *zide* (getting it oneself) as a latter-day manifestation of the same heuristic instinct, an instinct which he identifies as both individualist and liberal. In a recent collection of his essays, de Bary justifies the application of these modern, Western terms because they correspond to what he finds in the native texts:

> The question of the individual in Confucian thought is one I stumbled into some years ago while pursuing other lines of inquiry, historical and political, which, it turned out, could only be dealt with adequately by addressing first the problem of the Neo-Confucian self. In doing so, I found myself using terms like "individualism" or "liberalism," not because of any predisposition to read Western values into Chinese thought but because, against my original assumptions and preconceptions, certain resemblances could not be ignored.[22]

De Bary is not just concerned with providing an adequate description of Chinese thought, of course. He is also engaged in building a connection back to the world of the Neo-Confucians, a world whose culture was vibrant, innovative, and changing, and full of the very values that Westerners hold dear. It is the resemblance of the Western liberal self and the *lixue* disciple who discovers the meaning of a passage, for himself, *zide*, that is remarkable. All men, it seems, are brothers. Just as with classicists like Zhu Xi, who explicitly identified a responsibility to seize the moment of the past before it disappeared and to preserve it through transmission, de Bary, inspired by the humanity of ancient example, commends himself to the task of its recollection:

> Today no people can look to their own traditions alone for this kind of learning and understanding, any more than could the Confucians earlier. The latter at least understood the need for dialogue and discussion as essential to "advancing the Way," even though they were unable to sustain it, much less broaden it, in the given circumstances. Now the time

has come for us to extend and expand the discourse, as a dialogue with the past, with other cultures, and even with future generations, who cannot speak for themselves but whose fate is in our hands.[23]

Arguments such as these, with their message of the enduring relevance of medieval Chinese beliefs and of the continuing vitality of a tradition deemed dead earlier in this century, are inspiring in that they offer proof of the vitality of the *ru* tradition of scholar-officials. Nevertheless, such accounts also reveal much about the desire of the interpreter. All interpretations and translations involve intention, and accounts of *ru* or Confucianism have been no exception.[24] De Bary's account of the contemporary relevance of Zhu Xi's thought, then, is in this sense his own and not Zhu Xi's construction. Although such a construction may rescue *lixue* and Zhu from the contempt in which they were held by early-twentieth-century Chinese nationalists, what the account salvages should not be taken as simply restoring the tradition it purports to uphold.

Though we can never entirely restore the true principles of *lixue*, Neo-Confucianism is significant because of the demonstration of its contemporary relevance. After more than thirty years, de Bary's manufacture of an individualist, humane, and liberal Neo-Confucian tradition remains controversial, perhaps because it often seems to claim to be above intellectual debate, to have some special claim to authenticity or truth.[25]

But even those who attempt to avoid claims of authenticity and truth find it difficult. In *Thinking through Confucius*, David Hall and Roger Ames have provided an intriguing construction of Confucius through an "experimental dialogue" in comparative philosophy.[26] While the authors make it clear that their endeavor to reveal the thinking of Confucius requires the translation of concepts across differing cultural contexts and times, they do not see that their enterprise is in fact fabricated. Their book, however, is a significant rejoinder both to previous contemporary interpreters/translators of Confucian texts such as de Bary and Wing-tsit Chan and to the Anglo-European philosophical tradition.

Their result in *thinking through* Confucius is, first, an understanding of the principal issues in his thought and, second, the application of his "take" on these issues to a reshaping of the philosophical premises that ground our way of thinking in the West. In announcing their comparative interpretive advantage, Hall and Ames state:

> We are *convinced* that our exercise in cross-cultural anachronism will provide us *a truer account* of Confucius for the following reason: current Western understandings of Confucius are the consequence of the mostly unconscious importation of philosophical and theological assumptions into primary translations that have served to introduce Con-

fucius' thinking to the West. These assumptions are associated with the mainstream of the Anglo-European classical tradition. In point of fact, as we shall demonstrate directly, these assumptions have seriously distorted the thinking of Confucius. Our thinking through Confucius therefore must be in its initial phases an unthinking of certain of the interpretive categories that by now have come to be presupposed in understanding Confucius.[27]

The authors' objective is an accurate linguistic and conceptual translation; thus, they presume it is possible hermeneutically to recover the "true" Confucius. By considering their account of Confucius to be truer than preceding ones, Ames and Hall fall victim to the Anglo-European philosophical paradigm of commensurability against which Richard Rorty, whom they hold in high regard, has so eloquently written.[28] The consequences of this thought experiment are the elevation of Confucius to world-philosophical significance and a message of Deweyan moral rebuke to contemporary Western philosophy—philosophy has no meaning if ripped from its moorings in public life.

Looking back over this high- and low-culture catalogue of the imaginative constructions of Confucius/Kongzi and Confucianism/*ru* it may seem obvious which are fabricated and which are fictitious. Surely Confucius was not the author of the platitudes he is portrayed as creating in Gary Larson's cartoon. Nor did the Confucius of Warring States (479–221 B.C.E.) China appear with the darkened skin and white robes of a man from the Levant (least of all because his wearing white would suggest that he was in mourning) or the headpiece of an ancient Egyptian ruler, as he does in the iconography of Freemason orientalism. The Confucius of these two imaginations is an invention, more obvious, perhaps, to our eye than the views of a Beijing businessman or the thoughts of the teeming throngs at the national shrine of China's *Zhongguo wenhua de daren*, "the great man of Chinese culture."

We are right to consider these as examples of a commoditizing manufacture of Confucius, and believe that postmodern Confucianism, de Bary's Neo-Confucianism, and Ames and Hall's rethought Confucius are less so. The latter examples are, however, no less manufactured, regardless of claims of continuity with the tradition as handed down from Zhu Xi, or of the contention that one offers an "understanding of Confucius's thinking." Each of these interpretations is a metaphorical wager on coherence and succeeds insofar as it is able to command contemporary assent.

Thus, in juxtaposing these very different cultural phenomena, low-brow and high-brow, as examples of invention, I am suggesting that they are functionally similar. They are reminiscent, moreover, of a plasticity evidenced by Kongzi himself in antiquity. Throughout Chinese history, Kongzi and the name assumed by the followers inspired by his example, *ru*, ran a similar gamut of parodic extremes that may be observed in native texts from the pre-Qin (579–221 B.C.E.) to the Tang (618–906 C.E.) eras.

Ru: Storied Truth and Symbolic Plasticity

For early followers of the *ru* tradition, Kongzi was the sage exemplar of a proper life. Praise of the sort uttered by Mengzi (Mencius) when recalling the virtues of Kongzi, Bo Yi, and Yi Yin (all sage heroes) is neither uncharacteristic nor inordinately fulsome: "All were wise men of antiquity. I as yet have been unable to follow their path; still, what I desire is to emulate Kongzi. . . . Since the birth of humanity there has been no one like Kongzi."[29] Kongzi and *ru*, however, much as they were honored by such latter-day followers, were ridiculed and denounced by contemporary adversaries. Indeed, *ru* and Kongzi traveled widely through the imaginations of other literary traditions, as hypocrites, shallow thinkers, liars, and panderers. We find them in the texts of adversarial groups like the Daoist, Mohist, Legalist, Eclectic, and Utilitarian schools, where they stand for sentiments consistent with, as well as contrary to, those expressed in the *Lunyu*.[30] From the frequent citations of Kongzi and *ru* in traditions antithetical to them it is clear that in the late Warring States period, Kongzi and *ru* functioned as tropes of excessive ritualism, or traditionalism.

By calling them "tropes" I mean that they were figurative expressions of diverse symbolic character and a certain authority, as shown in this passage from the philosophical Daoist *Zhuangzi,* typical in its treatment of Kongzi and *ru* as coded concepts:

> On water it is most convenient to travel by boat, on dry land in a carriage; if you were to try to push a boat on land because it goes well on water, you could last out the age without traveling an inch. Are not the past and the present [Kongzi's] water and his dry land? And Zhou and Lu his boat and carriage? At the present day, to have an urge to get the institutions of Zhou running in Lu is like pushing a boat on dry land, there's no result for all your labor, you're certain to bring disaster on yourself.[31]

Inspired by the morbidity of *ru* ritual service at funerals, these same adversaries used grave robbing as a grisly metaphor for the *ru*'s obsession with antiquity, as in this memorable vignette:

> *Ru,* taking up the [Book of] *Odes* and the [Record of the] *Rites,* rob graves. The big *ru* announces to his subordinates: "In the East, the day begins, how is the work going?" The little *ru* reply: "We have yet to remove the graveclothes, but there's a pearl in his mouth!" . . . [They] push back his

sidelocks, pull down his beard, and then one *ru*, using a metal gimlet, pries into his chin, [and] delicately draws open the jaws, never injuring the pearl in his mouth.[32]

Kongzi and *ru*, as tropes, could be worked to denigrate as well as to lionize, and thus were instantly recognizable to aficionado and adversary.

The effectiveness of this trope, like that of any other, depended entirely on the reader's familiarity with Kongzi and *ru*—an obvious presumption of the *Zhuangzi* authors. And from the frequency of their appearance in these texts it is evident that Kongzi and *ru* were very well known, although their significance was not uniform. At the same time that Kongzi was bandied about in this way by rhetorical proponents and opponents, cycles of stories grew around him that were repeated generation after generation and came to resemble a transmission text inscribed on the memories of raconteur and audience. A collected body of lore attested before the Han era included stories of Kongzi's magical birth, the heroics of his father (Shu Liang He), the travail of his mother, the illicit nature of his parents' union, the physical deformity of his older brother, and tales relating to his later travels among the kingdoms of the Zhan'guo era. Indeed, fragments of this legend cycle can be found in a number of such early literary works as *Mozi, Lüshi chunqiu, Mengzi, Yanzi chunqiu, Lunyu, Huainanzi,* and *Zhuangzi* and were authoritatively assembled in the first official biography of Kongzi in the *Shiji*.[33]

In the book of *Mozi,* for example, there is an entire chapter, "Fei ru," or "Contra-*ru*," one of many disputations of principal rhetorical categories. Here *ru* ritual obsession, extolled in their texts as devotion to *gu* (antiquity), is represented as self-serving and, like the *Zhuangzi* passage above, this *Mozi* text declares that the real motivation for *ru* insistence on elaborate funerals and a three-year mourning rite is not the preservation of ancient practice, but the collection of revenue. Near the end of this "Contra-*ru*" chapter, Kongmou, or "So-and-so Kong," appears with increasing frequency, usually in connection with the telling of a tale that we also know from the *ru* story traditions. In these instances Kongmou is a narrative marker, and it identifies the single figure from *Lunyu* lore, Kongzi, as a congeneric invention of the era. By comparison of these two tellings of the same story, we can observe the semiotics of Kongzi as trope and glimpse some of the symbolic plasticity common to our postmodern culture.

In a well-known account from *Lunyu* 15.1 that depicts the fledgling fellowship on the edge of extinction in the course of one of their many sojourns following Kongzi's exile from his native kingdom of Lu, the *ru* narrative reads:

> In Chen when provisions ran out, the followers became so sick that they were unable to stand upright. Zilu approached him [Kongzi] and said

querulously: "Is it proper for lordlings [*junzi*] to be reduced to straitened circumstances [as we are]?" He said, "A lordling can endure hardship; however, it is the lesser man who, when subjected [to such hardship], dissolves."[34]

Now compare this passage with a parallel account from the *Mozi*, where the tale of *ru* destitution is told with the same raw story material worked up to a very different effect:

> Once, So-and-so Kong was destitute between Cai and Chen having only vegetable soup without rice to eat. [After] ten days, Zilu roasted a pig for him. So-and-so Kong did not inquire from whence the meat came and simply ate. [Zilu, then] took a person's clothing and bartered it for wine. So-and-so Kong did not inquire from whence the libation came and simply drank. [Yet when] Ai Gong [Duke Ai of Lu] received Kongzi, Kongzi refused to sit on a mat that was not properly placed and would not eat [meat] that was not properly sliced. Zilu approached [him] and asked: Why the obverse of what was done between Chen and Cai? So-and-so Kong replied, "Come, I will tell you. Then our objective was to remain alive [while] today our objective is righteousness."[35]

Using the same tale, the *Mozi* passage emphasizes a situational ethic and lampoons the application of an uncompromising ethical standard that could result in death with honor. In this account, two separate events are condensed into the one retelling to achieve an effect of insincerity and falsehood. This "Fei ru" chapter of the *Mozi* was assembled circa 375 B.C.E.—at least a century following the putative death of Kongzi. Therefore, it is significant that its account would so accurately reproduce the story from the *Lunyu*. As a narrative device "Kongmou" testifies to the existence of a larger collection of stories or at least of multiple renderings of the same story.

In fact, portions of the *Lunyu* and later hagiographic works like the *School Sayings of Kongzi* (*Kongzi jiayu*) and the *Kong Transmission Record* (*Kong congzi*), though replete with remarks attributed to Kongzi, were nonetheless produced from just such a wider, popular lore. In other words, in native texts Kongzi was not simply the ancestral teacher of classically educated followers, called *ru*, as Han redactors believed and as we have conventionally assumed. Indeed, by the Tang dynasty he was a well-worn tool of narrative invention, in virtually the same manner that Emperor Yang of the Sui (589–617 C.E.) served as a protagonist in the historical romances of the seventeenth-century Chinese novel.[36] Thus Kongzi appeared, as Arthur Waley has shown, as a protagonist in satirical and even pornographic popular ballads, some of which have been preserved in the grottoes of Dunhuang.[37] In his study of Chinese scholars and the state in the Tang, David McMullen notes that Kongzi was the focus of "an official cult of satire and ribaldry" associated with court entertainment by the mid–ninth century.[38] Moreover, in a dramatic example of the loosening of sectarian ties, Kongzi, along with his most cherished disciple, Yan Hui, entered into popular Buddhist cults as a bodhisattva (*pusa*), a compassionate semidivine being—an honor visited most recently on the late Chairman Mao Zedong (1893–1976).

As we see from these and many other examples, the name "Kongzi" may recur over time, but the individual it designates is anything but consistent or continuous; the history of Kongzi, like that of Confucius, is one of differential invention and local manufacture.

In Defense of a Title: The Meaning of "Manufacture"

A question that I have deliberately hesitated in answering is, why "manufacture"? There are many reasons why "manufacture" is an appropriate term for describing the processes of conceptual invention with which I am concerned and of which we have already considered some examples, past and present.

"Manufacture" conventionally means "make by hand." It derives from the Latin "manufactus," literally, "handmade." And "handmade" is an apt term for a tradition, that discrete transmission of custom, habit, stories, and the rights to the telling of them. In this way, "manufacture," with its connotation of "manyhandedness," captures the palimpsestic labors of a cumulative tradition of local knowledge of rite, text, and the strategies for using them that we associate with Confucianism.

Although "manufacture" was widely used in the West in the eighteenth century because of the increasing definition of industrial work as manufacture, the word first appeared in the final decades of the sixteenth century, when it was used to describe a product of "the artificer's hand"—an image formed by human agency, rather than something naturally occurring.[39] Less than two decades later, two continents away, Chinese provincial officials were considering granting several Jesuit fathers in Macao the right to build their first mission in southern China.

"Manufacture" functions as a temporal marker in a cultural chronology that, in defining me (for example) as an interpreter living in the era of industrial civilization, identifies my place in relation to the texts of the works and lives I have elected to study. I am a latecomer to these texts, but then so were the Jesuits in studying Kongzi, and as Kongzi was in studying the Zhou.

But more than chronology and handmadeness favor my use of "manufacture"; it is the doubleness of its meaning that makes it suitable for disclosing the construction of communities of sense that emerges from these texts. The early meaning of "manufacture" emerged from the interstice between something made by hand and the natural object. What was made by hand was, ipso facto, not God-given. Such an artifact, while it was not natural, was no less real than nature. The significance of "manufacture," like so many other words, comes from the ambiguity of its cognate associations, in this case from the slippery distinction between natural and artificial. We will see in each of the chapters below that ambiguity is the most prominent characteristic of both Confucianism and *ru*, and it is responsible, moreover, for invention.

The equivocal significance of manufacture as both "made" and "made up" recalls the ambiguity of "fiction," from the Latin *fingere*, to fashion, to fabricate, or to form.[40] Yet such emphasis on "fiction's" madeness does not prevent it from having the connotation of "false," for *fingere* is also the root of "feign." In the popular consciousness, fiction is work that is feigned in the same way that "manufactured" refers to something made up. In the specific context of Kongzi's celebrated remark (*Lunyu* 7.1) "Shu er buzuo" ([I] receive but do not invent), the ambiguity of our modern term is also evident, as Kongzi implies that it is better to accept what is handed down than to make up something new. Perhaps madeness always bears the disparaging significance of "false." Certainly, it is easy to see how the sense of "manufacture" as fraudulently or fictitiously invented derives from the fact that the products of such fabrication are manmade and thus in a sense unnatural. As the term increasingly has been glossed with reference to modern industry, the use of mechanical power, the assembly line, the division of labor, and even robotics, the unnaturalness of its resonance is very pronounced for us.

"Manufacture" appears in this book usually in the sense of fabricating from raw material, that is, from culture: what we receive as categories for interpreting the world and what confronts us in everyday life that must be shaped in accord with what is received. The product of this conjuncture is manufacture. By "manufactured" I mean created, invented, fabricated, each of which is consistent with the Chinese word *zuo*,[41] which they are meant to represent. The gloss of *zuo* as "invent" fits the general theme of this book; yet it does not stray from traditional definitions such as Xu Shen's reading, *zuo: qi ye*, "to start." Furthermore, the meaning of *zuo* in passages from Zhou bronze inscriptions and from the *Shi jing* (Book of Odes), "to make," "to open up," "to erect," "sprouting," is unmistakably inaugural or foundational. Thus "invent" works as a gloss for *zuo*. Given that Kongzi himself has been transmitted through invention, it is necessary for us to preserve in our own translation something of the difference and similarity of these meanings. "Manufacture," I think, accomplishes this with an impressive linguistic economy, and my use of the term is motivated by the sense of "fiction" as an enterprise of forming significance.

I should point out that I do not consider such fictiveness problematic in the way that, for example, Gu Jiegang (1893–1980) did seventy years ago when he followed a path pioneered by Cui Shu (1740–1816) and discovered that Chinese antiquity was intricately and reiteratively layered by the inventions of later scholars.[42] Of course, it is difficult to escape the associations, common in our day and emerging in Gu's, linking fiction with the untrue, but I insist on making the ambiguity more pronounced by emphasizing the productive fictiveness of "manufacture." Both "Confucianism" and *ru* are ambiguous terms, and when I speak of them as manufactured entities I exploit the ambiguity of "manufacture"—an ambiguity contained in the *Lunyu*'s use of *zuo*—because the meaning of the term can be determined only in the context of what is being made and how it is being made. Yet I do not claim that there is no meaning, no real world, no real past. Concepts are not endlessly fungible. There are lines within which sense may be constructed and beyond which sense is lost. It is a dialectic of works and lives, or as we will soon learn, a dialogue between texts and interpretive communities that is responsible for the charting of these lines.

My use of the gerund "manufacturing" in the title of this book is intended to accentuate the essential and continuing conceptual processes by which *ru* and Confucianism have been made and remade. "Manufacturing" is used to stress the action of manufacture so as to distance this project from any attempt to characterize it as simply another meditation on a dead tradition. "Manufacturing," thus, suggests that this corporate enterprise of making sense of China by way of Confucianism continues. Though as this three-hundred-year-old tradition called Confucianism continues by reinvention today in some of the ways discussed above, it does so, some argue, with an implicit sense of an earlier "failure," the failure of Confucianism to endure as the socioethic of the Chinese people authorized by a living dynasty.

To speak of the failure of Confucianism is, however, to betray a lack of understanding of tradition. Moreover, such talk announces our distance from the ground we aim to represent. In fact this sense of Confucianism's failure is quite prevalent among Western and Chinese scholars whether they are defending or attacking it. Such fatalism also reflects the doctrinal persistence of the denigrative interpretation of *ru* and the dynastic state as decaying obstructions of modernity, which was first put forward by student nationalist advocates of "new culture" in 1915 and which was a salient concern of those demonstrating against the inequitable terms of the Treaty of Versailles in Tian'anmen Square on May 4, 1919. In this May Fourth Movement, as it came to be called, *ru* and Kongzi were singled out as cultural symbols of death, prominent figures of the past that had long outlived their usefulness and which an iconoclastic generation in pursuit of enlightenment was challenged to destroy, as summed up in the slogan "pohuai Kongjia dian" (Smash the shop of the Kong family). The virtual synonymy of *ru*, Kongzi, and China's imperial past in this critique provided an effective framing device for generational revolt, but there is little reason for us to continue to subscribe to such an indiscriminate interpretation today.

There should be no defensiveness of tone in our account of earlier manifestations of the practices we have elected to call Confucian. Reiterative invention of the concept *ru* and the communities represented by it throughout Chinese history, or the more recent multiple mutations of Confucianism and Neo-Confucianism show plainly that tradition is a process of constant reinvention. Thus, to take one moment in this process, say the *ru* scholarly practice of the last years of the nineteenth century, as emblematic of the whole ensures misunderstanding. While I have considerable doubts as to the representative value of Confucianism and Neo-Confucianism as interpretive fictions, doubts very similar to those expressed by Roger Ames and David Hall, I cannot subscribe to the notion, popular with some, including them, that Confucianism "failed" in the early twentieth century.

Lastly, through the use of the terms "manufacture" and "manufacturing," I seek a vocabulary that, while essentially a contemporary Western one, still might be used to describe the cultural processes, not of our era but of an earlier one, and yet functionally homologous with our own. "Manufacture" is intended to serve as a metaphor of interpretation and of the construal of sense. It is meant to describe the reiterative reproduction of meaning within the native tradition, *ru*, before the widespread use of industrial machinery, and, if effective, to join past and present, native and foreign on common metaphorical and similar cultural ground.

The appropriateness of the metaphor will be determined in the course of the book's argument, which proceeds in two parts. Part 1, "The Manufacture of Confucius and Confucianism," analyzes the foreign manufacture of Chinese identity, and part 2, "Making Sense of *Ru* and Making Up Kongzi," examines the native manufacture of national Chinese identity. For both, the lines of manufacture draw from *ru*. I explore two moments at which Confucius/Kongzi and the tradition identified with him were reinterpreted, made important, yet *made* to conform to the specific needs and desires that prevailed among a community of interpreters at the moment these entities were fashioned. The moments are (1) the sixteenth-century Jesuit encounter with the Chinese and with the tradition that they deemed Confucianism, and which has been known ever since in the West by that name; and (2) the early-twentieth-century encounter of Chinese with themselves through the intermediary of the West, in which efforts to define and "organize a national Chinese heritage" (*zhengli guogu*) produced critical reflection on the meaning of *ru*, in the form of a Chinese equivalent (more or less) of Confucianism.

Chapters 1 and 2, "The Jesuits, Confucius, and the Chinese," and "There and Back Again: The Jesuits and Their Texts in China and Europe," examine the fictive roots of Confucianism. The inquiry is conducted through historical criticism and analysis of the Western inventions "Confucius," "Confucian," and "Confucianism," as these emerged in the texts—letters, catechisms written in Chinese, memoirs, a history of the China Mission, translations of and commentary on the *Sishu (Four Books)*, and a monumental summary of Chinese culture called the *Confucius Sinarum Philosophus*—of a century and a half of Jesuit life in China. These two chapters pose the question of reality and representation in the specific context of the Jesuit encounter with China. They treat the sixteenth- and seventeenth-century conjunction of European and Chinese cultures as an instance in which the adequacy of indigenous categories of thought (Chinese and Western) to a novel situation were tested.

The result of this experimentation was the successful representation of Christian monotheism, using the native language of *ru* restorationism, and the invention of Confucianism. The Jesuit invention also reveals the same mechanisms of canon construction and textual manipulation that were so critical to the *ru* tradition while displaying an essential tension between universal message and sectarian defense. The opening chapters of this book demonstrate our contemporary conceptual indebtedness to the early Jesuits while permitting us to distinguish the processes critical to the invention of any tradition.

In part 2, I evaluate the extent of indigenous reflection on *ru* to determine (1) how Chinese represented themselves in it; and (2) how in so representing themselves they reasserted the Jesuit metonymic equivalence of *ru* and Chineseness. In chapter 3, "Ancient Texts, Modern Narratives: Nationalism, Archaism, and the Reinvention of *Ru*," I show that it was only with Western economic expansion and the decline of Manchu political and cultural authority early in this century that the normative scholar-official definition of *ru*, through which the Jesuits manufactured their own native identity, was replaced by a conjectural history of socioreligious evolution in which *ru* were defined as priests.

Unlike the normative conception that was fashioned by Sima Qian (145–89 B.C.E.) and Liu Xin (43 B.C.E.–23 C.E.?) and that presumed *ru* were the *congzhe*, "the followers" who took Kongzi as their *zongshi*, "ancestral teacher/commander," this conjecture, the product of an impressionistic philology by Zhang Binglin (Taiyan, 1868–1936), established a pre-Kongzi meaning of *ru* that was linked to the patrimonial theocracies of China's Bronze Age. The bulk of chapter 3 and all of chapter 4 are dedicated to a critical presentation of the two twentieth-century interpretations of *ru*—that of Zhang and another by Hu Shi (1891–1962)—where the emphasis will be on the specific conditions between 1900 and 1934 that inspired the differing developmental histories each scholar constructed of *ru*. In these two chapters I am concerned as well with how their combined accounts of an ancient history of *ru* achieved the status of a master fiction for the Chinese and for us. So persuasive was this "take" on *ru* that most subsequent interpretations took this account as their fundamental premise.

Chapter 4, "Particular Is Universal: Hu Shi, *Ru*, and the Chinese Transcendence of Nationalism," shows that scholarly acceptance of Hu's and Zhang's explanatory fiction had much to do with the former's systematic representation of the history of Chinese and Western civilization as distinct moments in a unitary process of spiritual/material evolution. In this context, I will demonstrate how Zhang Binglin's effort to identify and then emplot the plural meanings of *ru* as moments in a narrative of evolutionary change from antiquity to the present provided the raw material that Hu Shi worked up into a cosmopolitan vision of the world's cultural evolution from a messianic past to a secular present. Such a vision was uniquely akin to the ecumenical understanding of sixteenth- and seventeenth-century Jesuits, who saw in China compelling evidence for the world's spiritual unity in God.

Most striking in Hu Shi's interpretation was, as we will see, the way he read the evolution of *ru* by means of the history of Christianity's emergence from the Judaic cult of the *Perushim*, or Pharisees, and in turn glossed this Christian history with respect to the generation of Kongzi's teachings from a vestigial cult of Shang religious observance. The Jesuits had insisted that Christianity and *ru* were highly compatible but offered little more than faith as proof. After the questions raised in part 1 about reality and representation with respect to the Jesuit construction of *ru*, it is ironic that Hu Shi would return us to these same questions from the native point of view, in his insistence that only Christianity provided the most appropriate symbolic fund for the meaningful interpretation of the episodic manufacture of *ru*.

Acknowledging that Western and Chinese imaginings of *ru* are indeed indissociable, the book concludes with a reprise of the specific impulses that conditioned these separate instances of manufacture—seventeenth-century Jesuit and twentieth-century Chinese—and a reflection on contemporary prospects for the realization of Hu Shi's effort to establish a fundamental identity of East and West on the basis of a shared pattern of civilizational growth.

The chronology of this study may seem rather odd in the sense that if my interest is in determining what *ru* was made of, then I should begin with the earliest texts in which there is a record of this term. Yet it should be obvious from the above discussion that my interest is not in what *ru* in fact may have been, largely because it is impossible to "authenticate" such a notion. My real interest is in what *ru* and Confucianism mean for us, and thus I am concerned with setting forth a reasonable historical conjecture of these two conceptual inventions. Given that neither *ru* nor Confucianism was ever one thing, I have tried to show how the plural interpretive constructions of the Jesuits and certain twentieth-century Chinese intellectuals in the names of these two surprisingly interchangeable entities have provided a uniform representation of *ru* as a secularized religion that continues to influence our comprehension of this term.

The interpretation advanced in this book is merely an interpretation, and so no argument is made for the exclusiveness of my claims. The readings consequent upon my engagement with texts of an earlier time are, like Hans-Georg Gadamer's understanding of hermeneutics, "horizontal."[43] I have obviously benefited from previous readings of the same literature, and this may be evident from my interpretations of them. If I differ from received interpretations or violate conventional readings, I do not denigrate them. Instead I have assimilated them, gathering such accounts into what I hope is a wider spectrum of understanding. Therefore, while my work is intended to stand alone, my findings are significant only in the context of a horizon of interpretations manufactured out of previous encounters with these texts. In this respect, my work is just the most recent inscription on a palimpsest that preceded my arrival by a number of centuries.

Thus, this book is not a defense of, nor an attack on, Confucianism. Rather, it is a defense of the creative impulses that have sustained centuries of invention in its name and that of its native equivalent, *ru*. Some may find this reading unconventional, even provocative, although the methods that enable my reading are conventional, even traditional. My aim is, rather, to draw historians of China, particularly intellectual historians and philosophers like myself, into a conversation that evaluates an implicit faith in our own interpretive conventions and in a continuity of Chinese culture made immemorial by us in the two-thousand-year marriage of Confucianism and the Chinese imperium. Simply, I ask for a conceptual reckoning that proceeds along two distinct but interwoven lines—the imagination of the interpreter in search of coherence, and the indigenous culture out of which the interpreter, foreign or native, hones a narrative. Proceeding in this way we will lose little but learn much, above all, about ourselves.

PART ONE

THE MANUFACTURE

OF CONFUCIUS AND

CONFUCIANISM

Verum et factum convertuntur.
(The true and the made are convertible.)
—*Giambattista Vico*

What you have as heritage,
 Take now as task;
For thus you will make it your own.
—*Goethe,* Faust

CHAPTER 1

THE JESUITS,

CONFUCIUS, AND

THE CHINESE

"He [Cook] is a god." But then recognition is a kind of re-cognition: the event is inserted in a preexisting category, and history is present in current action. The irruption of Captain Cook from beyond the horizon was a truly unprecedented event, never seen before. But by thus encompassing the existentially unique in the conceptually familiar, the people embed their present in the past.—*Marshall Sahlins*

In ancient times they followed the natural law as faithfully as in our lands; and for 1500 years this people was little given to idols, and those they adored were not such a wretched crowd as our Egyptians, Greeks and Romans adored, but a lot who were very virtuous and to whom were attributed very many good deeds. In fact, in the books of the *literati* which are the most ancient and of the greatest authority, they give no other adoration than to heaven and earth and the Lord of them. When we examine closely all these books we discover in them very few things contrary to the light of reason and very many in conformity with it.—*Matteo Ricci*

By the time the Italian Jesuits Michele Ruggieri (1543–1607) and Matteo Ricci (1552–1610) had established the first Christian mission of the modern era in China in September 1583, Zhongni, Kong Qiu, or Kongzi had been dead for over two millennia, but "Confucius" was about to be born. He was born, in a manner similar to that which Marshall Sahlins describes in his account of Captain Cook's incarnation as a Maori god, that is, in an instant reflexive translation of what was strange into a preexistent understanding. Cook was decidedly a man, not a god, yet he and his retinue from the British Royal Navy were not at first comprehensible to the Maori as men. If not men, then they were, says Sahlins, gods; thus Cook the man was appropriated as Lono, the god of fertility.[1]

For sixteenth-century Chinese, the native entity, Kongzi, was a man-god, a *shengren*, who was the object of an imperial cult, the ancient ancestor of a celebrated rhetorical tradition, and a symbol of an honored scholarly fraternity (the *ru*, or "Confucians") represented by a phalanx of officials who staffed every level of the imperial bureaucracy. But before the eyes of clerics newly arrived from the West he appeared as prophet, holy man, and saint (*santo*).

In Jesuit hands the indigenous Kongzi was resurrected from distant symbolism into life, heroically transmuted and made intelligible as "Confucius," a spiritual confrere who alone among the Chinese—so their version had it— had preached an ancient gospel of monotheism now forgotten. As the Italian fathers imagined him, this Chinese saint and his teachings on the One God, *Shangdi*, had presaged their arrival. It was with this presumption that they undertook a restoration of what they termed his "true learning" (*zhengxue*). In this way, Ruggieri, Ricci, and several generations of accommodationist fathers construed Kongzi through a timeless vertical relation with divinity, re-cognizing him as "Confucius" while inventing themselves, qua *ru*, as native defenders of the sage's "first Ru" (*xianru*) doctrine.

This Confucius was more than the cognitive adjustment of Sahlins's Maori and more than translation. It was a symbol manufactured by the early Jesuits in the course of their adaptation to China. Through their invention, these first missionaries overcame the cultural strangeness of late imperial China and, more surprisingly, within a decade of life among the Chinese, were able to represent themselves to the natives as the orthodox bearers of the native Chinese tradition, the *ru*. In the name of "the true learning" and its master, Confucius, Ricci, Ruggieri, and others were reincarnated as a Chinese fundamentalist sect that preached a theology of Christian/Confucian syncretism. In turn, the Chinese accepted the fathers as *ru* and even referred to them, in some cases, as *shengren menxia* (followers of the holy men).

Today the term "Confucius" and its derivative "Confucian" endure as the principal symbols of China, Chineseness, and tradition. For some time, Confucius has been seen as a legacy left us by the Jesuits, yet scholars have been unable or disinclined to identify an author or text that would confirm the presumption.[2] The figure was assuredly the Jesuits', but it was the second-order reinvention of "Confucius" in Europe, not merely its local invention by the Sino-Jesuit community, that made the term so potent. Our Confucius is in fact a product of both these moments of invention. Although it is proper to acknowledge the Jesuits' role in inventing Confucius, in doing so we tend to obscure the other historical conditions of its invention and reinvention, and thus overlook the term's differential functioning in two separate textual communities. This chapter queries this conflation of the two figures and begins by questioning the invention "Confucius."

It is not my objective to ascertain when and by whom "Confucius" was originally uttered, principally because there is no historically verifiable first use. Instead, I am concerned with the representational mechanics associated with the Jesuit strategy for their mission in China. Specifically, I wish to explore how they, as foreigners, were able to construct a native complex of reference according to which they made sense of both themselves and the Chinese. Secondly, I am interested in the manner in which a certain conceptual product of the local Jesuit conversion project, "Confucius," was received and interpreted in Europe within a collateral, universalizing complex of reference in a fashion contradictory to the intentions of the fathers, but productive of a rich array of fetishes bearing the aura of Chineseness.

What runs through both of these concerns is the fictive character of Confucius, examination of which inevitably opens a window onto the life of the community that created it and onto another one abroad in Europe, which reconceived it under very different cultural circumstances. In chapter 2 I will consider the consequences of the Jesuit assimilation in both China and Europe by examining the difference in the meanings of the missionary "Confusius" (the earliest Jesuit spelling of the name) and the "Confucius" of wide Continental celebrity with which we are more familiar.

However, in this chapter the focus will be the ecclesiastical community in China. This community was the cultural matrix from which a certain "Confusius" was brought forth; it remains the least well understood of the protagonists in this story, having been portrayed only as a mediator between historically given communities. But the first Jesuits were a self-constituting intellectual community, whose local identity was obtained through a lengthy process of translating themselves into native reference while translating Chinese texts into the language of their faith. Their translation was a complex negotiation of identity on native terrain in which they were assisted by Chinese while also helping themselves to the multiple symbolic resources offered by the culture that they quickly made their own.

Through study of this Jesuit enclave and its "engaged representation"[3] of the Chinese, we can reconstruct the making of a tradition, learning how communities of persons create communities of texts, all interrelated and mutually elucidating. We begin by retracing the route taken by those unusually pious priests who, in seeking to make themselves Chinese, constructed a path that for more than four centuries interpreters have used to cross over into China.

Cultural Wilderness and the Reach of Jesuit Imagination

A traveller who has lost his way, should not ask, "Where am I?" What he really wants to know is, Where are the other places? He has got his own body, but he has lost them.—*Alfred North Whitehead*

To arrive in south China in the last quarter of the sixteenth century must have been disorienting, as well as difficult and dangerous for Michele Ruggieri, Matteo Ricci, and the other missionaries who accompanied them on their respective journeys there in 1579 and 1582. While "Cina," as the Italian fathers called it, was not uncharted territory, it remained a wilderness for them, a place of fanciful European dreams and a spur to the imagination of adventurers and cartographers. Fathers like Ruggieri and Ricci who requested service in the yet-to-be-founded China Mission, elected to undertake a kind of boundary exploration, devoting themselves to pacing and measuring the contours of the line between this wilderness and their own civilization. The passage from Lisbon to Goa and on to Macao took at best one year, but there was always a considerable risk of maritime disaster en route. In their transit to China, the Jesuit fathers endured a lengthy apprenticeship in the unknown to arrive at a tiny outpost of European civilization on the tip of China's southern coast.[4] Macao was a fitting location from which to take the measure of the vast wilderness to the north. But it was strange nevertheless, and the largely European character of its public works could not neutralize its strangeness.

These circumstances must have been quite unsettling for the two men for, unlike many of their fellow residents in this polyglot entrepôt, they were not to return home soon. Macao was for them a way station propaedeutic to a greater enterprise, of which neither the perils nor the fruits could be known, only imagined. They were also virtually on their own. Their zeal to immerse themselves in the culture of China distinguished them from the other missionaries in Goa as well as their predecessors in the Mission of the Indies, who, unlike Ricci and Ruggieri, resisted the impulse to go native, preferring instead to preach in their own vernaculars with the assistance of local converts.[5]

On several counts, then, the experience of these two missionaries was one of cultural dislocation. They were isolated in Macao, where few would hear their message. More important, they lacked a language to convey what they could preach so effortlessly on the streets of Rome. To give voice to themselves, the fathers simply *wrote* themselves into existence. From the records they have left, they were engaged, it would seem, in a feverish self-inscription. During their first years, they generated, in short order, a great volume of letters, a Latin catechism, and a world map.

They wrote in Chinese, Latin, and Portuguese,[6] and between 1581 and 1586, there seemed no limit to their curiosity. In a letter of October 1581, three years after Michele Ruggieri arrived in Macao, Father Pero Gomes, another of the early missionaries, reports: "Father Rogerio [Ruggieri] and I who have been here these months, are employing our time in composing a brief history of the beginning of the world which will be used at the same time as a Christian doctrine and this in the form of a dialogue which will be translated into the Chinese language."[7] That same year, Ruggieri completed a catechism and a version of the lives of the saints, both written in Chinese with the assistance of an unnamed Chinese convert.[8] They had taken three years to write. By 1585 he had become a fair calligrapher and had already written a number of poems in conscious imitation of Tang style. He also completed much of a bilingual (Portuguese/Chinese) dictionary, which when finished comprised 189 folios.[9] In these years Ruggieri ranged across much of the cultural terrain before him, writing down and explaining the Chinese terms for the heavens, the twenty-four periods of the lunar cycle, and the *tiangan dizhi* (stems and branches) system of calculation. He identified the thirteen provinces of the empire as well as the northern and southern capitals of the Ming dynasty and even undertook preparations to assemble a globe with Chinese notations.[10]

The same sense of fervid acquisition of local knowledge can be seen in the first letters that Ricci and Ruggieri posted from China. These early letters were given (tirelessly) to the details of the quotidian: documenting what they could of Chinese custom; rehearsing their plans for a mission settlement in

China proper; chronicling the scholarly activities of the fathers, particularly their progress in language study; and reporting on their meetings with local Chinese officials, from whom they sought permission to enter the country. Of the last of these there is frequent mention, giving any reader of the letters the impression that the Jesuits were directing extraordinary effort at carving a niche, geographic and political, for themselves and for the mission volunteers they presumed would follow. Through this significant epistolary production, they were constructing a frame of reference, situating the China that loomed before them in relation to the known world. They were, like Whitehead's lost traveler, finding the other places.

When in the autumn of 1584 these first letters were sent via Portuguese carrack to awaiting Jesuit censors, the missionaries had already acquired a tract of land near the town of Zhaoqing, ninety miles west of Canton on the south bank of the Xi River, and Ruggieri was laboring over a series of maps that would be made into an atlas of China.[11] At the same time his colleague, Matteo Ricci, was completing his first *mappamondo*, or world map (see figure 4), which proved to be quite a novelty to the Chinese eye. The *mappamondo* was an established genre in sixteenth-century Europe; its conventions dictated that China be placed on the eastern edge of the map, with Jerusalem in the center, and Europe in the West. Thus the *mappamondo* charted the new reaches of known civilization, specifically marking the borders of the unknown and wicked, and all in relation to the ancient locus of the cartographer's faith, Jerusalem.

However, Ricci's *mappamondo* was different. He composed it in situ to chart his relation to the civilization he had left, but his cartography was most unconventional. In fact, it violated the conventions of the *mappamondo* genre, as if to indicate a drift toward native perspective or to portray the degree of his cultural displacement. For on Ricci's map, Europe was in the *far* West. And perhaps in unconscious deference to the regnant Chinese cultural conception of centrality (*zhong*), Ricci put China near the center; the Holy Land was represented in the western quadrant as an isthmus that linked Asia with North Africa.[12]

The first version of the map went through a series of editions and, owing to its great popularity among the Chinese, became a well-known symbol of Jesuit erudition, reiteratively redacted and reproduced over five decades by subsequent detachments of missionaries. This initial effort was obviously not made to assist Jesuit proselytism: the original map was stolen from their Zhaoqing compound not long after it was finished and was then reproduced by woodblock in multiple copies for an inquisitive Chinese audience. Consequently, unlike its many subsequent revised and annotated editions, this first map was intended exclusively for Ricci and his fellow missionaries, offering a visual, documentary testament of the wide reach of God and fram-

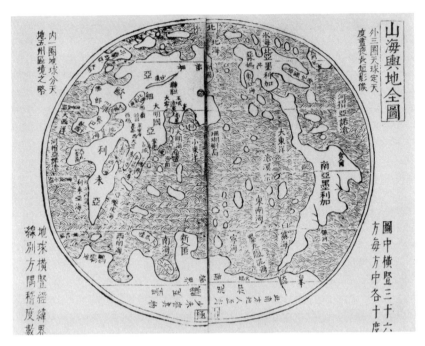

Figure 4. Li Madou (Matteo Ricci), "Shanhai yu di quan tu" (Complete Map of Mountains, Seas, and Land). This version of Ricci's celebrated *mappamondo* was completed with Chinese assistance circa 1602. Ricci unconventionally places China, not Jerusalem, at the center of the map. Moreover, the depiction of water recalls the woodcut illustrations of Ming dynasty *congshu* (gazetteers) rather than the cartographic depictions of European scholars.

ing these European men, both spiritually and physically, within the borders of a science they instinctively understood—cartography—and within a language they sought to master.

Such framing was inspirationally reinforced by the preparation of a Latin "catechism," the initial draft of which was completed in 1581 and called the *Vera et brevis divinarum rerum expositio* (A True and Brief Exposition of Divine Things).[13] This work is a heterogenous sampling of materials and genres so idiosyncratic that it is difficult to categorize. The first seven chapters consist of a dialogue between a European priest and an "ethnic" philosopher, followed, in order, by the Ten Commandments, the Articles of Faith, a selection of Christ's sayings, and the Sacraments. This catechism, like the map, acted to frame the Jesuits in relation to their immediate experience of the Chinese other. As the work was composed in Latin, its immediate audience was certainly not the Chinese, and it was not, by the Jesuits' own admission, so much a catechism as an explanation and defense of doctrine (*doctrina*).[14]

While it did serve as a very important though very imperfect template, from which was produced a second version in the Chinese language, the *Vera et brevis expositio* was clearly of greater value to the Jesuits in coping with cultural estrangement than it was to prospective Chinese catechumens. In drafting a Latin *doctrina* of this sort at the interface of the unknown, Ruggieri and Ricci were able not simply to reaffirm but to nourish and celebrate, in the language of their beloved church, the cardinal tenets of their faith. Thus, they steeled themselves spiritually for what God had asked of them by making a declaration of faith under duress.

While adumbrating the outlines of known civilization and locating themselves within its expanding perimeter, the Jesuits were also training their imaginations on the task of reaching Chinese souls. Yet, to acquire a more profound understanding of the China they had mapped and now entered, the fathers would need more than the assistance of the two well-connected southern officials—Wang Pan (1539–1600?) and Guo Zizhang (1543–1618)— who ceded them the land for the mission. As dictated by their missionary strategy of accommodation, entering the cultural horizon of the sixteenth-century Chinese required the Jesuits to seek out what was common in the experience of two very different cultures, to locate lines of filiation. These lines were ultimately manufactured—not discovered—among *ru*, or what Ricci designated "la legge de' letterati" (the order of the literati), and whose founder Ricci called "Confutius," a cultural patron on whose established native authority as Kongzi the Jesuits could present themselves to the Chinese.[15] But there was nothing inevitable in this analogical choice of *ru* or in the Jesuits' appropriation of a cultural patriarch; these were largely fortuitous consequences of an initial identification with Buddhist monasticism in which the fathers in accommodating themselves to China literally assumed the identity of Buddhist priests.

"Accommodation," a simple term, was in fact a very complex, even treacherous, process in which the men of the Mission of the Indies reinvented themselves, in effect abandoning their identity as European priests in order to, in the words of Ruggieri, "become Chinese." Within this bold experiment lies an understanding of the Jesuits' meaningful representation of themselves, of Chinese culture, and of the native tradition of "la legge de' letterati." It is a story of accident and misapprehension in which men of two different worlds, Chinese and Jesuit, become almost indistinguishable, one becoming more like the other.

Jesuit Accommodation: Constituting a Native Community

The topic of "accommodationism," a term invented by twentieth-century Jesuits to refer to the sixteenth-century evangelical operation in China, has received very thorough treatment in the works of Johannes Bettray and D. E. Mungello.[16] Rather than summarize their arguments, I will analyze accommodationism in three respects—culture, theology, and literature—in order to illustrate the manner in which the first missionaries constituted themselves as a local community. The reader, however, should recognize that these distinctions are heuristic and should try to imagine them as continuous links in a chain of personal experience, preexistent logic, and cognitive appropriation instinctually forged at the juncture of the two cultures.

In its widest application, accommodationism identifies a specific missionary method employed by the Society of Jesus to obtain, in Ricci's words, "entrata nella Cina" (entrance into China), and to bring the Chinese into the Christian fold. The accomplishment of either of these objectives was less than routine. Before the establishment of the Zhaoqing mission, Ricci and Ruggieri's Jesuit precursors had found it especially difficult to enter China, getting no closer than the Portuguese entrepôt of Macao—and that for only three months at a time.[17] The Jesuits' own Francis Xavier (1506–1552), after spending three years catechizing and converting the Japanese to the "Sacred Faith" (Santa Fede), sought passage to China, convinced that "all of the religious orders and rites of the Japanese originated in China."[18] However, before he could make further progress in propagating Christ's teachings throughout Asia, Xavier was marooned and died on the island of Shangquan—twenty leagues from the Guangdong coast—waiting to be ferried to China for a meeting with the emperor. Nevertheless, he succeeded in drafting a plan for the conversion of all of China and Japan, believing that a well-articulated imperial structure such as China's, where the emperor commanded absolute obedience, would embrace Christianity without hesitation.[19]

Through the politic judgment and direction of Father Visitor Alessandro Valignano of the Jesuit order in the East Indies (1539–1606), Xavier's plan "accommodationism" was pursued right down to the adoption by missionaries of indigenous dress and language, despite the vigorous objections of seasoned missionaries at the mission's headquarters in Goa.[20] As unaccustomed as an earlier generation of Jesuits might have been to such a strategy, for those to whom it was to be applied—the Chinese—accommodation was not unfamiliar. As many previous foreign cultures did, upon taking up residence in China—most recently the Mongols—the Jesuits adopted a strategy that could be termed "sinification."

Sinification and the Paths of Enculturation

Accommodation was in effect a form of sinification, of becoming Chinese, and in the first sense we may treat it as a cultural phenomenon, that is, the Jesuits' acceptance of China's foreignness and acclimation to it by diligent study of language, custom, and habit. Accommodation, however, was a more thorough form of cultural assimilation than was sinification and could not have been accomplished without significant Chinese indulgence. In retrospect, what is most striking about the accommodationist endeavor is its success in generating a native Chinese identity for the fathers: they conducted themselves in a Chinese manner and were, in turn, recognized as Chinese.

In this light, "enculturation," rather than "sinification," is the more appropriate descriptive term.[21] Over the course of this enculturation we can observe a pattern of two distinct phases: an initial phase from 1583 to 1595 in which the Jesuits carved a niche for themselves in China by assuming an identity as Buddhist monks, followed by a longer period symbolized by their second incarnation as *ru* and their subsequent engagement in doctrinal debates and polemics with Chinese scholars over the meaning of the *ru* teaching. Obviously the success of such a bold program required both a significant weakening of European cultural habits and Christian sectarian superiority as well as a distinct Chinese magnanimity.

In contrast to earlier missionaries and most of their contemporaries, the Jesuits divested themselves, as much as was practicable, of a belief in the superiority of their message. They shed as well an unrealistic expectation that conversion would follow immediately on the heels of exposure to the message of God's envoys—even if those envoys spoke only the languages of God's favored cultures and not the language of the people they hoped to convert. Their proselytizing predecessors in Goa and Macao insisted on taking full advantage of King Sebastian's *Padroado*,[22] or patronage, and limited their preaching to Portuguese residents, relying on interpreters to catechize prospective converts. The Jesuit fathers selected by Valignano, by contrast, conscientiously pursued a meticulous cultural imitation of the Chinese. The extent of their willingness to undergo acculturation in the name of conversion was nothing short of remarkable, for their colleagues at the mission headquarters in Macao were still "portugalizing" the natives, insisting that Chinese converts assume Portuguese names, wear Portuguese clothes, and practice Portuguese customs.[23] At the strenuous urging of Valignano, the China Mission was to operate in de facto autonomy from the Jesuit community and authority at Macao. The mission was, therefore, an outpost in two senses—foreign to Chinese terrain and exceptional in theory and practice within the larger Asian missionary community. Theirs was a novel and unique experiment countenanced by very few within the order, but Ruggieri and Ricci molded themselves on the example of their revered Xavier and adopted the clothing, tonsure, and native title (*heshang*) of Buddhist monks, or "bonzes" (the Portuguese term).[24]

Although Michele Ruggieri and Matteo Ricci stressed in their reports to mission authorities and their letters to friends the similarities between Roman Catholic priests and Buddhist monks, their actual assumption of Buddhist monastic identity entailed a major shift of strategy and a significant conceptual leap. And yet, correspondence preserved in Jesuit letterbooks and published in the formative period of early contact with the Chinese suggests that the fathers were hardly discomfited by this change. We see there a priestly enthusiasm, not for merely imitating the customs of the natives, but for *becoming* Chinese.

In a letter to Valignano of February 3, 1583, shortly before the founding of the mission of Zhaoqing, Ruggieri recounted the events of a critical meeting (held in December 1582) with the city's prefect and benefactor of the Jesuits, Wang Pan. At this time Wang agreed to cede property and to provide a small house in Zhaoqing for the missionaries' purposes. It was suggested that the members of the order attire themselves in the contemporary fashion of Buddhist priests. Wang, according to Father Ruggieri, "wished us to dress in the manner of their fathers, which is a little different from ours, and now we do so dress, and, *in short, we have become Chinese* so that we may gain the Chinese for Christ."[25]

Ricci's secondhand account of the same episode does not entirely corroborate that of Ruggieri. From him we learn more of Ruggieri's alacrity to adopt the appearance of bonzes, than of Wang's exhortation. In a letter posted from Macao on February 13, 1583, rather than confirm the interpretation of his senior colleague, Ricci depicts Wang Pan's recommendation somewhat differently, as an affirmative response to an offer made by Ruggieri, saying, "when the fathers said to him [Wang Pan] that they wanted to become vassals of the king of China, and that they would even change their mode of dress . . . he said that he would give them the habit of the priests of Peking, which is the most honored one could give."[26]

With different contemporary perspectives on what constituted the common ground of the missionaries and the Chinese, clearly there was more than one way to "become Chinese," or at least there were as many ways as there were theories on the most effective means of delivering the Christian message. Two theories of accommodation emerged from the first fifteen years of evangelical practice in southern China, with Ruggieri and Ricci as their respective proponents. The application of either theory required the Jesuits to remake themselves, in the former case as Buddhists and in the latter case as *ru*.

The Bridge of Buddhism

Early on, the Jesuits were impressed with China's masses of Buddhist believers. From his observations of the plurality of sectarian Buddhist practice—

Tiantai, Chan, Huayan, or Jingtu—in his history of the China Mission, Ricci concluded that Buddhist monks alone numbered in the millions.[27] If the objective was to preach among the people, then it may have been wise to become Buddhist monks of the Pure Land (Jingtu) sect, particularly in the last decades of the Wanli era (1573–1619 C.E.), when popular Buddhism was undergoing a renaissance of sorts. Tiantai monasticism presented another accommodative possibility, insofar as the Jesuits could exploit the theological similarity between their one omniscient and ubiquitous God and this sect's notion that all phenomena are manifestations of the one mind. Given such congruences, even the skeptical Ricci at first believed the Buddhist incarnation appropriate, if not natural. Indeed, writing to Giulio Fuligatti in November 1584, Ricci takes Buddhist costume to be indexical of Chineseness and appears excited by the prospect of having crossed over, when he reports: "*I have become a Chinaman. In our clothing, in our books, in our manners, and in everything external we have made ourselves Chinese.*"[28]

In assuming the identity of *osciani* (Buddhist monks) the fathers did not imitate the natives but "went native" and in a formal sense at least ceased to be priests, having exchanged their Catholic vestments for the homespun robes of Buddhist priests. Describing the change in habit to Fuligatti, Ricci made a distinction between external appearance and internal commitment, a distinction that is too facile, if not somewhat disingenuous; to have made themselves Chinese in everything external meant that Ricci and his cohort denied those very trappings that reinforced their identity as priests. Adopting the identity of the other challenged the fathers to reinvent themselves *in alio esse*, in another mode of existence. The testimony of Ruggieri and Ricci at the time of this image change makes clear that they were not simply stepping from one priestly world into another. Rather, they imagined Buddhist monasticism to be a vehicle for becoming Chinese. We cannot overestimate the significance of this act, particularly in light of the fact that men like Ricci were fully aware that the conclusion of their evangelical work was a meeting with their Maker, not a joyous homecoming in their native land. Their native land was now China.

The challenge for these men was to find themselves among the natives, trusting that as they traveled the path of enculturation in speech and in bearing, they would meet the Chinese coming back. The Jesuits could carry liturgy in their hearts, but liturgy must be applied, or enacted, to be meaningful. Indeed ritual enactment and liturgy are mutually reinforcing; the one will atrophy with the decline of the other. What would enactment of the liturgy mean in a world where the physical accoutrements of ecclesiastical life were nowhere in evidence? Moreover, how did the radical transformation of their physical appearance affect their internal disposition? The fundamental difference in their physical appearance and in the religious landscape meant that Jesuit identity, like their liturgy, would not mean what it did at home in Europe.

This they had to negotiate among the Chinese. Having cast away the trappings of their former identity and not yet having cleared ground upon which they could enact the rites of their faith, these men were without visible support. They were victims, like anthropologists in the field, of culture shock, and shock such as this could only be overcome through invention, invention based on analogy.[29] This is why the assumption of Buddhist identity was equated with Chineseness, for the Jesuits could project themselves into Chinese life on the basis of the structural homology they apprehended in Buddhist monasticism. Buddhism, thus, served as the tool with which the Jesuits first constructed themselves as Chinese, thereby mitigating the shock consequent upon their encounter with the native population.

The choice of monastic Buddhism as the initial mode of enculturation may have made sense to the fathers because it was, in a general sense, politically sound. If, as Ruggieri recalls, Wang requested that the Jesuits dress as Buddhists, such a suggestion was wise in that their appearance as *heshang* was not liable to draw the kind of official protest or suspicion of heterodoxy that would endanger the order and its Chinese benefactors. Indeed the Jesuits were aware of the risk of appearing in another, unfamiliar guise, as is obvious from this cautionary statement from Ricci's journals: "In order that the appearance of a new religion might not arouse suspicion among the Chinese, the fathers did not speak openly about religious matters when they began to appear in public."[30] Ruggieri shared his colleague's wariness and informed his superiors that he and Ricci were not practicing the rite of baptism, saying, "for now we do not move to make Christians in order not to give any occasion to the Demon to demolish this new plant."[31] Furthermore, although there was a small chapel on the grounds, Jesuit letters are silent about mass, giving one the impression (an impression confirmed in later letters, in which Ricci states that they will "open no more churches, but instead a preaching house and we will say mass in private in another chapel")[32] that the chapel was more like the *shu yuan*, or private academies, that proliferated in the late Ming.[33]

As long as they were recognized as Buddhists, there was much to recommend in this accommodation strategy and, from what Ricci reports here about the votive gifts of early visitors to the mission, the Chinese did, in fact, see them as Buddhist monks: "Many also began to offer perfumes as incense for the altar and also alms to the fathers for their food and for oil for the lamp that was lit before the altar."[34] In the late sixteenth century, Buddhist sects were already numerous, and, according to some scholars, they were on the rise; thus there could be little harm (even from the perspective of a suspicious government) in the appearance of yet another sect or subsect spawned from an increasingly indistinguishable mass.[35] Considering that pious Chinese honored the fathers with symbolic offerings such as lamp oil that were peculiar to Buddhist rite, it would appear that no distinction was made between the Jesuits as "Chinamen" and the Chinese *heshang.*

And why *should* Chinese have distinguished between these two monastic orders? Buddhist monks were not like most Chinese. They occupied a marginal symbolic plane, something made particularly clear by their generic socioreligious function as celebrants of the mortuary rite. The Jesuits were physically different from the Chinese and from Buddhist monks, but there was nothing to prevent the Chinese from taking them as pietistic travelers from the land of the Ganges—they lived as monks, had shorn their hair, wore robes, were celibate, and were known to have come from India. This was precisely how the Japanese had seen Francis Xavier and his fellow Jesuits, noting the same features and coincidences.[36] In China the fathers were as different and as marginal as Buddhist monks, so for Chinese observers little conceptual innovation was required to make them comprehensible. And, as these monks came from the West appearing in shapeless robes, hemp belts, and tonsures, bearing devotional icons peculiar to their worship, the structural similarities to Buddhist monasticism were compelling. The Chinese, to borrow again from Sahlins, "re-cognized" the Jesuits as Buddhist monks.

Such recognition was undoubtedly facilitated by the fact that the magistrate, Wang Pan, like many officials in late imperial China, was very partial to Buddhism. In fact, in one of his first meetings with Father Ruggieri and Father Francesco Pasio he donated a single tael of silver as alms for the mission. By bestowing the title of Buddhist monks on the fathers, it is clear that Wang believed he granted them a privilege of which they were particularly deserving. Within a year of the meeting between Ruggieri, Pasio, and Wang Pan, the Jesuits were given a residence with a chapel constructed on the new site.

Wang marked the occasion by presenting Ruggieri with two gilded plaques and a poem commemorating the mission's founding and honoring its founders. The first plaque read *xianhua si* (Immortal Flower Monastery), while the second read *xi lai jingtu* (From the West comes the Pure Land).[37] The allusions here are to tenets of the Huayan and Jingtu sects. Wang, like the other Chinese almsgivers, considered the mission to be a monastery, and Ruggieri and Ricci its abbots. And in this way Chinese reflexively translated the foreigners into familiarity. For Wang, the fit of foreign priests and Buddhist monks was particularly apposite, and so his assistance was inspired less by the demands of his office than it was by a belief that in so acting he accumulated merit for a future salvific moment when the goddess Guanyin would deliver him to the *jingtu* ("The Pure Land," for which the sect was named). The instinct of the Chinese, popular and elite, to see the Jesuits as Buddhist monks elicited their generosity, for in assisting these monks, they made spiritual gains.

There were as well unspecified others, "Chinese friends" as Ruggieri called them, who were moved to generosity on the fathers' behalf. Indeed without the financial assistance of these Chinese individuals, the mission's chapel would not have been built. Writing on January 25, 1584, to his superior, Ruggieri reveals that there had been difficulties in finishing construction at the mission compound, difficulties that were exacerbated by the refusal of Portuguese authorities in Macao to provide needed monies for the construction materials—more evidence of the troubled relations between the fathers and their Portuguese benefactors.[38] He goes on to say that the crisis was averted by the intervention of Chinese friends who donated one hundred silver dollars to defray the remaining expenses. What he doesn't say is that this subsidy was apparently used to complete the construction of the chapel, as the fathers' residence had been provided with the original grant of land.

This, of course, is a sizeable admission, conveying as it does the extent of native embrace of the Jesuits. Such local willingness to assist the missionaries in their enterprise, while greatly appreciated by Ruggieri, would have been anathema to Vatican authorities. This must have been evident to Ruggieri for though he acknowledged the Chinese contributions, he still insisted that they were used to complete the construction of the Jesuit residence. One gets the sense that Ruggieri did not wish to admit that unconverted Chinese had financed the construction of a dwelling place for the Christian God and that the Vatican was disinclined to admit any pagan responsibility in the making of the mission. Consequently, other significant details—that the Jesuits were, in effect, no longer Jesuits, but Buddhist monks and that unconverted natives had made possible the erection of God's dwelling place—were omitted in the epistolary accounts of the mission's founding or censored by church authorities prior to publication in the order's letterbooks. Conscious omission of this kind, while essential to the local success of the enterprise, would prove especially problematic later, as church authorities became aware of the difference between the reality of the missionaries' enculturation in China and its representation in Jesuit letters.

The fathers, accepted as Buddhists in China, remarked on certain obvious formal similarities between the two orders: an apparent trinitarian conception (i.e., the pledge of devotion to Buddha, *sangha*, and *dharma*); a notion of heaven and hell; temples and devotional statues; the *qinggui*, or "pure rules," governing monastic life; the practice of almsgiving; prayer and meditation; and vows of celibacy and poverty. Certainly the wide appeal of Buddhism in the late Ming provided a prescription for Jesuit success as an earlier religious culture that had migrated eastward into and across China. The course of Buddhism's adaptation had been so thorough, its practice so widespread, further-more, that it had come to seem—especially to the fathers—indigenous.[39]

In time, the Jesuits learned that it was not indigenous, and this fact proved significant, for in the decades after their official embrace of "*la legge de' letterati*" (*ru*) in 1595 the Jesuits did not tire of noting the essential foreign-ness of Buddhism. The fathers also later noted that the sect was not publicly appreciated by their well-placed Chinese benefactors; it was lacking in social status, and was viewed with contempt by many Chinese. Particularly in its popular Jingtu manifestations, they took Buddhism as corrupting China's archaic belief in the one God through a bewildering array of idols.[40] Near the close of book 1 of his *Storia*, Ricci seems astonished by the countless idols populating the Chinese landscape:

> One thing that is hard to believe is the multitude of idols that exist in this kingdom, not only in the temples, which are full of them, for in some of them several thousand have been set up, but also in private homes, where there are a great number, kept in a special place conse-crated to them. In the squares, streets, mountains, ships and public pal-aces, one sees nothing but such abominations.[41]

Beginning with the desultory description in Marco Polo's *Il Milione* ("The Million," later known as the *Travels*), idolatry was the most common charge made against Chinese religion, referring to practices as dissimilar as ancestor worship, geomancy, alchemy, and chanting the name of the Amitabha.[42] In the nearly three hundred years between Polo's putative last visit and the arrival of the Jesuits, the interpretive equipment of foreigners had become comparatively sophisticated; "idolatry" was no longer generically applied. For the Jesuits "idolatry," "idol worship," and "sect of the idols" were all terms strictly referring to Buddhism, with an occasional exceptional applica-tion to Daoism, all signaling heresy. It was more than heresy that disturbed Ricci, who denounced *Sciechia* (one of his terms for the Buddhists), abbots and acolytes alike, for their inability to abide by the monastic injunctions of sexual abstinence.[43]

The Jesuits may also have felt that Buddhism was not sufficiently "other." Buddhism, beginning with its monasticism, had much "in common with the Indo-European and Near Eastern sources of Catholicism."[44] Moreover, the space carved by Buddhism in the Chinese religious landscape was marked by claims of doctrinal purity and the necessary supersession of local practices, arguments very like those that the Jesuits used on behalf of Christianity. In a sense, by representing themselves as Buddhists the fathers were not suffi-ciently differentiated from other religious traditions including (perhaps more importantly) the Franciscans who were, at the same time, presenting themselves as *heshang* in their proselytizing work in the Chinese countryside. Thus, "the shift to representing missionary work as *ru* learning involves a many-layered differentiation from several not-quite-others (Buddhists, Franciscans) by identification with the group that historically does constitute a more convincing other."[45]

In the end, for the Jesuit missionaries in China the real sign of their cultural assimilation was their abandonment of the indigent trappings of the Buddhist cloister for the resplendent robes and headdress of the "literati."[46] After the spring of 1595, the Jesuits wore the apparel of *ru*, assumed the official, academic designation *xiucai* (licentiate), and even called themselves both *ru* and *daoren*, "men of the Way."[47] In doing so, they effectively transformed themselves again, from Buddhists into *ru*. To reason that the Jesuit embrace of *ru* culture is an example of accommodationism does not endorse their choice as "appropriate" but reflects a conclusion that the missionaries reached on native ground, a choice that has influenced centuries of subsequent scholarship. From this gradually acquired political perspective, the official *ru* tradition and the administrative vernacular at which they were becoming increasingly fluent provided the only real conduit to power for the Jesuits. Perhaps it was the legacy of Xavier as carried out by Valignano, but the Jesuits, particularly Matteo Ricci, knew that the mission could not succeed without the imprimatur of high-ranking dynastic officials, if possible the emperor (*huangdi*) himself.[48]

There were other troubles, too, which their superiors in Rome had learned of, though these problems were not specifically related to their becoming Buddhists—for example, a nocturnal raid on the Shaozhou mission in July 1592 by local youths that necessitated a desperate retreat from the compound, during which Ricci seriously injured a leg.[49]

Taken together, such difficulties might have been sufficient to recommend other kinds of strategies. But, above all, it seems that in Buddhism, the fathers found no "voice" or, rather, there was little fidelity in the Buddhist translation of Jesuit self-conception. With time and continued work in the Chinese language and on selected native texts, Ricci and his cohort were compellingly drawn toward a second accommodationist strategy, that of becoming scholar-officials. In this second incarnation as *ru*, the Jesuits seemed to find their voice.

Conversion to the Order of the Literati (*Ru*)

Invention is an enterprise of trial and error, as any history of great inventors or scientific discoveries demonstrates. In this sense of invention we can interpret the Jesuits' first native experiment as Buddhists, and in so doing we would not be unfaithful to Ricci's own perception of their Buddhist transfiguration, for he considered it a mistake.[50] As early as 1592 the missionaries were, by his account, already consciously distancing themselves from their incarnation as Buddhists in electing to travel by palanquin rather than, as they had in their first decade of residence, walk the streets. To his Jesuit superior in Rome, General Claudio Acquaviva (d. 1615), who may have questioned this modification of their public image, Ricci explains why such a change was necessary: "[We] have great need of this type of prestige in this region, and without it would make no progress among these gentiles: for the name of the foreigners and priests is considered so vile in China that we need this and other like inventions to demonstrate that we are not priests as vile as their own."[51] To the many Chinese who had taken them as *heshang*, the sight of these Buddhist-clad monks conveyed by sedan chair through the streets of Shaozhou must have been unaccountable, or worse, just more evidence of the inevitable corruption of monastic life.

The wording of Ricci's letter, one can only presume, would have vexed his superiors. He admits here that their efforts to convert the Chinese would be hindered by their identity as priests but facilitated by their public appearance as "men of rank," whose habit it is to be ferried by sedan chair. To become an official, or a "man of rank," was to abnegate one's role as priest and hope that such a presence would permit the Jesuits to show that they were not "priests as vile as their own." Yet this was no more than a gamble which, while the fathers waited for the outcome, acted to obscure rather than define Jesuit priestly identity.

Within three years of this letter, Ricci and his colleagues had completed the transformation and dressed in the style of what he termed, following an earlier Portuguese convention, the "*mandarinum*," remaining so attired until the mission ceased to function in 1773. Ricci's description of China's principal sects from the *Storia* (probably written in 1608), with its preference for *ru*, reiterated in script what the Jesuits now sought to understand in their imitation of native life: that the tradition of the "literatus," alone, "belongs to the Chinese."

Subsequent generations of accommodationists, beginning with Nicolá Trigault (1577–1628), consistently reaffirmed Ricci's definition of China's three principal religious teachings of *ru*, *dao*, and *fo*, stressing the undisputed antiquity, legitimacy, or propriety of the native *ru* tradition. Following Ricci, Trigault notes in this spirit, "Literatorum secta Sinarum est propria, & in hic regno antiquissima" (The sect of the literati is indigenous to the Chinese and in this kingdom is the most ancient).[52] Trigault's Latin uses the same reductionism that led Ricci and Ruggieri to equate Buddhist monasticism with Chineseness—only it is now the *ru* who are the genuine Chinese, and their intellectual devotion to a scriptural tradition, scholarly organization, and educational institutions are emphasized as reminiscent of those of the

Jesuits. What is explicit in these pleasing parallels are the mechanisms of meaningful projection that operate in any observer's overcoming of the strangeness of the other through the act of naming. At the interface of the European and the non-European, as Henri Baudet has observed, "the European's images of non-European man are not primarily, if at all, descriptions of real people, but rather projections of his own nostalgia and feeling of inadequacy. . . . They are judgments on himself and his history."[53]

In identifying *ru* as the principal religious order in China, the Jesuits, then, articulated their own best self-image, but in a context where the living cultural artifacts were Chinese. The essential "truth" of the Jesuits' reductionist representation was assuredly confirmed by what the prelates perceived as the formal identity of *ru* culture and Jesuit culture. The world Ricci and his brethren had left had been one in which academic degrees were conferred with religious ceremony and the university calendar was punctuated with Christian feast days and saintly observances, so the new world he beheld of Chinese imperial and academic regalia—the official cult to Kongzi and the Hanlin Academy—was a familiar fusion of the sacred and the secular.

Ruggieri, but to a much greater extent Ricci, found the superficial features of these *ru* reassuring, especially the nature and degree of their academic training—as well they should have, for they were, in a sense, enjoying the comforts of their own projections. Indeed, pointing to the ardent solidarity of scholar-officials, their collective literary accomplishment (evident in their successful completion of the metropolitan examination), and their disproportionate influence in matters cultural and political, Ricci described *ru* as a "legge," or law. This same term, *legge,* was used of the Society of Jesus, indicating that the early Jesuit missionaries understood *ru* by analogy with what they knew best, their own order. In the Latin summary of his catechism, *Tianzhu shiyi* (Real Significance of the Heavenly Master), Ricci refers to the Society of Jesus as "nostram Legem," or "our Order," and an identical reference, *nostri leggi,* is used throughout the *Storia.* Given, too, that the language to which they devoted themselves was *mandarino* (the language of *ru* scholar officials), the conceptual links between the Jesuits and the Chinese were fated to be forged along *ru* official lines. Ricci, Ruggieri, and the director of the East Indies missions, Valignano, read the surface similarities of *ru* and the Jesuit order as formal evidence of substantive likeness and presumed that *ru* doctrine had shaped, as did Christianity in Europe, the language, laws, customs, and literature of the empire.

Given that Jesuit life in China was increasingly circumscribed after 1592, remaining entirely within the culture of scholar-officials, all of them men bearing the official title of *ru,* one would expect that the features of this culture colored every perception. As a result, the presumption of identity with *ru* could hardly have seemed fortuitous to Ricci and his cohort who, in his estimation, "lived in amicable intercourse with the nobles, the supreme magistrates, and the most distinguished men of letters in the kingdom."[54] The Jesuits—who, by their own admission, spoke "the native language [i.e., guanhua] of the country," set themselves "to the study of their [Chinese] rites and customs," and devoted themselves "day and night to the study of their books"[55]—found in ru a term whose apparent ubiquity was evidence of a single thread binding the fabric of Chinese culture, a thread that also bound the fathers and ru.

More than this, through their insistence that the country had, in essence, but one language, the fathers were engaged in the production of a singular China. Although this invention was at odds with the reality around them, it was representative of the new reality they formed in conscious alliance with the native society on which they now depended, ru,[56] and symbolized the Jesuits' elevation from the quotidian of multiple dialects the mastering of which would have been essential to their success as local Buddhist priests:

> Even in the various provinces of China the spoken language differs so widely that their speech has little in common. . . . Besides the various dialects of the different provinces, the province vernacular so to speak, there is also a spoken language common to the whole empire, known as cuonhua [guanhua], an official language for civil and forensic use. This national language probably resulted from the fact that all the magistrates, as we shall explain later on, are strangers to the provinces which they govern, and to avoid the necessity of obliging them to learn the dialects of the provinces, a common speech was introduced for transacting government business.[57]

In this particular instance, Ricci articulates the view of a late Ming official and assumes a uniform culturalist definition of Chineseness characteristic of a growing number of Chinese elites in the early seventeenth century. And while such a singular image was critical to the missionaries' maintenance of ecclesiastical support, it proved even more important later to the lay and clerical devotees of the Clavis Sinica,[58] and ultimately to the practitioners of modern sinology. But here, on Chinese ground, for the Jesuits to articulate such an official definition of Chineseness was to admit membership, or the aspiration of membership, in a community narrowly defined by a culture that excluded Buddhist monasticism and whose sumptuary recognition was conferred in their assumption of the title xiucai (cultivated talent).

For the Chinese cultural conservatives drawn to the Donglin Shuyuan, (Eastern Forest Academy), with which the Jesuits had a tenuous connection through several of their converts, Buddhism's foreignness was perceived as an infection, one weakening the original vitality of Chinese culture. The militant restorationism of the Jesuits is reminiscent of the fundamentalist critique of political institutions put forward by Gu Xiancheng (1550–1612) of the Donglin Shuyuan. A scholarly controversy has arisen as to whether their anti-Buddhist sentiment stemmed from Jesuit alignment with the Donglin or was reached somewhat independently. Those who explain it as the result of direct intellectual ties between the two groups, including Father Henri Bernard, point to a remark found in Daniello Bartoli's history of the Jesuits written in 1663. "There had been founded in Vusuie [Wuxi] . . . a famous academy of Literati, who used to gather to discourse either on the moral virtues, or on the means most appropriate and useful for the government of the people. . . . Our doctors Leo [Li], Paul [Xu] and Michael [Yang] [the celebrated converts Li Zhizao (d. 1630), Xu Guangqi (1562–1633), and Yang Tingyun (1557–1627)] presided at some of them. The Fathers approved of the institute because of the great profit which the faith drew from it."[59]

The greater weight of the evidence does not corroborate Bartoli's claim. Instead it suggests that the Jesuits' anti-Buddhist sentiments were not the result of Donglin partisanship so much as the fathers' own appropriation of an indigenous revulsion against Buddhism, first evident in the nativism of the Southern Song period (1127–1279 C.E.). In this act of appropriation they made explicit the self-constituting status of their native textual community and the growing influence on them of a *ru* restorationist ideal.

Their awareness of native *ru* preeminence grew more keen the longer the mission operated in China, for the fathers' influential Chinese associates, we are told, found the Buddhist guise to be unacceptable. The conscious courting of favor with the powerful as opposed to the weak is unmistakable in Ricci's recollection (taken from the *Storia*) of Chinese response to their second incarnation as *ru:*

> Our friends were very pleased with us, seeing that they could use many more signs of respect to us than they used to their bonzes. Although from the first we were regarded very differently from the ministers of the idols, in view of the great difference in virtue between them and the fathers, nevertheless the ordinary people made little distinction between us and the bonzes.[60]

Access to political authority was indispensable to Jesuit success in a preceptoral system such as that of late imperial China. As the political mechanisms of the preceptor, the emperor, were in the hands of scholar-officials, it made little sense to pursue the approbation of "the ordinary people."

The status conferred upon the Jesuits by imperial approval greatly enhanced their contacts among scholar-officials and, therefore, increased the likelihood of conversions of those among whom Father Visitor Valignano felt the Jesuits should circulate. Further, since Ricci and his followers were drastically reinterpreting classic works in a manner hospitable to Christianity—work that was begun during their enculturation apprenticeship, as it were, as Buddhist monks—the social consequences of such reworking were significant. In the end, only the emperor could galvanize the political forces necessary to construct an alternative context within which the classics could mean what the Jesuits said they did. This dependence on Chinese officialdom, along with the desire to convey their teaching to the preceptor, became increasingly explicit in the seventeenth century and, as I explain in chapter 2, reflected a parallel relation at home between the Jesuits and European monarchies.

In these ways and for these many reasons, the fathers became *ru*. To Ricci, who must have encountered the term everywhere he turned in books and travels, *ru* would have appeared multifaceted. To the Chinese as well as Chinese-speaking foreigners of sixteenth-century China, the term *ru* designated at least descent from Kongzi. It was, however, used to represent a great deal more, being a strikingly polysemous symbol referring to any or all of the following: (1) the imperial cult and the diverse rituals of legitimacy, such as the *feng* and *shan* sacrifices; (2) examination candidates; (3) members of *shuyuan* (private academies); (4) scholar-officials (metropolitan, provincial, and local); (5) self-conscious local sodalities of scholarship, meditation, and worship, such as the *jingshe* (lodge of wondrous remembrance); (6) gentry—unsuccessful examination candidates, landholders, merchants—whose conscious pursuit of civility was marked by the term; (7) the practice of ancestor worship and the privileging of "central place" as such rites reproduced traditional hierarchy; (8) the orthodoxy of the Hanlin Academy and the official doctrines of the state; and (9) "the State Family Romance."[61] These referents might be better visualized as a stratigraphy in which certain layers of significance were closer to the surface and more accessible to the observer. Thus, even for the indigenous observer, not all meanings would have been available at any one time, constrained as they were by contemporary currency. In the late Ming period *ru* might elicit immediate associations with 2–4, 6, and 8. Given the common Jesuit rendering of "litteratorum secta" for *ru*, it appears that the fathers appropriated a favored native definition.

However, rather than take its many meanings as specific to certain practices of an earlier age, Ricci and his fellow Jesuits in effect, and perhaps not by intention, simply reduced all the significances of *ru* to a single symbol, in the same way they resolved the multiple vectors of Chinese vernacular into the single language of *guanhua*. Instead of seeing a history of plural episodes, the Jesuits took *ru* tropologically, as a metonym. Therefore, even if the various meanings of the term were known to them, they would have been read in the manner in which they understood the presence of God: as diverse manifestations of a single substance. In this fashion a new theology appropriate to this singular missionary community—not Buddhist, but "Confucian" and Christian—emerged.

Theology: The Sino-Jesuit Textual Community

In its second sense, accommodationism can be understood theologically as an effort to make explicit the common religious ground the Jesuits presumed they shared with the native Chinese. This common ground was what Ruggieri, who was more inclined toward Christian-Buddhist than Christian-Confucian accommodation, called the "prophetic intimations of the Christian religion."[62] This shared religious foundation was also the place where the Jesuits constructed a textual community eclectically bred of Jesuit Christianity and Chinese religious practice and so unique that it could only be called a cult (something that will become especially evident in the subsequent chapter).

Brian Stock uses the term "textual community" to describe societies of heretics and reformers in eleventh-century Europe. Such societies "demonstrated a parallel use of texts, both to structure the internal behaviors of the group's members and to provide solidarity against the outside world."[63] I use the term to describe microsocieties organized around, and justified by, a specific text or texts, whose members share a common understanding or agreement about the broad significance of the text: to organize or discipline group conduct, thus creating solidarity; to provide scope and dimension for the living of an individual life; to adjudicate rival claims to truth; and to establish a basis for the reform of contemporary practice or belief. One impulse for the formation of textual communities is the religious one, and such groups often resemble what is familiar to us as cults. The organization of individuals into such a textual community is usually the consequence of some perception or experience of a larger incongruity such as that caused by sudden social dislocation or willful abnegation of the conventional practices of society.

The emergence of such textual communities is common to an age in which archaic ritualism is eclipsed. Ancient rites can no longer be preserved simply in unmediated performance; hence, appeals to ancient precedent to authorize contemporary practice can only be advanced through a complex process of refraction through texts. In other words, to make a claim of legitimate descent from the exemplar of a particular tradition requires citation of text instead of performance. Indeed citation of text *is* performance, and as these communities employ texts to reproduce lives on the example of an inspired predecessor, texts become persons. The essential marginality of these groups causes them to be especially cohesive. Their cohesion is nurtured through the use of texts as scripts, the truth and effectiveness of which are often displayed in the life of an exemplary figure. Finally, textual communities are not only recipients of texts but also producers of them. The communal life of such groups is underwritten by engagement in a continuous normative exegesis that is necessary to defend their claims and that serves to historicize the community.

The Jesuits, in their cultural accommodation to Chineseness, conform particularly well to this model of a textual community. They produced a hybrid theology that moved them to identify themselves as a Chinese religious enclave. The monotheistic teachings of "Confucius" were predicated as a preexistent, "true" message which it was the Jesuit mission to recover. God's ubiquity was not in question, only the particular evidence of his presence among the Chinese. And all evidence pointed to his presence among the *ru*, or rather, as we shall see later, the genuine *ru*, Ricci's "i veri letterati" (the true literati).

As the fathers explored the conceptual parallels in Jesuit and *ru* discourse, they presumed the compatibility of the natural theology of the Chinese construed as "il lume naturale" and their own revealed theology, believing that the presence of divine light among the Chinese prefigured a subsequent embrace of Christianity. Any differences perceived by the Jesuits were simply the differential effects of a single divine light.

Recovering the homologies between Chinese beliefs and their own meant for the Jesuits that they would again preach among the Chinese, this time in alliance with the men of God they believed the "order of the literati" to be. However, such "preaching" would be written rather than spoken, given the fathers' oft-noted struggles with pronunciation, and so would resemble the *ars rhetorica* of their training at the College of Rome. Having constructed a Chinese identity as *ru* by reading their books and wearing their clothes, Ricci and his fellow missionaries began to sermonize a Christianized *ru* doctrine advocating the resurrection of the true teaching of Kongzi, in the contemporary spirit of restorationism. And this they did with a vengeance, it would seem, denouncing China's other sects with a convert's zeal. Even the structural similarities identified in Buddhism—like its trinitarian conception— that had been so critical to the Jesuits' first effort to become Chinese were now perceived as the work of Lucifer.

From Ricci's analysis of the two other major Chinese sects—an analysis based on the conventional condemnation of Islam's false trinity—we learn something of the passion of the fathers' commitment to their "legge de' letterati." Speaking of the Buddhists and Daoists, he says: "Both of these sects feign their trinity, in order to show clearly that the father of all falsehoods, who is the author of all this, has not forsaken the superb pretension of wishing to be the same as his Creator."[64] Here, on the common ground of "the order of the literati," the scions of the house of Confucius and the Society of Jesus met. Here, too, at least conceptually if not politically, their missionizing strategy would come to fruition.

There was yet another dimension of theological compatibility, intracultural rather than cross-cultural. Ricci's brand of apologetics was the mirror image of an early patristic tradition, that of the saints who had worked among the pagans at the time of the early church, a reductionist approach with its invention of formal and essential likenesses. Ambrose, the bishop of Milan (d. 397 C.E.), had similarly lent the imprimatur of his office to the popular but heterodox celebrations at the graves of martyrs that became the cult of the saints. The result of the bishop's indulgence was that in time the cult was reorchestrated with Ambrose as the celebrant. Thus the church appropriated pagan practice and practitioners.[65]

This approach, as set out in Paul's sermon to the Athenians, was to engage the natural religion of the pagan with the gospel. Apologetics—like the mission's first catechism, *Tianzhu shilu* (Veritable Record of the Heavenly Master), and the second catechism authored by Ricci, *Tianzhu shiyi* (The Real Significance of the Heavenly Master)—were drafted to reconcile natural theology and revealed theology on the ground of what John Henry Newman later called "the divinity of Traditionary Religion."[66] Ricci's emphasis on the proto-Christian natural theology of the Chinese as represented in "Confucius" and "la legge de' letterati" was fully consistent with this venerable missionary practice. While it is difficult to judge his success in terms of converts, there is little doubt that this approach gained him a wider audience.

Through their translation of *ru* texts, just like the translation of themselves into Buddhist costume earlier, the fathers believed they discovered lines of filiation in native belief. "During these last years," Ricci reflects, "I have interpreted with the aid of good teachers not only the Four Books (*Sishu*) but also the Six Classics (*Liujing*), and I have noted many passages in them which favor the teachings of our faith, such as the unity of God, the immortality of the soul, the glory of the blessed, etc."[67] Theological complementarity was borne out by the hallowed texts of the Chinese.

Alessandro Valignano's urging that the fathers align themselves with China's "homes letrados" was founded not so much on a premise of theological compatibility as it was on the assumption that *ru* were men of respected social status and lettered influence. But, these *ru*, along with other Jesuit missionaries and Catholic converts, could not help but be swayed by Ricci's insistence that *ru* was the original teaching of Confucius, the cultural backbone of Chinese civilization, and the "key"[68] to the ancient vault of Chinese monotheism. And Matteo Ricci demonstrated this belief through one of Confucius's own texts, *Lunyu*:

The fundamental duty of spirits is to execute the will of the Heavenly Master: to supervise the transformations. They do not possess absolute power over the world, thus Zhongni said, "By respecting spirits, the lordling [junzi] keeps them at a distance." With reference to happiness, prosperity, and the forgiveness of sin, the ability to grant them lies not with spirits, but with the Heavenly Master.[69]

The belief in theological similarity, of which the Jesuits thought there was empirical evidence, would remain unassailable in most missionary circles for over a century, furnishing critical justification for their enterprise and especially their native literary activity.

Accommodation was made possible by, but also eventuated in, a fervent belief in the ineluctable presence of God. To believe, as the Jesuits did, that all cultures were moments of God's presence, enabled them to deduce Chinese belief in God, in a Tianzhu (Heavenly Master). Thoroughly tautological, belief in the reducibility of all difference to monotheistic identity was both the inception and the culmination of accommodationism.

Ricci's Chinese catechism, the *Tianzhu shiyi*, is a textual portrait of this inspired tautology, for it is in this work that he tried to establish a logical ground for the Jesuits' unitary theistic conception. Having secured such ground the fathers would inculcate the fundaments of Christian doctrine—original sin, Christ as savior, the Ten Commandments, papal infallibility, the immortality of the soul, and so on. The underlying reductive apprehension of single cause with multiple effects is nowhere more apparent than in the hortatory exchanges between the *xishi* (Western scholar) and the *zhongshi* (Chinese, or ethnic, scholar) that make up the text. In this excerpt from the dialogues, the Western scholar effortlessly resolves the world's manifold difference into a theistic unity, saying:

> The individual originations of things are assuredly dissimilar, but the Lord who is the universal source of things is without second. Why? The reason is that the Lord who is the universal source of things is He from whom the many things come forth, who provides the virtuous natures of the many things, and whose superlative virtue cannot be superseded.[70]

The ontological presumption here was, in Ricci's day, an unquestionable datum of faith corroborated by science; however, the real issue for him as a missionary among the Chinese was whether these untutored but potential Christians indicate any awareness that the Christian God was the *primum mobile*. From Ricci's perspective this was hardly an issue, though, for no less a figure than "Confutius" himself displayed just such an awareness in his acknowledgment of *shangdi*.

Ricci felt certain he would find evidence of Chinese belief in the one God, if we give any credence to the few confessional remarks found in his introduction to the catechism. He presumed, or rather imagined, the existence of a Chinese natural theology even before he had left Lisbon for Goa in 1578. He confesses that:

> I, Dou [Matteo], left my village as a young man and roamed the world, [only] to find that ideas which poison men's minds reached to every corner. I thought that the Chinese, as they were the people of Yao and Shun and the followers of the Duke of Zhou [Zhou Gong] and Zhongni [Kongzi], certainly could not deviate from the Heavenly principles and the Heavenly doctrines and become infected [with poisonous ideas].[71]

Ricci's mission in China was necessary to uncover the "real significance of the Heavenly Master" concealed in the ancient culture of the Chinese. Whether artful or ingenuous, as a narrative device, the testimony placed Matteo Ricci, the interloper, squarely within the mythic history of Chinese antiquity out of which Chinese cultural identity was formed, wherein the institutions of the imperium were shaped by the loving hands of sage-king exemplars and passed down to the Duke of Zhou and to Kongzi.

Father Ricci's hypostasis of a single, eternal Chinese doctrine virtually identical to the Christian is startling because it is made in Chinese. It is not offered to shame a European audience for its misplaced cultural arrogance, as were the panegyric accounts of Chinese statecraft from the likes of Voltaire in subsequent decades.[72] Rather, it would appear that Ricci believed he could chastise the Chinese by an appeal to their apotheosized heritage. Whether his suggestion that China once possessed an unalloyed Christian belief was a rhetorical exercise or he genuinely believed the Chinese to be unique among the world's peoples in their pure preservation of "the Heavenly principles and the Heavenly doctrines," what is significant in his testimony is that China provided a spiritual answer for Ricci. Either as the last refuge of unsullied belief in the omnipotence of Heaven, whose existence would confirm his own faith, or as a former dwelling place of the truth that had been obscured by time and heresy, China—as Ricci saw it—was in need of his personal intervention.[73] The clever manner in which Ricci conveys salvation as implicit in Chinese culture distinguished him from so many of his colleagues and explains the accomplishments of accommodationism.

The Jesuits' belief in China's theological compatibility with Christianity was, therefore, structured tropologically, in a manner invisible to them, like a preapprehension guiding their organization of experience, whether in Europe or in China, and undergirding the literary construction of a unique, hybrid canon. Most importantly, in the effort to demonstrate this theological compatibility by proof, men like Ricci remade the canon of the "Sacred Faith" in the image of their new native embodiment.

Constructing a Sino-Jesuit Canon

Although I have distinguished them for the purposes of exposition, the theological and the literary dimensions of accommodationism were mutually reinforcing and complementary in the same way that Scripture and apostolic tradition are in Christianity, in that one learned the creed from the reiterative reproduction of traditional practice while appealing to the sovereignty of Scripture to justify the creed.[74] The third sense of accommodationism, its literary sense, refers to the Jesuit practice of canon formation, in which Chinese texts were selected and organized into a system of relations with other (Western) texts dear to the critics.

This canon, a heterogenous assemblage of Western and Chinese inspirational texts, was the scriptural complement to the apostolic tradition of Jesuit accommodationism. Here my use of "apostle" to describe Jesuit accommodationists is not just metaphor. Father Philippe Couplet (1622–1693) refers to the Jesuits who preceded him in the Mission of the Indies and to those who assisted him in the preparation of the *Confucius Sinarum Philosophus* as *apostolum gentium*.[75] The favored Chinese texts were *Lunyu, Zhongyong, Daxue,* and *Mengzi*—in other words, the Four Books. These were the first works the missionaries translated and, although they were cursorily familiar with the Five Classics (*wujing*), the Four Books remained the center of their curriculum. The *Zhongyong* (Doctrine of the Mean) and the *Daxue* (Great Learning) were found to be particularly inspiring: as many as six partial and complete translations of them were produced by the missionaries between 1588 and 1687. However, the Jesuit fathers read and organized the texts in a manner peculiar to them and clearly inconsistent with the canonical tradition of their study passed down from the texts' original compiler, Zhu Xi. Instead of reading the Four Books according to Zhu's prescription, "take the *Daxue* to begin, followed by the *Lunyu,* the *Mengzi,* [and] the *Zhongyong,*"[76] Ricci and his fellow padres read the *Lunyu* first, then the *Daxue,* followed by the *Zhongyong* and the *Mengzi.*

Not unlike twentieth-century Chinese intellectual historians and philosophers in the West, the Jesuits were spiritually aroused by the mystical vision of sociocosmic harmony found in the *Daxue* and the *Zhongyong.* Accorded the same esteem as other "ethnic" texts such as the works of Plato, Aristotle, Euclid, Epictetus, Lucretius, and Ptolemy, the Four Books took their place alongside cherished works like the Bible, the New Testament, St. Augustine's *City of God,* St. Thomas Aquinas's *Summa Theologica,* and St. Ignatius of Loyola's *Spiritual Exercises,* in forming something approaching a hybrid canon of revealed literature.[77]

Under Ricci's aegis and with the assistance of Xu Guangqi and Li Zhizao among others, the Jesuits made a number of the Western texts dear to them available to the Chinese. The *Jiaoyou lun* (Treatise on Friendship) of 1595, perhaps Matteo Ricci's best-loved work, was a translation of a heterogenous collection of sayings on friendship from numerous authors that he had committed to memory. Ten years later the *Ershiwuyan* (Twenty-five Sayings) introduced the Chinese to Epictetus in the form of a chrestomathy of his works. Shortly after, Epictetus's wisdom was followed by a Chinese rendering of Planudes' work on Aesop under the title *Qiren shipian* (Ten Discourses of a Strange Man). Lastly, the *Jihe yuanben* (The Elements of Euclid) was Ricci and Xu Guangqi's translation of Clavius's recension of Euclid's *Elements.*

Through translation of their cherished texts, it would appear that "Jesuit missionaries accommodated Western learning to the Chinese cultural scene,"[78] as David Mungello has observed. It may be more appropriate in light of this missionary canon to reverse Mungello's characterization and say that the Jesuits accommodated Chinese learning to the Western cultural scene. But the accommodative urges that gave rise to canon formation deserve even more subtle judgment, for the fathers did more than this. They made the texts of one Chinese scriptural tradition known in the West in terms their interested audience could understand, and in the process produced a distinctively eclectic canon. This, then, was the foundation of their cultural hybridity, textual evidence of the unique self-constitution of the Jesuits on new native ground.

Rather than "accommodating" Western learning to Chinese culture, the Jesuits manufactured a new mode of discourse that bestowed privileged status upon certain Chinese texts. Passages from Chinese works were indexed to passages from any of those texts formative of Jesuit understanding, as in Ricci's gloss on *ren* (humaneness) from a passage in the commentaries on the *Yijing:* "The meaning of *ren* can be summed up completely in the following two sentences: Love the Heavenly Master as there are none above Him; for [the sake of] the Heavenly Master, love others as you love yourself."[79] Excerpts from Chinese and Western texts pass through the sieve of a preformed Jesuit intellection. In this instance Matthew 22:34–40, Mark 12:28–34, and Luke 10:25–28 are used to gloss the most important of Chinese virtues.

Such indexing was certainly not the cynical casuistry that Jacques Gernet contends it was. The fathers were aligning their native scripture with that of the Chinese; there could be no greater symbol of respect. The hermeneutics here reveals more than the Jesuit presumption of theological compatibility with which we have become familiar. Indeed, the first translations of Chinese texts published in Europe in the seventeenth century indicate that the fathers' native language and their acquired tongue blended together, reflecting in script what was true in thought (a point discussed in greater detail in chapter 2).

To the Jesuits, all men were born of God and endowed with a soul, so they possessed a congenital awareness of him that was nurtured through prayer, worship, and the prosecution of an ethical life. The "Confucius" who authored the *Lunyu*, the *Zhongyong*, the "Xici zhuan" (Commentary) of the *Yijing*, the *Chunqiu*, and the *Daxue*[80] displayed just such an understanding of God and of the significance of decorum and pious worship in the broad, social cultivation of that understanding. In the staged theological debates of the *Tianzhu shiyi*, Kongzi is appreciatively cited for his obvious monotheism. The "Western scholar" states: "Our Heavenly Master is precisely what is called *shangdi* [Sovereign on High] in Chinese. . . . Our Heavenly Master is the *shangdi* mentioned in the ancient classic works. Citing Kongzi, the *Doctrine of the Mean* says: 'The rites of the [seasonal] sacrifices to heaven and earth are performed to the Sovereign on High.' "[81] In successive excerpts from the Chinese classical canon, the clever citation of which demonstrates the foreigner's extraordinary command of Chinese language and literature, the Western scholar illustrates the archaic theism contained in China's sacred books and preserved by the stewards of the canon, the *ru*. We will see below that Ricci lacked confidence in the ability of contemporary *ru* to steward the canon, and so he devoted himself to this very task, fortified in his presumption that he was doing the Lord's work.

It is necessary to note here something that was not mentioned in my earlier review of the missionaries' second Chinese incarnation as *ru*. There was a distinct, perhaps conscious, parallel between the chronology of their *ru* conversion and Ricci's study of the Chinese classics. Textual work paralleled the major episodes in Jesuit accommodation. The communal life of the Jesuits under Ricci's tutelage was characterized by engagement of the priests in the study and exegesis of Chinese classical texts, in particular the *Sishu*, since it was regarded by the Jesuits as a record of the scripture of Confucius, even while they were dressed in Buddhist garb. We can ascertain the *Sishu*'s status as canon in the history of the text beginning with Ricci's first use of it in 1592 as a text for language instruction. Between 1591 and 1594 Ricci was working on an annotated translation of the Four Books into Latin and during this interval began to instruct newcomers to the mission in Chinese through the text.[82]

The approach was very sound because the Chinese commentaries (whether those of Zhu Xi or of Zhang Juzheng [1525–1582]) were in an accessible vernacular and so the fathers were instructed in both literary and colloquial Chinese. Yet such instruction amounted to more than just inculcating the rudiments of Chinese, because the fathers were reading these texts for evidence of visible manifestations of God.[83] They were engaged in an endeavor to recover a lost truth; their textual labors were a hermeneutics of belief.

Something of this intimate relation of community and texts is evident in Ricci's correspondence, for it underscores that as he deepened his commitment to the study of the Chinese classics, he abandoned his Buddhist identity. In the fall of 1592 he informed General Acquaviva that the missionaries were now distinguishing themselves from the *bonzes*. From this time through October 1596, when the first draft of the *Tianzhu shiyi* was completed, and indeed until the end of the next century, the Jesuits devoted themselves solely to exegesis and translation of the Four Books. In 1595 Ricci took up the study of the classics, informing Acquaviva in another letter, of November 4, "I have noted down many terms and phrases in harmony with our faith," here speaking of specific places in the *Shi jing, Shang shu, Yijing,* and *Li ji* where he had found evidence of a primordial monotheism.

These passages were then used in the production of a new text, the *Tianzhu shiyi,* which was to be taken as a contribution in the tradition of Chinese classical commentary, not only as a catechism. In the second chapter, "An Explanation of the Erroneous Views of the Heavenly Master among Today's People," the Western scholar, Ricci's *doppelgänger,* comments:

> In the [Record of] *Rites* it is said: "When all these points are as they ought to be, the Sovereign on High will accept the sacrifice," and continues: "The Son of Heaven himself ploughs the ground for the rice with which to fill the vessels, and the black millet from which to distill the spirit to be mixed with fragrant herbs, and for services of the Sovereign on High." The Oath of Tang says, "The sovereign of Xia is an offender, and as I fear the Sovereign on High, I dare not but punish him." And it says: "The great Sovereign on High has conferred even on the inferior people a moral sense, compliance with which would show their nature invariably right. But to cause them tranquilly to pursue the course which it would indicate, is the work of the sovereign." In the "Metal-Bound Coffer" [Chapter of the *Shang Shu*] the Duke of Zhou says: "And moreover he was appointed in the hall of the Sovereign to extend his aid to the four quarters of the empire." . . . Having examined the ancient books, therefore I know that Sovereign on High and Heavenly Master are only different in name.[84]

By the time Ricci had run off this serial citation of ancient Chinese evidence of the Heavenly Master, he had been converted to the order of the literati, styling himself a defender of its canon. Through the formation of this canon and its personal transmission to successive generations of Jesuit missionaries, a textual community was organized that would endure for nearly a century following Ricci's death. The exegetical principles of the canon were spelled out in the Jesuits' presumption of the implicit theism of "il lume naturale," the natural light of divine reason to which all phenomena could be reduced.

Invisible to the Jesuits, this presumption, or rather preapprehension, is visible to us in the "fiction effect" of those texts produced by them to represent their accommodative other. The manner of their invention is clear because from our vantage there was no such religious similarity linking *ru* doctrine and the fathers' own Christianity. What is also visible to us, and was probably felt by the fathers, are the lines of interpretive difference that run like veins through their self-constituted intellectual/spiritual community reflecting the growing tension between the local necessity to accommodate and the ever-insistent demand of the Vatican for the demonstrable sovereignty of the Christian word abroad. The tension was most evident in missionary equivocation concerning the religious character of the "order of the literati" and their worship of Confucius; their representation of China was contested, but in many ways it was their vision that has endured to underlie Western scholarship on China.

Politics and Polyphony in Accommodationist Representation

In all the emphasis on Jesuit-Chinese similitude, differences inevitably appeared, not so much between the representation and the reality, but between the Jesuit interpretations from which the representation of theological similarity was drawn. Interpretive difference was most salient when the Jesuits undertook descriptions of native religious behavior or attempted to evaluate the religious character of the three principal traditions, particularly that of their favored *legge de' letterati*.

For instance, near the beginning of the first book of *De Christiana expeditione apud Sinas* (Of the Christian Expedition among the Chinese),[85] Father Nicolá Trigault's Latin rendering of Ricci's *Storia* published in 1615, we read a declaration, common among the early fathers in its encomium for "Confutius," but curious for what it does not say:

> The most learned of all Chinese philosophers was named Confutius. This great and learned man was born five hundred and fifty-one years before the beginning of the Christian era, lived more than seventy years, and spurred on his people to the pursuit of virtue not less by his own example than by his writings and conferences. . . . Even the rulers, during the past ages, have paid him the highest homage due to a mortal. He was never venerated with religious rites, however, as they venerate a

god. They gratefully acknowledge their indebtedness to him for the doctrines bequeathed to them, and even today, after so long a lapse of time, his descendants are held in the highest esteem by all.[86]

The effect of this reading is an equation of "Confutius" and "Chineseness" that was increasingly common to Jesuit interpretation the longer their stay among the Chinese, as well as critical to the conceptual foundation of chinoiserie in both its English and French incarnations. The reducibility of China to "Confutius" and his "law of the literati" implied here is made explicit later in the fifth chapter when Ricci, the narrator, and Trigault, the translator, say, "The sect of the literati belongs to the Chinese and in this kingdom is the most ancient . . . This sect governs the republic, abounds in books, and is renowned above all others."[87] We might consider, as we did above, whether such colossal reduction was purely a Jesuit fiction, or an appropriate representation of what they beheld but could not know was a preexistent Chinese fiction.

Why shouldn't Ricci, in other words, have conceived of "Confutius" as a controlling metaphor of Chinese culture? There was much to support such a view: there was an imperial cult dedicated to Kongzi and an imperial academy training and placing titular followers of his tradition, and "he" had authored almost all of China's classics. For the Chinese, Kongzi was already so exalted as an imperial icon, and the pervasive presence of his doctrine among the literati conditioned the Jesuits to take the tradition attributed to him on analogy with their own sacred faith, which was the spiritual backbone of European institutions.

But in this account of the rites to "Confutius," the early missionary practice of exalting natural theology as the seed of the true religion is explicit. Observation and imagination are delicately interwoven in this account; however, the accuracy displayed in some of Ricci's observations does not make the account any less fictive. His words do convey a rough, empirical familiarity with many observable items of contemporary Chinese culture: Sima Qian's chronology in his essay "Kongzi shijia" from the *Shiji*, the imperial ceremonies held annually in honor of Kongzi, the popular genealogical fiction of Kongzi as patriarch, the popular cults honoring him, and the rites of local worship critical to the choreography of daily life in private academies (*shuyuan*).[88] Still, in spite of the trenchant character of his observations and the breadth of his reading, Ricci emphatically denied the religious aspect of the ceremonies in honor of Kongzi. His perception, it would seem, was less accurate than his reading, given his insistence on the secular character of the state cult. A less charitable interpretation, like that favored by such recent scholars as Gernet, claims that Ricci created a deliberate inaccuracy, because it was useful for his purposes.[89]

The oversight did not prevent Ricci from articulating a metonymic conception of "Confutius" in which his "Chinese philosopher" and the latter's following represented China. Ricci says as much in his discussion of China's principal sects, forcefully conflating ethos, empire, and sect in his assertion that "this sect [the sect of the literati] rules the republic,"[90] and "all the territory [of China] is governed by the literati."[91] Through figurative reduction Ricci forged a union between the visible (the ineluctable symbolism of the state, the bureaucracy, and the religious sects) and the invisible (the dead "Confutius"), establishing the reality of "Confutius" as the exclusive symbol of China's archaic natural religion, in the visible manifestations of China.

In this clever part/whole relationship, then, the order of the literati (ru), the Chinese state, and the emperor were seen as effects of "Confutius," virtual equivalents that permitted one to represent the other. The symbolic integrity of this reduction was inviolable so long as one shared the tropic predisposition to metonymy.[92] And it was this strategy supplemented by ecclesiastical order that internally reinforced the Jesuit interpretation in spite of its contradictions while transforming the Chinese reality it authoritatively represented, as in the account of Confutius's secular veneration above.

The Jesuits' unwillingness to identify the religious aspects of the state cult was the result of both political and tropological considerations. It is not difficult to understand why the fathers might have read heathen practices out of the state cult, for then their involvement with the cult would amount to apostasy and subject them to censure at the hands of Inquisition authorities. To admit that Confutius was worshiped as a god or even an ancestor was to brand the Chinese, despite the quality of their civilization, pagan. Prominent features of the everyday in China, such as ancestor worship, ritual sacrifice, mortuary rites, geomancy, and numerology, simply could not, from the perspective of church authorities, be accommodated within accommodationism, and so a transformation of the text of Chinese life was assimilated to the inventive equivalence of "Confutius" and "Cina." This modification did not occur at the point of Ricci's apprehension, however. Instead, it was introduced posthumously as a supplement to the original narrative, as the space narrowed between the marginal Chinese missionary community and papal authority.

Comparison of Trigault's Latin translation with Ricci's original Italian manuscript shows that an emphasis on the secular character of the imperial and regional cults was added by Trigault in the translation (see figure 5). In contrast with Trigault's rendering, Ricci's original is explicit in its account of both the animal sacrifice and the incense burning that mark celebratory worship of Confucius (whom he calls "Confutio") "in every city and academy at which the literati congregate":

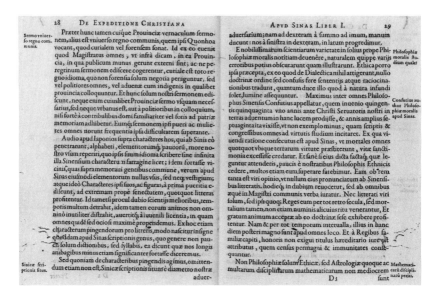

Figure 5. Pages 28–29 of Nicolá Trigault and Matteo Ricci's *De Christiana expeditione apud Sinas*. This Latin translation of 1615, published in Augsburg at the request of the Vatican, was the first version of Matteo Ricci's history of the mission's founding in China. This passage introduces "Confutius," but the translation omits a section of Ricci's original Italian manuscript (see figure 6) where the religious significance of Kongzi and his cult are noted. (Photograph courtesy of the Bancroft Library, University of California, Berkeley)

Oltra di ciò, in ogni città e scuola, dove si congregano i letterati, per lege antica vi è il tempio del Confutio molto sumptuoso, dove sta la sua statua e il suo nome et titulo; et tutti i novilunij et plenilunij e quattro tempi dell'anno i letterati gli fanno una certa sorte di sacrificio con profumi et animali morti che gli offeriscono, sebene non riconoscono in lui nessuna divinità, nè gli chiedono niente. E così non si può chiamare vero sacrificio.

[Besides this, in every city and academy where the literati congregate, in accord with ancient law, there is a most sumptuous temple to Confutio, where one finds his statue, his name and title; and at every new moon and full moon (as well as) four times a year the literati perform a certain kind of sacrifice with incense, in which dead animals are offered to him, even though they do not recognize in him any divinity, nor do they ask him for anything. Thus, it cannot be called a true sacrifice.][93]

Trigault's "translation" eliminates an entire paragraph from the original, taking Ricci's temporizing over the religious quality of such practice—"the literati offer up to him [Confutio] a kind of sacrifice with incense and dead animals, although they acknowledge no divinity in him and ask nothing of him"—and converting it into a blanket assertion of the secular quality of the cult.

So Ricci, it turns out, never misrepresented the state cult. At least he did not distort it in the manner cited above, because he was not the "author" of the passage in question. His superiors, having encountered Ricci's history without mediation, were undoubtedly discomfited by the "pagan" religious character of Kongzi's popular appeal. The original text of the *Storia* must have been especially unsettling to Catholic authorities: it was not seen outside the Vatican until 1911, when Father Pietro Tacchi Venturi published the first volume of his *Opere Storiche*.

Moreover, the very passage redacted out of Trigault's translation that permitted an expressly secular reading of the state cult had already been crossed out in Ricci's handwritten manuscript. Lines are drawn through the four lines in the Italian original containing a description of the animal sacrifice offered to "Confutio" (figure 6). Was this the act of Ricci or Trigault? Regardless, the politics of representation is explicit, as is the fact that Trigault managed here in his translation to defer to higher authority while maintaining fidelity to his deceased colleague's depiction of the national worship of Kongzi. Thus, disentangling the foreign narrative from what it signified becomes extraordinarily difficult when one is reminded, as one is here, of the unstable quality of the received text, or of the many layers that constitute a text assumed to be homogenous.

Ricci and his followers navigated a very narrow passage between what they observed and what they believed it meant, gauging the interpretive risks noted above and being mindful of censorial superior authorities who did not want Christian truth compromised by pagan ritual. No matter how consistent with Ricci's accounts later Jesuit interpretation seemed, the volatility of seventeenth- and eighteenth-century religious politics (to wit, the rites and terms controversy) effected subtle shifts in the manner and content of Jesuit representation of the Chinese. The fathers held in common their membership in the Society of Jesus and in the Mission of the Indies; however, such solidarity was not purchased at the expense of creativity. Their interpretations of China were not monolithically uniform.

The reasons for the missionaries' plurivocal responses to the strange world they struggled to comprehend were not entirely due to the unstable politics of the Vatican. There was coercion from the Holy See; this was evident to all and never taken lightly.[94] But, as I will show in the following chapter, it was the interpretive consensus of a unique textual community of missionaries that held greater claim on the mechanisms of Jesuit representation. This community evolved through successive deployments of prelates and like a

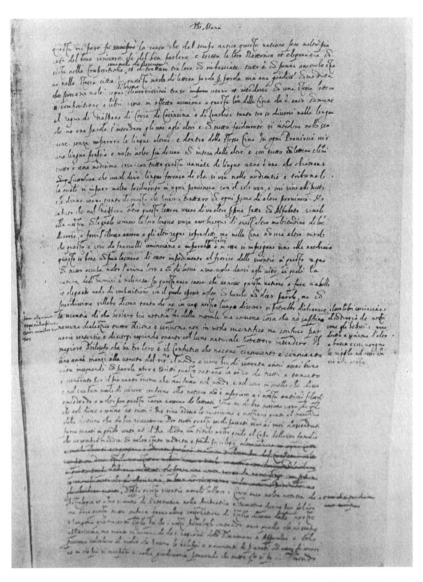

Figure 6. Matteo Ricci, "Della entrata della Campagnia di Giesù e Christianità nella Cina," p. 30, in Ricci's handwriting. Note that lines 36 to 41 have been crossed out. The struck passage reads: "Besides this, in every city and academy where the literati congregate, in accord with ancient law, there is a most sumptuous temple to Confutio, where one finds his statue, his name and title; and at every new moon and full moon (as well as) four times a year, the literati perform a certain kind of sacrifice with incense in which dead animals are offered to him, even though they do not recognize in him any divinity, nor do they ask him for anything. Thus, it cannot be called a true sacrifice." (From Matteo Ricci, *Fonti Ricciane*, ed. Pasquale d'Elia, vol. 1, fig. 3, facing p. 40. Photograph courtesy of Edward L. Davis and the University of Hawai'i Library)

living palimpsest produced a more comprehensive articulation of their invention, that preserved the invention as it safeguarded their community.

In this instance what Ricci appropriated as *legge de' letterati* was reappropriated by his translator, Trigault, in the word "Literatorum" and the phrase "Literatorum Secta."[95] And it was the latter's redaction, not Ricci's account, that was expeditiously completed for ecclesiastical authorities and made available to an interested European audience. Obviously, Trigault "translated" the original text in a period much more sensitive to the potential heresy of Ricci's accommodation and, consequently, widened or narrowed the interpretive field of selected passages so as to make his senior colleague's testimony unimpeachable. By identifying *ru* as *secta* and not *legge*, Trigault chose to stress the sect-like character of this group, thus putting them on par with the more obvious sects of Buddhism and Daoism, yet mitigating the preeminence they displayed in Ricci's account as *legge de' letterati*. However, at the same time, he tried to deliver the *ru* tradition from a purely religious significance by insisting on the Latin term "literatorum secta" rather than "legge de' letterati" as its equivalent. Editing of this kind would be considered censorship by some—and Trigault has been pilloried for this tampering—but I would like to suggest that it is not necessary to treat such an emendation as a perversion of the *Storia*. Instead, Trigault's editing should be understood as an elaboration of Ricci's text, one that preserves its message while concealing the full extent of Jesuit accommodation to the Chinese and their practices.

First, by drawing out the sectarian character of *ru* while branding Confucius as the generic symbol of genuine Chinese culture that he was for Ricci, Trigault merely said explicitly what his predecessor had implied. Secondly, even if Trigault altered Ricci's manuscript under duress,[96] he transformed the highly charged passages in a manner that would elude proscription, thereby preserving the integrity of the Jesuit tradition of accommodation. Given the central place of Confucius and Confucianism in subsequent accommodationist compilations such as the *Confucius Sinarum Philosophus*, Trigault, in salvaging most of the letter but all of the spirit of Ricci's work, may be solely responsible for the continued development of accommodationism in the seventeenth century.

Ricci, therefore, did not so much displace religion as redefine it, emphasizing its character as an ethical system governing all of Chinese social and political life without neglecting to mention the full range of observances in honor of Kongzi. And yet the only conceptual likeness Ricci could consistently draw of *ru* was a religious one. He deemed them *legge*, as his own order was called. Furthermore, he acceded in the designation of Confucius as "shengren," a term he in turn employed to describe the Christian saints. For the early Jesuits, Confucius did more than dispense a needed patronage. They imagined him in a very special relationship with them, as a holy man who bequeathed the inspirational texts, the Four Books.[97] For this reason the communal life of the Jesuits under Ricci's tutelage was underwritten by engagement in study and exegesis of the Four Books, which they took as a record of the scripture of Confucius containing visible manifestations of God.

These inspired scholarly endeavors took the fathers far beyond the identification of parallels between themselves and *ru*. Indeed, as we have seen, they *became ru*. It is in considering this Jesuit conversion to *ru*, and not the baptism of Chinese,[98] that we may draw closer to an understanding of the function of Confucius and the power of his claim on this community. From this local, late-sixteenth-century metaphorical conduit, the Jesuits, with significant native conceptual assistance, became Chinese while being seen at home as the mediating interpreters of a China the meaning of which was to be found in Confucianism.

The Joint Invention, "Confusius"

As we have seen, in order to "cross over" the Jesuits had to borrow generously from the cultural products of the Chinese in order to invent a self-conception consistent with this foreign world. And, most importantly, such invention had to be sustained by Chinese generosity and embrace. This required, as Ricci and his superior, Alessandro Valignano, knew, mastering the language. Nevertheless, Ricci also knew, in contrast to so many others—especially his superiors—that even a decade of laborious linguistic exertion could not secure passage from the Jesuits' known world to the Chinese unknown. Getting around among the Chinese was more a problem of conceptual logistics than accomplished linguistics, and neither would have been achieved without the fortuitous help of natives, both lettered and unlettered. This essential "jointness" of the Jesuit enterprise was evident in their earliest efforts to convey the *Santa Fede* (Sacred Faith) to the Chinese through catechism.

The *Tianzhu shilu* (Veritable Record of the Heavenly Master), composed by Michele Ruggieri, was the first of two catechisms prepared by the Society of Jesus for devotional work among the Chinese. This primary educational text was completed in 1584 and was also the first Western work written in Chinese that was printed in China using woodblock technology. Between 1579 and 1581 a preliminary draft was prepared in Latin, perhaps because Ruggieri, like most neophytes, lacked the confidence or sufficient skill to compose in a language he had just begun to learn, and, by some accounts, learn poorly.[99] The draft, *Vera et brevis divinarum rerum expositio*, was produced at a time when mission activities were confined to Goa and Macao;

this text was alternately drafted in Macao and Canton and printed in Goa, not in Zhaoqing.

There was something very appropriate about the circumstances of the catechism's production—composed in Latin and printed in India for use in China—that made it the emblem of an era in transition. The Latin draft and its ensuing Chinese version, which was completed with the assistance of Matteo Ricci, symbolize the tentativeness with which the mission at first undertook the task of assimilation. This catechism, in both Latin and Chinese, was the first text generated in China at the initial interface of the two cultures, and thus stands as a limit or a backdrop against which an early evidence of Confucius should be visible.[100]

Though the *Vera et brevis expositio,* according to Ricci, was organized as "a dialogue between a Gentile and a Father from Europe,"[101] neither of whom would seem to have reason to invoke the name of the Chinese sage, it contains two mentions of "Confusius"—apparently the first textual documentation of the Jesuits' earliest Latin name for Kongzi. Yet even Ricci's brief characterization is less than accurate, for Ruggieri plotted the catechism as a dialogue between an "Ethnicus Philosophus," or ethnic philosopher, meaning a non-Christian, and a "Sacerdos Christianus," or Christian priest. "Ethnic" philosophy in some sixteenth-century circles was understood as a reference to the Greeks, specifically Plato and Aristotle. Here I believe "ethnic" should be taken as a designation for the non-Christian other, a term maintained in the nineteenth century by Goethe and Hegel, both of whom deemed those religions other than Christian "the ethnic religions." In this way, "ethnicus" can be used to describe religions as various as Greek and Etruscan, or even Chinese. Clearly it refers to a non-Christian, yet one would have to read through at least seven chapters of the catechism to discover that the "Ethnicus Philosophus" is, in fact, Chinese. This kind of ethnic and/or identity confusion can be seen in the catechism's first Chinese edition, where Ruggieri concluded his preface with the remark, "guoseng shu" (written by a monk from India).[102]

In chapter 7 Ruggieri employs the dialogue to introduce two divine laws—to believe in the one God, and "not to do unto others what you do not want them to do unto you." Both protagonists, native and foreign, here debate the ancient sage's uncanny awareness of these laws:

Ethnicus Philosophus:
Illud posterius caput ego *Confusij* nostri libris traditum recognosco; prius vero nequaquam ab eo expositum fuisse miror.

That latter point I recognize as handed down in the books of our *Confusius;* [as for] the first point, I truly marvelled that it had been propounded by him at all.

Sacerdos Christianus:

Hoc prius etiem caput naturae lumine cognosci posse nostrates sapientes asserunt; an vero a vestro *Confusio* agnitum non omnino mecum statuo.

Indeed men dwelling in our country allege that even this first point can be recognized by the light of nature, but whether this by your *Confusius* [has] been recognized I am not altogether decided.[103] (emphasis added)

This exchange, specifically its flattering attribution of Christian wisdom to "Confusius," was the product of multiple collaborations. Ruggieri had conceived of the project by the time he had arrived at Macao in 1578; then, with the help of Father Pero Gomes, he worked on the Latin version of the dialogue in 1581. Finally, through 1583 and 1584 he went over the text with Ricci and was assisted in the Chinese translation by a *xiucai* from Fujian who was preparing for the *juren* examination and who was baptized by Francisco Cabral as "Paul."[104]

Though we might be inclined to identify Ruggieri as the "inventor" of "Confusius," it is more likely that such invention, while indexed to a teleology of conversion, was largely fortuitous, even accidental, and not the action of a willful authorial impulse. Considering that Ruggieri's oral and aural abilities in Chinese were, by his own admission, poor,[105] "Confusius" might have been his best Latin approximation—cases and all—of what he heard in the local patois of those Chinese enlisted to assist him in his study of the language. There is little evidence to indicate that the Chinese residing at the Jesuit quarters in Macao were accomplished in what the fathers called *mandarino* or that they were more than marginally literate.[106] Therefore, I cannot help but wonder how Ruggieri could know that there was in "the books of our Confusius" an aphorism similar to "do unto others as you want them to do unto you," familiar to his Christian priest or to any reader of Leviticus (19:18). One presumes in this regard that the ethnic philosopher alludes to book 12, chapter 2 of the *Lunyu*, but I doubt that Ruggieri learned of his "Confusius" here.

This is because from 1579 to 1581 Ruggieri was unlikely to have understood the *Lunyu* well enough to draw a parallel on his own between one of its passages and a passage from the Bible, or so we would conclude from the testimony of Valignano and Ricci. On Ricci's authority we have it that none of the other Jesuits stationed at Macao could read Chinese literary texts or converse in the vernacular and the "interpreters" provided for Ruggieri were, according to his fellow fathers, functionally illiterate. However, even a Chinese of questionable literacy was likely to know of the contents of the first chapters from book 12, as these constituted a fundamental rote-acquired lesson in the native catechism of personhood in late imperial China. And yet, we now know that Ruggieri was more accomplished in Chinese than we have been led to believe by his confreres; indeed his skills with the language were adequate enough to permit him by 1585 to compose rudimentary Chinese verse, one example of which bears the phrase, "du sishu" (study the Four Books).[107]

But the Latin text had been completed by 1581 and thus Ruggieri had only to understand a modicum of Chinese, Portuguese, or pidgin to converse with his interpreters and servants. I believe that one of these functionaries, either in sympathy or skepticism, introduced him to Kongzi's celebrated dicta on humaneness and reciprocity. When considered in light of the conditions surrounding the Jesuits' Chinese neologism for God, *Tianzhu* (Heavenly Master), such joint construction seems very likely. Tianzhu, the Chinese name for the Christian God, was in fact the gift of a Chinese convert, a certain "Cin Nicò" in Ricci's account, who, when left as caretaker of the Zhaoqing compound in the fall of 1583, erected a spirit tablet above an incense-festooned altar on which he had inscribed the characters "Tianzhu."[108] The god who protected the grounds of the mission from baleful influences had to be appeased even in the absence of the normal celebrants of the cult. And so "Cin" produced the proper accoutrements of local cult worship and paid tribute to the Jesuits' God.

As the Jesuits had yet to offer a Chinese nomination for their God, "Cin" 's invention was immediately appropriated by Ruggieri and employed in his Chinese translation of the *Decalogo*, or Ten Commandments.[109] In Chinese the complete title of the original version of the *Decalogo* is "Zuchuan Tianzhu shijie" (The Ancestrally Transmitted Heavenly Master's Ten Admonitions). Explicit in the very title of this translation is the hybrid semiotics that characterized Jesuit self-conception among the Chinese. Thus, even the fathers' presentation of the *Decalogo* as "ancestrally transmitted" conformed to the preexistent native logic of the religious rite of ancestor worship, according to which "Cin" had conducted sacrifice to Tianzhu—a single god, double understandings.

I imagine, returning now to the catechism, that the exchange between the ethnic philosopher and the Christian priest occurred very much as it was recorded, like so many of the real conversations Matteo Ricci worked into his later catechism, the *Tianzhu shiyi*. From a brief account of Ruggieri's first years of Chinese study at Macao contained in Father Francisco Pirez's memoir, *Pontos do que me alembrar o anno de 79 o Nosso Pe Geral Everado ao Pe Pero Gomez*, we learn that there was an early Chinese convert whose assistance in preparing a Chinese catechism had been secured in 1579. It would not be unreasonable to presume that this person was the model for the *Ethnicus Philosophus*. In the *Vera et brevis expositio*, the Christian priest explains the second Divine Law, only to have his prospective catechumen retort, "That last point I recognize as handed down in the books of our Confusius." But the text goes beyond this recognition of comparability in principle to bestow even greater esteem on "Confusius."

Piling on more evidence for the close identity of "ethnic philosopher" and "Christian," Ruggieri, in his rebuttal qua *sacerdos christianus*, admits that "Confusius" knew of the One God—that ultimate principle, knowledge of which was radiated by the light of nature. It is this revelation that startles the ethnic philosopher, Ruggieri's interlocutor, prompting the response, "I truly marvelled that this first point had been propounded by him at all." And here we can discern the influence on Ruggieri's presentation of Paul's Epistle to the Romans in which both messages, the Christian duty of mutual love and the presence of God among the unanointed, are found. Moreover, in the portrait of "Confusius" as the ancient Chinese bearer of these essential truths, particularly his possession of *naturae lumine*, we may also recognize the apologetic imagination of Ricci.

Though Ruggieri was the principal "author" of the catechism, in this one very significant exchange he gave textual form to the imaginative construction of his silent partner, Ricci. Thus the textual evidence of the Latin construction of "Confusius" recalls the Jesuits' Chinese manufacture of God as Tianzhu: both inventions began in Chinese impulses conceptually reappropriated by the fathers to represent the native religious culture that was being represented to them. In Jesuit eyes the existence of a Chinese term revealed to them that there was indeed an implicit awareness of the One God among the Chinese. For "Cin," however, this was not invention so much as a symbolic transaction wherein a new god was appropriated into a preexistent understanding of spirit worship and sacrifice to local tutelary deities.

It was as if Ruggieri, hoping to make contact with another soul, shouted his familiar divine laws into the darkness before him and back came a response. In both instances of fabrication, that of "Cin Nicò"'s Tianzhu and that of Ruggieri's "Confusius," the text preserves a moment of joint invention of the sort that Roy Wagner has identified as inevitable in cultural encounter: the outsider "invents 'a culture' for people and *they* invent 'culture' for him."[110] The representation of the native through translation was impossible, then, without a mutual, coordinated construction by both Chinese and Jesuits. The fact that both parties were responsible for the invention of Tianzhu and "Confusius" did not mean, however, that their relations were transparent and unmediated. What it meant was that they saw themselves through the prism of their respective representations of the other. The culture of the Jesuits and that of the Chinese were like two circles partially overlaid and partially separate; what joined the circles at their points of intersection were inventions like *la legge de' letterati*, *naturae lumine*, Tianzhu, and above all Confucius.

The difficulty of determining responsibility for the invention of Confucius is exacerbated, then, by more than just the centuries that lie between the sinified fathers and ourselves. As we have seen, the work of the mission, much like Chinese imperial history, was voluminously documented: in letters to superiors, friends, and colleagues; paraphrases and translations in various languages of scriptural Chinese works; memoirs of missionaries; publications by the mission in China; and commissioned (Whiggish) histories of the Christian evangelical project. That what is perhaps the earliest textual reference to "Confusius" occurs only now in this account tells us something about the nature of Jesuit experience in China, as well as our approach toward understanding it. The problem is not one of scarce materials; indeed the archival mass is huge, and many later works have effaced the contributions of earlier ones, like overlapping tracks in the snow. One cannot be certain of retracing one's steps but can only follow someone else's path in returning. The problem is one of conception—the assumption that the Jesuits are more like us and less like the Chinese they lived among and that texts, alone, are determinative of the true.

Thus we must be aware that the text does not take priority over context, just as literacy does not negate orality. Text—what is preserved in the records of the mission—and context—the social, intellectual, and cultural circumstances within which these records were produced—are mutually essential to understanding. This is not a relationship of priority so much as one of complementarity, and, in the case of the Jesuits, this critical complementarity points, counterintuitively, to a community more like the Chinese and less like us. We will see in the next chapter that the texts produced by the Jesuits in China were written registries of sense made among them as a community of indigenous interpreters. What these texts meant for the Jesuits in situ and how they were received by ecclesiastical and lay authorities in Europe in the decades following the missionaries' native self-constitution in China are matters to which we now turn.

CHAPTER 2

THERE AND BACK AGAIN:

THE JESUITS AND THEIR TEXTS

IN CHINA AND EUROPE

When *jinru* condemn the Heavenly Master, still more do they turn their backs on the injunctions of Kongzi and Mengzi. If you ask whether Christianity is the same as or different from Confucianism, I say, examine the preceding work and judge for yourself. Xu Wending of Wusong says, "Christianity banishes Buddhism, but complements Confucianism" and Prime Minister Qian Saian of Wutang also says, "By replacing what our *ru* have lost, Christianity is unique, and conserves and reforms the other sects."—*Father Joao Monteiro*

The problem can be shown in multiple and sometimes inverted forms. For instance, American Indians or Chinese "Sages" are granted the role of representing a truth (a "natural" truth, but bound to revelation through a regress of biblical chronology) which may have been corrupted among the colonizers. The positive pole is an elsewhere, opposed to a corrupt and "infidel" Europe. Here we can locate another form of the hidden, since civilizations thus acquire a mystical meaning and constitute the immense allegory of God who is under veil in the West. Thus begins a nostalgia—soon to become philosophical—for truth which rises, masked, in the East, and which is tarnished in the mirrors where the West had believed it could take hold of it.—*Michel de Certeau*

The introduction and opening chapter introduced the hybrid Jesuit/Chinese community and its reconciliation of natural theology and revealed theology in the name of Confucius. The present chapter will effect a more detailed description of this community and the simultaneous translation of itself into China and of selected Chinese inspirational works into Latin, because understanding the extent of Jesuit self-constitution on indigenous ground requires an assessment of their capacity for local invention.

Beginning with a closer analysis of "Confucius" and its purported native equivalent, Kongzi, the chapter rehistoricizes the Jesuits, bringing into view the many contingencies that dictated interpretive choices about themselves as missionaries and about the Chinese as potential converts to the *Santa Fede*. In the course of obtaining a better understanding of the early Jesuits in China, we uncover a critical difference, in fact a divergence, between this local Chinese community of sinified prelates and the Vatican, the foreign, ecclesiastical host of the China Mission.

From this divergence, the focus shifts from Jesuit invention in China to foreign reception of it as we consider the theoretical consequences for the late-seventeenth-century European scientific community of the publication of selected Jesuit translations from Chinese texts, specifically the classics. Here the objective will be to recover the accidental, internally divided character of the intellectual conditions favoring enthusiastic European reception of these texts—particularly the works of Confucius and his school and the classic *Yijing*—as data of "real," unmediated indigenous experience of the "true." Following this chapter is a meditation on the significance of Confucius as a universal emblem of seventeenth-century civilization and as a metonym of "real" Chineseness. It examines the making and meaning of Confucianism and concludes with some thoughts on the analytical utility of this construct.

The difference between what the Jesuits were actually doing in China and what church authorities at home believed they were doing has been overlooked in previous studies, owing to a tendency to identify the Jesuit missionaries as "interested" informational conduits between the historically given communities of Europe and China. In this way, the early Jesuit missionaries are customarily portrayed as prefigurative agents of colonialism, guilty of insinuating a subversive foreign doctrine into the conceptual stream of Chinese life by means of cynical manipulation of native texts in the service of conversion. What chapter 1 demonstrates is that we must abandon this customary portrait and recognize the Jesuits as a hybrid community.

To speak of the Jesuit missionary community and its efforts to become Chinese in terms of hybridity is a conscious inversion of the use of the term in recent works in cultural studies,[1] where it represents native, "postcolonial" movements that resist the essentializing narratives made of indigenous peoples by the colonist. Such inversion of contemporary convention is intended to help identify this group as a self-constituting entity on native Chinese ground. Knowledge of the Jesuits' historically situated invention of themselves as the true followers of Kongzi will enable us to uncouple the links presumed between the Vatican and missionaries in the field and thus question the common understanding of the Jesuits as mere mediators of ecclesiastical authority or spiritual colonizers of the Chinese. Furthermore, an understanding of Jesuit Chineseness will mitigate the harsh oppositions of foreign/native, European/Chinese, and white/colored that are instinctive in our era of revived nationalism, but not so self-evident to people of the sixteenth century.

The Jesuits were pious inventors of an indigenous tradition they called *xianru* in Chinese, *i veri letterati* in Italian, and *homes letrados* in Portuguese. The patriarch of their tradition was Kongzi or Kong Fuzi, who was known by a cluster of Latin and Europeanized names: "Confusius," "Confutius," "Confutio," "Confuzo," "Cumfuceio," and, of course, "Confucius." These significant aspects of their native embodiment were not known to Jesuit authorities in Goa or in Rome, but were concealed in the very complex and confusing process by which the Jesuit fathers accommodated themselves to China. Because the Vatican took its missionaries as mediators, it presumed that what was translated out of China textually—letters, memoirs, ethnographies, histories, scriptures—to Europe was faithfully represented in the language of the interpreter. Yet the meaning of Jesuit translation was not unequivocal, because translation is never a simple re-presentation but a careful selection and retelling in another guise. Fidelity may be a goal, but one accomplishes it in one realm at the expense of another.

The Latin "Confutius" was, from the vantage of church authorities, identical to the Chinese, "Kong Fuzi"; however, the identity was never queried, but taken on the authority of the church's Chinese-speaking missionaries. The most cursory investigation of this presumption would have shown that these terms were not marks of equivalence but symbols of conversion: "Kong Fuzi" was an icon of Jesuit nativeness, "Confucius," the fictionalized European exemplar of reason and civility. To understand how the Jesuit missionaries' symbolic nomination of "Confusius" eventuated in their undisclosed reinvention as the orthodox followers of the ancient saint and how later generations of sinophiles learned of China through Confucius, we turn now to an examination of what is for us a familiar consequence of their Chinese conversion experience—the equivalence of Confucius and Kong Fuzi.

Confucius, Kong Fuzi, and the Assimilated Interloper

For over three hundred years Western scholars, missionaries, and travelers have used the term "Confucian," holding that "'Confucian' derives from 'Confucius,' the Latinization of K'ung Fu-tzu, or Master K'ung."[2] This is not a definition but an assertion of representational accuracy based on the presumption that "Confucius" is a phonetic transcription. And given the weight of scholarly presumption and the centuries of habit that support it, the equivalence appears beyond question. However, time, presumption, and habit have all been sustained by a meagre inheritance, as the assertion is never backed by evidence.

This equivalence of Confucius and Kong Fuzi is not recent and it is documented—most notably in the cumulative magnum opus of accommodationism, the *Confucius Sinarum Philosophus, sive Scientia Sinensis* (Confucius, Philosopher of the Chinese; or, The Chinese Learning) of 1687.[3] Opposite the first page of the "Confucii Vita" (The Life of Confucius) that makes up part 2 of the work there is a French artisan's woodcut rendering of Confucius, complete with a caption bearing the following words (see figure 7):

> CUM FU ÇU sive CONFUCIUS, qui et honoris gratia CHUM NHIJ dicitur, Philosophorum sinensium Princeps; oriundus fuit ex oppias KIO FEU Provinciae XAN TUM.

> CUM FU ÇU [Kong Fuzi] or CONFUCIUS, who also for the sake of honor is called CHUM NHIJ [Zhongni], the leader of the Chinese philosophers; originating from the city of KIO FEU [Qufu], the province of XAN TUM [Shandong].[4]

The identity of Kong Fuzi as Confucius, right down to the characters, is unequivocal.

Certainly, "Confucius" would appear the natural Latin equivalent of "Kong Fuzi"; simply sounding the two words out will confirm this. And since the nineteenth century, such European scholars as M. G. Pauthier were as convinced of the identity of these terms as they were of the Jesuits' responsibility

Figure 7. "Cum Fu Çu sive Confucius." The first Western portrait of "Confucius," by an unknown engraver in Philippe Couplet et al., *Confucius Sinarum Philosophus* (Paris, 1687), a hybridized image of him as still point of the bibliographic world. This woodcut was inspired by the popular Ming hagiography, *Shengji zhi tu* (Portraits of the Sage's Traces), as well as the Jesuit imagination of Kongzi informed by the *Lunyu* and the *Li ji*. The French artisan's woodcut relied on established motifs for the depiction of royalty as congeneric with the cosmos, and as "Confucius" was worked into this artistic framework, his features became more Western. The image was the source for all subsequent illustrations of Confucius. (Photograph courtesy of the Special Collections Library of the University of Michigan)

for the neologism "Confucius": "*KHOUNG-FOU-TSEU* [que les missionaires européens, en le faisant connaître et admirer à Europe, nommèrent *Confucius*, en latinisant son nom]."[5] Ten years later there was no need to provide an etymology, and it was clear that Confucius was our invention: "Khoung Fou-tseu, que nous appelons, Confucius, naquit 551 ans avant notre ère."[6]

Most textbooks on Chinese history, and many books and monographs today, while ignorant of the conditions of the name's production so familiar to Pauthier, all note that "Kong Fuzi" is the Chinese name approximated by the Western convention "Confucius." And, as we recall from the introduction, this convention has acquired an impressive universal currency. So it is that this equivalence simply "makes sense" and nothing can gainsay its appropriateness. Nevertheless, implicit in this apparent equivalence is the further assumption that the name "Kong Fuzi" was the common Chinese term of address for the sage at the moment the Jesuits conferred the Latin nomination. Specifically, it is this assumption of fidelity that invites further questioning and that, in turn, will bring us closer to the significant differences between Jesuit representation in situ and the later reception of their native translations in Europe.

The proper name "Kong Fuzi" is not the popular Chinese expression we have assumed it to be, and it appears that it has never been common. Indeed "Kong Fuzi" is inconsistent with linguistic protocol from the post-Zhou through the Han (ca. 650 B.C.E.–200 C.E.), as well as foreign to the fellowship known as *ru* with which the Jesuits so earnestly identified themselves.[7] For example, in the heterogenous fascicles that comprise the extant *Lunyu* (familiar to us as the *Analects*), Kongzi's presence is usually heralded by the signal phrase *zi yue* (he said). There are occasions in which he is called by other names, but it is *zi*, literally meaning "eldest son," that is most common throughout what we believe are the earliest sections of the text.

However, *fuzi*, an honorific that is common to pre-Han literature, occurs with some regularity in the *Lunyu*—thirty-seven instances altogether, twelve of which are located in the first, and older, half of the text. In all but five of these cases *fuzi* is used as a form of address for Zhongni, one of Kongzi's names, and is never employed together with the master's surname Kong.[8] Assuming frequency of occurrence to be an indication of the linguistic salience of an expression, the sixty-eight instances of "Kongzi" make it more common than *fuzi*.[9] As with *fuzi*, the majority of the occurrences are found in the latter portion of the work. Increasing evidence of both names in the second ten books of the *Lunyu* suggests that they are products of late accretion, circa fourth to third century B.C.E.[10]

The term "Kong Fuzi" is also unprecedented in the literature of other Warring States rhetorical traditions, and is absent from the later classical commentaries of Han era erudites and loyal Confucians (*ru*) like Dong Zhongshu

(195–105 B.C.E.) and Zheng Xuan (127–200 C.E.). We do find *fuzi* used with some frequency in pre-Han texts such as the *Zhuangzi, Han Feizi*, and *Yanzi chunqiu*, usually in the sense of "gentleman" or "sir." In these same works there are many forms of reference to the sage, such as "Zhongni," "Kongzi," and "Kong Qiu," but not "Kong Fuzi." Of course, one might justly contend that the *Zhuangzi, Han Feizi*, and *Yanzi chunqiu* are not *ru* texts; still, even the fictive genealogical literature of the *Kong congzi* and the *Kongzi jiayu*, which is salient in its reverence for Kongzi, contains no evidence of the name "Kong Fuzi."[11] The literature of antiquity, *ru* and contra-*ru* alike, offers no instance of the name, and so it is hardly surprising that "Kong Fuzi" was not used in the rituals of the imperial cult honoring the sage. In these rites, he was worshiped as *xianshi* (first teacher), *zongshi* (ancestral teacher), or, increasingly from the Song era on, *xiansheng* (first sage).[12]

If "Kong Fuzi" was the native substrate of "Confucius," then it must have been an honorific of late provenance. Some scholars have stated as much— "K'ung Fu-tzu [Kong Fuzi, Great Master K'ung] [was] the name and appellation by which the instructor of the sixth century B.C.E. had come to be known in the sixteenth century C.E. when the Jesuits went to China"[13]—but, unfortunately, supply no evidence. So where, if not in the aforementioned texts, might Ricci, or for that matter, Inácio da Costa (1603–1666), Prosper Intorcetta (1625–1696), and the many other Jesuit translators who followed his lead, find the "Kong Fuzi" from which they made "Confucius"? Should there be an answer satisfactory for us, it can only be in the other native texts they used and the texts they themselves made. When we examine the indigenous texts dear to the first three generations of accommodationists it becomes more, not less, difficult to answer this query. Indeed, a review of Chinese books read by the Jesuits and of works they produced while in China suggests that "Kong Fuzi" and "Confucius" were both created by the fathers.

Comments by Matteo Ricci in his *Storia* and in the bibliographic discussion preceding the translations that comprise the *Confucius Sinarum Philosophus* make clear that the first three generations of Jesuit missionaries in China particularly esteemed two works: the Yongle era (1403–1425 C.E.) compendium on Song philosophy, the *Xingli daquan*, and a recension on the Four Books called *Sishu zhijie*[14] by the Grand Secretary of the Wanli emperor, Zhang Juzheng (1525–1582 C.E.). "The Great Compendium on Nature and Principle" (*Xingli daquan*) was a rather eclectic anthology of the writings of 121 different Song and Yuan era *ru* on a range of topics whose diversity is not reflected in the collection's title.[15] It was, of course, required reading for all examination candidates and, along with the *Sishu daquan* (Great Compendium of the Four Books) and the *Wujing daquan* (Great Compendium of the Five Classics), constituted a government-authorized curriculum that endured into the twentieth century.

Considering the Jesuits' close relations with Chinese provincial officials, all metropolitan degree holders, and their intimate ties with important national intellectual figures like Xu Guangqi of the Hanlin Academy and Li Zhizao of the imperial Board of Public Works, it was inevitable that they would learn much about works so critical to the academic certification of these men. Philippe Couplet and the other authors of the *Confucius Sinarum Philosophus* confer great favor upon this text and its author, for it proved fundamental to a century of Jesuit exegesis and translation.[16] The thirty-eighth chapter of the *Xingli daquan* is the one most likely to contain honorable recognition of the sage in the form "Kong Fuzi," since it is concerned with retracing the development of the *ru* tradition. Yet in the chapter's initial section, one devoted to *daotong* (the legacy of the way), the ancestry of *ru* is charted not from "Kong Fuzi," but from "Kongzi." Immediately following *daotong* in this chapter is a section titled "Shengxian conglun" (Collected Discourses on Sages and Worthies), and although the *ru* founder is lionized here, he is referred to as Kongzi. Even the compendium's prefaces, notorious for their lionizing temper, consistently refer to him as Kongzi, *xiansheng* (first sage) and *xianshi* (first teacher).[17] Regardless of this work's significance for a century-long Jesuit translation project, the text contains no evidence of the honorific "Kong Fuzi."

The *Sishu zhijie*[18] is also a likely source for the title "Kong Fuzi," for it was the text from which Matteo Ricci worked in preparing what he called his Latin paraphrase of the Four Books. From 1591 to 1594 Ricci labored over an annotated Latin translation of the Four Books and during this interval began to instruct newcomers to the mission in Chinese through the text.[19] Subsequent detachments of Christian soldiers to the eastern mission all learned Chinese by means of Ricci's paraphrase, and it was this very translation that comprised the body of the *Confucius Sinarum Philosophus*.[20] The Four Books was the most important native text studied by the Jesuits.

While Zhang's *Sishu zhijie* may have been the foundation of missionary study, it does not contain evidence of the honorific, as the commentary it contains on the *Lunyu* and *Mengzi* reveals a preference for the form "Kongzi." For that matter, the absence of the term "Kong Fuzi" from these Ming (1368–1644 C.E.) collections is consistent with its dearth in the very texts to which Zhang's commentary is an addendum. Indeed, "Kong Fuzi" cannot be found in any standard edition of the *Lunyu*. Neither in Zhu Xi's *Lunyu jizhu*, upon which Zhang based his own reading of the *Lunyu*, nor in the earliest extant redaction, *Lunyu jijie yisu* by Huang Kan (d. 545 C.E.), do we encounter "Kong Fuzi."[21] Moreover, "Kong Fuzi" does not appear in even one of the twenty-four standard dynastic histories. In effect, "Kong Fuzi" conveyed the essential otherness of the Jesuits, marking their distance from the native culture they appeared to represent by making it the Chinese source of their Latinization.

In admitting that "Kong Fuzi" was a distance marker, it is interesting that the only native evidence of Kong Fuzi preceding Jesuit entrance into China appears to be from an inscriptional record of a state ceremony held during the Yuan dynasty on the occasion of Temür's (1265–1307 C.E.) adoption of a second reign title. At the time of the renomination, the emperor (*huangdi*) Chengzong received a memorial from his cabinet ministers wherein he is addressed as "zhisheng wenxuanwang Kong Fuzi zhi disun," "legitimate descendant of the most holy, literary king, Kong Fuzi."[22] In the annals of state sacrifice to Kongzi there probably has never been an honorific of such inflated acclaim or quite such an effort to appropriate a powerful legacy of legitimation. In other words, "Kong Fuzi," though a rare Chinese term, might best be considered the designation of the interloper, Jesuit or Mongol, desirous of making a legitimate claim on an otherwise uncontested will.[23]

My surmise is that the Jesuits felt compelled to confer an incomparable respect upon Kongzi and, for this reason, granted him the superlative honorific "Kong Fuzi." Without this ennobling formality, the Kongzi they found in native texts like the *Sishu* would be indistinguishable from a host of other, less esteemed (because, in the early Jesuits' eyes, unorthodox), masters such as Guanzi, Laozi, Zhuangzi, Zengzi, Xunzi, Han Feizi, and many more. More importantly, the title "Kong Fuzi" placed the sage above a group of figures whom Matteo Ricci and his followers loathed as "false literati," but who had already secured the *zi* suffix along with popular acceptance: Zhangzi (Zhang Zai, 1020–1077 C.E.), Zhouzi (Zhou Dunyi, 1017–1073 C.E.), Chengzi (the Cheng Brothers, Cheng Yichuan, 1033–1107 C.E., and Cheng Mingdao, 1032–1085 C.E.), and, most notoriously, Zhuzi (Zhu Xi).

Thus, "Kong Fuzi" was an uncommon title and even more uncommon term of address. As the putative native equivalent of "Confucius," it, too, was a Jesuit fiction. For the early fathers, who were outsiders and who were not familiar with the native context wherein the sage was known by plural but specific references, this absence of "Kong Fuzi" from the Chinese texts they studied was a condition for its invention. The Chinese honorific, therefore, represented Jesuit nativeness, not Chinese, and conveyed something of the extent of missionary enculturation, an enculturation regarded with growing suspicion by the Vatican, but which would be highly valued by lay scholars in Europe.

Confucius: Orthography, Ambiguity, and Difference

Before Ruggieri and Ricci founded the mission there was no textual evidence of "Confucius," yet by the time of Ricci's death in 1610 this was no longer true. This is why for over four centuries Matteo Ricci has borne the responsibility for conferring the Latin title "Confucius" on "Kong Fuzi." Inasmuch as his orthography may have served as the basis for the other nominal permutations, we might consider Ricci the principal inventor of "Confucius." Yet there is not in Father Ricci's letters, translations, catechisms, or memoirs a single use of the Latin name in this particular form; we also know that Ruggieri's Latin version of the first catechism bears the name "Confusius." An examination of works on China published before the establishment of the Jesuit mission confirms the absence of "Confucius" prior to the publication of the catechisms of Ruggieri and Ricci and demonstrates the crucial link between the center of local Jesuit invention and the broad periphery of European cognizance.

Two of the earliest European publications on China, Gaspar da Cruz's *Tractado em que se cotam muito por esteso as cousas da China* (A Treatise in Which Many Aspects of China Are Presented, 1569)—a narration of Portuguese discovery based on personal experience—and Bernardino de Escalante's *Discurso de la navigacion que los Portugueses hazen à los reinos y provincias del oriente, y de la noticia q́ se tiene de las grandezas del reino de la China* (Discourse on the Navigation of the Portuguese to the Kingdoms and Provinces of the Orient, and Information They Held on the Riches of the Kingdom of China, 1577)—a synthesis of the sum of European knowledge on China—were published before Ricci had completed his instruction at the Jesuit college in Rome. Neither work makes mention of anyone by the name "Confutio," "Confuzo," "Cumfuceio," or the like, although the terms *mandarim* and *bonzo*, which would figure so prominently in the experience of the Jesuit mission after 1583, do appear to have been already incorporated into European consciousness.[24]

Over a decade later, in 1585, as Ruggieri and Ricci began to catechize Chinese through their recently completed *Tianzhu shilu*, Father Juan González de Mendoza (1545–1618), a Spanish Augustinian, published *Historia de la cosas mas notables, ritos y costumbres del gran reino de la China* (A History of the Most Notable Things, Rites and Customs of the Grand Kingdom of China).[25] González de Mendoza's account was derived in large part from the previously unpublished narratives of several missionaries, Augustinians and Franciscans, who had entered China as early as 1577—a full two years before Michele Ruggieri was posted to Macao. Conspicuously absent are "Kong Fuzi," "Confucio," "Confutio," or "Confuzo," and the like, as are such terms as *letrados* or *mandarines*, both of which were early equivalents for *ru* and are amply in evidence in Luis de Guzman's *Historia de las Missiones de la Compagñia de Jesus* (History of the Missions of the Society of Jesus) of 1601 and Diego de Pantoja's (1571–1618) *Relacion de la entrada de algunos padres de la campagnia de Iesus en la China* (An Account of the Entry of

Some Fathers of the Society of Jesus into China) of 1605.[26] Thus when the Jesuit mission was established in southern Zhaoqing, "Confucius," as we might expect, had not yet entered European awareness.

For modern Jesuit scholars of the Chinese expedition, this meant that Ricci was responsible for the invention of "Confucius." The presumption is a commonplace, securely rooted in the claims of Fathers Henri Bernard and Pasquale d'Elia, that he was the first to Italianize the sage's Chinese name.[27] Their contention is founded on the textual authority of the history of the Chinese mission that Ricci was ordered to undertake by his superiors in 1608, *Della entrata della Compagnia di Giesù e Christianità nella Cina* (On the Entrance of the Society of Jesus and Christianity into China). Yet one must carefully distinguish Italian and Latin versions of this term. The initial appearance of "Kong Fuzi" in his Italian, but not Latin, guise comes early in the first book, amid an introduction to the science and the arts of the Chinese. "Padre Ricci," as he calls himself throughout the work, reports:

> Il magiore filosofo che ha tra loro è il Confutio, che nacque cinquecento e cinquanta uno anni inanzi alla venuta del Signore al mondo, e visse più di settanta anni assai buona vita, insegnano con parole, opre, e scritti questa natione.

> The greatest philosopher among them is Confutio, who was born 551 years before the coming of the Lord to the world [Christ] and for more than seventy years lived a very good life teaching this people through words, works, and writings.[28]

Ricci's "Confutio" is not our "Confucius," and since the lion's share of Ricci's extant corpus is in *Italian* it is not entirely sensible to expect him to be the author of the *Latin* "Confucius." More importantly, there is no reference here to a Chinese equivalent of the Italian term and no suggestion of transliteration. Instead, "il Confutio" stands iconlike as "the greatest philosopher among them."

Ricci appeared to know of Kong Fuzi's fictiveness. In the *Tianzhu shiyi* he consistently maintained a distinction between the Jesuit invention (Kong Fuzi) that formed the Chinese substrate of the Confucius dear to his European audience, on the one hand, and the indigenous names for the sage immediately recognizable to Chinese (Kongzi, Zhongni), on the other.

This awareness is easily demonstrated with a selection from the *Tianzhu shiyi*. Near the end of the catechism the "Chinese scholar" challenges his Western counterpart to account for the virtue of Jesuit celibacy in light of Mengzi's statement that "there are three kinds of unfiliality; the greatest of these is no posterity."[29] The query occasions a series of references to "Kongzi" (not "Kong Fuzi") as the Western scholar argues that the words in question were not handed down from the sage, but spoken by followers of Mengzi. He continues:

> The esteemed kingdom [China] takes Kongzi as a great sage. In the [Great] *Learning* [*Daxue*], the [Doctrine of the] *Mean* [*Zhongyong*], and the *Selected Sayings* [*Lunyu*], the discourses of Kongzi on filial piety are extremely detailed, [and so] why would this heinous violation of filial piety escape the comment of his disciples and his grandson only to be first remarked by followers of Mengzi? Kongzi took Bo Yi and Shu Qi as worthies of antiquity, and took Bi Gan as the most humane of these three [men] of the Yin. Since [he] praised these three men saying 'humane' and 'worthy,' he must have believed that the virtue of each was complete and without shortcoming. However, all of these men were without progeny. Thus, the followers of Mengzi considered [them] unfilial and Kongzi thought them humane, so is this not a contradiction?[30]

To the *Chinese* catechumen, the sage could only be known as Kongzi, yet among the Jesuits, and in particular for their superiors in the Vatican, it was the Latin, "Confutius," that was recognized.

Indeed, when Ricci sent one of the first copies of the *Tianzhu shiyi* to Claudio Acquaviva, he enclosed a detailed chapter-by-chapter summary in Latin in which the genitive singular, "Confutii," appears.[31] In listing the points of chapter 2, Ricci attempts to convince his audience of the fundamental divinity of Taiji (Supernal Ridgepole) as Confutius understood it:

> Europaeus interpratur hic quendam locum Confutii, qui maxime est apud eos autoritatis et sanctitatis, qui quingentos ante Christum natum annos floruit, et multa optime scripsit, et usurpatum est hoc nomen Taikiei in quibusdam commentariis, et ait intelligendum esse de materia prima de qua pollicetur se alibi acturum.

> The European interprets here a certain position of Confutius, who is especially of authority and sanctity, who flourished five hundred years before the birth of Christ and wrote many things very well, and this name Taiji has been taken over in certain commentaries that it should be understood in terms of the intelligence of prime matter from which it is promised it acts elsewhere.[32]

Recapitulating a critical point in his demonstration that God has always been among the Chinese, Ricci introduces his superiors to the man called Confutius, locating his lifetime in relation to that of the Lord, while, in the official language of the church, noting his prestige. Obviously this, the first mention of Confucius among the many letters and reports Ricci made to Jesuit authorities, is not literally Confucius, but simply a Latin noun in the genitive singular case, "Confutii." The dative case of "Confutius" would be "Confutio." Such a Latin construction of the name, while consistent with Ricci's Italian "Confutio," which appears often in his journals, is not consistent with our presumption that "Confucius" was *the* Latinization. "Confutio" lived in the Italian vernacular of the fathers and his Latinization as "Confutius" followed the logic of their vernacular until 1689, when "Confucius" replaced all other forms.

It was some time (nearly a century) before the variant "Confucius" was standardized. It was particularly common in both the Latin and the Italian renderings of the name to find a lack of distinction between *c, z,* and *t*. This was due to several factors, not the least of which was the newness of the name itself. The Jesuit community was made up of people from many lands, employing different vernaculars. Each of these adopted their own native Chinese terms, insofar as they could be reproduced as heard, and thus the orthography of Jesuit translations out of Chinese into Latin and into their native vernaculars yielded a profusion of different reproductions. In the case of transliterating Kongzi there was certainly a range of possible European pronunciations for the "zi" in Chinese—"ci," "ti," "ts," and "ch" in Italian, German, and church Latin would all be pronounced with a "ts" initial very similar to the target sound. Consequently, such multiple rough correspondences would naturally yield a variable orthography, even more so because it is likely that many of the fathers were trying to reproduce the sounds of a southern dialect, according to which Kongzi would have sounded like "Kongji."[33]

A third barrier to consistency in spelling was the popular acceptance of Amato Lusitano's (1511–1568) idiosyncratic Portuguese transliterations of certain Chinese words. As a consequence of this practice, it was possible for Lusitanized words to be adopted alongside Latin phonetic appropriations of Chinese terms. The same was true for the many transliterations introduced by Marco Polo that had by the sixteenth century become permanently affixed to Ptolemy's revered but obsolete world map. Fourth, a great quantity of Chinese words were orthographically confused because they "entered Europe through the medium of the Portuguese language," and then "filtered, through translations primarily, into the other languages of Europe."[34]

A final, and conceivably the most important, consideration in this regard was the decline in the sixteenth century of Latin's linguistic hegemony. The late sixteenth century saw the emerging independence of vernacular languages, and Italy and Portugal (whence many of the mission's fathers came) were the first to declare their national languages suitable for scholarly endeavor.[35] The elevation of vernacular was encouraged by the Jesuits. The interval between church Latin and an evolving Sino-Italian or Sino-Portuguese was deceptively large; it was the space of successful accommodation.

Thus, during the first twenty years of missionary publication from China, the orthography shifted from "Confusius" to "Confutius" to "Confucius" without pattern. In Portuguese, which incidentally was the lingua franca of the first wave of missionaries, the Jesuit sage was represented as "Cumfucio" or "Cumfuceio";[36] in Latin "Confucius," "Confutius," "Confusii," "Confusio," "Confucio," "Confucii," "Confucium," identified the sage, in forms that changed according to declension; and in Italian he was "Confutio," but just as often "Confuzo."[37] These slight orthographic differences notwithstanding, it was clear to the missionary Jesuits of whom they were speaking when any of the names was used.

"Confutius" (Latin), however, stands alone, as did the "il Confutio" (Italian) of Ricci's *Storia*. It does not refer beyond the context of the outline of the catechism's argument and its meaning is clearly indexed to Christian theology. Certainly Claudio Acquaviva or any officer of the Society of Jesus in Rome knew nothing of the Chinese terms "Kongzi" and "Kong Fuzi" that were represented by the Latinization, because their awareness was constrained within a Latin summary they presumed was faithful to the Chinese text. "Confutius" had already secured a distinct epistemological status independent of the presumption of native equivalence.

And without the native referent, "Confutio," "Confutius," or "Confucio" was similar to many other Chinese words like "mandarin," "bonze," and "Cantao" or "Canton" that were adopted into the European lexicon through derivative forms in the sixteenth century. What they had in common was their status as things of great value or familiarity to merchants, missionaries, and explorers—ports of call, official titles, products.[38] They were marvelous found objects or, rather, fetishized entries in an expanding Western lexicon whose appeal was sustained by a self-contained foreignness.

Such fetishization of "Confutius" was the legacy of Matteo Ricci and Nicolá Trigault, who sought a particular European representation of the missionaries' experience in China, knowing that the theological and practical consequences of accommodation with *la legge de' letterati* would be of grave concern to the Society's authorities and ultimately to the pontiff. Ricci, as superior of a mission that had demonstrated success in working with the natives, could preserve the accommodationist program only by navigating a very narrow passage between what he observed and did and what he believed it meant, mindful of censorial higher authorities who did not want Christian truth compromised by pagan ritual. The narrow aperture created between their native, in situ representation and the representation intended for export to the Holy See was wide enough to permit the first generation of Jesuits to remake themselves in the image of their Chinese scholarly other without drawing a censorial response from their superiors in Rome. Thus a dual representation of the Chinese sage and his legitimate apostles was constructed from which would develop the two distinct complexes of reference that have been effaced ever since by the facile equivalence of "Kong Fuzi" and "Confucius."

The first missionaries, then, were responsible for much more than Kong-zi's Latin cognomen. Jesuit invention began with the use of a Chinese proper name without precedent in the texts bearing the signature of his school and not evident even in the numerous commentaries generated by pious descendants seeking to construe the words of their "ancestor." "Kong Fuzi" was the Jesuits' invention as much as was "Confucius," and yet these mutually reinforcing inventions were not fully disclosed to Vatican authorities, in part because they were contained in texts that were supplements to the native cultural field of missiology in which "Confucius," "tianzhu," and "la legge de' letterati" operated as linguistic integers within a combinatorial calculus of expression.[39]

Jesuit texts, like the Latin/Chinese *Sishu*, and the *Tianzhu shilu*, were produced and circulated continuously within a local signifying system. Ruggieri's "Confusius" was but one very significant sign among many others constituting this system. Thus, the significance of the term (like all terms) was semiotic and was to be found in the currents of Jesuit thought and speech as much as in their writings. But even as local imaginative constructions, "Confusius" or "Confutio" and "la legge de' letterati" acquired a history of broader significance when they were received in Rome and in Goa by ecclesiastical authorities desirous to understand the activities of the China Mission. In what follows I will consider the reasons for, and the consequences of, the difference in meaning of this fungible corporate concept by examining in greater detail the Jesuit microsociety in China and the specific, extraordinary claims it made for itself as a native tradition. Only after we have a better understanding of this Sino-Jesuit context will the epistemological significance of Confucius for seventeenth-century Europeans and for us today be apparent.

The Jesuit Saint, Confucius, and Native Identity

Name, though it seem but an outward and superficial matter, yet it carrieth much impression and enchantment.—*Francis Bacon*

"Confucius," then, was more than mere Latinization; its significance was not merely literal. By pronouncing Kongzi "Confucius" and identifying his followers, *ru*, as the literati, Ricci did more than classify them; rather, he was admitting them into the realm of the knowable, a realm accented by the visible presence of the holy. As the order of the literati, *ru* were made brethren of Ricci's beloved Society of Jesus in also being a sect and in effect symbolically christened.[40] Indeed the two *legge* were essentially interchangeable.

Li Zhizao, in one of the prefaces to his collection of Christian literature, the *Tianxue chuhan*, admits that Ricci "encountered Qu Rukui [Taisu (fl. 1595–1623), his first Chinese convert] and turned against Buddhist monasticism; afterwards growing his hair and designating himself *ru*."[41]

Ricci and a succession of later fathers consistently displayed a striking sympathy with the order of the literati, as we noted in discussing Jesuit conversion to *ru* identity in chapter 1. To be sure, there are moments in Ricci's narration of the mission's history where he appears convinced that these men are in essence the mirror image of the Jesuits. To support his observation, Ricci cites evidence both real and invented, the most obvious being the scholasticism of *ru* as evident in their organization of study societies (*shuyuan*), their descent from a privileged patriarch (taken on the analogy of charismatic transmission from St. Ignatius of Loyola to his Christian soldiers), their belief in heaven, and their moral ministrations to the Chinese populace.

In a letter written a year after he began work on the *Storia*, Ricci would draw yet another qualified comparison in saying, "Though the literati do not set out to speak of supernatural things, in morals they are almost completely in accord with us."[42] Ricci concludes that "this academy [*ru, la legge de' letterati*] could well become Christian, since their [doctrinal] essentials contain nothing contrary to the essence of the catholic Faith, nor does the catholic Faith impede it in any way, but, on the contrary, would very much work for the quiet and peace of the republic to which their books aspire."[43] Chinese literati converts like Qu Rukui considered Ricci and his cohort to be almost completely in accord with them. In his preface to Ricci's *Jiaoyou lun* (Treatise on Friendship), Qu observes: "Duke Li [Ricci] cites the texts of the sages, abides by the kingdom's regulations, displays the cap and belt [of the scholar], performs the sacrifices at spring and autumn, [and] respects and executes Heaven's charges [thus] promoting orthodoxy."[44]

It appears from this cross-cultural testimony that what Matteo Ricci and his accommodationist sympathizers experienced among the high-culture Chinese was, to borrow an image dear to the astronomical system with which they brokered connections with that world, a harmony of spheres. They believed, as Chinese like Li Zhi (1527–1602) and later Dai Zhen (1723–1777) believed of the Jesuits, that there were structural/functional homologies linking the fathers and *ru*. The practical economy and consistency of Western astronomical models, Dai believed, were a reflection of a more refined moral intelligence. Chinese recognition of this higher moral sensibility, in turn, prompted a vigorous examination of their own culture,[45] while Ricci was led to investigate Chinese religion more fully because the practices of *la legge de' letterati* "conform[ed] to the light of nature and to catholic truth."[46]

Confucius—as the Jesuits constructed him—offered testimony through his writings of the natural theology of the Chinese and the prospect of its union with the Jesuits' own revealed theology. The Jesuits did not see similarities of this sort as coincidence. In fact, resemblances of the slightest degree (the trope of similitude) could not for them be fortuitous, because they were the intentional signs of a divine semiotics through which God was made visible to his subjects, ensuring that "Confucius" was their Christian other. The Jesuits believed that "on the authority of the Bible itself . . . *all* knowledge of religion is from Him, and not only that which the Bible has transmitted to us."[47]

Throughout Ricci's *Storia*, "Confutio" was exalted in an almost patristic sense as the former prophet of Chinese monotheism whose teachings perished along with the classics in the infamous Qin era Burning of the Books.[48] In fact, Ricci, to the evident dismay of Niccolò Longobardo (1565–1655), said that Kongzi's official title of *shengren* was best rendered in the Italian as *santo* (saint), rather than *sapientissimo* (wise man).[49] The equation was no accident; Ricci used the same term—*shengren*—to describe Christian saints to Chinese catechumens.

While in Chinese *shengren* may be understood by either of the dyads, wise person/holy person, or sage/saint, in seventeenth-century Italian *santo* and *sapientissimo* were far apart in meaning. Pagan philosophers like Aristotle, who was much appreciated by the Jesuits, were nonetheless considered *sapientissimo*, while *santo* was reserved for the visionaries of the early church like Augustine and Jerome. Thus the issue was not terminological, nor was it one of proper representation. "Confutio"'s identity as *santo* placed him squarely in the Christian pantheon. Still, what other title would be appropriate for a man who, in the estimation of Ricci and his fellow Jesuit and translator, Trigault,

> through his congresses and meetings has incited all to a zeal for virtue. He is believed among the Chinese to have exceeded, by means of the holiness of life, all mortals, as many as have been outstanding in virtue anywhere in the lands. We shall say that he yields to few of the Ethnic Philosophers in our own country, indeed that he overcomes many. No proposition of his may be called into doubt not only by the Chinese literati, but by all equally it is sworn according to the words of the common Master. Not only the literati but the kings themselves venerate him through so many centuries measuring backwards in time, nevertheless by the right of mortals, not by some *Numen*, and they avow that they themselves display a soul grateful for the doctrine received from him.[50]

He must have been a saint.

That Trigault considered it necessary to distinguish the "holiness of life" (*vitae sanctimonia*) of Confutius as that befitting a mortal and not a god (*Numen*) suggests something of Confucius's status in the Jesuit community. It is important to remember, too, that these are Trigault's words, not translations of a generic Chinese hagiography of the sage, and thus they must have fallen hard on the ears of Vatican censors. So, in reading this description, one could swear that the Jesuits, no less than the Chinese, regarded him as a holy man and were no less "grateful for the doctrine" received from him. In this light it is less difficult to understand either the fathers' insistence that "Confutius" could not be placed in the same category as "the literati of recent times," or the passionate rigidity with which Ricci drew the line between *i letterati*, (the literati) and *i veri letterati* (the true literati).

The Jesuits sincerely believed that they had something in common with "Confutius," for all that he did and said resonated loudly with their own experience: the importance of undying fraternal affection, the role of rites in the molding of meaningful lives, elected service to the wise in the interest of achieving social harmony, study as a fundamental method of moral self-fashioning. So close was their attachment to him that, as the fathers labored over his writings to recover in public practice the message of his teachings, they came to resemble disciples more than brethren, and their use of "Confutius" and "Confutio" enabled them to draw a very small circle around their saint and his accommodative congregation.

In all the records of the accommodationists, beginning with the *Storia*, "Confutio" commanded an entirely different significance than the respective founders of China's other two principal sects. Ricci devotes the tenth chapter of his introductory book to a discussion of the *varie sette* (various sects) of the Chinese, including the *tre leggi diverse* (three different orders) of *ru, fo,* and *dao*.[51] For their points of similarity with the Jesuits, the *ru*, or *letterati*, are esteemed above all others, which, though accurately described, are none-theless denounced as products of the devil.

Of the three traditions, only that founded by Kongzi is identified through the use of an Italian term. The other *sette*, in meaningful contrast, are simply transliterated. Buddhists are *leggi di Sciechia* (*shijia* [Shakyamuni]), or *legge degli Fatochei* (*fojiao*), and Daoists are *Tausu* (*daoshi*), or *setta è di Laozu* (Laozi). Indeed, from the first mention of "Confutio" and his sect, no transliteration is attempted and no effort is made to explain the proper pronunciation of the Chinese name, as if this figure was already a known quantity. There *were*, according to Pasquale d'Elia, rough Italian equivalents for each of the sounds of "Kong Fuzi." Kong was reproduced as "Ccom" while Fuzi was represented through a variable orthography: "Fuze," "Fuzu," or "Fucu." Furthermore, Kongzi's given name, Qiu, was rendered as "Cchieu" and his style name (*zi*, a name of courtesy given by one's family and used by one's friends), Zhongni, was pronounced as "Cionni."[52] That these equivalents were not used suggests that "Confutio"/"Confuzo" had, by the time of Ricci's writing, been adopted into the language of the Jesuits as a native Italian form. And herein lies the earliest evidence of the instincts behind the later Western appropriation of "Confucianism" I gave in the introduction.

Donald Lach testifies to the epistemologic security of the Jesuits' Confucius when he says, "The names of Asian deities ('Shaka' [Buddha], Ganesha, Confucius) . . . were all used after a time in European writings without explanation."[53] The Jesuits now beheld Chinese culture through the lens of "Confucius," and China, in turn, beheld them. These inventions, guarded so dearly by the fathers in China, soon became the fundaments of a sectarian grammar of "we" and "they" in which the definitive native qualities of the Jesuit community became especially salient.

The Textual Community as Scripturalist Sect

The fathers acknowledged differences between Jesuit learning and that of the *ru* fellowship on which the fathers molded themselves—"the science which among them is especially noticed is moral science, yet because they know nothing of dialectics all of what they say and write [in this regard] is not in a scientific mode, but confused, in many sequences of various sayings and discourses [which] through the light of nature they are able to understand"[54]— but only to emphasize the clarity of the Jesuit vision of similitude. Ricci dwelt at length on resemblance, as did all Jesuit accommodationists, constantly seeking structural similarities residing beneath the differences of *ru* and themselves.

In this relentless search for homology, Ricci seemed unaware that the verbal pyrotechnics that he performed in the service of disclosing structural identity were the stuff of invention, and not merely the labor necessary to penetrate the opacity of Chinese culture and language. Moreover, in the course of persuading the Chinese of the universality of Christian theology, his apologetics blurred distinctions between foreign and native belief, making him as recognizable to contemporary Chinese scholars as he was to the members of his own order. Writing in 1604 to the father general, Ricci defends Chinese belief in Taiji (Supernal Ridgepole) as conducive to, not obstructive of, monotheism. In so doing he gives us a glimpse of Jesuit functional revaluation (by way of Aristotle) of indigenous Chinese concepts:

> They say it [Taiji] is not a spirit and that it is not endowed with understanding. And although some people say it is the reason for things, by reason they do not mean something substantial or intelligent, and it is a reason that is closer to reasoned reason than to reasoning reason. . . . Accordingly, we have judged it preferable in this book, rather than attack

what they say, to turn it in such a way that it is in accordance with the idea of God, so that we appear not so much to be following Chinese ideas as interpreting Chinese authors in such a way that they follow our ideas. . . . And if, in the end, they come to understand that the Taiji is the first substantial principle, intelligent and infinite, we should agree to say that it is none other than God.[55]

Rather than arguing that Chinese difference from Christianity constituted falsehood, as would later Catholic and Protestant missionaries, Ricci presumed their complementarity and drew the metaphysical presumptions of contemporary *ru* into dialogue with his own faith. The legitimacy of this dialogic conception is made explicit in the *Tianzhu shiyi*, the work that, above all, symbolized Jesuit passage from priests to *ru*. To Ricci his success as a catechist was in direct relation to his ability to reproduce the *habitus* of sixteenth-century *ru*.[56] The *Tianzhu shiyi* was testament to the success of cultural crossing, for unlike its precursor (*Tianzhu shilu* which had been drafted first in Latin), it was written in Chinese for a Chinese audience and enjoyed monumental popularity, passing through numerous subsequent editions and printings between 1603 and 1966.[57] The effect of the catechism and the immensely popular *Jiaoyou lun* (Treatise on Friendship), written by Ricci and Xu Guangqi, was, the former admitted, to "establish our reputation as scholars of talent and virtue."[58]

So the dialogic content of Ricci's argument in the catechism was evidence of his search for common premises. The effort to demonstrate an original Chinese monotheism, with *ru* as God's native servants, was advanced through use of a technique uncustomary for the missionary, but familiar to the Chinese literati. Instead of employing the common literary convention of exposition (as did Ruggieri in the *Tianzhu shilu*) in which the regnancy of the Christian message is assumed by the omniscience of the third-person narrator, Ricci engaged the practice of disputation, drawing on the rhetorical stock of Scholasticism. In this respect, the disputation of the *Tianzhu shiyi* broke free from the *expositio* of the *Tianzhu shilu*. Indeed, Ricci's Latin translation of the catechism, prepared in 1603, was described by the author as "De Deo verax Disputatio" (A True Disputation Concerning God).[59] At the same time, argument by disputation was a practice dear to the Chinese. Known as *shui* (persuasion), it was a form of rhetoric common to the Warring States and the foundation of classical Chinese oratory.

In the catechism Ricci took advantage of these formal rhetorical similarities and presented a logical proof of a native Chinese understanding of fundamental Christian concepts: Heaven and Hell, the Supreme Being, just reward and punishment, the existence of an immortal human soul, and God's creation of all things. All of these were teased out of indigenous Chinese culture as the "Western scholar" gradually awakens in his iconic interlocutor, the "Chinese scholar," a re-cognition of the truth of an ancient Chinese natural religion, now obscured. There is no better demonstration of this rhetorical strategy than an exchange that occurs at the close of the seventh chapter.

This chapter, titled "Lun renxing benshan er shu tianzhu menshi zheng-xue" (A Discussion of the Original Goodness of Human Nature, and the Transmission of the Correct Doctrine of the Followers of the Heavenly Lord), is itself a marvelous invention in the native vocabulary. The term *menshi zhengxue* is delightfully ambiguous: it may refer to the apostolic transmission of Christ's teaching, or to the transmission from Kongzi of the true teachings of the Heavenly Master through his disciples, as *menshi* is the term commonly used for the followers of the sage. With some prompting from his argumentative adversary, the *ru* scholar realizes the grave error of the current (and popular) belief in the unity of the three teachings—*fo, dao, ru*—and exclaims: "Dear me! Thieves have injured the people coming in the depth of night and we have yet to rouse ourselves in defense. Hearing your words I have been awakened from my sleep as if by a thunderclap."[60]

The "thieves" in this instance are those of increasing number who advocate the religious eclecticism of *sanhan jiao* (the three sects' teaching). It is they, particularly its *jinru* (contemporary *ru*) followers, who have squandered the heritage of the true doctrine, blending historically distinct native and foreign traditions, thereby collapsing the necessary distinctions between orthodoxy and heterodoxy. *Jinru*, by stealth of their confident assertion of intellectual descent from Kongzi, have taken possession of *zhengdao* (the true way).

Displaying an impressive command of *ru* philosophical vocabulary, it is the "Western" and not the "Chinese scholar" who condemns the *sanhan jiao* as *yiduan*, or heterodox, while explicitly stating the orthodox, *zhengdao*. "Now the moral effort [*gongfu*] that our Heavenly Master bequeathed to us," he says, "is neither the teaching of Daoism on nothingness nor of Buddhism on *nirvana*, but is concerned with guiding the mind [*xin*] through sincerity [*chengshi*] to the mystery of the humane way [*rendao*]."[61] While differences could be used to accentuate the fundamental similarities between the fathers and the Chinese, they were also employed, as here, to segregate proper from improper native belief.

In this talk of the Heavenly Master's bequest there is something conceptually odd at work, and it is this very strangeness that reveals the extent of Jesuit indigenousness as a *ru* cult. The fundamentalist instinct to defend the *zhengdao* of Kongzi is expressed in a language taken from the lexicon of Song era *ru* and, in light of Ricci's distaste for the metaphysical narration of the ancient *ru* tradition by Zhu Xi and the other Song figures who used these terms, one must conclude that he was unaware of the contradiction. We find here all the signature phrases of the Song/Ming metaphysical construction of *ru* tradition, better known as *lixue: rendao* (the way of humanity), *gongfu* (moral effort), *xin* (mind), *chengshi* (sincerity). As well, in his denunciation of contemporary *ru*, the scholar reiterates *lixue*'s clichéd reproach of Buddhism and Daoism. Yet these *lixue* concepts are wielded simultaneously as tools to define the orthodox and as weapons to defend this orthodoxy from the very *ru* sects responsible for contemporary understanding of these specialized moral terms.

The provenance of these ideological terms must have been unknown to Ricci, I suspect, because they were learned as part of the Jesuits' own training in *guanhua*, having been assimilated to the commentaries on those texts (like the *Sishu*) upon which they depended. This is the obvious conclusion one may draw from the fertile, misconceived conflation of separate moments in the history of *ru* explicit in Ricci's notion (noted above) that the Song cosmic principle, Taiji (Supernal Ridgepole), was an ancient term for the first principle uttered by Kongzi. Ricci read the *Sishu*, Zhu Xi's redacted anthology, as the work of "Confutio," and, while criticizing Zhu for his atheism, redeployed the rhetorical infantry of *lixue* against the *yiduan* of Buddhism and Daoism.[62] In using the image of an ancient, doctrinally correct *ru* to displace *ru* (*lixue*), Ricci inserted his Sino-Jesuitical conception into a contemporary stream of sectarian images, where he and his fellow Jesuit *xiucai* could not help but appear marginal.[63]

Their liminality was the enabling condition of their jeremiad against contemporary Chinese who had turned away from the true teaching of which they, the Jesuit fathers, were the purveyors. To a question about the efficacy of chanting Buddhist sutras, the "Western scholar" responds in a succession of familiar native metaphors, sounding much like the *ru* restorationist Zhu Xi when he says,

> A clan can have only one head, having two is a crime. A kingdom can have but one prince, having two is a crime. The universe is in the grasp of one master. To say there are two—is this not the most heinous crime in the world? *Ru* wanted to banish the two families [Fo and Dao, Buddhism and Daoism] from China; however, today they [contemporary Ru] construct temples of the two clans and worship their images.[64]

This is but one example of the persuasive consequences of the fathers' identity as *ru*. Passages of this sort reveal the considerable depth of their commitment to native discourse, for "the clan has one head" trope echoed the common refrain of Chinese political debates—"There is only one sun in the sky."

In the guises of "Western scholar" and "Chinese scholar," Ricci advanced a rival claim to legitimacy of the Confucian way, one rooted in an earlier *ru* tradition, putatively prior to its corruption by the metaphysical superstitions of Buddhism and Daoism. The refutation of *houru* (later *ru*) or *jinru* as schismatics indistinguishable from Buddhists or Daoists, was encased within the Jesuit canon, which, as we have seen, explicitly excluded the metaphysically speculative interpretations of the classics peculiar to the Song and Ming *ru* traditions, but which were the good coin of Hanlin orthodoxy at the time of Ricci's writing.

Throughout the *Tianzhu shiyi* the "Western scholar" (*xishi*) and the "Chinese scholar" (*zhongshi*) speak of *xianru, guzhiru, guru,* and *qianshi zhiru* (former *ru, ru* of antiquity, ancient *ru,* and *ru* of a previous era). By way of this interpretive code, Ricci and his priestly cohort distinguished orthodoxy from heterodoxy, as in this debate concerning the appropriateness of identifying oneself as one with the single body of the universe, where the term *xianru* first appears:

> Mo Di [Mozi] loved man without distinction; however, the former *ru* (*xianru*) disputed this as untrue. Today if you prevail upon people to treat earth and mud with humaneness, contemporary *ru* (*shiru*) would be in accord with [Mo Di]—how bizarre! When the Heavenly Master created heaven, earth, and the ten-thousand things each had its own form and appearance, some having the same ancestor but a different kind, some being the same kind but with different bodies, some having the same body but with different functions. Today, desirous to insist that it is one body, [they] rebel against the one who made all things.[65]

The distinction drawn here between ancient and modern was not chronological but doctrinal, and what may have been understood as a philosophical difference by *ru* of late imperial China was taken as a marker of orthodox or heterodox theology by Ricci. The criticism of contemporary *ru* as inauthentic or deceitful represented a sound critique of the orthodox *ru* tradition. Indeed Ricci's insistence that modern *ru* are indistinguishable from Buddhists and Daoists and that there was no single transmission of *ru* doctrine from antiquity to the present was later taken up in Gu Yanwu's (1613–1682) *Rizhi lu* (Record of Daily Learning) and most persuasively in Dai Zhen's *Mengzi ziyi shuzheng* (Evidential Commentary on Meanings of Terms in the *Mengzi*).

"The doctrine that is most commonly followed here [among the literati] seems to me to have been taken from the sect of idols (Buddhism) about five centuries ago," observes Ricci. In the last five hundred years the three teachings had become confused, causing Ricci's Chinese scholar to lament that "there are even *ru* disciples who, led by their selfish wisdom, forcibly accommodate the doctrines of the two clans [Buddhism and Daoism] and, like beggars eating in excess simply to fill themselves, have confounded the true learning [*zhengxue*]."[66] Through his literary conceit of the Chinese scholar,

Ricci was proclaiming the righteous distinction between the true and orthodox (*zheng*) and the false and heterodox (*xie*).

He does not hesitate to condemn this contemporary doctrine, borne forward in the teachings of both the Cheng/Zhu and Lu/Wang *ru* traditions, for its monistic premise "that the whole world is composed of only one substance, and that its creator, together with heaven and earth, men and animals, trees and plants, and the four elements all make up one continuous body."[67] For Ricci, the logical, and disturbing, consequence of this premise is that "man can come to be like God by being of one and the same substance with him."[68] And such heresy must be refuted "not solely by reason but also by the authority of their ancients who quite clearly teach a very different doctrine."[69]

The defense of the *ru* tradition on the basis of its self-sufficiency and primordiality resembled the primitivist argument of sixteenth-century Protestant reformers, who based their arguments on scriptural inerrancy. The fundamentalist contention of these reformers, most notably the biblical scholar Matthias Flacius Illyricus, was that the Bible was inherently noncontradictory and fully intelligible; thus, there was no need for commentarial or interpretive intervention.[70] Similarly, Ricci urged his brethren to devote themselves to the study of the classic works unencumbered by the commentaries of latter-day *ru* like Zhu Xi whose interpretations violated the intentionality of the sacred texts.

For the Chinese, in contrast, *xianru* and *houru* were chronological distinctions and certainly not loaded ideologically in the manner they were for Ricci. He insisted on dividing the "order of the literati" into two: the ancient and the modern, or the true and the false.[71] "*Ru* today invariably misinterpret ancient writings, too quick to cite the text and too slow to interpret it."[72] This is just a variant of the eleventh-century Song critique of scholarship that became a standard in the vociferous scholarly debates over *guwen* (ancient prose) and *shiwen* (contemporary prose)—all style and no substance—and which had become the stock-in-trade of professional scholars. Though the instincts of Sino-Jesuit fundamentalism may have been acquired from the fathers' theological disputes with Protestant reformers, their insistence on a return to a Chinese scripture unvarnished by commentary was more evidence of their successful "crossing over."

It is difficult to imagine at first how such powerful lines of filiation could develop between the missionaries and *ru*. There were many surface similarities about which the Jesuits themselves remarked early in their encounter and which were discussed in the previous chapter. But there is a considerable leap from noting similarities in function, education, and organization, to claiming legitimate possession of the *dao*. This was in fact what the Jesuits had done in protesting against the idolatry of contemporary *ru* practice and in holding out for a complete restoration of the tradition inaugurated by Confucius. In another selection from the catechism Ricci reveals himself as the proper interpreter he has become, and not the interloper he once was, as he permits his Chinese scholar to separate orthodox wheat from heterodox chaff:

> Thus, man is not yet enlightened of the truth of himself; how much less can he understand other truths? Yet those who follow the Buddhist tradition, those of Laozi's following, and imitators of Kongzi have fragmented the universal mind into three parts. Again there are yet other officious persons who have established their own sects, inventing new teachings so it will not be long before the three teachings have divided into at least three thousand. Although each cries "the correct way!, the correct way!," the more paths there are in the world, the more strange and confused they become.[73]

Therefore, in saying such things Ricci was more the servant of contemporary debates on the reform of the *ru* by imperial scholars than he was the missionary seeking converts through the reinterpretation of Confucius. Of course, he was actively engaged in the latter, but he was keenly aware that conversion was impossible without conversation. Thus, it is not surprising to learn from Xu Guangqi, Father Ricci's most celebrated proselyte, that the *Tianzhu shiyi* along with other Jesuit works in Chinese were effective tools in late Ming sectarian debate, as they worked to *"bu ru yi fo"* (supplement *ru* while excising Buddhism).[74]

Adversarial positions against Buddhism in favor of a reassertion of *ru* teachings of this sort have been identified with the reform movements of the Donglin and Fushe associations in the late Wanli era. The fathers and their Chinese converts have been so associated with the reform fundamentalism of these groups. As we learned in the last chapter, however, such association was fortuitous. Gu Xiancheng and Gao Panlong (1562–1626) organized the Donglin shuyuan in Wuxi to eliminate corruption from the highest echelons of Ming imperial life, but in doing so they called for a return to the *shixue*, or solid learning, of Zhu Xi's *lixue* tradition, the very tradition considered "atheist" and repugnant by Ricci. So, against the backdrop of late Ming restorationism, the Jesuits' Chinese self-image was remarkable, and we can learn more about it from contemporary Chinese reaction to them.

Chinese Embrace of Jesuit Sectarianism

Their native self-definition was singular in the most obvious sense because, like their insistence on the use of Kong Fuzi, the Jesuit definition of *xianru* was out of tune with contemporary Chinese understanding. There are native precedents for the term, but they occur rather sparsely in Chinese literature before the Yuan and Ming, where it is used almost exclusively in the imperial cult to refer to certain followers of Kongzi. In a preface to his commentary on the *Chunqiu* (Spring and Autumn Annals) Du Yu (222–284 C.E.), in criticizing the commentaries of his contemporaries, complains, "that which the *xianru* passed on was not at all like this."[75] Here the value-laden distinction between ancient and new is reminiscent of the Jesuit definition of *xianru*, as is the contrast between *xianru* and "what has survived them" made a few centuries later by Kong Yingda (574–648).[76] In subsequent eras *xianru* and *jinru* would be commonly used to mark the chronology of past and present habit, the former term losing its prescriptive significance.

By the Ming, *xianru* had become more of a descriptive than a normative expression, used as an invocation in ritual and as a designation of rank for placement of spirit tablets in the Kong temple (Kongmiao).[77] In this latter respect it was barely distinguishable from *xianxian*, or "former worthies," the title reserved for ten of Kongzi's honored disciples, including Yan Hui and Zeng Dian. *Xianru* designated the transmission of Kongzi's teaching from Zuo Qiuming, the alleged *ru* disciple and putative author of the *Zuo zhuan*.

In fact, *xianru* was an imperial temple title for those men considered transmitters of canonical learning (*jingxue*). According to the *Mingshi lizhi* (Ming History Catalogue of Rites), it was in the ninth year of the Ming emperor Jiajing (r. 1522–1566) that the title *xianru* was applied to *ru* followers, beginning with Zuo Qiuming and extending to Hu Juren (1434–1484) in the fifteenth century.[78] These titles were changed in 1642 under the emperor Chongzhen (r. 1628–1644) and were in effect at the time of Ricci's work on the catechism. Not included, to be sure, in either the *xianru* or *xianxian* pantheon was Kongzi. Kongzi is always identified as *xiansheng* (first sage), and an altar bearing this title is found at the head of the Kongmiao, while the *xianru* and *xianxian* altars stand along the sides. Hence, while there was a term, *xianru*, familiar to educated Chinese in the late Ming, it did not refer to what the Jesuits intended it to refer to. Its significance was limited to the ceremonial function served by distinguishing members of the *ru* tradition within the imperial cult and rarely occurred alongside *houru* and *jinru*, those vernacular references for contemporary scholars.

The choice of *xianru* as the native exemplar of the Jesuits' work as Chinese scholars and foreign missionaries also reflected something of the delicate negotiation of the fathers' place in China vis-à-vis the authority of the church. We have learned that with "Kong Fuzi" the Jesuits accorded the sage a superlative status in the pantheon of Chinese philosophers and officials and that in Chinese they called him *shengren*, insisting on translating it as *santo*. Yet, they deliberately chose not to abide by the Chinese title for their saint, *xiansheng*, as it appeared in every temple of the land. However well the

Jesuits had merged with Chinese life, their representations of native experience and their interpretation of its meaning had to be justified before their superiors in Goa and in Rome. How could Kongzi be the *primo santo* when none other than Christ could be so identified? Justification of this Italian equivalent of *xiansheng* exceeded the possible, I suspect, and so *xianru* was chosen as their Chinese term for an ideal teacher and his ancient ethical teaching.

Their choice was intelligible to their fellow Chinese, but in Ricci's criticism of modern developments in the *ru* tradition, particularly the work of Zhu Xi, the Jesuits' *xianru* conception even broke rank with the late Ming cultural front of classical restoration and became independently sectarian. It was not enough for the fathers, especially Ricci, to refute the theories of Buddhists, Daoists, and contemporary Confucians by an appeal to "the natural light of reason," *il lume naturale*. Instead, Ricci was compelled to defeat these doctrines in a manner wholly consistent with the ethos of the tradition he so enthusiastically adopted. And in this way he carried out the argumentative dictates of his role as assimilated interloper while provoking visceral reaction from such contemporary Chinese scholar-officials as Wang Qiyuan, who said: "The barbarians first attacked Buddhism. Next they attacked Daoism, next later *ru* [*houru*]. If they have not yet attacked Kongzi it is because they want to remain on good terms with the literate elite and officials, in order to spread their doctrine."[79] Another Chinese scholar, Zeng Shi, vigorously queries the legitimacy of the Jesuits' claims on behalf of *ru*, saying:

> How can it be claimed that their doctrine is in accord with our *ru* when, in "The Real Significance of the Heavenly Master," Ricci explains that Kongzi's idea of cosmic origin is false, that Zisi's statement that one should follow nature is unfounded, that Mengzi's statement on the three contraventions of filial piety is wrong, that the commentaries by Zhu Xi on the sacrifices to Heaven and Earth are unacceptable?[80]

These polemical excerpts from the infamous 1639 anti-Jesuit tract, *Shengchao poxie ji* (The Sacred Dynasty's Collection Exposing Heresy), confirm the viability of the Jesuit community's invention as a native scripturalist sect. The language of these Christian critics reveals an exchange of insults and interpretations on the ground of a common culture, that of *ru*. The mutually acceptable premises Ricci established between Christianity and *ru* in the *Tianzhu shiyi* are affirmed here, in a contrary spirit and from an opposite direction. The authors whose writings are assembled in these chapters seem especially aggrieved by the claim of Jesuit preservation of Kongzi's teachings and demonstrate logical inconsistency or contradiction in the arguments the fathers advance in defense of their *zhengxue*. Such rhetorical embrace through denunciation is explicit in a selection from Chen Houguang:

Kongzi speaks of serving men and rectifying daily conduct. They, contrarily, speak of serving Shangdi and holding onto fantasies. Kongzi speaks of understanding life and knowing how to stay in one's place. They, in contrast, speak of knowing death and winning favors in the next world. Kongzi takes the Supernal Ridgepole [Taiji] as the governor of the cosmos, considering it the most venerable and most noble. [They], however, judge Taiji to be dependent, low, and profoundly despicable. . . . Believing care for one's parents to be of little importance, they reject fathers and in this way show that they are more culpable than Mozi. . . . Consequently, their obedience and respect for Tian and Shangdi are only a pretext for advancing their own deceitful ideas. The men from the far west, using *ru* as an ally, come into our land armed with weapons. Unfortunately, half of those who esteem their teaching are prominent figures and educated men. Thus, if humble men like myself decide to stand up and fight them, there are many who will spit upon us and insult us.[81]

Inasmuch as he states here the problems with accommodationist interpretation, Chen also makes clear that the Jesuits were able to represent themselves as fierce defenders of native ground and, more importantly, indicates that Chinese from the region were persuaded by the teachings of the foreigners. It is perhaps not an accident that this text originated in the southeast province of Fujian, an area that had witnessed an impressive growth in the popularity of accommodationist Christianity in the early decades of the seventeenth century. Much of this successful dissemination of the faith was due to the work of missionary followers of Ricci like Giulio Aleni (1582–1649), who were favored with both local and national attention from officials and who were able to negotiate theological inroads into the kin-based ancestral cults that were the firmament of the Chinese religious universe.

Chinese of all classes, the *Poxie ji* texts complain, were much impressed with the curative effects of the fathers' holy water, the magical efficacy of the Latin language, as well as the ubiquity and omnipotence of Tianzhu (the Heavenly Master). They were particularly captivated by the image of the Madonna and child and assorted artifacts of Christian iconography, above all the crucifix, which Aleni permitted Chinese converts to use in conducting the familial cult of the dead, so that the efficacy of prayer could be translated from the cross to the ancestral shrine.[82] Local critics were well aware of the growing presence of Christianity in Chinese life and measured it in several ways: the increasing accumulation of European books and Catholic churches throughout the country, and, according to the calculation of Huang Zhen, the "tens of thousands of families," who had taken up *tianzhu jiao*.[83]

Indeed, the text fairly bristles with resentment of the appallingly wide dissemination of *tianzhu jiao* among both the educated and the uneducated: "In the exalted ranks they have obtained allies among officials, while below they sow discord in the hearts of the common people";[84] "Their poison is spreading everywhere and threatens to contaminate myriad generations . . . Respected literati and people of reputation follow their views, printing books of the doctrine of the Heavenly Master and composing prefaces for them."[85] Yet, in these angry reactions there is significant evidence of the foreign faith's convergence with the plural streams of native practice, if not a confirmation of Jesuit nativeness, because the animadversion is conveyed in the context of a common culture and language and in the very manner that one would address the rhetorical weaknesses of any adversary in persuasion. For all of their use of the term *man* (barbarian) in speaking of the missionaries collectively, the critics represented in the *Poxie ji* still labor to exaggerate the distinctions between what is Chinese and what is not.

These concerned scholar-officials must "expose" (*po*) this doctrine as heresy (*xie*) and "discriminate its teachings" (*bianxue, bianjiao*) from those native to China, but in the process show that an accommodative Christianity was grafted onto the root of indigenous practice and was syncretically joined with certain traditions of *ru* discourse. Another passage offers a tendentious, but telling, explanation of how Ricci in particular was able to invent a Christian doctrine still consonant with indigenous tradition. Accusing Li Madou (Ricci) of deceit, Huang Wendao holds that:

> The words and sounds of his language were not like those of Chinese and [some] feared that his ideas would confute those of our *ru*. Therefore, he invited Chinese scholars to teach him the Five Classics. Ignoring the abstruse in these works, he fashioned his own doctrine so that there appeared little difference between what he was saying and what was said by Yao, Shun, Zhou Gong, and Kongzi. Yet in fact he was furtively inventing his own doctrine. Renouncing *fo*, criticizing *dao*, and disparaging *ru*, he, at the same time, used Yao, Shun, Zhou Gong, and Kongzi to convey his teaching.[86]

Huang could denigrate Ricci's motives, but there was no denying that the Jesuit, with the assistance of very capable Chinese scholars, had made a native Christianity that, according to some Chinese, was indistinguishable from *ru*. These rhetorical discriminations were the reflex of a persistent impulse to recapture the native identity of *ru* teaching, for the Jesuits are never called by either of the titles they assumed *apud Sinas*—*xiucai* and *ru*. Instead they are *man* and *yeman* (barbarians), while by means of a host of nativist neologisms such as *wu ru*, (we *ru*, or our *ru*) and *wu rusheng* (our *ru* saints), the various authors through conscious invocation of tradition seek to reclaim legitimate, native ground believed lost to the Jesuits.

At every turn, rhetorical phrasings punctuate the sectarian syntax of native and foreign, the most effective of these being the term *xuemai* to designate the authentic intellectual traditions of China.[87] The expression is a homophonic pun on *xuemai* meaning "artery"; thus, proper teachings are distinguished by appeal to anatomy, to the ultimately inalienable—blood. However, the symbolic capital, as it were, of *xuemai* exceeded anatomy, reaching from native self to authoritarian state, as it was a common late Ming metaphor for the waterways over which coursed the sustenance of the empire.[88]

In this way the narrow differences between Jesuit *ru* and Chinese *ru* were dramatized. At the same time anti-Christian critics sought to frame their invective as an appeal for official sanction against the foreigners in the name of what one of them called "love of ruler and country." The appeal to the imperium was a desperate plea for official discrimination of the strands of native and foreign that had become so unselfconsciously intertwined in the minds of Jesuits and, more importantly, the Chinese. This could only mean one thing: that, on the ground, the vocabularies of one tradition merged indiscriminately with those of another. Only the power of the state could vanquish such arrogant misrepresentation by challenging the ancient indigenous authority upon which the Jesuits made good their claims for the preservation of *zhengxue*. But such authority was beyond the reach of the state and resided exclusively within a community given to the acquisition and transmission of sacred texts. Through these labors the Sino-Jesuit community was repeatedly constituted, translating itself deeper into Chinese life and, after 1660, translating itself back to Europe, as we will see.

Authority and the Textual Apostolate

When the fictive Western scholar spoke of the identity of "Shangdi," the ancient term for deity attested in the Chinese classics, and "Tianzhu," the Sino-Jesuit neologism for God, he defined Chinese antiquity as the space of monotheism. This fiction, Ricci believed, would serve "to draw over to our opinion the principal of the sect of the literati, that is Confutio, interpreting in our favor some things that have been left uncertain in his writings."[89] It was from this ambiguity in ancient writings that the fathers obtained the necessary warrants to style themselves defenders of *xianru*, yet questions remain: How did they obtain the "true way" (*zhengdao*) if not through Zhu Xi and the Masters of the Song? On what authority did they present themselves as defenders of orthodoxy? Given that their reading of the tradition was unconventional and contrary to the imperially sanctioned conception of the *ru* tradition, how did the fathers avoid persecution? Was it because the restorationist claims of the Jesuits were considered so ludicrous as to be undeserving of review? Or did their avoidance of imperial rebuke reveal a severance of the formerly intimate ties between *ru* doctrine and state administration?

Certainly one reason that the Jesuits could advance themselves as an independent sect was the environment of intellectual pluralism and cultural questioning coincident with the political decline of the late Wanli era. By the first decade of the seventeenth century it was common for even certain aspects of Cheng/Zhu orthodoxy to be queried by the orthodox as new communities of intellectual authority developed. Consequently the Jesuit claims of possession of the "true way" of Kongzi were not so extraordinary. Their confidence in such declaration of native faith was, at the same time, a reflex conditioned by the specific history of the Society of Jesus as one of a number of new Roman Catholic reform sects that appeared in response to the Catholic Reformation of the mid–sixteenth century.[90] Thus, the authority for the Jesuits' variant *ru* was construed in two complementary respects, one Chinese and one Catholic, both sustained by and sustaining of the Jesuits' textual community.

That critical reaction to the catechism *Tianzhu shiyi*, for instance, was late in coming suggests that its message, rather than seeming ludicrous or heretical, was generally accepted. Nevertheless, when Chinese scholars took issue with Jesuit interpretation, as we noted, the criticisms fell squarely on the question of the legitimacy of their defense of an archaic *ru*, *xianru*, against all remaining sects, including *houru*, or later *ru*, of the Song and Ming.

Ricci's invention of *xianru*, while justified in conventional Chinese rhetoric by appeal to classical authorities, called for a redefinition of the authoritative canon of contemporary interpretation. Of course the ultimate justification for Ricci's special advocacy on behalf of archaic *ru* and against contemporary *ru* was his confidence that the former were divinely inspired. It was God the ultimate inventor, visible through the natural light of reason trapped in the surviving texts of China's ancient practices and beliefs, who granted Ricci the authority to define heterodox and orthodox. Thus, in obedience to this authority whose presence was for him implicit in the sacred works of the Chinese, Ricci mixed and matched texts and traditions, tailoring them to the specifications of his fundamentalist design.

But on native ground the authority of the neologism "Tianzhu" was insufficient to command assent in argument. The key to Jesuit nativeness as a sect was indigenous authority, a mastery of Chinese principles of argument. In a brilliant hermeneutic contention that history was often—accidentally but not necessarily—corrosive of memory, Ricci cited as his authority ancient writings claiming that the discontinuity in the transmission of the monotheism of China's ancients arose because "traditions are incomplete [literally, not exhausted]. . . . either they were delivered orally and not completely recorded in writing, or they were recorded but later lost; or later, stupid scribes did not believe that they were authentic and destroyed them."[91] In this apparent break in the line of transmission, Ricci and his catechism entered to lay sole claim to the legitimacy of the tradition of the *xianru*.

Here, in a few inspirational thoughts written for the connoisseur Cheng Yubo (1541–1616), he spells out the hermeneutics of belief underwriting his claim of legitimate defense of the ancient *ru* tradition:

> At a distance of a hundred paces, voices do not carry, but when they are confided to writing for communication, then two men, although they live more than ten thousand miles apart, may converse, exchanging questions and answers, just as if they were sitting face to face. I cannot know what kind of men there will be a hundred generations hence, who are not yet born, but because of the existence of this writing I can let those of ten thousand generations later penetrate into my mind, just as if they were of my own generation, and moreover, although former masters of a hundred generations ago have already vanished, yet we, of these later days, because of the writings they left, still may hear their authoritative words, look up to their admirable behavior, and know about the order and disorder of those times, exactly as though we were living in that age. The establishment of the sacred doctrine, the work of the hundred schools, the skill of the six cultivations, how could they, without writing, ever have reached the present perfection?[92]

The authority for his restorationist conception was derived, above all, from a belief in transmission, specifically what Ricci termed *shuwen*, or "transmission by writing." In a manner prefiguring the biblical hermeneutics of Schleiermacher, Ricci believed that the text had a spiritual life, that writing in fact conveyed the spirit of previous ages.

He may have anticipated later biblical exegesis in making normative claims for a particular reading of a text based on its spirit, but Ricci was only reproducing a version of what he saw around him. The inspiration for *shuwen*, as in the Jesuit elevation of Kongzi to the status of a saint, came from indigenous traditions of redaction that presumed writing's transmission of intent, as in this statement attributed to Mengzi about the meeting of ancient and modern minds in the reading of the *Shi jing:* "One who interprets the *Shi* [*jing*] should not let the words damage the phrases, or the phrases damage the intent. . . . To encounter the author's intent with one's own idea—this is the way to get it."[93] A formulation virtually analogous to Ricci's *shuwen* may be found in Yang Xiong's (53 B.C.E.–18 C.E.) commentary on the *Yijing*'s "Xici zhuan," where we learn:

As for encompassing and enwrapping the things of the world, recording what is long past to make it clear to the distant future, setting down what the eye could not see in antiquity and transmitting across a thousand *li* what the mind cannot understand, there is nothing better than writing. Therefore, speech is the voice of the mind and writing is the picture of the mind.[94]

But, ironically for Ricci who was such a redoubtable critic of *lixue*, it was Cheng Yi, more than Mengzi or Yang Xiong, who anticipated the father's belief in the mysterious link between recorded language and ancient spirit:

There may have been some who have understood the words and not attained their meaning; but there has never been anyone who has not understood the words and still was able to acquire the meaning. The most subtly attained is principle. The most obviously attained is the image. However, substance and function have a common origin. There is no separation between the subtle and the manifest. If we observe and completely understand [the *Classic of Change, Yijing*] so as to execute its canonical ceremonies, then there is nothing which is not completely contained in its words. Therefore, if a good student is in search of the words [of the ancients], he must bring himself close [to the ancients]. The *Yijing*] [allows us] to draw close, [even though] we do not know the speech [of the ancients.] [A]ll that I can comment on are the words themselves. If the meaning can be acquired through the words, then it will be [restored] to man's possession.[95]

There is a sense here, as in Ricci's *shuwen*, that time is an accident; thus, the distance between ancient text and contemporary reader may be overcome by the intention of the latter to go "in search of the words." Consequently both recognize that doctrine is passed solely through texts and not through an apostolate. Instead, it appears as if texts themselves were the apostolic tradition.

To appropriate a certain text or texts was to admit that one could perform a reading of such works consistent with the intentions of the authors. The passages from Ricci, Mengzi, Yang Xiong, and Cheng Yichuan all admit of the inventive role of the reader. Indeed, the vision of Mengzi and Yang Xiong of an ageless conveyance of meaning asserts the active role of the reader/inheritor's intellect in receiving the intention of the author. Thus, innovation is presumed but couched in a filial aesthetic of reception broad enough to include even an avid "foreign" reader of native texts.

"Interpreting in our favor some things that have been left uncertain in [Confucius's] writings," Ricci had said, in explaining how it was that the Jesuits managed to communicate their message to the Chinese. This may be read as an admission of Jesuit struggle to understand the ambiguities common to any text, especially one as equivocal as the *Lunyu.* Indeed there may be little distance between Ricci's "interpreting in our favor some things that have been left uncertain" and the counsel of Kongzi himself that true learning consists in *zide,* or "getting it oneself": "To reanimate what has gone before and thus to learn it anew; [this] may be taken as one's teacher."[96] In this act, one decides what is authoritative in a text while laying claim to a reading, which, by being asserted, locates one within a preexistent horizon of interpretation.[97] This I take as the meaning of Ricci's comment "procuro molto di tirare alla nostra opinione . . . Confutio" (we have acquired much by pulling Confutio over to our opinion). What they acquired was an authoritative, normative position within a historically expanding horizon of Chinese interpretation.

Though authority was invested in the classics and the symbol of Confucius, it was generated nonetheless by the Jesuits, and was an expression of the needs and values of their community among the Chinese. This authority, privileged by the invocation of Kongzi and *xianru,* and the citation of selected texts, was critical to the maintenance of the Sino-Jesuit community among the Chinese. As such it was a local necessity that bound the early missionaries to their texts, to the Chinese, and to each other and that was transmitted through successive generations of Jesuit recruits. However, in the course of this privileged transmission the composition of the mission community and the nature of its enterprise changed, the latter in increasing sympathy with the tumult of Europe's seventeenth-century intellectual climate.

Jesuit Translation: From Chinese
Sectarians to European Scholars

In the years following the publication of Ricci's catechism (1603) the Jesuits became less self-conscious of the local necessity of an authority that sustained their relations with Chinese and the Chinese scriptural tradition, for they were no longer a community of immediate moment bound by shared jeopardy. By 1610 Ricci and his Jesuit confreres had navigated, with considerable native assistance, a spiritual and political path from Shaozhou to Beijing, erecting missions all along the way. The authority of their interpretation of a primordial, monotheistic *ru* tradition was recognized by Chinese and would be sustained through four generations of missionaries, several of whom would receive imperial appointments as servants of the emperor himself.

The Chinese may have accepted the Jesuits and their claims, but the same could not be said of other nonaccommodationist fathers and certain officers of the Holy See who contested the authority of their methods, and above all, their conclusions. These opponents aggressively challenged the strategy of accommodation and even repudiated Ricci's judgment of ancient Chinese texts and the proof of an originary Chinese monotheism.

Immediately after Ricci's death in 1610 through the end of the century, the Society of Missions and European ecclesiastical authorities debated his accommodationist construct, especially his insistence on the comparability of Christianity and the *zhengxue* of Kongzi. Niccolò Longobardo, Ricci's successor as the superior of the China Mission, rejected his precursor's claims for an indigenous Chinese name for the Christian God, and contested his assertion that the message of archaic Chinese monotheism could be found only through study of the Five Classics and Four Books and the studious rejection of their accumulated commentaries.[98]

Through the seventeenth century at least, accommodationism was not deterred by this internal squabbling, and those Jesuit fathers who preserved a fidelity to Ricci's project were rewarded by royal recognition in Europe as well as China: Ferdinand Verbiest (1623–1688) was director of the Chinese Bureau of Astronomy and a close associate of the emperor Kangxi (1654–1702); Père François de La Chaise (d. 1709), an accommodationist, was the confessor of Louis XIV. Against their ecclesiastical opponents, the accommodationist missionaries defended the validity of their interpretations, insisting on their authority, and turned their rhetorical skills to translating themselves and their hard-won native understanding back into Europe. They made public to their secondary audience at home what they had produced privately among the Chinese. This was accomplished through translations of the *Sishu*—Latin and bilingual Chinese/Latin—etymologies of the Chinese word for God, a biography of Confucius, an explanation and reproduction of the hexagrams of the *Yijing*,[99] and a host of other representations of native culture.

Though their intention was to justify the original experiment of Xavier and Valignano by placing before European eyes the textual evidence of theological complementarity (*ru*/Christian), the fathers succeeded in enraging the Vatican while offering an unexpected solution to troubling epistemological queries of seventeenth-century science. The revelation of the products of their textual work on native Chinese ground did not garner for the accommodationist Jesuits the approbation they sought from their superiors, but it did draw the attention of monarchs like Friedrich Wilhelm, Elector of Prussia (1688–1740), and Louis XIV (1638–1715), as well as a number of scientists, among them Leibniz and Newton.

Thus, a principal, if unintended consequence of the defense of accommodationism by Ricci's followers was their acquisition of a dual authority: local and international, theological and ethnological. The former governed the small group ritual of missionary redactors in China; the latter organized a form of knowledge production valuable to science and justified by ethnographic authority that was intentionally drawn into a formal information complex joining philosophers and scientists in France, Germany, Italy, and England.[100]

The success of the Jesuit community in going native was critical to its transformation from a fledgling order of ascetics to trusted advisers of royalty and respected technicians of a highly prized local knowledge, that of China. They were "between-takers," located in the space between Europe and China, bearing authentic knowledge of the unknown, and they brokered their knowledge and access to China for an expanding market in personal libraries, political strategy, and economy. This knowledge and access accounted for the interest that statesmen and rulers had in them, but more important than their prospective contributions to the political and economic shape of the new nations that formed after the Peace of Westphalia (1645) was the contribution of their translated texts in offering evidence to contemporary scholars of a semiotic form (Chinese), representative of nature itself. It is in this latter respect that Confucius and Confucianism acquired the universal life they have enjoyed for many centuries. On the authority of their translations and their role as bearers of "the wisdom of China" the Jesuits insinuated themselves into the plural streams of European self-consciousness; this is why the story of our Confucianism is a narrative made from both of these distinct but inseparable complexes.

The remainder of this chapter will chart a course between the Sino-Jesuit translation project in China and the European reception of its textual products. The Vatican will be less salient in this presentation, not because it was insignificant—in fact, it was more tempestuously involved in the life of the Jesuit order in the mid–seventeenth century than at any other time—but because there were many powerful bidders for the missionaries' talents who could provide subsidies for their travel and for the publication of their works. The purpose of the narrative that follows is to call attention to the accidental quality of Confucius's introduction to Europe, particularly how the very specific features of the Sino-Jesuit community—their native experience, translation, and their reconciliation of the science of investigation with theology— proved well suited for inclusion in the rivalrous cultural politics of Europe on the eve of modernity and amidst a scientific revolution.

The Translation Project

Throughout their work in China in the seventeenth century the accommodationist fathers passed the local knowledge of text and tradition hand to hand. According to what can only be called a system of apprenticeship, new

volunteers to the mission worked with their senior colleagues on translations and commentary, thereby becoming familiar with the canon bearing
God's mystery as they progressed in their study of Chinese. Language study,
for the purpose of translation and commentary, comprised a Jesuit rite of
passage, in fact, the principal rite joining missionary predecessors and successors in the production of knowledge. Ricci, for example, assisted in the
last phases of the preparation of the *Tianzhu shilu*, and in a preliminary
translation of the *Daxue* (The Great Learning), both projects having been
initiated by Ruggieri before Ricci's arrival at Macao in 1582. Ruggieri had
completed a draft Latin translation of the Four Books by 1588, the year he
was recalled to Rome, and Ricci, five years later, finished what he modestly
termed his Latin paraphrase of the Four Books, having mastered Chinese in
the course of its preparation. His labors in this regard were made less oner-
ous, I suspect, by Ruggieri's earlier work on the same texts.

Working side by side with native informants and esteemed scholar-
officials, the Jesuits and their assistants resembled the translation teams of
fourteen centuries earlier that were responsible for the invention of a Chinese lexicon of Buddhist terms.[101] Subsequent detachments of Christian soldiers to the eastern mission joined such teams upon their arrival. All of them
learned Chinese through the study of Ricci's paraphrase of the Four Books,
and it was this very translation that comprised the body of the *Confucius
Sinarum Philosophus*, as d'Elia has pointed out in his annotated translation
of Ricci's mission history.[102] From 1593 to 1687, as the number of Jesuit
publications from China increased, the apprenticeship in knowledge transmission became more explicit.

Prosper Intorcetta assisted Inacio da Costa in the compilation of the *Sapientia Sinica* (Wisdom from China, 1662), a translation of the *Daxue* inherited from Ricci, along with an abbreviated biography of Confucius, and
the first five books of the *Lunyu*.[103] This text was the first truly bilingual
Chinese-Latin translation available in Europe: the characters of the *Daxue*
and the transliteration of their sounds were displayed (figure 8). An obvious,
because curious, feature of this text was the way Chinese merged into Latin
and Latin into Chinese, with virtually no distinction between the literal
translated text and the Jesuit commentary. The Latin renderings of Chinese
graphs are underlined in the text which, in the case of the first paragraph,
shows that a good portion of the "translation" was interpolation.

The blending of Latin and Chinese may be taken as a textual remnant of the
hybrid Sino-Jesuit community. Yet for many European readers this literary
creole meant something very different, owing to the popular seventeenth-
century conception that Chinese, whether pictographic or ideographic, was a
natural language of "real characters." Chinese, in contrast with European

Figure 8. "Lib. Tá Hiô." The first page of Inacio da Costa and Prosper Intorcetta's translation of the *Daxue*. Titled *Sapientia Sinica* (Wisdom from China), this work was the first translation of its kind seen in Europe. The combination of Chinese characters with Latin shows that the fathers made no distinction between Latin and Chinese. (Photograph courtesy of D. E. Mungello)

languages that were seen as constructed systems of representation inadequate to the task of describing the physical world, was taken to be a natural reflection of the fixed laws governing the universe. Considered the lost language of Adam, Chinese was believed to embody what it named and, thus, Jesuit translation of such real characters was appreciated because it brought translator and reader alike closer to the hand of God.

Evidence accumulated with each subsequent publication of the fathers' possession of the real knowledge of a Chinese semiotics, that, like mathematics, was a natural representation of the universe. The *Sapientia Sinica* was followed several years later by another work by Intorcetta, the earliest and most primitive Latin translation of the *Zhongyong* (Doctrine of the Mean). This work, which included an expanded *Confutii Vita* (Life of Confucius), was published in 1667 and 1669 by the mission centers at Goa and Canton as *Sinarum Scientia Politico-Moralis* (The Politico-moral Learning of the Chinese).[104] This latter text, too, was a collective effort, one that benefited from the editorial review of Inacio da Costa, Antonio de Gouvea (1592–1677), François de Rougemont (1624–1676), Christian Herdtrich (1625–1684), and Philippe Couplet, men who were also credited with assembling the *Confucius Sinarum Philosophus*. The textual evidence of an enduring tradition conducted through face-to-face transmission of knowledge and authority is explicit, as we learn from David Mungello:

> The list of seventeen contributors in *Sinarum scientia politico-moralis* not only conforms to the collective nature of the work's production but also supports the contention that *Sapientia Sinica, Sinarum scientia politico-moralis,* and *Confucius Sinarum Philosophus* of 1687 all represent part of an interlinked and evolving translation project. The linkage is shown by the presence of certain names such as da Costa, who was listed as the primary author of *Sapientia Sinica.* When *Confucius Sinarum Philosophus* was published at Paris two decades later, four names were listed on the title page as authors: Intorcetta, Herdtrich, Rougemont, and Couplet. All four of these names were among the *Sinarum scientia politico-moralis* contributors.[105]

As we will recall from chapter 1, the Jesuits established a canon in the name of Confucius and formed authoritative interpretations, which were then appended to newly redacted texts like the *Daxue* and the *Zhongyong*. These texts, the interpretations, and the Chinese language were personally transmitted to subsequent generations of disciples; it was this process that sustained Jesuit solidarity and the conceptions they invented. On Chinese ground these activities were responsible for the Jesuits' impressive acculturation; back in Europe it was their success as a cult of *ru* restoration that obtained for these missionaries respect as experts, specifically as ethnologists.

The Consequences

The cultic qualities of the accommodationist translation project followed naturally from the fathers' membership in piety sects within their own faith. Matteo Ricci and many of the other early Jesuit missionaries had been members of the Marian sodality (cult of the Virgin) in Rome. Francesco de Petris, the first of the Fathers to study Chinese language with Ricci, was an ardent devotee of the cult of the Virgin, as was Ricci's superior, Claudio Acquaviva, who heartily encouraged the formation of such groups within the order. Consequently, as Jonathan Spence notes, "the strength of the bonds that could be forged by those who shared this common experience was carried over into China, reinforcing the ties of shared hopes and dangers."[106] These were the same ties that bound Petris and Ricci as readers of China's classical texts and perhaps the source of the passion with which they defended their construction, "Confucius."

This point of bonding, nurtured in the name of their exemplar and more befitting of sectarians, became a locus for the generation of a science of the ethnic concrete, as Jesuit interpretation, by accommodationists and dissenters alike, moved toward the conclusion that Confucius and Chinese civilization were synonymous. The "rites and terms controversy," which involved the Jesuits in continuous internal disputes, conflicts with brethren Franciscan and Dominican prelates, and disagreements with papal authority, had no effect on the status of Confucius as a metonym for things Chinese. Even Longobardo, in his treatise on Chinese religion (a systematic refutation of Ricci's contention that Tianzhu was the Chinese name for God), did not question this significance of Confucius. Indeed, he considered the foundation of the Chinese religion to be "Confucius and his doctrine."[107]

Among the Jesuits the terminus of this reductionist course was figurism, a protoscientific hermeneutic that creatively preserved Ricci's original notion that China's ancient culture held the key to God's plan. Figurists like Joachim Bouvet (1656–1730) and Jean-François Foucquet (1665–1741) believed that China's most ancient works (*Yijing* and *Shang shu*) contained allegorical vestiges of Christian teachings and even maintained that Christ's revelation was prophesied in the abstruse symbolism of such texts. In this later phase of accommodationist evolution, it was the text, specifically the *Yijing*, and not the words of the prophet Confucius, that contained divine wisdom. Yet, the figurist pursuit of antiquity was fully consistent with, because inspired by, the insistence of Chinese *kaozheng* scholars of the late seventeenth century that an authentic reconstruction of *gu* (antiquity) could only be accomplished through the *Yijing*.

Furthermore, the authority claims for figurism's hieroglyphic decipherment were bound to the political authority invested in the emperor himself—a sign that Jesuits had internalized the contemporary politics of imperial appeasement that engaged the energies of much of their Chinese scholarly cohort in the mid–seventeenth century. The intimacy of royal authority and Jesuit classical exegesis is supremely evident in the frontispiece of Father Louis le Comte's (1655–1728) *Nouveaux mémoires sur l'état présent de la Chine* (Recent Memoirs on the Present State of China), where the emperor Kangxi (r. 1662–1722) is pictured. This royalist imagining of the *Clavis Sinica* reflected the Jesuits' assimilation of Manchu metropolitan culture and their tacit acceptance of the "divine right of kings," and made clear that these later priests, as members of the Missions Étrangères, were the servants of their paymaster, Louis XIV.[108] But, above all, this Europeanized image of Kangxi (CAM HY,

Figure 9. CAM-HY, Empereur de la Chine (Kangxi emperor). Woodcut frontispiece of Louis le Comte, *Nouveaux mémoires sur l'état présent de la Chine*, vol. 1 (Paris, 1696). The image of the emperor has replaced Confucius as the controlling symbol of China, reflecting the accommodation of Jesuit "figurism" to the contemporary politics of imperial appeasement. In 1699 the image was copied and reproduced in the second edition of Leibniz's *Novissima Sinica*. (Photograph courtesy of the Bancroft Library, University of California, Berkeley)

figure 9) from le Comte's text, as it was copied and reproduced in the second edition of Leibniz's *Novissima Sinica* (Latest News from China, 1699), signaled accommodationism's successful translation back to Europe.

The Foreign Reception of Native Invention

Cette perpetuelle erreur, qui est précisément la vie.—*Marcel Proust*

In the last decades of the seventeenth century, the fundamental mechanisms of meaningful invention, canon construction, and authority generation that had enabled the reiterative reproduction of *ru* identity from the Warring States era forward and that sustained the Sino-Jesuit community proved valuable in contributing to schemes to resolve what Robert Markley has called "a crisis of representation" in Europe.[109] The Jesuit translations of Chinese texts that were published from 1662 until the end of the century and which had been undertaken in a spirit of disclosing the latent Christianity of the

Chinese, ironically, were now taken up in Europe to reconcile troubling contradictions brought on by an effort to make science the complement of theology. As the message of these texts had been reduced to the symbol of Confucius, so it was that the Jesuits and their symbol passed from particular to universal significance, a passage effected through the publication of the *Confucius Sinarum Philosophus.*

From the moment the first translations of selected texts from the Chinese canon appeared in seventeenth-century Europe, Confucius, the cherished Jesuit symbol of archaic monotheism, became a lightning rod of speculation among the continent's educated. Confucius was now Europe's sagely uncrowned king, not just China's. His significance was not restricted to an ecclesiastical readership, as he enjoyed a much wider celebrity evidenced by the hasty re-publication, even popularization, of very technical translations and interpretive works produced by the China Mission. Many of these texts, translated from Latin to native vernaculars and republished, circulated widely.

It was in the greater interest of both the Vatican and the China Mission for Jesuit works to find a larger audience. Church authorities, from the inception of the Chinese expedition, scrupulously tended the public image of the mission through the selected publication of Jesuit letters from the field. It was believed that these letterbooks, as they were called, were valuable in soliciting contributions and as well might draw the interest of pious young men and coax them into missionary service. Publishing letters from the field was unusually risky from Rome's vantage, for such documents were as likely to reveal a healthy intellectual curiosity as they were a pious dedication to do God's work among the heathen. More often than not and to the great frustration of men of the China Mission, letters were strenuously edited, even bowdlerized, evidence of the general popularity of Jesuit texts.[110]

For example, the *Sinarum scientia politico-moralis* was translated into French as "La Science des Chinois" and republished in 1672 by Melchisedec Thévenot in a popular four-volume work of travel literature titled *Relations de divers voyages curieux.*[111] The difference in the reception of the two works reflects a shift in modalities for representing individual experience, wherein canonical and theological allegory gave way to protoethnography, to the real. Travel literature became increasingly popular in the late seventeenth century because something akin to ethnographic authority was developing, which was, in turn, part of a larger epistemological shift away from faith and insight to experiment and observation as the basis of reliable knowledge.[112] In this intellectual context the Jesuits and their Chinese texts were construed as scientific authorities providing testimony on behalf of the *universality* of divinely authored creation. The local, self-constituting character of the Jesuit mission in China (described above) has been largely overlooked, even as their texts were widely read. Paradoxically, the authority of the Jesuits lay in their having been there "among the Chinese," while the message they were believed to convey transcended the particular.

When the *Confucius Sinarum Philosophus* appeared in 1687 it was greeted by intellectual excitement from its lay audience, despite its conceptual sophistication and awkward Latin equivalents of Chinese terms. The work was immediately abridged and translated into French, appearing the following year in Amsterdam as *La Morale de Confucius, Philosophe de la Chine.* An English translation of the French abridgement, *The Morals of Confucius, a Chinese Philosopher,* was published in 1691 in London. Both books were reprinted and, like the first editions, were published as leather-bound parchment pocket books. Each was fewer than 125 pages long and offered an abbreviated sampling of the translations of the *Daxue, Zhongyong,* and *Lunyu,* a shortened biography of Confucius, a preface by the editors, and an introductory essay titled "On the Antiquity and Philosophy of the Chinese."[113] This abbreviation and publication of significant portions of the *Confucius Sinarum Philosophus* occurred alongside the abridgment and re-publication of the *Philosophical Transactions* of the Royal Society, which were translated into national vernaculars. So, in the same way that the multilingual European scientific community was sustained by the rapid circulation of the summary volumes of the Royal Society, an educated lay community was joined through the movements of an information network. In the coincidence of the scientific and the popular abridgment of the works of a new experimental science we may recognize the high and low culture complexes of Confucius's significance that were observed in the introduction to this book.

The popular abridged tracts were compendia of the Jesuit translations and commentaries. A glance at the format of these works, or at the preface accompanying the translations, confirms that their audience was not scholarly. They were intended as Baedekers of the moral life of the Chinese, read through the wisdom of Confucius, a man consistently lauded for the depth of his ethical sense. The reader was encouraged to ponder the lessons of Confucius and note their relevance to contemporary life, rather than wonder patronizingly about the impressive wisdom of a pagan primitive.

Not only did such books satisfy and further whet the curiosity of Europeans about China, but they functioned as guides, collections of inspiration to which one could turn when necessary. There was, however, a distinct political message in the English incarnation of Confucius, his celebrity following rather quickly after the Glorious Revolution and the end of the Commonwealth. "After a divisive civil war characterized by a breakdown of censorship and a cacophony of voices struggling to articulate the rights of various factions,"[114] certain segments of English society would have wanted a rational exemplar of the status quo, especially one so given to toleration. Confucius and his moral sayings served, then, to buttress the Restoration, representing the virtue of the universal against the scourge of factionalism. In an age of nascent nationhood, where rulers confronted the challenges of linguistic, cultural, and religious pluralism to the ideal of a cohesive state, the purported empirically attested cohesiveness of Chinese life under the aegis of Confucius proved inspirational in the imagining of new communities.

Confucius could offer more than a political vision of reasoned stability and civil order; in fact, Confucius and the written language of which he was the most learned representative were conceived of by some natural philosophers and scientists as features of a semiotic system analogous to mathematics, a universal system of "real characters." As an unmediated reflection of nature or the universe, the cogency of this system was dependent on textual evidence of the very sort provided by Couplet and his colleagues in the *Confucius Sinarum Philosophus*.

Confucius Sinarum Philosophus and the Seduction of Science

A product of the best Jesuit scholarly endeavor, the *Confucius Sinarum Philosophus*, or *Scientia Sinensis* (Chinese Learning) was published in the same year as Newton's *Principia* (1687), and like the *Principia* sought to establish one-to-one correspondences between God's providential order and signifying systems. It represented the accumulation of one hundred years of translation and exegesis in demonstration of China's archaic monotheism and, as we will see, offered the first documented use of the descriptive term "Confucian." Earlier individual products of missionary scholarship were similar in their focus on history and geography, cartography, or language and grammar, but this work was different; it was a massive, annotated translation. The cost of the work was subvented in large part by Louis XIV (r. 1661–1715), and therefore appeared in a conspicuously elaborate format—412 folio pages along with illustrations including a full-page stylized portrait of Confucius—complete with fleur-de-lis at the head of most sections. It comprised detailed comparative chronological tables of Christian and Chinese history, an incomplete translation of a recension of the Four Books by Zhang Juzheng, the *Sishu zhijie*, an exhaustive critical introduction, and a biography of Confucius.

More significant than the translation, though, was the "Preliminary Discourse" ("Proëmialis Declaratio") which, in 113 pages, introduced the reader to the Chinese classics, a broad history from distant antiquity to the present, the major religious sects, the etymology of Shangdi and *tian*, an analysis of the concepts *li* and Taiji, and the customary religious practices of the Chinese. But the "Proëmialis Declaratio" was more than this. It was a highly original contribution to contemporary debates on natural philosophy; the

Latin translations from the Chinese served as empirical proofs of the claims advanced in this section of the *Confucius Sinarum Philosophus.*

The presentation of the principal sects, *brevis notitia sectae,* borrowed heavily, both in organization and in tone, from Ricci's account of the *tre leggi diverse* from the *Storia.*[115] The latter was a "fieldnotes" impression of the beliefs and practices of the three religious traditions cobbled together for the Society of Jesus, but the compilers of the *Confucius Sinarum Philosophus* organized this inherited account into a rhetorical presentation proper to their lay European audience. The title of this section recalls the *oratio brevis* of medieval rhetoric, a conventional practice in the art of etymology consisting of a brief narrative of the method employed in deriving the etymon of a word. Here, Couplet and his colleagues intended their *brevis notitia* as a defense of the derivation of Chinese religion from three distinct sects explaining origins, just like an *oratio brevis.*

Even as they organized their etymologies and narratives in a manner intelligible to their European contemporaries, these fathers of the Missions Étrangères still transmitted, mutatis mutandis, much of the taxonomy of Ricci's charter text, the *Storia.* That the conceptual foundations of this account were laid by Matteo Ricci cannot be doubted, for the editors follow Ricci's division of China's religious sects and resort to terms like *Sinicas vero litteres* (China's true literati), which were simply Latin versions of Ricci's Italian designation (*i veri letterati*).[116] Plaudits for the *secta literatorum* (sect of the literati) are immediately followed by a vitriolic critique of Buddhism, Daoism, and the teaching of the *Neoterici Interpretes* (neoteric interpreters, and called *i letterati* or *jinru,* today's *ru,* by Ricci and the early Jesuits). Within their denunciations one finds a fascinating parallel, drawn by the authors and discussed for six pages, between these Chinese "neoterics" and the "atheist Christians" of Europe—a confirmation of our earlier suspicion that the Jesuits reproduced the categories of their familiar experience among the Chinese. A new category within the literati sect is "manufactured," that of the *Modernii interpretes* (modern interpreters), in order to describe contemporary *ru* who have upheld the legacy of Confucius.

The "Proëmialis Declaratio" is succeeded by a short biography of Confucius, "The Life of Confucius: Prince of the Chinese Philosophers." The translations from the *Daxue, Zhongyong,* and *Lunyu* follow in order, and the book concludes with an impressive chronological table of Chinese monarchs, beginning with Yao. The effect of this work, even on today's reader, is astonishment, not only at the authors' detailed scholarship but at the fully drawn portraits of Confucius, the charismatic ethical scholar, and of the Chinese, his morally sensible followers. Indeed, so much material is crammed into the pages of this book that the reader draws comfort from the imposing woodblock print of Confucius (figure 7) preceding the biography, as the image seems to contain within its orderly bounds the monumental mass of culture, history, and religion related by the authors.

Remarkably, the Jesuits assembled this heterogenous cultural mass of plural contemporary schools, practices, texts, and interpretations into a system identified as the legacy of the mythic philosopher-hero. It was just this metonymic reduction of the many to the one that was responsible for the political significance of the *Confucius Sinarum Philosophus* for new states seeking to articulate, justify, and enforce absolute claims to nationhood. Confucius was, in effect, China, and so too was Louis XIV France or William III (r. 1689–1702), England. The fathers could not have foreseen such an interpretation of their work, but they did believe that China could be reduced to Confucius, offering at least two reasons that would justify this equivalence.

First, they argued that because he was the author of the *libri classici* (The Classics), which are the literary summation of China's ancient culture, Confucius has been immemorially honored. While he was described by Ricci and Trigault as the Chinese equal of "ethnic philosophers" like Plato or Aristotle, a living icon of a system of thought,[117] the authors of the *Confucius Sinarum Philosophus* compared Confucius to the Oracle at Delphi,[118] though he was held in higher regard than was the Delphic Oracle because he enjoyed more authority among the Chinese than the Oracle did among the ancient Greeks. The comparison serves a higher objective. Just as all the pagan gods lie down before Christ in Milton's poem "On the Morning of Christ's Nativity," the Chinese and their indigenous religion, Couplet and his colleagues believe, will yield to Christian evangelism.[119] In fact, as they see it, Confucius's teachings are a good propaedeutic to Christianity.

Second, and here too they extend the reasoning of the early accommodationists, Confucius's teaching, *ju kiao* [rujiao], was a distillation of the ancient belief in Xan ti [Shangdi] or what the authors now call *Religio Sinensium* (the Chinese religion).[120] Here they exceed the ground-level ethnographic notations on religious practice made by Ricci, as they also demonstrate a compelling cognate philological link between Xan ti, Deus, Elohim, and Jehovah. In an impressive gesture toward theological ecumenism, the authors claim that these terms are etymologically derived from the same source. It was just such ecumenism that especially appealed to Leibniz, whose efforts to create a *characteristica universalis* (universal system of characters) were justified by the fathers' testimony.

Revealing something of the indistinguishability of theology and contemporary politics, the authors remind us that the Chinese monarchy has been in place for more than four thousand years, seventeen hundred of which were continuously under the magistracy of Confucius (*Magistratum Confucium*).[121] Support for their conviction is provided by "Siu Paulus," or Paul Xu (Guangqi) who, according to the fathers, testifies that Christianity "fulfills what is lacking in our teacher Confucius and in the philosophy of the literati; it truly removes and radically extirpates nefarious superstitions and the cult of the demons."[122] There were, then, limits on theological ecumenism even in China. In an unstable Europe after the religious wars of the sixteenth century, a reasoned defense of national faith in a single religion or ideology such as the fathers advocated by way of Xu Guangqi's formulation could do much for political idealism. The politics of nationhood, rather than the search for a universal language, was best served by the fathers' argument for theological complementarity, but both the political and the scientific readings of the *Confucius Sinarum Philosophus* would together account for its universal significance.

Here the Jesuits again affirmed the fundamental compatibility of their doctrine and that represented by their Confucius. However, more than seventy years after the death of their patriarch, Ricci, Jesuit invention exceeded the limits of what he thought possible. Couplet and his colleagues did more than point up the compatibility of Chinese natural theology and Catholic theology. While Ricci had contributed the idea of theological compatibility through reliance on the concept of the light of nature (*il lume naturale*), the authors of the *Confucius Sinarum Philosophus* proposed with their invocation of the Delphic Oracle the necessary evolution of one into the other. Now the contact between Chinese natural religion and Jesuit revealed religion acquired a conceptual mechanism for the transmutation of the former into the latter.

This same mechanism would soon be found in a host of works on pagan religion and world chronology written by scholars such as Newton and Hume, as the quarrel between the ancients and the moderns raged among European philosophes.[123] Ironically perhaps, as Ricci's first conceptual inventions like *legge de' letterati* enabled his passage from self to other, the interpretations of the late-seventeenth-century accommodationists entered the stream of European ideas and secured their conceptual return passage from Chinese self to European self.

For the Jesuit accommodationists of the late seventeenth century, the concept Confucius acquired a different significance. Or, at least, that is what we can infer from the effects produced by the *Confucius Sinarum Philosophus*. China was by this time not the wilderness it had been for Ruggieri and Ricci. The landscape of China's interior had not only been charted, but also was now punctuated by Jesuit missions extending from Macao to Nanchang and from Nanjing to Beijing.

This was no longer the marginal community of shared jeopardy that undertook the task of crossing over into Chinese society. Fathers of this generation, like Couplet, were metropolitans at home as well as in China. More than their predecessors of a century before, they were accepted and, furthermore, accepted as learned men. Indeed they were integrated into a formal, multilingual complex of information exchange joining experimental scientists, natural philosophers, and mathematicians through correspondence, personal visits, and the professional journals and reports produced by newly founded scientific societies and academies in London and Paris.

Jesuit texts were much talked about in the late seventeenth century, and their authors, like Couplet, were greatly admired. For example, before the *Confucius Sinarum Philosophus* actually appeared, Leibniz had learned of its imminent publication and something of the content of the work from correspondence with Daniel Papebroch, a Jesuit. The spirit of the missionaries' work was still inspired by Ricci's example, but owing to the success of the Jesuit enterprise, they were unable to engage themselves as fully in Chinese life as their patriarch, Ricci, could. Nonetheless they were recognized by the courts of Europe and the emerging scientific community as experts who had successfully navigated the space between faith and experience in their work among the Chinese.

In saying that Couplet and his colleagues were less engaged in the Chinese quotidian, I pass no judgment on their piety or their commitment; I only wish to point out that historical conditions for the Jesuits, at least those responsible for the *Confucius Sinarum Philosophus*, were quite different from those when Ricci wrote the first history of the mission. Another feature of the life of these later Jesuits that illuminates the difference in these conditions was their comparative mobility. Men like Petris, Cattaneo, and Ricci, who received mission posts in China in the sixteenth century, remained there until their deaths, learning the language, catechizing natives, translating their hybrid canon from Chinese to Latin and from their native vernaculars to *guanhua*. Couplet and his cohort often received several different mission appointments in their careers, and, most importantly, virtually all of them returned to Europe for extended periods after assignment in the East.

Unlike Ricci and his colleagues, who it might be said did the interpretive spadework that made China, its esteemed classical heritage, and the "order of the literati" comprehensible, Couplet's generation were inheritors who appropriated this complex of understanding as given fact and worked with it to produce a systematic "learning of the Chinese." In this respect, they were engaged in a different endeavor, organizing all the knowledge produced in the mission since Ricci. Like Ricci, they operated according to a metonymic apprehension, systematically pruning the many branches of elite Chinese life—imperial families, books, scholars, ideas—in relation to the trunk they called Confucius. These accommodationists were as much technicians of knowledge as missionaries; although translation work continued to be critical to the life of the Jesuit textual community, it was increasingly taking on a less devotional, more scholastic meaning. This was especially so in Europe, where science and Christianity joined to construct a coherent picture of the world, while reaffirming the truth of biblical chronology.

Indeed, with the publication of the *Confucius Sinarum Philosophus*, we may say that at this juncture, the accommodationist community was reconstituted in relation to the contemporary intellectual fashions of Europe where most of the authors returned. This work, I believe, forged the critical link between the discourse about knowledge-production of the Mission of the Indies and European scientific debates, including those of Newton, Isaacson, Scaliger, and Freret on the synchronization of all "ethnic" histories into a continuous stream of biblical time. The conjuncture of Jesuit texts from China and developments in the "physicotheology" of European science may be demonstrated with reference to the chronological "Table of Chinese Monarchs" that concludes the compilation.

Couplet's *Tabula Chronologica Monarchiae Sinicae*, completed in 1686 and published again as an appendix to the *Confucius Sinarum Philosophus*, anticipated the work of the great Christian chronologists in the first three decades of the eighteenth century and followed in the wake of works such as Reuchlin's *De arte cabalistica* and Isaacson's *Saturni Ephemerides: Tabula Historicochronologica*.[124] The "Table of Chinese Monarchs" (figure 10) is constructed in double columns, so that all moments of historical importance in the Chinese record are indexed to events in the Christian chronology, the purpose being to offer "both a visual scheme of metaphysical order and an incentive to conduct further research."[125] The inference of linkage between Christianity and Chinese history in this spatial arrangement, however, required further research into Christian chronology.

Thus, following the chronology of the Septuagint, Yu, who controlled the waters of China's *Zhongyuan* or central plain, the locus of its culture, was identified in this table as Noah's contemporary. This was because Jesuits discovered very early on that the accepted chronology of China's culture heroes Fu Xi, Yao, Shun, and Yu conflicted with that of the Vulgate text of the Bible then in use: Fu Xi's reign began in 2952 B.C.E. and the Flood, it was calculated, occurred in 2349 B.C.E. If the Chinese chronology was correct, then all of these figures would have antedated Noah. The Septuagint translation, unlike the Vulgate, which depended on Hebrew texts, was based on a Greek version of the Bible and yielded a chronology which made all the Chinese heroes postdiluvian.[126] And with this modified chronology the accommodationist compilers offered compelling taxonomical evidence of the theological compatibility of Chinese religion and Christianity.

More than this, in accord with their own genealogical mapping of the descent of "Christian" peoples from "Adam through Noah, through Abraham, through the Babylonian captivity on through Christ,"[127] Couplet and his colleagues painstakingly reconstructed the central and collateral lines of

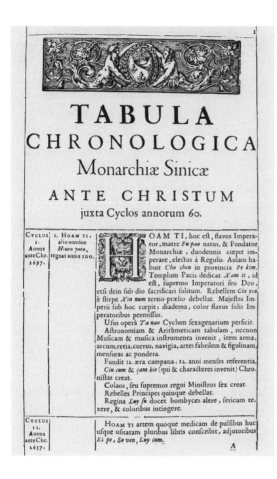

Figure 10. "Tabula Chronologica Monarchiae Sinicae," from Philippe Couplet et al., *Confucius Sinarum Philosophus* (Paris, 1687). The double vertical columns index the narrative of Chinese history to biblical and Christian chronology. The *Tabula Chronologica* was inspired by the *Chronological Canon* of Eusebius of Caesarea (ca. 260–ca. 340 C.E.) and was consonant with the new scientific experiments in chronology by Scaliger, Freret, and Newton, among others. (Photograph courtesy of the Special Collections Library of the University of Michigan)

descent of the Chinese imperial families from "Hoam Ti" (Huangdi) to "Cum Fu Çu seu Confucius" (Kong Fuzi or Confucius) (figure 11). The Jesuit belief that similitude was not fortuitous but divine is as clear here as it was in Ricci's work, with the only exception being that the similarities are not seen as serendipitous but as scientific. Couplet and his fellow missionaries were not only men of God but men of science. And thus they took their place alongside European scientists, now engaged in making the world as comprehensible as it had always been regarded as divine.

The Eponym "Confucian" and Its Universal Significance

The semiotic taxonomies of the imperial genealogy and the *Tabula Chronologica* were readily admitted into the rhetoric of authentic representation of the physical world that occupied the energies of seventeenth-century lay

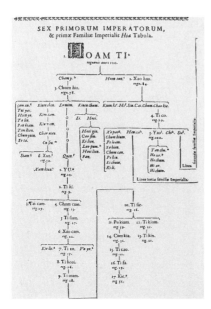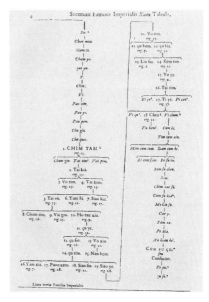

Figure 11. "Sex Primorum Imperatorum et primae Familae Imperialis *Hia* Tabula" (Table of the First Six Emperors and First Imperial *Hia* Family), from "Tabula Genealogica Trium Familiarum Imperialium Monarchiae Sinicae," in Philippe Couplet et al., *Confucius Sinarum Philosophus* (Paris, 1687). This genealogical table demonstrates that "Cum Fu çu *seu* Confucius" was a descendant of the Shang dynasty (see lower right of second page). No other figure in Chinese antiquity was given a Latin name. (Photographs courtesy of the Special Collections Library of the University of Michigan)

intellectuals.[128] The perplexing chasm between the fallen languages of man and the work of God provoked a search by way of linguistics, experimental science, mathematics, and natural philosophy to invent new semiotic forms capable of representing God's creation while avoiding the sin of hubris.

Newton's calculus, Cave Beck's "universal character," Leibniz's "universal system of characters," John Wilkins's "real character" were all rhetorical strategies invented to justify experimental science as a pious deduction of the work of the Deity. And, once Chinese texts were understood as semiotic forms representative of nature, then the Jesuits' translations and interpretive commentaries could serve the same pious function as the strategies of Leibniz and Newton. Moreover, Jesuit translations of the "real characters" of Chinese offered evidence of the reasonableness of the contention of European scientists that real characters, the calculus, or a universal language could be deduced from the "natures of things" as unmediated expressions of God's intention.

Through correspondence and personal contacts, the fathers of the China Mission were drawn into the expanding information network of Europe's scientific academies, contributing to the morally serious, but intellectually quixotic, program to find a metalanguage capable of conveying the beauty of God's creation. In so doing, the Jesuits named the Chinese system that some Europeans believed was isomorphic with nature and about which they had expounded. They called it Confucian.

It was in inventing this eponymous term that the accommodationist compilers of the *Confucius Sinarum Philosophus* exceeded the imagination of Ricci, who had implied but never stated the reduction of China to Confucius. This implication was exaggerated by Couplet and his cohort and resulted in the neologism "Confucian." The *Epistola* or dedicatory letter addressed to Louis XIV asserts that "by the blood of Chinese rulers, he who is called Confucius . . . is the wisest moral philosopher, politician, and orator."[129] Elsewhere Couplet and his coauthors chronologically document the transmission from the heralded moral philosopher to themselves when they write, "the lineage of [Confucius] has been propagated with a not-uninterrupted series in this year 1687."[130] At the close of the *Confucii Vita*, the fathers summarize Chinese dynastic descent from the Han dynasty to the present, taking care to note the millennial tribute to Confucius paid by a succession of dynastic families. Further, in obvious deference to the self-conception of *le roi soleil*, they report that, although Confucius was symbolic of Chinese religion, the rites performed to him were thoroughly secular—"civiles sunt honores ac ritus illi Confuciani" (civil are the honors and those Confucian rites)[131]—and here the authors deliver for the first time the neologism "Confucian" (figure 12).

A paragraph below this phrase, a similar formulation appears: "vero magis confirmat ritus illos Confucianos merè esse politicos" (he confirms those Confucian rites are truly political), again affirming the secular character of the rites in honor of Confucius. These were assurances that the revering of Confucius was not idolatrous and therefore worthy of comparison with the cult-like adulation rendered to Louis XIV by his people. Consequently the invocation of Louis XIV, *Magni Ludovici*, "Louis the Great," in the summary paragraph of the "Life of Confucius" was intended as a way for Couplet and his colleagues to pay homage to their monarch and benefactor by deliberately drawing a comparison between the undying symbol of the Chinese people and the living icon of the French and their enlightened culture.

These two symbols—the sage and the sun—thus acquired the properties of each other in the eyes of those who engineered the comparison and for everyone else, particularly the later chinoiserie coterie, who considered it appropriate. Confucius was the Eastern ideal of wisdom, good government, and civilization, and the Jesuits were his self-appointed envoys, come all the way around the world to bestow these gifts on their king. In turn, Confucius acquired the symbolic trappings of a Bourbon monarch, his metonymic func-

cxxij   CONFUCII VITA.

ipsos idem est) eximia quadam sapientiâ ornato , aliisque similibus ,
quibus hunc gentis suæ Doctorem Imperatores Familiarum Han , Sui , Tam,
Sum , Yven (fuit hæc Tartarorum occidentalium) tantum non supra lau-
des humanas evexerunt. Quamquam illius familiæ (quæ hodiernam Tartarorum orientalium Cim proximè antecessit) Mim dictæ Fundator vetuit
ritu Regio honores deferri Confucio , in eo dumtaxat permisso , quo olim
solebat memoria Sien su , hoc est , vita functi Magistri celebrari , atque adeo
non cum aliis muneribus , quam , quibus eos , dum viverent , discipuli sui
prosequi consueverant : ad hæc in Gymnasiis statuas Confucii , aut discipulorum erigi vetat (neque enim , inquit , eodem ritu quo reliqui
spiritus, aut idola honorandi sunt) sed sotas tabellas , quibus tituli &
nomina singulorum inscripta sint , mandat exponi : sunt igitur tabellæ fu-
nebres istæ signa merè memorativa Magistrorum (& eadem est ratio de ta-
bellis majorum) ne vitâ functorum de litteris sic meritorum , aut paren-
talis familiæ pia memoria apud posteros intermoreretur : neque magis er-
rori cuipiam gignendo tabellæ hujusmodi obnoxiæ , quam nostræ Europæo-
rum tabulæ , quæ nobis vivas avorum effigies venustissimè depingunt ,
quas amicis & hospitibus ostendentes hunc avum , illum Doctorem nostrum,
haud dubitanter & venerabundi quoque dicimus. Quocirca nec offendi nos
oportet, licet videamur Sinas ante tabellas istas curvare poplitem more inter Sinas usitatissimo , non magis quam offendimur , si Europæum quem-
piam , dum is forte ante patris aut Regis sui effigiem transit , caput ape-
rire videremus quemadmodum nuper vidimus D. D. Legatos Regni Sia-
mensis , quotiescunque ante imaginem MAGNI LUDOVICI transi-
ibant , gradum illicò sistere , junctisque in altum manibus , eas cum totius,
corporis inclinatione demittere veluti ad pedes tantæ majestatis. Etenim planè
civiles sunt honores ac ritus illi Confuciani ; qui adeo non in Templo sano-
ve idolorum (quod lege Imperatoriâ vetitum est) sed in gymnasio , qui
locus tantum litteratis patet , exercentur , à litterariæ facultatis præfectis,
quos inter etiam sunt Mahometani (ut de atheopoliticis non loquar) qui
nec divini aliquid hîc agnoscunt , & superstitiones Gentilium atque idola
detestantur. Imo si loquimur de litteratis idololatriæ Toxico à teneris jam
afflatis (cujusmodi sunt infima fortis homines) cum jam tempus appetit
examinis subeundi ad gradum aliquem obtinendum , vel ii domesticos suos
penates prius consulunt , & horum Numen & opem implorant , vel optati
successûs gratiâ publica dæmoniorum sana supplices adeunt , nequaquam verò cogitant de adeundo gymnasio Confucii , quem uti Pu su (nomen hoc
est idolis commune) habere aut nominare , aut ab eodem aliquid petere,
aut sperare , apud ipsos inauditum est & inusitatum.

Quod vero magis confirmat ritus illos Confucianos merè esse politicos
ex eo patet , quod non tantum in iisdem gymnasiis tabula Confucii oblon-
gior (quam duorum & septuaginta Discipulorum tabellæ utrinque am-
biant) sit collocata , sed & aliorum Sapientum, de quorum doctrinâ,

Figure 12. "Confucii Vita" (Life of Confucius) in Philippe Couplet et al.'s *Confucius Sinarum Philosophus* (Paris, 1687), p. 122. The underlined phrases—"civiles sunt honores ac ritus illi Confuciani" and "Quod vero magis confirmat ritus illos Confucianos merè esse politicos"—mark the first textual evidence of the Jesuit neologism "Confucian." (Photograph courtesy of the Special Collections Library of the University of Michigan)

tion as the symbol of Chineseness reminiscent of Louis XIV's famous remark, "L'etat c'est moi."

A comparison of the woodcut of Confucius (figure 7) with a depiction of Louis XIV (figure 13) reveals, in fact, conceptual/technical similarities in the imagining of monarchy and astrology, wherein Confucius and Louis appeared as icons of the universe. Confucius is portrayed through the popular post-Renaissance metaphor of illustration, wherein royal power and the order of the heavens are coincident. Indeed this epic illustration literally frames Confucius within such coincidence by placing him in an archway whose right column bears the two graphs, *tianxia* (the world, or as the Jesuits read it, "below heaven"), while the left column displays his imperial honorific, *xianshi* (first teacher). Both expressions are symmetrically lined up beneath the two graphs of his given name, "Zhong" and "ni." Thus his birthright is registered in the universe and the legacy of a scholarly tradition.

The firmament of Confucius is a bibliographic universe, in contrast, but his peculiar headdress is made of a bank of clouds and the sun, very similar to those appearing in the astrological depiction of Louis XIV's birth. Confucius's head contains the heavens, the cosmos in miniature. Rays emanating from the sun of the headpiece appear to illuminate the face of the sage—a depiction of Ricci's "lume naturale." The two horizontally projecting crucifixes each resemble the fleur-de-lis that marks the chapter breaks of the *Confucius Sinarum Philosophus.* Hanging vertically from his palm is a cord from which is suspended a jeweled ornament suggestive of a crown. Indeed, it is an inverted crown and recalls the Han legend that Kongzi was a *suwang* (an uncrowned king). Confucius, furthermore, is holding a jade tablet, *gui,* the symbol of Lu feudal investiture, in a posture imitative of the one described in book 10, chapter 5, of the *Lunyu:* "He holds it at the highest as though making a bow, at the lowest as though he were making an offering."[132]

Though executed by a French artisan unaware of the meaning of the Chinese graphs he inscribed, or of the purpose of the spirit tablets with the names of Kongzi's disciples, or of the significance of the titles of the books on the shelves of this biblio-cosmos, the portrait of Confucius still conveys the depth of Jesuit understanding of the tradition of the sage. This is the image that spawned countless imitations in the century following the publication of the *Confucius Sinarum Philosophus,* yet there is a vestige of the special

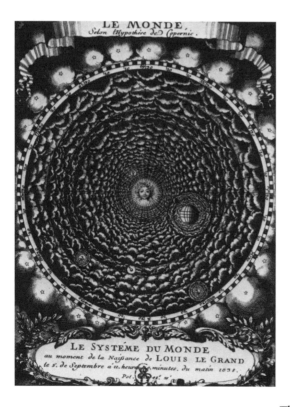

Figure 13. "Le Système du monde au moment de La Naissance de Louis le Grand" [The World System at the time of the Birth of Louis the Great], woodcut illustration from Cabinet des Estampes, Bibliothèque Nationale, Paris, with its depiction of the mutual entailment of monarchy and astrology, illustrates the imaginative technics of late-seventeenth-century royal portraiture that were responsible for the woodcut illustration of Confucius. (See figure 7)

identification of the fathers with the teachings of Kongzi visible to us even amid this reification. On the shelves to the right and left of Confucius are placed the classics, ten texts in all. On the right of the figure from top to bottom we can see "Li Ki" (*Li ji*), "Ye Kim" (*Yijing*), "hi cu" (*Xici*), "Xi Kim" (*Shi jing*), and "mem cu" (*Mengzi*). To the left of the figure the texts are "Xu Kim" (*Shu jing*), "chun cieu" (*Chunqiu*), "ta hio" (*Daxue*), "chum yum" (*Zhongyong*), and "Lun yu" (*Lunyu*).

The authorized Chinese "classics" are marked by the use of uppercase—that is, "Ye Kim," "Xi Kim," "Li Ki," "Xu Kim"—while the books of the *Sishu* are in lowercase, that is, with the exception of the *Lunyu*, which bears a hybrid uppercase/lowercase orthography. Moreover, the *Chunqiu* ("chun cieu"), one of the Five Classics purportedly authored by Kongzi, remains in lowercase, possibly suggesting that the *Lunyu* had replaced the *Chunqiu* as a classic for the Jesuits. All the titles are romanized and written from left to right, while the Chinese characters are presented in a right-to-left vertical orientation in deference to Chinese custom. The one exception to this convention is the *Lunyu*, which is romanized and written from left to right. It is as if the appropriation of Kongzi/Confucius by the Jesuits was transmitted through the hand of the illustrator. Even as the eponym and its image became universal public property, the Sino-Jesuit intimacy with the *ru* transmission was retained.

Ricci had resisted the temptation to invent an eponymous designation because he knew that it was more than mere conjugation. By the time he had spent twenty-seven years in China he was aware that the tradition of Kongzi was very much a faith of the educated, privileged, and politically well-placed and, thus, did not reach from center to periphery, without period or comma, as did Christianity in his native Italy. So, *ru* in his estimation was cultlike, a sect, albeit a rational, monotheistic, and powerful one. The authors of the *Confucius Sinarum Philosophus* spoke of *ru* as a sect, yet defined it as Chinese religion and this, too, was to exceed Ricci's claims. To identify *ru* as a Confucian religious system would have placed it on equal ground with his own faith. Even if he had accepted a conception in which Christianity and Confucianism were simply identical moments in world religion, he would have been extremely hard-pressed to state it. Ricci, perhaps for the very reasons Wilfred Cantwell Smith has articulated, considered the designation "Confucian" inappropriate, even blasphemous.[133]

There is one final and very likely reason why Ricci did not transform "Confucius" into "Confucian," leaving it instead for his accommodationist successors. To call *ru* "Confucian," Ricci knew, meant to invert the proper order of relation between ethos and exemplar. Kongzi was the living embodiment of an ethos, yet he was not synonymous with it. The same was true of the Jesuits' Confucius who was the inspiration for their textual community.

The meaningfulness of this ethos derived from the poignant recollection of his exemplary life. Kongzi, like Confucius, exemplified a particular complex of moral and physical attitudes, of textual strategies dear to the *ru* and the early Jesuits alike.

For Kongzi to be synonymous with *ru*, "Confucius" with "Confucian," or for them to be interchangeable, was to diffuse the exemplary power of the sage. Followers, inspired by the life of their master, read this life as a code of conduct that they struggled to replicate. The record of his life and sayings provided a paradigmatic narrative structure according to which followers molded themselves. The moral vigor, and so the meaning of this enterprise, came from the incessant tension between Kongzi's exemplary life and the *ru* ethos. However, if *ru* was ipso facto equivalent to Kongzi, then by merely calling oneself *ru*, a follower could himself invoke identity with the exemplar, thereby averting the strenuous discipline of moral self-fashioning.

This special local knowledge of the private lines of inspiration by which a scriptural tradition was transmitted was borne forward as a vestige of the Jesuits' earlier assimilation. The eponymous transformation of Kongzi through "Confutio," "Confucio," "Confuzo," "Confutius," "Confusius," and ultimately "Confucius," while preserving the memory of the Sino-Jesuit community, at the same time served to define, either by complement or contrast, the identity of the modern, scientific West. Through the history of the Jesuits' double invention as native Chinese sectarians and as European men of science, we can now understand the undecidable symbolic connections between religion, ethics, and science in our Confucianism. In what follows we take stock of the consequence of this understanding for the representation of China, before we consider the complex Chinese conditions that generated an ancient religious significance for *ru*, the putative indigenous other of our Confucianism.

INTERLUDE

THE MEANING AND END OF

CONFUCIANISM: A MEDITATION

ON CONCEPTUAL DEPENDENCE

I have not found any formulation of a named religion earlier than the nineteenth century: "Boudhism" (1801), "Hindooism" (1829), "Taouism" (1839), "Zoroasterianism" (1854), "Confucianism" (1862). . . . The transition to a specific name did not take place in any of those cases where a people's religious life remained integrated and coterminous with their social existence. . . . [W]e may simply observe once again that the question "Is Confucianism a religion?" is one that the West has never been able to answer, and China never able to ask.—*Wilfred Cantwell Smith*

For the translation too must have a life of its own, one that breathes to its own rhythms; it cannot exist without its nourishing atmosphere. Thus, the process of translation is a to-and-fro voyage, toward and away from the shores of the text, until finally one disembarks on new land. . . . Translation entails risks—with departure as the first step in a largely unforeseeable sequence of movements.—*Marcia Falk*

Concepts and Communities

Writing in the century following Matteo Ricci's death, Giambattista Vico (1668–1744) argued for the crucial interrelation of concept and context, insisting that we can know only what we can make. He stressed that concepts are not inherent in the nature of things but are invented by and transmitted through culture. Even though they are binding, concepts remain susceptible to transformation, enduring not as mere archaeological artifacts but in subtly evolved forms. Others have elaborated upon Vico's formulation that "the true and the made are convertible," reasoning that certain concepts persist because they embody the values, expectations, and understanding of specific communities.[1] Recently, the social anthropologist Ernest Gellner has argued this line persuasively, remarking:

> A concept is, of course, far more than a "mere" concept: it encapsulates and communicates and authorizes a shared way of classifying, valuing, a shared range of social and natural expectations and obligations. It makes cooperation and communication possible. It limits behavior and sensibility, otherwise endowed with a potentially infinite diversity, into circumscribed bounds, and thereby establishes a "culture."[2]

Gellner's thoughts shed considerable light on the reasons for the endurance of the concepts Confucius and Confucianism.

Like all concepts, Confucius implies a specific set of social relationships. In chapters 1 and 2 I accounted for the significance of this invention and its derivative Confucianism, describing how they were used.[3] The later European inventions Confucius and Confucian developed out of a Jesuit desire to comprehend a foreign other. Since the missionaries' cultural categories were religiously inspired, their understanding reflected that source of inspiration. To this extent, their interpretations may be taken as self-serving or ideological in offering justification for their evangelical work.

Nevertheless, the Jesuits' translation of themselves onto Chinese ground, and the translation out of China of selected canonical texts, were significant events. It is common to speak of what gets lost in translation, but rare to acknowledge what is gained. Matteo Ricci's accounts, for example, of language, science, the arts, government, and religion among the Chinese were extremely impressive "metaphorizations" of lived experience, a "way of describing others as one would describe ourselves."[4] He and his fellow priests resymbolized what they perceived in translating their observations into a complex that was meaningful to them and those around them, and even to their supervisors and benefactors a half a world away. What they could not do or, better, what they have left for us to do, is to reflect critically on their (and our) continued manufacture of Chinese culture and to find a way of disclosing the process.

Confucianism is not, therefore (contrary to the assertion of scholars bound by this convention), simply "a generic Western term,"[5] but, as we have noted, a complex of meanings central to the project to accommodate Chinese culture and Western culture on the ground of the common religion of Christianity. "Confucian" and "Confucius" sometimes still resonate with the intentions of the later Jesuit missionaries, for whom the most pressing concerns were the conceptual mapping of foreign spiritual territory and the demonstration through ethnology of the scientific evidence of God's ubiquity.

Yet, knowing the peculiarities of the Jesuit reading of *ru* and of China, how can we continue to use "Confucian" to describe systems in Chinese culture—whether they be tradition, empire, bureaucracy, civilization, or family? The relations between "la legge de' letterati" (in Ricci's native Italian) and the care of the empire (including the activities of the emperor and the legal-bureaucratic apparatus) were structured in a specific, analogous manner by Ruggieri, Ricci, and their followers to sustain an ideological program justifying the costly pursuit of conversion. But, Jesuit accounts of what they perceived among the Chinese—their "metaphorizations"—were, at root, genuine attempts at understanding. So though "la legge de' letterati" derived its comprehensiveness as a system from its function as a primitive natural religion amenable to evangelization, it was a "historically specific organization of the field of cultural relations"[6] on local Chinese ground.

Reinterpreted by a later generation of Jesuits more intimately linked to Europe's growing scientific community, "Confutio," "la legge de' letterati," and even "mandarino" acquired a critical classificatory value that made them significant within a very different field of cultural relations. Once this had occurred, the image of Confucius was widely plagiarized, as we have learned, and the term "Confucianism" was uttered in all the vernaculars and new, unsettled nations of Europe. These unforeseen consequences of Jesuit accommodationism that brought "Cina," "Sinas," and "la Chine" squarely into the light of a new intellectual dawn in Europe are the reason I believe that to pronounce *ru* "Confucian" or Kongzi "Confucius" awakens the long history of the Jesuit project of accommodation responsible for these inventions.

To follow Marshall Sahlins's conception, discussed in chapter 1, by embedding "the existentially unique" (Chinese culture, specifically *ru*) in "the conceptually familiar" (Christianity), the Jesuits effected a synthesis of their Western present and China's past that justified proselytism as it distorted, to some Chinese eyes, the culture of late Ming China,[7] allowing the Jesuits to embed their present in China's past. Moreover, by way of a similar dialectic of inherited categories and novel experience, European scholars embedded "China" and "Confucius" in the fearful symmetry of their then struggle to reconcile the plurality of God's vast creation with the unity of science.

At the same time, we must not forget that the Chinese of Ricci's day and beyond refunctioned the symbolism of their encounter with generations of missionaries by making the existentially unique (the Jesuits) a part of the conceptually familiar (the ethos of *ru* and *fo*). This was the context of the early Jesuits' work in translation—the mutual occurrence in situ of the existential and conceptual adjustments requisite in cultural encounter—and it was in this moment that their translation had its greatest fidelity. Ironically it was just this wonderfully inspired and courageous translation that generated Confucianism, both as a systematic doctrine and a religion while elevating *ru* above *fo* and *dao* as the only legitimate indigenous faith, and delivered *ru* from local eminence to international prominence, so that today we are aware of Confucianism and its diverse manifestations to such an extent that the name conveys nothing precise anymore.

However, it is not the mere profusion of terms bearing the adjective "Confucian" that causes this loss of meaning. Instead, it is the divided burden of our seventeenth-century intellectual heritage, half translation, half taxonomy, that renders our contemporary Confucian formulations senseless. Alasdair MacIntyre, in an entirely different context, has spelled out the way the language may develop internal contradictions that cripple the meaningful interpretation of experience, as when a form of discourse is constituted out of equal parts of contradictory philosophies.[8] Our contemporary use of "Confucian" seems a particularly good example of the kind of contradiction that MacIntyre has argued undergirds the Western language of moral sentiment. It is used in manifold, apparently unrelated ways: Confucian thought, Confucian spirituality, Confucian humanism, Confucian education, Confucian learning, Confucian religiousness, Confucian studies, Confucian values, Confucian ethics, Confucian project, Confucian tradition, Confucian culture, Confucian teaching, Confucian philosophy, Confucian enlightenment, Confucianity.[9] The term is swiftly approaching meaninglessness, and the current predicament may be considered an epistemological one wherein the language of representation is inadequate to stand for what is signified. The difficulty of the West's continued reliance on "Confucius" and "Confucianism" is, however, more than a matter of the politics and mechanics of representation.

A Commingling of Representations

The question of accuracy is a critical one in any discussion of representation, yet the what and how of representation may not be entirely distinguishable. This is particularly true in the case of Confucianism, because for the last three centuries it has been taken to be something "out there" in the history that the Chinese have made and continue to make. This reality does not stand alone objectively before words; it exists for us and for the Chinese insofar as it is mediated through those linguistic categories peculiar to the distinct forms of cognition we call Chinese and Western. To say this is not to deny that there is a world external to language, only that all knowledge of that world is the consequence of instinctual, mediative operations of conceptual construction.

The history of Confucianism's conceptual construction does not make the Jesuits alone responsible for the difficulties of establishing accurate representation. Any claim of representative accuracy for Confucianism, or even by the Chinese for *ru*, is problematic in itself because Confucianism and *ru* alike are *significations* of reality. Recognizing this, one might conclude that the concept must be abandoned altogether, especially if we intend to be more precise in our description of Chinese culture and intellectual life. But abandonment of Confucianism is a very radical interpretive move, largely because in doing so we may lose China's intelligibility for us. So it is that "Confucianism" endures in any or all of its qualified permutations.

In this light, the challenge to contemporary interpretation is to disentangle the Chinese traditions symbolized by *ru* from the later Jesuit reductive metaphor, "Confucian." The distinction is more than semantic. Extrication of one from the other has proven extraordinarily difficult, because of a willingness of historians of China to treat "Confucius" and "Confucianism" as referential values, on the assumption that the latter term is just a Western designation for a preexistent corpus of ritual and belief common to the *ru*. The positivist inclination here carries a logic that may be identified as follows: "Confucian" or "Confucianism" may be Western neologisms; however, they do refer to some factual body of intellectual, social, or political expression antedating the "Great Encounter" with the West, a body that would be apparent to any observer of Chinese culture and even to the Chinese themselves. Thus, the terms, though lacking literal Chinese equivalents, have a descriptive adequacy sufficient to enable foreign understanding. Positivist logic insists that China, including the imperial state, its ideology, the emperor, his bureaucracy, existed before contact with the Jesuits; hence, "Confucian" and

"Confucianism" stand as identifying descriptions of this. But, I suggest, it is just such insistence on the adequacy of the relation of word and object that undermines the more faithful representation of Chinese experience at which we aim.

The problem with the positivist reading described here is that it operates on a presumption that "Confucian" and "Confucianism" are facts; but since what we know to be Confucian and Confucianism come from specific texts and communities, the reality we are presuming is at root what Brian Stock calls a relation, not an event. Objective facticity is not questioned by the historian of texts, and it should not govern the effort of sinologists to represent native Chinese experience. Stock has eloquently critiqued the positivist assumptions of much contemporary history:

> The historian in the positivistic tradition assumes that the event is related to fact rather than to relation—that is, to an assumed objective reality, not to a system of independent factors, some subjective, some objective. As a result, a text, even one that treats events alone, cannot itself be an event: it is something that is *derived* from real or imagined events. The obvious problem with this approach is that events assumed to have taken place objectively only occupy a meaningful position in a "history" to the degree that they are perceived, either by the original participants, by the later historians, or, potentially at least, by a series of intervening interpreters. In other words, they have been subjectivized. They are not as subjective as a text of pure fiction created for an occasion, but have more in common with such a narrative than with the event-structure of the external world. Let us not be deceived by the skepticism of much historical writing, that arid criticism of documents that pretends to take the reader behind their historical facades [*sic*] and into a world of sober facts. Historical writing does not treat reality; it treats the interpreter's relation to it.[10]

A logic of the sort Stock criticizes, essentially a *post hoc ergo propter hoc* fallacy, lends the peculiar inventions of Confucianism an opacity that leads even a critical intellect to understand them as "translations." "Confucius," and its attendant nomenclature, cannot be understood, even by twentieth-century Chinese scholars, as translations in the sense that they render into one language something written or spoken in another. They are, above all, interpretive constructs, rather than representations of native categories. They are representations of the seventeenth-century European reading of the Jesuit missionary experience among late Ming Chinese, representations that were employed, and have been preserved, as elements within a universal system of classification by language, chronology, science, and faith.

Of course, a persistent belief in the *reality* of Confucianism says something very important about interpretive authority, for it is on the authority of the Jesuit work among the Chinese and its European appropriation as Confucianism that we continue to articulate what we have determined are its central features—filial piety, respect for tradition, dedication to public service, conscientious regard for the other, love of family, ancestor veneration, and the notion of sociocosmic harmony. Yet, as definitive cultural traits, these features could more reasonably be identified as Chinese rather than Confucian. Certainly, the Chinese term for Kongzi's tradition, *ru*, was not exclusively identified with this range of practices; however, because of the Jesuits' preference for *ru*, it was this tradition, above all others, that has been taken, in a manner reminiscent of Clifford Geertz's work, as a critical symbol under which all such features of the Chinese quotidian are subsumed. "Confucianism," as *ru* teaching, may never have enjoyed such symbolic authority in Chinese life, a point that was eloquently made by Wilfred Cantwell Smith in the epigraph to this interlude, in which he queries Confucianism's status as a religion; nonetheless, it still enjoys authority as a critical symbol among the contemporary community of Western interpreters.

The condensed, manifold significance contained by the seventeenth-century Jesuits' Confucianism persists today in *our* Confucianism. The term endures by default, and its implicit valorization of *ru* over all other traditions is even more troubling. Obviously there are risks in using the term; it assumes much, conveys little, and by its simplicity conflates too many former meanings, thereby preventing a productive modern reading of the Chinese texts. However, the European conceptual wager on Chinese culture continues to organize our interpretation in the same way that a frame orders a painting, and it implicitly governs our appropriation of this other as did the early Jesuits' representational strategy of similitude.

Nothing is more demonstrative of the continued presence of Jesuit interpretation in our reading of Confucius than the late Herrlee Creel's *Confucius and the Chinese Way*. Creel's was a self-conscious attempt to discover "the real Confucius," and he cites the Jesuit interpretation of Confucius approvingly. Perhaps because of his labors at the elbows of Dong Zuobin in the reconstruction of the ancient Shang dynasty (1576–1046 B.C.E.) capital at Anyang, Creel reads the Jesuit effort to recover an original Confucius through the archaeological metaphor of excavation. In the book's introduction, titled "Tradition and Truth," Creel recalls the long history of narrative embellishment surrounding Kongzi. His intellectual precursors in this search for the real Confucius are the missionary fathers of the Society of Jesus, whose restorationist spirit Creel admires:

> There were almost always a few scholars, however, who were capable of discernment. So were the number of the Jesuit missionaries who entered

China and became scholars and even officials at the Chinese court in the seventeenth and eighteenth centuries. They brushed aside as so much chaff the accumulation of recent interpretation and sought to go back to Confucius himself.[11]

Creel, furthermore, identifies the Jesuit denunciation of "Neo-Confucianism" for its Buddhist and Daoist conception as the inspiration for China's Hanxue revival in the late seventeenth century, saying:

> It would seem that when he [Ricci] and other Jesuits began to propagate this opinion, it was not held widely (if at all) among Chinese scholars. The Jesuit contention became generally known, and was widely debated in Chinese intellectual circles. Subsequently, the proposition that Neo-Confucianism was not original Confucianism, but a distortion deriving much of its content from Buddhism, became a basic tenet of the important "school of Han learning."[12]

Creel did not find strange the impact the Jesuits had on Chinese considerations of their own intellectual history. Indeed, by all appearances, the Jesuits were treated as one more subsect in the sixteenth-century conversation. Their orientation was especially fundamentalist—a stance that Creel admires because it aims to restore "the real Confucius."

Translation and Taxonomy

Today, we have come some distance from Creel's "real Confucius," and though our age is tempered by skepticism, Confucius, nonetheless, endures. Western scholars who are wary of its use but unaware of its peculiar religious history invoke "Confucian" with either qualifications or apologies. Most note, as did Jordan Paper recently in a translation of the *Fuzi*, that " 'Confucianism' is a most misleading translation; but because the term is now an entrenched part of the English language to use any other term would cause confusion."[13] The fact that "Confucianism" is "now an entrenched part of the English language," however, is the very reason there is so much confusion. The term's entrenchment in our language conditions axiomatic and uncritical use, which, in turn, buttresses the illusion that "Confucianism" actually represents, rather than constructs, reality, a native Chinese reality.

Note as well that, for the skeptical and linguistically sensitive Paper, "Confucianism" is merely a bad translation and has to be retained as an unfortunate, unfaithful representation. Owing to a continued misunderstanding that the term translates something indigenous, "Confucianism" has acquired a false transparency that, in placing it beyond criticism, ensures the continued reproduction of the term and its disabling contradictions.

However, as linguists and anthropologists since Ferdinand de Saussure have shown, language, Western or Chinese, is never neutral. The relationship between signifier and signified—"Confucianism" and what it represents—is a product of convention, in which sound patterns in speech and the means by which these are represented in writing signify the concepts of things.[14] With a figure as prominent as "Confucianism" in our epistemological landscape, one in large part synonymous with China, it is necessary that we have a lucid definition. Such lucidity depends upon accounting for "Confucianism" as a conceptual object with a particularly long history of mediating our knowledge of China.

Thus, I would contend, pace Jordan Paper, that to employ the term "Confucianism," which we know lacks representational accuracy, in situations where accuracy is desired, is to create confusion. There is as much that is genuinely Chinese in Confucianism as there was in chinoiserie. For interpreters whose concern is ethnographic and who aim to articulate accurately in a familiar language what is foreign, "Confucianism" does not get them closer to the object of their inquiry. And this is because the term is a product of seventeenth-century European taxonomy, not of sixteenth-century Jesuit translation. Therefore, an uncritical use of "Confucianism" consigns the scholar, and for that matter the modern reader, to the closed space of later Jesuit interpretation, where all that can be known is heard as echoes of intertextuality—Chinese words and texts translated into Italian, from Italian into Latin, from Portuguese into Latin into French, from French into English, from Latin into German to English, and so on.

Common accounts presume the textual activity of the Jesuits to be ideological in nature, and understand their labors to be in the service of a procrustean proof of the omnipresence of God's word. Thus they could not have properly "represented" the Chinese, their customs or their beliefs, and so Jesuit accounts of life among the Chinese are necessarily distorted. Yet if we consider their accounts to be *interested* rather than distorted, the ideological qualities of the Jesuits' constructions do not make the Jesuits the cynical practitioners of legerdemain that scholars like Jacques Gernet have described.

Knowing what we do today of the history of the mission in China following the death of Ricci—the long-running controversy over the Chinese practice of ancestral rites and over the proper Chinese term for God, as well as the juggernaut of military and economic colonization of China in the final century of Manchu rule—it is tempting and easy to characterize the Jesuits as cultural imperialists. There is no pristine culture left today, largely because of Western expansionism. We may bemoan such a development and disparage the Jesuits as its harbingers, yet the lamentations of twentieth-century historians over the violation of China's cultural pristineness by unscrupulous European expansion is misplaced. Scholars of ancient China such as K. C. Chang have pointed out that the integrity of China's culture was vitiated, not with the inception of imperialist social subversion, but in the Neolithic.[15]

Instead of focusing on the self-serving features of Jesuit interpretation, denouncing it for lacking representative accuracy, we would do better to consider the ideological nature of all textual production, Chinese no less than Western, and to acknowledge that the Chinese embraced the fathers as fellow Chinese. Ideology is inscribed in every discourse: "It inheres in words because they themselves represent significations capable of mobilizing people to act or perceive their world in specific modalities, either to conform to forms of domination or to contest them."[16] Therefore, by holding to an inappropriate definition of ideology as false consciousness we would deny ourselves a splendid opportunity: to understand how the Jesuits on their side manufactured Chinese culture; and to attempt to reproduce in our contemporary understanding the manner in which Chinese culture also manufactured itself.

What we can do, however, is to segregate the work of Ricci and his cohort in creating a Sino-Jesuit textual community from the Jesuit "encyclopedists," Couplet and his colleagues, with an understanding that the contextual differences between these two groups were made more dramatic by political, theological, and scientific crises of seventeenth-century Europe. Because their construction of a Chinese moral science was governed by the conceptual resources of the crisis of representation and theological strife that occupied Europe in this period, the reception of this science and its founder, Confucius, discovered among Chinese natives was intellectually effortless. For seventeenth-century scholars the Confucius and Confucianism conveyed to Europe through Jesuit translations were not marvels, but new, creditable contributions to an expanding inventory of evidentiary objects of natural philosophy. As "matters of fact,"[17] attested to by the work of the Jesuits among the Chinese, Confucius and Confucianism proved uniquely valuable to the seventeenth-century search for a common language, a stable monarchy under an inspired leader, and a rational science whose moral certainty was equal to mathematical certitude while inspired by God. In short, it was a search *against* the explicit diversity and conflict of contemporary life in a post-Westphalian age of nascent nation-states, and *for* an overarching or underlying unity, be it language, law, absolutism, or culture.

Thus what made Confucius and Confucianism so compelling, even if one was to use them, like Montesquieu, in a comparative calculus that favored European ideas and institutions by contrast, was their remarkable suitability to the resolution of Europe's disabling but quintessentially modern diversity. However, Confucius and Confucianism had no scientific status for Matteo Ricci and his cohort of early missionaries who knew them as "Confutio" and "la legge de' letterati." For them, the significance of these words was definitively local, not universal. Their task was to find the absolute in local, foreign ground; their effective passage into Chinese life was evidence of the successful completion of this task.

Our legacy as sinologists is a commingling of both of these moments. We are divided—emotionally aligned with Ricci and accommodationism, but intellectually bound to the canons of our Enlightenment heritage. And it is this schismatic quality that accounts for the curious persistence of the notion of Confucianism as translation. The language of our interpretive craft is borrowed from the seventeenth-century scientific appropriation of Confucius and Confucianism in the name of moral universals like the perfect language. At the same time, the spirit of our endeavor is more akin to the work of the first Jesuit missionaries in that we most want to understand the Chinese as they understood themselves. Like all good translators, sinologists want to cross over to Chinese ground, but the language through which our desire is conveyed is that of the distancing classification of taxonomy, not the intimate poetry of translation. Language and desire are in conflict, but the struggle is not visible to us, owing to our presumption that Confucius and Confucianism are translations of native entities.

This, of course, they are not, and the understanding of the Chinese brought by the conversion of Ricci and his colleagues to *ru* and through their translation of the *Sishu* was not carried across to the *scientia sinensis* project of Couplet and the Jesuit members of the Missions Étrangères. Ricci and the early missionaries, on the one hand, and Couplet and his confreres, on the other, had diametrically opposed responses to a common object: the former tolerant, the latter compulsory. Yet, both were enmeshed in the common assumption that Confucius and Confucianism were objects of real Chinese experience. Both attitudes, like two estranged interpretative cultures, remain entangled in the inventory of our Western intellectual heritage.

The persistence of the conceptual reification of Confucianism is, I believe, testament to a Western scholarly hope (the exertions of the better angels of our nature) that the formal complex of the term's significance still bears the spiritual imprint testified to by Ricci and his accommodationist epigones. We see in Confucianism the values that we most want our own philosophy and our own social body to display—that it be well-reasoned, morally coherent, explicitly responsible, and dedicated to truth, but not at the expense of mystery. Oddly enough, these particular aspects of the Confucian ethos were those that the early Jesuit missionaries also believed especially noble and esteemed throughout their translations and letters: *ren* (humaneness), *xiao* (filiality), *li* (rites), *dao* (way), *yi* (righteousness), and *zhengxue* (true teaching).

This was the Jesuits' invention and our legacy; however, our Confucianism must be one in which the episodic invention and reinvention of Chinese culture by the *Chinese* is the interpretive focus. The remainder of this book will demonstrate what we have already observed in the Jesuit/European construction of a Confucian China, that is, how, at their outward limits, Jesuit and Chinese techniques of invention turned into each other, disclosing similar properties of reading and production of texts. What I intend to show in the chapters that follow is that these cultures could speak across their divide because the mechanisms of manufacture were not the province of the foreigner but the common tools of Jesuit and Chinese. I will show how the Chinese in the first decades of this century were able to separate the two strands of Western representation and thus recuperate the early Jesuit understanding that the local was universal. Ironically, the twentieth-century Chinese would segregate the cultures of translation and taxonomy and restore the sovereignty of the local through grand theories of Western provenance—nationalism, evolution, and Christianity.

The following two chapters emphasize the dialectic of invention and restoration that the Chinese themselves engaged in as we consider the question of what the native entity *ru* (represented to us by the fathers as *letterati* and *Confucianos*) was made of. We turn now to the Chinese territory shown in Jesuit maps, its representation, and the Chinese who so represented it by reliance upon the metonym *ru*, where it becomes clear that the unstable quality of this indigenous term made impossible a faithful, uniform translation in the name of Confucianism, but did make possible a nationalist fiction revolutionary in its defense of Chinese ground.

To reanimate what has gone before
and thus to learn it anew; [this] may
be taken as one's teacher.—*Kongzi*

Leopards break into the temple and
drink the sacrificial chalices dry;
this occurs repeatedly, again and
again: finally it can be reckoned on
beforehand and becomes part of the
ceremony.—*Franz Kafka*

The seeing eye is the organ of
tradition.—*Franz Boas*

CHAPTER 3

ANCIENT TEXTS, MODERN

NARRATIVES: NATIONALISM,

ARCHAISM, AND THE

REINVENTION OF *RU*

The explanation that has become most influential says that the word [ru] has the basic semantic value of "weak" or "yielding." It was applied to the learned aristocracy of the Shang court who, after the conquest by the martial Zhou dynasty, had to serve new overlords as compliant, subservient experts on the ritual and the techniques of government. In contrast with the self-confident knights (shi) of the Zhou, the ru of the Shang were a powerless group who were aware of their intellectual superiority, but were still willing to perpetuate their literate high culture because of their devotion to its intrinsic values and use it in the service of the new dynasty.
—Frederick W. Mote

The yarns of seamen have a direct simplicity, the whole meaning of which lies within the shell of a cracked nut. But Marlow was not typical (if his propensity to spin yarns be excepted), and to him the meaning of an episode was not inside like a kernel but outside, enveloping the tale which brought it out only as a glow brings out a haze, in the likeness of one of these misty halos that sometimes are made visible by the spectral illumination of moonshine.—Joseph Conrad

In the first years of the twentieth century, China was no longer the wilderness that had inspired the exotic imaginings, wanderlust, and curiosity of Jesuit missionaries and European scholars of previous centuries. Not strange, but familiar, the Celestial Empire was officially opened to the West, though some would say rather that it was opened *by* the West. Following the resolution of the millenarian uprising of the Righteous and Harmonious Fists (*Yihe quan*), or Boxers, in 1901, a group of new sovereign Western nations had established a commanding economic and political presence in China and, impelled by the dictates of imperialist fancy, secured extraterritorial concessions in the treaty ports of the south and east coast, as well as the capital of Beijing.

China, too, had opened to the West, as thousands of Chinese made passage far beyond the Ocean of Great Peace (Taiping Yang) to destinations such as Jiujinshan (Old Gold Mountain [San Francisco]), Yingguo (England), Faguo (France), and Deguo (Germany) in search of wealth or in satisfaction of scholarly and political objectives. Matteo Ricci's rather protean *mappamondo* had been filled in by this time—great expanses of the globe had drawn together in webs of familiarity, linguistic and cultural, that were made thicker with the now common two-directional flow of peoples and products. And, most important of all, the character of the conversation in which China and the West had been engaged since the Jesuit fathers' arrival changed dramatically. As Confucius and Confucianism, Kongzi and *Ru* had been critical mediative forces in the dialogue of cultures; it was inevitable that their significance would be transformed in this tumultuous course of world history that Karl Polanyi once called "the great transformation."

For the Jesuits and their European lay interpreters, the world had been a vast cultural space made continuous through the omnipresence of God, with Confucius and Confucianism marking the eastern reaches of that ubiquity. By the early twentieth century, however, Confucius and Confucianism had become symbols of local obstruction of a vast cultural space made continuous through the operation of the market. The Jesuit melding of native Chinese practice and Christianity, which undergirded the seventeenth-century search for the perfect language[1] and drew China and the West closer, had been replaced by contemporary ideas of greater currency and weightier scientific presumption—nationalism, imperialism, and evolution—which made the imaginative space between China and the West as great as their geographic distance.

China was still enclosed within a universal space first articulated by the Jesuits, but that space was now defined in terms of a new complex of global struggle and "the survival of the fittest," to use a biological metaphor. However, in the nationalist racial biology of the day, China was also identified as a lower life form. Ironically, nativist Chinese intellectuals were greatly inspired by the comprehensive quality of this taxonomy and embraced it, appropriating metaphors of struggle, extinction, genus and species classification, the primitive, and inevitable progress with alacrity. They took up its interpretive tools but confounded its intended results, by taking advantage of China's position within this system to begin a debate on the significance of *ru* that would redefine Chinese identity and reestablish China as a site of ecumenism. This restoration of China's ecumenical cultural status and the reassertion of its role in resolving the modern West's divisive pluralism were accomplished through a meticulous philological reconstruction of *ru* and historical defense of its antiquity. The present chapter tells the story of this unexpected restitution of China's global historical significance in the translation of foreign concepts into the language of Chinese national identity, and much like the yarns of Conrad's alterego, Marlow, its meaning is to be found in the accumulated record of conceptual manufacture by which East and West have been bound. It is a story of the enabling conditions of obscurity and the heroism of a few who believed, unlike ourselves today, that art, the art of Chinese invention, could transform the world; it begins with *ru*.

Interpretive Preliminaries: The Keyword *Ru*

After learning of the imaginative manner in which the Jesuit fathers manufactured a native identity as *ru*, it might come as a surprise to find that the Chinese conception of *ru* is just as constructed, no less fabulous, and of more recent provenance than that of the Jesuits. Knowing of the "ideological" character of Jesuit interpretation, we tend to disparage their claims of allegiance to the *zhengxue*, "true teaching," of the *xianru* (the first *ru*), of Kongzi as inauthentic, even preposterous. Foreign priests, especially ones zealously seeking the conversion of natives to the Sacred Faith, simply could not be *ru*. And yet testimony from many Chinese observers and most converts, some of which we have read in chapter 2, instead confirms the unexpected—the fathers were indeed *ru*.

Acknowledging this prospect causes one to wonder how an indigenous Chinese term, culturally distinct and historically venerated, could describe the bearers of such a foreign language and oppositional faith. This question contains another—what does *ru* really mean—and both questions lie at the heart of the inquiry to which the second part of this book is devoted. The obvious answer to the first question is that there was more than simply one way to be Chinese. In addition to the obvious ethnic definition of Chineseness, there was a broader, inclusive culturalist understanding of identity that regarded spoken language, dress, and citation of classical texts as definitive.[2] *Ru*'s native definition was predicated on these culturalist criteria, a social category defined by effects rather than essence. However, beginning with the energetic exchanges between Zhang Binglin (Taiyan, 1868–1936) and other early nationalists on the subject of *ru*, this culturalist definition was overcome by the criteria of race and blood. Consequently, their debates over *ru* were inextricably bound to national politics and to the politics of scholarship among intellectuals competing over the preservation of Chinese culture and civilization in the face of its imminent demise. This insistence on an exclusively ethnic definition of Chineseness, furthermore, helps to account for our skepticism when faced with Jesuit enculturation.

As for the second question, what does *ru* really mean, we may answer that for over two thousand years *ru* (see glossary) has been a salient term in the common fund of practices, words, and meanings that make up Chinese culture. Nonetheless, it is a term of uncertain provenance and meaning that engaged an entire culture's communication with itself and, because of this, is assuredly one of a handful of what Raymond Williams, in a different context, called "keywords."[3] Such terms are particularly significant because we believe that any culture or society is fundamentally defined by means of them.

As a Chinese keyword *ru* has enjoyed a metonymic status, akin to the one it held for the Jesuits, throughout the history of imperial China, apparently functioning as an emblem of the culture's central value system. As early as the reign of the third Han emperor Wu (Liu Zhe, 153–87 B.C.E., r. 141–87 B.C.E.), when imperial patronage was probably first conferred on men of this title, the referents of *ru* reached far enough that it symbolized a familial sociocosmic harmony keyed to the living emperor, in which respect for the past and a sense of the individual as an ensemble of ritualized social relations were foundational.[4] But regardless of the meaning it acquired from this imperial association, the term was especially prominent during the two centuries preceding Qin unification (221 B.C.E.), and even before this *ru* was already synonymous with Kongzi, Kong Qiu, or Zhongni, as texts such as the *Zuo zhuan, Zhuangzi, Mozi,* and *Yanzi chunqiu,* among others, attest.

While it may seem strange, the textual salience of *ru* in early literature is matched only by the term's semantic ambiguity. *Ru* is, by all accounts, "a name of obscure origin,"[5] and debates about its *locus classicus* among Chinese, Japanese, European, and American scholars have become routine in this century. Such debates are not easily resolved, because in the native vocabulary *ru* is bathed in obscurity.

The uncertainty that has surrounded the term, then, is inherent and not solely the product of clumsy Western interpretive hands, although it must be noted that it was these hands that introduced an element of primordiality into discussion about *ru*. And certainly one reason for the elusiveness of this term is the presumption, not evident in Chinese works until this century, of a definitive archaic moment out of which *ru* was spawned. The Jesuits, with their constructions *xianru* and *guru*, "ancient *ru*," were perhaps the first to suggest that the term had an originary significance preceding its association with Kongzi. They presumed the teachings of Kongzi were distillations of monotheistic rites plainly attested in the odes of the *Shi jing* and the proclamations of the *Shang shu*.[6] The fathers took very seriously Kongzi's claim in *Lunyu* that he was a transmitter, assuming that it was with him that the liturgy and ritual forms of an earlier era survived. On this—presumption more than empirics—rested *ru*'s archaic antecedence. Of course the captivation of the "modern" intellect with origins has only affirmed the existence of an authentic point from which all meanings of *ru* may be traced. Yet the ambiguity endures.

There are at least several other causes for the persistent ambiguity in native texts, possibly the most significant one being the dubious historicity of Kongzi, that semifictional invention of the corporate compilers of the *Lunyu*, and his symbolic association with *ru*.[7] There is also the matter of the semantic obscurity of *ru*, the oldest definitions of which are frustratingly paronomastic, puns on the sound of the word rather than definitions as *we* construe them. The intimacy of the links between Kongzi, a mythical figure, and *ru*, a figure of uncertain meaning, succeeds in reinforcing ambiguities of the respective terms. Another and previously unremarked reason for the enigmatic quality of *ru* has to do with the numerousness of its applications. It has been the title of a large number of philosophically distinct and dissimilar traditions, naming many different schools at different times and at the same time. To be sure, it is this essential protean quality of *ru* that makes it particularly susceptible to reinvention and even vulnerable to symbolic appropriation by foreigners like the Jesuits.

The ambiguity of *ru* is what made it possible for Jesuit missionaries to invent themselves in its name; it has also provoked a history of invention by Chinese seeking to overcome this same ambiguity. The ambiguity is not easily resolved, because to do so requires one to confront the historical imaginations of previous centuries where one learns, like a character from L. P. Hartley's novel *The Go-Between*, that "the past is a foreign country; they do things differently there."[8] Hartley's wisdom is more than a caveat for the inquirer; it dramatizes the importance for those "going back" of finding common ground with the object of their desire and implies that such common ground is more likely the result of the seekers' manufacture than of the hosts' offering.

If the past is a foreign country, then how does one get around at all or get around well enough to comprehend what one sees there? Knowing the language, of course, is indispensable, which is why so many Chinese interpreters in this century have employed philology as a method of getting into the foreign country wherein they presumed *ru* resided. Practitioners of such philological reconstruction, as we see in this chapter, sought to establish unity with a historical past by isolating an ostensible ancient purity of the written language, the endurance of which offered incontestable evidence of the continuity of ancient and contemporary. Nevertheless, even complete mastery of the ancient language (*guwen*) does not bring one satisfactorily closer to the world of ancient Chinese. So, "getting around" is more, as we saw with the Jesuits, a problem of conceptual logistics than of proper linguistics. Here we put aside the question of context, and this is where the "foreignness," as it were, of the past is most pronounced.[9]

To get around requires imagining, by means of a textual artifact, the context within which that artifact was produced. An appreciation of context is comparable to appreciating a painting: what one needs, as in a Chinese landscape, say Fan Kuan's (ca. 990–1030 C.E.) *Travelers among Streams and Mountains*, is a place to enter. The most effective method I can imagine for entering the horizon of a foreign context is to locate lines of filiation, to seek out what is common in the experience of two different countries—the present and the past—at two very different times.[10] Filiative links of this sort never simply disclose themselves, as the Jesuits discovered and as the Chinese have found in subjecting their past to study. But, while previous interpreters in China have come to the same conclusion about the importance of finding common ground while facing the challenge of making sense of what preceded them, they have entered the foreign country of their past without recorded comment. Confronted by doubt, they chose to do the only thing they could do: invent in the image of what they knew, to reproduce their contemporary concerns in the obscurities of a text. Where commonality was suspect or even nonexistent such interpreters assumed, even manufactured, conceptual common ground, and thus, following Hartley, booked passage from one country to another.

Emphasis in this chapter and the one that follows will be on the indigenous Chinese readings of *ru* that were produced by two communities of scholarly discourse in the first three decades of this century. To get at the distinctiveness and to understand the importance of these readings we must first explore the essential paradox that despite its prominence *ru* is troublingly ambiguous. Thus we will first consider the internal heterogeneity of *ru*'s meaning, its lack of representational uniformity, and query our presumption of its stable identity. From here we will proceed to analyze the heightened interest in *ru* and Kongzi spurred by the late-nineteenth-century revival of "New Texts" (*jinwen*) of the Han era that portrayed Kongzi as a visionary and the Qing government's advocacy in 1907 of a state-sponsored national religion, *guojiao*, based largely on the *jinwen* account of a prophetic Kongzi.

From this resurgence of interest in identifying *ru*, we will look, in the second half of the chapter, at a narrative explanatory fiction of it manufactured by the twentieth-century Chinese scholars Zhang Binglin and Hu Shi (1891–1962). In an inventive response to an interpretive situation of uncertainty, both men drafted a conjectural history of *ru* and posited its ancient origins. This native scholarly fiction, which I call the "originary fable of *ru*," though spawned from contentious intellectual debates over race, identity, and cultural heritage, proved particularly valuable to Western sinologists and has been assimilated to our understanding of this tradition as well as of Chinese antiquity in general. In an examination of the essays out of which this fiction was fashioned, we will see how, in reworking ancient texts, Zhang and Hu produced a new reading of the term, one that appeared to overcome the ambiguity of *ru*.

By selecting texts of this century and not those of the Warring States or the Han as evidence, I mean to mitigate the historical abstraction of *ru* and its perilous identification with the greater whole of China, both of which have made it possible to presume that Confucianism is authentic. I have also chosen these twentieth-century works because they set out rather nicely the principal texts, the philological arguments, and some fruitful speculation from which one might imagine what *ru* could have meant in ancient China. In this respect the Chinese reconstruction of ancient practices is strikingly akin to the work of the Jesuits in inventing the lost orthodox tradition of the *xianru* (first *ru*).

It is not because a great deal was known about *ru* that there has been so much discussion, even explication, of it in the last few decades. It is, rather, an awareness of the persistent obscurity of the term and continued doubts as to why *ru* named the fellowship of itinerant persuaders associated with Kongzi that have incited this profusion of explanation. I would insist in this regard that the troublesomeness of *ru* is our problem and is caused by the presumption that *ru* and Kongzi *are* stable, known entities instead of historical products whose significance is generated from a delicate dialectic of ambiguity and invention. Let us take up this dialectic by considering the vagueness of *ru*, its persistence in Chinese cultural vocabulary, and its putative role as a symbol of Chineseness.

Few scholars today are convinced that what we know of *ru* from the earliest glosses is sufficient to explain why it has endured. This is because the light shed by such glosses on the meaning of the term is diffused by scholarly conventions of an unfamiliar historical imagination. Things are said about *ru* by early commentators (in fact there are definitions), but what is said in them makes negligible sense to us even with the assistance of a good dictionary. The *Er ya, Guang ya,* and *Shuowen jiezi,* all early etymological works, are either silent or confounding on the subject of *ru*.[11] Scriptural texts of the *ru* tradition like *Lunyu* and *Mengzi* offer scribal evidence of the character, but yield no insight into its meaning. Appended commentaries on these scriptures only ratify their interpretive quiet concerning this name by which the tradition would later be known.

There is, as would befit elected custodians of the canon, a canonical gloss of the term as "scholar" (*shi*), vouchsafed us by Han dynasty redactors, themselves "scholars" and *ru.* The common Jesuit rendering of the practitioners of *ru* as *literati* and *homes letrados* has ensured the endurance of the Han gloss in the West while the early gloss has been sustained in China. East and West, the *ru* are *shi,* the equation of scholar and *literatus* being reproduced endlessly in popular and academic literature. Thus, we have every reason to presume that *ru* is a stable, known entity. Yet, as soon as we question the meaning of *ru,* that is, pursue it beyond the common post-Han readings of "scholar" and "gentleman of wide learning" (*shi, boshi*), and beyond the post-*Confucius Sinarum Philosophus* reading of *scholae Confuciani* (Confucian school), we are confronted by a daunting vagueness and a lack of agreement even among the Chinese scholars who have attempted to define it.

Out of this ambiguity, veiled by the facile equivalence of *ru* and *shi,* a conceptual invention was shaped in the twentieth century. It negates yet preserves, in an elaborate explanatory theory, the once unproblematic Han gloss of *shi* in stating that men called *ru* began as priests and shamans and ended up as teachers and canon redactors. This is the gist of Zhang and Hu's originary fable to which I alluded previously; it is a tale of the beginnings of a world written by those living at its end. As we shall see, it grows from a depressed or oppressed nobility theory of *ru,* a name that is again personified, this time as the noble cultural ancestry of a great civilization in crisis.

By "originary" I mean a significance that predates Kongzi and the *Lunyu,* which, as I will show, is still the source for the earliest use of this term in pre-Han literature. The efforts of Zhang and Hu to establish a precedental significance for *ru* were directed not at restoration of the true teachings of Kongzi, but at defining the term in a manner independent of the mythology that had grown up around the sage and his traditions. Above all they sought scientifically to construct a narrative historical frame that prefigured the later cultural significance of Kongzi as an imperial icon, building this frame from the earliest meaning of the graph, *ru*. In this philological manner they aimed at making *ru* mean something that authorized its present use and justified its previous significance, not as the mere title of those who assumed Kongzi as their ancestral teacher but as a symbol of Chineseness. A distinct degree of historical self-consciousness and national pride was prerequisite, therefore, to such an effort.

The identity of these inventors is well known, even if we know little of how their interpretations have seeded our intellectual historical consciousness. Zhang Binglin in 1910 and then Hu Shi in 1934, both relying upon selected Han era texts, attempted to elucidate this term.[12] What they produced gave rise to a consensus on the primordial significance of *ru:* that it was, even before Kongzi, a specialized term that referred to an elite corps of priests, shamans, and sorcerers, in service to the ruling lineages of the *Zhongyuan* (north central plain), the cradle of ancient Chinese civilization.[13]

Zhang's essay, titled "Yuan ru," was an exercise in linguistic stocktaking in which the author scrupulously reproduced the stages in the term's etymology to demonstrate that its meaning had changed considerably. One might fix its meaning in the present, but this would do nothing to bring one close to the linguistic protocol of *ru* in the time of its earliest use, Zhang pointed out. So, he intended to chart a course from this earliest use to its contemporary application through a simple etymology. In so doing he revealed a pattern of semantic evolution that suggested incontrovertibly that *ru* had developed from tribal priests into a free-floating intelligentsia.

More important than Zhang's etymology, however, was the implicit claim that past and present meanings of *ru* were not alike and that this dissimilarity could be explained through a vague, evolutionary metaphor of secularization. In addition to its account of the semantic peregrinations of the graph/word, "Yuan ru" offered a distinct sociology in which *ru* began as magicians (*fangshi*) and ritual practitioners, later becoming teachers and scholars (*shi*) who, because they were the bearers of the canon, imagined themselves descendants of China's legendary sage-kings.[14]

The many speculations that accompanied Zhang's etymology were lifted up out of their context and driven forward by Hu Shi's theoretical elaboration on "Yuan ru," which he called "Shuo ru." The essay was a clarifying addendum to Zhang Binglin's piece, one which followed the implications of its argument in principle. While seconding the assertive guesses and reasonable philological reconstructions put forward by Zhang Binglin, Hu reaffirmed that the meaning of *ru* had changed from a religious to a secular one, and concurred that it was Kongzi who initiated this shift in significance, but in accord with a prophecy contained in the *Yijing* (Classic of Change) and a single ode from the *Shi jing* (Book of Odes).[15] These essays, particularly Zhang's "Yuan ru," will be examined in greater detail below; here I wish to emphasize only how these scholars manufactured an ancient pedigree for *ru* and narrated a history of descent from this fictive point that laid a romantic, but authoritative, claim on the modern imagination, whetting the hopeful presumption that *ru* did have a very ancient significance that presaged the arrival of Kongzi.

While these two essays may stand as an effective summary of wisdom ancient and modern, their preeminence should not obscure the fact that Zhang's and Hu's interpretations were advanced in a historical context where different meanings ceaselessly competed for concrete expression.[16] Ambiguity has always inspired invention, but what is different about the modern historical narrative of these scholars is its absorption of all previous accounts and thus its definitive claim of knowledge. The work of Zhang and Hu is consistent with a previous history of the manufacture of *ru*. But despite their convincing historicist explanation of the term's evolution, I will show that it does not permit them to assert a definitive understanding, just a different understanding, one functionally in concert with the work of preceding interpreters. We must not forget what Zhang and Hu both knew very well—that their originary fable of *ru* emerged from an implicit doubleness, negotiating its interpretive place in dialogue with a received normative conception constructed in the Former Han period. The consensus that followed from their accounts was not present in the time of the Jesuit mission. It is the product of these more recent and very specific interpretive developments of the last half century.

For centuries what was said of *ru* was not expressed in an explanatory narrative, and what narrative there was certainly was not keyed either to etymology or to historical conjecture, but stated as declaration. It is with the twentieth century that narratives of *ru* reappeared, albeit as conjectural histories derived from an etymology of the word and its cognates. The most influential of these recent narratives were more than imaginative reemplotments of the traditional *ru* narrative put forward by Sima Qian in the *Shiji*. They depended upon techniques of figurative predication[17]—metaphorical construction of an ancient historical predicate of the later attested *ru*—and are qualitatively distinct from earlier narratives.

These constructions are different because they are genetic and even more so because they have been employed in representing *ru* in a grand cultural inventory, explaining it as a metaphor of the inevitable passage of Chinese culture from its religious beginnings to its modern secular present. Though these interpretations are Chinese, they are, nevertheless, the constructions of outsiders, whose narrative voice is ironic more than sympathetic. Constructions in the name of *ru* made in the early Han are, in contrast, sympathetic and are ancestral to the modern equivalence of Chinese and Confucian that portrays the interdependence of *ru* and the state as natural and necessary. The early Jesuit missionaries and, of course, an array of seventeenth-century scholars appropriated, as the reader will recall, this peculiar representation of government and ethos as the essence of *ru* and their "Confucianism." The twentieth-century Chinese narratives, however, first question and then reject the naturalness of this equivalence, thereby causing us to wonder how fixed the meaning of *ru* was.

Zhang Binglin and Hu Shi went about establishing the unnaturalness of the traditional interdependency of *ru* and *zhi* (government) by investigating the term *ru*. The scholarly apparatus of their narrative inventions, then, was essentially linguistic. Yet when one considers the challenges of historical phonology in Chinese (which will be discussed later in this chapter), the prospect of authentic reconstruction of its ancient meaning is very doubtful. Perhaps it would be preferable to trace the ancient meaning of *ru* from the current language, in the same way that linguists like Jerry Norman have suggested that we might do better to reconstruct the ancestral forms of popular Chinese by working back from contemporary spoken dialects.[18] What keys to an earlier significance can be found in the contemporary Chinese understanding of *ru?*

There has been considerable variation in its significance since the appearance of the term in texts from the fifth century B.C.E., but this semantic diversity provoked little conclusive comment, as we have suggested, until the first years of this century. Although in China today *ru* lacks its former prominence in the cultural vocabulary, it is hardly unknown. For many Chinese, *ru* is vaguely understood as either a symbol of the late imperial state or just another name for the mandarinate.[19] If *ru* persists as a keyword at all it is because it remains a symbol in terms of which the larger cultural life of imperial China has been, and continues to be, construed. However, it is among Western scholars of Chinese philosophy and intellectual history, rather than Chinese, that *ru* continues to be so understood, albeit in the interpretive constructions known to us as Confucianism and Neo-Confucianism. In most works from this genre, the native referent, *ru*, has been superseded by the Western neologism "Confucianism."[20] Even when speaking of the "tradition" of Kongzi or Zhu Xi scholars display a reluctance to use the term *ru*, which says much about the difficulty of employing it as a descriptive term. Instead they tend to rely on *daotong* (legacy of the way), which, like "Confucianism," operates with a mental economy that summarizes an otherwise untidy ambiguity.

In vernacular Chinese, *ru* may be found in some colloquial compounds like *rusheng*, now meaning "scholar" or even "student," but it is infrequently used. Contemporary Chinese intellectuals tend to equate *ru* with "scholar," and compounds like *daru* or *hongru* retain a traditional meaning of "great or learned scholar." As a symbolic vestige of the Chinese imperium, *ru* conjures in some regions of the popular imagination an image of an oppressive, despotic state, specifically that of the Manchus.[21] Neither with *ru* nor with Kongzi, however, can we point to a community in China today that claims identity under these rubrics. *Ru* today is marginalized, insignificant, at best providing a theoretical counterpoint to a world that has little real use for it.

The formerly synonymous terms *ru* and "Kongzi" have bifurcated and are no longer linked in the minds of contemporary Chinese. No longer so closely associated with *ru*, Kongzi stands alone as a symbol of Chinese civilization and antiquity, and of the greatness of the nation's tradition of learning, being so honored in 1990 on a set of commemorative postage stamps. In this manifestation he functions more as a commercial equivalent of, rather than as metonym for, *chuantong* (tradition) in its most general sense of cultural legacy or artifactual bequest. Commerce is pursued with the fervor of religion in China—such religion being encouraged more than tolerated—and so, as recounted in the introduction, citizens are urged in school and in public service advertisements to follow Kongzi's ethical example. Seen in this way, the contemporary Kongzi appears to possess the same symbolic capital that "Confucius" did for eighteenth-century Europeans: that of the moral exemplar, the great humanist philosopher, the symbol of Chinese civilization.

Ironically, this contemporary marginality, however, more than *ru*'s former role as a symbolic paraphrase of China's central values, recalls the qualities of the term in the time before the imperial era. At that time, *ru* designated a strict order of men who lived on the fringes of contemporary social life, outside the same authoritarian political structures with which they would be associated after the end of the Former Han dynasty. But our lack of awareness of *ru*'s earlier, unwritten history is simply a consequence of Han redactions, which delivered the fellowship from this life to another, rewriting the memory as much as the texts that preserved that indistinct past. These redactions were the work of Sima Qian and Liu Xin, for whom *ru* were unquestionably scholars and officials whose history had yet to be written.

Ru: The Normative Interpretation

If it is with the *Shiji* that a genuine Chinese narrative history begins, wherein the technics of chronology and theme were worked to unite past events and transmitted speech,[22] then it is probably here that the story of *ru* begins. Sima Qian's particular chronology for *ru* covered the interval from the decline of the ruling clan, Ji, of the Zhou, through the unrecognized and desperate wanderings of Kongzi and his seventy disciples, to service by the disciples descended from those first followers as counselors and attendants of the emperor. The narrative frame was actually narrower than this, because it was a history of the ascendance of *ru* from the dark days of the fledgling fellowship after Kongzi's death to their imperial prominence under Dong Zhongshu (ca. 195–105 B.C.E.) and his alleged three hundred disciples. This chronology contained a theme—the passage from chaos to order and the inevitable supersession by *ru* of their former ignominy. When the *Shiji* was completed near the close of Han Wudi's reign (ca. 90 B.C.E.), *ru* meant *shi*, "scholar, gentleman" or, more commonly, *boshi*, "gentleman of wide learning," something evident throughout Sima's history and quite explicit in the one chapter (chapter 67) devoted to the *ru* fellowship, the "Rulin liezhuan," or "Tales of the *ru* Forest."[23]

Most of the text is prosaic, predictably interspersed with memorials, anecdote, and serial listing of the names and offices of the *ru* elect, yet there is one vignette so poignant that it rises up out of the chronicle. It is an account of *ru* desperation during and after the terror of the Qin emperor Shi Huangdi's (r. 221–210 B.C.E.) rule when the *Shi jing* and *Shang shu* were supposedly incinerated and the scholars buried alive. And it is the story of *ru* on the verge of extinction at the hands of Liu Bang (Han Gaodi, r. 202–195 B.C.E.) in the last days of his fight against Xiang Yu (233–202 B.C.E.). The Burning of the Books marked the nadir of the *ru* tradition, for, as Sima Qian tells it, "[T]he six disciplines from this time were damaged and incomplete,"[24] so that when Chen She (248?–206 B.C.E.) stumbled into rebellion against the Qin (221–208 B.C.E.), the *ru* took up with him. Sima recounts how the "assembled *ru*," *zhuru*, of Lu departed their native state, how through a powerfully symbolic translation of relics they "moved the ritual vessels of the Kong clan and aligned themselves with Chen She in Chu." "Thereupon," the narrative continues, "Kong Jie [purportedly a direct descendant of the master in the eighth generation] became Chen She's *boshi* and was buried with him at death."[25]

Chen She was, however, executed and the rebellion crushed, while Liu Bang and Xiang Yu raised armies to contend for what was left of Qin territory. Sima Qian, the "Grand Historian," barely notes the failure of the uprising, recording it only when he records the homeless *ru*'s vain hope that Chen would avenge their humiliation at the hands of the Qin. He makes much of their having given up everything and how, with complete disregard for Chen's now lower social status, they presented him with gifts dedicating themselves to his service.[26] They risked all and received nothing. Sima presumes that the reader is aware that *ru* quietly favored Xiang Yu in the rebellions against the Qin and so wagered even more steeply than before; hence, he says nothing more about their political sympathies following the collapse of Chen She's rising.

In the space of a single line, the narrative jumps forward several years to the defeat of Xiang Yu and the subsequent siege of Lu. This time the *ru* do not seek alliance or proffer assistance to either of the combatants. Instead they remain sequestered within the ancient walls of the capital awaiting the outcome of the slaughter outside. Sima Qian's account of what follows is one of the few passages from early literature that conveys so powerfully the unique qualities of *ru*. Knowing that their adversary is just beyond the gates of the city, they await their fate in a spirit consistent with the words of their master:

> The Supreme Lord (Liu Bang) executed Xiang Yu and [then] advanced his troops to surround [the ancient city of Lu]. From the center of [the city of] Lu [there came] the sounds unending of strings and voices where the assembled *ru* were still discoursing and chanting, practicing rites and music. Was it not because of the sage's surviving influence that [Lu] was a state that loved rites and music? Therefore, Kongzi, [when] in Chen, said, "Return, I must return home! My little village of young boys are wild and reckless. They are accomplished at the display of refinement, yet do not know how to refine themselves." People from the regions of Qi and Lu have since antiquity displayed a native talent in literature. Thus with the ascendancy of the Han it followed that *ru* began to make a living [through] their canon and cultivations, and to recite and practice the rites of the Great Archery Contest and Drinking Ceremony.[27]

Here in these ten sentences of Sima's text we have an expressive summary of the essential features of early (preimperial) *ru* life: strange wisps of song, echoes of lutes filling the air above the ancient city as Liu Bang's troops prepare for assault. The image is, I think, unforgettable. The troops may well have been so dumbstruck by the din of recitation, dance, and song that their martial urge was stilled, as a later gloss on *ru* by Zheng Xuan might suggest: "The words of *ru* are excellent, comforting, and can pacify man."[28] Perhaps this passage suggested to Zheng a possible gloss for *ru*, yet I suspect the pacification of Liu Xiang's hordes was not the point the Grand Historian wanted to stress, as he does not elaborate on it.

Sima probably intended several effects, the first being the description of the plight of *ru* under the Qin, in order to contrast this with their fate under the succeeding Han. Second, he wished to depict *ru* as honorable for their unlikely preservation of ancient practice in a benighted age. In this respect it is a paean to *ru* virtue, learning, and courage. Third, and this would seem the chief effect, Sima Qian attempted to construct a narrative of the rise of *ru* that paralleled the restoration of culture under the Han. To this end, the tale of *ru* desperation—the chanting of scripture in the face of imminent destruction—acts as a thematic hinge on which ignominy and near extinction turns into celebrity. For this reason the early image of tribulation was superseded by Sima's detailed account of what he knew by personal experience—the progress of *ru* success in officialdom from Shusun Tong (fl. 2d century B.C.E.)

through Gongsun Hong (200–127 B.C.E.) to Dong Zhongshu.[29] Nevertheless, it seems appropriate that this image of a community in jeopardy should be intimately connected to a narrative of the triumph of the *ru*, for that achievement encloses and preserves the image of *ru* solidarity that captures its pre-Han identity. We should not forget that Sima Qian himself said that these strange behaviors were the surviving influence of Kongzi. It is from this almost surreal and yet extremely poignant vision of *ru* that the normative interpretation of *ru* as "scholars" retreats.

Indeed, for all of Sima Qian's homage to the desperate heroism shown by Kongzi and the ancient *ru* fellowship, the text of his chronicle reports scarcely anything of their earlier existence and instead records an early Han "Whiggish" history of this group's inevitable administrative achievement. For the Grand Historian, the *ru* are not so much followers or descendants of Kongzi as they are powerful administrative functionaries (Dong Zhongshu being one of the exemplars of this ethos contemplated by Sima), as this very characteristic passage from the "Rulin liezhuan" (Tales of the *ru* Forest) suggests: "When the present emperor came to the throne there were a number of inspired [figures] such as Zhao Wan and Wang Zang at court who were engaged in *ru* learning. The emperor was greatly attracted to their ideas and accordingly sent out a summons for *shi* of moral worth and literary ability to serve in the government."[30] *Ru* here is the particular type of learning characteristic of the scholar-official; it resembles more a technique than a way of life. There certainly is no suggestion of a close-knit community, or more specifically of a fellowship of ne'er-do-wells joined in filial devotion to a master and committed to the pious reenactment, through chanting and dancing, of ancient rites. *Ru* in this case denotes an official biography, a biography of officials who are without clear antecedents, or whose antecedents are not official.

The "Rulin liezhuan," being a chapter in Sima Qian's accounts of the notable, was the first chronicle of the rise of the *ru* from the humble—living in alleys and wearing ragged garments—to the prominent, serving as ministers to the emperor.[31] It, too, was a narrative that organized Chinese understanding of Kongzi and his tradition, just as the chapter organization of the *Shiji* became the paradigm for all subsequent official histories, for nearly two thousand years. Yet this understanding so familiar to us, at the moment of Sima Qian's writing, represented a new and different meaning of *ru*, one which betokened a reconstitution of its native community. The Han linguistic protocol of *boshi* (gentleman of broad learning) signaled a change in significance appropriate to the changed community that embraced this new title, just as the meaning of "Confucius" changed for the Jesuits as the constitution of their accommodationist solidarity was altered.[32] The change is further reflected in the literature subsequent to the putative "victory of Han Confucianism,"[33] where *ru* paramountcy is a *fait accompli*.

No works written after this period, for instance, engage the common criticisms of *ru* from the Warring States era nor do they provide passionate countercriticisms by *ru* in defense of their customs and dress. In post-Han literature we encounter no chapters such as we find in the *Li ji* ("Ruxing"), where Kongzi's extensive protestations to Duke Ai (r. 494–469 B.C.E.) about the sensibleness of *ru* attire affirm the very salience he sought to deny.[34] The texts of subsequent centuries simply seem less alive with regard to the status of *ru*; in them, the meaning of *ru* is as unquestionable as its status.

Thus, this normative interpretation, which stresses the natural links between *ru* as *boshi* and the Chinese imperium, brings us around to a question implicit in my treatment of the Jesuits: Should and can Chinese culture be reduced, as it was by the later Jesuit accommodationists, to a conceptual nexus of "Confucius" and *Confucianos*, so that all of what is traditional about China is, ipso facto, Confucian? The question is not inappropriately put to the Chinese, for in native accounts *ru* and Kongzi have been indistinguishable as symbols of cultural heritage and as with Sima Qian, an effort was made to establish the necessity of the ties between *ru* and imperial government *in statu nascendi*. Certainly, we understand how this reduction of China to "Confucius" was accomplished by the Jesuits and also how we continue to reproduce it today; however, now we can see that this reduction was not only peculiar to the Jesuits. Their heroic reduction may have been a faithful foreign rendering of a Chinese reality in lives and texts. Confucius and *Confucianos* in this light seem like a Latin mirror-image of Kongzi and *ru*.

To our way of thinking, *ru*, of course, cannot symbolize all of Chinese culture, and some Western scholars, most notably the late Michel Strickmann,[35] have challenged the metonymic status of Confucianism by pointing out that the most likely candidate for this symbolic role is Daoism, China's oldest indigenous religious tradition. A strong case can be made that from 215 C.E. onward the *tianshi dao* (Way of the Celestial Master) was the "true" official religion of China, with a priestly hierarchy, an elaborate scriptural tradition textually assembled in the Daoist Canon, wide popular acceptance, and most importantly, a close relationship with the state.[36] As these are the very grounds upon which the metonymic cultural status of Confucianism is invariably defended, Strickmann contended that all the talk about socioethics and orthodoxy in the rites and observations of Chinese defined in terms of Confucianism suggests a systematic misrepresentation of traditional China. Contentions such as this, while well reasoned and supported by a growing weight of epigraphic, ethnographic, and ethnological evidence,[37] nevertheless keep the argument in the court of the "Confucianism as cultural essence" advocates. It would be better to get outside this game altogether by abandoning the tendency to compare the traditions *ru* and *dao* as adversarial competitors for legitimacy.

So instead of fighting among ourselves as interpreters for what, at best, is a Pyrrhic victory, sinologists might ask again of the Chinese and their texts if the cultural hegemony of *ru* is defensible. The answers are counterintuitive. For example, we can assert that the Chinese language is not ideographic and fulminate against Pound and Fenollosa[38] for deriving so much imagistic poetry and prose from this notion, and yet, there is no escaping the fact that the Chinese themselves often explain their language as if it were ideographic or even pictographic.[39] The native view of *ru* follows the same paradoxical path, as much as we might insist that the term cannot perform the broad symbolic duties placed upon it by the Chinese and, of course, ourselves. The wide symbolic reach of *ru* and Kongzi is plainly evident even in the early literary texts where these two entities represent something greater than the beliefs and practices of a single tradition.

There are other, more difficult epistemological questions raised by the inquiry thus far. Is it possible to reconstruct *ru* tradition as it might have been before the advent of its Han manifestation? Can we imagine *ru* as anything other than classical exegetes and imperial advisers, and moreover, can we, with adequate evidence, support such a contrary conception? Why should we be unsatisfied with the meaning of *ru* found in the first systematizing texts? By looking beyond the *Shiji* and the first official history of the early Han, the *Han shu* (History of the Former Han, ca. 100 C.E.), as we obviously do in asking questions of this nature, do we then reject their definitions of *ru* as inauthentic or wrong? Asking these questions, we enter the same unreported dialogue that occurred earlier between the normative interpretation received from classical antiquity and the newer philological readings of twentieth-century Chinese. I now consider these questions and examine the broader historical sense that has been made of *ru*.

The Missing History of *Ru*

To inquire of the origin of *ru* is a troubling affair for the modern scholar, for much the same reason that locating the earliest appearance of "Confucius" was in chapter 1—the path back is not clear. Rather than the confusing abundance of texts with which we were confronted in the latter case, here we are faced with a paucity of contemporary sources from the twelfth through the fifth centuries B.C.E., the interval during which the *ru* fellowship was likely to have begun. The earliest literary texts speak of persons who lived and events that took place some seven to ten centuries before they were compiled, and yet we have virtually no additional textual evidence of them, other than a few Zhou ritual bronzes bearing inscriptions that match or are directly relevant to charges recorded in specific books of the *Shang shu*.[40]

Reconstruction of these works is further made difficult by the fact that extant texts are not homogenous, but are "layered" and composite. And this is not simply an accident of modern history or of carelessness in the recovery of ancient documents. The books of the Chinese canon were never homogenous.[41] In almost every instance when we speak of the provenance of a text, we are speaking *figuratively* of the entire text, but actually of only a fascicle or fascicles of it. Among these heterogenous shards there is some scribal evidence of *ru;* however, its meaning in these few cases is less than clear.

But the problem is even more one of interpretation, or lack of it, than of evidence. In ascertaining the meaning of *ru,* perhaps more disconcerting than the sparse evidence is that until the close of the last century the few efforts to define *ru* yielded explanatory fictions that, from our "scientific" perspective, explained little and presumed much. In these instances the Chinese appear unconcerned with the origins of *ru.* Among the available contemporary sources from the era of the fellowship's emergence before the dawn of imperial history, there is simply no recorded self-conscious reflection on the term. Furthermore, Chinese readings of *ru,* whether historical, philosophical, or philological are, like our "Confucianism," similarly framed by preexistent interpretations so that indigenous understanding is seamlessly intertwined with representation.

When we look to native texts to locate the meaning of *ru* we find that, much like the storytelling of Joseph Conrad's Marlow, described in this chapter's epigraph, *ru* is already enveloped by previous episodes in interpretation including even the Jesuits' fictional *xianru.* There is no definitive kernel of truth or reality lying beneath the storied manufacture of sense made in the name of *ru.* To understand *ru* is to appreciate all that has been made of it. This does not mean, however, that between the fifth century B.C.E. and the twentieth century that the Chinese were not interested in *ru;* they were just not concerned with *ru* in a manner satisfactory for our modern sensibility, where origin and cause are the sources of certainty. For a good portion of this interval, there was a consensus derived from the first narrative of *ru* and which was produced in an age when Chinese historical self-consciousness blossomed. The authority of this Han narrative ensured its perpetuation as consensus even as subsequent interpreters pondered the meaning of *ru* in very different historical conditions.

Later Considerations on *Ru:* Supplements to
Interpretive Closure

There was, during the Three Kingdoms period (220–288 C.E.) for instance, a commentary on the *Shuowen* in which a slightly different etymology of *ru* was given. According to the *Shuowen jiezi gulin*, Chen Jie (3d–4th century C.E.) said that the meaning of *ru* in *Shuowen* was "weak," *rou*. He also asserts that "the word *ru* means timid [*nuo*],"[42] and quotes supporting passages from the *Li ji* and the *De dao jing*, the latter of which equates timidity with femininity: "To know the male side, but to hold onto the female side is the same as timidity [*nuo*]." Chen's work was more a footnote to Xu Shen (ca. 30–124 C.E.) than it was a new determination of *ru*'s meaning; moreover, his contribution was conceived in the tradition of paronomasia as both *rou* and *nuo* were partners with *ru* in a phonetic cluster. Explication again eludes us, not because Chen said nothing, but because what he said cannot be construed by us as explanation, for paronomasia is, as Aristotle pointed out, a form of literary entertainment. But as one presses on through the written record in search of a native explanation of *ru* one finds explication of a different kind that, like the paronomastic offerings, is less than satisfactory.

Near the end of the Yuan dynasty (1279–1368 C.E.) several essays and meditations on *ru* appeared. At this juncture two celebrated figures and literary competitors, Song Lian (1310–1381) and Wang Wei (1323–1374), commented on *ru*. Their interest in the term did not engender a genetic study of its meaning, as these efforts were the product of Chinese reorientation within a novel cultural situation—a dynasty founded by conquerors.[43] The evident self-consciousness of their writing on this topic suggests that the creation of "*ru* households" (*ru hu*) by the Mongols for their new taxation registry system provoked some Chinese to consider what defined *ru* status.[44]

Writing in the fourteenth century in a disquisition bearing a title identical to that of Zhang Binglin's later essay, Wang Wei reflected on the different senses of *ru* and concluded that its contemporary significance was incompatible with its archaic meaning. The essay was documentary rather than philological, and no precedental meaning of *ru* was adduced beyond his assertion that the ancient learning transmitted by Zhou Gong and Kongzi was not the same as the learning of the Five Masters of the Northern Song era—Zhou Dunyi, Shao Yong, Zhang Zai, and the brothers Cheng.[45]

For Wang and his fellow *ru*, what *ru* meant was a given. It was a name that really described several kinds of learning, the only true one being that of "the sages and worthies." Though it was also used by those who recited texts and crafted essays, the idea of an ancient *ru*, as Wang Wei understood it in his "Yuan ru," signified the learning of Kongzi and Zhou Gong, an ideal not transmitted beyond Xunzi and only aped by the Northern Song masters. The disquisition was clearly an exercise in contemporary cultural criticism, for the difference in the past and present meanings of the term was lamented as deviance. Borrowing heavily from the vocabulary of *daoxue* (learning of the way) with its presumption of a contemporary relation to receding sagely ideals, Wang said that the self could infer the regulation of the world in Zhou times by grasping the heaven-endowed principle revealed through "illumination of the mind and exhaustion of the nature" (*mingxin qiongxing*).[46]

In "Qiru jie" (The Seven [Types of] *Ru* Explained), a more thorough discrimination of the plural significance of *ru* by Wang's contemporary, Song Lian, the synonymousness of Kongzi and *ru* was presumed. Song's effort here produced not much more than an explication of contemporary types derived largely from the distinctions made in book 8 of the *Xunzi*, "Ruxiao" (On the Achievements of *Ru*) and in the "Shujie pian" of Wang Chong's *Lunheng*.[47] In Song's case this dearth of explanation is particularly striking, in light of a definition of *ru* put forth in another of the essays from his collected works, the *Song wenxian quanji*.

In "Hetu shu" (Pivot of the River Chart), where he assumed an alter existence as Master of Dragon Gate (Longmenzi), Song says that "*ru* is a name for the weak (*rouru*) [those incapable of manual labor]; prior to the Three Dynasties, it was not a specialized name."[48] By saying this he indicates his awareness of the gloss by Xu Shen from the *Shuowen jiezi* (Explanation of Pattern, Elucidation of Graphs)—that place where all subsequent philological efforts to define *ru* would begin.[49] Yet it is significant that Song's cognizance of the *Shuowen* gloss did not lead him to posit a genetic account of the antecedents of Xu's definition, though his definition did reflect an understanding of the semantic difference between contemporary and ancient uses of the term. As Song Lian pointed out in "Qiru jie," *ru* was now a specialized name, the many referents of which were to be distinguished through observable differences in public practice.

In the same way that a gravitational field is inferred by its visible effects, so the public demeanor, gestures, expressions, and the scholarship of the person, for Song, as for Xunzi, or even Sima Qian, revealed his identity as *ru*.[50] To *be* a *ru* was one thing, but to *define it* in a manner other than just stating the self-evident aspects of one's existence as *ru* was quite another. There was no "origin" to find in order to explain the term; what was known had been transmitted—the meaning was manifest. But Song Lian was also reaffirming the inherited meaning of this order in a transitional age, in the same way that Sima reinforced the emerging definition of *ru* as textual specialists in a period of relative uncertainty. In the fourteenth century it would seem that custom, the transmission achieved through imitation, was sufficient to preserve ancestral values. The reasons for *ru* behavior were not distinct from its practice, even though the authors were conscious of a fundamental difference between *ru* of antiquity and those of the present day. An "explanation" of *ru* was immediately available, for it was regarded as a visible feature of the intelligible cultural universe, conveyed through the very sinew of the cultural organism. The unselfconscious equation of *ru* and the public practice of the scholar-official class—one wholly lacking in genetic presumption—is confirmed as well by some of the early glosses on it from the Han and Tang eras.

A review of any one of these glosses certainly would have quelled speculation on a pre-Kongzi significance of *ru*. Examining the etymology of Xu Shen from the *Shuowen* and the commentarial glosses of Zheng Xuan (127–200 C.E.) and Huang Kan (488–545 C.E.), it is evident that their explanations do not refer beyond the immediate context in which *ru* is defined.[51] In fact the definitions of the term advanced by these justly celebrated redactors are, as so many early glosses, paronomastic, mere puns on the sound *ru: ru ru ye* (ru means wet), or *ruzhe ru ye* (the ru are wet). Such definitions naturally tell us more about an accepted style of early rhetorical practice than about the original significance of a term. Nonetheless, these puns are clearly intended to provide a practicable definition of *ru*; hence, it is incumbent on the later readers of a gloss of this kind (later readers such as the late imperial Chinese, the Jesuits, and ourselves) to recover the context in which such a paronomastic definition makes sense.

Beyond, and perhaps because of, this, even *kaozheng* (evidential research) scholars partial to the *ru* tradition like Jiang Yong (1681–1762), Duan Yucai (1735–1815), and Cui Shu (1740–1816) were not moved to query the term's meaning beyond that provided by these inherited glosses. This, incidentally, is very telling, as both Jiang and Cui were committed to a thorough reconstruction of the man Kongzi and his text the *Lunyu*.[52] Of course, the fact that in their ruthless examination of texts such men were not given to skepticism about the meaning of *ru* may have been a consequence of the movement of *kaozheng* studies away from the *Sishu* toward the *Wujing*.[53]

Leafing through the voluminous eighteenth-century critical reconstructions of the canon and finding no commentary on *ru* might suggest that any clues to its meaning were excised along with forged chapters and commentaries by scholars intent on recovering the core of the received tradition. The absence of scholarly comment from this era on *ru*, or lack of interest, is significant and helps to explain why the first efforts to identify the original meaning of *ru* were undertaken only by early-twentieth-century scholars, some of them followers of *kaozheng*, who renewed an eighteenth-century commitment to the study of the so-called noncanonical thinkers (*zhuzi*) of the Warring States era.[54] They emphasized the acknowledged intellectual pluralism of the Warring States, for they found in such a portrait a faithful reproduction of their own contemporary climate of opinion where the *jinwen, guwen*, Tongcheng, and Songxue coteries rivalrously coexisted. And while this commitment to *kaozheng* eventuated in a rediscovery of *zhuzi* thinkers by scholars of many stripes in late Qing China, it was among a particular group of such scholars that the renaissance of *zhuzi xue* brought forth an ancient image of *ru*.

In 1910 in the waning moments of Chinese imperial time, Zhang Binglin—Han studies scholar, Ming loyalist, cryptoanarchist, and archnationalist—completed work on a volume of essays that included an unusual meditation on *ru*. "Yuan ru" (The Etiology of *Ru*), as the piece was called, was an intellectual watershed both for what it uncovered about the meaning of the graph and for the manner in which its revelations were made. "Etiology," rather than "origin," from the Greek *aitiologia*, meaning a statement of causes, best conveys the tone of this piece, for it was not solely concerned with the etymonic origins of *ru*, but, more importantly, with the term's semantic development from its earliest uses to the present. Furthermore, as Zhang considered the contemporary understanding and practice of *ru* to be a significant deviation from its beginnings, etiology's association with illness makes it an especially apt rendering of *yuan*. *Yuan* also connotes "primitive," as in the contemporary social scientific usage, *yuanshi* (primordial).[55] The beginnings or origins of *ru* in this sense would constitute a statement of its primordial manifestation, a form now superseded by the current meanings as a proper classification for a specific discourse.

Never before had the plural and confounding significances of this prominent term, which most Chinese presumed they knew, been set out so cogently. With the publication of this essay, Zhang became "the first person to put forward a historical observation [*lishi jianjie*] of the differences between past and present, causing us to understand that this word [*ru*] that ancient people used had three broad, narrow, and dissimilar interpretations."[56] Yet, on a deeper, less discernible level, *ru*'s semantic variations were defined through a developmental history derived from Zhang's creative appropriation of the geopolitical racialism of Terrien de Lacouperie (1844–1894) and a Spencerian theory in which the world's social forms passed through stages of necessary supersession.[57] Such theories of inevitable progress were intellectually endemic to his generation and were often swept up into contemporary reflection on native texts and traditions of interpretation, so that Chinese debates over traditional scholarly subjects like the canon displayed a distinctly foreign conceptual phrasing.

It may have been just this hybrid quality of Zhang's theorizing on *ru* that drew the attention of a skeptic like Hu Shi who, in the spring of 1934, completed a work that was inspired by "Yuan ru." In a preface to his "addition and correction" (*buzheng*) of Zhang's earlier essay, Hu wrote that in "Yuan ru" Zhang had "bored through mountains," adding that the essay's historical conjecture in particular was unprecedented:

> Mr. [Zhang] Taiyan's [Zhang Binglin's] great contribution was in enabling us to know that the meaning of this character *ru* has passed

through historical transformations, from a broad one encompassing *ru* as the practitioners of magical and scholarly technē, to a narrow one of *ru* as those who follow the example of Yao and Shun, write about the civil and the martial, and [take] Kongzi as their ancestral teacher.[58]

But there were revisionist scholarly objectives that also united the two figures. Inquiring into the meaning of *ru* only to show that its meanings were multiple, dissimilar, and incompatible was consonant with an intellectual tendency Zhang shared with Hu Shi and of which Hu was a most articulate proponent.

Zhang Binglin and Hu Shi were the first to define *ru* with respect to a pattern of continuous semantic change that extended from the Shang to the present. The pattern was presented as a developmental history of the term's significance: in Zhang's view inherent in the character itself; in Hu's, revealed in certain texts of the post-Zhou (771 B.C.E.–); and from our contemporary vantage, one reminiscent of the evolutionary social theory that galvanized both Western and Chinese scholarly intelligence in the first decades of this century. And yet these essays, while their theoretical edifice was shaped out of broader intellectual currents, including those generated by theories of evolution, racial competition, and progress, were above all reactive impulses stimulated by a wholesale revision of Chinese antiquity and the canon of its documentation brought on in the *jinwen* (New Text) revival.[59]

It was not the revival itself that occasioned this reflection so much as the profound changes during the period from 1895–1910, of which the aggressive reassertion of New Text scholarship under the aegis of Kang Youwei was the most dramatic intellectual consequence. From the humiliation of the Qing dynasty and its thirty-year program of modernization called *ziqiang* (self-strengthening), symbolized by the Treaty of Shimonoseki of 1895, to the proposal of a Qing imperial commission for a national constitution, electoral laws, and a parliament, educated Chinese lived amidst radical change, where customary status and, indeed, all that was familiar was in doubt. Some have characterized this era as one of crisis, others as one of transition,[60] but talk among Chinese intellectuals of this time, including those interested in the ancient significance of *ru* and especially those writing for the Tongmeng Hui party's journal, *Minbao*, was of representative government and the making of a Chinese republic in the image of France or the United States.

The former imperial Chinese society, groaning in dilatory response to increasingly peremptory calls for substantive educational and political reform, gave way to wholly new institutional complexes more proper to a modern nation-state than a crumbling empire. Abolition of the system of national, provincial, and local examinations for civil service recruitment was the first and most celebrated step.[61] More important, however, were several decisions that followed in the wake of this development and the constitutional deliberations of 1905–1906 that profoundly influenced the thinking of active, yet academic, republicans like Zhang Binglin and Liu Shipei.

The government announced in July of 1908 that provincial assemblies and elections were to be established. A month later, a nine-year period for the drawing up and implementation of a constitution, electoral laws, and a national parliament was promulgated.[62] Suddenly, like accelerated fate, ideas and propositions soundly rejected in 1898 as seditious were becoming, quite rapidly, government policy in 1908. This year, as proclamations of the imminent formation of provincial assemblies (ironically, a political vision dear to Tan Sitong [1865–1898] that had earned him death as a reward) and the drafting of a state constitution were made, the Manchus were poised to transform China's national heritage. They were prepared to remake antiquity in the image of *jinwen* ideology embracing the political advocacy of reformers, as it appeared to revolutionaries. With official policy beginning to resemble the once-ridiculed program of Kang Youwei (1858–1927) and Liang Qichao (1873–1929), Zhang, Liu, and others like Deng Shi and Wang Jingwei (1883–1944) who believed that the government's embrace of Kongjiao ("Confucianity") would be China's cultural undoing, rushed to reaffirm the fundamental correctness of *guwen* antiquity as the sole reservoir of the country's "national essence" (*guocui*).

To revolutionaries and revolutionary scholars whose opposition to the state grew chiefly from an increasingly virulent ethnocentrism or racism, the government's flirtation with constitutional reform suggested that this lesser race, the Manchus, might actually survive as China's overlords, accomplishing the feat by placating republican and national religion conservatives. Zhang, once a staunch advocate of republicanism, reacted on both political fronts, decrying republicanism and opposing the officialization of Kongjiao.[63]

While *jinwen* reformers like Kang Youwei attempted to forge an organic link between the Chinese people, the emperor, and a visionary tradition they believed was mystically pronounced by Kongzi, educated Chinese were challenged from many areas to evaluate the meaning of their culture. The most enlightened and progressive scholars and activists among them, while not all susceptible to *jinwen* sanction, did look to *ru* and Kongzi in the representing of the past that helped them reconstruct their contemporary native identity. It is difficult to say whether the instability of a steadily changing society, the cognitive dissonance produced by the prospect of a hybrid political system with a hereditary monarch overseeing the workings of an elected parliament, or simply the growing popularity of Kang Youwei's advocacy of a national religion was responsible for this renewed interest in Kongzi and his *ru* fellowship. However, it was obvious that the confluence of the old society China had been and the new society it had not yet become engendered a systematic reflection from many intellectual quarters on Kongzi and the name given to his tradition.

The turn by intellectuals, believers and skeptics alike, to these "cultural roots" was evidence of an effort to fashion a new identity amidst the conceptual dislocation caused by the suddenness and intensity of social change. Racialists and *guocui* partisans especially were engaged in making a "new age man," something that required, Zhang believed, the honoring of a proper sense of the past.[64] The intemperate debates brought on by the search for these roots were nothing less than culture wars fought in front of a backdrop of politics. And theirs was an argument about the precise context in which to understand themselves perhaps through reflection on *ru.* For none of them, however, was the interest in the ancient meaning of *ru* a plea to restore its authentic former existence. And for all of them the debates were political.

The early salvos launched in these wars assumed the form of a dispute over the ancient significance of *ru* and what it might imply about a contemporary political role, not only for men assuming the title but for all Chinese. These salvos were fired at the beginning of this century by Kang Youwei and Liang Qichao for the *jinwen* reformists, and by Zhang Binglin and Liu Shipei for the *guocui* coterie. All were patriotic activists, but they lacked agreement on the effective methods of political action, on political objectives, on the proper classical training of an intellectual, on the authenticity of the received canon, and especially on the place of Kongzi and his legacy in the definition of Chinese nationality. They did agree that Kongzi was a significant aspect of that legacy; however, there was apparently no agreement on what he meant.[65]

These men lived in an age of increasing national self-consciousness, a self-consciousness fomented by duress, and even when several others chose to enter the debate over *ru* in subsequent decades—among them Feng Youlan (1895–1991), Guo Moruo (1892–1986), and Fu Sinian (1896–1950)—they found that pursuing the questions raised in these debates was part of a process of national self-definition that had only grown more intense following the fall of the Manchus.[66] All of them witnessed, and most championed (with the obvious exception of Kang Youwei), the collapse of China's traditional imperial system, but all were threatened immediately by the imposition of another imperialist one that denigrated China and its cultural heritage as "sick" and "weak."[67] Zhang Binglin, certainly the most strident of these cultural critics, described his country's predicament as one in which it had become a double slave, chattel of both the Manchus and the Western powers of the treaty ports.[68] Raised in the traditional examination culture, these scholars looked unanimously to classical texts—recently and authoritatively redacted and made authentic—as weapons in a larger battle for national identity.

For them national identity was about history, and their reconstructions of *Chinese* history required them to come to terms with Kongzi and *ru,* those symbols with respect to which so much of the national culture had been defined. There was irony in this consequence—that radical nationalist scholars considering the rejection of *ru* and Kongzi as the ideological tools of Manchu overlordship would have to come to terms with and even reaffirm both—and it was not lost on Joseph Levenson (1920–1969), who said: "Even when clearing the ground, the Chinese wanted desperately to own the ground they stood on. They wanted to continue making *Chinese* history even when—or rather, by—making the products of Chinese history *history.*"[69]

As desperate efforts to clear Chinese ground by cultural conservatives and political radicals brought forth *ru* and Kongzi, Kang Youwei's contention that the prophet from Lu was the only symbol capable of overcoming China's cultural diversity and inspiring a unified drive for national community appeared justified. The return to Kongzi as an instinct of cultural defense generated by an urgent search for Chinese ground, not trivialized by its recent imperial past and also not the conquered subject of Western civilization, was linked, furthermore, to the new researches of *guocui* scholars into *guwen* texts in order to advance a scientific and not a religious defense of antiquity. Whether scientific or religious, the contentions of *guwen* and *jinwen* scholars alike defined Chineseness through Kongzi. And so the critical scholarship of the early-twentieth-century Chinese, in effect, reproduced the seventeenth-century Jesuit equation of *Confucianos* and Chineseness. Kongzi, regardless of the judgment one made of him in this capacity, remained the symbol of China's inherited traditions.[70]

The native reproduction of this Jesuit reduction was explicit in the revisionist works of Kang Youwei and Liao Ping (1852–1932), which succeeded in establishing Kongzi, the *Chunqiu,* and the *Weishu* (Apocryphal Texts) as principal objects in the visual field of late-Qing cultural criticism. Kongzi was, for them and for some others—even *jinwen* adversaries—a totalizing icon, the measure of China's entire civilization, the transmitter of its ancient cultural heritage, the maker of both the classics and history. But more than this, Kongzi was a visionary whose *weiyan dayi,* "abstruse words and great meanings," conveyed a prescient understanding of global history and geography and hinted at the impending unification of the world. Liao Ping tells of the prophet's remarkable wisdom in his *Huangdi jiangyu tu,* stating:

> The evolution of the world, culturally, is from barbarism to civilization and, geographically, from lesser to greater. During the Spring and Autumn [period] the Nine Provinces [*jiu zhou*] totaled only a square of three thousand miles and, going back to the time of Shun and the Xia, conditions were even more primitive and obscure. When Kongzi sagaciously edited the writings [*Shang shu* (Book of Documents), *Shi jing* (Book of Odes), *Yijing* (Classic of Change), *Chunqiu* (Spring and Autumn

Annals)], he attributed the institutions promulgated therein to antiquity, and thus furtively inserted the term "province," current in his own day, into his charts of sovereigns and emperors, in which he looked ahead to what would become current in later times. [These judgments] stored up are like Mount Sumeru in the mustard seed; spread out, they extend to everything within the four seas. Yet in each case they remain equally applicable.[71]

Jinwen ideology seized the contemporary imagination, and if accounts such as this one of Kongzi's omniscience were not entirely persuasive, the discourse of this brand of reformism was certainly pervasive. Western, Japanese, and Chinese vocabularies intermingled, yielding many new ideas, ideas that would help the Chinese chart a course out from their nation's dilemma. Evolution, progress, and the increasing popularity of the linear trope proved indispensable in articulating these new ideas, and all three imported conceptual technologies are in evidence here in the comfortable native confines of Liao Ping's first sentence. An almost seamless conceptual braid of foreign and indigenous notions characterized the theoretical constructions of scholars of this era, *jinwen* and *guwen* alike.

From 1890 to 1915, *jinwen* theory and practice affected both reformers and revolutionaries, and this is evident in the intimations of the signature prophetic conception of Kongzi found in the writings of antagonists. Zhang Binglin was just such an antagonist, who in 1895 joined the Qiang Xuehui (Strength Study Society) in sympathy with Kang's reformist sentiments and who seven years later, after he had vehemently rejected Kang Youwei, still regarded Kongzi as the figurative ancestor of all China's dynastic houses.[72] There was a widespread, nativist appeal rooted in the unconventional *jinwen* interpretation of Kongzi as reformer-messiah. The image caused most men of this generation to take an inventory of their inherited conceptions of the sage and his tradition. Such a reckoning was, of course, critical to contemporary efforts to define the features of Chinese identity while preserving the material and immaterial culture of a newly articulated "national heritage," *guogu*. And this native cultural identity was, like that of Kongzi and *ru*, not monolithic, but divisively plural, with the principal divisions falling between the scholars of New Text and Old Text hermeneutics.

Kang Youwei and his activist New Text followers believed that China's cultural rejuvenation could be facilitated through what might be termed a "muscular" Confucianism capable of uniting the Chinese population against its enemies while proselytizing foreigners to its religious mission. As originally envisioned by Kang and partially implemented by Liang Qichao in Changsha in 1897, the state religion of Kongzi, Kongjiao, was to mimic the Christianity of the treaty ports down to a program for missionizing. A year before the inauguration of the *Wuxu bianfa* (One Hundred Days Reforms), Liang put forth a set of ten guidelines for study at the Shiwu Xuehui, the tenth of which called for *chuanjiao* (preaching the faith), one of the Chinese terms used for the work of Christian missionaries. The tenth regulation was directed at the senior members of the study society who were expected to disseminate the doctrine they had learned among ignorant Westerners. Liang's final benediction reads:

> On the day when you finish your studies and graduate, it is our desire that the final point of your studies will be transmitting to all nations of the world Kongzi's teachings of the Great Peace [*taiping*] and the Great Equality [*datong*]. The job of preaching the faith belongs to the period following the completion of studies. Because all the work in this study society focuses on the principle of glorifying the Sage's teaching, this final assignment may in fact be termed the job of "preaching the faith."[73]

The *jinwen* tradition offered just such a muscular Confucianism where Kongzi was more than the redactor of the received canon; he was a political reformer, an uncrowned king (*suwang*), and a prophet whose message of the impending unification of the world was kabalistically coded in the sparse words of the *Chunqiu*.

In 1896 Kang Youwei published his *Kongzi gaizhi kao* (Researches on Kongzi as a Reformer), a more focused supplement to his wider-reaching, withering critique of Hanxue (Han Learning), the *Xinxue weijing kao* (A Study of the Forged Classics of Xin Era). In it, Kang dismissed nearly two centuries of empirical scholarship on the canon, when he suggested that this new, muscular reading of Kongzi and his tradition was the only authentic one. Practicing a double hermeneutics of suspicion and belief[74] wherein the prevailing *guwen* readings of the canon were rejected as obfuscatory while the true voice of the sage was restored in the genuine language of *jinwen*, Kang remarked:

> The spurious antiquity theories emerged, and then [the new text] was obstructed and concealed and [no one] understood the meaning of *ru*. [They] considered Kongzi to be merely a person who had assembled and [then] handed down the Six Classics and treated him as an erudite and accomplished man of refined conduct, like Duke Zheng [Xuan] or Master Zhu [Xi] of later generations. How could [he] be a great sage? Zhang Xuecheng went so far as to consider the Duke of Zhou [Zhou Gong] the great synthesizer, not Kongzi.[75]

Here Kang voiced his objection to Zhang Xuecheng's celebration of the Duke of Zhou as the last figure who combined *jiao* (teaching) and *zhi* (rule). It was Zhou Gong rather than Kongzi who provided the inspirational agency for the active transformation of the masses as his example engendered movement from the state of *suoyi ran* (that which therefore is) to that of *dangran* (ought). In this respect Zhang Xuecheng simply proffered an ontological gloss on Zhou Gong's precedence over Kongzi, a precedence presumed for most of Chinese imperial history. On the page following the quotation cited here, Kang demonstrates his awareness of the fact that until the early Tang, it was the Duke of Zhou and not Kongzi who was apotheosized as the great sage of Chinese antiquity and the man responsible for the institutions formative of China's cultural character. Consequently, his criticism of Zhang Xuecheng on this count is hardly fair, as he was stating what was, by most accounts, obvious.

Fair or not, within a decade of Kang's self-justifying complaint, Zhang Binglin wrote what could be taken as a scholarly *guwen* rejoinder to this emotional diatribe. In his onomastics, "Yuan ru," Zhang made it clear that there were some among Kang's contemporaries who did in fact understand the meaning of *ru* and were willing to go to some length to demonstrate it, especially if such demonstration was disadvantageous to the interpretive, and thus political, objectives of the *jinwen* coterie.[76] Thus, while Kang and his cohort were "pleading antiquity for reform," *tuogu gaizhi*, in service to the establishment of a new religion of Kongzi, Kongjiao, Zhang Binglin advanced his own nativist appeal to the language of antiquity to reform current understanding of the tradition identified with Kongzi. He, Liu Shipei, and Kang each believed in the necessity of cultural preservation, yet the identity of this indigenous culture was hardly unequivocal.[77]

It was as if Chinese culture had acquired in the "self-strengthening" (*ziqiang*) disputes that preceded their debates a capital "C" and become, for both revolutionaries and reformers, a court of appeal before which they presented their respective defenses of its integrity.[78] For Kang this defense was the presentation of the living embodiment of this culture—the emperor—and so he founded the Baohuang Hui (Protect the Emperor Society) following his escape to Japan.

For Zhang and Liu, in contrast, national survival entailed the nurturing and preservation of *guocui*, and this was the sole objective of their devotion to *guoxue* (national studies). In this spirit they organized the Guoxue Baocun Hui (Society for the Preservation of National Studies)—a society dedicated to what Zhang termed *zhengli guogu* (the organization of the national heritage), an ambitious task of philological and philosophical criticism aimed at establishing the authentic literary lineaments of Chinese cultural identity as these extended unbroken from antiquity to the present.[79] The success of Zhang's endeavor to put the national heritage in order can be seen in his reconstruction of *ru*, the original meaning of which he joined to contemporary arguments over Chineseness, authentic antiquity, and political transformation.

All these constructions of figural precedents—Warring States fabrications of sage-kings, Jesuit fictions of "orthodox teachings" of ancient monotheism, Chinese fables of an originary *ru*—were engendered by a perception of difference or loss that gives rise to a representation/narration of meanings that permits the present to be linked imaginatively with the past. Understanding this should make us skeptical of the authenticity of Zhang Binglin's representation, yet at the same time help us to recognize what we share with earlier commentators simply by putting the question once again. However, we must further explore the paradigmatic revolution brought by Zhang Binglin in the inspired intellectual climate of the early twentieth century.

Nativist Politics and Historical Reconstruction

Thomas Kuhn pointed out some time ago that a scientific revolution may occur when scientists revisit questions presumed to have been adequately answered by "normal science"; a paradigm shift away from this normal science will occur because these questions have again become prominent and in this state of salience they are more satisfactorily answered by a new science.[80] Thus, it is the historical record rather than willful paradox that prompts me to assert that all written speculation on the genesis of *ru* begins with the formation of this new paradigm, out of which an interpretive palimpsest on the subject of *ru* took shape. Questions never previously asked of *ru* were posed, and Zhang's "Yuan ru" offered a coherent response that organized a welter of citations concerning *ru* from respected ancient texts.

In this essay Zhang accomplished a historical reconstruction of the meaning of *ru* from pre-Qin and Han texts, logically accounting for its semantic passage from the second millennium before the common era to the present. His brief sketch exemplified *zhengli guogu* and, though Zhang's reconstruction made sense and was made out of materials known to all of his contemporaries, it was comparable to a paradigm shift. Zhang offered his genetic account as a corrective to prevailing contemporary uses, which, as he claimed near the end of the essay, he felt had "pared down and confused the proper name *ru*,"[81] and yet his response represented an entirely new way of looking at the term. Because there was before this no such study of the origin of the graph, and also because it seemed to assemble in a convincing, scientific manner the diverse meanings of *ru* over four millennia, Zhang's "Yuan ru" might have achieved the status of a Kuhnian paradigm, providing the interpretive frame through which the intellectual history of China could be organized. The essay did effect a paradigm shift, but not until it was rediscovered and reworked by Hu Shi twenty years subsequent to its publication.

Since this time "Yuan ru" has endured as the standard reference tool used by all who are interested in a meaning of *ru* other than the conventional meaning of "scholar." In a manner reminiscent of the framing significance of *guanhua* (official words; administrative vernacular) for the Jesuits, which predisposed them to favor *ru* over *fo* and *dao* in constructing their Chinese self-image, "Yuan ru," with the help of Hu's reading, has constrained all previous inquiry to yield conclusions not very different from its argument and implications. In this capacity the essay has inspired considerable scholarly speculation—Chinese, Japanese, European, American—on the originary significance of *ru* and on the precise nature of its historical development.[82]

What one learns of this rather late appearance of a widely documented *ru* history puts one in mind of Gu Jiegang's once startling discovery that the earlier a figure is seen in the mythic strata of China's past, the later it is invented or appears in texts of certain antiquity.[83] Just as figures like the ancient culture heroes Yao and Shun are inventions of the Warring States (479–221 B.C.E.) but appear in the received chronology before Yu does, whose mythic existence took shape in the Zhou (1045–771 B.C.E.), the ancient history of *ru* is of recent provenance. It is difficult not to see that Gu's observation, "The earlier [mythic] figures appear in the accepted chronology, the later they actually emerged in history,"[84] fittingly characterizes the essential modernity of the endeavor to ascertain the earliest meaning of *ru*. Beginning with the primitivist constructs of the Jesuits and extending to the twentieth-century etymologies and developmental histories put forward by the Chinese, we must concur with Gu "that our traditional knowledge of Chinese antiquity was built up in successive strata, but in an order exactly the reverse of the actual occurrence."[85]

"Yuan ru" was probably written in the last few years of the nineteenth century but did not appear until 1910, in the first edition of Zhang's *Guogu lunheng*, a work whose title revealed its twin sources of inspiration—*guogu* (national heritage), and *lunheng* (critical evaluation of doctrine, which Wang Chong used as the title of his celebrated criticism of the prevailing beliefs of the Han dynasty).[86] *Guogu*, a coded term, was, like so many of the expressions of the new nativism, borrowed from the vocabulary of Japan's *kokugaku* (national studies) and referred to the antiquity of the Chinese—their language, myths, beliefs, practices, artifacts—and not the Manchu people.[87] As for the term *lunheng*, it aptly conveyed Zhang's own sense of his scholarship. Just as Wang Chong had criticized received *ru* doctrines and the popular beliefs of his day, in particular disparaging its auguries and numerous incredible legends, Zhang was concerned to demystify the New Text interpretation of Kongzi, his teaching, and the classics and to push China's cultural chronology back beyond Kongzi to the Yellow Emperor, Huangdi.

And Zhang was not the only scholar of his generation whose thoughts in the final decade of the Chinese empire had turned to the genesis of *ru*. In these objectives he was joined by his erstwhile colleague Liu Shipei who, motivated by similar concerns about the destructiveness of *jinwen* criticism, published the first reconsideration of the origins of *ru*. In his essay "Rujia chu yu situ zhi guan shuo" (An Explication of the *Ru* School's Emergence from the Office of the *Situ*), published in August 1908 in the journal *Guocui xuebao*, Liu revealed a reading of Han and pre-Qin texts very similar to that of his comrade in *kulturkritik* and the journal's founder, Zhang Binglin.[88] The essay, though lacking the philological flashiness of his colleague's work, did offer a novel reading of *ru* based on Liu Xin's account of the fellowship in the "Yiwen zhi" (China's first bibliographic catalogue) in which he said, "Rujiazhe liu gai chu yu situ zhi guan" (Those of the *ru* family came forth from the [Zhou] office of steward of the masses [*situ*]).[89] In reiterating this account, Liu Shipei was advancing an eloquent defense of Liu Xin, the much-vilified Former Han bibliographer, against the egregious claims of *jinwen* scholars that he had singlehandedly forged the *guwen* classics.

Liu Shipei was merely stating what one can presume most scholars of his generation and the eighteenth-century scholars from whom he claimed intellectual descent took for granted: that *ru* was, as the *Han shu* attested, an official designation of unmistakable pedigree. Why *ru* should be so understood, however, was not made clear in Liu Xin's "Yiwen zhi"; that task was left for Liu Shipei to complete. He did so by joining Liu Xin's own account with selected passages from the *Zhou li* (Rites of Zhou) bearing the term *ru* and from Zheng Xuan's commentary on the same text. In this manner he substantiated the claim that *ru* did indeed emerge out of the Zhou official post of *situ* (steward of the multitudes, leader of the footsoldiers). But more than this, Liu put historical flesh on the Han interpretive skeleton of *ru* by constructing an ancient *ru* company, the *gudai zhi ru* of the "Western Zhou," that inaugurated a set of teachings, an ethos later made famous by Kongzi. According to Liu's imaginative reconstruction:

> In the Eastern Zhou, the official duties of the office of the steward of the multitudes gradually flowed into the nine streams. Each of the one hundred families (*baijia*) held a different theory [of teaching]. Only Kongzi's theory of teaching [the people] . . . bore the slightest similarity to that of the learning of the *guru* [ancient *ru*]. Therefore, Kongzi's learning was known as *rujia* [the *ru* family]. In fact, Kongzi's words drew near those of the ancient *ru*, but his actions diverged from them.[90]

Liu Shipei's "Eastern Zhou," then, marked a historical turning point where the ancient *ru*, once secondary officials residing in rural hamlets and teaching the people of their customs, gave way to a novel social class of the same name whose pedagogy was indissociable from the classical canon, *jing*. Furthermore, Liu believed that the national essence of the Chinese—perhaps idyllically preserved in that last moment from the *Zhou li* where *guru* were stewards of the people—was lost in the "Eastern Zhou." This explains why, in Liu's estimation, Kongzi had attempted to emulate, but did not preserve, the legacy of the *guru*, a lost arcadia.

Oddly enough, Liu Shipei's exposition of the *Han shu* account of *ru* beginnings restated the epochal significance of Kongzi, even though it was offered as an implicit critique of the learning of Kang and his *jinwen* devotees whom Liu, acerbically but memorably, characterized as "wordsmiths from the Jiangnan who, endowed with little knowledge but great self-esteem, explored the New Texts of the Western Han."[91] For Liu Shipei it was Kongzi, as the great redactor, who was responsible for the compilation and transmission of the *Shi jing* (Book of Odes), *Chunqiu* (Spring and Autumn Annals), and perhaps the *Yijing* (Classic of Change). Thus, it was with Kongzi that the ancient *ru* practice of rural instruction in the *daoyi* (cultivations of the way)—farming, customs, loyalty, fidelity, charity, and filiality—gave way to the narrower, and scholastic, transmission of the canon.[92]

Thus, *ru* was not synonymous with Kongzi, as the *jinwen* advocates might have it, or, at least there was a primordial *ru* whose practices Kongzi imitated but did not transmit. The ancient *ru* were not rhetoricians or political advisers, but farmers and gentleman scholars, who dwelt among the people and found their principal obligation in popular instruction. This would have been the tradition of *ru* known to Kongzi, yet it was transformed by his hand and remade as canonical study so that by the time of Sima Qian, Liu states, "*ru* were those who penetrated and transmitted the canon."[93]

Liu's characterization of Kongzi was thus as a man acting as the linchpin upon which the archaic turned into the new, yet who was firmly situated outside a tradition of specialized practices (all of those pertaining to the *situ*, "leader of the footsoldiers") that he reworked, innovated, and then presented as his inheritance. *Ru* by this account designated a tradition of stewardship, one that surely antedated Kongzi. Kongzi and his teaching signaled a departure from that tradition. Moreover, in Liu's reconstruction Kongzi was robbed of the originality, the inventive power granted him by *jinwen* reformists like Kang, who believed that whatever sense could be made of the classical canon was a direct result of Kongzi's imaginative interventions, for he, in effect, had authored the Six Classics.[94] Also, in Liu's interpretation of his role as inaugurator of a new tradition in the name of the old, Kongzi bore a negative significance. Liu clearly believed that *guru* were the authentic representatives of the tradition, in large part because it was in this image that he saw himself as a national essence activist—as a man of the people living, teaching, and working among the unwashed but veritable essence of China.

In addition to reiterating the early Han consensus, corroborated with passages from selective texts, Liu also suggested that the social function, and along with it the cultural significance, of *ru* had undergone considerable change from distant antiquity to the present. What *ru* meant for his late Qing contemporaries—manning government posts, serving the imperial clan, memorizing and redacting the canon—was considerably removed from Liu's vision of ancient practices where the *guru* acted as the natural conscience of the countryside. The remarkable consequences of Liu's populist redefinition of Chinese antiquity would be worked out by Zhang Binglin who, at almost the same time, was busy rigging the philological foundations for a much more original conjecture in his *Guogu lunheng.*[95]

Zhang Rescues *Ru* from the Nation and Its Apologists

In two collections of his essays, Zhang laid the groundwork for a revolutionary nationalist redefinition of *ru: Guogu lunheng* (1910), a critical reflection on the state of contemporary Chinese cultural understanding, and *Qiu shu* (1900, 1904), an intriguingly diverse miscellany in which Zhang tried his hand at etymology, historical phonology, philology, and intellectual history. Though publication of the collections was separated by ten years, the essays were extraordinarily consistent in method and in message, so much so that they may be treated together. Among the pieces in the earlier miscellany, *Qiu shu* (Peremptory Book), was a series of interpretive sketches of the traditions inaugurated by the Warring States *zhuzi,* wherein *ru* was redefined in the context of the *jiuliu,* or "nine streams," of pre-Han persuasion: "Ru Mo," "Ru Dao," "Ru Fa," "Ru Xia," and "Ru Bing."[96]

Qiu shu also contained a number of etymological études on particular Chinese terms such as *ren* (humanity), *bian* (change), *xue* (learning), and *jiao* (teaching, or religion).[97] "Yuan ru" was very similar to these studies in title and composition and took its place alongside them as an attempt at contextualizing a term, *ru,* that, like *ren, bian, xue,* and *jiao,* was marked by philosophical abstraction in the late nineteenth century. In each of these efforts it was Zhang's aim to bring his readers back to the earliest literary texts (meaning *guwen* texts) where they might learn something of a targeted character's defining history. His enemy in this enterprise of context restoration was not the contemporary uses to which a term was put per se—he was not a linguistic revanchist—but rather the commonsense transparency that encrusts the language so that only a contemporary use seems natural, immutable.

Zhang believed, says Charlotte Furth, that "by a process of analogy and association of ideas, words branched out historically to encompass widening layers of nuance and additional meaning, spawning in the process new vocabulary which revealed its links with earlier stages through phonetic family resemblance and ideographic form alike."[98] Thus the work of philology was, as he would later say in his denunciation of Esperanto, "to make words flow appropriately from their beginnings."⁹⁹ Zhang was convinced that in the revisionist exegeses of *jinwen* scholars, certain terms had been defined far beyond the reach of their beginnings and deserved a rectifying clarification that he was particularly able to provide.

With the essay "Yuan jiao" (Genesis of Teaching), for example, he tried to demonstrate that the contemporary reading of the term *jiao* in the sense of "religion" was untenable.¹⁰⁰ What undoubtedly troubled Zhang in this context was the increasing popularity of Kongjiao (the religion of Confucius, or "Confucianity") and the fact that the *jinwen* mysticism inherent in this conception had acquired a commonsense transparency. Zhang Binglin's dislike for New Text interpretation and its growing popularity was an incentive for the founding of the National Studies Society (Guoxue Hui) and of the *National Essence Journal* (*Guocui xuebao*). His disposition on *jinwen* was well known. Gu Jiegang, in the preface to his seven-volume work *Gushi bian* (Critiques of Ancient History), recalls a lecture of Zhang's given before the newly founded Guoxue Hui in which he castigated those who presumed *ru* was a religion and pointed out the intolerable interpretive extremes to which such true believers would go:

> First, he discoursed upon the conflict between learning and religion, asserting that those who then promoted Confucianity did so with ulterior motives. He brought up the many noncanonical theories put forward by such critics of the "modern text" school as Wang Kaiyun, Liao Ping, and Kang Youwei, reminding us how these critics explained the graphs representing the word Jesus [*Yesu*] as meaning "The Father arisen"; how they explained the phrase, "the foremost disciples of Modi" [*Mozhu juzi*] as referring to the Christian cross; how they explained the passage [from book 1, chapter 12, paragraph 1 of the *Lunyu*] *junzi zhi dao si wei mei* as meaning "Russian is being Americanized" . . . and how they falsely invented miraculous events in connection with Kongzi's [birth and life] in order to portray him as a religious founder [*jiaozhu*].¹⁰¹

When in 1907 Kongjiao ceased being the minority interest of a select group of southern Chinese intellectuals and became an official, Manchu-promoted tradition invented and transmitted by Kongzi,¹⁰² Zhang's "Yuan ru" corrected the errors in *jinwen* scholarship while recovering Kongzi for the Chinese "as the fountainhead of the people's well-being."¹⁰³

In making this remark he was not claiming an exclusive affinity with the tradition inaugurated by the sage; these were not the words of a restorationist *ru* sectarian, but those of a nativist concerned to reappropriate Kongzi as a national treasure, the "Big Dipper of China" (*Zhina de daxiong xing*), as Zhang called him. Rather than imagine himself an inheritor of *ru* practices, a self-legitimating claim common to this tradition, Zhang felt no particular loyalty to *ru* and merely displayed the changing meaning of *ru* from a novel reading of ancient literary texts. Personally Zhang was not favorably disposed toward the *ru* tradition, and from 1911 to 1936 when he was increasingly influenced by Yogacara Buddhism, he even grew contemptuous of it.[104]

At the same time, it was probably the considerable personal distance between Zhang and this tradition that enabled him to articulate the different meanings of *ru* and to adduce these semantic differences as evidence in support of an explanatory theory. Despite this distance, Zhang recognized Kongzi as an exemplary cultural figure in Chinese history. In his passionate refutation of the proposal to establish a national religion of "Confucianity" Zhang maintained that to make of this tradition a state-revealed religion as the New Text reformers and the Jesuits did was absurd, for to do so "impedes reason's road to progress and is a source of discord in the great way to peace." Zhang offered instead what he evidently considered a reasoned reflection on Kongzi's significance for the Chinese, saying:

> The reason that Kongzi is the Big Dipper of China lies in the fact that he created history, disseminated written texts, promoted scholarship, and eliminated status differences between men. . . . Kongzi was a pillar who protected the people and caused civilization to flourish. He was not the founder of a religion. Had a man we have come to know as Kongzi not appeared in the world, political standards would not have been transmitted, scholarship would not have flourished, the state would have been destroyed by barbarians and never revived, and the people once fallen into degradation would not have been able to rise up. It would have been impossible for his name to rank among the civilized countries of the world. It is indeed because of this former sage that we have not yet perished. For this reason, Kongzi ranks far higher than Yao, Shun, Wen Wang, or Wu Wang.[105]

Zhang's admiration of Kongzi may be regarded as subversive, for he conferred upon him a ranking greater than the most esteemed cultural patriarchs such as Yao and Shun. By design, Zhang's etiology, like Russian formalist techniques that seek defamiliarization (*ostranie*), dislocated conventional understandings of *ru*.[106] Zhang's confrontational prose indulged a proclivity to use ancient, variant graphs of common characters throughout. For example, in referring to the Eclectics or *zajia* of the Warring States, he chose to use the ancient *za* instead of the more common, contemporary *za* (see glossary).[107]

Judging from his liberal reliance on noncanonical texts, primarily the *Mozi*, Zhang was undoubtedly aware that for some his essay would be more provocative than expository. And yet the net effect of the essay was not subversive but revelatory because he succeeded in laying out an entirely different and more coherent understanding of *ru*. This unfamiliar though convincing coherence grew from Zhang's reliance upon *zhuzi xue* (studies of the "noncanonical masters), a minor genre within the broader field of Hanxue (Han learning) with which he was identified by contemporary critics.[108]

Zhang Reconstructs *Ru:* A Conjectural History from Sound and Sense

A good deal of Zhang's work, much like his politics, defies simple categorization. However, "Yuan ru," though idiosyncratic, did bear the signal traits of *zhuzi xue*. The method associated with this genre is consistent with that found in the philological studies in Zhang's earlier collection, *Qiu shu*, where he places texts of competing Warring States schools on an equal interpretive footing.

Many of the essays in this collection, as well as "Yuan ru," seem to draw from this genre, one normally associated with its founding eighteenth-century practitioners, Zhang Xuecheng (1738–1801) and Wang Zhong (1745–1794), both of whom attempted independently to return Kongzi to his rightful place in the currents of the *jiuliu* or of the pre-Han period.[109] There is one very significant theoretical difference, however: Zhang Binglin, by the practice of this technique, did not mean to restore Kongzi to history where through hard exegetical work one could recover his teaching. *Zhuzi xue*, in Zhang's hands, was used to ground a purely semantic, and not romantic philosophical, exercise—the determination of the meaning of *ru*, the graph. His choice of this analytical approach to the literature of the pre-Qin era was more than one of elective intellectual affinity. Rather, his decision to take it up was a consciously political one, rooted in a belief that eighteenth-century *Hanxue* had been an intentional, coerced misdirection of Chinese scholarly industry away from questions of politics to questions of textual veracity.

In this vein, he offered the judgment that Manchu despotism had terrorized Chinese intellectuals, discouraging them from political engagement.[110] Thus Zhang's forays into *Hanxue* were intentional efforts to repoliticize this discourse that had acquired, against its will, an identity either as antiquarianism or as scholasticism.[111] *Zhuzi xue* was, for Zhang Binglin, the academic mechanism of such repoliticization. In his hands study of the "noncanonical thinkers" was to be a scholarly vehicle of aggressive Chinese self-affirmation within a political environment that was increasingly ethnically conscious. At the same time, this politics of scholarship was directed beyond a settling of accounts with the Manchus to the countering of *jinwen* scholarship and its apotheosis of Kongzi, one that delivered him and his fellowship, the *ru*, far beyond the historical context that produced them.

In just the organization of "Yuan ru" one finds subtle, but distinct, evidence of Zhang's devotion to the eclipsed genre of his namesake, for it is built from a single passage in the logical canons of the [Book of] *Mozi*. With the use of this excerpt, Zhang organized an explanation of *ru* to brilliant effect, each sentence of the excerpt serving to articulate the different levels of meaning operating within this one term. While he does not explicitly elevate Mozi (the Warring States utilitarian philosopher [ca. 5th century B.C.E.]) to equivalence with Kongzi, as did Wang Zhong, his use of the logic of one officially dishonored tradition to explain the meaning of *ru*, the name of the orthodox, indicates that Zhang, as was typical of practitioners of *zhuzi xue*, took *mo* and *ru* as coeval constructions of the pre-Qin era.[112] Canonicity, in other words, was a product of the Han, the interpretive closure of which limited the intelligibility of a reading of ancient texts. There were in fact no restrictions on antiquity's records in an inquiry into the etymology of a word, especially one as salient as *ru* in the intellectual pluralism of the Warring States. Such a study had to be ecumenical, not parochial, in order to convey the full range of the term's meaning; it also had to challenge the hold of interpretive convention on contemporary minds enough so that an alternative reading of *ru* could be contemplated. Zhang Binglin's "Yuan ru," as dense as it is terse, achieved these objectives.

By way of his inspired application of *zhuzi xue*, Zhang "restored" *ru*—for him a cultural concept, not a living tradition—to a context that was of his own construction, but which set the terms for what remains of my examination of native representation in the rest of this section. Dividing "Yuan ru" into four parts roughly corresponding to conceptual breaks in Zhang's argument, I examine this construction, taking care to draw out the manner in which he reworked ancient texts and terms for the purpose of demythologizing *ru*, so he could develop alternative metaphors for nationalist consensus.

"Yuan ru" is a very complex piece of work: its complexity a product of Zhang's obscure vocabulary, a great weight of ancient literary presumption conveyed in ambiguous allusions, and inscrutable speculation. As it appears in the first edition of the *Guogu lunheng*, the essay has approximately 1,400 graphs in fifty-one lines of text. It is a compendious summary to be sure, marred somewhat by the author's exclusive dependence on texts from the Han era, especially the testimony of Sima Qian, Liu Xin, and Wang Chong. The sole pieces of non-Han evidence are two references to the *Zhuangzi*, a couple of allusions to incidents in the *Lunyu*, an excerpt from the *Zhou li*, and some unconventional application of the *Yijing*. That Zhang would ascertain a primordial meaning for *ru* through reliance upon Han texts compiled as much as seven centuries subsequent to the term's earliest use is an irony befitting the difficulty of trying to establish precedent in ancient Chinese literature. So, considering that the earliest narrative of ancient *ru* descent begins in the early Han and is already evident in chapter 121 of the *Shiji*, the explicit Han character of Zhang's account is appropriate testimony to the difficulty of getting at the earliest significance of the term—that is, if one presumes that such an ancient meaning can be captured.

Betraying no sense of the elusiveness of the term, Zhang seems convinced the meaning could at least be reconstructed from context, as is clear from the first sentence of "Yuan ru" where he declares: "[Of] the name *ru* there are three categories [*ke*]: generic [*da*], class [*lei*], and proper [*si*]."[113] His penchant for wordplay is evident here in his use of *ke*, a character of established antiquity meaning "classification" or "order" in the *Shuowen*, which he intends primarily—but not exclusively—to convey its emerging contemporary significance as "scientific," as in *kexue* (science). Indeed it is not farfetched to regard these categorical distinctions as those of genus, species, and type. So, in this simple beginning, Zhang Binglin stated, implicitly, a commitment to *zhuzi xue*, while subtly manipulating concepts in a manner reminiscent of the Jesuits, as he borrowed the words of an ancient text to produce an unexpected contemporary significance.

Specifically, his analysis of a name (*ming*) according to the three categories, generic, class, and proper, was taken from chapter 41 of the *Mozi*, where it is stated:

> A name, as in "thing," is unlimited. If there is an object it necessarily requires this name. To designate something "horse" is to classify [it]. For what is "like an object" it is necessary to use this name. To designate someone [by the surname] "Zang" is proper; this name is limited to the object. The sounds which are emitted from the mouth all have names, as in surnames and style names.[114]

As for the "sounds emitted from the mouth," the text is referring to the common belief at this time that one of the "Five Sounds" (*wuyin*) was associated with every surname. This theory, among many others, is criticized by the Han skeptic Wang Chong, who in so doing elucidates the significance of the last line in the *Mozi* passage:

> The experts of the Five Sounds articulate the surnames, personal names, and style names with their mouths by using the surname to fix the personal name, and the personal name to determine the style name. *By opening and closing the mouth, they produce outward and inward tones, and thus fix the Five Sounds.*[115]

What we have here is a discussion, through descriptive example, of the appropriateness of language use, one very common in the rivalrous disputations of the era of the *baijia* (Hundred Families). While it is not uncommon, says Chad Hansen, for descriptive terms to be used in the *Mozi* "to support evaluative conclusions,"[116] such terms in Zhang's hands were marshaled for an even weightier objective that is revealed as the essay unfolds.

Ru: The Generic Name (*daming*) and the Genesis of *Ru*

With the *Mozi* passage providing a frame for his analysis, Zhang proceeds to articulate the most important part of his argument—a philologically grounded conjecture on what he calls, as Matteo Ricci did, the *guzhiru* (*ru* of antiquity). First he attempted to demonstrate the early semantic breadth of *ru* by way of a serial citation of various passages from early literature, all indexed to a part of the definition of *ru* offered in the *Shuowen jiezi:*

> The generic name is *ru* as in "the *ru* are scholars of received skills (*shushi*)." The Grand Historian's "Tales of the *Ru* Forest" says: "In the waning years of the Qin [they] interred the scholars of received skills"; and generation after generation has referred to this as "the burial of the *ru.*" Sima Xiangru said in enumerating the immortals of *ru:* "[They] live between mountains and marshes."[117]

Anyone familiar with Xu Shen's gloss would know that the citation here of the *Shuowen* definition was incomplete, as Zhang ignored the first sentence of that text which reads: *ru rou ye* (*ru* means weak). Ironically it is this first sentence that provoked Yuan-era scholars and has aroused the interest of interpreters since Zhang who have relied upon *rou* in the sense of "weak" as a key to the understanding of *ru*'s earliest meaning.[118]

Zhang ignored this definition but was obviously struck by the frequent occurrence in ancient literature of *shushi* alongside *ru*. He marshaled these co-occurrences in support of the broad (*da*) currency of the term. The often unspecified techniques (*shu*) in these texts were, for him, definitive of this group and thus the key to understanding the name they had acquired. By presenting diverse authorities—*Shuowen, Shiji, Zhuangzi, Mengzi, Yantie lun, Lunheng,* and the *Yijing*—in reverse chronology, Zhang illustrated the generic character of *ru*. At first, he did little, in restating relevant anecdotes from these miscellaneous texts, to flesh out the technē of these *ru* experts beyond simply implying that they were esteemed for their erudition and engaged in service to a lord.

Through a mechanism of textual collage that combined diverse passages having no more in common than a single instance of the graph *ru*, Zhang reproduced numerous contexts (regardless of sect or school) in which *ru* was used. As in this passage, the effect of such a method was to substantiate *ru's* general character while breaking down its conventional circumscription within what we call "Confucian," that is, within a single sectarian line of transmission authored by Kongzi:

> Crown Prince Kui of Zhao also said to Zhuangzi, "Sir, if you must wear *ru* attire to see the king [King Wen of Zhao], then your mission will be greatly opposed from the outset."[119] These, although the words of Daoists and sorcerers, are *ru*. In the *Yantie lun* (Discourses on Salt and Iron) it is said, "King Xuan of Qi praised *ru* and esteemed learning. The followers of Meng Ke [Mengzi] and Shunyu Kun received the emolument of high ranking ministers and though they did not obtain office, they discoursed on the affairs of state. Then below the Ji gate of the Qi capital these gentlemen numbered more than one thousand. King Min boasted of his accomplishments without cease, [while] the assembled *ru* [of his court] remonstrated [to no avail] and did not follow him, but each divided off and scattered. Shen Dao and Jie Zi vanished, Tian Pian left for Xie, and Sun Qing went to Qu."[120]

The passages making up this collage, in their certification of *ru* prominence, were, I am sure, familiar to Zhang Binglin's contemporaries. So it would seem that the essay hardly deserved Hu Shi's praise, as it simply reiterated the obvious. But these first six lines of "Yuan ru" are for Zhang, as Hu well understood, a prelude to an original formulation that must await the setting out of a broader textual history.

The demonstration of *ru's* polysemy in early texts concludes with an image of diaspora—the myriad *ru* in the service of the once majestic King Min scattered, each going his own way near the close of the Warring States (ca. 284 B.C.E.)—that symbolizes the geographic breadth of the term.[121] The diaspora also symbolically prefigures the splitting up of the *ru* tradition that Zhang considers the essential precondition of its modern manifestation as a proper name. All that remained after this diaspora, as Zhang presents it, were the various mythic story traditions claimed by *ru*, many of which were preserved and critically retold by Wang Chong in the *Lunheng*:

> Wang Chong [in] "Ru zeng" [The Exaggeration of *Ru*], "Daoxu" [The Vacuities of *Dao*], "Tantian" [Talking about the Ascendant], "Shuo ri" [Explaining the Sun], and "Shiying" [Verifying Omens],[122] commends those that are praised in *ru* writings. Like Lu Ban, who carved a kite out of a pear tree; Li Guang, who shot an arrow [so deep] into a stone that only the feathers could be seen; Qing Ke, who using a dagger to assassinate the King of Qin, [instead] drove it a foot into a pillar; Nü Wa [Snail

Maid], who melted stones; Gong Gong [Flood Laborer], who alone shook the pillar of heaven; the single-horned she-goat that rectifies the wicked; the mimosa that points at the guilty; the Yellow Emperor who rides the dragon; the dog of King Huainan that barks; the chicken above the sky that crows in the clouds; the three-footed bird in the sun; and the rabbit and the toad in the moon. These names are registered. Other than the classifications of *daomo, xingfa, yinyang,* and *shenxian,* there is what the *za* [Electics] recorded and what the biographies documented. One word compasses them all—*ru.* They were all an undifferentiated clan of the noble.[123]

Wang Chong was a skeptical dispeller of superstitions; he sorted out the fantastic from the reasonable through a "balanced" reexamination of the textual evidence (if any existed) upon which such conceptions were based.[124] Indeed such sorting out is particularly salient in those chapters from the *Lunheng* cited above by Zhang, who not coincidentally considered himself a dispeller like Wang, living in an age where augury and apocrypha passed for wisdom.

From the record of incoherence salvaged by Wang Chong and reproduced by Zhang, we know that *ru,* the bearers of ancient legend, were, like the other native rhetorical traditions, a clan of noble descent (*gongzu*). With his native skepticism, here Zhang was recalling stories about *ru* legend derived from all the traditions of the late Zhou era. He was suggesting that Wang, in attaching these fables to the *ru* tradition alone, had lent a sectarian air to his recollection. He was going beyond Wang Chong to suggest that *ru* was the ancient title of all gentlemen of received skills, *shushi,* a corps of specialized technicians. *Ru* did not mean what Wang presumed it meant; it was not one of several traditions, but the general term that named them all. All the myths Wang retold in these sections of the *Lunheng* were indefeasible mythic components of China's newly conceived national heritage, the heroic figures that were employed for symbolic advantage by all practice traditions—*ru, dao, fa, za, nong, ming,* and so on. *Ru* was simply their name before they were dispersed.

Still, at this juncture the essay displays no proof for this revision of Wang Chong, the importance of which derives from Zhang's assertion that the many rhetorical families of the Warring States (the large number of which were figuratively enumerated as "the Hundred families") were *ab origine* one figurative family, *ru.* If the *shushi* who were called *ru* were in fact one great noble clan, the implication is that the *jiuliu* (Nine Streams) flowed forth from the royal houses of the Zhou or the Shang. Following this suggestion, Zhang's text pursues an astute historical reconstruction of *ru* built from philological and phonological tools tempered by his boundless imagination.

No texts were offered in support of *ru*'s generic identity, probably because
there really were none, save the *Shiji* where Sima Qian used terms like *rushu*
and Huang-Lao *zhishu*, although not interchangeably. I presume it is for a
lack of adequate literary proof that the mechanism of the essay shifts at this
point, almost imperceptibly, away from textual collage to historical phonology and a modified graphemic analysis of the character itself. Zhang attempts here to push his analysis back beyond what the texts will warrant and
has no recourse other than to analyze the scribal form of the character, belief
in the sovereignty of which he held religiously. His objective is not merely to
establish the earliest meaning of *ru*, but to make convincing the argument I
have just adumbrated for the lack of differentiation in its meaning. His analysis is further linked to a hermeneutic of *ru* creatively derived from the fifth
hexagram of the *Yijing*, *xu*, meaning "waiting."

"Yuan ru" 's next eight lines flesh out the implications of the noble descent
and the common identity of *ru*. Zhang borrows the language and syntax of
the Han bibliographer Liu Xin to describe the official genealogy of *ru* in the
"Yiwen zhi,"[125] taking up philology (*xiaoxue*) to manufacture an engaging
account of the inherited techné represented by the common name, *ru*:

> The name *ru* came from *xu*. *Xu* signifies clouds above the sky, and so it
> is that *ru*, already knowing the pattern of the sky [*tianwen*], can forsee
> drought and flood.[126] How can we understand this? Birds that know of
> the sky's impending rain are called *yu* [turquoise kingfisher, or snipe].
> Those who performed [the rain dance] in drought and were immolated
> wore a cap and costume made of the feathers of the turquoise king-
> fisher. Turquoise kingfisher caps were also called caps of the *shushi* clan
> [*shushi guan*] and round caps [*yuanguan*]. Zhuang Zhou said that *ru*
> were "the ones who wore round caps and foreknew the timeliness of the
> sky, who wore crooked sandals and knew topography, and who suspend a
> half-disc of jade from their girdles, so that at the appropriate time they
> can act decisively."[127] Those who perform the vernal sacrifices to Jupiter
> and Venus and who, in seeking rain, chant *xujie* are called *ru*. Therefore,
> they formerly set aside the possessed and specialized in the sacrificial
> dance to the rain gods; they originally conferred order on the reckless
> and wore the *hua* cap. They were all treated as shamans because they
> incensed the world. Recoiling in fear, they set their minds on the path of
> the spirits. Ancient *ru* [*guzhiru*] knew the pattern of the sky and [on
> the basis of this] divined. [And this is why] it is said they had many
> talents.[128]

There is a great deal to unpack here, all suggestive of practices whose history is quite old and of which we have come to know much through scholarly work on the oracle bone inscriptions of the Shang and the bronze inscriptions of the Zhou. Considering that Zhang rejected extant ancient epigraphy as spurious, I presume that he obtained this information from the *Shi jing, Shiji, Zhuangzi, Shuowen,* and *Han shu.* The mechanism of this part of the essay is basically philological but there is much conjecture. In a matter of four lines of his text, Zhang situated *ru* in the geographical, mythical, and religious core of Huaxia civilization and enabled the reader to date, however vaguely, the era of the common name's currency—Shang/Zhou.

The entire reconstruction rests on two implicit philological assumptions, at least one of which is quite sound. First, as there were no semantic classifiers or "radicals" in the Shang and the early Zhou, the increasing complexity of the language was accomplished through a process of phonetic borrowing (*jiajie*). In fact, it was not until very late in the Warring States, indeed some two centuries or so after Kongzi, that these classifiers were used to distinguish similar-sounding but different-meaning terms (homophones) such as *ru* and *xu.* During the post-Zhou most new terms were composed by means of paronomasia, an equivalent of the rebus method, in which an established and homophonous graph was used to represent another word of similar sound. As written Chinese was linguistically elaborated in this manner, paronomasia became an archaistic rhetorical convention (just as it did in medieval and early modern European etymological practice) and was the principal method of etymology in imperial China. With the application of this convention, Zhang argues that *ru* originally was pronounced as *xu* (see glossary), which is considered the etymonic nucleus of the modern character *ru.* His second presumption is a bit more problematic and the reasoning generated from it tendentious, as it runs counter to the inherited tradition of *Yijing* interpretation. Zhang reasons that *yu* (rain), comprising the upper portion of the graph for *xu,* is determinative of its meaning—a claim made on the basis of a most unusual reading of the hexagram *xu* (see glossary).

The equation of *xu* (the hexagram) with *xu* (the graph) works to corroborate his description of the skills of the *ru* of antiquity; nevertheless, it is quite unusual because he intends his reader to accept that the composite construction of the hexagram explains the *huiyi* (joined meanings) construction of the character.[129] A presumption such as this not only contravenes previous *Yijing* interpretation, but is refuted by the surface dissimilarity in the compositions of the hexagram and the graph.[130] *Xu,* the character Zhang considers the etymonic nucleus of *ru,* is literally composed of *yu* (rain) over *er* (and), and not *yu* over *tian,* as Xu Shen himself noted in glossing *xu: "Xu* means *xu* [to tarry], as when one encounters rain and, unable to proceed, stops. It is a phonetic compound composed of *yu* [rain] and *er* [and]. According to the *Yijing*, the trigram for *yun* [clouds] over the trigram denoting *tian* [sky] yields *xu*."[131] So while citing the *Shuowen* as an authority, Zhang puts forward a definition disallowed by that same authority—a curious fact, considering that he evidently believed Xu Shen's etymology to be the most genuine record of the ancient language. The fortunate interpretive consequence of this unconventional reading of *xu* was the definition of *ru* as a clan of sorcerers with a specialized knowledge of astronomy. Thus, by exploiting phonetic similarities between three characters and redefining the composition of the etymonic nucleus of *ru*, Zhang constructed a context within which the Han definition of *ru* as *shushi* became meaningful. He cleverly asserts that the skills that the *ru* inherited were those of the mantic arts—prophecy, divination, homeopathy—and that this is what both Xu Shen and Sima Qian must have meant by *shushi.*

By linking *xu* with *ru*, Zhang (perhaps unwittingly) invoked a host of further philological associations of *ru* and a cognate *ru* (pronounced with a rising tone and bearing the semantic classifier for water) meaning "to wet," "to soak," or "to moisten." These semantic links appear to be quite old; nevertheless it is not possible to determine if the linguistic protocol in Kongzi's day permitted such associations. But of course that is not as important as the presumption, one Zhang shared with all *kaozheng* scholars, that neither phonological nor philological links were entirely fortuitous. Zhang assumed that *ru* and this cognate were indissolubly linked. Thus the *ru* of Kongzi's fellowship, which is graphically different from *ru* meaning "to soak," might be treated as a scribal error and therefore an instance of metaphor as mistake.

In other words (the interpretation goes), the original *ru* of the passage was written with the water radical, but over the period during which the text was assembled, this *ru* was transcribed—erroneously or intentionally—as the *ru* of Kongzi's fellowship (see glossary). Reasoning such as this might then permit Zhang's philological point that *yu* (rain) determines the ancient resonance of the character.[132] Considering the evolution of the Chinese language between 1200 and 500 B.C.E. (an approximate interval stretching from the oracle bone inscriptions to the first independent texts of the Warring States era) "scribal error" of this kind, though hypothetical, was not entirely unlikely, as we can now see.[133] But Zhang did not consider this, I believe because the character *ru* had been the mystical scribal conveyance of the ancient sound *xu*. I have made the effort here to follow through the wider reaches of a philological inquiry, encouraged by the earliest glosses, to illustrate that Zhang could have gone further with texts that he undoubtedly knew to certify the validity of the links he made between cognates and homonyms.

The idea that *ru* may have been at one time the rainmakers for the tribes of the Zhongyuan territory (where rain tended to fall only in summer and always in torrents) is a most interesting notion, particularly because glosses of *ru* from early imperial times suggest that in making this claim Zhang was onto something. Indeed a long line of filiation joins Zhang's meditations on the wet qualities of *ru*'s ancient significance and the paronomastic definitions of previous exegetes; his speculations in this regard were not without foundation and deserve further comment.

The *Hanshi waizhuan,* the *Guang ya,* and Huang Kan's *Lunyu jijie yisu* identically assert that "the *ru* are wet" (*ruzhe ru ye*) and thus, by implication they confirm Zhang's curious philology.[134] Though the essay does not indicate Zhang's awareness of this cognate link, it is reasonable to suspect that he learned of these earlier glosses from his study of the *Shuowen jiezi zhu* of Duan Yucai. Here under the etymological citations listed for *ru* in this recension there is one from Zheng Xuan's *Li ji zhengzhu,* which says "*ru* means wet." In his elaboration on the gloss Zheng attempted to reconcile the connotation of wetness with the established definition of *ru* as "scholar" by putting forth the claim, at first inscrutable, that *ru,* "through the way of the Former Kings, were able to wet their bodies."[135]

Zhang Binglin's insistence that *yu* (rain) determined the meaning of *ru,* then, is not entirely capricious, since so many of the early commentaries define it as "wet." These comments further corroborate the consistency of the association of *ru* and wetness in early texts. And the *ru* were wet because they were responsible for entreating the heavens for rain, the homeopathy of this ancient enterprise embedded in the phonological and philological recesses of the character. So this is what Zhang presumes. These silent presumptions do much to reinforce the cognate affiliations upon which he depends so heavily. Yet these archaic philological links that I present here as implicit in Zhang's construction seem more like echoes cast out by voices long silent—vague, muffled, mysterious, and quite difficult to integrate into a coherent narrative of the term's travels.

The links that join *ru, xu, wu* (rain dance), and *yu* are even less visible than those of Kongzi's *ru* and the "to soak" *ru;* however, Zhang implies a connection, perhaps assuming that *wu* (an unbalanced right-footed shuffle) was akin to the "yielding" (*rou*) attitude that defines *ru.*[136] Of course, the Sage-King Shun's legendary appointment of Yu, the alleged founder of the Xia dynasty (legend, 1953–1576 B.C.E.), to regulate the flood waters of the Zhongyuan did establish a mythological and symbolic link between Yu and water. But for Zhang, the union of Yu and *ru* is forged as much out of their dress as their dance, as one gleans from his insistence that the *ru* wore caps, and possibly even an entire garment, made of the feathers of the turquoise kingfisher (the *yu*) when performing the ritual dance for rain, *wu.*

In his interlinear commentary Zhang further suggests that the feathers of this unusual bird, the *yu*, were the stuff from which the caps (known as *yuguan*) of the ancient capping ceremony were made.[137] Given what Zhang states is the popular conception, that the *yu* knew heaven's future rain impulses—a belief recorded in the *Shuowen* but, according to Zhang, first mentioned in the *Zhuangzi*—the feathers of the turquoise kingfisher represent a form of homeopathy capable of inducing precipitation.[138] Chapter 12 of *Zhuangzi* ("The World") does supply oblique confirmation of Zhang's speculation as *yu* appears here in the compound *yuguan* in a context insinuating that it refers to *ru*. There is no suggestion of their powers of meteorological forecasting,[139] and in fact most of this discussion of rain dances, feathered caps, and homeopathy could have been found in chapter 74 of Dong Zhongshu's *Chunqiu fanlu*, in an essay titled "Qiu yu" (Seeking Rain).[140] However, Zhang did not consult the *Chunqiu fanlu*, and though it is difficult to deny the genuinely "old" flavor of the reconstruction, the indexing of *wu* (the term for the shaman) to *ru* (meaning "wet") was, like the primordial impulses undergirding all nationalisms, archaistic.

There were good, even if apocryphal, reasons to presume that *ru* was a term referring to men of Shang (otherwise known as Yin)[141] descent (like Kongzi) who lived among the Zhou, though such reasons pulled no weight with Zhang. The Chinese have always considered Kongzi to be a descendant of the Shang, a belief resting on several passages from the *Li ji* (The Book of Rites) and on the mythology of sagehood symbolized by the *qilin* (unicorn) near the end of Kongzi's life, when its appearance signified the master's imminent demise and prophesied the coming of Liu Bang, the founder of the Han. If the "Tan gong" chapter of the *Li ji* is to be believed, then Kongzi was, by his own admission, descended from the Yin: "The Yin people placed the coffin in the space between two pillars, so that the steps for the host and those for the guest were on opposite sides. . . . I myself (Qiu) am a man of the Yin and last night I dreamt I sat with the ancestral offerings at my side between two pillars."[142] In a later chapter, "Ruxing" (Ru Deportment), Kongzi again refers to his Yin lineage when he recalls wearing the ceremonial Yin headdress, the *zhangfu*, when he lived in Song.[143] Much of this apocrypha was resurrected in the late-nineteenth-century *jinwen* (New Text) revival and was current at the time Zhang wrote his interpretation of *ru*.[144]

By the nineteenth century there was a wealth of inherited knowledge of Kongzi's life—his parentage and lineal descent, details of his unsuccessful political career—collected in the cultural memory of Chinese. What the popularity of New Text interpretation produced was an enhanced recognition of the mystical, prophetic aspects of this memory, but without invoking the received traditions of his connections to the Shang. Zhang's *jinwen* rival, Kang Youwei, was not particularly interested in the question of Kongzi's descent, seeming to regard him as the sui generis mythical locus of Chinese culture itself. If *jinwen* adherents were at all concerned with origins, they believed they could stop at Kongzi.

The popular presumption of Kongzi's Shang descent may have informed the intellectual climate of Zhang's philological reconstruction; however, the mythology within which this belief in his royal lineage was buried portrayed Kongzi as a noble descendant of the ducal house of Song—and not the legatee of a ritual corps of shamans. In *jinwen* mythology, Kongzi was a nobleman, and certainly not a hereditary attendant of the ruling class; but this presumption of pedigree was simply unfounded. Zhang's reconstruction of ancient *ru* identity may not have favored this inherited myth, yet it was grounded in the scribal form, evidence he considered more palpable than a pair of disputed passages from the *Li ji*.[145] Zhang Binglin, however, did not go further and take *ru* as the name of Kongzi's fellowship. He described the ancient practices known as *xu*, then *ru*, a name that became inextricably bound to Kongzi (since he was the patriarch of both the *guwen* and *jinwen* traditions) only in the Han, and what he assumed and exploited in order to construct a primordial functional meaning for *ru* was the phonetic similarity in the graphs *ru*, *shu* (of *shushi*), *xu*, and *yu* (rain).

This kind of philological analysis, moreover, had the value of establishing evidentiary support for an ancient meaning of *ru* that was independent of the texts of the rhetorical traditions of the Warring States, which, with respect to this term, display a confounding vagueness. He also demonstrates his sense that there was a clan of technical specialists, *shushi*, who were the *guzhiru*, the *ru* of antiquity and thus the predecessors of Kongzi. This, then, is the ancient technē of *ru* and, unlike in Zhang's earlier discussion of the term, this particular meaning is embedded in the scribal form of the character *ru*. And, as if by insisting on the graphic artifact itself, Zhang delivered himself from the charges of invention he was so willing to level at Kang Youwei.

The exegesis of *ru* as a common term is both technical and sophisticated. Yet for all of his empiricist devotion "to ferret out truth from facts" (*shishi qiushi*)—that *kaozheng* (evidential research) slogan cited with evident approval in "Yuan ru"—Zhang remystified the culture out of which the fellowship emerged, but in a manner very different from, and even inimical to, the mystical portrait offered by *jinwen* advocates of a national religion. Herein Zhang Binglin's developmental history took shape as he went on to examine texts of a later date, in which the *leiming* or class name of *ru* could be found.

Ru: The Class Name (*Leiming*)

The interpretation in this section follows less abstruse and more predictable lines, as Zhang turns to *ru*'s second semantic category, the *leiming*.

Like the generic name, the *leiming* is defined functionally, and is taken as a term referring to mastery of the Six Cultivations (*liuyi*)— rites, music, archery, charioteering (horsemanship), calligraphy, and numbers. *Liuyi* is not found in the formative texts of the *ru*, there being only one mention of it in the *Zhou li*. The Six Cultivations as a standard of expertise or accomplishment are in evidence later in the Former Han, although here it is reflexively used to describe *ru*. The conventional rendering of *liuyi* is "the Six Disciplines"; however, I translate it as "Six Cultivations" in deference to Xu Shen's gloss of *yi* as "to plant" or "to cultivate." The basis of Xu's gloss is probably the "Jiu gao" of the *Shang shu* where *yi* obviously describes the planting of millet, the sacred grain of the Ji clan, the Zhou dynasty founders. *Yi*, then, is an agricultural term. It suggests a bucolic past for *ru* who, by most accounts, were members of the *shi* class, a class that lived on the produce yielded from parcels given them in recognition of service to a lord. I believe there may have been a conscious play on words here in which an aptitude for working the land was used as a metaphor for cultivating the self. "Six Cultivations" permits us to imagine this resonance and recognize the social ground traversed by *ru* from the Warring States to the Han. There are suggestions, too, in the term of the numerology of which the Former Han imagination was captive, or at least of the *jinwen* concern with symmetry—the *liuyi*, Six Cultivations as the companion of the *Liujing*, the Six Classics.[146]

Zhang suggests that specialists in the *liuyi* were the Zhou descendants of the priestly *shushi* of the Shang. They were people of many talents, as were the *guzhiru*; however, these different skills were the practices of a different era. Here Zhang turns away from the speculations of the first definition and returns to reiterating a few passages from the *Zhou li* and its commentaries where *ru* may be found. He implies that the specialized mantic techniques of the *guzhiru* have given way to a broader, secular expertise of protecting noble clans and educating the rural populace:

> The class name is *ru*. *Ru* are accomplished in rites, music, archery, horsemanship, calligraphy, and numbers. In the ascendant offices [of the *Zhou li*] it is said: "*Ru* by means of the path affect the people." The commentary [by Zheng Xuan] states: "The assembled *ru* are those who protect the clans, and with the fruit of the Six Cultivations they are able to teach the people." In the earthly offices [of the *situ* (leader of the foot soldiers) in *Zhou li*] it is said: "[He] unites the commanders and the *ru*." The commentary reads: "*Shi* and *ru* are the ones who live in the countryside and give instruction in *dao* and *yi*." . . . As it is said in the *Lüshi* [*Chunqiu*]: "They are all men of the Six Cultivations."[147]

Indeed *ru* was, according to the *Zhou li*, a classification of a specific social order of experts under the auspices of the second-rank *diguan situ* (earth office of leader of the footsoldiers). Thus Zhang draws a line of technical descent from the *guzhiru* of the Western Zhou to all men accomplished in the Six Cultivations of the late Warring States, stressing that despite these historically and functionally distinct meanings, it is still the same word: "It is quite sufficient to consider that the two characters we have illustrated as *ru* are thus its foundation."[148] In fact the *da* (generic) and *lei* (class) uses of *ru* act like two posts (Zhang's image) upon which stands the ancient meaning of *ru*, that of the practitioners of a received tradition.

Of course the texts upon which Zhang relied in this instance to define the class name of *ru* were Han era conceits and somewhat romanticized ones at that. Although he cites two relevant passages from the *Zhou li* to establish an early post-Zhou understanding of the term, the passages really do nothing to explain the expertise of *ru* and only vaguely suggest that it may have had a broader meaning. Consequently, Zhang used the commentaries of Zheng Xuan (127–200 C.E.) and Zheng Sinong (5 B.C.E.–8 C.E.) to point out that at this time *ru* meant those accomplished in the Six Cultivations. The Six Cultivations, he presumed, were the later manifestation of the ancient *ru* technē, a presumption confirmed by a reference to the *Lüshi chunqiu*. His analysis of the class name simply reaffirms the traditional identification of *ru* with the Six Cultivations, but implies that *liuyi* was not an exclusive *ru* designation. Instead, *liuyi*, like *shushi*, could have referred to any of the other rhetorical families, practice traditions, and skills of the Zhou—*dao, mo, mingfa, yinyang, xiaoshuo*, and *xingfa*—which have come to be differentiated according to these class names. To be sure, it did not refer exclusively to Kongzi, and this can be gleaned merely from the sparse mention of his name in Zhang's text. Zhang identified the change in *ru* as an evolution in techniques from *shushi* to *liuyi* and stressed, the analysis following the gradations of the *Zhou li* offices, that *ru*, who were practitioners of *liuyi*, were functionally distinct from *shi*, instructors. With this contention Zhang sharpened the gaze of his criticism at the most recent embodiment of *ru*, the *siming*, or proper name.

From Classics to Polemics: The Proper Name (*Siming*), *Ru*

Through two-thirds of Zhang's discussion of *ru*'s various names and even through a reconstruction of the ancient social and religious functions represented by it, he makes no mention of Kongzi. Zhang, it would seem, did not accept the popular view that identified Kongzi with *ru*. Indeed he never refers to the celebrated passage from book 6 of the *Lunyu* where Kongzi is said to have told his disciple Zixia, "Be a lordling *ru*, and not a plebeian *ru*."[149] This is strange, considering that the exchange may provide the earliest evidence of the term. It is this association, nevertheless, that Zhang chooses not to accentuate. He seeks instead to disaggregate these two entities so as to transcend the contemporary sectarian consciousness that has been read back onto earlier texts. By placing the word *ru* above the man, Zhang intends to counter the contemporary apotheosis of Kongzi, a myth, with the science of *ru*'s semantic progress. But this does not mean that in this typology of *ru* meanings there is no role for Kongzi. He stands, by Zhang's account, for the proper name *ru*, most importantly and paradoxically, a symbol of the break between its ancient and modern meanings.

Just as Liu Shipei had argued that the post-Zhou (or "Eastern Zhou") represented a turning point in the meaning of *ru* and justified his claim with the identical *Zhou li* passages, Zhang contends that the foundational meaning of *ru*, a tradition of specialized technical practices, was not transmitted past the the post-Zhou. The discontinuity was fundamental, more a rupture than an incomplete transmission. The profoundness of the gap between the *ru* of ancient practices and the *ru* of the imperial imagination is explicit in Zhang's treatment of the proper name, *ru*, and it is by implication unfortunate.

As Zhang takes up this final band of meaning it seems that, while appropriating selected Han provenance texts, he assimilated the vanished arcadian trope of the Han imagination as well. Sima Qian and Liu Xin had both prefaced their biographies of the *rulin* (forest of *ru*) with a stylized lamentation of the disorder that ensued with the fall of the Zhou and put a challenge to *ru* to recover the former dynasty's identity of names and things and its unity of *zhi* (rule) and *dao* (way). In the spirit of this prescribed lament, Zhang pronounces the difference between past and present, but asserts that such difference is fundamental, reading it as unrecoverable loss.

It is in Kongzi's voice of immemoriality that the continuousness of *ru* is ironically revealed as conceit. When his name suddenly appears halfway through "Yuan ru" it is in the guise of lamentation, complaining that history has failed to transmit custom: "Therefore, Kongzi said: 'I reach back to a time when scribes left blanks and when one who had a horse would lend it for another man to ride. Today, such times are no more, [they are] lost.' "[150] The excerpt stands in counterpoint to the citation of Liu Xin's description of *ru* from the *Han shu* that Zhang offers as the gloss of the proper name and which states that the transmission has come down inerrantly from the heroes of the culture:

> In the *Seven Outlines* (*Qilue*) it is said: "Those of the *ru* family were descended from the office of the *situ*. They are those who assist the ruled and the ruler in accord with the yin and yang by elucidating the teachings and transformations. [They] roam in the midst of the writings and the Six Classics. They focus on meaning at the conjunction of benevolence and righteousness. Their great ancestral transmission is from

Yao and Shun; their charter from [kings] Wen and Wu; their ancestral teacher, Zhongni, whose words they value. They hold *dao* in highest esteem."[151]

What Zhang wants his audience to know by way of this juxtaposition is that the semantic changes reflect real historical changes, in fact, irreversible ones. At the time of Liu Xin's account and in late Qing China, *ru* were *shi*, scholars and instructors, and in this capacity they were political operatives and experts on certain classical texts, not the skilled craftsmen of the Six Cultivations. Furthermore, Zhang decidedly points out, in the time between the Zhou and Han there were many traditions of instruction, all of them bearing the mantle *ru* so that to speak of *ruxing* (*ru* deportment), for example, described fifteen different kinds of *ru*.[152] As a proper noun *ru* is polymorphous, its referents ambiguous—in Han Feizi's time it designated eight distinct practice traditions and in early imperial accounts, as Zhang recalls, the title of fifty-two schools.[153]

The notion that there was an ancient heritage, presumed transmitted to Kongzi who, in turn, passed it on to the *ru* of the Han era, could not be sustained. Kongzi grieves that former times are no more, that the transmission missed him. With Kongzi, then, we have nothing more than the dregs of the past, the *guji*, shards from which we might at best imaginatively construct descent from the culture heroes Yao, Shun, Wen, and Wu.[154] Viewed in this different light, we understand Liu Xin's official genealogy of *ru* as simply a report and not a claim. He merely stated the current *ru* self-conception where descent from Yao and Shun and the presumption of Kongzi as ancestral teacher were definitive, but at the same time, fictive.[155] This seems to be the way that Zhang intends for us to understand it; he says as much when he judges that nothing of the ancient technē of *ru* survived the end of the Zhou:

> [When] the Zhou declined, the guardian clan failed in its defenses. The writing of the large seal by scribes, the peerless calculation of the Shang, the archery of the wasp followers, the charioteering of the cap clan—all of these were not handed down from *ru*. . . . Names were truncated and disordered. The skill of holding the reins to train the chariot was also washed away. . . . The *Seven Outlines* set it straight: the [proper] name was not derived from *ru*.[156]

Therefore to define oneself genealogically by positing descent from the ancients was to make a false claim. With the Han, *ru* became the normative tradition, its coherence secured by the narrative of Sima Qian and the catalogue of Liu Xin. As this tradition achieved official status, so did the *ru* self-image as the progeny of sage-kings and their readings of the texts that testified to their sagely pedigree. I believe Zhang is suggesting that as *ru* became officialized in the Han they justified their status [which was purely fortuitous] through false declarations of a broader, ancient significance because men of this title were in fact only instructors, officials, or *boshi* (learned scholars) in a certain text. In subsequent ages the contradictory Han legacy endured as the standard, and thus confusion and misrepresentation became doctrine.[157]

From this point on, the present-mindedness of Zhang becomes increasingly apparent as he argues that *ru* is, and has been, a term of limited scope and certainly not the all-embracing metaphor it was when it referred to *shushi*. Beginning with the Han (although the conditions for this development are to be found in Kongzi's day), *ru* is endlessly contradictory, even false, clearly not fit to serve as a broad symbol of Chinese culture. Also its present definition can in no way be followed back to its phonological source, as this path of recovery was washed away in the Han. Zhang is emphasizing the essential Han-constructedness, as it were, of the official *ru* image and reminds his reader in this regard that it is with the Grand Historian, Sima Qian, that the association of *rulin* with men of Qi and Lu begins.[158]

Not only is there no continuity in the meaning of *ru*, but the equation of teacher or scholar, *shi*, as *ru* was a category mistake. Modern-day *shi*, teachers or specialists in certain classics of the canon but certainly not all of the Five Classics, possessed skills that did not extend to the Six Cultivations. There is only individual specialization, as in someone being considered *boshi* in a work like the *Chunqiu*, a practice which we know began in the Qin. One might claim identity on the basis of a nominal continuity, Zhang suggests, but *ru* does not name the same thing. The distinction between the first two bands and the third band of meaning, furthermore, is not simply that of differing crafts; in fact, he seems willing to concede that there is an insurmountable epistemological barrier that runs the length of the interface of pre-Han and post-Han antiquity, dividing truth and falsehood.

Since the Han era, *ru* has also referred to the art of redaction, yet this is not a techne. This is not to say that there is no talent in working the canon, only that such labor is more the product of rote mastery than a skill hard-won through repetitive practice. Although he does not admit it, the epistemological wall between the ancient and modern understandings of *ru* is the same one conveyed by Zhuang Zhou in the parable of Wheelwright Bian, which showed that knowledge can be gained, not from studying the words of dead sages, but from working the material of one's craft, feeling it in the hand and responding in the heart.[159] Bian's is the learning of the *guzhiru*; outside of this everything else is, as Zhang Binglin and Zhuangzi would have it, an endless rite of pious necromancy. However, the silence of the dead proved uniquely productive of claims of continuous transmission, made authoritative through the invocation of *ru*, whose three semantic categories were hopelessly confused.

There were, indeed, people who were canon redactors and teachers who acquired the title *ru*; but "this category [of person]," as Zhang tells it, "in the offices of the Zhou are called *shi*,"[160] implying they did not come by their *ru* name legitimately. He then states the conclusion he has been inching toward, charging not only his contemporaries but Han scholars as well with a willful misappropriation of *ru* made possible by the semantic fragmentation of the term: "*Ru* were shattered and under these circumstances, *shi* falsely took up their name."[161]

Thus we are reminded again that this mostly philological reconstruction of Zhang's was not directed at restoration of the genuine *ru* fellowship or the founding of a new community of faith around Kongzi as exemplar. The critical stylistic components of the primitivist claim—originality, authenticity, exclusivity—were evident, yet he believed recovery impossible, absurd. Zhang's hope in such a philological undertaking was, as Michael Gasster has said, "to have ancient practices understood and appreciated but not imitated."[162] Instead, building a semantic context within which the term *ru*, and not the sage Kongzi, operated as a historical individual, Zhang sidestepped altogether the emotional issue of Kongzi and the contemporary reworking of his image as a religious symbol. He was most concerned with current practice and wondered what the utter confusion of a term so critical to the history of Chinese civilization said about the contemporary condition of China's national heritage. Kongzi was significant in these musings, as it was with him that the fundamental incongruity of past and present practice was first asserted. Kongzi, therefore, announces the modern, secular conception of *ru*, which was concomitant with the disarticulation of the earlier understandings of the term, an irreversible consequence beyond the ken of the *jinwen* scholars of Zhang's day—the real target of his final benediction.

As for men like the Han *jinwen* redactor and official, Dong Zhongshu, who have been looked to as representatives of a "glorious exaltation" of *ru* tradition new and old, Zhang judged that in Dong's hands the three categories of *ru* were made "reciprocally chaotic."[163] It is Dong's false conflation of these three categories that lies behind our present inability to understand the proper distinctions between the different meanings of *ru*. Consequently, it is now the practice to use the "common name" for the "proper name" and the "class name" for the "proper name." Against this historically transmitted failure of *jinwen*, Zhang says, "lately the ancient text school has emerged, and in seeking truth from facts has found proof in writings, [and] not proof in currying favor."[164] The "proof" here is textual evidence of *jinwen* error of the kind Kang Youwei had laid at the feet of Liu Xin. The issue, then, is not really Dong Zhongshu's misuse of the language but the state of Zhang's own culture, insofar as this may be inferred from the current use of a single graph. What he saw was that although "the name *ru* from antiquity has been conveyed as *shushi*, it is today only the preserve of teaching clans, just as the name *dao* from antiquity was conveyed as virtuous action and *dao* skills, now only refers to the followers of Laozi."[165]

This was, however, the complaint of an outsider, the words of someone enraged, as was Liu Shipei, at the undue influence exercised on national policy by those "wordsmiths from the Jiangnan [Southern Yangzi delta]," the *jinwen* reformers. The political influence of *jinwen* scholars would only increase—in fact, even Liu would in 1916 offer his services to the Hongxian emperor (Yuan Shikai, 1859–1916) in the promulgation of the state religion (*guojiao*). Even after the downfall of their Manchu benefactors and the formation of a republic, advocates of *jinwen* religion still laid claim to real political power in the traditional sense of ideological technicians of the imperial state.

Thus, Zhang and his *guocui* (national essence) comrades rightly "saw themselves," says Kent Guy, "as intellectuals out of power, entrusted by accidents of history with the task of preserving their heritage."[166] Such preservation, for them, was decidedly not an abstract intellectual exercise of redacting texts that *jinwen* scholars had converted into a religion (*jiao*), but was an act of learning (*xue*). And by "learning" Zhang meant that it was the work of specially trained individuals, just like the ancient *shushi* in whose construction he represented men of his own nativist kind, who were not opposed, as had been Kongzi, to lowly matters (*bishi*).

Zhang Binglin placed heavy emphasis on Kongzi's remarks at *Lunyu* 8.4 and 9.6 that the *junzi* (lordling) should stay clear of lowness and that he must not have a great variety of abilities, like someone of low status who, by dint of economic necessity, must choose survival over a discriminating application of his skills. With Kongzi's accentuation of the avoidance of *bishi* (lowly matters), which Zhang identifies with the exorcism and sorcery of the *shushi* as a defining aspect of the *junzi*, sectarianism grew. Now men of many talents (or at least six) abandoned the practice of a variety of skills for specialization. The record of this sectarian consequence is obvious, Zhang points out, in the fifty-two *ru* fellowships identified in the *Qilue*.[167]

It is at this juncture of Zhang's text and of his recounting of the history of *ru* that his reconstruction reveals a polemical claim for the moral necessity that intellectuals unite with the unrepresented, laboring populace of China. Indeed, Zhang's populist political leanings were explicit as in this characteristically acerbic dismissal of the Tongzhi era reform advocacy of Feng Guifen:

> Feng Gueifen was on intimate terms with the great houses of Suzhou. With some, he was even related by marriage. But the agonized cries of

the toiling masses never reached his ears. . . . For his troubles on their behalf, Feng was rewarded by the worthies of Suzhou with a personal shrine, in tribute to his reputation as a scholar. Would it not have been more just if, in his stead, they had deified an ordinary farmer from the fields?[168]

As Zhang sees it, there was, beginning with Kongzi, a turn away from truth (of the sort exemplified by Feng) in which the lowly matters of service to the people definitive of the *shushi* were abandoned for the obsequiousness of the life of the scholar-official.

Ultimately, I believe, Zhang Binglin's intention was to reconstruct the Chinese intellectual heritage as one of service, of practice, and of engagement in skills that sustain communities and their leadership. The immediate embodiment of this notion was the group of similar-thinking activist scholars who made up the *guocui* coterie, but the objective was to make a larger national community on the model of the specific features of this group. Occupying the moral/intellectual high ground in this way, Zhang was the quintessential political outsider, far more like Kongzi than he ever could have imagined. So Zhang was implicitly calling for a contemporary *zhengming*, a rectification of names, of which the chief consequence would be the disestablishment of the mystical claims of continuity made by *jinwen* followers on the basis of their understanding of a canon of Kongzi's creation and the reestablishment on a pure racial ground of the natural links between *guwen* texts, their advocates, and the state.

The "facts" of Zhang Binglin's reconstruction, then, were rather adversarial in their opposition to the *jinwen* self-conception. Kongzi could not be the founder of a religion, for according to Zhang's presentation, the religious significance of *ru* was bound to the shamans (*wu*) of the Shang royal family and by Kongzi's time had passed. Zhang even went as far as to declare that "there was not one Father Kong," the patriarch of the many practice traditions grouped under the *ru* umbrella. Also to the dismay of the *jinwen* contingent was Zhang's revelation that the evolution of *ru* did not favor a *sanshi* "third age" utopia, but rather a linguistic dystopia reflecting the disrepair of Chinese culture. The narrative he offered, far from telling a followable story of development from antiquity to the present, was a tale of chaos, of incoherence, and of fraudulence and misrepresentation very much at odds with commonsense understanding.

From a contemporary Chinese perspective where the "sense" of things was increasingly made by the conceptual technology of evolution, Zhang's "Yuan ru" was more like an antinarrative. He did consistently affirm that as a term *ru* was indefeasibly Chinese, having emerged at the dawn of Huaxia (urculture) civilization with the Shang, to be understood not through teaching and redaction, but through work. Only writing and mathematics remain from the Six Cultivations by which *ru* had been defined, and these have been rejected. In the end "Yuan ru" was an empirically grounded disavowal of the legitimacy claims of both the Manchus and *jinwen* ideologues, who depended greatly on the presumption that Kongzi and his message had been vouchsafed them in the classics.

"Yuan Ru" Retrospect: Pleading Antiquity for the Present

There was much that was innovative and inventive in this reconstruction of *ru*, beginning with the basic structure of the essay by which Zhang plotted his interpretation of *ru*, built from logical coordinates taken from the *Mozi*. But as I have shown, Zhang appropriated this post-Zhou nominalism as the frame for a historicist conception of *ru*. He articulated, in fact fabricated, the different meanings subsumed within this one term so that the generic (*da*), the class (*lei*), and the proper (*si*) names might be understood as standing in stratigraphic relation in time. Textual citations betrayed the stratigraphy or chronology that subtly organized an interconnected set of assumptions. In this manner, he reworked a passage from a text lying outside official culture, and certainly not favored by the new "orthodox" discourses of the *jinwen* and Tongcheng schools.

More than just clarifying the multiple functions of naming and distinguishing semantically between *ming* (command) and *ming* (name), which is the obvious objective of the *Mozi* passage cited above, Zhang used this discussion as a mechanism that he applied in a manner wholly different from that of the original text. Whereas the *Mozi* passage provides a simple nominalist explanation of the differential functions of naming, Zhang's reading takes the distinctions *da*, *lei*, and *si* as discrete developmental moments in the meaning of a single proper name. Consistent with this implicit evolutionary logic is Zhang's insistence that the modern use of *ru* as a proper noun cannot retroactively describe the generic name in use in remote antiquity. Thus he implies but never introduces an agency through which this name evolved from general to specific significance in the interval from antiquity to the present. An obvious consequence of this ex post facto demonstration of the drift of *ru*'s meaning was the establishment of a meaning more ancient than the one asserted by Liu Shipei. This, it would turn out, was a significant even if unintended consequence of Zhang's essay. By speculating that the broad, *da* significance of the *term* was the earliest, Zhang pushed the time of *ru*'s emergence back before the era of the *baijia* (Hundred Families) to the Bronze Age Shang, thereby creating a precedent whose antiquity was unquestionable, borne as it was by the language itself in its earliest form.

"Yuan ru" was not directed exclusively at the problem of *ru*'s original meaning in the sense familiar to us from medieval rhetorical practice, and thus it was not about the establishment of the *vis vocabuli* (authentic, original force of a word) beyond which there could be no debate about meaning. That enterprise, a quest for a single unequivocal originary moment, is the etymological quest so dear to Renaissance rhetoricians. Whether in China or the West, etymology is ideological, operating according to an exclusionary authority that claims to disclose the true force of a word by identifying its original root (etymon). Therefore it presumes an originary significance of a word, privileging that significance above all subsequent variations. Our appreciation of "Yuan ru" is the appreciation bred from a tradition (a Western tradition) in which it is presumed that language has a continuous identity and that the moment at which language began is divine. Since the nineteenth century, etymology has become for us a science, no longer a persuasive art, through which the divine originary power, the ultimate cause, of a word and thus the root of its meaning can be definitively established.

Etymology, then, is not disinterested. This is true for Zhang's as well as for ours; etymologies are fables of power[169] in any culture, but how that power is construed is certainly not identical. For us, Zhang's essay was a way of getting to the root not only of a word but of an entire intellectual and cultural tradition in terms of which Chinese tradition has been conventionally understood. If we could ascertain *ru*'s primordial significance, then we could understand why it has attained in Chinese history its singular cultural significance. But these are concerns produced by a science and subtly linked to vestiges of Renaissance rhetoric; they are not exactly Zhang Binglin's concerns.

He was actually much more interested in what happened to *ru* after its precedental significance was posited. Unlike our mentors of etymology, Cicero and Aristotle, Zhang believed that no original force of a word could be obtained by identifying its earliest appearance in the language. He did identify a continuous linguistic identity, presuming the scribal form of Chinese to be a mysterious essence of the Huaxia people. On closer analysis, however, we can see that "Yuan ru" is like an etymology in reverse, as is underscored by Zhang's devotion of half his essay to criticism of contemporary understanding of the term. Consequently, this essay did nothing to reconcile Kongzi and his fellowship with the ancient priestly class of the same name to which *ru* first referred in Zhang's account. Emphasis here is on the different meanings of the one term, not a single ultimate meaning which denied the validity of those meanings that arose in the course of history.

Zhang believed these different meanings were reflections of the different conditions of the "social aggregate" of China at those times. That explains why he fulminated so at contemporaries who confused the different names, who did not recognize that it was impossible for one band of meaning to explain another. In this diatribe, Zhang seemed to be insisting, in a fashion consonant with the nominalism of the *Mozi*, that words were appropriate to things and that to violate this natural relation was to confuse reality and names and thus to truncate the weakened ties of Chinese cultural patrimony. This broad-brushed contemporary criticism was the culmination of "Yuan ru"'s argument, yet this message has been lost.

Through his pointed historical speculation, Zhang was attempting to make prominent the diversity of skills that had defined *ru* in antiquity while showing that the term's contemporary manifestation was, by contrast, uniform. Zhang intentionally contrasted this ancient definitive diversity, in order to demonstrate that current *jinwen* and state efforts to confine *ru*'s meaning to the Kongjiao univocity of the mystical and the religious ran counter to the very sources of its ancestry. Ancient intellectual pluralism was an interpretation anti-absolutist and anti-monarchical in impulse. At the same time, Zhang Binglin was an essentialist; he believed passionately in the *guocui*, "national essence," of the Chinese as a people whose heritage was transmitted from the culture heroes and this, of course, as a shibboleth brandished against the despotic, ethnic minority rulers of his nation. Nevertheless, his understanding of what was essentially Chinese was not singular, monolithic, and timeless, but plural, variable, and contradictory. This, too, is what the Jesuits had understood so well centuries before when they were embraced by the Chinese as Buddhist monks and as native defenders of the *ru* tradition.

Between 1910 and 1935 speculation concerning the precise nature of *ru*'s historical development was increasingly common, most of it inspired by the argument of "Yuan ru," and all of it unmindful of the subversive politics of its reconstruction of antiquity. Substantive critical essays by the Chinese scholars Fu Sinian, Hu Shi, and Feng Youlan, and even a book by Kitamura Sawakichi titled *Jūgaku gairon* (A General Outline of *Ru* Learning) appeared during this time, making clear that the question of *ru*'s beginnings was of historical importance.[170] Besides large fragments of Zhang's text, which they all quoted, and a common commitment to the kind of "interested" etymology by which an ancient history of *ru* was adduced, what all these scholars shared was the opinion, promoted by Hu, that the essay was an intellectual watershed.

And it was a watershed—no mean feat for an essay of five pages' length— but not until Hu Shi drew public attention to it in the preface to his own attempt to pin down the meaning of the word. In fact "Yuan ru" would have had significantly less effect and would probably have been unknown to us had it not been for Hu's fulsome praise and his articulate application of Zhang's basic argument. Reviewing today the contents of the journals *Min-*

bao or *Guocui xuebao* from this period, one is struck by the lack of acknowledgment of this essay. If "Yuan ru" was a work of unparalleled intellectual significance for this "breakthrough generation," as Benjamin Schwartz has trenchantly characterized Zhang's activist scholarly cohort, then knowledge of the essay must have been this generation's best kept secret.[171] Why did this small but momentous piece of Zhang's work draw so little attention? The answer to this question brings us to the close of this chapter and closer to the reasons why in this century Chinese and Western imaginings have been rejoined in the manufacture of *ru*.

The Curious Legacy of "Yuan Ru"

Although controversy surrounded Zhang as an incendiary figure in the tumultuous first three decades of China's experiment in nationalism, none of it was provoked by his idiosyncratic historicization of *ru*. We could consider the lack of response to be evidence for the general acceptance of the argument of "Yuan ru," a possibility abetted by the popular perception among urban intellectuals that Zhang Binglin was a man of profound intellect and exacting empirical scholarship. It is also possible that Zhang's etymological essays were read as a form of entertainment for the lettered who might have read them anagrammatically as texts bearing coded criticisms of contemporary scholars. Perhaps a more likely explanation for such scholarly tranquility is that there was something simply uncontestable about the logic of "Yuan ru," having little to do with the impressive breadth of Zhang's erudition and more to do with his conceptual appropriation of the broad logic of evolutionary theory. Maybe "Yuan ru" was simply seen as a commonsense restatement of scholarly opinion on the matter, obvious to, but never previously documented by, his contemporaries.

Such a contention presumes, however, that the article was read or, if read, understood, and there is good reason to be wary of such presumption. It is well known that many of Zhang's contemporaries did not understand Zhang's scholarly compositions (some might say virtually no one understood them, including Lu Xun by his own admission). Indeed, most found it difficult to comprehend the language, not to mention the literary allusions that were packed into every line of his prose. Perhaps at the time of its publication "Yuan ru" was received among potential readers as just another of Zhang's very trying, traditionalist scholarly productions replete with impenetrable archaic verbiage. And we must remember that even very capable students like Gu Jiegang confessed that the articles written by Zhang and Liu Shipei for *Guocui xuebao* were at first difficult to comprehend.[172]

Yet "Yuan ru" was not published in the stigmatized journals of *guwen* activists but in Zhang's book, *Guogu lunheng*, a volume of substantial and instant popularity. Considering the order of the book's contents it is possible that "Yuan ru" was overlooked due to its brevity and its location in the volume between two longer essays on learning ("Yuan xue") and the word *dao* ("Yuan dao"), essays that were cited occasionally by other scholars. This is why, in the end, I am persuaded that contemporary inattention to "Yuan ru" reflected the essay's status as entertainment, a more sophisticated and politicized "wordsmithing." Perhaps another reason for this salient inattention was that the moment for "Yuan ru"'s effectiveness had been lost. By the year of its publication in 1910, the matter of redefining *ru*'s origins as a means of disestablishing *jinwen* hegemony and undermining a failing government's desperate ideological ploys, however inspired, was monumentally irrelevant. The politics of the piece were evident, but not compelling.

The popularity of the essay among Chinese and particularly Western scholars in the last few decades, even just the last decade, provides some further understanding of the reasons for contemporary Chinese neglect of "Yuan ru." Recent academic interest in it has been exclusively philological, with only a passing acknowledgment of the historical conjecture within which this philology was embedded. Inquiries into the meaning of the term habitually begin with Zhang's essay and especially include consideration of the historical phonology we have examined above. This tendency as much as anything confirms why "Yuan ru" was lost among the reams of nationalist literature produced in the first years of the Republic. What Zhang Binglin's contemporaries missed in "Yuan ru" was missed also by later scholars, none of whom could recognize the unprecedented nature of his argument and its implications for his contemporary combatants of the Tongcheng and *jinwen* schools. But this was largely a consequence of how later scholars learned of, and how later scholars read, Zhang's essay.

The inspired scholarly speculation on *ru* of this century, with the exception of Kitamura's, was brought about almost exclusively by Hu Shi's "Shuo ru," not by "Yuan ru" itself. This is why, after 1935, a growing number of scholars in China and the West offered their considerations on an ancient *ru* and, in the course of doing so, took note of Zhang's earlier essay. The earliest Chinese respondents, Fu Sinian, Feng Youlan, and Guo Moruo, were engaged in intellectual debate with Hu Shi over the authenticity of the texts he used and the validity of the interpretation he advanced on the basis of these texts; yet in beginning their critiques none failed to make some reference to Zhang Binglin's work.

"Shuo ru," furthermore, was far from obscure, piquing the interest of Western scholars who loyally appropriated the outline of its argument. At the same time that the Chinese were assessing its validity, Western awareness of Zhang's "Yuan ru" was being acquired in a fashion very similar to that by which Chinese readers of his era learned of it—through Hu Shi's essay. Hu's "Shuo ru" was translated into German in 1935 (a year after its publication in China) by Wolfgang Franke for a special issue of *Sinica* and a digest in English of Franke's translation appeared right after the *Sinica* issue.[173] Thus there was something about Hu's further theoretical considerations on *ru* that was of great interest to Western scholars, and the summary effect of their reading of this native palimpsest was a belief that the original meaning of *ru* had been ascertained.

These are the facts governing "Yuan ru"'s aesthetics of reception, and they tell us much about how it was drawn into a wider readership and thus appropriated by interested seekers of an original meaning of the ever-elusive *ru*. It was in this way that the academic exchanges of a coterie of Chinese intellectuals on a topic of immediate and urgent cultural relevance produced an analysis of broad scope, one that Western scholars undoubtedly found convincing because it was consonant with the characterization of their own transition from the nineteenth to the twentieth century. However, while we might see how these theories of *ru*'s origins were made intellectually saleable by way of their unconscious application of a developmental logic, we do not, at the same time, acquire any insight into the timing and the form of Chinese interest in the origins of *ru*.

In Zhang's case, the argument of "Yuan ru" just "seemed right," but, in insisting that the essay should be so seen, I reveal more about the reasons why it commands my assent. I contend that the latent developmental logic of "Yuan ru" permitted it to be accessible to both Chinese and Western scholars, yet to understand its popularity among such individuals we must look beyond its implicit evolutionary scheme. The longevity of Zhang's provocative piece has been ensured because it posits a philologically grounded *fons et origo* of *ru* and situates this locus within a protean, but coherent, narrative historical framework. Nevertheless, if this is the source of the essay's interpretive authority, we must understand that this authority derives from uses to which the text has been put by a very different cohort of inquirers: ourselves of course, but also Hu Shi, who put its argument in the service of a strikingly different agenda.

The contentious intellectual pluralism of his own era—multiple *guwen* schools, and equally numerous *jinwen* and *gongyang* factions, persuaders all of either the populace or the government—I'm certain must have resonated deeply with Zhang's historical sense of the era of the *guzhiru*. His researches on the past lives of a single graph left for us in "Yuan ru" was a celebration of that diversity against the increasingly total administration of cultural life by politics. The logic of evolutionary progression that underlies Zhang's historical conjecture of *ru* acted, like Darwin's account of the species, to disclose a pattern of change implicit in the evidence of biodiversity. Rather than achieve a reductionist conclusion about *ru*, the intellectual consequence of Zhang's theory of origins was testament to plural shapes of experience summarized by a single graph, in the same way that Darwin's unifying theory gave life to the pluralities of speciation. It was this testament that inspired Hu Shi to advance a more eloquent defense of China's native diversity, a diversity that would offer a model for the world.

How did it come about that the meaning of *ru* changed so that by the end of the nineteenth century it referred to, in Zhang Binglin's words, "canon commentators and instructors"? What remained unsaid in "Yuan ru," particularly the historical reasons for the semantic transitions made evident in the increasing specificity of the name, was taken up for the first time by Hu Shi more than twenty years later. This agenda will become clear in the next chapter as I address how Hu took the inarticulate agency of the changes in *ru*'s meaning and drew convincing links between semantic variation and historical context.

Chapter 4, consequently, will be concerned with the interpretive details by which Hu filled out "Yuan ru"'s implicit "historicoevolutionary standpoint,"[174] thereby granting it a needed narrative coherence. It was this particular coherence, with its liberal borrowing from Christian theology and the early history of Christianity, that drew fire from other Chinese while also attracting the immediate attention of Western scholars. In this reaction we can understand how a consciously nativistic manufacture of the history of *ru*, irrelevant in one historical context, becomes immensely valuable in another. By the time of China's political crisis of the 1930s, unlike twenty years before, *ru*'s ancient origins were again relevant. Western powers were now embroiled in a Chinese civil war and Western scholars abroad sought evidence of that three-century-old compatibility of Chinese and Western cultures invented by the Jesuits, so that a native tradition could be restored to prominence and justification could be found for the support of liberal alternatives to the Nationalists and the Communists. For these hopeful observers, such a restoration of *ru* was found in the inspired reading by Hu Shi of Zhang Binglin's "Yuan ru."

The squabble over texts and interpretations in contemporary Chinese scholarship that was resolved by Zhang in favor of an ancient noncombative diversity of schools was with Hu Shi's "Shuo ru" opened out onto a broader interpretive field, where the question of the evolution of *ru* was elevated to world historical significance. In examining Hu Shi's theory in some detail, this inquiry into the paradox of the modern invention of an ancient *ru* will show, as was suggested at the close of part 1, that Chinese and Western imaginings are indeed intertwined, mutually implicated in the sense that has been made of *ru*. However, one conclusion certainly not anticipated by the direction of our inquiry to this juncture is that *ru* and its purported founder, Kongzi, would stand as native emblems of a global civilization of tolerance and understanding bred from loss. It is this ironic conclusion worked out by Hu Shi—that the particular is universal—toward which we now turn.

CHAPTER 4

PARTICULAR IS UNIVERSAL:

HU SHI, *RU*, AND THE

CHINESE TRANSCENDENCE

OF NATIONALISM

An equally telling fact is that relations to tradition change. The "return to origins" always states the contrary of what it believes, at least in the sense that it presupposes a *distancing* in respect to a past (that space which precisely defines history: through its effected mutation of lived tradition by which one makes a "past," the "ob-ject" of study), and a will to *recover* what, in one fashion or another, seems lost in a received language. In this way the "return to origins" is always a modernism as well.—*Michel de Certeau*

Hu Shih developed the exciting theory that not only the Jews but the Shang people had been animated by messianic ideas. He further suggested that the Shang had also transferred these messianic hopes to the religious sphere after they had been disappointed in the political arena. Hu Shih's starting point was the self-designation of the "Confucians" which is indeed much older than Confucius. . . . they did not simply resign themselves to the decline of the Shang but hoped for a restoration of their rule and thus of their own position of dominance. Hu Shih seems to have believed that many prophecies to this effect were hidden in the classical writings. —*Wolfgang Bauer*

Joseph Levenson, the intellectual historian of China, had a fondness for contrastive complexes such as tradition/modernity and *meum* (mine)/*verum* (true), but in characterizing the "modern fate" of "Confucian China" in the early decades of the twentieth century he spoke of China's wrenching struggle with national identity in terms of the contrast of *tianxia* (the world, the universe) and *guo* (nation). Once a cultural universe unto itself, imperial China had numerous tributaries, but no peer. But with the proclamation of the Republic of China in 1912, China became a nation among numerous peers and entered the volatile currents of international politics, encountering obstacles that it negotiated only with considerable difficulty.

Levenson reasoned that China's survival could be reduced to a tale of conflict between universe and nation. The Chinese traded their immemorial cultural world for a less satisfying, but imminently real, role as one nation in an international chorus—"joining the world on the cosmopolitan tide." This tale forms the narrative backdrop of the present chapter; however, in the Chinese debates over *ru* incited by Hu Shi's eccentric reading of Zhang Binglin's "Yuan ru," scholars in the 1930s labored toward a formulation of national identity and found, pace Levenson, that *tianxia* and *guo* were not opposed but congeneric. At least, that was the critical conclusion reached by Hu Shi in narrating a history of *ru*.

As we learn more of the specific intellectual ancestry of our understanding of the term *ru* in this final chapter, the cultural lines of West and East again intertwine, for Hu's vision of *ru*'s genesis is retold in the language of conflated Chinese and Christian imaginings. From Zhang Binglin's effort to define a singular Chineseness by means of a semantic evolution of *ru*, Hu Shi would inscribe a redemptive moral arc enclosing all of civilization. In performing this ecumenical feat, Hu made explicit a truth fundamental to the Sino-Jesuit encounter: that it is the local and not the universal that is sovereign. We now close an interpretive circle by discovering on Chinese ground, in the Chinese language, a universal significance for *ru* reminiscent of yet critically different from the seventeenth-century Jesuit and lay elevation of "Confucianism" to global relevance.

Chinese Icon of the Oecumene

There could have been no more suitable (or, rather, no other) historical representative of the conflated cultural imaginings that have spawned the genesis of an ancient *ru* than Hu Shi. A native of Anhui, he could claim a common territorial origin with the critical philosophical tradition of Dai Zhen, unlike Zhang Binglin, who could merely claim an intellectual affinity for it.[1] In fact, Hu averred both a territorial and intellectual connection, and we may presume it was this identification and his rigorous commitment to the empirical study of received native texts and traditions that earned him recognition as an exemplar of *Hanxue* in Liang Qichao's survey of Qing intellectual history.[2] Also, like growing numbers of intellectuals of his generation, Hu had the advantage of studying abroad, but in this respect he excelled and was given opportunities in a way unmatched by his contemporaries. An exception that comes to mind is Y. R. Chao (1892–1982), who matriculated at Cornell in September of 1910. Like Hu Shi, he made passage to the United States for undergraduate study through the auspices of the Boxer Indemnity Scholarship.

Still, Hu was unusual by the standards of his cohort, and this fact was certainly not lost on the Chinese at home; when Hu returned to China in 1917 he was selected by popular vote as "The Greatest Living Chinese," an honor he did not greatly appreciate. He was admitted to Phi Beta Kappa at Cornell and won the coveted Hiram Corson Browning Prize in the Department of English in his senior year. A year after graduation from Cornell, he began graduate studies in philosophy (his major as an undergraduate) at Columbia University with John Dewey. It would be fair to say then that by the end of his academic sojourn to the United States, Hu had reaped the rewards of wide exposure to and familiarity with what we would call the "Western intellectual tradition." Indeed he was a man between two worlds, with a traditional Chinese scholarly temperament and an intellect bred from a passion for the humanistic ideals conveyed through "Greek and Roman literature, sculpture, science, and politics."[3]

In the West he had become a philosopher in his own right, developing a distinctive reading of the pragmatic and experimentalist fundamentals of Dewey's philosophy. In China, following his return, he was a revered figure of its literary renaissance who effectively combined indigenous *kaozheng* philological techniques with the experimentalist methodology learned from Dewey, by which, for example, he established the literary merit of traditional novels written in the vernacular.

It was these intertwined intellectual impulses and professions that were responsible for the unusual interpretation he ventured in his essay "Shuo ru." The essay, however, was unusual not only in the character of its argument, as emphasized by Wolfgang Bauer in the epigraph to this chapter.[4] Bauer's comment suggests that what Hu did was to identify an adventist strain in the culture of the Shang, that Bronze Age tribe of whom Guo Moruo wrote in a critical response to "Shuo ru," "Chinese culture may be traced in its origins."[5] Admittedly such an interpretation was novel, yet Hu did quite a lot more than gloss Chinese antiquity by reference to Christian millenarianism. His interpretation, as we will see, was a singular invention. For in this essay, Hu Shi, through a very sophisticated analysis that compared the ancient messianic religious beliefs of the Shang and the Jews with the humanitarian teachings of Kongzi and Jesus, used indigenous texts to identify what was common in the historical paths of China and the West, and thus to bind their futures in a common universal civilization.

From the history of the Jews in enslavement and of the Shang under the yoke of the Zhou in which there arose among both peoples a prophecy of liberation, he adduced a pattern of mythical misappropriation of the true instruction of Jesus and Kongzi. To accomplish this, Hu had to undertake criticism of both the Chinese and the Western religious traditions, and he could not be satisfied with merely employing the logical methods of modern Western thought to illuminate what the two traditions did and did not hold in common. In a manner of speaking this is what he had done in *The Development of the Logical Method in China*, but as culture broker of the West to China and of China to the West, in "Shuo ru" Hu advanced a thorough, critical conflation of the cultural history of the two worlds he straddled.

There are several reasons why this long, commendably researched and wildly imaginative essay requires our study, the most obvious of which I have just mentioned—that it was "Shuo ru" that introduced Chinese and Western scholars to the first genetic reckoning of *ru*. Hu's essay, together with Zhang Binglin's "Yuan ru," made an enormous contribution to the twentieth-century image of Chinese antiquity. Indeed the influence of "Shuo ru" may account for the particularly "Confucian" gloss we have applied to that antiquity. The chief contribution of these two scholars was their provision of a way back to the foreign country of China's past, a path down which native and foreign inquirer alike might move.

We must not underestimate the fact that both of these men, especially Hu Shi, were accomplished scholars, very influential individuals who served as prominent members of the faculties of Chinese universities and research institutions. By dint of the circumstances of their intellectual situation—having disciples and students, considerable foreign contacts, and a national reputation—the academic production of these two men displayed an impressive authority.[6] This point is effectively summarized by Jerome Grieder, writing about Hu:

> During his long association with China's modern institutions of higher learning and research—Peita [Beida, i.e., Beijing University], Academia Sinica, the China Foundation—Hu did much to broaden the horizons of scholarly opportunity. In his own scholarship he served as preceptor and inspiration for many younger men, opening to them wide and inviting new vistas. Among those who have recorded their debt to Hu are Ku Chieh-kang [Gu Jiegang], the historian and folklorist; Yü P'ing-po [Yu Pingbo], literary critic and historian; and Lo Erh-kang [Luo Ergang], a specialist in the history of the Taiping Rebellion, to name only a few of the more eminent.[7]

Similarly, the environment in which Zhang and, especially, Hu conceived and wrote their pieces on *ru* was one of intellectual ecumenism that began at the turn of the century, reached enthusiastic extremes in the 1910s and 1920s, but by the 1930s had become an unconscious presence. This ecumenism was partly a result of the geopolitics of scholarship in the 1930s. Many Chinese were of the May Fourth generation that had championed "Westernization" and had studied abroad, and increasing numbers of Western intellectuals were working in China. More importantly, many Chinese intellectuals had embraced the linear tropes of evolution, progress, and modernization, which had the conceptual effect of flattening the normally rocky ground that separated one culture from another. In a new world community of scholars convinced of the truth of the developmental paradigm and the inevitable passage in social evolution from the religious to the secular, Zhang Binglin's and Hu Shi's developmental histories of *ru* probably appeared quite cogent. Consequently, these interpretations were drawn up into the conceptual vortex of the early Western efforts to secure an interpretive hold on China and have been reiteratively reproduced.

For more than sixty years the Zhang/Hu consensus that *ru* originally was a title for religious attendants who evolved into classical scholars and civil servants has remained undisturbed by revisionism commanding assent among Chinese scholars of very diverse politics whose works are particularly valued by Western interpreters. Subsequent scholarly treatments of *ru* among the Chinese were essentially elaborations on this consensus and usually considered the work of Zhang and Hu to have defined the perimeter of debate. For instance, in the acclaimed histories of Chinese thought written by Hou Wailu and Hsiao Kung-ch'üan [Xiao Gongquan], this secularization thesis forms the basis of their accounts of the *ru*, accounts that are, at least in this respect, strikingly alike.[8] In turn, given the extent of Western scholarly dependence on these two comprehensive intellectual histories, the authors' reiteration of the Zhang/Hu-based consensus has consequently exerted considerable influence on Western interpreters, Frederick Mote being one of the more notable; an example of his appropriation of this reading appears as an epigraph to chapter 3. This interpretation has indeed seeped down into the depths of sinological consciousness and is reproduced without comment in many works. Given the reach and the persistence of this explanation, it might be more appropriate to consider it a master fiction through which *ru* has been identified as a continuous presence in the lengthy passage of Chinese civilization. For this reason alone Hu Shi's essay is worthy of our attention.

Secondly, "Shuo ru" was regarded as the first genuine historicist construction of *ru* and as such did a great deal theoretically to open up scholarly debate at home and abroad about Chinese antiquity while also working to make Chinese culture less esoteric for the Westerner. In a certain way the essay acted to undermine the perception of China as exotic, much as Feng Youlan had attempted to do with Chinese thought, by defining it as "philosophy" in its familiar Western sense.[9]

Contemporaneously both Feng and Hu sought to overcome China's intellectual exclusiveness by situating its intellectual history in a broad philosophical context. Their use of analogies from Western intellectual and religious tradition greatly facilitated understanding of the complex philosophical manipulations and encyclopedic recollections of ancient texts that had become standard intellectual fare in China since the eighteenth century. "Shuo ru" was exemplary of this new technique of illuminating native texts, defending interpretations of those texts through comparative evidence and analogical constructs.

Thirdly, the essay also exemplifies the enterprise of reiterative meaning construction that we have stressed throughout this book, which enabled the Jesuits to make sense of the Chinese and to make themselves Chinese, which permitted Zhang Binglin to invent a *ru* of ancient sorcerers, and which operates in the work I have undertaken here. In juxtaposition with "Yuan ru," its avowed parent text, the subtle differences in interpretation and emphasis of Hu's essay are especially evident, and we can see just how men of this same culture and nearly of the same generation can manufacture sense from ambiguity. We may also see how Chinese contemporaries may belong to different modes of cultural production and how the texts of these different modes are worked (in the case of classical or ancient texts, reworked) for a significance relevant to their respective spheres of production, spheres that only partially intersect.

One way of talking about this kind of textual productivity at the hands of the author is familiar to us from Derrida's *jeu*, as the play of texts and interpretations.[10] Hu Shi did not live in a canonless universe; although he was from a generation that excoriated the ossification of classical study, he still respected the texts of ancient history and literature. Nonetheless, there is an obviously playful element in his interpretation of *ru*, in the choice of texts used in defending points, in the glosses of obscure terms, and in the drawing of cross-cultural comparison. But such play is not unrestrained. Rather, it is committed and transpires among unspoken loyalties to native identity and place—loyalties from which derive intellectual and moral values of great depth. This we can recognize as a characteristic of our own urge to make sense of *ru* in a manner satisfactory to a late-twentieth-century historical imagination.

Fourth, Hu's representation of ancient *ru* and Kongzi in terms of the revolt of an oppressed and marginal nobility was nothing short of a revision of the conventional understanding of Chinese antiquity and the symbolic service of *ru* in standing for the traditional culture handed down from it. Furthermore, "Shuo ru" "deconstructed" the received interpretation of the Judeo-Christian tradition and thus challenged the accepted worldview of both the Chinese and Westerners. In Hu's account Kongzi appears as a lineal descendant of the Shang, who departed from rather than upheld the ancestral practices so definitive of their tribal character. But Kongzi was no less a maverick than was Jesus Christ, and both were misunderstood by their own people, and the interpretations of them that were left for posterity were category mistakes. Thus "Shuo ru" reinforces the argument of this book that *ru* has endured as an exquisitely fertile, fabricated symbol and makes clear that in what has been vouchsafed us the inherited canonical understandings of either of these celebrated figures is neither natural nor necessary.

Lastly, "Shuo ru" makes explicit something that was only implied in Zhang Binglin's earlier, largely semantic, reconstruction. That something is the cultural "interwovenness" of our understanding of *ru*, the fact that the sense that has been made of it for the modern mind and which purports to be "the most ancient wisdom" is a product of Chinese and Western imaginings. This product is a confluence of native Chinese impulses for cultural self-definition and Western conceptual technologies of science and religion. We might separate these impulses here for the purposes of identification, but it is obvious when one looks at "Shuo ru" that Hu Shi experienced them as continuous. It is this belief in an interpretive continuum stretching from West to East that enabled Hu to imagine a twentieth-century Chinese renaissance and to declare that such a cultural rebirth was prefigured by Kongzi's ancient revolt against parochialism and weakness in favor of a new ecumenical world of humaneness. But I am getting ahead of myself in saying this; we will return to these considerations after a selective examination of a narrative that Hu would have been likely to characterize as "historicoevolutionary."[11]

"Shuo Ru": Reading Hu Shi on Chinese Antiquity

Just as an excerpt from chapter 41 of the *Mozi* framed Zhang Binglin's expanded etymology of *ru*, so did Zhang's "Yuan ru" frame the theoretical foundation of Hu Shi's essay on the origin and development of *ru*. His now well-known exegesis of *ru*'s evolution, "Shuo ru" (An Elaboration on Ru) was completed on May 19, 1934, and published by the Academia Sinica that fall.[12] Perhaps in deference to Zhang and the intellectual heritage he had claimed, the essay followed the eighteenth-century tradition of *kaozheng* scholarship, and was written as an "addition and correction" of "Yuan ru." However, as one may glean from Wolfgang Bauer's impressions, quoted in the epigraph at the beginning of this chapter, "Shuo ru" involved a far wider conjecture than Zhang's essay could reasonably bear.

Because Hu intended his essay to be understood as fleshing out Zhang's "Yuan ru," we should treat the two pieces as a single interpretive endeavor, essentially a palimpsest. (I will develop this characterization further in the course of this chapter.) Nevertheless, "Shuo ru" more than stands on its own through its ingenious use both of Zhang Binglin's earlier work and of the great array of conceptual technologies Hu possessed as a result of his being an intellectual "citizen of the world." It is this ingenuity that we presently consider.

It should be clear that "Shuo ru" was really not a supplement to, so much as a reinvention of, "Yuan ru," one that exceeded even Zhang Binglin's uncommon imaginings. Still, Hu kept to the notion that his new interpretation grew from Zhang's earlier essay and devoted the first three pages to a thorough recapitulation of his forerunner's argument and its corroborating sources.

After a number of compliments on Zhang's critical intellectual spadework, Hu confessed that "looking now at Zhang Taiyan's theory there are, however, places that may be revised and supplemented,"[13] implying that with the passage of a quarter century aspects of the work required some editorial intervention. Merely glancing at the essay's table of contents makes clear just how far beyond his precursor Hu's elaboration took him. It can also tell us a great deal about the ingenuity of this reinvention, while revealing Hu's presumptions and the trajectory of his argument. Five distinct sections comprise the body of essay, each of which could stand alone as an exposition of the topic announced in its title:

[Section 2] On *Ru* as the Missionaries[14] of the Yin Tribe [*minzu*]:[15] Their Clothing Was Yin Clothing, Their Religion Was the Yin Rites, Their Philosophy of Life[16] Was That of Weak, Resigned Survivors of a Vanquished Nation.[17]

[Section 3] On the Life of *Ru:* Their Profession as Funerary Directors and Ritual Assistants.

[Section 4] On the Prophecy of the Vanquished Nation of the Yin/Shang Tribe That a King Arose Every Five Hundred Years; Kongzi Was Considered by People of That Time Born as a Sage to Realize the Prophecy.

[Section 5] On Kongzi's Great Contributions: (1) Magnifying the Tribal Character of the *Ru* of the Yin/Shang Tribe into the *Ru* of "Humaneness Is My Responsibility"; (2) Transforming the Weak *Ru* into Tough and Aggressive *Ru.*

[Section 6] On the Relationship between Kongzi and Laozi; On Laozi as the Founder of *Ru.* A Supplementary Essay on the Relationship between *Ru* and the Fellowship of Mo.[18]

Section 1, which precedes all these, is called "Raising the Question," the question being the meaning of *ru* as construed by Zhang Binglin. Zhang, as we know, had merely adumbrated a development in *ru*'s meaning from a generic name for mantic technicians to a proper name for instructors who worship and work the canon. This conclusion provided Hu Shi with his objective—to provide a plausible theory of the evolution of *ru.* Hu construed his essay as a further consideration of questions raised though not answered by Zhang, questions which required the marshalling of more ancient evidence and fewer elliptical allusions.

In this section, quoting generously from "Yuan ru" and with obvious pride, Hu faithfully reviews the same three-stage argument we analyzed in the preceding chapter. He enthusiastically concurs with Zhang's reconstruction of *ru*'s ancient meaning and credits him with enabling his contemporaries to understand what the term meant when it was used by Kongzi in book 6, chapter 13, of the *Lunyu:* "Ru wei junzi ru wu wei xiaoren ru," (Be a lordling *ru*, not a plebeian *ru*). Hu contends that Zhang's explanation of *ru* as a broad, common name (*daming*) for gentlemen of received technē (*shushi*) provides the key to understanding this much-queried phrase and surmises:

> Thus we can see that in Kongzi's time the social status of *ru* was quite varied; there were lordling *ru* and there were plebeian *ru.* Later people have often been prejudiced, and were not able to deduce the latent meaning of that sentence. But using Zhang Taiyan's explanation, seeing that in the time before Kongzi *ru* already had a broad significance, this sentence is then very understandable.[19]

Still, Hu admits "feeling unsatisfied" with Zhang Binglin's account of the *leiming*, the "class name," in which they are identified as "the kind of *ru* who were men of the Six Cultivations" and opines that this constitutes a "very big weakness" in the argument.[20]

Here the criticism was not of the theory in which these two things were equated, but of Zhang's use of passages from the *Zhou li* and from Zheng Xuan's commentary, passages that were entirely too thin, Hu contended, to support the weight of such a significant notion:

> The foundation of this theory is only two phrases from the *Zhou li* and Zheng Xuan's commentary. It is not a matter of whether the *Zhou li* is or isn't reliable; the original text of the *Zhou li* [in which *ru* appears] is only in the sentence, "*Ru* by means of the *dao* affect the people," and the phrase, "unite the *shi* and *ru*." In these the graph *ru* has no fixed definition. Zheng Xuan in his commentary explains that *ru* are "those of the Six Cultivations, who with it teach the people." This is only an explanation of scholars in the waning years of the Eastern Han; but we cannot on the basis of this believe that in antiquity there really were only *ru* who practiced the Six Cultivations.[21]

The excerpts from these texts are so elliptical, he is claiming, that they are of little value as evidence, and, beyond agreeing with Zhang's irrefutable assertion that *ru* in ancient times meant *shushi*, Hu believes that too many unanswered questions lingered after what Zhang explained. Hu maintains that

> Mr. Zhang said that the name *ru* that was passed down from antiquity was gentlemen of received skills (*shushi*); nevertheless, the sources that he quotes as proof are all Qin and Han. He still cannot explain in the end in what era this broad meaning of *ru* arose, what their antecedents were, what their lives were like, what their historical relationship was with the more narrowly defined *ru* of Kongzi and with the intellectual currents between the Spring and Autumn and the Warring States periods.[22]

As he put forward his reservations in asking these questions, Hu Shi adumbrated the argumentative path of his "revised supplement," for his questions were the keys to the exposition in each of the remaining five sections. What the title of section 2 does not announce, however, is that it begins with a return to Kongzi's utterance in book 6, chapter 13, of the *Lunyu*, with Hu stating the very thing that Zhang undoubtedly knew but avoided acknowledging, "as for the designation, *ru*, the earliest appearance is in the *Lunyu* where Kongzi says, 'Be a lordling *ru*, not a plebeian *ru*.'"[23] In his own account, Zhang had carefully disassociated Kongzi from the *guzhiru* (*ru* of antiquity), as we previously noted, but in his own reading Hu Shi employed Zhang's definition of the earliest meaning of the graph, the *daming*, to gloss the troubling *Lunyu* passage, thus revealing the mechanism of his reworking of Zhang's text.

From the start Hu grounded his inquiry in the normative, "natural" conjuncture of *ru* and Kongzi—the very association Zhang identified as accidental and unnecessary—assuming that there must have been good, but previously undisclosed, historical reasons for the linkage of these two entities. "As a way of more fully expounding on Mr. Zhang's theory," Hu aims to track down these reasons and begins his pursuit with the question, "What kind of people were these *ru*?"[24] Hu was convinced that there was evidence in the canon that would put historical flesh on the bones of his inspired predecessor's philology. If Kongzi could speak so unselfconsciously about two different types of *ru*, then logic dictated that there was in fact a kind of person at that time represented by the name, Hu probably reasoned.

The next step in such reasoning, however, was not a fuller examination of the context in which Kongzi's remarks were allegedly made, but the establishment of the ancient meaning (*guyi*) of the character. Just as Zhang Binglin had done, and for that matter what most Chinese and Japanese scholars perplexed by the ambiguity of *ru* have done, Hu eschews defining *ru* by ascertaining its meaning in parallel texts of other rhetorical traditions of the Warring States and instead turns to the *Shuowen*. To proceed in this fashion—establishing the genuine antiquity of a term that first appears in the *Lunyu* by taking the definition of it from a text of a different genre and some five centuries after Kongzi—might seem, to us who are concerned with authenticity, methodologically questionable. However, given that philology is less a science than an aesthetic that apprehends the world through a veil of specific sentiments and values,[25] we must remember that to consult the archaic reconstructions of the *Shuowen* is an enterprise of faith, sustained by the belief that what one finds glossed there is the meaning of the script in its earliest form.[26] Yet for men like Zhang and Hu, who considered dubious claims for the authenticity of the oracle bones and who were indebted to the scholarly traditions of the eighteenth century, Xu Shen's pun-replete text was the logical point of embarcation.

Thus, the case for an ancient meaning is made by reliance on the paronomastic offering "ru rou ye" (*ru* means "weak") from the *Shuowen*, that had been ignored by Zhang Binglin. Hu treats *rou* (weak) as the *vis vocabuli* of *ru*, the genuine source of its originary power; thus the task he sets for himself is to ascertain the earliest meaning of "weak." He aims to account for why weakness as opposed to any other quality has been used to gloss *ru*. The search for philological clues takes him along a slightly different path than that followed by Zhang in his reconstruction. Hu asserts that "the character *xu* in antiquity was interchangeable with *ruan* [which] according to the *Guang ya* means 'weak,' (*ruo*)."[27] Zheng Xuan and Zheng Sinong separately attest to the identity of *xu* and *rou*, the former commenting that in ancient writings *xu* was written differently (see glossary), while the latter notes that this ancient *xu* was understood as "the *xu* of *rouxu*, as in the saying 'The thick fat of a tamed hide is weak.' "[28] The sense of *xu* as "weak" is evident as well in the tendency to contrast it with *jian* (solid or firm), and in another gloss in which it is defined as the "*ruan* of *rouruan*," meaning "dilatory," or "slow."

The redundancy of these phonological links between *xu, rou, ruo*, and *ruan*, and the contrastive semantic coupling of *xu* and *jian*, do suggest a semantic field—how ancient we cannot be certain—in which *xu*, the etymon of *ru*, carries the meaning of weak or slow. Of course, this demonstration, as Hu knows, does not disclose why this important etymological root would have been so glossed in early commentaries or other sources. Consequently he turns, as did Zhang Binglin, to the *Yijing* in an effort to construct a more intelligible context for the weak and dilatory qualities associated with *ru* by way of its derivation from *xu*. Yet Hu Shi pushes his interpretation further by using the text not merely to confirm the *Shuowen*'s gloss, but to draw out another meaning critical to his hypothesis of *ru*'s ancient history. Given that so much of the theory Hu puts forth in this essay is based on his interpretation of clues deduced from the fifth and forty-third hexagrams of the *Yijing*, I quote in full his intellectual meanderings among the text's oracular utterances. Hu states:

> The Commentary on the Decision [of the fifth hexagram, *xu*] in the *Zhou yi* [*Yijing*] says, "*Xu* means 'to wait.' " The Miscellaneous Notes on the hexagram say, "*xu* means 'not to advance.' " In the *Zhou yi* "marsh rises to heaven" [*ze shangyu tian*] is *guai* [to decide; decision], while "clouds rise up to heaven" [*yun shangyu tian*] is *xu*. *Guai* is "rain already having fallen," thus it is the image of a completed decision. Moreover, *xu* is "dense clouds that have not yet rained," thus it is an image of hesitation or tardiness. In the *Zuo zhuan* in the chronicle of the sixth year of Ai Gong [it is said]: "Delay [*xu*] is the poorest of methods." And again in Ai Gong's fourteenth year, "Delay [*xu*] is the thief of affairs." The [examples] above are derived from the character *xu*, the great majority of which involve meanings of "weak" or "slow." "*Ru* means 'weak' [*rou*]."[29] "*Ru* means 'a suckling.' " "*Nuo* means 'incompetent' or 'timid.' " The *Mengzi* has "how dilatory and hesitant." All of these are from the character *ruan* and all have the meaning "weak" [*ruoyi*]. According to the *Shuowen*, "*nuan* means 'weak.' " [In his commentary] Duan Yucai says, "*Nuan* is identical with the character *nuo*," . . . . as in today's "glutinous rice" [*nuomi*]. [It is said in] the *Guangya shigu*, "*Nuan* means 'feeble.' " So in antiquity *xu* and *ruan* were the same word, and in ancient pronunciation they were both read like *nu* as in crossbow or like *nuo* as in "glutinous rice." . . . [Thus] it seems that it is not without reason that the character *ru* is derived from *xu* and is glossed as "weak."[30]

Such intratextual glossing—using the hexagram *guai* (see glossary) to explain the hexagram *xu* (see glossary)—has the advantage of standing clear from the well-established tendency to read the graph *xu* exclusively by way of a late Han etymology. By taking *guai* and *xu* as a linked conceptual pair, both elements of which share the base trigram *qian* meaning sky (*tian*) (see glossary), Hu also avoids Zhang Binglin's unconventional practice of using the fifth hexagram to interpret the graph *xu*. If *guai*, as an integer in this divinatory calculus, represents a situation in which rain has previously fallen, then *xu* (its upper trigram standing for water) must convey the imminence of rain. The former stands for completed action, the latter for action deliberated but not completed.

This novel approach brings Hu to a conclusion that resembles in part that of Zhang's earlier exercise in *xiaoxue* (philology), as he emphasizes, too, the significance of impending rain for an understanding of *ru*. Of course they do both presume that the earliest meaning of *ru* is to be found in the oracular ruins of the *Yijing*, but Hu does not from this conclude that *ru/xu* referred to sorcerers and exorcists. What we are left with instead is simply a composite meaning of *ru* as "weak" and "waiting" derived in equal measure from the commentary on the fifth hexagram and the gloss in the *Shuowen*. And yet one is hard-pressed to recognize *ru* in this chain of philological links and prophetic, symbolic shorthand.

However, this presentation is tied to an unstated latticework of linked assumptions and is followed immediately by the regurgitation of some passages from the *Mozi* and the *Xunzi*, where *ru* begins to take on a certain historical visibility. *Xu* characterized the attitude of these people, but from the later Warring States texts we learn that *ru* are identified as men who wear distinctive clothing called *rufu* (*ru* garments), with wide sleeves, broad belts, and high caps. This unusual attire was, Hu claims, worn by "the most ancient *ru* and displayed an air of the weakness and sluggishness of the lettered, thus they had the name *ru*."[31]

The immediate juxtaposition of passages concerning the appearance of *ru* enables Hu to confer a particular significance on *rufu* as the clothing of the weak. Further, the clothing is linked to *ru* not by philology but by a kind of associative symbolism, so that the garments worn by people of the Shang, people identified by Hu as a distinct "tribe," become the visible evidence of the weakness of *ru* attested in the earliest glosses. Presuming the retiring and saturnine qualities of the intellectual in his own day to be exportable to antiquity, Hu sees weakness in the very clothing of the earliest *ru*, all of whom were Yin (Shang) people. They were, in other words, priests, not warriors. The weakness conveyed in *ru* clothing, he claims, is the second ancient meaning of *ru*. Thus Hu Shi, relying on much the same evidence as Zhang, placed the *ru* of Kongzi with their denigrated hats and garments in a direct line of descent from the *shushi* with their distinctive raiment.

To this juncture Hu Shi repeatedly emphasized the weak qualities associated with *ru* and a number of other graphs that form a phonological cluster of similar sounding morphemes. This definitive weakness of *ru* is, in turn, symbolized by the specific clothing worn by members of the fellowship that Hu contends was the same as that worn by the Shang people, or at least what they were believed to wear after subjugation by the Zhou. Lastly, Hu's own analysis of the *Zhou yi* suggests that, given the presumption that the character *ru* was written first as, or at least first pronounced as, *xu*, in the time following the defeat of the Yin it meant "to wait" or "waiting patiently." The last of these clues is the most curious. Still, after another several pages of conjecture dealing with ancient cultural geography, the enduring problem of the pacification of the rebellious Shang, and the ancient role of *ru* as specialists in mourning and funerary rite (*sangli*), one cannot help but wonder, "Waiting for what?" Like the queries raised in the mind of the reader of suspense, the answer must follow the disclosure of a greater number of clues near which violence always hovers.

The historical context constructed out of these clues in the first ten pages of his essay is of an ancient history of violent struggle, of oppression and ethnic conflict, not resolved but frozen in the moment of subjugation of one tribe by another.[32] Against this background of cultural resentment, Hu paints an image of *ru* as an interloper, spawned by Shang, but the servant of Zhou. Hu's reconstruction of the social situation in the first several hundred years of the Zhou or what he refers to as "Yin-Shang wangguo shi" (the era of the vanquished nation of the Yin-Shang) may be summarized in the following manner:

It is, in essence, the well-worn narrative of steppe-sown conflict. The Yin/Shang and Zhou were originally two separate tribes with distinct cultures, histories, heroes, habits, and geographies. The two tribes remained distinct, peacefully occupying the north China plain (*Zhongyuan*)—Shang in the east and Zhou in the west, the two growing more alike in conscious and unconscious ways. The Yin/Shang were the fervently religious, indigenous people of the *Zhongyuan*, the cultural center of antiquity; the Zhou were the eastern-migrating, less-civilized arrivistes, a nomadic, martial tribe from west of the plain. It was, of course, to be expected that two tribes with long-term contact would become more alike culturally. This situation did not endure, as we know from reading the *Shang shu*, and as Hu Shi reminds us,[33] and the conscious aspects of this cultural assimilation of the two tribes had more serious ramifications.

The culturally more rudimentary Zhou conquered the Shang (henceforth called Yin),[34] whose tribal practices were preserved in the eastern four kingdoms (*siguo*) of Wei, Qi, Song, and Lu. Aggressive assimilation pursued under Zhou Gong (r. 1042–1036 B.C.E.) ensured conflict, as the Yin refused to be pacified and continued to resist overlordship. But as much as they may have wanted to extinguish the Shang, the Zhou found Shang ancient tribal culture to be impressively resistant to their efforts to force its assimilation. Zhou leaders were compelled by the staunch persistence of the religious traditions of these people to esteem their rituals, even as they divided up the six clans of the Shang tribe.

It is at this historical juncture of cultural assimilation that *ru* appears, or rather that it becomes significant for us as its twentieth-century interpreters. Hu claims that the conscious assimilation by which the two tribes "little by little became identical had a great deal to do with the class and occupation of *ru*."[35] As aggressive cultural assimilation proceeded along with territorial annexation, *ru*, together with two other groups of Shang noble attendants, *buwu ren* (diviners) and *zhuguan* (officers of invocation and sacrifice), were taken as captives and enslaved and scattered among the people. The *ru*, former elite religious functionaries appended to the Shang ruling clan who were skilled in both ancestral invocation and traditional mortuary rite, although similarly displaced, could exchange their abilities for food and clothing.[36] *Ru* specialists survived the encounter to serve new overlords because as custodians of the dead they were also stewards of the living memory of the Shang as preserved in their rites. Thus they evolved into experts on antiquity as well as ritual.

And because, as Hu alleges, the Zhou ruling class needed them for two linked purposes—as advisers to the nobility and consolers of the majority—they were not destroyed in the violent phases of the conquest and instead came to be favored, achieving equal status with the Zhou's own warrior class, *shi*, occupying the bottom rung on the nobiliary hierarchy. This status equivalence was registered in the tendency among the Zhou to call them *shi* (instructors), as opposed to *ru*. They acquired a position of special significance for the Zhou in that they were to assist them in the learning of Shang ritual and at the same time in conducting the appropriation by the Yin of Zhou custom.

Ru, then, converted a living understanding of their own Shang people into knowledge purveyed among the conquerors for their edification. As so depicted, they were culture brokers who abetted what Hu believes was an inevitable absorption by the Zhou of a cultural foundation provided by their Shang hosts. Hu explains: "It really is that the ancient culture of the eastern region [the preserve of Yin culture] assimilated the new tribal history of the Western Zhou . . . [and] the new construction of the Western Zhou tribe was built upon the foundation of 'the Zhou follow the rites of Yin.' "[37] And so was summed up the most recent of a succession of conquests—a process of "*super*stratification"[38]—that began with the absorption of the Xia by the Shang, and ended with Zhou assimilation of the Shang through the assistance of *ru*.

Indeed, as assistants in cultural assimilation, they were collaborators in the conquest and in this role acquired a measure of upward social mobility within Zhou society. This was reflected, as we noted above, by the conqueror's habit of referring to them by the noble rank of *shi*, which in reference to *ru* bore a civil rather than martial connotation. Despite this apparent collaboration, they were, at the same time, perceived by their own people as holy men, their sanctity embodied in their continued wearing of the old garments and caps of the Yin, and in their preservation of their tribe's ancient religious rites, centuries after assimilation. *Ru*, according to this characterization, were between two worlds: religious authorities (guarantors of the rites of the Yin) and men of talents and intellectual and administrative skills of value to the Zhou. The characterization could as well be applied to intellectuals like Hu Shi, who might have seen themselves as guardians of the spiritual qualities of Chinese civilization and advisers to the new, militaristic power élite of the Guomindang (National People's Party). We cannot know if the parallel may have been intended, but what we do know is that this "creative minority," to use a term of Karl Jaspers favored by Benjamin Schwartz and Tu Wei-ming[39] in describing *ru*, were holy men and factotums, tribal leaders and slaves. And as bearers of the name *ru* they were, as was their native tribe, "in waiting."

Ru: Guardians of Ancestral Cult, Agents of Cultural Redemption

This summary establishes the context for the substantive questions put forward by Hu Shi in the body of his essay. Our query may again be raised, "Waiting for what?" The answer, it turns out, can be found in the life of *ru* as a Shang class living under Zhou occupation. Apparently under the belief that there were no indigenous parallels by which an understanding of the *ru* might be arrived at metaphorically, Hu Shi offers a cross-cultural analogy in terms of which he believes it is possible to "visualize" (*xiangjian*) *ru* at this moment in antiquity. The analogy seems apt, and I suspect it seemed especially so in 1934 for many Chinese scholars who had come of age in the era of Manchu domination and feared an imminent conquest of China by its "pan-Asian" brother, Japan. Hu remarks:

> We know that Greek intellectuals served the Roman victors as slaves, often from this enslavement clambering up to the position of clerks, or

teachers in the home of their masters. After doing battle with the imperial army of Rome, the barbarian tribes [yeman minzu] of northern Europe were finally conquered by the long-robed missionaries of Roman
Catholicism and in turn became their followers. Yin/Shang intellectuals[40]—the diviners, invokers, astrologers of the ruling family and including many scholars of the nobility—were under the western Zhou
tribe which had newly taken power. Although theirs was a tragic slaving
life, there was one thing that constituted the core of the Yin unifying
strength. And it was also their weapon in subsequently vanquishing
those who were victorious [over them] in war. This was nothing other
than their religion.[41]

The message here is unambiguous, and, provided the analogy holds, so is
the fate of the oppressed *ru* servants of the Zhou. They will, in time, conquer
the victors by the spread of the word, for *ru* are, as Hu repeatedly avers,
jiaoshi, the "missionaries" of the religious culture of the Yin. Their teaching,
like a soothing ointment, will soften the martial soul of the conquerors,
acclimating them to the nobler ways of Shang worship, and converting them
into followers and servants. The agents for this religious conquest will be, of
course, *ru*. Certainly it is not difficult to imagine the Shang tribe's *ru* through
the analogy with Greek intellectual enslavement to the uncultured Romans.
Considering the consequences for "Western civilization" (in its conventional
sense) of the staggering cultural efflux generated by this encounter, its value
as metaphor of the development of Chinese civilization is manifest. Just as
the cultural achievements of the Greeks were the foundation for those of the
Romans so it was that the Zhou elaborated upon the basis provided by the
Shang: patrimonial government, cities, writing, bronze metallurgy, ancestor
worship, pyromancy, shamanism.[42]

The comparison drawn between ancient *ru* and Greek intellectuals was
not entirely novel. There were other figures of the May Fourth generation
who had stumbled upon a similar comparison, Chen Duxiu being one of
them. Although he was a Marxist, Chen at one time favored the adoption of
Christianity by the Chinese, because he believed that the cultural strength
of the West derived from modern Western philosophy, whose roots were in
Greek and Christian thought. Comparisons of ancient China and Greece
were common before this time, and Hu's particular emphasis on the sociological and philosophical similarities between Greek and Chinese *zhishi
fenzi* (intellectuals) recalled earlier cultural comparisons such as the one
essayed by Liu Shipei and Zhang Binglin when they described the pre-Han
zhuzi ("noncanonical" masters) as the Chinese equivalents of classical Greek
philosophers like Plato and Aristotle.[43]

By way of his Sino-Hellenic parallel, Hu does more than expound on the broad correlations. He adumbrates a scheme of inevitable cultural emancipation in which *ru*, teachers of their overlords, will become their masters in the same way that Catholic missionaries tamed the bestiality of northern European barbarians with words. What is particularly striking about this comparison is its assertion of inevitable redemption by words that have the effect of violence. Other than the metaphor of the inevitable conquest of the European soul by Christianity, what reason do we have to accept that *ru* will be the liberators of the Shang, the agents of redemptive vendetta? The answer requires more clues, some philological, some analogical, some interpretive and all manufactured by Hu.

Ru first had to be established as religious actors—in effect, made into missionaries of Shang rites among the uncultured Zhou.[44] This can be done but not without some inventive manipulation of artifactual and textual evidence. If the *ru* are the Chinese analogue of the fathers of Roman Catholicism, then how are we to understand the specific nature of their missionary duty as potential liberators of the Shang people from the grip of the truculent Zhou? Hu says that when one looks at *Yinxu* (the wastes of Yin) at Anyang (the final royal capital of the Shang), the artifacts of this people reveal that theirs was a truly religious culture and that their religion was based chiefly on the worship of ancestors.[45] Divination (*bu*), ancestral invocation (*zhu*), and mortuary rites (*sangli*) were the religious activities by means of which the life of the Shang community was choreographed. According to Hu, each of these religious functions was overseen by a specialist (*zhuanjia*) bound, perhaps hereditarily like the *be* of ancient Japan,[46] to the ruling lineage: "This religion required a batch of specially trained men. For divining they used diviners; for sacrifice and invocation they used invocation specialists; [and] for funeral rites they used ministers of rites [*xiangli*]."[47]

Again the sources for this reconstruction are not in evidence in Hu's text. Like Zhang Binglin's identification of *ru* (weak), *shushi* (scholars of received skills), and *ru* (wet), these assertions are part of a larger, but "reasonable" historical conjecture. Such claims may not be reasonable in themselves, but they do not stand alone. They are interconnected assumptions subtly organized in support of conclusions as yet invisible. It is in light of these conclusions that even questionable, uncorroborated assertions seem reasonable. With the fall of the Shang the need for diviners and invokers declined and gradually the *xiangli* (assistants at the rites), those who were responsible for mortuary rites, became the preservers of Shang custom and the custodians of the tribal memory.[48] *Sangli* duties are never defined by Hu but we can only presume that in their early, Shang incarnation they probably consisted of preparing the body for burial, disciplining space in accord with interdictions against defilement of the corpse or the living community, orchestrating lamentation, sealing and disposing of the coffin, directing the funeral procession, exorcising demons or pestilence encountered along the course of the procession, and arranging the deposit of "valuable" objects to accompany the dead. The *sangli* were preserved by the *xiangli*, and the Zhou, having assimilated Shang rites, were dependent upon these custodians to instruct them in the proper prosecution of ritual, specifically the burial of the dead. It was from this specialized ritual profession that *ru* and Kongzi came.

A knowledgeable reader might be inclined to reject this claim as unattested, particularly because there is considerable doubt as to the antiquity of the mourning customs associated with *ru*. Moreover, what we know of the office of *xiangli* is that it was a post of secondary rank at best, as described in sources of late post-Zhou provenance. The preponderant evidence of *xiang* or *xiangli* comes from the *Zuo zhuan*,[49] where it is clearly the name for a ritual officer, or more correctly, a ritual attendant, *xiang* meaning "assistant."[50] I presume this is where Hu came by his knowledge of this ritual company, although he cites no text in support of his contention. What is certain is that although Hu's knowledge of the *xiangli* was acquired from the *Zuo zhuan*, he presents these attendants as the sole specialists entrusted with the customs of the Shang mortuary rite, who, following the conquest, preserved the surviving culture of the Yin people while becoming the compliant servants of the Zhou in the pacification of the Yin. Several entries from the text even record that Kongzi, referred to by his style name Zhongni, served as a *xiang* for his native state of Lu.[51]

Even if we assume like Hu Shi that his *xiangli* and the office of *xiang* so frequently cited in the *Zuo zhuan* are identical, Kongzi's tenure as one does not establish the Shang provenance of these ritual assistants. For example, as *xiang*, Kongzi would have been one of three different officials responsible for the negotiation of covenants, or *meng*, certifying friendship between Lu and other competitive Warring States satrapies as they vied for the spoils left in the wake of the collapse of Zhou suzerainty. *Meng* is more accurately defined as "blood oath." The solemnizing of such oaths was a highly ritualized process requiring the following of a rigid script by the parties involved. The ceremony was very sanguine, entailing the slaughter of an animal, usually a sheep, sometimes an ox, the affixing of the written text of the oath (*caishu*) to the corpse of the headless animal, and the anointing of the lips of the signatories with the blood of the victim. We are just now beginning to understand this Warring States convention, with the excavation of Houma in Shanxi, where numerous records of these blood oaths were discovered. In large part the archaeological find has substantiated impressively what we know from the *Zuo zhuan*.[52] The *meng* was a quasi-legal contract conceived in an age of dwindling Zhou royal authority and, thus, was peculiar to post-Zhou culture. There is no reason to assume that its ritual choreographers, the *xiang*, were the remnants of a class of Shang religious specialists, although scant textual evidence in the *Zuo zhuan* indicates that *ru* was a term peculiar to the kingdom of Lu and acknowledged as such by contiguous satrapies.

The chronicle from the twenty-first year of the reign of Ai Gong (Duke Ai, r. 494–468 B.C.E.), for example, records a meeting at which Duke Ai, the marquis (*hou*) of Qi, and the prince of Zhu gathered to negotiate a *meng*, on neutral ground at Gu (the Fan prefecture in present-day Henan). In general outline the situation resembles one found in much of the *Zuo*, where a blood oath of common defense, or *canmeng*, is drawn up and solemnized by three parties. Ritual assistants (*xiang*), whose role it was to ensure the proper negotiation of each of the four consecutive steps, presided over every detail and may have been joined by other officers in the preparation of the document. If any of the parties should diverge from the terms of agreement stipulated in the *caishu* prepared before the oath was taken and solemnized or, should they fail to be scrupulous in their adherence to ritual, then the *xiang* would rescind the covenant. The slightest ritual lapse—perhaps because the entire transaction was extralegal—necessitated annulment of the agreement.[53]

The *Zuo zhuan* abounds in evidence of such broken covenants, some of which, as in this instance, were intended to join Lu and Qi in friendship. On this occasion the *canmeng* rather than being sealed was invalidated, as the commentators tell us, by the marquis of Qi's tyrannical demand that the representatives of Lu and Zhu prostrate themselves before him in recognition of the political supremacy of Qi. The men of Qi insisted that the presumed intent of the oath, the acknowledgment of friendship, should be superseded by a recognition of Lu and Zhu of subsidiary political status. For Qi to seek formal acknowledgment of political superiority in a context where the parties met as equals on neutral ground contravened the stipulations of the agreement drawn up between the three states. Consequently, Ai Gong and the prince of Zhu refused to comply and, it is assumed, the oath was dissolved. The reluctance of the two states' representatives to concede Qi's paramountcy provided the inspiration for a Qi poem—the point of this digression—that begins in sarcasm but ends in lamentation, holding obsessive Lu ritualism responsible for the lack of diplomatic accord:

> How bogged down are the men of Lu!
> So many years pass yet they do not awaken.
> They make us beside ourselves with anger.
> Alas [it is] those *ru* terms [*rushu*] that vex [our] two states.[54]

A history of difficulty in solemnizing such covenants preceded this poetic plaint. Owing to objections by Lu to various Qi improprieties, there were at least two previous instances during the reign of Ding Gong (r. 508–495 B.C.E.) when *meng* were abrogated. One such abrogation occurred in the Duke's tenth year when Kongzi himself assisted in preparing the document. This particular *meng* was revoked because Qi had brought its army and a threat of force to the ceremonies. The covenant was redrawn—"warmed" with the sacrifice of another animal—but not before Kongzi admonished Qi of its singular ritual dereliction.[55] This second covenant was nearly consigned to an identical fate when the men of Qi suggested that a schedule of celebratory entertainment follow the swearing. This suggestion, considered unconscionable by Kongzi, brought on another rebuke.[56]

The final condemnatory line of the Qi lamentation may be understood in light of this history of reiterative revocation. Du Yu remarks that *rushu* are ritual manuals of the *ru* school that were obstinately adhered to in Lu.[57] Du's commentary, however, may be too generous in its explication. *Ru* is descriptive, I believe, not of "books," but of *shu*, the stipulations or conditions set out in the written text of a blood oath that specify the obligations of the signatories. Each time a covenant between Lu and Qi was dissolved it was because of violations of the intent or the letter of the document, *caishu*, which meant that the parties never succeeded in completing even the first of the four required steps.

What troubles the two states is the ritual meticulousness of the *ru* who insist on undeviating compliance with the specific conditions within which the ritual acknowledgment of legitimacy is framed. The bit of verse just quoted from the *Zuo zhuan* appears to confirm the equivalence of *ru* and *xiangli* so dear to Hu Shi's conception of *ru*, while depicting men of Lu as the stalwart defenders of ritual epitomized by Kongzi, men who were slow and deliberative, judging each situation by an appeal to ritual precedent, as opposed to simply innovating in the face of contingency.[58]

Nevertheless, we still have no reason to associate these ritual attendants with mortuary rites, since their responsibility in the drawing up of such agreements was limited to the drafting of the *caishu*. The belief that *xiangli* were engaged in mortuary rites is a conjecture of Hu Shi's, uncorroborated save for recent scholarly speculation that the original victims of the solemnizing ritual were human. In this case, *xiangli* could have acquired its association with funerary rite.

There is one other, though tenuous, link unremarked by Hu. It involves Kongzi, or, rather, popular myths associated with him that would permit us to identify him as a ritual practitioner of *sangli*; it leads us along a shamanic trail. In numerous Warring States and Han texts it is said that Kongzi had the face of a dog, and there is a connection between *sangli* and dog-mask-bearing *fangxiangshi* (exorcists, sorcerers). It is not always clear from these received texts whether Kongzi possessed canine features or that his face resembled the kind of canine mask worn by *fangxiangshi* in funeral processions and during the yearly *danuo*, or great exorcism.[59]

The earliest written account is probably that of the *Xunzi*, where Kongzi's face is described as looking like the mask of an exorcist, *qi*. Traditional descriptions of the mask explain that it was made of bearskin and, following the *Shuowen* definition, was used "to expel pestilence." The *Hanshi waizhuan* also has an account of Kongzi's appearance, clearly intended as an augury of his sagehood, that reiterates the description in the *Xunzi*. From the mouth of Gubu Ziqing, a well-known physiognomist, and therefore probably an exorcist, comes a fantastic description that brings together the distorted features of King Yan of Xu, the Duke of Zhou, Yao, Shun, Yu, and Gaoyao from their physiognomies as described in *Xunzi*, book 5. The text reads:

> Gubu Ziqing also said, "My disciples, pull my chariot aside, a sage approaches." Kongzi descended and walked. Gubu Ziqing came and met him, for fifty paces observing him. Then he followed behind him for fifty paces, staring. He turned to Zigong and said, "Who is this man?" Zigong said, "He is my teacher. His name is Kong Qiu of Lu." Gubu Ziqing said, "So, this is Kong Qiu of Lu. I have indeed heard of him." Zigong said, "What do you think of my teacher?" Gubu Ziqing said, "He has the forehead of Yao, and the eyes of Shun, the neck of Yu, and the beak nose of Gaoyao. Seen from the front, he is so complete that he resembles those who possess territory. Seen from the back, he has high shoulders and a weak back. Zigong sighed. Gubu Ziqing said, "What concerns you?" Because of his sunken face he is not hated, nor is he employed for his bullrush-like mouth. Seen from a distance, he seems unsettled just like a dog in a house of mourning.[60]

From being described as having a face like the dog-faced mask of an exorcist, Kongzi is now described as a dog in a house of mourning, the implication being that the dog, like the mourners, is saddened, but not so much for the deceased as for all the attention that is directed at the deceased and not at it.[61] Texts in which these bizarre descriptions appear are identifiable as Ruist, and their accounts are all quite fabulous. I concur with D. C. Lau that such a trope of the marvelous is employed in these texts to affirm unequivocally Kongzi's true nature as sage. Though this hardly makes a convincing case for a native association between *xiangli* and *sangli*, it is no less likely than the explanation put forward by Hu Shi, who also believed that *xiangli* was a Shang office for which only descendants of these religious functionaries were eligible. So, inasmuch as his claim is legitimate, the conclusion is ineluctable: since Kongzi was a *xiangli*, we have more evidence that he was of Shang stock, a lineal descendant of the *xiangli* corps.

It is not clear how Hu intended to extrapolate about Shang practice from a post-Zhou text. We cannot easily place a group such as the *xiangli* back in the Shang unless by some principle of overinterpretation we could treat this evidence as testimony of a higher antiquity, as Hu apparently does. Such literary misprision, bolstered however slightly by Kongzi's service as a *xiang*, permits Hu Shi to construct a Shang pedigree for the office. With evidence more suggestive than conclusive, Hu reasons that under the Shang and early Zhou, these specialists were known as *ru*, in its sense of *rou* (pusillanimous).

The interpretive economy of this conception is impressive and may explain its persuasive quality for some; however, I believe this alone is not sufficient to account for the enduring scholarly assent it has commanded. Questions remain: Were *ru*, in fact, *xiangli*? And, if so, why? Hu's response in such a situation is predictable. He looks to later, less ambiguous evidence that can be drawn on to establish his point. To understand why his explanation was compelling it is necessary to reflect a bit on the analogies Hu employs, even more effectively than textual evidence, as proof of the validity of his more arguable assertions.

In fact, the three-year mourning rite (*sannian zhi sang*) was, he says, identical with, albeit a descended form of, the Shang/Yin tribe's own mortuary rite called *sangli*. The three-year mourning rite is a well-established ritual in *ru* tradition, particularly touched on by the principal and Latinized luminaries, Kongzi (Confucius) and Mengzi (Mencius).[62] Yet neither of these figures suggests that their advocacy of this practice is based upon its being a received tradition; their discourse on these matters, particularly that of Mengzi, is embedded in ritual proclamations linked to filiality, *xiao*. Nevertheless this religious practice identified with *ru*, and which Hu himself at an earlier time believed was invented by Kongzi and his following, was actually inherited from the Shang.[63] In a single lengthy sentence, Hu sums up his conclusion that *ru* may be linked to Shang by philology, attire, weak posture, and their practice of the three-year rite of mourning. With a certain degree of special pleading, he says: "The three-year mourning is the mourning rite of *ru*; however, it is not their invention; it is simply the mourning rite of the Yin tribe, just as *ru* clothing and *ru* caps are not their invention but only the Yin tribe's native clothing."[64]

And *ru* are, to Hu's satisfaction, the inheritors of what he argues is the most important of the religious rites of the Shang. Yet he adduces another link more compelling than this bit of speculation when he argues that philology as well corroborates his assertion that *ru* would inevitably vanquish those who had been victorious over the Shang in war. *Ru* were more than simply descended from the Shang. They were destined to restore it, and this was because of an obscure, "organic" link between *ru* and the Shang tribe: the two names came from the same root. Thus, in spite of their apparent collaboration, *ru* were incapable of relinquishing their allegiance to the Shang, for their loyalty was embedded in their class like a brand, in their very name. Or, at least this is what Hu attempts to convey by way of a rather strange logic, when he says:

> The name Shang arose from *gu* (trader), just as the name *ru* came from *Yinshi* (Yin Knights). These survivor *shi* [with] old clothing and old words themselves formed a unique class—theirs was a long-robed, tall-hatted, aggrieved one, and all with a refined knowledge of the rites were survivors of a vanquished nation accustomed to the "ignoring the offenses against themselves" of nonresistance.[65]

Even here as he describes the apparent uniqueness of the Yinshi, Hu's images draw us back into the Christian religion. The description of "survivor *shi*" reads more like an account of the Jesuits in their seventeenth-century native costume—long, billowing purple robes and tall black hats—than of ancient Chinese mortuary specialists, however these might appear.[66] The comparison of *ru* with Christian priests or with the first apostles is constant, an involuntary association bred, we can only presume, by the uncanny similarity of the two groups in Hu Shi's mind. Both form and content, however, are similar, for it is Christ's teachings on pacifist resistance, returning good for evil, and not Laozi's recommendation of nonpurposive action, *wuwei*, that is used to convey the attitude of *ru*.[67]

The procedure involved in this extended comparison is best likened to masonry, as Hu adds one brick at a time to a growing edifice of argument, the mortar of the construction made of the subtle analogies he draws from Western intellectual and religious tradition. Having just set the bricks of his interpretation of the life of *ru* "under a very difficult state of affairs," he begins in this instance to lay the mortar of another level of comparison as his thought again segues into early Christianity.

Ru were the living exemplars of the religious core of a proud but defeated tribe, and they were ritual instructors to the newly risen, the masters of a world in which martial imperatives governed society. Not only were they survivors of a vanquished nation, their very learning, Hu asserts, was constituted out of a semiotics of remembrance that he interprets as the epiphenomenon of a philosophy of nonviolent resistance. Accordingly, the difference of *ru* robes and headdresses, so manifest in the eyes of their subsequent Warring States contemporaries,[68] was for their wearers a badge of honor, physical evidence of their resistance to the cultural assimilation of the Zhou. The weakness and the femininity of their appearance, like their strange clothing, was a conscious form of symbolic opposition waged by the survivor against the martially superior Zhou conquerors. *Ru*, meaning "weakness" or "weakling," was then a term of derogation in Zhou society that stigmatized this surviving class of the Shang. However, as Hu describes them, *ru* aggressively repossessed this insult as a strident criticism of the warlike culture within which they were subsumed.[69]

In this reading of *ru* distinctiveness one can recognize, I think, something more than the persistent conceptual influence of Christianity. One can see Hu Shi's former appeal to his own generation to adopt extreme individualism in defense against society's inherent autocratic tendencies such as he made in 1918 in his essay on the individualist philosophy of Henrik Ibsen.[70] The aggressive individualism, even eccentricity, of *ru* grew from the courage and self-sacrifice of reverently honoring a tradition threatened with daily extinction. The inspiration for his description of *ru* under Zhou overlordship could just as well have come from Hu's days as an intellectual firebrand as from his former life as a Christian.[71] They were, in this particular respect, reinforcing.

But, there were shades here, too, of Christ's oft-quoted, but frequently misunderstood remarks about turning the other cheek in his Sermon on the Mount, where the apparent victim (or collaborator) is in fact an aggressor who renders violence farcical by "dwarfing the demands of the wicked with the sheer volume of his compliance."[72] The logic of the sermon must have been transparent to Hu Shi when he first studied it, and no doubt compelling in an era when China was again threatened by foreign conquest and its national politics had turned violent. Clearly Christ's words on the moral integrity of voluminous defiance were part of his intellectual store.

It is difficult to say whether this characterization of *ru* as Zhou slaves and imminent victors derived from the famous parable or if the situation that Hu Shi constructed from ancient texts of *ru*'s proud enslavement naturally drew comparison with Jesus's instruction in nonviolent resistance. The inspiration for this depiction can only be speculated on, not confirmed, yet as Hu advanced his argument for the genuine antiquity of *ru* attire and religious practice, Christianity was not far from his thoughts. Indeed, it is near at hand as Hu notes in one of his many summaries of *ru* character: "Weak compliance was one surviving custom nurtured vigorously by the Yin people under the conditions of being a vanquished nation. [When] compared with the non-resistance teaching of the Christian religion which comes from Jesus of the vanquished nation of the Jewish tribe, it seems there are similar historical causes."[73]

The analogy made here was not merely heuristic; Hu was deeply committed to the philosophy of nonresistance that he believed emerged from Jewish theology under duress. Given the inexorable expansion of Japanese militarism and the ceaseless inefficacy of the Guomindang as the governing national party, it is not difficult to understand how centuries or even millennia could be leapfrogged in a gust of sympathy blown up by the emotional symmetry of the Jews, with their nonresistance, and the Chinese, with Hu and his pacifism. Writing just over a year after he finished "Shuo ru," Hu made a remarkable confession that revealed the extent to which native conceptual vocabulary and foreign doctrine were inextricably intertwined:

> However, in Judaism there is a curious doctrine that encourages people to "love your enemy." For twenty-five years, I have believed profoundly in this Jewish doctrine. Nonetheless, I am ashamed that my belief in *dao* is not adequately sincere and that my faith in *dao* is not sufficiently firm. In recent months, I have had doubts about whether this doctrine is really something that I, a person of ordinary flesh and blood, may adhere to for life.[74]

That Hu could so effectively link the philosophies of Jesus and Kongzi, thus, has a great deal to do with the fact that for him a Judeo-Christian ethos offered the fullest representation of his understanding of the *ruist dao*.

Nonresistance, then, was derived from the historical situation of the Jewish exile and diaspora. So with this Hu adds another historical layer to the kind of extended analogy for which he was well known, and the essay seems transported beyond reflection on the meaning of *ru* to a comparison of intellectual traditions, Western and Chinese. This particular cross-cultural comparison was drawn through the changing function of a group to whom the name *ru* was applied and who shared little with other native traditions but much with the teachings of a prophet from the Levant. Knowing as we do of the history of the origin and the consequences of the revolt brought by Christ within ancient Judaism, the scenes subsequently depicted by Hu Shi of the revolt of *ru* are easily anticipated. To this point in the argument, however, he had not yet worked out from indigenous texts of some antiquity the greater implications of this comparison. These implications are those emphasized by Wolfgang Bauer: that the Chinese shared with Western culture a messianic myth that presaged the appearance of the savior of ancient China—Kongzi.

Something else that Hu Shi revealed in this comparative moment was his conviction, so lucidly expressed in 1917, that, "when the philosophies of ancient China are reinterpreted in terms of modern philosophy and when modern philosophy is interpreted in terms of the native systems of China, then, and not until then, can Chinese philosophers and Chinese students of philosophy truly feel at ease with the new methods and instrumentalities of speculation and research."[75] So Hu, shuttling back and forth from native texts to interpretations of these texts based on Western analogies, hoped to illuminate the method and content of both cultures simultaneously, so that each might recognize itself in the other. The issue was one, as it is for us and as it was for the Jesuits, of finding common ground.

In the history of the Jews in exile, and under the yoke of the Romans, Hu found what he considered the best means of imagining the ancient cultural conflict between the Shang and the Zhou. Both the Hebrews and the Shang/ Yin were noble peoples who were defeated and enslaved and more "cultured" than their oppressors, and their oppression spawned a compensatory prophecy of deliverance in which a holy man would in righteousness slay their masters. In defense of his repeated assertion that the Jews and the Shang were kindred ancient tribal spirits who longed for freedom, Hu Shi quotes the Book of Isaiah where, alluding to David, God says to the Israelites, "Behold, I have given him for a witness to the people, a leader and commander to the people."[76] This establishes the context that Hu Shi declares for a prophecy of inevitable salvation, God's words here indicating that the Jews would be blessed with a leader. Without figurative period or comma, Hu follows this quotation immediately with another citation from the Book of Isaiah: "And he said, It is a light thing that thou shouldest be my servant to raise up the tribes of Jacob, and to restore the preserved of Israel: I will also give thee for a light to the Gentiles, that thou mayest be my salvation unto the end of the earth."[77]

The important place of Christianity in Hu Shi's historical imagination of Chinese antiquity cannot be denied, and his effortless recourse to it as a symbolic fund demonstrated that as the Jesuit missionaries had glossed Chinese classical texts by instinctual reference to the Gospels, so too did he interpret China's past. In this instance the Book of Isaiah was used not only to define the condition of the Jews in enslavement but also to set forth the lineaments of their liberation by a prophet who would deliver them from oppression just as he would be an inspiration for their conquerors. This image, and for that matter the Bible's many other memorable stories, clearly enabled Hu by analogy to imagine that past and to reconstruct it as a parallel narrative of the release of ancient humanity from a self-incurred tutelage to outworn ideas and customs. In short, this is what Jesus as renascent Hebrew and Kongzi as renascent Yin represented to him. Both the Jews and the Shang prayed for deliverance from their overlords even as they served them, but until the arrival of Jesus and Kongzi their ideas of redemption were only, in Hu's words, "daydreams."

Ru were, as he portrayed them, the principal agents of cultural assimilation, priests to their people, teachers to the Zhou, and in this way the forgers of a new hybrid Chinese civilization, familiar to him and to us as *huaxia.* Out of this context of tribal warfare and enslavement, just as with the Jews, conditions for prophecy were created. Assimilation was promoted as a consequence of the new role *ru* assumed under the Zhou; however, the consolidation of this fusion of the two cultures never came about completely and the legacy of this failure was bred into the bone of ancient mythology. An elliptical record of a pathology produced by this cultural conflict was preserved by subsequent generations of Shang people living under the Zhou, and was to be found in the *Yijing* and the *Shang shu*.

Intimations of Universal Prophecy
in Ancient Chinese Texts

The text to which Hu Shi turned by instinct to disclose the meaning of native systems of thought, particularly *ru*, was the *Zhou yi*, or *Yijing* (Classic of Changes). From this text it was possible to learn of the life of *ru* in the time after the Zhou conquest but before the birth of Kongzi.[78] The reason for this, Hu says, is that "the so-called *Zhou yi* [*Yijing*] was originally a kind of divinatory text of the Yin tribe."[79] Furthermore, when one reads the text of the *Zhou yi*, particularly that of a hexagram such as *xu*, one can feel the anxiety and dread of a people oppressed, and this angst is additional proof of Shang authorship during the years following the conquest. Given that Zhang Binglin's assertion that the single character *xu* was the earliest written form or the earliest pronunciation of *ru*, it was logical to look, Hu Shi believed, at the fifth hexagram, *xu*, for information concerning the life of the ritual core of this same name before the Spring and Autumn period. What Hu finds in the commentary on this hexagram is more a clue about the prophecy of retaliation and tribal redemption alluded to in his comparisons with Christianity than it is a clue to the former existence of *ru*.

Hu repeats that *ru* are a group in waiting, and while waiting they pass the time following "the path of drinking and eating," "yinshi zhi dao," unable to move forward because of danger. The six lines, broken or unbroken, that make up the hexagram are said to characterize *ru* who in biding their time for a later propitious moment simply "guo rizi," "pass the days" as the saying goes, by doing only what is necessary to survive—drinking and eating. Hu quotes in full the gnomic text of each line of the hexagram to bring home his point that what is described by them is "very much like *ru* after the subjugation of the Yin/Shang tribe":

Beginning nine: Waiting on the periphery. It furthers one to abide in what endures. No blame.

Nine in the second place: Waiting on sand. There are few words; but in the end there is good fortune.

Nine in the third place: Waiting in the mud. The enemy is brought on.

Six in the fourth place: Waiting in blood. Leave your pit.

Nine in the fifth place: Waiting on wine and food. Persevering is favorable.

Six at the top: Enter [into the] pit. Three uninvited guests arrive. Respect them. In the end there is good fortune.[80]

Using the six lines of the hexagram, Hu shows that "this sort of person," in other words, one whose situation is symbolized by the hexagram, is one who is in great difficulty, with danger lying in the future. But by persevering rather than forging ahead, peril is averted and adverse fate is reversed.

Xu on the periphery is a person in the wilds who has lost his position (i.e., the ritual attendants of the Shang who have become the *jiaoshi*, missionaries to the Zhou), who has no choice but to preserve himself on the margins. *Xu* on sand cannot stand firmly, so it is said that he is uneasy at standing in the middle, meaning the insecurity that results from the conflicting roles of priest to the Shang, teacher to the Zhou. *Xu* in mud has fallen into danger; if he is assaulted but is careful and respectful, he will not necessarily be defeated. *Xu* in blood is the image of conflict. In this situation, he struggles listlessly, so it is best to come out timidly from his refuge and submit to the other. *Xu* in wine and food is simply having food to eat, and this is the most appropriate position from which he may return to his cave; even if trouble persists he can dispatch it by maintaining a respectful attitude. "*Xu*," Hu reiterates, "is the image of waiting patiently; he is necessarily able to be forebearing in waiting for the proper time. The time arrives, other people have patiently awaited him; they are like *xu*; he indeed has food to eat."[81]

Hu reads the *Yijing* text as a script for action, as well as a divinatory document, an oracle for the timeliness of response; thus it serves two purposes in his interpretation. The first is to confirm the antiquity of *ru*, or *xu*, reconstructing their life from the hexagram with which the term has a homophonic relationship. The second is to put forward an unannounced prophecy, *yuyan*, that will offer an explanation of their waiting. The word "prophecy" is not mine but Hu Shi's, and with this reading of the hexagram *xu* we have intimations of such prophecy. What we discover in the next layer of argument is that it is Kongzi and what Hu will call his followers, *xinru*, the "new *ru*," whose arrival is prophesied in ancient texts, just as the sacrifice of Isaac by Abraham figuratively anticipates the crucifixion of Christ.[82]

Ru bide their time as ritual specialists, surviving on their wits as *zhu* (invokers) or as the directors of funerals, offering instruction in the proper ritual choreography of burial and mourning. The image thus constructed owes much more to the common criticisms of *ru* from later Warring States texts such as the *Mozi* and the *Zhuangzi* where their excessive punctiliousness in funerary rite is either denigrated or lampooned. In a clever reworking of these texts, Hu offers the evidence they provide of *ru* involvement in piacular rites to show that they were indeed passing their days as funeral directors, merely going through the motions. He suggests further that it was

Mozi's more fervent commitment to the older religious aspects of these rites, their effective properties of ancestral communication as opposed to their aesthetic formalism, that is at the root of his harsh criticism.[83] Thus he contextualizes many remarks in oppositional texts of the Warring States about the dubious merit of *ru* service at funerals, but in a fashion that historicizes this role as a vestige while providing a larger chronology against which we might make sense of these criticisms.

Five hundred years following the Zhou conquest, *sangli* (mourning rites) possess merely aesthetic significance, and therefore their practitioners are similarly eviscerated. They are no longer critical to the administration of politics. Ancestors are simply less present, and thus this rite to which the *ru* were hereditarily bound has become like *ru* themselves a vestigial survivor. Continued devotion to the proper ritual forms in observing such rites as was common among *ru* of Mozi's and Zhuangzi's day was perceived consequently and correctly, Hu would say, as hypocrisy.[84] However, even as a vestige, the ancient organic links of *ru* to the Shang would prove, like the summary judgment of the fifth hexagram, a means of overcoming danger and affliction for good fortune. The argument again turns to prophecy, although it is increasingly anchored to Kongzi, not by Hu Shi but by the desperately hopeful Shang survivors remaining in the eastern states.

All the emphasis on the religion of Shang tribal culture and thus on *ru* as the surviving bearers of the specialized knowledge of its otherworldly ancestral religion creates an interpretive mood for a transformation of this ancient culture to a "modern" this-worldly social sanction. My use here of Weberian language to describe this aspect of Hu Shi's analysis is deliberate, for I believe it most appropriate to an understanding of the kind of global meditation on the transition from religious to secular forms of life that Hu Shi was considering by way of this reflection on *ru*.

Against contemporaries like Liang Shuming (1893–1986), who propagated a theory of China's historicocultural distinctiveness grounded in its unique intuitive rather than rational apprehension of the world, Hu was prepared to argue that Western and Chinese antiquities were equally religious and that the history of both civilizations had been shaped by a universal dialectic of secular and religious forces.[85] Although "Shuo ru" was written over a decade after the initial flurry of intellectual debate concerning *kexue* and *rensheng guan* (science and view of life) in 1923, it is perhaps a most effective rejoinder to the spiritualist cultural conservatives Hu opposed in these discussions. Their vision of a China that affirmed its global cultural significance through appeal to an "accommodationist" mindset that could facilitate a third path in the material development of a civilization, neither world-renouncing like the Hindu, nor world-destroying like the Western, did not in fact, according to Hu, redeem China. As Hu saw it, these ideas simply perpetuated the already entrenched Western judgment of China's inscrutable and thus insignificant character. In other words, rather than elevating China to world historical significance, the philosophy of *rensheng guan* enthusiasts only marginalized it, at their worst providing indigenous testimony in support of a continuation of chinoiserie. Writing in 1931, Hu summed up his philosophical differences with cultural conservatives and at the same time offered a glimpse of the reasoning that lay behind his construction of an originary fable of *ru*:

> It has been said that the Chinese people are the least religious among the civilized races, and that Chinese philosophy has been most free from the domination of religious influences. Both of these observations are not true in the light of history. A study of history will convince us that the Chinese people were capable of highly religious emotions. . . . Chinese philosophy has always been so much conditioned by the religious development of the different periods that the history of Chinese thought cannot be properly understood without being studied together with that of the Chinese religions. If our people today do not appear as religious as the other races of the world, it is only because our thinkers, our Voltaires, and our Huxleys had long ago fought hard against the forces of religion. And if China has so far failed to achieve a truly humanistic civilization, it is only because the rationalistic and humanistic tendencies of Chinese thought had been frustrated more than once by the too great powers of religion.[86]

If Hu intended to set the record straight on this issue, then "Shuo ru" may be taken as a well-researched defense of this position. In the dialectic of the religious and secular, Hu placed *ru* and Kongzi as forces aimed at the transvaluation of the mantic religious values of the Shang. By "religion" Hu meant devotion to ancestor worship, sacrifice, invocation, and divination. The lineaments of Hu's secularization thesis are evident in the summary of his argument that precedes his interpretation of Kongzi as "misaiya," a messiah of his vanquished ancestral tribe who rises from the ashes of their cultural disgrace as the harbinger of a new age:

> *Ru* were the missionaries of the ritual religion of the Yin tribe. Under this very difficult state of affairs, they continued preserving the canonical corpus of the Yin people's religion, and continued wearing the clothing and headdress of the Yin people. They were the missionaries of the Yin people. Over six to seven hundred years, they metamorphosed little by little into the religious instructors of a great number of people. Their occupations were still regulating mourning, assisting at the rites, and tutoring; however, their ritual religious teachings had already gradually entered into the ruling class, their disciples already had disciples from

the noble families of Zhou and Lu. Their talents constituted the broad meaning of *ru*. *Ru* was an ancient religious instructor [and] outside of regulating mourning and assisting at the rites, they still performed other religious obligations.[87]

To understand what made China special required that its culture be placed on the same footing with that culture, which had swiftly and aggressively commanded the terms on which cultures could be appraised. In this context China was in step with the rest of the world and yet retained its specialness, the case of Kongzi and his new *ru* demonstrating this brilliantly.

From this point Hu's argument becomes a little more complex and requires the reader to consider simultaneously two independent historical phenomena. First, we must pay attention to the changing functional significance of *ru*, specifically that six centuries after the initial conquest of the Shang in 1046 B.C.E. these priests had become pedagogues and, as such, sold their purely formal knowledge of the rites to the Zhou as a means of survival. This is why they were weak and listless: because in merely preserving the formality of such rites they were constantly reminded of their failure to genuinely uphold the spirit of their people. They were also weak because, just as Zhang Binglin had pointed out in his criticism of the new *ru* of the Han, they were no longer actively engaged with their tribe but were technicians of knowledge whose expertise presumably derived from traditional transmission but in fact was acquired by and protected in the arts of reading and writing. The new *ru* of Kongzi, as they are called by Hu Shi, are the revitalizers of this weak tradition, and Kongzi himself was "the leader of *ru* renaissance." Following his novel teachings about nurturing one's moral sense in an immoral world through *ren* (humaneness), the meaning of *ru* was transformed. Weakness was replaced by vision and fortitude, as men from Kongzi's class gained political prominence later in their service as principal advisers to the competing satrapies of the central states (*Zhongguo*).

This analysis greatly resembles what some have termed Max Weber's theory of the "routinization of charisma," from his general study of the sociology of religion, and is in step with his notion of "die Entzauberung der Welt," "the disenchantment of the world," as outlined in the latter sections of *The Protestant Ethic*.[88] This was no coincidence, I think, for by the time of Weber's death in 1920, the Chinese were avidly engaged in reflection on rationalization and the particular form it would take in their country. Weber's account of the rise of intellectualism in Europe, in which original priestly figures whose power grew from charisma gradually trade magic for knowledge in the civilizing process, was parallel to Hu Shi's theory of the historical development of *ru*. The only distinction between them was the extent to which Weber's theory was conducive to broad application. Even more than Weber,

Hu considered institutional rationalization to be a universal phenomenon, insisting that secularization was a path of life inevitably walked by all peoples, albeit at varying speeds and usually with advantageous consequences.[89]

A second parallel aspect of the argument has to do with the transmission among the conquest's survivors of a desperate hope, which first crystallized as a prophecy of deliverance from Zhou oppression and the recovery of their splendid tribal dominance. Through successive attempts in the first few centuries of their enslavement, the prophecy was not realized, but this failure generated a presumption among the Shang survivors that "every five hundred years a sage inevitably appears" (wubai nian you shengren zhi xing). There was no more confirmation of this presumption than there was realization of the earlier prophecy, and so the survivors waited yet never abandoned what soon became an augury of universal salvation. It is in the context of these unrealized prophecies and vainly preserved hope that Kongzi appeared. Fortuitously, his arrival coincided with several decades of nativist Shang revival, promoted in the state of Lu by Xiang Gong (r. 573–542 B.C.E.), who was especially conscious of the fact that he was living in the fifth century after his people's defeat.[90]

It is very important that we maintain a sense of both of these aspects as we retrace the messianic interpretation Hu Shi lifts out from his twin sources: his reading of the *Shang shu* and his rather clear knowledge of the history of Christianity. Recent scholars, such as Wolfgang Bauer, not recognizing the two levels on which the analysis operates, misread Hu's interpretation and consequently take Kongzi as the religious equivalent, in Chinese history, of Christ.[91] Such a misreading would, of course, be good news for advocates of Confucianity like Kang Youwei, but it is only a misunderstanding, perhaps bred from the hope that on this common identity the foreign interpreter could enter the foreign country of Chinese culture.

The two situations are also analogous in the changes that occurred in the original prophecies of deliverance anxiously held by the Jews and the Shang. Hu Shi points out that both Kongzi and Christ possessed a new vision not easily reconciled with the conventional religious themes familiar to the people from whom they were descended. More important, however, was the fact that the Jewish and the Shang conceptions of the messiah were originally visions of a renaissance hero, in the sense of a full political restoration of these two tribes to their former positions of dominance.[92] The language of the prophecy changed for both the Hebrews and the Shang so that after several centuries it had been transformed into an apocalyptic vision of world renewal. The difference in the early and the later prophecies was profound, Hu Shi notes, and suggests that this expressed oppressed peoples' intensified hopes for liberation from their enslavement, the Shang no less than the Hebrews.

With the use of this analogical construct of prophecy, Hu directs us to consider the conjecture that the Shang anticipated the coming of a tribal hero who would slay their adversaries and deliver them from oppression. The prefigurative structure of this strange wisdom was built out of Christian revelation and the ode "Xuan niao" (The Black Bird), from the *Shi jing*,[93] so jealously guarded by the Shang during their bondage. Hu believes the prophecy is found in the legend of the Ascendant's (*tian*) command to the black bird to give birth to the Shang:

> The Ascendant commanded the black bird,
> To descend and give birth to Shang.
> [His descendants] dwelt in the land of Yin, and became great.
> [Then] long ago God appointed the martial Tang
> To regulate the boundaries throughout the four quarters.
>
> [In those] quarters he appointed princes,
> And grandly possessed the nine regions [of the kingdom].
> The first sovereign of Shang
> Received the appointment without any element of instability in it,
> And it is [now] held by the descendant of Wuding.
>
> The descendant of Wuding
> Is a martial king, equal to every emergency.
> Ten princes, [who came] with their dragon-emblazoned banners,
> Bear the large dishes of millet.
>
> The royal domain of a thousand *li*
> Is where the people rest;
> But there commence the boundaries that reach to the four seas.
>
> From the four seas they come [to our sacrifices];
> They come in multitudes;—
> King has the He for its outer border.
> That Yin should have received the appointment [of the Ascendant] was
> entirely right;—
> [Its sovereign] sustains all its dignities.[94]

The general import of this ode is unclear, in fact puzzling. What we do know for certain is that the black bird has always symbolized the Shang in ancient mythology even in representations from early imperial times.[95] The Shang king Wuding's existence has been attested to in the oracle bone inscriptions; indeed, a great number of the inscriptions analyzed so far are concerned with Wuding, his ancestors, his consort, and events that transpired in the time in which he was regarded as *yu yi ren* (I, the one man).[96] In his translation of this particular ode, Bernhard Karlgren takes Tang, the founder of the Shang, as the martial king and identifies the descendant of the martial king as none other than Wuding.[97]

· According to Hu Shi, the exact identity of the martial king remains an issue of some dispute, and consequently it is conceivable that this mythological script could be worked for a new significance, even a millenarian one. In addition, the received text is grammatically unspecified as to tense, so it is possible that the martial king who extended the borders of the Shang to the "four seas" had already done so. Hence the ode was just as likely an ancestral invocation, perhaps addressed directly to this martial figure in the form of praise, the invokers representing themselves as descendants of Wuding.[98] However, Hu Shi suggests that the expression "Wuding sunzi" (the descendant(s) of Wuding) is a way of referring not to the subsequent generations of lineal Shang descendants, but to a monumental hero of the Shang who has yet to appear. For Hu, the tense of the poem is decidedly future.[99]

For centuries the "hero of the Shang tribe's restoration" (Yin minzu de zhongxing yingxiong) was anticipated—but no great warrior, no chariots, and no dragon banners were ever seen. Xiang Gong's dream of Yin/Shang restoration was extinguished, the result being a deliberate transmogrification of the original prophecy, with the Shang survivors of the Eastern Kingdoms longing for the advent of a savior:

> Therefore their prophecy of a tribal hero gradually changed into a prophecy of a sage who would save the world. The *Zuo zhuan* records Meng Xizi summoning his minister on the verge of death and saying: "I have heard that there has arisen one of vast [wisdom] named Kong Qiu [Kongzi] who is the descendant of a sage who was killed at Song."[100]

Thus just as the Hebrews remade their prophecy as a consequence of its failure, the Shang transformed the prophecy of their tribal hero into the prophecy of a sage who would come to save the world. In the words of a certain Zang Sunhe to Meng Xizi: "If a sage-like man of illuminating *de* [power] is not distinguished in his time, then from among his posterity there will arise someone of vast wisdom."[101] "This is now to be confirmed in Kong Qiu," reasons Meng, and Hu Shi concurs that the patriarch's last wish for his sons, Yue and Heji, demonstrates that in the minds of the ruling class of the state of Lu (i.e., *ru*) Kongzi was the sage whose arrival had been prophesied.

Messianism, Cultural Renaissance, and the Iconoclasm of Kongzi

From a different direction, we have come full circle in the consideration of the religious invention "Confucianism" begun in part 1 of this book. Hu

Shi, by equating a hero of cultural restoration and especially a *shengren* (sage) with the Christian messiah, returns us, in a sense, to the Jesuits and seventeenth-century debates within their order about Confucius's status as *sapientissimo* or *santo* ("wise man" or "saint"). One might say that Hu resolved the debate in favor of saintliness over wisdom and thus, in his own way, upheld a sincere conviction of Ricci and the early accommodationists. It is the insider, though, and not the foreign Jesuits, who tells us of Kongzi's Christlike significance, thus placing native Chinese religion on an equal footing with Christian. It appears as if the Chinese were capable of generating their own Confucian/Christian synthesis.

There are noteworthy differences, however. The Jesuits sought to elevate China to world historical significance on the basis of its culture and religion, first because its culture was so admirable and so similar to their own. Secondly, the significance of the indigenous religion of "la legge de' letterati" derived from its comparability with the ethnic religion of the Greeks and with certain practices of the Jesuits themselves. Furthermore, the religion based upon the teachings of Confucius, like the simpler ethnic religions, was considered propaedeutic to the genuine higher religion of Christianity.

From Hu Shi's direction, however, Kongzi did not prophesy the arrival of Christ nor did he prefigure the Jesuits' teaching among the Chinese. China stood on level ground with the West, on the basis of a remarkable comparability in the development of its historic civilization with Judeo-Christian civilization. In other words, as Hu reconstructed the histories of China and the West, they had run along a parallel trajectory since the late Bronze Age, and Kongzi and Jesus Christ were the respective representatives of a five- to six-hundred-year historical trend away from archaic religion.[102]

And yet, just as Hu Shi seems to join the Jesuits from a reverse direction, he steps back. He resists the impulse, which for them was creed, to conclude that Kongzi is a messiah. In his own day, Kongzi must have been seen as such, given Meng Xizi's final words to his sons. Furthermore, Hu points out that, in several passages in the *Lunyu*, Kongzi himself appears to concur with this popular mythology. Mengzi, likewise a man from Lu, carried with him the prophecy of the inevitable arrival of a sage and reworked the mythology so that Kongzi appeared five centuries following the rule of Wen Wang, the founder of the Zhou. There is no doubt that Kongzi was effectively appropriated as the wished-for apocalyptic figure of the mythology of Yin survivors. It is also true that this mythology lived far beyond Kongzi and was even passed beyond Mengzi to the *ru* erudites of the Han dynasty. It is Hu Shi's contention, nonetheless, that Kongzi was *not* a messiah.

He is at pains to point out that the meaning of Kongzi and of *ru* was manufactured in antiquity; it was reworked in response to a particular historical situation and made into a narrative of desire. Kongzi's great contribution, according to Hu, was that of a new ethos in which ritual was exalted as a moral structure of relations among the living and not the dead. *Ren* (humaneness) was the ideal of this new ethos and was the philosophical basis for a renaissance of *ru*. Yet, Kongzi's constant appeal to ritual and his emphasis on the proper prosecution of mortuary rites was read as an appeal to the ancient ancestral rites of his own tribal people in his capacity as a descendant of its ruling priestly class. Thus, he was *recognized* as a messiah by the later generations of conquest survivors. In this way his radical reform of *ru* in function and self-conception was explained away as an assertive continuation of ancient Shang practice.

We might say there are, then, two images of Kongzi and his fellowship here, one constructed by Hu out of received texts, and the other constituted in the post-Zhou out of fragments of a myth of cultural redemption and retold by Hu. It is Hu Shi's sophisticated theoretical claim that the popular conception of Kongzi as a messiah is the result of a symbolic abduction of Kongzi into a preexistent myth of retaliation and redemption. As Hu sees it, this is the root of Kongzi's transcendental significance, and consequently, it is from this immensely productive misappropriation that Kongzi is to be seen, like Christ, as a messiah. In its suggestion that there is neither a natural nor a necessary relationship between the historical Kongzi and his new *ru* and the common mythology of him as sage, or messiah, this argument is similar to that put forward by Max Weber about the dialectical relations between capitalism and Puritanism. The ancient myth that appropriated Kongzi as messiah is an example of what Weber called "an attitude of mind," which happened to find its most suitable expression in the historical fact of Kongzi and his teaching. The myth and the man are independent phenomena, but they were fused by hopeful Shang tribesmen anxious to acquire a hold once again on their coveted homeland, the Zhongyuan. It was in this manner that the meaning of Kongzi and *ru* became ideological.

Hu pays homage, almost fervently, to the received adventist myth of Kongzi the visionary, the one reworked so brilliantly and tirelessly by Kang Youwei on the analogy of the Buddhist bodhisattva. At the same time, however, in advancing such an analysis, Hu actually demythologizes Kongzi. This act has certain repercussions for his immediate intellectual cohort—but also for us. His relegation of the messianic premise to a symbolic misappropriation of Kongzi by his own people certainly did not uphold the New Text reworking of this myth in the interest of a national religion, but we should not find this troubling. Still, the implications of this argument are unsettling for more than just the aficionados of *jinwen* messianism. By exposing the links between Kongzi's actual life and teachings and the desperate Shang mythology of deliverance as fortuitous, Hu calls into question the very validity of the imperial reconstruction of Kongzi as uncrowned king and of the recognition of his teaching as a summary of the imperium's principal values. His interpretation has the effect of loosening the sediment of the official inherited interpretation of Kongzi, *ru*, and their relations to the imperial Chinese state.

Considering that this official interpretation has greatly shaped our own perception of Kongzi and his tradition, not to mention Chinese culture itself, and has encouraged those native inclinations first shaped by the Jesuits to identify *ru* as the foundational ethic, its discrediting by Hu should be troubling. Even more troubling is the reasoning that Hu Shi employs in arguing for the untenability of the messianic reading of Kongzi. Having already established that the principal responsibility of the *ru* was the proper regulation of mourning rites and invocation of ancestors, Hu proceeds to argue that Kongzi's foundational teaching of *ren* was directed solely at the living. More than this, he shows that although Kongzi and his followers did uphold a practice that they called *sangli* (mourning rites), their understanding and practice of these rites was wholly inconsistent with the *sangli* of the Shang. The "sannian zhi sang" (three-year mourning rites) advocated by *ru* was an inherited but significantly remade version of the Shang *sangli*.

And it is in this respect that Hu accomplishes much more than the illumination of a "historicoevolutionary" outline of China's spiritual civilization by way of his novel Judeo-Christian narration of Chinese antiquity. In the last pages of "Shuo ru" he appears to invert the order of the cross-cultural comparison that governed his interpretation by first establishing the fundamental change from a religious to a social consciousness symbolized by Kongzi. He reminds the knowledgeable reader that there is but one statement attributed to Kongzi in the *Lunyu* where ancestor worship is mentioned. This is the well-known expression "Ji ru zai, ji shen ru shen zai" (Worship spirits as if they were among you). By pointing out that ancestor worship is a topic not frequently discoursed on in the *Lunyu*, Hu identifies another way in which *xianru* are not *ru* of antiquity.

Moreover, he offers up Kongzi's philosophy of ancestor worship as something radical more than new, the implications of this statement by Kongzi being, as Hu interprets it, an admission that the spirits are not in fact present. In this regard, Kongzi is describing worship as an aesthetic or theatrical presentation rather than an authentic ritual of communication with ancestors.[103] For this reason, what disciples of the sages say about mourning rites in the "Tan gong" chapter of the *Li ji* only *appears* to be the words of Shang spiritual invocation, but is actually devoid of genuine religious feeling. In these passages, the sagely followers are only performing. In a world governed more by relations among the living than between the living and the dead, such ancestral worship has become a purely aesthetic enterprise, bearing only vestiges of its former mantic power.

So how are we to understand the fact that for centuries we have believed Kongzi to be the unerring transmitter of the remnant ancient practices of China's past? Although Hu Shi does not explicitly state the reasons for this misunderstanding in the text of "Shuo ru," he did provide a perfectly suitable explanation in a letter written to a Christian friend and colleague in which Hu defended his feeling that the death of Socrates appealed to him more than the death of Jesus. In this letter, Hu Shi in effect stated the idea behind his analysis of the fortuitous conjuncture of a Shang messianic prophecy and Kongzi's individual effort to revitalize a moribund *ru* tradition by confessing: "I admit that *to the Christian* the death of Jesus does mean a great deal more than the death of Socrates. But why? Because centuries of powerful tradition have made it so."[104]

Against a background of this shift away from the ancestral complexes of the Shang and Zhou exemplified by Kongzi's teaching on *ru*, Hu portrays revolt by Christ against the Pharisees and the scribes. However, in this particular comparison, it is Kongzi and the secularization revolt of the Chinese that glosses Christ, and the association is to Hu's sensibility a natural one. Commenting upon the lack of "fit" between the historical presumption of Kongzi's transmission of the mortuary rites of the Shang and the textual evidence of his understanding of ancestor worship, Hu writes:

> This mindset is merely that of sympathizing with the emotions of a living person, and not the common idea people have of a religious attitude. Therefore when we read the ritual writings of Kongzi's disciples, we always feel [*zong juede*] that this group of esteemed sages and worthies who knew the rites is very much like the Jewish scribes [*wenshi*] and Pharisees [*falisairen*] against whom Jesus inveighed in the Gospels of the Christian religion. The Jewish scribes and Pharisees were all skilled and familiar with the ancient rites; they were all great teachers practiced at the rites; they were all *ru* of the Jewish people. Jesus was unsatisfied with them simply because they clung to the letter of the law and did not have true religious feeling. China's ancient *ru* in terms of knowledge, surpassed the religion of the multitudes, and moreover with respect to profession they could not but assist the multitudes in the carrying out of burials and mourning. Therefore they really could not have much religious emotion toward the rites of mourning and burial.[105]

The naturalness of the comparison Hu draws here by using the phrase "zong juede" (we always feel) shows just how much wider a field the imagination could work in the 1930s than in the first decade of the twentieth century. One could say it was more natural for Hu Shi to illuminate Kongzi's departure from the venerated rituals of his own people by extended analogy with Jesus Christ and the Jews, than it was for Kongzi to be explained indigenously as the sage of his people come to fulfill their prophecy of "wubai nian bi you wang zhi xing," that every five hundred years a king appears.

The two figures were functionally similar in their transvaluation of inherited traditions of worship and in their emphasis on bettering relations among the living as a means to personal fulfillment. Yet this is not simply an analogy, for Hu appears to believe that Kongzi and Jesus were part of a worldwide religious movement, the twin pillars, east and west, of what Karl Jaspers deemed the *Achsenzeit* (the Axial Age).[106] From this extended comparison implicit throughout the essay comes the explicit sense that the cultural heroes of China and the West share maximum common ground.[107]

The analogy seemed plausible in its specifics: that as Jesus had revitalized and empowered an ancient, moribund Judaism and thus was the hero and messiah of the Hebrew nation, so Kongzi, who reinvigorated the tribal rites of the Shang, was the messiah of the Chinese nation. But the analogy breaks down under closer examination, for the Jews reject Jesus as *moshiach* (Hebrew for "messiah") and his creed, which they insisted was an unprecedented interpretation of the Tanakh (their sacred scriptures).[108] In the context of Jewish theology, Jesus is not considered the redeemer of Judaic faith in a new muscular manifestation—which is the obvious assumption of Hu Shi; instead, he is the inaugurator of a strange and new faith, one that broke more ground than it shared with the teachings of the Patriarchs. There is no denying that this new faith was a Jewish heresy, later manufactured by Paul into a new orthodoxy that superseded its ancestral religion for its converts.

From the Christian perspective, as well, we can intuit an understanding of Jesus's work as a significant, even repudiating, departure from the agnatically transmitted religion of Moses' Pentateuch. "New Testament" alone announces itself as superseding to the point of annulling the "Old Testament" of the Jews, and it is clear, furthermore, from a comparison of the Jewish Tanakh and the Christian Bible, that partisans of this new faith consciously repudiated the religion of their forebears as violent, deceitful, and inhumane.[109] Jesus certainly spoke the language of the covenant God made with his chosen people, but he was surely not the hero of the Hebraic tribes that Hu Shi imagines him to be. He was the inventor of a new unheralded religion, a subcult reaction to the dominant faith it negated yet preserved.[110] The comparison of Jesus and Kongzi as saviors of their respective peoples, who delivered them from ignominy at the hands of oppressors, appears injudicious and wrong in this light. But what I would like to suggest is that Hu's mistaken metaphor conveys something very important about Kongzi, something that is never seriously considered when we think of what the sage customarily represents. The analogy is eerily appropriate (whether or not Hu Shi would concur I cannot say) because it implies that Kongzi, like Jesus, in a spirit of restoration—what we might today term "fundamentalism"—broke away from the tradition that inspired his teaching. Both spoke an archaic or archaicized tongue, but their message and the institution by which they perpetuated it were unconventional, new, and—if I may say so—manufactured.

Kongzi may have been linked by blood to the Shang, and he may have claimed that he followed the Zhou or that he was only a transmitter, not an inventor, but he was clearly a rebel and also a man, not a messiah. In making this point and explaining the similar rebelliousness of Christ's teaching, Hu deliberately frames the significance of these teachings and of their transmitter within the interpretation of Kongzi as a man. By implication Christ, who is descended from the house of David, insists that he acts in accord with the law of Moses and says nothing that is not already said in the Scriptures, but he is also a man. He is not the king of the Jews any more than Kongzi is an uncrowned king. To make Christ just a man is more than demythologization, it is blasphemy. But by this equivalence of Kongzi and Christ on the ground of their common humanity, Hu intended to make them even more remarkable than they seemed to Chinese and Christians as gods.

I cannot help but feel that Hu's retelling of Christ's life through the record he constructed of Kongzi's was intended for an audience other than those we can presume he was addressing in his desanctification of Kongzi. In 1914, in an exchange of letters with Henry E. Jackson, a New Jersey pastor and producer of Christian tracts, Hu said: "I have greater admiration and love for Jesus if he were a man than if he were the Son of God. It would not be remarkable at all for the Son of God to act as Jesus did act. But it *was* and will always be remarkable that a *man* should have acted as Jesus did."[111] Hu was, nevertheless, no blasphemer, for in separating history from myth he actually amplified the heroism of both Kongzi and Jesus.

What was greatest in both these figures was their challenge of tradition, their deliberate diversion from the path of the ancients which was, to Hu's mind, a decision inspired by what was best in the spirit of their received culture, yet requiring the ultimate Ibsenian heroism of standing against the current of its ossified letter. And in a certain way this is how Hu imagined his own role, and the image would be repeated in his appreciation of Dai Zhen, Ibsen, Kongzi, and Christ. The tale he told of Christ and Kongzi mirrored his own self-conception, a familiar story of the individual straitjacketed by tradition. Of course this was 1934 and not 1919, so it was more difficult to imagine the circumstances that incited Hu's individualist reflex. Certain conditions, specifically the increasing likelihood of Japanese colonization of China, the political incompetence of the Guomindang, and a conservative shift in the political culture in which he moved, all contributed to Hu's considerations on *ru*; however, "Shuo ru" was actually the intellectual product of a decade of internal debate about the meaning of modern civilization. The conclusions Hu reached on this question have been adumbrated above. I will try now to make them more visible by analyzing certain features of Hu's essay in light of his own development and the political culture in relation to which Hu was again an outsider.

"Shuo Ru": Cultural Construction or Cosmopolitanism

Proceeding from the well-known and indisputable premise that "any reading of the past—however much it is controlled by the analysis of documents—is driven by a reading of current events,"[112] I close this chapter and approach the conclusion of this book wondering just how we might understand "Shuo ru" as a reading of past and present organized in relation to problems imposed by Hu Shi's contemporary situation.

The effect of reading "Shuo ru" is powerful; I am not sure if this is because of Hu's indexing of critical moments in the history of Chinese culture—the Zhou conquest, the Warring States era, and the emergence of Kongzi and the *baijia* (Hundred Families)—to the history of the Jewish exile, enslavement of the Jews by the Romans, and the appearance of Jesus, or if it is only the unsettling feeling brought on by the persuasiveness of comparisons that by instinct I believe untenable. But like it or not, by the 1930s Jesus and Kongzi were standard intellectual integers in the mathematics of Chinese calculation of their place in a modern world. I would not, however, want to place too much emphasis on the shock value of an extended comparison between Jesus and Kongzi, for Christianity and *ru* had been fellow travelers for over three hundred years in China and the Christian and Chinese prophets were joined in the Chinese imagination forty years before Hu Shi put pen to paper.

Most intriguingly, in his *Renxue* (The Natural Science of Love), the 1890s nationalist revolutionary Tan Sitong had frequent recourse to comparison of Kongzi and Jesus, believing their teachings on *ren* (which Tan understood as "love" and not "humaneness") were virtually identical. Tan, like Hu, found the Sermon on the Mount to be an especially valuable source of analogy and personal inspiration, considering Christ's words before the multitude an admirable crystallization of Kongzi's own teaching on *ren*.[113] For many, after Tan Sitong's *Renxue*, Kongzi and Jesus were conceived of as the dual symbols of an untrammeled, democratic expression of love. And even in the tracts of anti-Christian, anti-*ru* partisans of the May Fourth era, where they were the equally despised voices of regressive contradictory ethics and theology, they were often linked.[114] Hu Shi presumed that the analogy, the metaphors drawn from the Bible, and his studies of Christian history would not be lost on his fellow intellectuals; otherwise, his presentation of the evolution of *ru* would not have depended so heavily upon such Christian ideas. That he could reason in this way and be understood—and understood he was, given the immediate furor caused among his colleagues—is testimony, I think, to the considerable degree to which Christian themes had become an integral part of the Chinese intellectual infrastructure.

What I have suggested is that in this culturally focused meditation, one deliberately situated in a specific, preexistent nationalist context, Hu was making a universal point. The parallels he drew between Western and Chinese civilization on the basis of an implied messianism weren't really about religion at all; they were evidence of grand patterns of cultural processes, of explicit stages of cultural growth in world civilization. The fortuitous messianism of Kongzi and Christ were critical to this divining of larger processes of growth, but the intention, it would seem, was for Hu to settle accounts with himself and to try once again through the use of a native vocabulary to expand the referents of Chineseness. In this light, "Shuo ru" could be considered an instance of reinvigorating Chinese history by making it like Western history.

Describing Hu Shi's work in this way I invoke my teacher's teacher, Joseph Levenson, who made just this point nearly forty years ago when explaining the appeal of evolution to *jinwen* advocates working to wring the last drops of legitimacy out of Confucianism:

> Since Confucianism could neither exclude nor absorb Western ideas, since neither *t'i-yung* [tiyong] nor *chin-wen* [jinwen] could really save the Chinese *t'i* [ti, essence], then Chinese thinkers must cease to feel that equivalence with the West was staked on it. And a new possible defense for China, a new sanction for innovation, could be salvaged from the *chin-wen* doctrine. For if evolution is the way of the world, as the *chin-wen* school had taught, an ancient *t'i* is properly superseded. Men may turn, if they lose the heart to compare the values of Europe and China, to comparing their histories and see a morphological analogy between the life of China and the life of the West. These may seem to evolve with similar sequences, as the dismal stages of their pasts are succeeded by stages to a brighter future, as their bondage to intellectual orthodoxies gives way to intellectual freedom.[115]

The final sentence seems a perfectly apt characterization of the intellectual resolution of Hu Shi—and yet it is not. Hu was not engaged in an entrenched, rearguard action to defend the vestiges of Confucian respectability, as was Liang Qichao. Perhaps because they differed by one generation, Hu needed nothing of the compensatory universalism naturally generated from the *jinwen* sanction, or of the culturally narcissistic excesses of the apologist Woren (1804–1871). His comparison of cultures was, in the final analysis, not mere "morphological analogy." There was buried in the scholasticism and specificity of "Shuo ru" a universal theory of the development of civilization in its material and spiritual components. In instructive ways, Hu's account stands in contrast to those of the earlier Chinese intellectuals Woren and Zheng Guanying (1842–1923), who had claimed that all of the advances of the West were fully developed in Chinese antiquity, and Kang Youwei, who identified a progressive evolutionary logic consistent with that of the evolution of Western political institutions implied by Kongzi and first articulated by He Xiu (129–182 C.E.). Hu Shi, unconcerned with an eloquent nativist defense of Chinese culture, instead described the history of ancient Near Eastern and Chinese civilization as paradigmatic moments in the development of a "scientific and technological world culture."[116]

It is not difficult to recognize the wider significance of "Shuo ru" when its message of shared cultural and religious patterns is lifted out from the pages of the *Bulletin of the Institute of History and Philology* and placed in the context of a revivalist movement inspired by the imminence of Japanese takeover, the Westernization of the academic curriculum, and the Guomindang's renewed interest in "tradition." The context I am alluding to is the movement that began among selected Chinese academics in late 1934 to facilitate "Zhongguo benwei de wenhua jianshe" (cultural construction on a Chinese basis).[117] In an excerpt from a response Hu drafted to this call for "construction on a Chinese basis" we can see very clearly how the idiosyncratic reading of native texts in terms of a foreign religious tradition is fully intelligible in the context of a continuing debate on the meaning of Chineseness. Hu's remarks, although lengthy, deserve to be heard:

> Culture itself is conservative. . . . When two cultures come into contact, the force of competition and comparison can partially destroy the resistance and conservatism of a certain culture. . . . In this process of survival of the fittest, there is no absolutely reliable standard by which to direct the selection from the various aspects of a culture. . . . There is always a limit to violent change in the various spheres of culture, namely, that it can never completely wipe out the conservative nature of an indigenous culture. This is the "Chinese basis" the destruction of which has been feared by numerous cautious people of the past as well as the present. This indigenous basis is found in the life and habits produced by a certain indigenous environment and history. Simply stated, it is the people—all the people. This *is* the "basis." There is no danger that this basis will be destroyed. No matter how radically the material existence has changed, how much intellectual systems have been altered, and how much political systems have been transformed, the Japanese are still the Japanese and the Chinese are still the Chinese. . . . Those of us who are forward-looking should humbly accept the scientific and technological world culture and the spiritual civilization behind it. . . .

There is no doubt that in the future the crystallization of this great change will, of course, be a culture on the "Chinese basis."[118]

This grander vision was apparently lost on his academic contemporaries, as it went unremarked. There was criticism, particularly from Feng Youlan and later Guo Moruo and Qian Mu, but scholarly debate focused on Hu's tendentious interpretation of the three-year mourning rite, his reading of pre-Han texts, Kongzi's possible knowledge of the *Yijing*, and the likelihood of Laozi's having been a *ru*. Particularly striking was that critics did not take issue really with Hu Shi's insistence that the knowledge of ancient rituals displayed by Kongzi and his disciples was nothing more than pretension, nor did they seem to notice his implied argument that there was no natural, self-evident relation between Kongzi, the mythology that grew up around him, and the imperial patronage lavished on his descendants. Although recently his theory that *ru* were the marginal aristocratic survivors of the Zhou conquest has been contested,[119] none of his fellow scholars considered it untenable.

Moreover, not one of the many critics of "Shuo ru" have even remarked on the close symbolic parallels that he drew between Jesus and Kongzi, and Christianity and *ru*. In fact, one of the critics most exercised by Hu's essay, Qian Mu, appears to have been persuaded by the analogy. Some thirty years following a rebuttal of "Shuo ru" in which he reproved Hu for his inability to see that *ru* who were engaged in *sangli* were *suru*, or vulgar *ru*, and that *ru* were not all descended from the Yin, Qian could still say, "I personally feel that the role played by Confucius in China is similar to that played by Jesus in the West."[120]

When writing in the 1930s, Hu was nearing the end of a decade of reconsideration of his earlier iconoclastic rejection of Confucianism, while China was nearing the end of a decade of struggle to establish national unity. Yet, by the time he worked out his interpretation for "Shuo ru" prospects for the kind of domestic political stability requisite to the formation of democratic institutions may have been more bleak than in the heyday of the warlords. For observers of perspicacity like Hu, two other startling developments were noticed. The first, the apathetic resignation, cynicism, and existential angst of his academic colleagues grew with the increased presence of Japan on the mainland. The second and even more alarming was the realization that violence had become the principal means of effecting change in Chinese society and thus was destroyed the hope of men of Hu's temperament that China could be stewarded to democracy.

"Shuo ru" was written at this juncture, which, as it turns out, was a time when Hu had achieved an impressive reconciliation of the sometimes contradictory lessons of his dual intellectual parentage. In this piece we can see a clear outline of the resolution Hu obtained between these conflicting influences: we read his plea for cultural tolerance and learn of his faith in the salvific effects of the cultural encounter inevitable in the passage of modern civilization. To emphasize its significance for him and for us intellectually, I quote from his first, and perhaps most eloquent, formulation of the encounter of foreign and native cultures:

> This larger problem is: How can we Chinese feel at ease in this new world which at first sight appears to be so much at variance with what we have long regarded as our own civilization? For it is perfectly natural and justifiable that a nation with a glorious past and with a distinctive civilization of its own making should never feel quite at home in a new civilization, if that new civilization is looked upon as part and parcel imported from alien lands and forced upon it by external necessities of national existence. And it would surely be a great loss to mankind at large if the acceptance of this new civilization should take the form of abrupt displacement instead of organic assimilation, thereby causing the disappearance of the old civilization. The real problem, therefore, may be restated thus: How can we best assimilate modern civilization in such a manner as to make it congenial and congruous and continuous with the civilization of our own making?[121]

In "Shuo ru" Hu found the middle ground, hoped for but unstated in this book, between the new and the old civilizations. He simply recast the terms of the debate, placing them outside the heated exchanges over native *ti* (essence) and foreign *yong* (application), and identifying modern civilization as a pattern of global evolution. Thus China "with a glorious past and a distinctive civilization of its own making" and the West were collapsed into a single process of civilizational growth, the self-same identity of which was explicit in the patterned variation in the biographies of their spiritual exemplars, Kongzi and Jesus.

What was also clear about "Shuo ru" was the continued importance of "New Testament" history as an interpretive mechanism—so important, in fact, that Hu imagined the antiquity of his native land through it. The essay was almost explicitly about redemption in both the weak sense, meaning that which comes from settling accounts with your former self (as Hu did), and in the strong sense of the messianic advent. The messianic premise permitted Hu an innovative reading of Kongzi's radical significance and reveals how inseparable from the Christian was the Chinese genetic instinct for *ru*. What conditioned this messianic reading of *ru*? The near extinction of China at the hands of the Japanese contributed, to be sure. Prospective foreign adversaries again threatened China at the time of Hu's writing, adversaries who easily conformed to the implicit racial conception of Zhang Binglin's essay.

Yet this is not why Hu deliberately chose to construct his theory of the patterned change of civilizations as a supplement to Zhang Binglin's more narrow nativist considerations. Hu's personal sorting out of the national heritage was directed at expanding—or exploding—the framework of such enterprise. His universalist, cosmopolitan message of an inevitable and humane evolution of the world's two principal cultures, Chinese and Western, buried in the constricted anti-Manchu and anti-Western frame of Zhang Binglin's "Yuan ru," acted to destroy the self-imposed intellectual constraints of Chinese nationalist discourse. On the common ground of *ru*, Hu implied, China and the West had met before, and in the intervening centuries much was lost in the cultures of both. However, by way of his intertwined tales of Christian and Chinese cultural redemption, Hu proposed to do much more than recover the moment of Sino-Jesuit cultural conjuncture with which this book began. Instead, he intended to exploit the imaginative Chinese/Western commonality in *ru* for the purpose of attaining an ecumenical objective greater than theology—universal civilization. This was an intended consequence of "Shuo ru." But the significance of its universal urgings for this study of the manufacture of *ru* and Confucianism is contemporary and is discussed in the epilogue that follows.

EPILOGUE: AT CENTURY'S END—

ECUMENICAL NATIVISM AND

THE ECONOMY OF DELIGHT

Enlightenment is man's release from his self-incurred tutelage. Tutelage is man's inability to make use of his understanding without direction from another. Self-incurred is this tutelage when its cause lies not in lack of reason but in lack of resolution and courage to use it without direction from another. *Sapere aude!* "Dare to know"—that is the motto of enlightenment. . . . Laziness and cowardice are the reasons why so great a portion of mankind, after nature has long since discharged them from external direction, nevertheless remains after lifelong tutelage, and why it is so easy for others to set themselves up as their guardians.—*Immanuel Kant*

"I have got lost: I am everything that has got lost," sighs modern man. *This* modernity was our sickness: lazy peace, cowardly compromise, the whole virtuous uncleanliness of the modern Yes and No. This tolerance and languor of the heart, which "forgives" all because it "understands" all is *sirocco* for us. . . . Rather live in the ice than among the modern virtues and other south winds.—*Friedrich Nietzsche*

We have completed a four-century passage in the episodic history of an idea and the communities created through it only to find that the journey begins and ends at the same point—on native Chinese ground. We arrive, in this apparently circular transit, at the subjects of this final meditation: ecumenical (Chinese) nativism and the economy of delight.

The first term refers to the confluence of local and universal effected by Hu Shi in his historical reconstruction of *ru*. Recalling, as it does, the invention of the Jesuits as defenders of Chinese faith, this apparent oxymoron subverts the common Western presumption of the singularity and essential otherness of China and suggests that native and foreign are but tropic positions along a single cultural spectrum. I use it here to encourage a retrospective reflection, not on the compatibility of native and foreign, but on the many meanings of Chineseness.

Such reflection, it is my hope, will permit us to recognize that the figures of "China" and the "West" have served, to borrow a term from Richard Rorty, as "alleviative geometries" that in effect have continued to render the former mystical and the latter rational, but both opaque. A review of the enculturation of sixteenth-century Jesuits, Zhang Binglin's seamless weaving of the argumentative strands of Warring States texts and Spencerian evolution, and Hu Shi's declarations on behalf of a "scientific and technological world culture and the spiritual civilization behind it" should compel us to see Chinese culture as ecumenical rather than esoteric. Thus, as Zhang and Hu tirelessly contended, it is the logic of our conceptual portrait of *ru* and, most of all, "Confucianism" that prevents us from representing China's diversity.

The second term, "the economy of delight," serves to disarrange conventional assumptions and engender reflection on contemporary culture. It is an expression, borrowed from John U. Nef's *Cultural Foundations of Industrial Civilization*, that returns us to metaphors of production while emphasizing the aesthetic sources of our modernity. Nef, like Hu Shi, believed that the engine of Europe's quantitative economy of science and industry was fueled by spirituality. Indeed, in Nef's view, industrial manufacture was the quantitative offshoot of a Renaissance impulse toward human perfection, an aesthetic urge supremely evident in the artistry of the Gothic cathedral. These qualitative and quantitative economies were complementary in the sixteenth century, but with the rapid industrial development of northern Europe in the following centuries, the art of workmanship and delight in consumption was overtaken by a devotion to calculable goals, those of "labor-saving and the multiplication of output."[1] The term is also intended to imply that the meaningfulness of human endeavor cannot be measured by the rational, quantifiable calculus of objective laws or "clear and distinct ideas" alone. Instead, meaning is found in the engaged study of the rather untidy cultural and intellectual diversity of local communities that delight in the manufacture of texts and traditions. Specifically it is found in those native communities, sixteenth-century Jesuit and twentieth-century Chinese, whose delight in the manufacture of value in the name of an exemplar, Kongzi, and his tradition, ru, has had global consequences.

It may seem like a willful paradox that we should have learned so much of the diverse manifestations of ru through close philological examination of ancient Chinese in order to arrive at a modern conception of universal civilization. But if so, this paradox is a measure of the distance we must still traverse to form a properly critical self-image of our age. It is our remaining task, one that offers a critical perspective on contemporary culture while indicating a direction for the renewal of the dialogue of cultural intimacy begun by the late-sixteenth-century Chinese and Jesuits but silenced by the din of industrial civilization.

Chinese Civilization and the Economy of Delight

In early 1933 Hu Shi accepted an appointment as the Haskell Lecturer at the University of Chicago, an appointment brokered (most aptly) by the university's Department of Comparative Religion. He prepared six lectures on what he termed "The Chinese Renaissance," the controlling idea of which was China's cultural revitalization as effected through the dissemination of "the scientific and democratic civilization of the new world." The series was presented in the narrow framework of an essentialist portrait as revealed in the foreword written by A. Eustace Haydon for the published edition of the lectures in which the West was the bearer of scientific advance and China was the spiritually exceptional recipient of science. "Professor Hu," Dr. Haydon asserts, had "the background and the detached vision necessary to an evaluation of the processes of intercultural penetration at work in his native land."[2] Hu, according to Haydon, exceeded these strictures of challenge/response and subtly portrayed a culture reignited by Western ideas, which, owing to this inspiration, was capable of acquiring a "spirit of the new world" that transcended the nation and yet was indefeasibly Chinese.

Reviewing the millennial ebb and flow of cultural influence in China's history, Hu worked to portray his homeland as a collective symbolic fund, an ecology of diverse representations and thus an emblem of contemporary cosmopolitanism:

> In this way practically all of our ideas and beliefs and institutions have been freely allowed to come under the slow contact, contagion, and influence of the Western civilization. . . . If anything is retained of the old, or any of the old things are thrown overboard, both the conservation and the change have been voluntary and probably practical and reasonable. We have not concealed anything, nor have we dogmatically withheld anything from this contact and change through "long exposure" and slow permeation. In this way China has also succeeded in bringing about a cultural transformation, which, though painfully slow and piecemeal, and often lacking co-ordination and coherence, may yet culminate in solving some of our pressing and basic problems of life and culture, and achieve a new civilization not incompatible with the spirit of the new world.[3]

Notice how Hu's intellectual inclination leans away from the nation and to the "world," and so moves beyond the narrow relativist confines of Haydon's interpretive frame. The message of this gesture is that China may be conceived of as exemplary of the new civilization, its ancient sources reanimated through long exposure and sufficient to conduct the civilizations of the new world forward.

This is not the sentiment of a defensive nationalist; the prevailing emotion is delight at a new understanding of the native resourcefulness of Chinese culture and at the prospect of a world beyond nations. I would contend that the vision of global civilization developed by Hu in the darkness of China's near extinction was an emphatic expression of his discovery of an "economy of delight"—the necessary, but rarely represented constitutive force of what Hu termed "the scientific and technological world culture." A people living out the values of their day provided the spiritual medium without which industrial civilization was unsustainable. Local was sovereign, and it was the qualitative resources of local traditions of depth and diversity that alone could provide direction and dimension to a boundaryless new world culture. If the world was to be unified, it would have to occur through the stirrings of creative hearts, not through technology, or the expansion of the market.

Hu's transnational conception of civilization sounds familiar today in a "world which can no longer be contained within the limits of 'nation' and 'nation-state.'"[4] But postmodernism has made it difficult for us to accept the promise of a reasoned tolerance in Hu's scientific and technological culture, or to see the emancipatory prospects in what remains of twentieth-century China's nationalist experiment. Nor will it allow us to recognize China, or any nation for that matter, as a model for a spiritual civilization. For our culture's postmodern celebration of the diversity of texts and readings valorizes the present as emancipatory and rails against science and systematicity in favor of interpretive anarchy.

Today, as in late-seventeenth-century European amended chronologies, the West is sovereign. If we in the twentieth century are also to valorize the present, then we must do so for the reasons and prospects that exist in the present, because only in this way can we arrive at an intelligible redefinition of the "true"—one that exposes the destructive limits of the scientific-industrial form of life and makes explicit our even more ruinous, cowardly compromise with its promises of progress and the greater satisfaction of global human need. However, there is no reason to celebrate the present, where the West and China are the polar points of "globalization," the former zealously monitoring the economic growth of the latter, and the latter envying the economic and political power of the former. Our contemporary heralding of the unlimited productive possibilities of texts, authors, and trade excites the imagination and engenders thoughts of an unprecedented melding of cultures in a "New Age" civilization. Yet as the West and China draw closer in enterprise and imagination, they become more insistent on their respective distinctiveness. The West remains the world's only "superpower" and the guarantor of its human rights, while China remains the "world's longest continuous culture" and its fastest growing economy. And both are self-consciously postmodern and globalized. However, there is little—especially when placed within the context of a larger, inclusive history of China and the West—that is distinctive about this frenetic moment, as a comparison of our contemporary Western, postmodern criticism and ancient Chinese literary culture can demonstrate. I think it proper, and necessary, to revisit the plural local impulses of ancient textual communities that inspired the Jesuits' passionate defense of *zhengxue* ("true learning"), as well as the reassertion of China's economy of delight by Zhang Binglin and Hu Shi against the increasing uniformity of the twentieth century. Here we will learn of the antiquity of the postmodern and find perhaps a better model for the "diversity" of our nationless age. We go now, as Matteo Ricci did in his translations, in search of words and find not a single essence but plural meanings that envelop the present, the near and remote past, all on Chinese soil.

Chinese Antiquity, the Postmodern, and Tradition

We now know that from wherever one looks at Confucius and Confucianism, Kongzi and *ru*, one encounters a tendency toward imaginative construction, as if the stability of these entities could be measured by their potential for metamorphosis. For us in the West and for the Chinese, Confucius/Kongzi can be all things equally—one no more preposterous or wrong than the other—because it, like so many other symbols strewn willy-nilly about postmodern culture, is a fetishized historical figure delivered from any native context in which it might embody a specific range of values or sentiments.

West or East, Confucius/Kongzi's value today is socially detached, and has reference entirely within the fictions of his remakers. This essential fungibility is, of course, what accounts for his value as symbol. The symbolic promiscuity underlying Confucius's commercial success might seem especially appropriate today amid a contemporary cultural criticism that revels in the irreverent manipulation of real historical material, taking records of lived experience, literary or artistic products, and spinning them round like a wheel of fortune. Such preponderantly self-conscious "play" is one of the hallmarks of our contemporary age. In this ironic cultural interval, there are no received or organic contexts, just newly made ones. There is only the adventitious constellation of random symbolic material in the "petit récit," the "little narrative" of the reader/narrator.[5]

"Metanarratives" of the nineteenth-century historiographic kind or of the quasi-Darwinian sort that inflamed the imaginations of Zhang Binglin and others of his nationalistic bent or of the theologicohistorical one embraced by Hu Shi are unfashionable and have given way to a recognition of plural, playful profusions of individual "construction." Yet, in the multiple uses of the symbols "Confucius" and "Confucianism" we may discern a current manifestation of events three centuries previous rather than a mere symptom of postmodernism. There is a certain cultural filiation, I think, between "Confucius"'s recent omnipresence as world commodity and the symbol's earlier global popularity as emblem of reason and the symbolic promiscuity of Kongzi as trope in Chinese antiquity. We are, then, returned to native Chinese ground to locate an economy of delight that precedes postmodernism.

I have intentionally drawn the discussion of the multiple manufacture of this native and foreign symbol into the currents of contemporary culture to remind us that we, like the Jesuits or the Chinese of the preimperial age, do our interpreting in a context. By placing an academic practice next to a contemporaneous popular one, or by juxtaposing the representation of *ru* in native texts with its representation in foreign interpretive ones, I aim to defamiliarize the philosophical, religious entities Confucianism/*ru* and Confucius/Kongzi. The effort may be considered an attempt to loosen the grip of conventional understanding on our imaginations so that we can consider other ways of seeing the objects of our study and, more importantly, ourselves.

Sinology, no less than other disciplines, is threatened by the contemporary drift of cultural criticism away from fixed texts and historically authorized readings. Textual indeterminacy constitutes a threat, as I explained in the interlude, because of our indebtedness to a positivist presumption that texts are objects, not relations. The fallacy of the presumption has been demonstrated in each of the instances of *ru*'s invention. Thus, there is no need for sinologists to retreat from current scholarly trends and ply their craft as if they were in a cloister. The debates within current literary theory and cultural criticism can prove useful for scholars of China because such debates reveal, in the recesses of Chinese antiquity, the very ideas that sinologists have been reluctant to consider.

Rather than read deconstructionist distrust of meaning and its apparent linguistic nihilism as signs of the death of history, we should take these as counsels for creation. In a sense, postmodernism has released the historian from the Rankean obligation to "give the past its due." As we write history today we do so amid a paradigm shift away from commonsense history to narrative invention. The shift, of course, was effected by the tumult of postmodern criticism, which, given its investment in evanescence and fracture, could never constitute the basis for a new historical discipline. Discontinuity and rupture are the conceptual tools of this new discipline, although one wonders if this discontinuity represents a legitimate grasp of past experience, or if it is but the product of intellectual fashion, the result of a disturbance within established scholarly opinion.

Today, on a less heroic scale than in Ranke's time, the historian's craft is governed by what Maruyama Masao has described in a different context as *sakui*, "the logic of invention."[6] The field of the historian's vision is overwhelmed with images, symbols, signs, interpretations—a concatenation produced by the collapse of the regnant linearity of historical significance. Sense does not inhere in events; instead, it must be created, and once created it must eschew prescription or general application. Texts, the classics and the histories, are the stuff we work in producing sense, albeit without the assumption of exclusive authority that would make our reading "right" and another interpreter's "wrong."

For the sinologist, the text is the origin; it is the foundation by means of which, with the careful use of philology, historical reconstruction is possible. Nevertheless, as close as we may get to a "text" such as the *Shi jing* and as much as we may identify the nuclear meaning of graphs by way of etymology, we still have to read its poems or, for that matter, to determine if they are "poems" at all. Even with the commentarial companions and prefaces provided us by Mao Heng (fl. 2d century B.C.E.) and Zheng Xuan (127–200 C.E.), making sense of a text like the *Shi jing* remains a solitary endeavor. Making sense is reading, which is, in turn, invention, because our own generation of coherence is all that we have when the communities that produced the texts and their earliest readings have vanished. Harold Bloom's contention that we live in a textless universe, where there are only readings, strong or weak, is a nightmare for the sinologist.[7] It need not be. However, it is time for us to acknowledge that our hallowed conception of an ancient work, as if it were some ur text upon which all correct readings can be established, is probably less faithful to the age in which these texts were generated than Bloom's image of "textlessness." Redactions like the *Lunyu* or the *Shi jing*, for instance, are texts, but they are decidedly not primordial.

Texts in ancient China, of course, were not simply books. They were part of an intimate dialectic of self-fashioning and narration. And, because texts were lives and lives were texts, it is very difficult to treat a work as a mere reflection of social and historical processes. Instead it is important to understand that such processes occur in, or through, texts. In an age such as ours where the authority of a text and the primacy of the author have been subverted and the reader correspondingly "empowered," it may be startling to discover that Chinese of the Warring States period are at the end of the road we have been traveling in literary criticism for nearly thirty years. A postmodern questioning of text, author, and reader, while new to us at least since the decline of New Criticism, was already familiar to ancient Chinese. Moreover, Chinese familiarity with these integers of interpretation did not produce the penumbra of doubt and difficulty that has paralyzed a great deal of contemporary literary criticism, because the spirit of their textual work was not suspicion but belief.

Authorial intention never acquired in China the same primacy it did in the West, perhaps because there was no undergirding essentialist metaphysics of parousia. Parousia is the notion of the "one behind the many" upon which, Derrida holds, Plato's epistemology was based. Derrida himself is aware of this "différance" between China and the West, it would seem. The Chinese language, with what the French continue to believe is its "ideographs," is invariably used as the limiting case in the attack on the representativist conception of writing in the West. Indeed, Derrida appears to be describing texts like the *Lunyu, Mozi, Zhuangzi, Laozi,* and others when, in criticizing the age of metaphysics in the West, he says:

> The names of authors or of doctrines have here no substantial value. They indicate neither identities nor causes. It would be frivolous to think that "Descartes," "Leibniz," "Rousseau," "Hegel," etc., are the names of authors, of the authors of movements or displacements that we thus designate. The indicative value that I attribute to them is first the name of a problem.[8]

Aside from a persistently jejune understanding of the Chinese language that denies its critical phonetic aspects, the best reason for rejecting the Derridean "reading," or rather construction, of Chinese is its explicit Orientalist bias. By elevating Chinese as a civilization on the basis of its "absence" of logocentrism, Derrida succeeds in exoticizing China as a fertile fund of contrasting effects that draw out the utter incoherence of the Western intellectual tradition. Vestiges of the Enlightenment fetishization of China as the reasoned "other" of flattering contrast remain in the very structure of Derrida's philosophical sensibility.

Yet Derrida's radical contention of authorial indeterminacy is, as I say, quite conventional in the Chinese case. Indeed, it is often impossible to establish the provenance of an archaic Chinese text; not only are the authors unknown but the history of the work's production cannot be reasonably attested to. Furthermore, the earliest literary records, those of the *Shi jing* and the *Shang shu*, are not homogeneous texts but later written reconstructions of oral traditions. This obviously makes authorship or authenticity extremely problematic; however, matters are made worse for anyone seeking the words of Chinese antiquity, because the phonological reconstruction of these texts, as pointed out in chapter 3, is based upon the linguistic conventions of an era a millennium subsequent to the time in which they may have been spoken. China's classical canon, its "Great Books," were not *written* so much as *assembled* or palimpsestically transmitted. Warring States literature, especially a work like the *Lunyu*, although revered by Western and Chinese scholiasts, was not homogeneous and certainly not the product of a single author's vision.

Authorial intention (in its familiar contemporary Western sense) might be imputed to a text—the well-known case being Kongzi's purported authorship of the *Chunqiu*—and a "text" such as the *Zuo zhuan* may be nothing more than an ad hoc collection of conversational moments, anecdote, legend, dream, poetry, contracts, and aphorisms received from antiquity. Consequently, the early history of Chinese literature is littered with questionable attributions. Such imputation of authorship undoubtedly enabled the Chinese to "fix" a text amid the kind of rivalrously pluralistic stream of rhetorical practices and story traditions that ran through the culture of the Warring States. But which Chinese? Certainly the way a text was fixed by the people of Qi was not the same as the way it was understood by people in Lu, for example. In fact, over fifty years ago in his book *Rongo no kenkyū* (Studies on the *Lunyu*), Takeuchi Yoshio argued masterfully that the textual strata of the *Lunyu* reflect changes in its transmission as it passed from Lu through Qi, where there was significant variation in dialect and interpretation of the text.[9]

Kongzi allegedly authored the *Chunqiu* (a Lu text), and thus it became a text associated with the *ru*; however, it certainly was a "text" (or transmission, rather) prior to the nomination of Kongzi as its author, and it is difficult to determine his authorship from examining the elliptical notations that comprise the text. The sacerdotal character of such works did not infringe upon a reader's privilege to lend them an appreciable coherence otherwise lacking. The *Chunqiu*, for example, is an extremely terse and ambiguous text, even by Chinese admission, and one tradition of its reading asserted that the *Zuoshi* (Zuo Qiuming's commentary) was indispensable to an understanding of it. The *Chunqiu* made sense because of Zuo's reading, and so his commentary, the *Zuo zhuan*, offered ample testimony to the license of the reader and to the cultural approval of placing flesh upon the skeleton of an ancient text. Yet, Zuo Qiuming's identity and his role in assembling this commentary remain uncertain; and nonetheless, the text is attributed to him.

Reading was, *ab origine*, "empowered," to use a contemporary term. Therefore the Chinese reader (particularly one living during the Han dynasty, where, as the introduction and chapter 3 recount, significant literary capital was spent on the construction of a coherent narrative of ancient experience) had always been an actor and never the passive, credulous recipient of authorial wisdom. Instead of disestablishing a presumed primacy of the author, Chinese readers exploited the ambiguity of literary creation, establishing a dynamic shared authority of text and reader, through which invention, as opposed to disclosure, operated as the fundamental hermeneutic premise. This is why the assumptions that frame our reading of a text must now be questioned as rigorously as the text itself. It is not the text that prescribes a specific reading and in proscribing others spawns orthodoxy. Readings are the products of an interpretive community's meaningful manipulation of a work, whether that be the lives of ancestors or the lines of classic commentary.

This aleatory world of ancient texts, readers, and readings would appear to resemble our contemporary world, where, we believe, the reader is liberated, uniquely enabled to "deconstruct" the text and to cast out the urge for transcendence or authorial intention that conspires to limit the permutations of reading.[10] This "empowerment" has been trumpeted by Richard Rorty who, following Heidegger, has termed such an act of creative reading, "poetry."[11] Contemporary ascendance of the "poetry" of invention, while it follows from the disestablishment of universals and the deconstruction of systems, is (ironically for the postmodernist but happily for the sinologist) a reiteration. Our contemporary enabling of the reader and the implicit counsel to produce meaning mark our arrival at the point reached long ago by Zhuangzi, Mengzi, and the countless *zhuzi* of the Warring States. The plural, combative, and incompatible narratives produced in the rhetorical disputations of this era were the efflux of the very textual indeterminacy and playfulness celebrated by Derrida himself, and revisited by Zhang Binglin in "Yuan ru."

A similar interpretive play can be observed in the plural portraits of Kongzi from the Warring States (discussed in the introduction), but more telling evidence can be offered. For example, with a common fund of apocrypha and an array of mythical elements surrounding the culture heroes Yao, Shun, and Yu, Warring States interpreters produced various oppositional narratives of the fictive genealogy that is reproduced in a series of exchanges between Mengzi and Wan Zhang in book 5 of the *Mengzi.*[12] Whereas Mengzi insisted that the Ascendant (*tian*) conferred rule upon Shun on the recommendation of Yao, the *Han Feizi,* a slightly later text, asserts that "Shun bi Yao" (Shun forced Yao). The *guben* ("ancient text") version of the *Zhusu jinian* offers a gloss for *bi* declaring that Shun arranged for the imprisonment of Yao and usurped the throne.[13] Indeed the nature of the questions put by Wan Zhang to Mengzi concerning the transfer of rule from Yao to Shun suggests that Mengzi's account was advanced against an established lore in which there was great doubt as to the legitimacy of the inheritance.

The popular doubt surrounding the legitimacy of mythic transmission is made more evident when we consult the *Zhuangzi,* the "Robber Zhi" chapter of which reports that "Yao was unfatherly and Shun was unfilial [*bu-xiao*]."[14] The significance of these disparate readings is in their message to historians that it is not the "past" so much as the "text" that is the object of their work. If we understand this, then as workers of these received texts and story traditions, we exist in homologous relation to Zhuangzi, Mengzi, Han Feizi, and Kongzi, which, of course, was the enabling claim of Matteo Ricci's *shuwen.* While we cannot experience texts as the *zhuzi* and the Jesuits did, it is evident that they worked them as we do—as tools for the construction of meaning and community. So it is then that our contemporary justification for the universal play of symbols and contexts may be found on Chinese ground, ancient, medieval, and modern.

Hence, in this light our understanding of tradition, too, is challenged, but made more vital and probably more consistent with the way it was understood in texts such as the *Lunyu.* "Tradition" (*chuantong*) is for the Chinese a relatively recent word, having been admitted into the language by way of the Japanese "*dentō*" barely a century ago.[15] But it is important to recognize that tradition as a concept need not be taken simply as monolithic transmission. Nor is it something that, as Karl Marx wrote and Lu Xun and his modernist May Fourth cohort would have concurred, "weighs like a nightmare on the brain of the living." Tradition is, rather, a process of selection and judgment of what will be handed down and what will be received. As Roxana Waterson has eloquently remarked, tradition "really describes a process of handing down, and as such is just as dynamic and as historical as any other social process. . . . Tradition, like history, is something that is continually being recreated and remodelled in the present, even as it is represented as fixed and unchangeable."[16]

Consequently there are no passive partners in the transfer and no two generations reproduce their culture identically, even if they reenact that culture in a spirit of profoundest piety and devotion. Alasdair MacIntyre further refutes the common assumption of tradition's passivity by pointing out that "an adequate sense of tradition manifests itself in a grasp of those future possibilities which the past has made available to the present. . . . Living traditions, just because they continue a not-yet-completed narrative, confront a future whose determinate and determinable character, so far as it possesses any, derives from the past."[17] Instead of an uninterrupted transmission of value through successive generations of undeviating practices, tradition is more like a frame within which invention is contained, wherein the past serves as cultural stock that informs present invention.

This, in fact, appears to be how the collected lore of the *Lunyu* would have us believe Kongzi understood it, judging by certain passages. The *Lunyu* contains a number of statements indicating that the strength of tradition was in innovation, not in blind, inerrant transmission (if that is even possible). Speaking about music with the Music Master of Lu, Kongzi is reported to have said: "This can be known about music: it commences with playing in unison, then with improvisation it is [still] mellifluous, clear, and unbroken, [and] then it concludes."[18] The message is less cryptic in book 2, chapter 11 of the *Lunyu*, "He, who by reanimating the old can gain knowledge of the new, is fit to be a teacher." The *Zhuangzi* criticizes *ru* for being "blissfully unmindful of the fundamental unsameness of past and present,"[19] but the criticism is off the mark. This is because *ru* emphasis on *li* (rites), the self-conscious scripting of their lives in accord with verses from the *Shi jing*, and even their anachronistic dress, were the concomitants of an effort to manufacture a coherent ritual order out of a contemporary cultural detritus of which they were quite mindful.

There is for us a considerable difference, I hope, between tradition and traditionalism, and Zhuangzi fellowship criticisms to the contrary, the Kongzi of the *Lunyu* appeared to believe the bond between himself and antiquity to be established through a homology of coherence, in making order out of what is at hand under the influence of the inspiration of ancient exemplars like the Duke of Zhou. The challenge for *ru* and Kongzi, as Stephen Owen has recently argued, was to manufacture, on a small scale, a culture of antiquity from the traces (*guji*) of its former existence.[20] One was to attempt to reproduce the rites as they were practiced by the Zhou, yet what one made was clearly of one's own hand.

In another statement attributed to Kongzi, where he speaks of ancestral sacrifice, a ritual critical to the maintenance of Zhou royal authority, the "unsameness of past and present" is unceremoniously announced: "Someone inquired of ancestral sacrifice. He said, 'I do not know. Anyone who understands ancestral sacrifice could deal with all affairs in the world as easily as I place this here.' He placed his finger in the palm of his hand."[21] There were, then, acknowledged differences between past and present, not so much in the rites themselves, although Kongzi was said to have remarked that the records of previous eras were incomplete or lost,[22] but in how they were to be understood, as in this comment attributed to Kongzi in book 3: "With the rites it is better to err on the side of frugality than on the side of extravagance, and with the mourning rites, they should be dictated by grief rather than by fear."[23] The distinction between grief and fear may be a subtle one in ancestral rite, but its significance is monumental in this instance, as it conveys the distance between Kongzi and the practices of the ancients, where awe and fear were essential to the rite.

In this respect, we should note as well that while the *Shi jing* may have been used praxeologically as a script for the ethical and aesthetic styling of *ru*, its use did not militate against innovation. Indeed, virtually every one of Kongzi's citations of odes from this scripture is in support of an interpretation at odds with the grammar of the text itself, as when it says: "He said, 'Of the three hundred odes in the *Shi jing*, one phrase covers them all, that is: "no deviating thoughts [*si wuxie*]." ' "[24] *Si wuxie* is a mere portion of a phrase from a line in the fourth stanza of one of the odes, "Jiong" (Stout), where it appears to describe the gait of horses as "unswerving," but Kongzi has "interpreted" it for another purpose. Thus, innovation preserves the vitality of text so that it may serve as a source for the scripting of a community's ethos, as we observed in Trigault's interpretation of controversial passages in Ricci's *Storia* and Zhang Binglin's use of the *Mozi* to frame the concepts of genus, species, and type. This, again, is not traditionalism, and it is not the tradition of our imagination of Kongzi and *ru* as bearers of the immemorial cultural practices handed down from distant antiquity; rather, it is something like "traditionary invention."

Distant antiquity, incidentally, need not be "real" to be of value to a living transmitter, as we saw in chapters 1 and 2, where the Jesuits successfully narrated themselves as adjudicators of the true learning of Confucius. In fact, in most instances, the precedental authority of the ancients is justification, not for mere transmission, but for invention.[25] Authoritative narrative need not correspond to actual events, only imagined ones. Obviously, this does make authenticating our understanding of Chinese antiquity and of *ru* as symbolic of it rather difficult; however, in the context I have just presented this is *our* unique problem. Thus we have recourse to reconsider our own understanding of tradition, inasmuch as tradition has for the last two centuries in the West acquired a negative valence as the significant, super-seded other of modernity.[26]

The apprehension of tradition as the monolith of undeviating transmission occurs, I think, in periods of enhanced social instability during which inherited doctrines or practices are seriously questioned and, in most cases, jettisoned. This may explain why the conception is favored today in China as it was in the Warring States and the late Qing dynasty by *ru*, who, in insisting that they were transmitters, not creators, defined tradition as immemorial. Kongzi's alleged self-characterization, "shu er buzuo" (I receive but do not invent), was a claim by means of which *ru* imagined themselves the inheritors of a tradition they had in fact manufactured by taking the raw material of myth, anecdote, and imperial cosmology and working it up into a claim of descent. The Jesuit fathers of the sixteenth and seventeenth centuries followed a similar path, one that opened much to them as they deepened their native Chinese commitments. Twentieth-century Chinese nationalists, both ethnic and cultural, imagined their community in terms similar to the Jesuits and in a manner reminiscent of the *baijia* (Hundred Families) of the Warring States.

At the close of this inventory of our inherited conception, "Confucianism," it may seem that the chief consequence of this study is the placing of restrictions on our creative agency as modern interpreters and the suggestion that the language of sinological and popular discourse on China remains harnessed to a proselytizing project and a theologicoscientific schema now defunct. If this creative constraint is the principal outcome, then the present interpretative context is both ironic and unsettling. By ignoring the conceptual beginnings of our interpretation of China through Confucianism—a consequence of the term's transparency—we displace from our consciousness the human, historical sources of what we have made and continue to make through an economy of delight. In this way, we, moderns all, indulge a proclivity considered traditional—that of apprehending one's own creation as something inherited from esteemed, and more able, predecessors—and best exemplified by Kongzi's "shu er buzuo." Yet, Kongzi, no less than the Jesuit missionaries, European scientists, Zhang Binglin, Hu Shi, and ourselves, did invent, faithfully reproducing his immediate concerns in the records of his predecessors.

Invention, Value, and the Future

I come to the end of this study of texts, traditions, communities and constructions with thoughts more ethicopolitical than scholarly, oddly enough, and more contemporary than archaic. This episodic history has enabled me to recognize that I also am an inventor, despite a natural reluctance to imagine myself in what is in our culture a heroic role. Furthermore, my study of the Jesuits among the Chinese and the Chinese among themselves, all of them seeking self-definition in situations of great complexity, has made me intimately aware of my complicity in the construction of a narrative of *ru*/Confucianism and has also revealed the extent to which such endeavor is personal rather than academic.

Attempting here to put forth some summary reflection, I find I am more concerned about how I might live a morally sound life in a world where the possibilities for doing so seem to recede by the day. Saying this—admitting my contemporary place, and identifying my interests, my fears, my hopes—I believe, actually brings me much closer to the individuals whose lives and works I have analyzed in these chapters, because like them, my manufacture of the sense they made of their respective worlds through *ru* and Confucianism is conditioned by the specific demands of a contemporary situation. However, my contemporary situation is much less disposed to reasonableness and toleration, more "religiously unmusical" than theirs, and thus less inclined to accept that native and foreign as "matter-of-fact" usages are positions along one continuous cultural spectrum.

By representing in a spirit of piety the plasticity of Confucianism/*ru*, I did not mean to suggest that we must abandon what knowledge we acquired, through our conventional understanding of Confucianism, into the cultural foreignness of China. I wanted to show that when we reconcile the plural discourses common to an economy of delight with the singular representation of tradition as "Confucianism" favored by Western and Chinese modernity, we must choose either to accept the obvious or to criticize it. However, this recasting of the familiar should prompt us to seek a more cogent explanation of exemplar (Kongzi) and ethos (*ru*). In misunderstanding the Jesuits in China, we have, I believe, suffered from the tyranny of the obvious, rather than a tyranny of Jesuit reading. Unlike individuals in Chinese traditions, we have passively accepted what was bequeathed us, the obvious epic portrait of culture conflict initiated by the Jesuits and resolved only very recently by China's "embrace of capitalism." The fathers were *obviously* the forerunners of Western expansion that would prove ruinous to China in the nineteenth century, just as it has been *obvious* that Zhang Binglin was an anti-Manchu racist and Hu Shi a despondent liberal.

In part 1 of this book the language of my explication was strong because I meant to bring home the point that one *must* criticize the obvious. I have wanted us to reconsider what we and the Chinese have made of Confucianism and of *ru*, not in the interests of objective truth—a goal far beyond our collective reach in this life—but in the interests of disclosing that economy of delight sustained by the value we and the Chinese have placed in these constructions and received in the name of authoritative knowledge.

So I must emphasize, as I did at the beginning, I am not making a polemical point in all this emphasis on the definitive fungibility of *ru* and Confucianism. Mine is a heartfelt encouragement that we be more self-critical, perhaps like the eighteenth-century *ru* whom Hu Shi and Zhang Binglin so admired, to doubt the "truth" of what has been received, or rather doubt it enough to see that it is our own construction, and our assertions of its truth an expression of our piety and our play.

Recognizing the "madeness" of Kongzi and *ru*, the "inauthenticity" of the normative conception vouchsafed by Han redactors, we understand perhaps better than we once could that to articulate an understanding of *ru* is to perform an act of faith. It is this faith that *ru*, beyond the conflicting texts and the contradictory readings, means something that guides us as it did our predecessors, Chinese and Western. My work throughout this book has been constituted out of this faith and depends upon a previous and enduring community of individuals for whom the tradition named by *ru* and its patriarch is eminently meaningful.

This study has questioned the coherence of *ru* and the history made of it by the Chinese from both ancient and modern texts. Such questioning of *ru* has disclosed discontinuities and contradictions in its representation that are initially disturbing if we presume *ru*'s uniformity. But *ru*, like "tradition," which is simply a characterization of the intersection of custom and creation, has always signified a negotiation between an inherited meaning and the present circumstances of the descendant or interpreter who defines the reception of that meaning.[27]

In the present inquiry I have not sought to reject earlier instances of coherence but to disclose them in light of a new era—my own. Therefore, I have interposed myself among selected texts of and about what the Chinese and later Western scholars have identified as the *ru* tradition, hoping to produce a new reading, born out of what has been declared as well as denied in these texts. Such a hermeneutics of toleration may be carried out only if we take *ru* on an analogy with Max Weber's construction of the "historical individual," as it appears in works like *The Protestant Ethic and the Spirit of Capitalism*.[28] Casting the *ru* as a historical individual will help deliver us from the belief that the only true reading of *ru* is that which identifies what users of the term felt at the moment they first called themselves by this name. Weber urged that the modern interpreter recognize that value was imputed to the objects of interpretation, not discovered within them, and that historical reality was a product of the ceaseless constitution of values. In such a context the interpreter's real quarry is not historical representation in the traditional Rankean sense of "giving the past its due," so much as a value-oriented reading.

Our best chance of understanding the historical individual *ru*, then, is to acknowledge what has been demonstrated above in the particular case of the Jesuits and which was grandly reiterated by Hu Shi: value is a constitutive force in history. Recognizing this, we may align ourselves with previous interpreters, native and foreign, who have constructed *ru* in the course of expressing changing historical values. The different meanings that *ru* displays over time can tell us much about the cultural conditions of its evolution, the identity of groups for which it was meaningful, and lastly the values imputed to it by previous interpreters. These are assuredly not the same. We can see how meanings of *ru* are constructed and received by specific communities of individuals who seek to represent themselves in such constructions. Though there has been wide variation in the meaning of *ru*, one feature of it has remained constant—its invariant ties to community, a textual community.

I acknowledge my place among these interpreters, recognizing our common conceptual indebtedness to theology, evolution, and a need to make sense unconstrained by culture or nation. I admit as well the fundamental newness of the endeavor to account for the origins of *ru*, realizing that it is engendered by difference or loss and has given rise to a representation of meanings that permits the present to search for origins, a fabric interwoven by dual strands native and foreign. So we may move now to stake out *our own* claim on the troubling, but enabling, ambiguity of *ru*, having taken the measure of, but not having adopted, the necessitarian logic of the developmental history advanced by our precursors. Today, we should look for no overarching scheme according to which a putative *truth* of the tradition may be disclosed but simply recognize that in the effort to make sense we have invented—and in so doing, take our place among other previous inventors and their productive communities, whose historical product, *ru* or "Confucian," was the expression of need and desire.

The long history of our contemporary concatenation of cultures and peoples, East and West, has been told episodically in this book through specific attention to the construction of foreign and native identity by means of a single but greatly condensed and diverse symbol, *ru*. For citizens of the late twentieth century the cultural conjunction of East and West is a given. Indeed, given the immediacy of global communication, the world's cultures appear fused. This, however, is the consequence of a very complex, interrelated, and as yet not completely understood set of factors. But two things are clear: that the common ground that Chinese and Westerners share began in a conversation initiated in the late sixteenth century when certain southern Chinese officials saw fit, for reasons not entirely clear to us, to invite a small contingent of Jesuit priests to establish a mission within China, and that our inherited understanding of China as a place essentially different than the West defies the historical record. Chinese scholars, like Zhang Binglin and Hu Shi, could reconceive and rededicate their cultural and national self-images by way of intellectual currents from the West, knowing all along that such reconception was truly Chinese. Jesuits, like Matteo Ricci and Michele Ruggieri, could become Chinese, yet never be aware of how much they had relinquished their hold on the faith they came to China to propagate.

Though, metaphorically speaking, the conjunction of the two cultures began as a conversation, the cultural, religious, and intellectual agreements discovered in this way were never seen as accidental. Chinese and Jesuits met as equals, and conceptually metamorphosed one into the other, but always preserving, perhaps with greater clarity, their identity. Their interaction was organized according to a logic of relationship, in which neither lost sight of what was native or what was foreign. And yet understanding was possible. As *ru* and "la legge de' letterati" became "Confucianism" and were assimilated into a European discourse of modern self-fashioning in the seventeenth and eighteenth centuries, this understanding was lost. But with Hu Shi's inventive redefinition of civilization as a nondenominational spiritual striving, it was restored in a manner similar to that favored by contemporary Western critics of modernity such as Stephen Toulmin and Alasdair MacIntyre, who have stressed that the epistemological program of modernity must be "humanized" by returning to the oral, the local, the particular, and the timely.[29]

Today we stand at the end of a way traveled first by the Jesuits, the path of cultural conjunction formerly governed by relationship but now apparently fused. The Jesuit logic of relationship, in which the nobility, the dignity of the Chinese was not condescendingly but admiringly upheld, has been replaced by one of subsumption, in which the specific features of these cultures, Western and Chinese, are commoditized as products available for purchase. China now is manufacturer to the world, and the Chinese long for the politically unencumbered prosperity of the West. Considering this simultaneous occurrence of "Orientalism" and "Occidentalism," it is more difficult today, in an era in which we celebrate ourselves as "empowered" by the recognition of our complicity in the cultural constructions we have received and now make, to get at China as the Jesuits did. However, it is not necessary for us to enter China and apprehend it as did the Jesuits; we need only to draw from it a serviceable means of living in the world of the next century.

I consider this mutual fetishization—a commercial "Confucius" and an economically magical West—the consequence of an earlier Western appropriation of Chinese evidences for theological and scientific debate. These are fetishes of the industrial economy that courses over the globe, vestiges of our unfortunate Enlightenment inheritance. At root, the most generous reading of the Enlightenment's insistence on commensurability in the ratiocinative calculation of the other acknowledges that the inspiration for the objective measurement of the world was not at all about colonization, but instead grew from a desire to extend the reference of the term "we" on the presumptive ground of a common rationality. There was in it a desire for solidarity, not unlike that which characterized the Jesuit sodalities among the Chinese, or the coteries of twentieth-century Chinese intellectuals. This seems to me the point of Kant's implication in the epigraph to this epilogue: that Enlightenment is *potentia* in all, and it is the onus of the already enlightened to engineer the *praesentia* of reason. The consequence of this humane premise, as we know today, over four hundred years since the beginning of Sino-Western conversation, was not tolerance of diversity—multiple "we's" alike only in their *potentia* and unalike in their *praesentia*—but an affirmation of univocity, where extension of the reference of "we" was transfigured into plural reflections of "me." This is our legacy, and the world's burden, a record of the failed hopes of an "enlightened" age.

Hu Shi stood on the cusp of that moment in which cosmopolitanism could still applaud the advances of the scientific-industrial form of life, knowing as he did that the industrial economy was sustained by the productive life of local communities, not by modernity's sovereign claims of nationalism and imperialism. Despite the violence of his age, he was optimistic about the possibilities of broadening the cultural meaning of "we" and, like the Jesuits, for whom he may have harbored some fellow-feeling, he sought to expand cultural understanding in the name of a universal pattern of civilization. His was a secular and not religious apprehension of this pattern, but again like the Jesuits, he divined this pattern by means of *ru.* He was a cosmopolitan in the moment where to the native mind such thinking was the sentiment of a foreigner. In fact, in this respect, he resembled our popular academic perception of Confucius, as a prophet without honor in his own country but whose later truths would illuminate the land. Unfortunately, the light of his transnational conception of civilization as the collective expression of plural cultural values has yet to dawn.

What Hu Shi, Zhang Binglin to a lesser extent, and certainly the Jesuits understood and some critics of modernity among us recognize is that the specific is the route to the universal. To be a good cosmopolitan is to be a fierce defender of native ground. It was no longer necessary, following Hu Shi's theoretical work in "Shuo ru," to consider how China might assimilate modern civilization "in a way congruous with a civilization of our own making." In the end, this is what "Shuo ru" is about for me, although as a citizen living near the end of this century, and perhaps the world, I might contest the depth of Hu Shi's optimism about the outcome of the civilizational pattern he had adduced as universal. But there is little else I would quarrel with, for my world is one in which we have the freedom to invent gloriously and yet to destroy unimaginably, both of which in this century we have succeeded in doing. We must not turn our attention away from science and technology, the bearers of quantitative authority, only to recognize the qualitative economy of delight that has sustained our communities even as they have been ravaged by the excess of our faith in progress. Instead we must restore the balance of art and science, by reestablishing the regnancy of delight.

Taking the full measure of this contemporary commingling of great virtue and great violence, I join Hu Shi, Zhang Binglin, and the Jesuits in hoping that through the manufacture of sense I may find the object of my understanding's desire, banish the darkness of ambiguity and moral doubt, and summon the courage to admit that in the satisfaction of this desire I discover myself and the other. *Mundus senecit.* The world grows old. And the humane "science" of manufacture, with its implicit manifesto of valuation, seems to disappear under the weight of scientific-industrial detritus.

As interpreters, scholars, but most of all as human beings, we may, by explicitly stating our needs and desires in the course of our making sense of what at first is senseless, honestly reinvent ourselves in a manner more deeply spiritual than is possible in an otherwise bloodlessly objective life under the tyranny of the obvious that constitutes the everyday. This could be accomplished. If the prose of our work is guided by the poetry of China's ecumenical nativism, we may chart a course away from the narrow judgment of the scientific temper and the destructive impulses of nationalism, toward a more inclusive definition of China and the West—an open space where we might, by way of our differences, continue a dialogue begun centuries ago in the name of understanding. Thus, "one way or another," to rephrase Levenson, the world will join *China* again on the cosmopolitan tide, leaving "Confucius" and "Confucianism" adrift near the shoal.

GLOSSARY

baijia, 百家 "Hundred Families": collective name for the plural rhetorical fellowships of the Zhan'guo era, including *ru*

Baohuang hui, 保皇會 Protect the Emperor Society: founded in 1898 by Kang Youwei while in exile in Japan

bian, 變 "Change," "transformation"

bianjiao, 辨教 "Discriminate between the teachings": expression common in the anti-Christian tract *Poxie ji* 破邪集 of 1639 stressing the need to elucidate the differences between the genuine native Chinese *ru* traditions and that of the Christian missionaries

bianxue, 辨學 "Discriminate learning": another phrase from the *Poxie ji* with the same meaning as *bianjiao*

bishi, 鄙事 "Lowly or demeaning affairs": characterization by Kongzi (*Lunyu*, book 9, chapter 6) of his earlier years

boshi, 博士 "Scholar of wide learning"; a common post-Han gloss for *ru*

bu, 卜 "Divination"

buluo, 部落 "Tribe"

"*buru yi fo*", 補儒易佛 "Supplements *ru* and confutes *fo*": Xu Guangqi's oft-quoted formulation describing the complementary relation between *ru* and Christianity; enthusiastically adopted by the Jesuits themselves

buwu ren, 卜巫人 "Diviners," "shamans"

buzheng, 補正 "Addition and correction": terms of textual recension used by Hu Shi to characterize his elaboration on Zhang Binglin's "Yuan ru"

canmeng, 參盟 A form of blood oath binding two or more signatories to mutual assistance and common defense in the post-Zhou era

Chan, 禪 "Meditation" sect of Chinese Buddhism

changcheng, 長城 "Long wall": the Great Wall; long an idea but not an artifact, it is a recent invention of the Chinese and a highly commercialized nationalist symbol of the state and of civilization; a global fetish

chengshi, 誠實　"Sincerity"

chuanjiao, 傳教　"Hand down a teaching," "disseminate a faith," "proselytize"

chuantong, 傳統　"Tradition"

cun guojiao, 存國教　"Preserve the national religion"

cun guxue tang, 存古學堂　Preservation of National Learning Pavilion built by moderate reformer Zhang Zhidong after the educational reforms of 1907

Cuonhua,官話　Italian romanization for *guanhua*, administrative vernacular, used interchangeably with *mandarino* by Matteo Ricci and the early Jesuit missionaries

da nuo,大儺　"Great exorcism": pre-Han rite of expulsion traditionally conducted following the winter solstice

Dade, 大德　"Great Virtue": Second era name of the emperor Chengzong (1297–1308 C.E.) of the Yuan

daming, 達名　"Generic name," "genus": earliest classification for *ru*, according to Zhang Binglin, referring to scholars of received technē (*shushi* 術士) and including a vast number of other practice traditions that would later acquire independent status as Warring States fraternities

dangran, 當然　"Ought": conventional philosophical complement to *suoyi ran*, "that which therefore is"

dao, 道　"Way," "road," "path": a normative Warring States expression common to virtually all rhetorical fellowships; diversely interpreted, but the eponym of the tradition made from the *De Dao Jing* (or *Laozi*) and the *Zhuangzi* known as "Daoist"

daoren, 道人　"Men of the path": a term of self-reference used by the Jesuit missionaries in the early 17th century C.E.

daoshi, 道士　"*Dao* scholars": educated followers of the teachings of Laozi

daotong, 道統　"Legacy of the way": characterization by Zhu Xi in 1189 of the authentic transmission of the *dao* from the culture heroes of antiquity to the present

daoxue, 道學　"Learning of the way": a restorationist *ru* subcult founded by Zhu Xi in the late 12th century C.E.

datong, 大同　"Great Harmony": Kang Youwei's vision of utopia

de, 德　"Mana," "power," "virtue"

dentō (Japanese), 傳統　"Tradition"

diguan situ, 地官司徒　"Earthly Office Leader of the Footsoldiers": office of secondary rank in the *Zhou li* believed by the Han bibliographer, Liu Xin, to be the ancient office from which the *ru* came

dui, ☱　last of the eight trigrams, believed to be an image of a lake

er, 而　"And," "but": a conjunctive particle that comprises the lower half of the graph *xu* 需

fa, 法　"Methods": title of a rhetorical fellowship of the Warring States (Legalists) associated with the traditions of Guan Zhong and Shang Yang; it is a term that refers to techniques of discipline and control through reward and punishment that governed the administration of the Qin state

falisairen, 法利塞人   Pharisees: a transliteration by Hu Shi

fangshi, 方士   "Magician(s)"

fangxiangshi, 方相士   "Exorcist(s)"

feng, 蜂   "Bee": contemporary graph

feng, 蠭   "Bee": archaic graph preferred by Zhang Binglin

feng shan ji, 風山際   "Imperial sacrifice" to wind and mountains initiated in the Han era

fenpai, 分派   "Faction": used to distinguish political and scholarly divisions

fo, 佛   "Buddha": Generic term for all forms of Buddhist practice; one of China's three principal religions and identified as one of the *tre leggi diverse* (three different orders) by Matteo Ricci in his *Storia*

fuzi, 夫子   "Master": a term of respect used by students for their teacher in Warring States; a common form of address for Kongzi in the *Lunyu*

geming, 革命   "Overturn the command": revolution, a term brought to national prominence in 1903 with the publication of Zou Rong's *Geming jun* (Revolutionary Army)

gongfu, 功夫   "Moral effort": refers to the exertion of the self toward the goal of realizing inner moral goodness; common philosophical refrain of Ming idealism

gongguoge, 功過格   "Ledgers of merit and demerit": Ming era personal records of transgression and achievement valued by Jesuit missionaries

Gongyang zhuan, 公洋傳   Commentary on the *Chunqiu* favored by the New Text school of the Han and revived by the New Text schools of the Qing

gongzhu, 公主   "Common lords": denigrative characterization of the Manchus found in Zhang Binglin's writings

gongzu, 公祖   "Noble descent": Zhang Binglin's characterization of the fellowships of the *baijia*

gu, 古   "Antiquity," "past," "old": a conceptual invention of the Springs and Autumns and Warring States periods made in the wake of the collapse of royal ancestral cults

gu, 賈   "Trader": graph that Hu Shi argues the name *shang* 商 of the Shang people was derived from

guai, ䷪   Forty-third hexagram of the *Yijing*: the upper and lower trigrams, *dui* (lake) and *qian* (creative), conjure the image of "resoluteness" (*guai*); considered by Hu Shi in "Shuo ru" to define the undemonstrative decisiveness of *ru* under Zhou overlordship who have decided to restore their people

guai, 夬   "Decide": taken by Hu Shi to gloss the hexagram *xu*, which he believes may offer clues to the earliest meaning of the term *ru*

guanhua, 官話   "Official language": Chinese administrative vernacular believed by Matteo Ricci to be the unifying standard language of the Chinese that the Portuguese had called *"Mandarins"*

guji, 古迹 *"Traces of antiquity":* vestiges by which the past may be reconstituted in memory

gujing jingshe, 詁經精舍 Refined Lodge for the Explication of the Classics: celebrated *kaozheng* academy on West Lake in Hangzhou founded by Ruan Yuan in the late 18th century C.E. and with which Zhang Binglin was affiliated in the 1890s

guocui, 國淬 *"National essence":* inspired by the Japanese concept *kokutsui,* it was the obsession of a coterie of nationalistic ancient prose enthusiasts

guofu, 國父 *"National Father":* posthumous honorific for Sun Yat-sen used in both Taiwan and the People's Republic of China

guogu, 國古 *"National heritage":* term common to late-19th- and early-20th-century C.E. discourse referring to Chinese mythology, folklore and the classics

guojiao, 國教 *"National religion":* after 1908 the term used to refer to Kongjiao or Confucianity

guoxue, 國學 *"National learning or studies"*

Guoxue baocun hui, 國學保存會 Society for the Protection and Preservation of National Learning formed by Zhang Binglin

Guoxue hui, 國學會 National Studies Society: a cohort of nationalist intellectuals devoted to both scholarly and political defense of China's cultural heritage

guru, 古儒 *"Ancient ru":* an ambiguous term used by 20th century C.E. nationalists to refer to *ru* before the Warring States and Kongzi, but also used by the Jesuit missionaries to speak of the *ru* of Kongzi's time

guwen, 古文 *"Ancient prose," "ancient script":* the script of the oldest extant texts of the classics and believed to contain the spirit of antiquity; at least since Ouyang Xiu (1007–1072 C.E.) it was believed that *guwen,* mastery of which was required for examination success, had a unique capacity to instruct morally

guyi, 古意 *"Ancient meanings"*

guzhiru, 古之儒 *"Ru of antiquity":* one of the terms favored by the Jesuit missionaries for the exemplars of the authentic *ru* transmission and also used by early-20th-century nationalist scholars such as Liu Shipei and Zhang Binglin

Han minzu wenhua, 民族文化 *"The culture of the Han race"*

Hanxue, 漢學 *"Han learning"* (18th century C.E.)

heshang, 和尙 Buddhist priest or acolyte; role name assumed by the Jesuits in their first years among the Chinese

hongru, 鴻儒 *"Grand ru":* title of favor used by Wang Chong in his *Lunheng* (ca. 80 C.E.) to distinguish categories of *ru* scholars

houru, 後儒 *"Later ru":* a derogatory term used by the Jesuits to distinguish authentic bearers of the *xianru* transmission

huangdi, 皇帝 *"Supreme Lord";* emperor

huangdi zhidu, 皇帝制度 "Emperor system": contemporary Chinese gloss for *ru*—
that it is part of the culture of the imperial past

Huang—Lao, 黃老 Pre-Han rhetorical fellowship

Huang—Lao *zhishu*, 皇老之術 Techniques of Huanglao

huaxia, 華夏 An ethnonym, deliberately archaic, employed by Zhang Binglin to
designate China's ur-culture

Huayan, 華嚴 "Wreath" sect of Buddhism

huiyi, 會意 "Joined meanings": a composite method by which Chinese graphs
were assembled from two graphic components the meanings of which suggest
another word

ji, 籍 registry of the birth order of a noble household's males: used by Zhang Binglin
to describe the *baijia*

"*ji ru zai, ji shen ru shen zai*", 祭如在祭神如神在 "When conducting worship,
sacrifice to the spirits as if the spirits are there": celebrated phrase attributed to
Kongzi in the *Lunyu* that suggests that the rites of ancestral cult had become
authentic

jiaguwen, 甲骨文 Oracle bone inscriptions: earliest Chinese script inscribed on
bovid scapula and tortoise plastrons, ca. 1200–1000 B.C.E.

jiajie, 假借 Phonetic loaning or borrowing

jian, 堅 "Solid," "firm": offered as an antonym of *ru* 儒 by Hu Shi

jiao, 敎 "Teaching": religion, faith

jiaoshi, 敎師/敎士 "Missionaries": Hu Shi's characterization of Shang era *ru* after
the Zhou conquest

jiaoyao, 焦僥 A legendary tribe from China's Southwest that grew to a height of
three feet and was philologically associated with *ru*

jiaozhu, 敎主 "Founder of a faith" such as Kongzi and Jesus

jieji, 階級 "Class"

jingshe, 精舍 "Lodge of wondrous remembrance": forerunner of Song *shuyuan*

Jingtu (jiao), 淨土敎 "Pure Land teaching": popular Buddhist millenarian sect

jingxue, 經學 "Classical studies"

jinru, 今儒 "Today's *ru*": a derogatory term employed by Ricci and his cohort to
distinguish lesser contemporary followers of *ru* from the authentic standard-
bearers of the transmission

jinwen, 今文 "New Text": a Han school of interpretation organized around Fu
Sheng's (3d–2d century B.C.E.) recension of the *Shang shu* and favoring the *weishu*
or apocryphal texts of pre-Han as bearing the "subtle words and larger meaning"
of the culture heroes' transmission

jinwen, 金文 Bronze inscriptions

jinwenjia , 今文家 "New Text School": formed by *ru* followers in the Western
Han; devoted to the study of texts written in the new *lishu* script of the period,
especially the Gongyang and Guliang commentaries on the *Chunqiu*

jiuguo, 救國 "To rescue the nation"

jiujing, 九經 "Nine Classics": the title conveys the expansion of the original "Six Classics" in the period between 200 and 600 C.E. and refers to *Chunqiu, Shang shu, Shi jing, Yijing, Li ji, Zhou li, Gongyang zhuan, Guliang zhuan,* and *Zuo zhuan*

jiuliu, 九流 "Nine Streams": Han metaphor for the plural fellowships of the Zhan' guo period

jiushi de ren, 救世的人 "Save-the-world person," savior: according to Hu Shi, the Shang people longed for the appearance of a savior and mistakenly identified Kongzi as one

junzi, 君子 "Lordling"; ethical exemplar of the *ru* tradition; a derogatory term functionally remade by the *ru* into an ethical exemplar

juren, 舉人 "Raised man," "promoted person": title of the second of the three ranks of examination accomplishment

kaishu, 楷書 "Standard script"

kakumei, 革命 "Revolution"

kan, ☵ "Abysmal": the second of the eight trigrams; believed to be an image of water

kaozheng, 考證 "Evidential research": 18th-century textual criticism movement to authenticate the works of Chinese antiquity through philology and historical phonology

kaozheng xue, 考證學 Evidential research and textual criticism

ke, 科 "Category"

kexue, 科學 "Science"

kogaku, 古學 "Ancient studies": learning associated with Ogyū Sorai (1666–1728 C.E.), intellectual architect of the Tokugawa era, grounded in study of the Chinese classics and reverence for the senō (Former Kings)

kokugaku, 國學 "Native studies": nativist scholarly tradition advanced in opposition to *kogaku* and stressing the phonetic majesty of Japanese language and its organic links to the soil

kokutsui, 國淬 "Native essence": a *kokugaku* term for the mysterious essence of the Japanese

Kong Qiu, 孔丘 "Mound" Kong: name given to Kongzi at birth; "mound" refers to a raised dirt altar at which his mother prayed for the birth of a son; *qiu* traditionally has been understood as a reference to Kongzi's signal head deformity

Kongjia dian, 孔家店 "Shop of Kong family": May Fourth–era term for tradition

Kongjiao, 孔敎 "Confucianity": national religion invented by Kang Youwei for the purpose of the vitalization of China in a manner imitative of Christianity's resourcefulness for Western civilization

Kongzi, 孔子 "Son who passed through"; also known as "Master Kong"

leiming, 類名 "Class name," "species": second and more narrow category of *ru* significance in Zhang Binglin's taxonomy and referring exclusively to mastery of the *liuyi* 六藝

li, 禮 "Rites"

lishi jianjie, 歷史見解 "Historical observation": Hu Shi's characterization of Zhang Binglin's essay "Yuan ru"

lishu, 隸書 Official clerical script of the Han dynasty

Liujing, 六經 "Six Classics": *Yi* (*jing*, Classic of Change), *Li* (Rites), *Shi* (*jing*, Book of Odes), *Shu* (*jing* or *Shang shu*, Book of Documents), *Yue* (Music), *Chunqiu* (Spring and Autumn Annals); though the Music classic was "lost," the other five works were presumed in the Han to have been either authored or edited by Kongzi

liuyi, 六藝 "Six Cultivations": term representing the diverse abilities of the accomplished man in the Han—music, rites, archery, charioteering, numbers, and calligraphy

lixue, 理學 "Learning of principle": a rhetorical fellowship formed in the Northern Song under the aegis of Cheng Yichuan; one of the Chinese inspirations for our Neo-Confucianism

lunheng, *Lunheng* 論衡 Critical evaluation of doctrine; also the title of Wang Chong's celebrated demystification of popular belief and practice (ca. 80 C.E.)

Lunyu, 論語 "Selected Sayings" of Kongzi and other teachers of the *ru* fellowship (ca. 479–249 B.C.E.); since James Legge's translation of 1868 also known as "The Analects"

meng, 盟 "Blood oath"; quasi-legal instrument employed to constrain hostilities between competing kingdoms in the post-Zhou era

menshi zhengxue, 門士正學 "True learning of the scholars at the gate": apostolic transmission of Christ's teaching; the transmission from Kongzi through his disciples of the true teachings of the "Heavenly Master"; ambiguous phrase used by Ricci in the *Tianzhu shiyi*

ming, 名 "Name": a rhetorical focus of Warring States disputation concerning the relationship between language and the real; also the name for a rhetorical fellowship

ming, 命 "Command," "mandate," "decree": interchangeable with *ling* 令 in oracle bone inscriptions and bearing a martial significance, it may refer to the directives of a high god that certified the rule of each of China's ancient clans, Xia, Shang, Zhou

mingxin qiongxing, 明心窮性 "Illumination of the mind and exhaustion of the nature": Song and Ming era expression stating that enlightenment could be obtained by relentless investigation of the phenomenal world

minzu, 民族 "Race," "tribe," "people"

minzu guangfu, 民族光復 "Renascence of the Chinese race"

misaiya, 彌賽亞 "Messiah"; Hu Shi's transliteration of the Christian version of the Hebraic "moshiach"

mo, 墨 "To mark," "a convict"; pre-Han rhetorical fellowship of craftsmen and strategists; perhaps the name of the fellowship's founder, Mo Di 墨

Mo Di (Mozi), 墨翟 "Convict Di": legendary founder of the *mo* rhetorical fellowship; experts in defensive warfare and logical argument, they were early adversaries of *ru*

Mozhu juzi, 墨諸巨子 The followers of Mozi

nong (jia), 農家 "Tillers family": one of the many rhetorical fraternities of the Warring States and adversaries of *ru*; associated with Xu Xing, a farmer

nuan, 渜 "Genial," "mild": a gloss of *ru*

nuo, 懦 "Timid," "weak": a gloss of *ru*

nuomi, 糯米 "Glutinous rice"

pi-Lin pi-Kong, 批林批孔 "Criticize Lin Biao and Kongzi" campaign of the 1970s

putong hua, 普通話 "Common speech," vernacular: the standard dialect, since the 16th century C.E. known in the West as "mandarino" or "mandarin"

qi, 期 Exorcist's mask made in the image of a dog or a bear

qian, ☰ "Dry": the first of the eight trigrams and believed to be an image of sky or heaven

Qiang xuehui, 強學會 Strength Study Society; founded by Kang Youwei in 1895 following the signing of the "Ten-Thousand-Word Memorial"

qianshi zhi ru, 前時之儒 "*Ru* of a previous time": another term favoring ancient members of the tradition by distinction from present-day followers

qilin, 麒麟 Unicorn; a fabulous beast, both magnificent and maleficent, legendarily associated with the birth and death of Kongzi

qimeng, 啓蒙 "Enlightenment": strident claim of New Culture activists from 1915 to 1930 justifying iconoclasm and the rejection of tradition; used again in 1978–1979 and 1989 by advocates of democracy

qinggui, 清規 "Pure rules" governing proper conduct in Chan monasteries

qinmin, 親民 "Loving the people": time-honored phrase from the *Daxue* defining the scope of the task for one seeking moral cultivation

qinru paifo, 親儒敗佛 "Draw close to *ru*, banish *fo*": four-character axiom of the early missionaries referring to the compatibility of Christianity and *ru*; see *buru yifo*

qixiong, 七兇 "Seven truculents": seven clans accorded independent fiefs in the east by Liu Bang at the founding of the Han dynasty in 202 B.C.E. and that led a rebellion against the imperial clan in 154 B.C.E.

ren, 仁 "Humaneness": considered the fundamental, defining virtue of *ru* practice

rendao, 人道 "Way of Humanity": philosophical complement of *tiandao* 天道 or "Way of the Ascendant"

rensheng guan, 人生觀 "View of life": characterization of the position held by

Chinese *Lebensphilosophie* advocates in a national debate with "scientists" in February 1923

rou, 柔   "Soft," "yielding," "weak"; standard definition in ancient texts for the term *ru*

rouxu, 柔嬬   "Weak, lesser wife": Yuan era rhyming gloss for *ru* 儒

ru, 儒   "Weakling"

ru, 孺   "Bastard son," "suckling"

ru, 乳   Human and bird parturition; "to suckle," "to nurture," breast milk

ru, 濡   "Moist," "wet"; to "immerse," to "soak": the most common early gloss for *ru* 儒

ru, 襦   "Short coat": another of the cluster of homophonous terms associated with *ru* 儒; it is the name of the eighteenth hexagram in the recently discovered Mawangdui version of the *Zhou yi* and is defined in that text as "moist" (*ru* 濡)

ru rou ye, 儒柔也   "*Ru* means weak": foundational gloss of *ru* from Xu Shen's *Shuowen jiezi*

ru ru ye, 儒濡也   "*Ru* means wet": early gloss of *ru* from the *Guang ya*

"*Ru wei junzi ru, wu wei xiaoren ru*", 如爲君子儒無爲小人儒   "Be a lordling *ru*, not a plebian *ru*" (*Lunyu* 6.13)

ruan, 耎   "Soft," "weak": one of the glosses for *ru* used by Hu Shi

rufu, 儒服   "*Ru* garments": wide sleeves, broad belts, and high caps; subject of derision in *Zhuangzi* and other Warring States texts and the reason for a defense of *ru* appearance by Kongzi before Duke Ai of Lu in the *Li ji*, chap. 38

ruhu, 儒戶   "*Ru* (scholar) households": category of population registry initiated in the 13th century C.E. under the Yuan

rujia, 儒家   "*Ru* family": Warring States characterization of the tradition associated with Kongzi, also found in the "Yiwen zhi"

rujia sixiang, 儒家思想   *Ru* fellowship thought

rujiao, 儒教   "*Ru* teaching"

rulin, 儒林   "Forest of *ru*": metaphor favored by Sima Qian for the tradition's followers in the Han with the implication that the *ru* were as numerous as trees in the forest

ruo, 弱   "Weak," "weakness": term commonly associated with *ru*

rusheng, 儒生   "Scholar," "academic": contemporary term

rushu, 儒書   "*Ru* terms": source of complaint against the state of Lu by the people of Qi in *Zuo Zhuan*

ruxing, 儒行   "*Ru* deportment"

ruxue, 儒學   "*Ru* learning"

ruzhe, 儒者   "The *ru*": another common collective reference to *ru* found in Warring States texts

ruzhe ru ye, 儒者濡也   "The *ru* are wet": common paronomastic gloss of *ru*

sakui (Japanese), 作   "Invention"

sandeng, 三等 "The Three Ages": *taiping* (great peace), *shengping* (ascending peace), and *shuailuan* (disorder); first outlined by He Xiu in his subcommentary on the *Gongyang zhuan* and later employed by Kang Youwei in reverse order to describe the evolution of culture and politics from antiquity to the present with *taiping* changed to *datong* 大同

sangli, 喪禮 "Rites of mourning"

sanhan jiao, 三涵教 "Three Confluence Teaching": late Ming era eclecticism of *ru*, *dao*, and *fo*; identical with *sanjiao yiyuan* 三教一原

sanjiao, 三教 "Three teachings": *ru*, *fo*, *dao*; the Chinese equivalent of Matteo Ricci's *tre leggi diverse*

sanjiao yiyuan, 三教一原 "Three teachings, single source"; "three teachings are one"

sannian zhi sang, 三年之喪 "Three-year mourning rites": an invention of *ru* followers in the early Han written into the *Li ji*; believed by some to be a vestige of a practice peculiar to the Yin-Shang people

sanshi, 三時 See *sandeng* above

shangdi, Shangdi, 上帝 "Lord above"; an honorific expression for higher forces that appears in early written texts and which was interpreted by the first Jesuit missionaries as evidence of an indigenous Chinese belief in the one God

shanshu, 善書 Ming era "morality books" that were of great interest to Jesuit missionaries owing to their resonance with the "Spiritual Exercises" of their order

shendu, 身獨 "Self-surveillance": a metaphor for the cultivation of the inner moral stirrings of the heart

Shengchao poxie ji, 聖朝破邪集 Sacred Dynasty's Collection Exposing Heresy: a vituperative anti-Christian tract published in Fujian in 1639; though its language is harsh and inflammatory, the denunciations suggest that the Jesuits had mastered the discourse of late Ming scholars; it reveals that differences between cultures are differences in kind and thus are the same as differences between theories in a single culture

shengren, 聖人 "Holy man," "sage ," "saint": Chinese term translated by Matteo Ricci as "santo"

shengxian, 聖賢 "Sages and worthies"

shenwei, 神位 "Spirit tablets"

shi, 士 "Warrior," "knight," "scholar," gentleman": purportedly the lowest rank of the Zhou era nobility and the class from which the *ru* putatively came

shi, 師 "Instructor," "teacher": early gloss for *ru* favored by Liu Xin

shijia, 釋加 Approximate Chinese transliteration of Shakyamuni, the name of the Buddha; Buddhism

shiru, 士儒 "Gentlemen *ru*": one of three categories of ru according to Xunzi (ca. 3d century B.C.E.)

shiru, 時儒   "Contemporary *ru*": disparaging term for putative contemporary followers of the *ru* tradition used by Matteo Ricci, the Chinese equivalent of his *i letterati*

"Shi shi qiu shi", 實事求是   "Seek truth from facts": 18th-century *kaozheng* expression appropriated by Mao Zedong and more recently employed by Deng Xiaoping to characterize the spirit of his reform of the economy

shixue, 實學   "Substantial learning"; Han studies definition of *kaozheng* empiricism

shu, 術   "Technique(s)," common metaphor for "legalist" teachings

shu, 述   "Received technē," to "hand down": cognate with *shu* 術 techniques or skills

"shu er buzuo", 述而不作   "[I] receive but do not invent"

shu shi guan, 術士冠   "Caps of technicians": synonymous with *yuan guan* of *ru*

shui, 說   "Disputation": referring to the rhetorical practice of Zhan'guo fellowships

Shun, 舜   One of the legendary Five Sovereigns (*wudi*); a sage-king who was allegedly raised up from toil in the fields and granted marriage to Yao's daughters and ultimately given rule of the *Zhongyuan* by Yao; the paradigmatic first succession predicated on merit and not ascription

shuo, 說   "To explain"; "explication," "elaboration"

"Shuo ru", 說儒   "An elaboration on *ru*": title of Hu Shi's "addition and correction" of Zhang Binglin's "Yuan ru" published in 1934

shushi, 術士   "Scholars of techniques," "gentlemen of received skills," "knights of received technē": name for *ru* in the era before the Warring States

shuwen, 述文   "Transmission by script": method by which Matteo Ricci claimed possession of the *zhengxue* of Kongzi

shuyuan, 書院   Private academy

Siguo, 四國   Four eastern kingdoms of Wei, Qi, Song, and Lu to which the legatees of the Shang were displaced following the Zhou conquest

siming, 私名   "Proper name," "type": narrowest classification of *ru* in Zhang Binglin's taxonomy referring to officers of the state, experts in texts not practitioners of a skill, such as contemporary bearers of the title

situ, 司土   "Leader of the footsoldiers," "steward of the multitudes" (see *diguan situ*)

Songxue, 宋學   "Song learning": an 18th- and 19th-century c.e. *guwen* (ancient prose) coterie that elevated the thought and criticism of the Song masters

suoyi ran, 所以然   "That which therefore is": conventional philosophical complement to *dangran* (ought)

suru, 素儒   "Vulgar *ru*": Xunzi's lowest category of practicing *ru*

suwang, 素王   "Common or plebeian king"; Han era hagiographic characterization of Kongzi taken by the Jesuits as evidence of a structural homology with their "Prince" Jesus

Taiji, 太極　"Supernal Ridgepole"

taiping, 太平　"Great Peace": first of the Three Ages (sandeng) following the subcommentary on the Chunqiu by the New Text scholar He Xiu, this moment was placed third by Kang Youwei and renamed Datong

ti, 體　"Essence/subsidiary function"

ti, 體/yong, 用　the strategic dyad that organized virtually all reform thought and activity in the 19th century; a defensive mechanism to preserve Chinese culture while making material improvements to the nation by selective importation and use of Western technology

tian, 天　"The Ascendant," "sky": pronounced "heaven" by Jesuit missionaries

tiangan dizhi, 天干地支　"Stems and branches": ancient calendrical system of the Chinese

tianshi dao, 天師道　"Way of the celestial master": name of the popular Daoist sect founded by Zhang Daoling (d. ca. 157–178 C.E.) in the Han

Tiantai, 天台　Buddhist sect founded in eastern Zhejiang's Tiantai Mountains; also known as the Fahua sect

tianxia, 天下　"Below the ascendant," the universe, the world

Tianzhu, 天主　"Heavenly Master," lord: name appropriated from a young Chinese convert by the Jesuits to represent the Christian God

Tianzhu shilu, 天主實錄　"Veritable Record of the Heavenly Master" by Michele Ruggieri: first "catechism" prepared by the Jesuits in the Chinese language (1584)

Tianzhu shiyi, 天主實意　"The Real Significance of the Heavenly Master" by Li Madou (Matteo Ricci): second catechism prepared by the Jesuits in the Chinese language (1603)

Tongcheng, 桐城　City in northern Anhui that was the site of a celebrated kaozheng tradition; in the late Qing the southern military modernizer, Zeng Guofan, claimed an intellectual affinity with this school and its appreciation for Song learning; adversary of the guocui coterie

tuogu gaizhi, 託古改制　"Pleading antiquity to reform the present"

wangguo, 亡國　"Vanquished nation": a self-deprecating term for China used by Zou Rong and Zhang Binglin stressing its double slavery at the hands of Western imperialists and the Manchu Qing dynasts

wanguo xinyu, 萬國新語　"New language of ten thousand nations": Esperanto

weiji, 爲己　"For oneself": a term found in the Lunyu that refers to the inspiration for learning and considered by Wm. Theodore de Bary to be the prefigurative liberal impulse for Zhu Xi's notion of zide (getting it for oneself)

wei renmin fuwu, 爲人民服務　"Serve the people"

weishu, 偉書　So-called apocryphal texts conventionally contrasted with jing "classics"

weiyan dayi, 微言大義　"Subtle words, great meaning": jinwen expression referring to the ponderous implicit significance of the words and phrases in the *Chunqiu*, designed by Kongzi to confound his contemporaries but convey his genuine meaning to later generations

wenhua, 文化　Culture

wenming, 文明　Civilization

wenru, 文儒　"Learned *ru,*" "cultured *ru*": gloss of *ru* favored by the Yuan era scholar Wang Wei (1323–1374 C.E.)

wenshi, 文士　"Scribes": Hu Shi's characterization of the Hebraic scholarly class that rebelled against the Pharisees

wu, 舞　"Dance": homophone of *wu* 巫 "shaman"; may refer to trance or exorcism

"Wubainian you shengren zhe xing", 五白年有聲人者興　"Every five hundred years a sage arrives": popular messianic mythology of Chinese antiquity believed by Hu Shi to have expressed the hopes of the Shang people for a restoration of their civilization

Wuding sunzi, 武丁孫子　"Descendant(s) of Wuding"

Wujing, 五經　"Five Classics"—*Chunqiu, Yi (jing), Li (jing), (Shang) Shu, Shi (jing)* believed to have been written and/or edited by Kongzi and officially authorized by the Former Han emperor Wudi in 136 B.C.E.; inscribed in stone in 175 C.E.

wu rusheng, 吾儒聖　"Our *ru* saints": possessive nativist claim on behalf of the *ru* patriarchs made by the Buddhists, against the *zhengxue* avowal of Matteo Ricci and other accommodationist missionaries in 1638–1639

wuwei, 無為　"Nonintentional action": a disposition described in the *De Dao Jing* (Integrity and the Way Classic) of the *daojia* ("Daoists") believed to effect spontaneity

Wuxu bianfa, 戊戌變法　The Hundred Days Reforms (June–September 1898)

wuyin, 五音　"Five Sounds": *gong, shang, jiao, zhi, yu*

xiang, 相　"Ritual assistant"

xiangjian, 想見　Inference

xiangli, 相禮　"Assistant at the rites"

xiangyue, 響約　Village covenant

xianru, 先儒　"First *ru*": by Ming times a term used to refer to the followers of Kongzi down to Zuo Qiuming, but appropriated by Matteo Ricci to designate Kongzi and his authentic teaching

xiansheng, 先聖　"First holy man," first sage: honorific for Kongzi

xianshi, 先師　"First teacher": Han era term of address for Kongzi

xianxian, 先賢　"Former worthies": designation of honor for *ru* followers of the second rank in the Kongmiao (Kong Temple)

xianwang, 先王　"Former Kings": reference to the culture heroes of Chinese antiquity, principally Yao, Shun, and Yu, all of whom acquired rule through merit and not ascription; also extended to Huang Di (Yellow Emperor, creator of civilization) and Zhuan Xu

xiao, 孝 "To feed" (the dead), "to feast," "filiality"

xiaoshuo, 小說 "small words": a pre-Han fellowship mentioned in Wang Chong's *Lunheng*; also the Chinese term for the novel

xiaoxue, 小學 "Small learning": philology

xie, 契 "Heterodox"; evil; heresy

xin, 信 "Faithfulness"

xingming, 形名 "Forms and names": critical rhetorical parameters of Zhan'guo persuasion

xingsi, 形似 "Form likeness": a term common to Chinese aesthetic practice referring not to the portrait of verisimilitude but to the mannered representation of the real

xinmin, 新民 "Renovating/renewing the people"

xinru, 新儒 New *ru*

xinrujia, 新儒家 New Confucian School

xinruxue 新儒學 New Confucian learning: contemporary academic formation favoring a restitution of the cultural nobility of the Chinese on the presumption that "Confucianism" is an enduring value system

xinxue, 心學 "Learning of the mind": a *ru* fellowship associated with the teachings of Lu Xiangshan (1139–1193 C.E.) and Wang Yangming (1472–1529 C.E.) that held the mind to be supreme in that it was congenitally moral and contained knowledge of the ancients; conventionally contrasted with the *lixue* 理學 (learning of principle) *ru* fellowship associated with Cheng Yichuan (1033–1107 C.E.) and Zhu Xi (1130–1200 C.E.); both *ru* traditions informed the academic élite of the last six hundred years of Chinese imperial history and both were denounced by Jesuit missionaries

xishi, 西士 "Western scholar"

xiucai, 修才 "Cultivated talent": signifies the first level of attainment in examination success and was one of the titles taken by the Jesuit missionaries for themselves after 1596

xu, 需 "Necessary," "requisite": etymonic nucleus of *ru* and thus the graphic source for its earliest meaning, according to Zhang Binglin and Hu Shi

xu, ䷄ The fifth hexagram of the *Yijing* traditionally identified as an image of waiting, *xu* (according to the *guaci* 卦辭 hexagram statement); it is composed of an upper trigram *kan* for water and lower trigram *qian* for the creative

xu, 刵 An early graphic variant of *xu* (bearing the knife semantic classifier), pronounced *ru*; an image of a shaman shorn of all body hair, according to Shirakawa Shizuka

xu (*ru*), 嬬 "Lesser wife," "second wife," "concubine": one of the rhyming associations with *ru* 儒 by means of which mid-imperial scholars glossed the term as "weak" (sometimes pronounced *ru*)

xuanniao, 玄鳥 "Black Bird": ornithological totem of the Shang; believed to have given birth to the ruling Zi clan of the Shang (as recounted in Ode 303 of the *Shi jing*) and linked to the birth of Kongzi in Han apocryphal texts

xue, 學 "Learning," "study"

Xuebu, 學部 National Ministry of Education: founded in 1905 following the abolition of the traditional examination system; after 1907 it became the institution that implemented the mandatory worship of Kongzi and national instruction in *guojiao* 國教 (national religion), previously known as Kongjiao 孔教 (Confucianity)

xuemai, 血脉 "Artery": Ming era term referring to the waterways over which imperial necessities—tax, tribute, and produce—moved; a homophonic pun *xuemai* 學脉 on this imperial metaphor was used by certain Jesuit antagonists in the diatribes of the *Poxie ji* 破邪集 as a means of reinforcing the legitimacy of their claims against the Jesuits

xujie, 吁嗟 Onomatopoeic rendering of the cry of a shaman according to Zhang Binglin

Yao, 堯 One of the celebrated *wudi* 五帝 (Five Sovereigns) of distant antiquity; a culture hero and paragon of meritorious rule, who, in choosing to grant succession not to his own son but to a misbegotten yet virtuous common man, the legendary Shun, symbolized the shift from ascription to merit as the basis for rule

Yazhou bingren, 亞洲病人 "Sick man of Asia": a term of derogation and self-loathing used by Chinese intellectuals to refer to China's lamentable political condition in the early decades of the twentieth century

yeman minzu, 野蠻民族 "Barbarian tribes"

Yesu, 耶穌 Jesus

yiduan, 異端 "Beginning of distinction"; heresy

yigu, 疑古 "Doubting antiquity": motto of the 18th-century textual criticism movement called *kaozheng*

Yin, 殷 Alternative name for the Shang

Yinminzu de zhongxing, 殷民族的中興 "Restoration of the Yin tribe"

Yin-Shang *wangguo shi*, 殷商亡國時 "Era of the vanquished nation of the Yin-Shang"

Yinshi, 殷士 "Yin knights": a term believed by Hu Shi to be the source for the name *ru* and describing a despondent but capable class of experts with knowledge of the rites who continued after the Zhou conquest to serve the Shang in their exile

yinshi zhi dao, 飲食之道 "The path of drinking and eating": the ethic of mere survival of the *ru* under the Zhou, according to Hu Shi

Yinxu, 殷虛 "Wastes of Yin": term that refers to the necropolis and cult center of the ruling Zi (子) clan of the Shang near present-day Anyang

yinyang, Yinyang, 陰陽 Female/male generative icons; pre-Han rhetorical fellowship associated with Zou Yan

Yiwen zhi, 藝文志   Record of Cultivations and Writings: the imperial bibliographic catalogue of the Han assembled by Liu Xiang (79–8 B.C.E.) and Liu Xin (46 B.C.E.–23 C.E.) in the last years of the Western Han; appears as chapter 30 of the *Han shu*; provides earliest claim for an early Zhou origin for *ru* in the office of *situ*; text displays a *ru*ist bias in its depiction of the *zhuzi*

yong, 用   "Use," "application," "function": employed to describe the technical trappings of Western civilization in contrast with the more profound cultural essence, *ti* 體 of China

yu, 鷸   Turquoise kingfisher; snipe: bird associated in Chinese mythology with power of foretelling

yu, 雨   "Rain": upper component of the graph *xu* 需 (the etymonic nucleus of *ru* 儒); believed by Zhang Binglin to determine the graph's ancient meaning and thus account for the repeated association of *ru* with wetness and moisture in etymologies and glosses

Yu, 禹   Last of the *wudi*; appointed by the sage-king Shun to succeed him because of his success in controlling floods that ravaged the *Zhongyuan*; legendary founder of the Xia dynasty (1953 B.C.E.), the first of the *sandai* 三代, or three foundational dynasties of historic civilization

yuanguan, 圓冠   "Round caps": purportedly worn by *ru* in antiquity

"Yuan ru", 原儒   "Etiology of ru": title of Zhang Binglin's essay of 1910 that offered a developmental history of the term that stressed its diverse, contradictory meanings and uses

yuanshi, 原始   Primordial; primitive

Yuanzhen, 元眞   Original era name of the Chengzong emperor of the Yuan (1295–1297 C.E.)

Yubu, 禹步   "The step of Yu": a rhythmic, uneven shuffle in which one leg advances while the other is dragged; believed to be an imitation of the walk of the sage-king, Yu; a magical, trance-inducing, exorcising dance performed by the shaman, *wu*

yuguan, 鷸冠   Kingfisher feather cap worn by ritual practitioners of prognostication, and associated with the ancient capping ceremony to mark the passage to manhood

yun shangyu tian, 雲上於天   "Clouds rise up to heaven": phrase from the *Yijing* statement (卦辭) for hexagram five, ䷄ *xu*, used by Hu Shi in "Shuo ru" to explicate the graph's and the hexagram's meaning of "waiting"; clouds have risen but rain has not fallen

yuyan, 預言   "Prophecy"

za, 襍   "Miscellaneous": more obscure graphic variant of *za* 雜 used by Zhang Binglin

zajia, 雜家   "Miscellaneous or adulterated family of teachings": Zhan'guo rhetorical fellowship *ze shangyu tian*, 澤上於天　"Marsh rises to heaven": phrase from the *Yijing* statement (卦辭) for hexagram forty-three, ䷪, used by Hu Shi in "Shuo ru" to explicate the graph's and the hexagram's meaning of "resolution"; marsh rises to heaven means that it has already rained and so the hexagram represents a completed action

zhangfu, 章甫　Headdress peculiar to the Shang people; it is said that Kongzi wore one when in the kingdom of Song, signaling his descent from the Shang

zhengdao, 正道　"True way": phrase used by Matteo Ricci in *Tianzhu shiyi* for the tradition of the *xianru* inaugurated by Kongzi

zhengli guogu, 整理國古　"Organize the national heritage": avowed goal of the Zhang Binglin *guocui* coterie, but one shared with other *guwen* advocates in the early 20th century; consisted in a scientific and historical reconstruction of the past texts and traditions, along with a defense of Chinese civilization against the Manchus and against Western imperialism

zhengming, 正名　"Rectification of names": common rhetorical salvo of the Warring States, one associated with the *ru* but reflecting a larger linguistic crisis of the 6th to the 3d centuries B.C.E.

zhengxue, 正學　"Correct teaching": title taken by the Jesuit missionaries for their fundamentalist defense of the *xianru* transmission of Kongzi and the justification for their recension of the Chinese text

zhi, 知　"To recognize," "to know one's worth"

zhi, 治　"Rule"

Zhina de daxiong xing, 支那的大熊星　"China's Ursa Major," "The Big Dipper of China": flattering alternative title for Kongzi used by Zhang Binglin

zhisheng wenxuanwang Kongfuzi zhi disun, 至聲文玄望孔夫子之嫡孫　"Legitimate descendant of the most holy, literary king, Kong Fuzi": honorific bestowed on the Chengzong emperor at the time of his change of era title in 1297 C.E.

zhishi fenzi, 知識分子　Intellectual(s): term used anachronistically by Hu Shi to characterize *ru* under the Zhou

zhong, 中　"Center of a target," "center," "middle"

Zhongguo, 中國　"The Central States": reference to the last remaining kingdoms arrayed in the *Zhongyuan* before the conquest by Qin; modern-day equivalent of "China"

Zhongguo fuxing, 中國復興　Restoration of China

Zhongni, 仲尼　"Second Son, Inverted Hillock": style name of Kongzi indicating his hereditary rank and recalling the *niqiu* 尼丘, "numinous hillock" where his mother prayed for his conception; a common term for him in the *Zuo zhuan*

zhongshi, 中士　"Chinese scholar": Matteo Ricci's rhetorical invention used in the effected dialogues of the Jesuit's second catechism

zhongxue wei ti yangxue wei yong, 中學爲體洋學爲用　"Chinese learning is the essence; Western learning is its (subsidiary) functioning": common phrase of the late 19th century attributed to Feng Guifen and to Zhang Zhidong

Zhongyuan, 中原 North China plain: territory near the alluvial confluence of the Huang, Huai, and Wei Rivers, considered the cultural womb of Chinese civilization

Zhou Gong, 周公 "Duke of Zhou": symbol of virtuous rule and moral probity; served as regent (r. 1042–1036 B.C.E.) to the third Zhou king, Cheng Wang (r. 1035–1006 B.C.E.), and is credited with forging the institutional structure of the Zhou cultic confederation; personal hero to Kongzi and for most of imperial history was ranked above him

zhu, 祝 Sacrificial prayer

zhuanjia, 專家 "Religious specialist": Hu Shi's description of *ru* under the Shang

zhuanshu, 篆書 Official script of the Qin standardization

zhuguan, 祝官 Office of Invocation and Sacrifice: a Shang and Zhou religious office believed by Hu Shi to have been filled by *ru*

zhuru, 侏儒 Believed by Hao Yixing (1797–1825 C.E.) in his commentary on the *Shanhai jing* to be a graphic variant of *jiaoyao*

zhuzi, 諸子 "Collective Masters," "noncanonical" masters: name for the plural, *ru* and non-*ru* traditions of the Warring States "thinkers" and their fellowships that appears in the Han imperial bibliography, "Yiwen zhi"; it includes Mozi, Zhuangzi, Yanzi, Guanzi, Kongzi, Mengzi, and Xunzi, among others

zhuzi xue, 諸子學 "Learning of the collective masters": one of the academic practices spun from *kaozheng* in the 18th century C.E.; associated with Wang Zhong (1745–1794 C.E.) and Zhang Xuecheng (1738–1801 C.E.) and taken up by Zhang Binglin and Liu Shipei in their researches in the early 20th century; one principal effect of *zhuzi xue* was the displacement of Kongzi from his apotheosized status

zi, 子 "Eldest son," "son"; "he"; "master"

zide, 自得 "Getting it oneself": a term used by Zhu Xi for moral self-mastery through learning, referring to the motivation for the labor of such accomplishment; stressed by Wm. Theodore de Bary as a critical foundation for liberalism

Ziqiang, 自強 "Self-strengthening": name of an incipient nationalist movement to fortify China against its external enemies that dominated political reform discourse from 1864 to 1895 C.E.

zong juede, 總覺的 "Always feel": expression used by Hu Shi in asserting that when Chinese read the writings of Kongzi's disciples, they "always feel" that these followers' obsession with the letter of the rites is "very much like" the Pharisees against whom Jesus inveighed

zongshi, 宗師 "Ancestral teacher": Han era honorific for Kongzi

zuo, 作 "Invent," "make," "create": graph found in early Chinese texts and bearing the same contrary significance (fashioning as well as feigning) as the English "manufacture"

NOTES

Abbreviations

CSP Philippe Couplet et al. *Confucius Sinarum Philosophus, sive Scientia Sinensis*. Paris: Daniel Horthemels, 1687.

DECAS Nicolá Trigault, ed. *De Christiana expeditione apud Sinas ab Societate Iesu Suscepta, es Matthaei Ricci Commentarus Libri*. Augsburg, 1615.

FR Pasquale M. d'Elia, S.J., ed. *Fonti Ricciane, Storia dell'Introduzione del Christianesimo in Cina*. 3 vols. Rome: Libreria dello Stato, 1942–1949.

Journals Louis J. Gallagher, S.J., trans. *China in the Sixteenth Century: The Journals of Matthew Ricci: 1583–1610*. New York: Random House, 1942.

OS Pietro Tacchi Venturi, S.J., ed. *Le Opere Storiche del P. Matteo Ricci, S.J.* 2 vols. Macerata: Giorgetti, 1911–1913.

SBBY *Sibu beiyao* [Complete Essentials of the Four Classes]. 351 titles in 2500 slips. Shanghai: Shangwu, 1920–1937.

SBCK *Sibu congkan* [Collected Editions of the Four Classes]. 468 titles in 3100 slips. Shanghai: Zhonghua Shuju, 1927–1937.

SKQS *Siku quanshu* [Complete Library of the Four Treasuries (1782)]. 3593 titles in 36,000 *juan*. Reprint, Taibei: Shangwu, 1983.

"SR" Hu Shi, "Shuo Ru" [An Elaboration on *Ru* (1934)], in *Hu Shi wencun* [Collected Essays of Hu Shi]. 4 vols. Taibei: Yuandong, 1953, vol. 4, pp. 1–82.

SSJZ Zhu Xi, ed. *Sishu jizhu* [Collected Commentaries on the Four Books (1189)]. Reprint, Taibei: Xuehai Chubanshe, 1984.

SSJZS Ruan Yuan, ed. *Shisanjing zhushu* [The Thirteen Classics, Annotated with Commentary (1815 woodblock of standard Song edition containing Han and Tang commentaries)]. 13 vols. Reprint, Shanghai: Guji Chubanshe, 1990.

TMLH Douglas Lancashire and Peter Hu Kuo-chen, S.J., trans. *The True Meaning of the Lord of Heaven* (complete English translation of *Tianzhu shiyi*). St. Louis, Mo.: Institute of Jesuit Sources, 1985.

TXCH Li Zhizao, ed. *Tianxue chuhan* [The Essentials of the Heavenly Learning (1609)]. 6 vols. Reprint, Taibei: Xuesheng Shuju, 1965.

TZSY   Li Madou [Matteo Ricci]. *Tianzhu shiyi* [The Real Significance of the Heavenly Master (1603)], in Li Zhizao, ed., *Tianxue chuhan* [The Essentials of the Heavenly Learning], vol. 1., pp. 351–635.

VDRE   Michele Ruggieri. *Vera et brevis divinarum rerum expositio* (1579–1581). Reprinted in Pietro Tacchi Venturi, ed., *Le Opere Storiche del P. Matteo Ricci, S.J.*, vol. 2., pp. 498–540.

"YR"   Zhang Binglin. "Yuan Ru" [The Etiology of *Ru*], in *Guogu lunheng* [Critical Exposition of the National Heritage (1910)]. 2 vols. Reprint, Taibei: Guangwen Shuju, 1967, vol. 1, pp. 151–155.

ZZJC   *Zhuzi jicheng* [Complete Collection of the Various Masters]: 8 vols. Reprint, Beijing: Zhonghua Shuju, 1990.

Introduction

1   Homer and Jethro, *Homer and Jethro's "Cornfucius Say" Joke Book: A Collection of Corn-temporary Wit'n Wisdom* (Battle Creek, Mich.: [Kellogg's Company, 1964]). In addition, Historical Products, Inc., of Cambridge, Mass., a maker of T-shirts printed with the likenesses of famous figures, includes a Confucius T-shirt in their inventory. I would like to thank David Keightley for the reference to Homer and Jethro.

2   Carol Osborn, *How Would Confucius Ask for a Raise? 100 Enlightened Solutions for Tough Business Problems* (New York: Morrow, 1994). I am grateful to Richard Burden for this reference.

3   "Accommodationism" is the term used to refer to a systematic apologist strategy conceived by the Jesuits under the aegis of Francis Xavier (1506–1552) for conversion of the Chinese. As a program of proselytism, directed by Alessandro Valignano (1539–1606), it called for rigorous grounding in the language and customs of the target population. See Johannes Bettray, S.V.D., *Die Akkommodationsmethode des P. Matteo Ricci S.I. in China* (Analecta Gregoriane, vol. LXXVI [Rome: Aedes Universitatis Gregorianae, 1955]), pp. 235–327; D. E. Mungello, *Curious Land: Jesuit Accommodation and the Origins of Sinology* (Honolulu: University of Hawai'i Press, 1989), pp. 13–19, 44–73, 247–299.

4   For examples of this religious nomenclature, see Henri Doré, *Recherches sur les superstitions en Chine*, vol. 13 (Shanghai: Imprimerie de la Mission Catholique, 1918); and Herbert A. Giles, *Chinese Biographical Dictionary* (Shanghai: Kelly and Walsh, 1898).

5   The masculine pronoun is needed here because all Jesuit missionaries and *ru* were men.

6   *Les Vies des plus illustres philosophes de l'antiquité, avec leurs dogmes, leurs systèmes, leur morale, & leurs sentences les plus remarquables; traduites du grec de Diogene Laerce* (Amsterdam: J. H. Schneider, 1758).

7   What these figures actually knew about China was less a reasoned conjecture grounded in "fact" than an invention inspired by the rapidly growing fund of information about the country. Nevertheless, Voltaire seems to have had a French

transcription of a Chinese disputation from the Warring States era (439–221 B.C.E.) from which he imaginatively constructed the "Chinese Catechism" that appears in his *Dictionnaire philosophique*. Montesquieu, it is known, had regular contact with a Chinese emigré, Arcadio Huang, a cataloger and translator of Chinese books in France who compiled the first Chinese/French dictionary. (While Montesquieu was drafting *De l'esprit des lois* he interviewed Huang.) Jonathan Spence, personal communication, April 13, 1990; and Jonathan Spence, "Claims and Counter-Claims: The Kangxi Emperor and the Europeans (1661–1722)," in *The Chinese Rites Controversy: Its History and Meaning*, ed. D. E. Mungello (Nettetal: Steyler Verlag, 1994), pp. 15–28.

8 The estimate of nearly 50 percent is taken from Frederic Wakeman Jr., *The Great Enterprise: The Manchu Reconstruction of Imperial Order in Seventeenth-Century China* (Berkeley: University of California Press, 1985), vol. 1, pp. 5–6. On the circulation of specie and precious metals in a global economy that favored China see William Atwell, "Notes on Silver, Foreign Trade, and the Late Ming Economy," *Ch'ing-shih wen-t'i* (December 1977): 1–33. On the movement of specie eastward in the sixteenth century and China's role within the developing world economy see Pierre Chaunu, "Manille et Macao, face à la conjoncture des XVI et XVII siècles," *Annales: économies, sociétés, civilisations* 17: 555–580; and Fernand Braudel, *The Mediterranean and the Mediterranean World in the Age of Phillip II*, vol. 1, trans. Sian Reynolds (New York: Harper and Row, 1972), pp. 462–510.

9 See Paul A. Rule, *K'ung-tzu or Confucius? The Jesuit Interpretation of Confucianism* (Sydney: Allen and Unwin Australia, 1986), p. 73; and Louis le Comte, S.J., *Nouveaux mémoires sur l'état présent de la Chine*, vol. 1 (Paris: Jean Anisson, 1697), p. 337.

10 Xu Yuanhe, *Ruxue yu dongfang wenhua* (Beijing: Renmin Chubanshe, 1994), pp. 47–58.

11 It was not very long ago that the campaign ended, for as Kam Louie points out in his history of contemporary criticism of Kongzi, polemics were still being written and protests organized in 1979, three years after the arrest of the Gang of Four, the four high-ranking and ultra-left-leaning Communist Party Politburo members—Jiang Qing (Mao Zedong's wife), Yao Wenyuan, Wang Hongwen, Zhang Chunqiao—who were officially credited with the excesses of the Great Proletarian Cultural Revolution (1966–1976). According to Susan Blum (personal communication, 1989), one could still hear echoes of the campaign in the streets of Nanjing in 1982. See Kam Louie, *Critiques of Confucius in Contemporary China* (New York: St. Martin's Press, 1980), pp. 97–136; and Jilin daxue lishixi, comp., *Yiqie fandongpai doushi zun Kongpai* (Beijing: Renmin Chubanshe, 1974).

12 In March 1986 an academic journal by the same name, *Kongzi yanjiu*, was begun at Qufu.

13 "Publisher's Note," in Kong Dema and Ke Lan, *In the Mansion of Confucius' Descendants* (Beijing: New World Press, 1984), p. iii.

14 Yu Ronggen, "Studies on Confucius in Our Country in Recent Years," in Etiemble, *Confucius (Maitre K'ong)* (Paris: Gallimard, 1986), pp. 285–291. Since the

Han dynasty, ceremonies were held (the Spring and Autumn Sacrifices) to honor Kongzi in the second and eighth months of the Chinese lunar calendar. To these seasonal days of celebration the Yongzheng emperor added, by ad hoc proclamation in 1727, an empire-wide observance of Kongzi's birth on the twenty-seventh day of the eighth lunar month. In Taiwan, this annual observance is maintained with great reverence and raucousness as Teacher's Day. On the history of memorial observance for Kongzi, see John K. Shryock, *The Origin and Development of the State Cult of Confucius* (New York: Century, 1932). See also Onogawa Hidemi and Shimada Kenji, eds., *Shingai kakumei no kenkyū* (Tokyo: Chikuma shobō, 1978), pp. 3–35. One estimate of the throngs in attendance at the 2,535th anniversary in Qufu was fifty thousand.

15   I say "disputed" because there are several other regions that have claimed to be the ancestral home of the Kong clan. There was an impromptu argument over the legitimacy of the Qufu claim at a recent gathering of scholars in the People's Republic of China (Frederic Wakeman, personal communication, fall 1990). The philosopher Li Zehou, for example, is of the belief that the authentic ancestral locus is near Suzhou; however, since the Tang (618–907 C.E.) there have been claimants of Kong descent in Gansu, not far from Dunhuang. Wolfram Eberhard has identified a Kong clan among twenty-nine clan names on a register of noble families of 634 C.E. and, according to this register, while they were originally from Lu, they had registered as a gentry family of Dunhuang before the Tang. It is very likely that this family was not of Chinese origin and that they had lived in western China since before the Han. See Wolfram Eberhard, "The Leading Families of Ancient Tunhuang," in *Settlement and Social Change in Asia* (Hong Kong: Hong Kong University Press, 1967), pp. 102–129.

16   My thanks to Michael Lindblom for these observations about beer and popular culture in central Shandong. The "three Kongs" refer to the Kong Mansion (Kongfu), the Kong Forest (Konglin), and the Kong Temple (Kongmiao).

17   Haun Saussy introduced me to the Kong Family brew.

18   For the term "hypergrowth" and an analysis of its functional value in defining the rapid expansion of certain Asian economies, see Edward K. Y. Chen, *Hypergrowth in Asian Economies: A Comparative Study of Hong Kong, Japan, Korea, Singapore, and Taiwan* (New York: Macmillan, 1979). See also Chalmers Johnson, *MITI and the Japanese Miracle* (Stanford: Stanford University Press, 1982), who argues that the political economies of the "Four Little Dragons"—Taiwan, Singapore, Hong Kong, and South Korea—represent a new form of industrial nation that he calls the "capitalist development state." The core value thesis of economic development in Asia is now a commonplace in academic and journalistic accounts and is well presented in Tai Hung-chao, ed., *Confucianism and Economic Development: An Oriental Alternative* (Washington, D.C.: Washington Institute Press, 1989). Lee Kuan Yew's pronouncements concerning the comparative rationality of a "Confucian"-grounded modernization are liberally cited in the press. See Fareed Zakaria, "Culture Is Destiny: A Conversation with Lee Kuan Yew," *Foreign Affairs* 73, no. 2 (March/April 1994): 109–126.

19   There has been more and more of this kind of interpretation of Confucianism in

recent years. A great deal of it has appeared in the Hong Kong political and cultural weekly, *Jiushi niandai* (The Nineties) with contributions from Tu Wei-ming, Liu Shu-hsien, and Li Zehou. For examples of this interpretation, see Tu Wei-ming, "A Confucian Perspective on the Rise of Industrial East Asia," *Bulletin of the American Academy of Arts and Sciences* 42, no. 1 (October 1988): 32–50; Tu Wei-ming, "The Rise of Industrial East Asia: The Role of Confucian Values," *Copenhagen Papers in East and Southeast Asian Studies* (April 1989): 81–97; Tu Wei-ming, "Wenhua Zhongguo chutan," *Jiushi niandai*, no. 245 (June 1990): 60–61; and Ezra Vogel, *The Four Little Dragons: The Spread of Industrialization in East Asia* (Cambridge, Mass.: Harvard University Press, 1992).

20 Tu Wei-ming, "Hsiung Shih-li's Quest for Authentic Existence," in *The Limits of Change: Essays on Conservative Alternatives in Republican China*, ed. Charlotte Furth (Cambridge, Mass.: Harvard University Press, 1976), p. 246.

21 Advocates of this interpretation distinguish themselves from, and are quite hostile to, the *guojiao* (national religion) conception of *ru* that was put forward by Kang Youwei and which the Qing government attempted to implement on a national level in the final years of its rule (see chapter 3). See "Ting Li Zehou, Liu Shu-hsien tan 'He Shang,' " *Jiushi niandai*, no. 227 (December 1988): 88–91.

22 Wm. Theodore de Bary, *Learning for One's Self: Essays on the Individual in Neo-Confucian Thought* (New York: Columbia University Press, 1991), p. xii.

23 Wm. Theodore de Bary, *The Trouble with Confucianism* (Cambridge, Mass.: Harvard University Press, 1991), p. 112.

24 For a scholarly treatment of tradition and invention in Europe, Africa, and India, see Eric Hobsbawm and Terrence Ranger, eds., *The Invention of Tradition* (Cambridge: Cambridge University Press, 1983).

25 See de Bary's recent defense of Confucianism against the particular charges of autocracy and sexism leveled by Anthony Yu on a panel at the Forty-fifth Meeting of the Association for Asian Studies in Los Angeles, March 1993. De Bary's remarks, along with the comments of Irene Bloom, Chang Hao, Frederic Wakeman, Yü Ying-shih, and Anthony Yu, were published as "A Roundtable Discussion of *The Trouble with Confucianism* by Wm. Theodore de Bary," *China Review International* 1, no. 1 (spring 1994): pp. 11–47.

26 David L. Hall and Roger T. Ames, *Thinking through Confucius* (Albany: State University of New York Press, 1987). See pp. 1–25, where the authors place themselves within the context of previous interpretations and approaches.

27 Hall and Ames, *Thinking through Confucius*, pp. 7–8. Emphasis added. See also pp. 29–43.

28 See Richard Rorty, *Philosophy and the Mirror of Nature* (Princeton: Princeton University Press, 1979), pp. 315–356; and Rorty, *Contingency, Irony, Solidarity* (Cambridge: Cambridge University Press, 1989). The authors appear amenable to Rorty's call for the abandonment of epistemology, where rigid laws of commensurability and paradigmatic truth hold, in favor of hermeneutics, because the latter creates a conversation and does not impose laws. Following this reasoning then there can be no philosophy with a capital *P* and no theistic concept of a single unvarying truth. These notions are (in this view) the legacy of a decrepit Anglo-

European philosophical tradition. Yet the urge for truth is very difficult to jettison, as we can see in this case. For a similar critique that emphasizes the singular incoherence of contemporary philosophical practice, see Alasdair MacIntyre, *After Virtue: A Study in Moral Theory*, 2d ed. with postscript (Notre Dame, Ind.: University of Notre Dame Press, 1984).

29 *Mengzi zhushu, SSJZS*, vol. 13 (reprint; Shanghai: Guji Chubanshe, 1990), pp. 56.2, 57.1.

30 One reason for the frequency of his appearance in the texts of competitive traditions might be that Mozi and Zhuangzi were, as Zhang Binglin once believed, members of the *ru* fellowship from the beginning—fallen followers of the same master. See chapter 3.

31 *Zhuangzi jijie, ZZJC*, vol. 3, part 2 (Beijing: Zhonghua Shuju, 1990), p. 91. See also A. C. Graham, *Chuang-tzu: The Inner Chapters* (London: George Allen and Unwin, 1981), pp. 192–193; and Burton Watson, trans., *The Complete Works of Chuang Tzu* (New York: Columbia University Press, 1968), pp. 159–160.

32. *Zhuangzi jijie*, p. 177; and Watson, trans., *Complete Works of Chuang Tzu*, pp. 296–297.

33 On the historical significance of this collected lore and the fictive quality of Kongzi's existence, see Lionel M. Jensen, "Wise Man of the Wilds: Fatherlessness, Fertility, and the Mythic Exemplar, Kongzi," *Early China* 20 (1995): 407–437.

34 *Lunyu zhushu, SSJZS*, vol. 10, pp. 136.1, 137.2; Pound, *Confucius: The Unwobbling Pivot, The Great Digest, and The Analects* (New York: New Directions, 1969), p. 263; Arthur Waley, *The Analects of Confucius* (New York: Vintage Books, 1938), p. 193; James Legge, *The Chinese Classics*, vol. 1 (reprint; Hong Kong: Chinese University Press, 1971), p. 294; and D. C. Lau, *Confucius: The Analects* (New York: Penguin Classics, 1962), p. 132.

35 See *Mozi jiangu*, in *ZZJC*, vol. 4, pt. 1, p. 187. A somewhat different recollection of this dark moment in the history of Kongzi and his following is repeated in several places in the *Zhuangzi*.

36 See Robert E. Hegel, *The Novel in Seventeenth-Century China* (New York: Columbia University Press, 1981), pp. 67–103. One cannot resist wondering in this respect whether it was the narrative ubiquitousness of Kongzi that inspired Chinese intellectuals of the late nineteenth and early twentieth century (especially May Fourth enthusiasts) to identify him so broadly with "tradition."

37 Arthur Waley, *Ballads and Stories from Tun-Huang* (London: George Allen and Unwin, 1960), pp. 89–96.

38 See David McMullen, *State and Scholars in T'ang China* (Cambridge: Cambridge University Press, 1988), p. 34.

39 *The Compact Edition of the Oxford English Dictionary* (Oxford: Oxford University Press, 1971), p. 1721. In his *Treatise on Images* of 1567, cited here as the first usage of "manufacture," the Catholic controversialist scholar, Reverend Nicholas Sander (1530–1581) writes, "Yet the image is rather a manufacture, to wit, a thing wrought upon a creature by the artificer's hand, then a seueral creature of it self."

40 *Oxford English Dictionary*, p. 991. See also Raymond Williams, *Keywords: A*

Vocabulary of Culture and Society, rev. ed. (New York: Oxford University Press, 1985), pp. 134–135.

41 See Xu Shen, *Shuowen jiezi* (Beijing: Zhonghua Shuju, 1963); Duan Yucai, *Shuowen jiezi zhu* (reprint; Taibei, 1984); Zhou Fagao et al., *Jinwen gulin* (Hong Kong: Chinese University Press, 1974–1975), nos. 1079, 1620. See also Bernhard Karlgren, *Grammatica Serica Recensa* (reprint; Stockholm: Museum of Far Eastern Antiquities, 1972), pp. 212–213, no. 8061; and Axel Schuessler, *A Dictionary of Early Zhou Chinese* (Honolulu: University of Hawai'i Press, 1987), pp. 874–875.

42 Gu Jiegang, *Gushi bian*, vol. 1 (reprint; Hong Kong: Taiping Shuju, 1962), esp. pp. 51–70; Arthur W. Hummell, *The Autobiography of a Chinese Historian* (Leiden: E. J. Brill, 1931), pp. 92–133; and Lawrence Schneider, *Ku Chieh-kang and China's New History: Nationalism and the Quest for Alternative Traditions* (Berkeley: University of California Press, 1971), pp. 18–52. See also Zhang Xincheng's notable analysis of the many different meanings of *weishu* ("forgery," "apocrypha"), in *Weishu tongkao*, vol. 1 (Taibei: Dingwen Shuju, 1973), pp. 16–17.

43 See Hans-Georg Gadamer, *Truth and Method*, trans. Garret Barden and William G. Doerpel (New York: Seabury Press, 1975), pp. 345–447.

Chapter 1

1 Marshall Sahlins, *Islands of History* (Chicago: University of Chicago Press, 1985).

2 While acknowledging that "Confucius is, in a sense, a Jesuit invention . . . and was introduced to Europe in the language of Rome," even Paul Rule avoids the identification of a text and an author. See Paul Rule, *K'ung-tzu or Confucius? The Jesuit Interpretation of Confucianism* (Sydney: Allen and Unwin Australia, 1980), p. ix.

3 "Engaged representation" is taken from Stephen Greenblatt, *Marvelous Possessions: The Wonder of the New World* (Chicago: University of Chicago Press, 1991). The phrase aptly describes Jesuit exercises in translation and commentary.

4 Ruggieri, Ricci, Francesco Pasio, and ten other missionaries departed Lisbon on March 29, 1578, and arrived in Goa on September 13, 1578. The transit to Macao (a city of more than five thousand, nine hundred of whom were Portuguese) could take another six months, but most of the fathers appointed to serve in the Mission of the Indies remained in Goa for study and/or preaching with the prospect of assignment in East Asia dependent on the judgment of the visitor of the mission, who held authority over appointments in China, Japan, and the Philippines. (The visitor's authority in such matters was negotiated with the Jesuit provincial at Goa, and both took their orders from the general of the Society of Jesus in Rome.) Ruggieri and Pasio were posted to Eastern missions within several months of their arrival at Goa and were ferried to Macao, while Ricci remained under the command of the provincial in India, Rui Vicente, until 1582, when he was summoned by the visitor of the Jesuit order in the East Indies to join Ruggieri.

5 I do not mean in this account to give the impression that Ruggieri and Ricci were the only priests assigned to the China Mission. By 1583 there were Jesuits in

Macao, Japan, the Philippines, and in Zhaoqing, many of whom circled through the East Asian missions in accord with their assignments. In the early years of the mission in China, Ricci and Ruggieri were joined by Francesco Pasio, Francisco Cabral (rector of the Jesuit college at Macao), Duarte de Sande (the actual leader of the China Mission in its early years), Pero Gomes, and Antonio d'Almeida. What made Fathers Ruggieri and Ricci's situation unusual was that their success in gaining admission into China for the Society of Jesus (because of their accomplishment in Chinese) ensured they would remain there.

6   On the significance of culture shock and the textual productivity occasioned by the observer's experience of dislocation, see Roy Wagner, *The Invention of Culture*, rev. and exp. ed. (Chicago: University of Chicago Press, 1981), pp. 1–70.

7   Fr. Pedro Gomez [Pero Gomes], letter to General Claudio Acquaviva, October 25, 1581, in Josef F. Schütte, S.J., *Monumenta Historica Japoniae*, vol. 1 (Rome: 1975), p. 117.

8   See Louis Pfister, S.J., *Notices biographiques et bibliographiques sur les jésuites de l'ancienne mission de Chine, 1552–1773*, vol. 1 of 2 vols. (Shanghai: La Maison Catholique, 1932), p. 20.

9   Pasquale d'Elia has given this work the title *Vocabularium Lusitano-Sinicae*; see Matteo Ricci, *Fonti Ricciane (Storia dell'Introduzione del Christianesimo in Cina)*, ed. Pasquale M. d'Elia, S.J., 3 vols. (Rome: Libreria dello Stato, 1942–1949), vol. 2, p. 32, n. 1 (hereafter cited as d'Elia, *FR*).

10 This account of the early activities of Father Ruggieri is drawn from Albert Chan, S.J., "Michele Ruggieri, S.J. (1543–1607) and His Chinese Poems," *Monumenta Serica* 41 (1993): 129–176.

11 On Ruggieri's atlas of China, see Eugenio lo Sardo, "The Earliest European Atlas of Ming China: An Unpublished Work by Michele Ruggieri," *Actes du VIe Colloque International de Sinologie* (Paris, 1994). Lo Sardo states that there are thirty-six maps of China, all drafted by Ruggieri.

12 The Chinese title of Ricci's map was *Shanhai yu tu quantu* (The Complete Map of the Mountains, Seas, and Land). The map may be found in Feng Mugang, *Yuelin guangyi, juan* 1, p. 60. Ricci reported to Acquaviva in November of 1584 that he had drawn a world map in the manner of European cartography at the urging of Wang Pan, the principal benefactor of the mission. See Pietro Tacchi Venturi, S.J. *Le Opere Storiche del P. Matteo Ricci S.J.*, 2 vols. (Macerata: Giorgetti, 1911–1913), vol. 2, p. 51 (hereafter cited as Tacchi Venturi, *OS*). On the initial drawing of the *mappamondo* and its subsequent celebrated history, see Pasquale M. d'Elia, S.J., *Il Mappamondo Cinese del P. Matteo Ricci S.J. (Terza Edizione, Pechino, 1602) Conservato presso la Biblioteca Vaticana* (Rome: Vatican, 1938).

13 It first appeared, along with Ruggieri's translation of the *Daxue*, as book 9 of Antonio Possevino's *Bibliotecha selecta qua agitur de ratione studiorum in historia, in disciplinis, in salute omnium procuranda* (Rome, 1593). See "Verum brevis divinarum rerum expositio" in Tacchi Venturi, *OS*, vol. 2, pp. 498–540 (hereafter cited as Ruggieri, *VDRE*).

14 On this genre distinction and its significance, see Rule, *K'ung-tzu or Confucius?* p. 7.

15 *Ru* are usually described as "the order of the literati" (*la legge de' letterati*) in Ricci's history of the Jesuit mission in China, titled *Della entrata della Compagnia di Giesù e Christianità nella Cina* or *Storia dell'Introduzione del Christianesimo in Cina*. In Nicolá Trigault's Latin translation one finds the terms *literatorum secta, secta literatii,* and, an expression conspicuously absent from Ricci's text, *secta Confutii.* See Nicolá Trigault and Matteo Ricci, *De Christiana expeditione apud Sinas ab Societate Iesu Suscepta, es Matthaei Ricci Commentarus Libri* (Augsburg, 1615), pp. 84, 105 (hereafter cited as Trigault and Ricci, *DECAS*). D'Elia says that *legge* was used by Ricci to convey a religious rather than a legal significance. Literally the term denotes "law," but I translate it as "order," as this seems to be how Ricci intended it.

16 See Johannes Bettray S.V.M., *Die Akkommodationsmethode des P. Matteo Ricci, S.J. in China* (Rome: Aedes Universitatis Gregorianae, 1955), pp. 235–327; and D. E. Mungello, *Curious Land: Jesuit Accommodation and the Origins of Sinology* (Honolulu: University of Hawai'i Press, 1989), pp. 44–73, 247–299.

17 Ruggieri was well apprised, as was every other servant of the mission, of the extreme difficulty met by the mission in its efforts to secure lodging within the borders of China proper, and this awareness is explicit in the first of his letters published by Jesuit authorities. He relates rather soberly that he has obtained permission from the Vicerè (viceroy), the provincial governor, to establish residence in China, saying, "There is no doubt that the Father Visitor [Valignano] is most thankful to the goodness of God for the grace and mercy given us in so difficult a matter. It was previously thought to be impossible to be able to enter this great kingdom, which in the forty years since our good Father Francis Xavier began the undertaking, has not been accomplished until now. May the Lord, in whom our hope is placed, be thanked forever." See Tacchi Venturi, *OS*, vol. 2, p. 417; and M. Howard Rienstra, trans., *Jesuit Letters from China, 1583–1584* (Minneapolis: University of Minnesota Press, 1986), p. 18.

18 These are Ricci's words, taken from his recollection of the early efforts of the Jesuits to gain entrance into the mainland. In the original the entire sentence reads: "E sapendo bene il Beato Padre che tutte le leggi e riti de' Giapponi hebbero origine dalla Cina, venne in pensiero che, se potesse prima convertere la Cina, non solo si farebbe bene ad un regno sì grande e nobile, ma in un medesmo tratto facilmente anco restarebbe convertito il Giappone." Xavier, furthermore, believed that Chinese was the linguistic root of Japanese and, in this light, his grand conversion strategy required that the fathers achieve native linguistic competence. See d'Elia, *FR*, vol. 1, p. 137.

19 Early in 1552 St. Francis Xavier wrote: "I hope to go there this year, and penetrate even to the Emperor himself. China is that sort of kingdom, that if the seed of the Gospel is sown, it may be propagated far and wide. And, moreover, if the Chinese accept the Christian faith, the Japanese would give up the doctrines which the Chinese have taught them." See H. J. Coleridge, ed., *The Life and Letters of St. Francis Xavier*, vol. 2 of 2 vols. (London: Burns and Oates, 1902), pp. 347–348. Apparently Xavier's conversion plan was common knowledge among the members of the society, for Ricci describes it in the second book of his journals with

corroboration from Xavier himself: "[S]e la Santa Fede che predicava era sì buona e conforme alla ragione, per qual causa il regno della Cina, che è tenuto per il più savio de tuti i regni orientali, non l'aveva anco pigliatta." See d'Elia, *FR*, vol. 1, pp. 136–137.

20 On Valignano and his uncompromising program of accommodation, linking Jesuit missionaries and native "men of letters," see Pfister, *Notices biographiques et bibliographiques*, vol. 1, pp. 13–14; d'Elia, *FR*, vol. 1, pp. 139–147; George H. Dunne, S.J., *Generation of Giants: The Story of the Jesuits in China in the Last Decades of the Ming Dynasty* (Notre Dame, Ind.: University of Notre Dame Press, 1962), pp. 17–20; and J. M. Braga, "The Panegyric of Alexander Valignano, S.J.," *Monumenta Nipponica* 5, no. 2 (1942): 523–535.

21 On the significance of the term "inculturation" in characterizing Jesuit accommodationism as well as the later Chinese assimilation of Christianity in the era following Ricci and Ruggieri, see D. E. Mungello, *The Forgotten Christians of Hangzhou* (Honolulu: University of Hawai'i Press, 1994), pp. 1–5.

22 The marginality of the China Mission was exaggerated by the ill-defined politics of the Jesuit presence in Asia. The Roman Catholic Church had made its way to Malacca, Japan, and China by way of Portuguese vessels, thanks to an earlier agreement between the papacy and the Portuguese crown. Until 1622 the *Padroado* was officially conferred upon the various Catholic orders by the Portuguese king. Institutionally centered at Goa, the *Padroado* was the religious authority in Asia through which the Vatican's ecclesiastical jurisdiction was negotiated. Though under the protection of the Portuguese crown, the Jesuits endeavored assiduously, and clandestinely, to obtain a monopoly over the Japan-China Mission, which they did by agreement in 1655 with the Holy See and not with the Portuguese. See Donald F. Lach and Edwin J. Van Kley, *Asia in the Making of Europe*, vol. 3, bk. 1 (Chicago: University of Chicago Press, 1993), pp. 168–200.

23 On "portugalizing" Chinese converts, see Dunne, *Generation of Giants*, pp. 16–20. For the specific request that the China Mission be segregated from the Jesuit community at Macao, see Alessandro Valignano, letter of 1582 to Father General Claudio Acquaviva, in Tacchi Venturi, *OS*, vol. 2, p. 111, n. 2.

24 The adoption of Buddhist monastic costume by Jesuit missionaries began in Japan under Francis Xavier; however, it seems that this was not the practice of envoys of the China Mission until 1583. Even then it seems that members of the order were divided over the issue, as Ruggieri endorsed the practice and Ricci, at least in hindsight, grudgingly accepted it. We do know from a catechism printed in Manila in 1593—*Tianzhu zhengjiao zhenchuan shilu* (A Veritable Record of the Orthodoxy of the Heavenly Master and Its True Transmission)—that the Jesuits posted in the Philippines also assumed the role of *heshang*, which suggests that this was a policy mandated by mission superiors. On the Jesuits' incarnation as *heshang*, see Daniello Bartoli, S.J., *Dell'Istoria della Compagnia di Gésù: La Cina* (Rome, 1663), vol. 4 of 4 vols., chap. 15. Ricci invented his own name for Buddhist monks, *osciani*, and often used this instead of *bonze* to refer to them and

himself during the first phase of Jesuit accommodation. See d'Elia, *FR*, vol. 1, p. 125, n. 3.

25 Tacchi Venturi, *OS*, vol. 2, p. 416. Emphasis added.

26 The language—"vassals of the king"—is fittingly emblematic of the Jesuit reading of Chinese culture through the prism of their inherited conceptions. See Tacchi Venturi, *OS*, vol. 2, p. 33. Although Ricci implies here that the Jesuits volunteered to change their appearance, elsewhere he notes that they shaved their heads and beards late in 1583, on the advice of Wang Pan. See d'Elia, *FR*, vol. 1, p. 337, n. 1.

27 See d'Elia, *FR*, vol. 1, p. 126, where Ricci says that Buddhist monks totaled "two to three millions."

28 Emphasis added. Tacchi Venturi, *OS*, vol. 2, p. 72. Ricci marveled at the ease with which he and the other fathers were converted from Jesuit priests to Buddhist monks, all the while not deviating from their customary Christian practices. See d'Elia, *FR*, vol. 1, pp. 124–125, 336–337. Note also the metonymic character of Ricci's interpretation as he takes Buddhist monks as emblems of Chineseness.

29 On the significance of culture shock in the production of texts "representing" foreign cultures, see Wagner, *The Invention of Culture*, pp. 1–70.

30 D'Elia, *FR*, vol. 1, p. 192.

31 Michele Ruggieri, letter of May 30, 1584, in Tacchi Venturi, *OS*, vol. 2, p. 423.

32 See Tacchi Venturi, *OS*, vol. 2, p. 211.

33 On this coincidence, see the discussion in Jacques Gernet, *China and the Christian Impact*, trans. Janet Lloyd (Cambridge: Cambridge University Press, 1985), pp. 16–17.

34 Nicolá Trigault and Matteo Ricci, *Histoire de l'expédition chrétienne au royaume de la Chine* (Paris: Desclée de Brouwer, 1978), p. 26, as quoted in Gernet, *China and the Christian Impact*, p. 74.

35 See Chün-fang Yü, *The Renewal of Buddhism in China: Chu Hung and the Late Ming Synthesis* (New York: Columbia University Press, 1981), pp. 1–8, 31–100, 223–231; and Judith Berling, *The Syncretic Religion of Lin Chao-en* (New York: Columbia University Press, 1980), pp. 33–61.

36 Henri de Lubac, *La Rencontre du bouddhisme et de l'Occident* (Paris: Aubier, 1952), pp. 68–70, n. 167; and Donald F. Lach, *Asia and the Making of Europe*, vol. 1, bk. 2 (Chicago: University of Chicago Press, 1965), pp. 674–688.

37 D'Elia, *FR*, vol. 1, plate 12, opposite p. 200.

38 See Michele Ruggieri, letter of January 25, 1584 to Acquaviva, in Tacchi Venturi, *OS*, vol. 2, p. 423. The 1586 Jesuit letterbook version of this epistle is bowdlerized and so conveys none of these circumstances. Instead it states that the viceroy granted Ruggieri a license to instruct the Chinese, "some of whom loaned me a hundred scudi," with the implication that the fathers would pay them back.

39 Paul Demiéville has stated this parallel in a different manner, noting that the Jesuit teachings, particularly those emphasizing the experimental method of European science, were implicated in the paradigm shift in Chinese epistemology from metaphysics to empirical criticism, or *kaozheng*. The interval between the Jesuit introduction of scientific techniques and their indigenous Chinese applica-

tion is explained by analogy with the great expanse of time that separated the introduction of Buddhism and its appropriation by Song-era *lixue* (learning of principle) and *daoxue* (learning of the way) cults. See Paul Demiéville, "La Pénétration du Bouddhisme dans la tradition philosophique chinoise," *Cahiers d'histoire mondiale* 3 (1956–1957): 36.

40 In his celebrated catechism, the *Tianzhu shiyi* (The Real Significance of the Heavenly Master), Ricci strenuously objects to the unhealthy proliferation of Buddhist statuary. See Li Madou (Matteo Ricci), *Tianzhu shiyi,* in *Tianxue chuhan,* ed. Li Zhizao, vol. 1 of 6 vols. (reprint; Taibei: Xuesheng Shuju, 1965), pp. 557–559 (hereafter cited as Ricci, *TZSY*).

41 D'Elia, *FR,* vol. 1, p. 131.

42 Marco Polo, *The Travels,* trans. Ronald Latham (New York: Penguin Books, 1958), pp. 213–239, especially the description there of native practices at Zayton (Quanzhou).

43 See d'Elia, *FR,* vol. 1, pp. 335–339, for Ricci's opposition to the Jesuit assumption of Buddhist appearance and his contention that Buddhist monks were frequently given to homosexual licence.

44 Letter to the author from Haun Saussy, April 2, 1994.

45 Ibid.

46 See Ricci's approving description of his mandarin dress in his letter to Edoardo de Sande of August 29, 1595, in Tacchi Venturi, *OS,* vol. 2, pp. 136–137, quoted in Jonathan D. Spence, *The Memory Palace of Matteo Ricci* (New York: Viking, 1984), p. 115.

47 On the Jesuits' referring to themselves as *ru* following their "conversion" to scholar-official dress, see Li Zhizao, *Tianxue chuhan,* vol. 1 (reprint; Taibei: Xuesheng Shuju, 1965), pp. 84–85 (hereafter, Li, *TXCH*). The administrative decision to alter the dress of the fathers, while not as soon as Ricci would have wanted, was handed down by the fall of 1594, not long after a meeting between Valignano and Lazzaro Cattaneo at the Jesuit quarters in Macao. In November of 1594, Father Valignano instructed Duarte de Sande, Ricci's superior, that the men of the mission should now grow their hair and cease referring to themselves as *bonsos.* Instead they would adopt the title *letrados.* On the specific circumstances leading to the adoption of scholar-official dress and Valignano's instructions to de Sande, see d'Elia, *FR,* vol. 1, p. 336, n. 1. For the Jesuits' self-nomination as *xiucai,* see d'Elia, *FR,* vol. 1, p. 338.

48 The more literal and more appropriate rendering of *huangdi* is "Supreme Lord." By noting the conventional tendency to identify it as "emperor," I am attempting to place myself outside a vocabulary of equivalence that has been encouraged since the eighteenth century. Given the Chinese, *huang* meaning "august" or "supreme" and *di* "lord" or "god," there is no reason to presume that in the native imagination *huangdi* was anything like our "emperor." We might understand our inherited sense of the fitness of "emperor" as a translation of *huangdi* by analogy with Arthur Waldron's demythification of the Great Wall. Although an invention of Western missionaries and travelers, this image of an unbroken three-thousand-mile-long defensive wall on China's northern tier has looped back into indige-

nous imagination as *changcheng*, and is today a cultural symbol of the Chinese and the focus of a patriotic cult. So too, "emperor" has entered the Chinese conceptual language through a similar feedback loop, as it is readily offered by the Chinese themselves as the meaning of *huangdi*. I have used "emperor" as a translation of *huangdi* throughout, in order to avoid the confusion of "Supreme Lord" with God. For some recent considerations on the meaning of the more literal term, the viability of the equivalence, and the history of its linguistic currency, see B. J. Mansvelt Beck, "The True Emperor of China," in *Leyden Studies in Sinology*, ed. W. L. Idema, papers presented at the conference held in celebration of the fiftieth anniversary of the Sinological Institute of Leyden University, December 8–12, 1980 (Leiden: E. J. Brill, 1981), pp. 23–33; and James L. Hevia, "A Multitude of Lords: Qing Court Ritual and the Macartney Embassy of 1793," *Late Imperial China* 10, no. 2 (December 1989): 72–105. See also Arthur Waldron, *The Great Wall of China: From History to Myth* (Cambridge: Cambridge University Press, 1990), pp. 1–10, 194–226.

49 On the raid and its consequences, see Spence, *Memory Palace*, pp. 57–58.

50 D'Elia, *FR*, vol. 1, pp. 335–337.

51 Ricci, letter to Acquaviva, November 15, 1592, in Tacchi Venturi, *OS*, vol. 2, p. 104. A different translation of this same letter appears in Spence, *Memory Palace*, p. 115. Note here, as in most instances when he is speaking of Buddhist monks, that Ricci refers to them as "priests." Such designation is consistent with the earliest Jesuit letters from the field wherein Buddhist clergy is identified as "priests." *Ru*, curiously, were never called by this name.

52 Trigault and Ricci, *DECAS*, p. 101. *Propria* here should be understood in the sense of "belongs to" or "is exclusive to." The implication, of course, is that the remaining sects are not exclusive to the Chinese, meaning that they are not native. Thus I have treated *propria* as part of an emphatic statement of the indigenous nature of *ru*. The term must not be understood in the sense of "proper," as some translators like Gallagher have rendered it.

53 Henri Baudet, *Paradise on Earth: Some Thoughts on European Images of Non-European Man*, trans. Elizabeth Wentholt (New Haven: Yale University Press, 1965), p. vii.

54 D'Elia, *FR*, vol. 1, p. 6. See also Nicolá Trigault and Matteo Ricci, *China in the Sixteenth Century: The Journals of Matthew Ricci, 1583–1610*, trans. Louis Gallagher, S.J. (New York: Random House, 1953), p. 5 (hereafter cited as Gallagher, *Journals*).

55 D'Elia, *FR*, vol. 1, p. 6. *Libri* does not refer to just any books, but to the *quatro libri*, or *Tetrabiblio* as Ricci designated them—the Four Books, *Sishu* (*Zhongyong, Daxue, Lunyu Mengzi*) anthologized by Zhu Xi (1130–1200). The *quatro libri*, naturally, were distinguished from the *cinqua doctrina* or the Five Classics, *Wujing* (*Yijing, Shang shu, Shi jing, Chunqiu, Li*), all presumed since the Han era to be authored and/or edited by Kongzi himself. For further explanation of these hallowed texts, see footnote 67.

56 Thus, as their accommodative choice was invisibly prejudiced by this linguistic choice, they were destined to borrow the mythic hero of Chinese official life,

Kongzi, in constructing their own native exemplar, Confucius/Kong Fuzi. The Jesuits may have become acquainted with the myths surrounding Kongzi even before their arrival on China's southern coast in 1579, for a certain "Confusius" was mentioned in the mission's first catechism, *Tianzhu shilu* (Veritable Record of the Heavenly Master).

57 D'Elia, *FR*, vol. 1, pp. 37–38. See also Gallagher, *Journals*, pp. 28–29.

58 *Clavis Sinica* was the "key to Chinese" by which certain European scholiasts (in this case Andreas Müller) intended to accelerate the mastery of Chinese in order to unlock the secrets of a universal language. Throughout the seventeenth century European intelligence was awash in reductionism, so much so that it may be proper to consider it the foundational trope of knowledge acquisition. The new and befuddling information that was transmitted to Europe about China was appropriated through this reductionist apprehension. The ideographic quality of written Chinese, for example, was read as evidence of a simpler language which, if mastered, might enable Europeans to restore the age of Adam. Decipherment and decoding were the intellectual operations of the day and were visible in all those who took special interest in China. What is intriguing in all of this is the consistent application of a dialectic of particular and universal, concrete and abstract, in which China as particular and concrete serves a European need to establish the universal by means of deduction. Whether it is Müller's work on the *Clavis Sinica*, Leibniz's on the mystical correlations of ancient Chinese numerology and his experimental binary system of arithmetic, or Bouvet's reconciliation of the chronology of the Septuagint with the dates of the *Yijing*, China functions as proof in support of the conceptual innovations of Europeans. Ricci's accommodationism bears all the signs of this seventeenth-century episteme. See Mungello, *Curious Land*, pp. 188–226.

59 See Bartoli, *Dell'Istoria della Compagnia*, vol. 4, p. 74. The passages quoted here are taken from the translation of Heinrich Busch in "The Tung-lin Academy and Its Political and Philosophical Significance," *Monumenta Serica* 14 (1949–1955): 156. See also Henri Bernard, *Le Père Mathieu Ricci et la société chinoise de son temps (1552–1610)*, vol. 2 of 2 vols. (Tianjin: Hautes Études, 1937), p. 173; and Dunne, *Generation of Giants*, pp. 372–373.

60 D'Elia, *FR*, vol. 1, p. 338, as quoted in Rule, *K'ung-tzu or Confucius?* p. 19. Note here the broad traditional Chinese class distinction between *zuoguan de ren* (officials) (the fathers' friends) and *lao baixing* (ordinary people) and the fact that the majority of Chinese continued to see the Jesuits as *heshang.*

61 "The State Family Romance" refers to the Han ideology of a self-regulating state conceived on an analogy with the family. The *wulun* (the five relations: sovereign to ruled, husband to wife, father to eldest son, elder brother to younger brother, friend to friend) and the *sangang* (the three net-ropes: sovereign to ruled, husband to wife, father to eldest son) form the conceptual basis of this definition of sovereignty as a parent-child relation in which the emperor is depicted as the patriarch. The principal ideological texts for this fable were the "Daxue" chapter of the *Li ji* and Dong Zhongshu's *Chunqiu fanlu*. Although the Chinese state was never actually run as a family, this ideological complex was the legacy of the Han

rulers, the Liu clan. The concept of "family romance" was put forward by Sigmund Freud in his studies of pediatric neurosis and describes the mythic narrative of parental love spun by neglected or abused children when asked by the analyst to characterize their family life. Almost uniformly, children subjected to maltreatment at the hands of their parents imagined a life vastly different from the one they had lived, as if their actual life and the romance were contiguous, contradictory narratives. China's State Family Romance was similarly constituted in contiguous incongruity, the state representing itself through a myth of self-regulating familiality while local lineages and their laboring dependents (especially among the *qixiong* [Seven Truculents] in the east under the Han) lived as extended families in opposition to the state. Freud's theory was formulated in the last years of the nineteenth century and was published as an unattributed essay in Otto Rank, *The Myth of the Birth of the Hero and Other Writings*, trans. F. Robbins and Smith Ely Jelliffe (New York: Vintage, 1964). Freud's essay is reprinted in *The Freud Reader*, ed. Peter Gay (New York: Norton, 1990), pp. 297–300.

62 Michele Ruggieri, "Archivum Romanum Societatis Jesu," Jap. Sin. 101, II, p. 310v., in Rule, *K'ung-tzu or Confucius?* p. 10.

63 Brian Stock, *The Implications of Literacy: Written Language and Models of Interpretation in the Eleventh and Twelfth Centuries* (Princeton: Princeton University Press, 1983), p. 90, passim.

64 "Ambedue queste sette finsero il suo ternario, acciochè si vegga chiaro esser il padre della bugia autore di tutte queste, il quale non ha anco lasciato la superba pretensione di voler essere simile al suo Creatore." See d'Elia, *FR*, vol. 1, p. 128.

65 See Peter Brown, *The Cult of the Saints: Its Rise and Function in Latin Christianity* (Chicago: University of Chicago Press, 1981), pp. 26–29, 36–41.

66 Cardinal John Henry Newman, *The Arians of the Fourth Century* (Westminster, Md.: Christian Classics, 1968), pp. 50–56.

67 Ricci, letter to Acquaviva, April 11, 1595, in Tacchi Venturi, *OS*, vol. 2, p. 207. Ricci's allusion here to the "Four Books and the Six Classics" was a common, archaistic refrain among educated Chinese of the imperial era and is meant to convey the breadth of his native erudition to General Acquaviva. The Six Classics (*Liujing*) were the *Yijing* (*Zhouyi*, Classic of Change); the *Shang shu* (*Shu jing*, Book of Documents); the *Shi jing* (*Maoshi*, Book of Odes or Poetry); the *Chunqiu* (Spring and Autumn [Annals]); the *Li* [*jing*] (The Rites Classic [probably the *Yi li*, "Decorum and Ceremonial"]); and *Yue* (Music [fragments of which it is alleged are found in *Yue ji*, "Record of Music," and *Yue zhi*, "Treatise on Music"]). The *Liujing* were the vestigial remains of the *liuyi* (Six Cultivations—music, rites, archery, charioteering, numbers, and calligraphy), skills specifically associated with the *ru* fellowship in the Warring States. It was presumed that these texts had passed from Kongzi's hand as the editorship or authorship of the *Chunqiu, Yi,* and *Shi* were attributed to him. By the time of the canonization of these works during the reign of Han emperor Wudi (141–87 B.C.E.), the Classic of Music was no longer (or had never been) extant. Thus, there were only Five Classics (*Wujing*), so that in 136 B.C.E., when official recognition was conferred on the classical traditions, the emperor appointed *ru* scholars to chairs in *Yi, Shi, Shu, Li,* and *Chunqiu*. In

175 C.E., in the waning years of the Han dynasty, an authorized edition of these classics was inscribed on stone tablets, fragments of which have survived.

By the Tang period (7th century C.E.), it was more common to speak of Nine Classics (*Jiujing*), the original *Wujing* now supplemented by the addition of the three commentaries on the *Chunqiu*—*Guliang zhuan*, *Gongyang zhuan*, and *Zuo zhuan*—and the extraction from the *Li* corpus of the *Zhou li* (*Zhou guan*, Rites of Zhou) and the *Li ji* (Record of the Rites).

In the Song dynasty (12th century C.E.) the official number of *jing* was increased to thirteen (*Shisanjing*) with the inclusion of the pre-Han etymology, *Erya* (Literary Expositor), the *Xiaojing* (Classic of Filiality), the *Lunyu* (Selected Sayings of Kongzi), and the *Mengzi* (Book of Mengzi). These last two Warring States collections, *Lunyu* and *Mengzi*, along with two chapters extracted from the *Li ji*—the *Daxue* (Great Learning) and the *Zhongyong* (Doctrine of the Mean)—had been anthologized in 1189 C.E. by Zhu Xi in the *Sizi* (Four Masters), later known as the *Sishu* (Four Books). The *Sizi* was created as a classical catechism for the students in Zhu's private academy, with instruction in these works intended as a propaedeutic to the proper study of the *Wujing*. Roughly a century after Zhu Xi's death, the *Sizi* had become the *Sishu* and was made the required syllabus for scholars training for the provincial and national examinations to enter the Chinese civil service. The *Sishu* remained a textual centerpiece of the examination system until 1905.

68 "Key" here is an allusion to the *Clavis Sinica*; see note 58.

69 Ricci, *TZSY*, p. 468.

70 Ricci, *TZSY*, p. 392.

71 Ricci, *TZSY*, p. 367.

72 See Voltaire, *Dictionnaire philosophique portatif* (Amsterdam: M. M. Rey, 1765), and *Essai sur les moeurs et l'esprit des nations et sur les principaux faits de l'histoire depuis Charlemagne jusqu'a Louis XIII* (Lausanne: J. H. Pott, 1780), pp. 13–31.

73 Undoubtedly each of the volunteers for the Mission of the Indies was similarly committed, driven by a salvific enthusiasm and convinced of the righteousness of their cause; however, some, like Francisco Cabral, while zealous, were far less sanguine than Ricci at the prospect of finding God amid "the people of Yao and Shun." Writing back to Acquaviva to report of a visit to Zhaoqing following the establishment of the mission, Cabral [Father Francesco (Francisco) Cabral to Acquaviva, December 8, 1584, Macao, in Tacchi Venturi, *OS*, vol. 2, pp. 52–53] presents a different understanding of the outlook for China's salvation, saying: "It remains only to pray to Your Paternity that you intercede much with our Lord God for this mission that is so important to His holy service and to the salvation of many thousands of souls, who, for the lack of those who will show them the way of salvation, will perish miserably." This letter was published in the 1586 letterbook of the Society of Jesus, which, although nominally devoted to correspondence concerning the activities of the mission in Japan, contained eight letters written by Jesuit missionaries in China. An English translation of Cabral's letter, along with the other seven, may be found in Rienstra, *Jesuit Letters*, pp. 25–28.

74 Jaroslav Pelikan, *The Vindication of Tradition* (New Haven: Yale University Press, 1984), pp. 23–32.

75 See Philippe Couplet et al., "Proemialis Declaratio," in *Confucius Sinarum Philosophus, sive Scientia Sinensis* (Paris: Horthemels, 1687), pp. lx–lxiii (hereafter, cited as Couplet, *CSP*).

76 Zhu Xi, *Zhuzi yulei* (reprint; Kyoto: Zhongwen Chubanshe, 1970), 397:1.

77 These works are randomly culled from the references found in the *Tianzhu shiyi*, *Jiayou lun*, and the *Jiren shipian* but should convey the diverse influences on Ricci's thought. *Jiren shipian* and *Jiayou lun* are also included in the first volume of Zhizao, *TXCH*, pp. 93–297 and pp. 299–323, respectively.

78 Mungello, *Curious Land*, p. 16.

79 Ricci, *TZSY*, p. 582. For contemporary Chinese examination candidates, *ren* was also known through a two-sentence axiom, taken from the opening lines of Zhu Xi's "Explanation of *ren*" (*Renshuo*): "Heaven and Earth take humaneness as mind and in the generation of man and things each receives this mind of Heaven and Earth as their mind." See Zhu Xi, "Renshuo," in *Zhuzi wenji*, Sibu congkan chubian jibu edition, vol. 7 (Shanghai: Shangwu Chubanshe, n.d.), p. 1244.

80 Consensus among the Jesuits held, as it did among many Chinese of their time, that Confucius was responsible for the *Jiujing*, or Nine Classics, along with the Four Books ("Confutio accomodò quatro libri antichi"). Furthermore, some of the metaphysical and cosmogonic conceptions of later *ru* thinkers like Zhou Dunyi (1017–1073 C.E.) and Zhang Zai (1020–1077 C.E.) were attributed to Confucius as well. For example, Matteo Ricci was convinced that Kongzi had spoken of Taiji, and the misunderstanding was transmitted to later accommodationists. See Ricci, *TZSY*, pp. 413–414, and Couplet, *CSP*, pp. xxxv–xxxvii. On Confucius's authorship of the Four Books, see d'Elia, *FR*, vol. 1, p. 42.

81 Ricci, *TZSY*, p. 415.

82 See d'Elia, *FR*, vol. 2, p. 33, and n. 5. By a clever inductive method, Ricci introduced new recruits to the target language through his bilingual handwritten translation of the *Sishu*, so that as they acquired facility in Chinese they mastered the teachings of Kongzi. This text was the first of its kind and part of a concurrent effort by Ricci to compile a Chinese/Portuguese lexicon.

83 Ricci's use of the Four Books as a language primer probably represents the first instance of teaching "Chinese by the inductive method," advocated by Herrlee Creel in this century. See Herrlee G. Creel, *Literary Chinese by the Inductive Method* (Chicago: University of Chicago Press, 1939).

84 Ricci, *TZSY*, pp. 416–417. See also Douglas Lancashire and Peter Hu Kuo-chen, S.J., trans., *The True Meaning of the Lord of Heaven* (St. Louis, Mo.: Institute of Jesuit Sources, 1985), p. 125 (hereafter cited as Lancashire and Hu, *TMLH*).

85 Among the papers found in Ricci's study after his death was a bound manuscript commissioned by Jesuit authorities titled "Della entrata della Compagnia di Giesù e Christianità nella Cina" (On the Entry of the Society of Jesus and Christianity into China), also known as *Storia dell'Introduzione del Christianesimo in Cina*. Under the direction of the Society of Jesus and executed in the literary hand of Trigault, this manuscript was edited and translated into Latin, appearing in

1615. For the history of the curious posthumous assembling of the work, see Mungello, *Curious Land*, pp. 46–48. On the questionable reliability of Trigault's edition, see Rule, *K'ung-tzu or Confucius?*, pp. 47–48. A cursory comparison of the first book of Ricci's *Storia* and Trigault and Ricci's *De Christiana expeditione apud Sinas* reveals the scope of the editor's distorting influence. Compare d'Elia, *FR*, vol. 1, pp. 115–117, and Trigault and Ricci, *DECAS*, pp. 105–108.

86 Trigault and Ricci, *DECAS*, pp. 105, 108. See also Nicolá Trigault and Matteo Ricci, *Histoire de l'expédition chrétienne au royaume de la Chine* (Lille: Pierre de Hache, 1617), p. 88. My translation follows that of Gallagher, *Journals*, p. 30.

87 Trigault and Ricci, *DECAS*, p. 101; Gallagher, *Journals*, p. 94.

88 D'Elia gives specific evidence on behalf of Ricci's observation of sacrifice to Kongzi at Beijing in March 1599 and Nanjing in March 1600. See d'Elia, *FR*, vol. 2, p. 70, n. 5. On the ritual choreography of the *shuyuan*, see Lionel M. Jensen, "Popular Cults and Confucian Paideia in Medieval China," paper presented at the Symposium on Religion and Society in China (750–1300), University of Illinois, Champaign-Urbana, Illinois, November 19, 1988.

89 See Gernet, *China and the Christian Impact*, esp. pp. 15–57.

90 Trigault, *DECAS*, p. 101; Gallagher, *Journals*, p. 94.

91 D'Elia, *FR*, vol. 1, p. 67.

92 Kenneth Burke, *A Grammar of Motives* (Berkeley: University of California Press, 1969), p. 503.

93 D'Elia, *FR*, vol. 1, p. 40, n. 3.

94 Ricci frequently expressed dissatisfaction with ecclesiastical authorities either over their censorship of Jesuit letters or their unreasonable intervention in the mission's publications. Particularly galling to Ricci was the requirement of the Vatican's imprimatur even for publication of the books he wrote in Chinese. He complains to his friend Girolamo Costa in reference to the *Jiaoyou lun* [Treatise on Friendship, completed in 1595], "I cannot publish it, because in order to publish anything I have to get permission from so many of our people that I cannot do anything. . . . Men who are not in China, and cannot read Chinese, insist upon passing judgment." Ricci, letter to Girolamo Costa, August 14, 1599, in Tacchi Venturi, *OS*, vol. 2, p. 250, translated by Dunne in *Generation of Giants*, p. 44. See also Ricci, letter to Acquaviva, August 5, 1606, in Tacchi Venturi, *OS*, vol. 2, p. 302, where a similar reproach is voiced.

95 D'Elia, *FR*, vol. 1, p. 120; and Trigault and Ricci, *DECAS*, p. 105.

96 Ricci's table of contents was redacted as well, the most noteworthy emendation being the title of chap. 10 of bk. 1. Ricci's *Storia* has "Di varie sette che nella Cina sono intorno alla religione" (Concerning Various Sects which in China are Religious) while Trigault has "Variae apud Sinas falsae Religionis Sectae" (Various Sects of False Religion among the Chinese). This, I take, as Trigault's response to duress.

97 See d'Elia, *FR*, vol. 1, pp. 42–44.

98 The point of this remark is to reverse our normal reading of the encounter between the Jesuits and the Chinese. It was the Jesuits who were "accommodated" within the native culture; this placed real limits on their efforts in catechism and

conversion. Moreover, the question of Jesuit success in proselytism remains open, given that some of the most celebrated converts, Xu Guangqi and Yang Tingyun (1557–1627) to name two, did not acknowledge their baptism. Xu's preface to Ricci's *Ershiwu yan* (Twenty-five Sayings) of 1605 contains a number of ambiguous remarks suggesting conversion, yet no mention of baptism. Also, in the posthumous literary collections and chronological biographies of these converts there is no record of the rite. This is not to say that these men were not baptized, for there is testimony from Ricci confirming the event and time. Nevertheless, a uniform absence of testimony about this most formative rite indicates that there were at least plural understandings of what the Jesuits believed was an unequivocal message. See Xu Guangqi, *Xu Guangqi ji*, vol. 2 (Beijing: Zhonghua Shuju, 1963), pp. 550–551; Liang Jiamian, ed., *Xu Guangqi nianpu* (Shanghai, 1981); see also Li Madou (Matteo Ricci), "Ershiwu yan," in Li, *TXCH*, pp. 326–329.

99 Due to no particular fault of his own, Ruggieri did not learn Chinese well. At least this is the claim of both Matteo Ricci and Alessandro Valignano. In 1579, Valignano instructed Ruggieri to undertake the study of Chinese, arranging at the same time for quarters in the rear of the Jesuit compound at Macao and a small cadre of local "interpreters" to "teach" him. Apparently none of them could speak Portuguese and it is not clear that they could use *guanhua* (administrative vernacular) or even write. See Father Antonio Monserrat, Annual Letter from Goa to General Everard Mercurian, October 26, 1579, in *Documenta Indica*, ed. Josef Wicki, S.J., vol. 11 (Rome: Institutum Historicum S.J., 1970), p. 641. On the highly improbable method by which Ruggieri was instructed in Chinese, see Michele Ruggieri, letter to Acquaviva, 1583, in Tacchi Venturi, *OS*, vol. 2, p. 411; and d'Elia, *FR*, vol. 1, pp. xcix, 155.

100 An initial run of twelve hundred copies of the Chinese version of the catechism was produced at the mission in the last week of November 1584. Another three thousand copies, according to d'Elia, were quickly produced thereafter, some finding their way to Cochin-China (Vietnam). This first catechism, *Tianzhu shilu* (The Veritable Record of the Heavenly Master), was deemed inferior, nevertheless, by Jesuit authorities, and Ricci was directed to complete a second catechism. The chronology of the many stages in the text's production is laid out in d'Elia, *FR*, vol. 1, pp. 194–195, n. 3, and p. 197, n. 2. See also Gernet, *China and the Christian Impact*, p. 8.

101 "Dialogo di un gentile et un padre di Europa," in Tacchi Venturi, *OS*, vol. 2, p. 51.

102 Ruggieri, *VDRE*, pp. 498–502.

103 See Ruggieri, *VDRE*, p. 520. Note that the "other" is conceived as a native "philosopher," much as Plato and Aristotle were regarded by the Catholic order. That the other was an educated Chinese individual indicates that from its inauguration the focus of the Jesuit conversion project was the social elite. This approach was consistent with Valignano's original advocacy that the fathers align themselves with what he called China's "homes letrados."

104 This information concerning the convert Paul and his role in the production of the Chinese version of the catechism is contained in a letter dated December 8,

1584, from Father Francisco Cabral to Acquaviva, in Tacchi Venturi, *OS*, vol. 2, pp. 52–53.

105 In another poem from the recently discovered cache of Ruggieri's works, he bemoans his poor knowledge of *Tang hua* (Tang words, meaning Chinese) and his inability to preach in Chinese. See Chan, "Michele Ruggieri, S.J.," p. 153.

106 Ricci believed that these men "knew nothing of Chinese letters" and not much Portuguese. See d'Elia, *FR*, vol. 1, pp. 154–155.

107 The text of this poem, titled "Yu man," may be found in Chan, "Michele Ruggieri, S.J.," p. 142.

108 The actual Chinese identity of this person has yet to be established, because of our inability to decipher the native sounds putatively represented by Matteo Ricci's "Cin Nicò." As his identity remains a product of Jesuit hands, I have put quote marks round the name.

109 In December 1583 the translation was printed at the mission and was the first text bearing the inspirational Chinese neologism, "Tianzhu." From this point forward "Cin"'s Tianzhu would endure as that name of the One God recognized by all Christians except those of Hong Xiuquan's (1813–1864) *Taiping tianguo* (Heavenly Kingdom of Great Peace). Indeed, the Jesuits would labor in subsequent years to establish an identity between Tianzhu, the nominal gift of their neophyte "Cin," and the ancient Chinese term "Shangdi." In the *Tianzhu shiyi*, for example, Ricci asserted that "Our Heavenly Master (Tianzhu) is precisely what is called Shangdi" and "Our Heavenly Master is the Shangdi mentioned in the ancient classic works." See d'Elia, *FR*, vol. 1, plate 9, opposite p. 194, and pp. 185–186. For Ricci's identification of Tianzhu and Shangdi, see Ricci, *TZSY*, p. 415.

110 Wagner, *Invention of Culture*, p. 11. Emphasis in original.

Chapter 2

1 For the conventional understanding of "hybridity," see Vicente L. Rafael, introduction to *Contracting Colonialism: Translation and Christian Conversion in Tagalog Society under Early Spanish Rule* (Ithaca, N.Y.: Cornell University Press, 1988); and Tejaswini Niranjana, *Siting Translation: History, Post-Structuralism, and the Colonial Context* (Berkeley: University of California Press, 1992), pp. 43–46.

2 Tu Wei-ming, "The Confucian Tradition in Chinese History," in *Heritage of China: Contemporary Perspectives on Chinese Civilization*, ed. Paul S. Ropp (Berkeley: University of California Press, 1990), p. 112. This belief is not peculiar to Tu, of course, but antedates him by more than a century. In his *Glossary of Reference on Subjects Connected with the Far East* (London: Curzon Books, 1878), p. 57, Herbert Giles offers the following explanation for "Confucius": "Confucius or Confutzee or Quangfoutchee:—K'ung the Master. The Jesuit missionaries took the Chinese sounds of these three characters, K'ung fu tzu, and Latinised them into their present form." Thus, we find the presumption complete in the works of earlier sinologists.

3   The volume appeared under its complete title, *Confucius Sinarum Philosophus, sive Scientia Sinensis latine exposita studio et opera Prosperi Intorcetta, Christiani Herdtrich, Francisci Rougemont, Philippi Couplet, Patrum Societatis Jesu* (Confucius, Philosopher of the Chinese; or, The Chinese Learning, a Latin exposition by Prosper Intorcetta, Christian Herdtrich, Francis Rougemont, Philippe Couplet, Fathers of the Society of Jesus). It was printed by Daniel Horthemels in Paris on Louis XIV's order in 1687. The work, a product of the labors of no fewer than twenty-seven missionaries, was assembled by Philippe Couplet (1623–1693), procurator of the Mission of the Indies, who appended a chronology of Chinese monarchs, the *Tabula Chronologica Monarchiae Sinicae (2952 B.C.–1683)*, which he had published independently in Paris the previous year.

4   Couplet, *CSP*, p. 116.

5   "Kong Fuzi [whom European missionaries, in making him known and admired in Europe, named Confucius in Latinizing his name]." See M. G. Pauthier, *Confucius et Mencius: Les Quatres Livres de philosophie morale et politique de la Chine* (Paris: Charpentier, 1841), p. vi.

6   "Kong Fuzi, whom we call Confucius, was born 551 years before our era." See *Pensées morales de Confucius*, 2d ed. (Paris: Victor Lecou, 1851), p. 1. It appears that this work is nothing more than a French translation of selected passages from the *Confucius Sinarum Philosophus*—which gives us some idea of the enduring popularity of the work.

7   Nonetheless, both the *Dai kanwa jiten* and the *Zhongwen dacidian* suggest that "Kong Fuzi" was a term of some currency during the Chunqiu period. No texts are cited in support of the claim, yet entries for "Kong Fuzi" state that *fuzi* was a title for older gentlemen in the Spring and Autumn period and, therefore, each of Kongzi's disciples addressed him as *fuzi*. See Morohashi Tetsuji, *Dai kanwa jiten*, vol. 3 of 12 vols. (reprint of 1977 Daishukan shoten edition; Taibei: Xuesheng Shuju, 1984), p. 3088; and *Zhongwen dacidian*, vol. 3 of 10 vols. (reprint; Taibei: Zhongguo wenhua daxue Chubanshe, 1977), pp. 3744–3745.

8   In the *Lunyu* the following passages contain "fuzi": 1.10, 1.10, 1.10, 4.5, 5.12, 5.12, 6.26, 7.4, 7.14, 7.14, 9.6, 9.10, 11.25, 11.25, 11.25, 12.8, 12.22, 14.6, 14.14, 14.14, 14.26, 14.26, 14.30, 14.38, 16.1, 17.4, 17.4, 17.7, 18.6, 18.7, 18.7, 19.18, 19.22, 19.23, 19.23, 19.25, 19.25. In the first ten books *fuzi* is used when disciples are speaking among themselves about him. It is common in the second ten books for *fuzi* to be used in the presence of the master or for direct address, with only one case in which it is applied in the third person. An interesting feature of these occurrences is that it is Zigong who most frequently employs *fuzi* when speaking of or with Kongzi.

9   The following passages contain the expression "Kongzi": 2.19, 2.21, 3.1, 3.19, 6.2, 7.18, 7.30, 7.30, 8.20, 9.2, 10.1, 11.6, 12.11, 12.11, 12.17, 12.17, 12.18, 12.18, 12.19, 12.19, 13.15, 13.15, 13.18, 13.18, 14.6, 14.20, 14.22, 14.22, 14.22, 14.26, 14.26, 14.34, 14.34, 15.1, 15.1, 16.1, 16.1, 16.1, 16.1, 16.2, 16.3, 16.4, 16.5, 16.6, 16.7, 16.7, 16.9, 16.10, 16.11, 17.1, 17.1, 17.1, 17.1, 17.1, 17.1, 17.6, 17.6, 17.7, 17.20, 17.20, 18.1, 18.3, 18.3, 18.4, 18.5, 18.5, 18.6, 20.2.

10 Cui Shu's critical reconstruction of the text, "Lunyu yushuo," remains the stan-

dard in determining the authenticity (and in the case of the *Lunyu* this is a very problematic notion) of the respective books of the *Lunyu*. See Cui Shu, "Lunyu yushuo," in *Cui Dongbi yishu*, ed. Gu Jiegang, vol. 5 of 6 vols. (Shanghai: Yadong tushuguan, 1936), esp. pp. 24–35. Since Cui, scholars have accepted the division of the text into two halves, one ancient, the other interpolated, although an argument could be made that the accepted reconstruction is flawed, as Robert Eno suggests in *The Confucian Creation of Heaven: Philosophy and the Defense of Ritual Mastery* (Albany: State University of New York Press, 1990), pp. 80–81. Nonetheless, Cui's judgment has been successively reaffirmed by H. G. Creel, Kimura Eiichi, D. C. Lau, and, more recently, Diane Obenchain. Now, however, we have a more impressive, because precise, chronological stratigraphy of the *Lunyu* texts, which, according to an accretional theory of the work, offers a date for each of the twenty books and reorders them in proper sequence. E. Bruce Brooks and A. Taeko Brooks have reconstructed the entire text and have demonstrated that it was palimpsestically assembled over the course of more than two centuries following the death of Kongzi. According to their reconstruction, the proper sequence and chronology of the *Lunyu* is as follows: Book 4 (479 B.C.E.), Book 5 (473 B.C.E.), Book 6 (460 B.C.E.), Book 7 (450 B.C.E.), Book 8 (435 B.C.E.), Book 9 (405 B.C.E.), Book 10 (380 B.C.E.), Book 3 (356 B.C.E.), Book 11 (337 B.C.E.), Book 12 (323 B.C.E.), Book 13 (321 B.C.E.), Book 2 (317 B.C.E.), Book 14 (310 B.C.E.), Book 15 (308 B.C.E.), Book 1 (301 B.C.E.), Book 16 (284 B.C.E.), Book 17 (272 B.C.E.), Book 18 (265 B.C.E.), Book 19 (252 B.C.E.), Book 20 (249 B.C.E.). See Kimura Eiichi, *Kōshi to Rongo*, pt. 2, chap. 3 (Tokyo: Sobunsha, 1971), pt. 2, chap. 3; H. G. Creel, *Confucius and the Chinese Way* (New York: Harper Torchbooks, 1960), pp. 291–294; D. C. Lau, trans., *The Analects* (New York: Penguin Classics, 1979), pp. 220–233; Diane Burdette Obenchain, "Ministers of the Moral Order: Innovations of the Early Chou Kings, Duke of Chou, Chung-ni and Ju," Ph.D. diss., Harvard University, 1984, pp. 18–19; and E. Bruce Brooks and A. Taeko Brooks, *The Original Analects* (New York: Columbia University Press, 1997), Appendix 1.

11 *Kong congzi* (reprint; Shanghai: Shanghai Guji Chubanshe, 1990); and *Kongzi jiayu* (reprint; Shanghai: Shanghai Guji Chubanshe, 1990).

12 Kongzi's honorary title varied considerably over the course of the history of imperial sacrifice. From the early Tang through the Ming he was consecutively referred to as *xuansheng Zhongni* (Propagating Sage Zhongni), *taishi* (Great Teacher), *wenxuan wang* (King of Propagating Culture), *zhisheng wenxuan wang Kong Fuzi* (Supreme Sage and King of Propagating Culture, Kong Fuzi), *dacheng zhisheng* (Supreme Sage of Great Completion), and *zhisheng xianshi Kongzi* (Supreme Sage First Teacher, Kongzi). See John Shryock, *The Origin and Development of the State Cult of Confucius* (New York: Century, 1932), pp. 137–195. See also d'Elia, *FR*, vol. 1, pp. 39–40, n. 6.

13 Obenchain, "Ministers of the Moral Order," p. 18.

14 Couplet, *CSP*, pp. xxxvii–xxxviii, xliii, cxiv. Praise of the work and its author was effusive twenty years earlier in Gabriel de Magalhaes's (1610–1677) *Historia de la China* and was repeated in several Jesuit works published in the century following the publication of the *Confucius Sinarum Philosophus*. See Gabriel Magail-

lans (de Magalhaes), *Nouvelle relation de la Chine*, trans. Benous (Paris: C. Barbin, 1688), pp. 102, 265–266; J. M. A. de Moyriac de Mailla, *Historie général de la Chine, ou annales de cet empire*, vol. 10 of 13 vols. (Paris: L'Abbé Grosier, 1777–1785), p. 336; and J. H. de Prémare, *Notitia Linguae Sinicae* (Malacca, Malaysia: Anglo-Chinese College, 1831).

15 The *Xingli daquan* was edited by Hu Guang (1370–1418), preceptor of the Hanlin Academy, and completed in October of 1415 at the anxious behest of Zhu Di, the Yongle emperor.

16 The transliteration of the title reads "Sim li ta çiven." See Couplet, "Proëmialis Declaratio," *CSP*, p. xliii.

17 See Hu Guang, ed., *Xingli daquan shu* [1597 edition] (reprint; Taibei: Shangwu, 1974), *juan* 38, pp. 1b, 13a–b.

18 This recension by Zhang Juzheng, tutor to Zhu Yijun, the Wanli emperor (r. 1572–1619), revised Zhu Xi's *Sishu jizhu* for use in the young emperor's instruction in the canon. It has been said that it was favored by Jesuits because of its greater simplicity and lack of the Song metaphysical glosses.

19 According to d'Elia, Ricci used his handwritten draft of the translation to teach Father Francesco de Petris Chinese from December 1591 to November 1593. He also states that the translation and commentary were completed by November 15, 1594, and points out that Ricci's description of it as a "paraphrase" was disingenuous. See d'Elia, *FR*, vol. 2, p. 33, n. 5.

20 D'Elia, *FR*, vol. 2, p. 33, n. 5.

21 See Zhu Xi, *Lunyu jizhu*, in *Sishu jizhu* (reprint; Taibei: Xuehai Chubanshe, 1984), pp. 53–193; and Huang Kan, *Lunyu jijie yisu*, 2 vols. (reprint; Taibei: Guangwen Shuju, 1968).

22 Temür ascended the throne as "Chengzong" in 1294, designating his era "Yuanzhen" (the Source of Truth). Two years later this *nianhao* (era name) was superseded by the appellation of the new era, "Dade" (Great Virtue). See *Zhongwen dacidian*, vol. 3, p. 3744. A search of the chronicle of Chengzu's reign and of the invocations of and sacrifices to Kongzi in the *Yuan shi* turned up no additional evidence other than that cited here from the *Zhongwen dacidian*. *Yuan shi* (reprint; Beijing: Zhonghua Shuju, 1976).

23 Another suggestive, but purely coincidental, link between the Mongol and Jesuit interlopers was their obsessive interest in the Four Books. By a proclamation in 1315 that marked the reestablishment of the metropolitan examination after a three-decade hiatus during the early years of their reign, the Mongols were the first to require study of the *Sishu* as the chief academic criterion of official eligibility. Moreover, it was at this same time that these four texts were given the title *Sishu*, having been known since 1189 as the *Sizi* (Four Masters)—a reference to Zhu Xi's understanding of the texts as his personal instructors.

24 Gaspar da Cruz, *Tractado de la China*, in *South China in the Sixteenth Century: Being the Narratives of Galeote Pereira, Fr. Gaspar da Cruz, O.P., Fr. Martin de Rada, O.E.S.A. (1550–1575)*, ed. C. R. Boxer (London: Haklyut Society, 1953); Carlos Sanz, ed., *B. Escalante: Primera historia de China* (reprint; Madrid: Libreria General Victoriano Suarez 1958). "Confuzo" and "Cumfuceio," Italian and

Portuguese vernacular terms for Confucius, were well attested in missionary letters and texts of the early years of the seventeenth century.

25 Juan González de Mendoza, *Historia de la cosas mas notables, ritos y costumbres del gran reino de la China* (Valencia, 1596). This edition was but a reprint of the original, one of eleven such editions produced in Spanish between 1585 and 1600. Consequently, the later editions, like the first, contain no references to Confucius.

26 Luis de Guzman, *Historia de las missiones que han hecho los religiosos de la compañia de Iesvs: para predicar el sancto evangelio en la India oriental, y en les reynos de la China y Japon*, 2 vols. (Alcalá de Henares: Buida de I. Gracian, 1601); and Diego de Pantoja, *Relacion de la entrada de algunos padres de la campagnia de Iesus en la China* (Valencia: Juan Chrysostomos Garris, 1606).

27 D'Elia, *FR*, vol. 1, p. 39, n. 1. "Il *fuze* ossia 'venerato maestro' Com [K'ung], o, in cinese, Comfuze, che il *Ricci fu il primo a italianizzare in Confutio o Confuzo*, aveva per cognome Ccom, per nome Cchieu [Qiu] e per agnome Ciomni [Chung-ni]" [emphasis added]. Father Henri Bernard, in fact, made the same claim five years prior to d'Elia in his *Le Père Matthieu Ricci et la Société Chinoise de son temps (1552–1610)*, vol. 1 of 2 vols. (Tianjin: Hautes Études, 1937). The first Jesuit assertion of Ricci's role in inventing "Confucius" and his "secta de' letterati" comes from the "Proëmialis Declaratio" of the *Confucius Sinarum Philosophus*. See Couplet, *CSP*, p. lxvii.

28 The account comes from the fifth chapter of the first book of Ricci's *Storia*. See d'Elia, *FR*, vol. 1, p. 39.

29 *Mengzi zhushu*, in *SSJZS*, vol. 13 (reprint; Shanghai: Guji Chubanshe, 1990), p. 138.1. See also D. C. Lau, trans., *Mencius* (New York: Penguin Classics, 1970), p. 127; James Legge, trans., *The Book of Mencius*, in *The Chinese Classics*, vol. 2 of 5 vols. (reprint; Hong Kong: Chinese University Press, 1971), p. 313; and W. A. C. H. Dobson, trans., *Mencius* (Toronto: University of Toronto Press, 1963), p. 140.

30 Ricci, *TZSY*, pp. 616–617; Lancashire and Hu, *TMLH*, pp. 429–431. Ricci's assertion concerning the inauthenticity of Mengzi's remark is a valid one. There is an earlier reference in the text (4B.30) to unfilial acts in which Mengzi enumerates five and not three such contraventions of propriety. The failure to generate progeny is not one of these five.

31 Owing to the manner in which Ricci framed the fictive conversation between the Western and Chinese scholars of the catechism, Jesuit authorities in Rome were not made aware of the degree of the fathers' embrace of native belief. The prefatory Latin summary of the text—point by argumentative point—was appended to the first Chinese edition of 1603. In 1604, Ricci sent a copy of this edition along with a summary postscript in longhand to his superiors in Rome. Here, Ricci detailed in legalistic prose the succession of arguments that comprise the work, repeatedly noting those beliefs, practices, and opinions of the Chinese that are appropriately confuted (*confutatur*) throughout. The preface, reinforced by the postscript, serves to disambiguate the many passages in the catechism that would appear to confer inappropriate respect upon pagan belief. See the reproduction of

the Biblioteca Casanatense Manuscript 2136, in Lancashire and Hu, *TMLH*, pp. 460–472.

32 The complete Latin summary is included as an appendix in Lancashire and Hu, *TMLH*, pp. 460–472. The above excerpt may be found on p. 463.

33 This linguistic point was brought to my attention by Don Price.

34 Donald F. Lach, *Asia in the Making of Europe*, vol. 2 of 2 vols., bk. 3 (Chicago: University of Chicago Press, 1977), p. 543.

35 Lucien Febvre and Henri-Jean Martin, *The Coming of the Book: The Impact of Printing, 1450–1800* (London: New Left Books, 1976), pp. 321–332.

36 The Dominican missionary, Domingo Fernandez Navarette, writing to Antonio de Gouvea on September 29, 1669, says, "En order al Cumfucio permittiremos . . . " In response de Gouvea refers to "Cumfuceio" and "ritos do Cumfucio." See C. R. Boxer, *A Propósitio dum livrinho xilográfico dos Jesuitás de Pequisu (Sécuo XVIII)* (Macau: Imprensa Nacional, 1942), pp. 1b, 5b, 6b.

37 In modern Italian, *confuso* means "confusion," and one cannot help but wonder if the similar-sounding nomination "Confuzo" for Kongzi conveyed something of the missionaries' doubts about the intelligibility of the term that may have been provoked by its multiple pronunciations. Undergraduate students today often make a similar expressive conflation in writing of "Confusionism" and "Confusious."

38 See Edgar C. Knowlton, "Words of Chinese, Japanese, and Korean Origin in the Romance Languages," Ph.D. diss., Stanford University, 1959, p. 53, where the author estimates that as many as sixty-five Chinese words, in Portuguese transliteration mostly, became part of the permanent vocabulary of the Romance languages.

39 Umberto Eco has said in this regard that language establishes "a 'cultural' world which is neither actual nor possible in the ontological sense; its existence is limited to a cultural order, which is the way in which a society thinks, speaks and, while speaking, explains the 'purport' of its thought through other thoughts." See Umberto Eco, *A Theory of Semiotics* (Bloomington: University of Indiana Press, 1969), p. 61.

40 My treatment of naming as christening was inspired by a similar analysis of the Spanish nomination of the "New World" other in Bernard McGrane, *Beyond Anthropology: Society and the Other* (New York: Columbia University Press, 1989), pp. 19–20.

41 Li, *TXCH*, p. 85.

42 Matteo Ricci, Letter to Vice-Provincial Francesco Pasio, February 15, 1609, in Tacchi Venturi, *OS*, vol. 2, p. 387, and quoted in Paul A. Rule, *K'ung-tzu or Confucius? The Jesuit Interpretation of Confucianism* (Sydney: Allen and Unwin Australia, 1986), p. 31.

43 D'Elia, *FR*, vol. 1, p. 120. See also Jonathan Spence's translation in *The Memory Palace of Matteo Ricci* (New York: Viking/Penguin, 1984), p. 210.

44 Qu Rukui [Taisu], "Daxiyu Ligong youlun xu," in Li, *TXCH*, vol. 1, pp. 295–296.

45 Nathan Sivin, "Copernicus in China," *Studia Copernicana* 6 (1973): 63–122.

46 "[T]utti conformi al lume naturale et alla verità catholica." See d'Elia, *FR*, vol. 1, p. 120.

47 The formulation is that of Cardinal John Henry Newman, as quoted in Jaroslav Pelikan, *The Vindication of Tradition* (New Haven: Yale University Press, 1984), p. 33.

48 This is the contention of Li Zhizao in his preface to the 1607 edition of the *Tianzhu shiyi*. Li, *TXCH*, pp. 9–12.

49 Ricci's use of the term *santo* continued to cause concern among the Jesuits in the twentieth century. Pasquale d'Elia devoted a two-page explanatory note to the first appearance of *santo* in Ricci's text. See Longobardo's response to Ricci's first use of *santo* in his Italian translation of a letter written to his original Chinese convert, Qu Taisu, on May 18, 1596, in d'Elia, *FR*, vol. 1, pp. 118–119, n. 7.

50 " . . . quàm scriptis & congressibus omnes ad virtutis studium incitaret. Ex qua viuendi ratione consecutus est apud Sinas, ut mortales omnes, quotquot ubique terrarum virtute praestiterut, vitae sanctimonia excessisse credatur. Et fanè si eius dicta factaq; quae leguntur attenderis, paucis è nostratibus Philosophis Ethnicis cedere, multos etiá eum superare fatebimur. Eam ob rem tanta est viri opinio, ut nullum eius pronunciatum ab Sinensibus literatis, hodieq; in dubium reuocetur, sed ab omnibus aequè in Magistri communis verba iuratur. Nec literati viri solùm, sed ipsi quoque Reges eu per tot retro secula, mortalium tamen, non etiam Numinis alicuius ritu venerantur, & gratum animum acceptae ab eo doctrinae sese exhibere profitentur." Trigault and Ricci, *DECAS*, pp. 28–29.

51 D'Elia, *FR*, vol. 1, pp. 108–132, esp. pp. 115–131.

52 See d'Elia, *FR*, vol. 1, p. 39, n. 1.

53 D'Elia, *FR*, vol. 1, p. 533.

54 D'Elia, *FR*, vol. 1, p. 39.

55 This is an excerpt from a letter of 1604 that accompanied Ricci's Latin outline and description of the argument in *Tianzhu shiyi*, which he sent to Acquaviva. D'Elia, *FR*, vol. 2, pp. 296–298, n. 2. It is translated and quoted by Jacques Gernet in *China and the Christian Impact*, trans. Janet Lloyd (Cambridge: Cambridge University Press, 1985), p. 27. Gernet gets the general overview in his translation, but a meaningful departure from the literal text of the letter enables him to cast doubt on Ricci's motives.

56 This term is borrowed from Pierre Bourdieu and is described in his *Outline of a Theory of Practice*, trans. Richard Nice (Cambridge: Cambridge University Press, 1977), pp. 72–86. The *habitus* consists of the unconscious structures of social reproduction, "the schemes of thought and expression [which] are the basis for the *intentionless invention* of regulated improvisation" (p. 79, emphasis in original). More than simply the inherited or learned self-conception of a specific group, the *habitus* is a miniature universe of practices, one's mastery of which is unselfconsciously evident in gesture, clothing, speech, and even inclination.

57 On the history of the repeated printing of the catechism, see Lancashire and Hu, *TMLH*, pp. 16–21.

58 Letter to Girolama Costa, 1598, in Tacchi Venturi, *OS*, vol. 2, p. 243, translated by George H. Dunne, S.J., in *Generation of Giants: The Story of the Jesuits in China in the Last Decades of the Ming Dynasty* (Notre Dame, Ind.: University of Notre

Dame Press, 1966), p. 44. *Jiaoyou lun*, literally, "Treatise on Friendship," was consistently described by Ricci as "Amicitia" in his letters.

59 The quotation is from the Latin autograph of Ricci's preface to his translation of the Chinese prefaces to the *Tianzhu shiyi* and to his Latin summary. The autograph, photocopied from the manuscript of the first Beijing edition in the Biblioteca Casanatense, Rome, may be found in Lancashire and Hu, *TMLH*, p. 459.

60 Lancashire and Hu, *TMLH*, p. 602.

61 Lancashire and Hu, *TMLH*, p. 591.

62 See Ricci, *TZSY*, especially pp. 597–602.

63 Of course, the *xiucai* as a class in local Chinese society were notoriously liminal in late Ming society and often were involved in local uprisings provoked by economic discontent or religious unrest. In urban areas of the South Yangzi delta (Jiangnan), according to Frederic Wakeman, *xiucai* "formed a newly expanded and eminently visible stratum in the cities of the Yangzi River delta, cultivating a flamboyant dandyism that was often associated in contemporaries' eyes with social and sexual deviance." Ricci noted this same phenomenon with disgust in the first book of the *Storia*, but seemed unaware that many of these men were *xiucai*. See Frederic Wakeman Jr., *The Great Enterprise: The Manchu Reconstruction of Imperial Order in Seventeenth-Century China*, vol. 1 of 2 vols. (Berkeley: University of California Press, 1985), pp. 94–95; and d'Elia, *FR*, vol. 1, p. 98.

64 Ricci, *TZSY*, p. 592. The complaint of closet heterodoxy in literati circles was common beginning in the Southern Song era. Indeed, Zhu Xi's most intemperate sectarian fulminations were not directed at Buddhists as were those of Cheng Yi chuan, but at self-proclaimed *ru* who succumbed to heterodox habit in their daily practice. See Zhu Xi, "Shishi lun," in *Zhuzi wenji*, supplementary collection, vol. 10 (Shanghai: Shangwu Chubanshe, n.d.), pp. 1934.2–1936.1.

65 Ricci, *TZSY*, p. 487.

66 Ricci, *TZSY*, p. 624.

67 D'Elia, *FR*, vol. 1, p. 116.

68 D'Elia, *FR*, vol. 1, p. 116.

69 D'Elia, *FR*, vol. 1, p. 116. See also Gallagher, *Journals*, p. 95, for a very different, because interpolated, translation.

70 See Matthias Flacius Illyricus, *Clavis Scripturae Sacrae* [1567] (new edition, Jena: Johannis Ludovici Neuenhans, 1674).

71 D'Elia, *FR*, vol. 1, pp. 115–116.

72 Ricci, *TZSY*, p. 551.

73 Ricci, *TZSY*, p. 425. As the catechism proceeds, "the Chinese scholar" ceases to be the foil for the argument of "the Western scholar" and rails against customary practices of his fellow Chinese, as he does here, becoming the enthusiastic proponent of Christian teaching.

74 Xu Zongze, *Ming-Qing jian Yesu huishi yizhu tiyao* (Taibei: Zhonghua Shuju, 1958), p. 309. Xu Guangqi, "Taixi shui fa xu," in *Xu Guangqi ji* (Beijing: Zhonghua Shuju, 1963), p. 61. The popularity of the phrase was so great among the Jesuits that it became for them a *chengyu*, a four-character axiom in the Chinese didactic

tradition. Indeed, this *chengyu* was reproduced in a Latin transliteration in the *Confucius Sinarum Philosophus* as "Pu ju; çive fe." See Couplet, *CSP*, p. xiii. Another version of the motto was *qinru paifo*, or "draw close to *ru* and repudiate *fo*."

75 "Xianru suo chuan, jie bu qi ran." Du Yu, "Xu," *Chunqiujing chuanji jie*, vol. 1 of 3 vols. (reprint; Taibei: Zhonghua Shuju, 1965), p. 2a.

76 *Chunqiu Zuo zhuan zhengyi*, *SSJZS*, vol. 7, pt. 1 (reprint; Shanghai: Guji Chubanshe, 1990), pp. 9.2–10.1.

77 On the ranked inner architecture of the Kongmiao according to enshrinement positions of *xian xian* (former worthies) and *xian ru*, see Thomas A. Wilson, *The Genealogy of the Way: Neo-Confucian Anthologies: The Construction and Uses of Confucianism in Late Imperial China* (Stanford: Stanford University Press, 1995), pp. 254–259.

78 Shryock, *Origin and Development of the State Cult of Confucius*, pp. 187–195.

79 Wang Qiyuan, *Qingshu jingtan*, as quoted in Chen Shouyi, "Sanbainian qian de jianli kongjiao lun," *Zhongyang yanjiuyuan lishi yuyan yanjiusuo jikan* 6, no. 2 (1936): 136–162.

80 Gernet, *China and the Christian Impact*, pp. 54–55.

81 Chen Houguang, "Bianxue chuyan," in *Shengchao Poxie ji* (reprint; Hong Kong: Jiandao Shenxue yuan, 1996), p. 244. My translation follows that of Gernet, with numerous modifications. See Gernet, *China and the Christian Impact*, p. 53. Chen actually slanders Ricci's interpretation of "Taiji" in this instance; Ricci merely pointed out that Taiji was not *sui generis* (*zili*) and thus could not be equivalent to the Heavenly Master, Tianzhu. On the Jesuit contestation of the divinity Taiji, see Ricci, *TZSY*, pp. 406–407.

82 This sort of magical efficacy of contiguity was common among the early missionaries and is described in Li Jiubiao, ed., *Kouduo richao* (A Daily Record of Oral Instructions). Aleni's encouragement of this practice is discussed in Erik Zürcher, "Giulio Alenis et ses relations avec le milieu des lettres chinois au XVIIe siècle," in *Venezia e l'Oriente*, ed. L. Lanciotti (Florence: Leo Olchki, 1987), pp. 105–135. Chinese fascination with holy water, Christian icons, and other mysterious objects of the missionaries is well documented throughout the *Poxie ji*.

83 Huang Zhen, "Qing Yan xiansheng pi Tianzhu jiao shu" (letter to Yan Maoyou, 1638) in *Poxie ji*, p. 152.

84 "Rangyi baoguo gongjie" (anonymous letter to Jiang Dejing), in *Poxie ji*, p. 292.

85 Huang Zhen, "Qing Yan xiansheng pi Tianzhu jiao shu," in *Poxie ji*, p. 152.

86 Huang Wendao, "Pixie jie," in *Poxie ji*, p. 267.

87 See Huang Zhen, "Qing Yan xiansheng pi Tianzhu jiao shu," in *Poxie ji*, pp. 150, 152.

88 On the metaphor of arteries for the waterways that joined imperial center and rural periphery, see Wakeman, *The Great Enterprise*, vol. 1, pp. 1–31.

89 D'Elia, *FR*, vol. 2, p. 296.

90 These new orders, the Jesuits and Capuchins among them, were spawned from internal impulses within the Catholic Church toward institutional reforms. The need for and the scope of these reforms was made evident with the promulgation

of the *Consilium de Emendanda Ecclesia* (Advice on Reforming the Church) in 1537. From this time old orders were suppressed and new ones such as the Society of Jesus were formed. The new orders competed with each other and provoked the resentment of the old hierarchy in their efforts to be accepted and, ultimately, accredited.

91 Ricci, *TZSY*, p. 551.

92 Li Madou [Ricci], "Shuwen zeng Yubo Chengzi," in *Sheyuan mocui*, ed. Tao Xiang, vol. 2 of 14 vols. (Beijing, 1929), pp. 1a–6b. See the translation in J. J. L. Duyvendak, "Review of Pasquale d'Elia, *Le Origini Dell' Arte Christiana Cinese (1583–1640)*," *T'oung Pao* 35 (1940): pp. 394–398. In this case I follow Duyvendak with few modifications.

93 *Mengzi zhushu*, in *SSJZS*, vol. 13, reprint, p. 165.2. See also D. C. Lau, trans., *Mencius*, p. 142.

94 Yang Xiong, *Fayan*, in *Congshu jicheng* (reprint; Taibei: Yiwen, 1967), *juan* 4, p. 14, as quoted in James J. Y. Liu, *Language—Paradox—Poetics: A Chinese Perspective* (Princeton: Princeton University Press, 1988), pp. 28–29.

95 Cheng Yichuan, "Yi zhuan xu," in *Er-Cheng ji*, vol. 1 of 2 vols. (reprint; Taibei: Hanjing wenhua shiye youxian gongsi, 1983), pp. 582–583.

96 *Lunyu zhushu*, in *SSJZS*, vol. 11, p. 16.2. See also Waley, *Analects*, p. 90.

97 Hans-Georg Gadamer, "Hermeneutics as Practical Philosophy," in *After Philosophy: End or Transformation?* ed. Kenneth Baynes, James Bohman, and Thomas McCarthy (Cambridge, Mass.: MIT Press, 1987), pp. 325–338.

98 Niccolò Longobardo, *Traité sur quelques points de la religion des chinois* (Paris: J. Josse, 1701). This tract was actually completed sometime between 1623 and 1625. It was written in Latin and bore the title *De Confucio ejusque doctrina tractatus* (A Treatise on Confucius and His Doctrine). Even among foes of accommodation like Longobardo, then, Kongzi's identity as "Confucius" was fixed by the first decades of the seventeenth century.

99 Hexagrams are the graphic vestiges of the oracular traditions of the Zhou era left from an earlier tradition of milfoil divination and now preserved as the *Zhou yi* (Zhou Changes). In an earlier time, it is alleged, someone wishing to interpret an omen would choose six stalks of varying length from which a pattern was formed. The diviner would then judge the auspiciousness of the resulting complex. A hexagram (a statement of which [*guaci*] opens each text) is composed of six lines, either broken (a space dividing the line in half) or unbroken, and each bears a distinct meaning recorded in an accompanying "line statement" (*yaoci*). Every hexagram has a name, often that of the image perhaps taken from the moment of the divination. Traditionally it was believed that the hexagrams were composite images made from a simple combinatorial calculus of any two of the eight trigrams that had been vouchsafed the Chinese by their revered Sage-King, Fu Xi, and yielding a total of sixty-four linear images. (Recently excavated texts dating to the pre-Qin period confute this conventional presumption in that the images are represented as hexagrams, not trigrams.) The line and hexagram statements of these sixty-four images represent the core of the text. The *Yijing* (Classic of Change) refers to this central text and the "Ten Wings" (*Shiyi*) of commentary

that have grown around the hexagram and line statements. This is how the Jesuits, as well as Zhang Binglin and Hu Shi, both of whom would rely on the *Zhou yi* to reconstruct certain ancient meanings of *ru*, understood the text.

In concert with widening European speculation in the late seventeenth century on the primitive language of the Chinese, the hexagrams were read as the hieroglyphs of ancient Chinese writing invented by Fu Xi, but soon they were taken, by the Jesuit Figurist, Joachim Bouvet, and especially by Leibniz in his *Discourse on the Natural Theology of the Chinese*, as the constitutive elements of a binary arithmetic. The instincts of this primitivist numerology resembled the interpretative urge of Zhang Binglin and Hu Shi in this century to look to the hexagrams to find the earliest meaning of the Chinese graph, *ru* (see chapter 3).

100 I. Bernard Cohen, *Revolution in Science* (Cambridge, Mass.: Harvard University Press, Belknap Press, 1985), pp. 82–84.

101 See Arthur Wright's discussion of the sinification of Buddhist terminology by translation teams, especially the analysis of *geyi*, "matching concepts," in *Buddhism in Chinese History* (Stanford: Stanford University Press, 1958), pp. 33–39.

102 See d'Elia, *FR*, vol. 2, p. 33, n. 5.

103 This Latin/Chinese translation by Intorcetta and da Costa was never seen outside the Vatican. On the *Sapientia Sinica*, see D. E. Mungello, *Curious Land: Jesuit Accommodation and the Origins of Sinology* (Honolulu: University of Hawai'i Press, 1989), pp. 250–251; and Knud Lundbaek, "The First Translation from a Confucian Classic in Europe," *China Mission Studies Bulletin* 1 (1979): 2.

104 The work was printed in installments at the mission headquarters at Canton and Goa. On the production of Intercetta's *Sinarum scientia politico-moralis*, see Mungello, *Curious Land*, pp. 250–252; and D. E. Mungello, "The Seventeenth-Century Translation Project of the Confucian Four Books," in *East Meets West*, ed. Charles E. Ronan, S.J., and Bonnie B. C. Oh (Chicago: Loyola University Press, 1988), pp. 257–260.

105 Mungello, "Seventeenth-Century Translation Project," p. 259.

106 Spence, *Memory Palace*, p. 242, pp. 238–250 on the popularity of Marian sodalities among the Jesuits.

107 Niccolò Longobardo, *De Confucio ejusque doctrina tractatus.*

108 On figurism in all of its permutations, see Mungello, *Curious Land*, pp. 300–328; and Rule, *K'ung-tzu or Confucius?* pp. 150–182.

109 Robert Markley, *Fallen Languages: The Crisis of Representation in Newtonian England, 1660–1740* (Ithaca: Cornell University Press, 1993). Stephen Toulmin offers a similar portrait of the epistemological contradictions of seventeenth-century science in *Cosmopolis: The Hidden Agenda of Modernity* (Chicago: University of Chicago Press, 1991).

110 On the politics and functions of letterbooks see Lach, *Asia in the Making of Europe*, vol. 1, bks. 1, 2.

111 Melchisedec Thévenot, *Relations de divers voyages curieux*, vol. 4 of 4 vols. (Paris, 1696), pp. 1–24. The translation of the *Zhongyong* as it appears in "La Science des chinois" is preceded by a preface and followed by a short biography of Confucius. On the fate of the *Sapientia Sinica*, see Louis Pfister, *Notices*

biographiques et bibliographiques sur les Jésuites de l'ancienne mission de Chine, 1552–1773, vol. 1 of 2 vols. (Shanghai: Maison Catholique, 1932), p. 328. On the difference between the *Sapientia Sinica* and the *Sinarum scientia politico-moralis*, see Lundbaek, "The First Translation from a Confucian Classic," pp. 2–4.

112 On this "paradigm shift," see Cohen, *Revolution in Science*, pp. 79–81.

113 This narration of the books' contents is based upon examination of original editions in the Bancroft Library at the University of California, Berkeley. The preface to the English translation appears to be nothing more than selected excerpts from the "Proëmialis Declaratio" of the *Confucius Sinarum Philosophus.*

114 Markley, *Fallen Languages*, p. 72. See also Christopher Hill, *Some Intellectual Consequences of the English Revolution* (Madison: University of Wisconsin Press, 1980).

115 On the *oratio brevis*, see Quintilian, *Institutio oratoria*, vol. 3 (Cambridge, Mass.: Loeb, 1959), X.vi.1.

116 In some instances the authors lifted whole passages from the *Storia*, modifying them only slightly, usually in emphasis. See Couplet, *CSP*, pp. lxi, c.

117 It was not Ricci but his successors, by way of Trigault's translation, who were the first to draw the favorable comparison of Plato and Confucius (which has been elaborated upon in this century by Feng Youlan in his *Zhongguo zhexue shi*), saying, "His self-mastery and abstemious ways of life have led his countrymen to assert that he surpassed in holiness all those who in times past, in the various parts of the world, were considered to have excelled in virtue." The paean continues, "Indeed if we critically examine his actions and sayings as they are recorded in history, we shall be forced to admit that he was the equal of the pagan philosophers and superior to most of them." See Gallagher, *Journals*, p. 30. See also Feng Youlan, *Zhongguo zhexue shi* (Beijing: Taipingyang tushu Gongsi, 1968), chap. 4.

118 "Delphici Apollinis Oraculo tantum fidei vel authoritatis prisca aetas tribuerit quantum China tribuit *Confucio* suo." Couplet, *CSP*, p. xiii.

119 John Milton, "On the Morning of Christ's Nativity," in *The Norton Anthology of Poetry*, ed. Arthur M. Eastman et al. (New York: W. W. Norton, 1970), pp. 299–304.

120 Couplet, *CSP*, p. xcix.

121 Couplet, *CSP*, p. c.

122 "Supplet illa et perficit quod Magistro nostro Confucio, nostraeque literatorum Philosophiae deest; nefarias verò superstitiones cultumque daemonum tollit ac radicitùs extirpat." Couplet, *CSP*, p. xiii. Although Xu was dead by the time Couplet came to China, his granddaughter became a convert, and she and Couplet enjoyed a warm and lengthy friendship during which she assisted him in his translations.

123 Father Noel Alexandre's *Conformité des cérémonies chinoises avec l'idolatrie grècque et romaine* of 1700 may have been an important bibliographic link between the work of the *CSP* authors and the new Enlightenment fashion of representing otherness. Noel Alexandre, *Conformité des cérémonies chinoises avec*

l' dolatrie grècque et romaine (Cologne: Les hautiers de C. l'Egmondt, 1700). See also Isaac Newton, *The Chronology of the Ancient Kingdoms Amended* (London, 1728); and David Hume, *The Natural History of Religion* [1757], edited with an introduction by H. E. Root (Stanford: Stanford University Press, 1957).

124 For a discussion and analysis of the relation between these two works, see D. E. Mungello, "A Study of the Prefaces to Ph. Couplet's *Tabula Chronologica Monarchiae Sinicae*," in *Philippe Couplet, S.J. (1623–1693): The Man Who Brought China to Europe*, ed. Jerome Heyndrickx, C.I.C.M., Monumenta Serica Monograph Series, vol. 22 (Nettetal: Steyler Verlag, 1990), pp. 183–199.

125 Kenneth J. Knoespel, "Milton and the Hermeneutics of Time: Seventeenth-Century Chronologies and the Science of History," *Studies in the Literary Imagination*, no. 22 (1989): 20.

126 Mungello, "A Study of the Prefaces to Ph. Couplet's *Tabula Chronologica*," pp. 192–194; and Van Kley, "Europe's 'Discovery' of China and the Writing of World History," *American Historical Review* 76 (1971): 360.

127 McGrane, *Beyond Anthropology*, p. 59.

128 The analysis of the epistemological crisis of seventeenth-century "physicotheology" that follows is derived from Markley, *Fallen Languages*, pp. 2–17, 63–75, 87–93, 99–101.

129 "Epistola," in Couplet, *CSP*.

130 Couplet, *CSP*, caption of woodblock print of Confucius, opposite p. cxvii.

131 "Philosophorum Sinensium Principis Confucii Vita," in Couplet, *CSP*, p. cxxii.

132 *Lunyu zhushu*, p. 86.1. See also Arthur Waley, *The Analects of Confucius* (New York: Vintage, 1938), p. 149.

133 Smith argues that the appearance of terms like "Judaism," "Christianity," "Islam," "Daoism," "Confucianism," "Buddhism," etc., is peculiar to a nineteenth-century reification of the concept "religion," and believes that the adoption of such abstract terms occurs only at the peril of the continuance of a living, cumulative tradition of piety. See Wilfred Cantwell Smith, *The Meaning and End of Religion: A Revolutionary Approach to the Great Religious Traditions* (New York: Harper and Row, 1978), pp. 1–19, 51–79, 124–152, 193–202.

Interlude

1 We have come to understand this especially well since Durkheim, whose analysis I follow here. See Émile Durkheim, *The Elementary Forms of the Religious Life*, trans. Joseph Ward Swain (New York: Free Press, 1965), pp. 121–140, 165–182, 217–236, 255–272, 462–496.

2 Ernest Gellner, *Plough, Sword, and Book: The Structure of Human History* (Chicago: University of Chicago Press, 1988), p. 55.

3 Peter Winch, "Concepts and Actions," in *The Philosophy of History*, ed. Patrick Gardiner (Oxford: Oxford University Press, 1974), pp. 42–43.

4 Roy Wagner, *The Invention of Culture*, rev. and exp. ed. (Chicago: University of Chicago Press, 1981), p. 30.

5 Tu Wei-ming, "The Confucian Tradition in Chinese History," in *Heritage of*

China: Contemporary Perspectives on Chinese Civilization, ed. Paul S. Ropp (Berkeley: University of California Press, 1990), p. 112.

6 Tony Bennett, *Formalism and Marxism* (London: Methuen, 1979), p. 167.

7 Marshall Sahlins, *Islands of History* (Chicago: University of Chicago Press, 1985), p. 146. Perhaps it is testimony to the success of Ricci's clever reading of Chinese texts as implicitly Christian, that he is so closely associated with the history of late imperial China. The official history of the Ming, *Mingshi*, compiled during the reign of Kangxi, contains a biographic entry for Ricci in *liezhuan* 214 (on foreign lands). The account is hostile and unflattering, consisting in part of two memorials from the Board of Rites citing a host of transgressions for which, they claimed, Ricci was expelled from both Ming capitals. "His speech is vague and unreliable," according to his accusers. Yet more damning, in the board's view, is what it saw as Ricci's infection of Chinese scholars with his teaching and the highly inappropriate tribute he presented to the emperor—portraits of Christ and the Virgin Mary, along with "the bones of immortals." *Bainei ben ershisi shi*, vol. 41 (*Mingshi*) (Taibei: Shangwu, 1967), pp. 17b–21a. A less libellous capsule biography appears in L. Carrington Goodrich and Chaoying Fang, eds., *Dictionary of Ming Biography, 1368–1644*, vol. 2 of 2 vols. (New York: Columbia University Press, 1976), pp. 1137–1144.

8 Alasdair MacIntyre, *After Virtue: A Study in Moral Theory*, 2d ed. with postscript (Notre Dame, Ind.: University of Notre Dame Press, 1986), pp. 1–75.

9 The expressions listed here, an incomplete catalog, are not mine, but are taken from the works of several scholars of Chinese religion, philosophy, and intellectual history. See Tu Wei-ming, *Confucian Ethics Today: The Singapore Challenge* (Singapore: Federal Publications, 1984), and "The Rise of Industrial East Asia: The Role of Confucian Values," *Copenhagen Papers in East and Southeast Asian Studies* (April 1989): 81–97; Irene Eber, ed., *Confucianism: The Dynamics of Tradition* (New York: Free Press [Macmillan], 1986); and Kwang-ching Liu, ed., *Orthodoxy in Late Imperial China* (Berkeley: University of California Press, 1990).

10 Brian Stock, *Listening for the Text: On the Uses of the Past* (Baltimore: Johns Hopkins University Press, 1990), p. 80.

11 Herrlee G. Creel, *Confucius and the Chinese Way* (New York: Harper Colophon, 1960), p. 5.

12 Creel, *Confucius and the Chinese Way*, p. 259.

13 Jordan D. Paper, *The Fu-tzu: A Post-Han Confucian Text* (Leiden: E. J. Brill, 1987), p. 6.

14 The analysis here follows that of Ferdinand de Saussure in his *Course in General Linguistics*, where he presents language as the force that signifies experience by conferring a conceptual complex upon it. It may appear that the order of things in the world and that of words in our language is identical; however, the relationships between signifiers in this conceptual complex is determined not by a relationship to the real but in an arbitrary manner, by similarities and differences in function between the other signifiers constituting this complex. More recently, Émile Benveniste has revised Saussure's insistence on the complete arbitrariness

of the sign, contending that unless a bond is forged between an object and a linguistic sign, communication is impossible. The bond between signifier and signified—for the speaker, not a "neutral" observer—must be recognized as necessary. See Ferdinand de Saussure, *Cours de linguistique générale* (Paris: Payot, 1972), pp. 98–113, 155–184; and Émile Benveniste, *Problems in General Linguistics*, trans. Mary Elizabeth Meek (Coral Gables: University of Miami Press, 1971), pp. 43–48.

15 Kwang-chih Chang, *Shang Civilization* (New Haven: Yale University Press, 1980), pp. 357–364.

16 H. D. Harootunian, *Things Seen and Unseen: Discourse and Ideology in Tokugawa Nativism* (Chicago: University of Chicago Press, 1988), p. 4.

17 A larger cultural turn away from classical allegory or biblical metaphor as sources for narration in favor of experience and observation (more broadly a shift from theology to ethnology) made the Jesuit records of life among the Chinese a valuable source. "Matters of fact" was an expression common among eighteenth-century English writers and conveyed their sense that the work of crafting a narrative was indistinguishable from history and depended heavily on empirical observation that now compassed the globe. See Robert Mayer, *History and the Early English Novel: Matters of Fact from Bacon to Defoe* (Cambridge: Cambridge University Press, 1997), esp. pp. 1–17.

Chapter 3

1 The phrase is Umberto Eco's from *The Search for the Perfect Language*, trans. James Fentress (London: Blackwell, 1995), pp. 1–33, esp. 73–193.

2 Prasenjit Duara, *Rescuing History from the Nation: Questioning Narratives of Modern China* (Chicago: University of Chicago Press, 1995), pp. 56–65.

3 See Raymond Williams, *Keywords: A Vocabulary of Culture and Society*, rev. ed. (New York: Oxford University Press, 1984). On prominent cultural symbols as keys to unlock the mysteries of a foreign culture, see Clifford Geertz, "Deep Play: Notes on the Balinese Cockfight," *Daedalus* 101 (1972): 1–37; and Sherry Ortner, "On Key Symbols," *American Anthropologist* 75 (1973): 1338–1346.

4 On this organizing institutional fiction see my discussion of the State Family Romance in chap. 1, n. 61. See also Hsü Dau-lin, "The Myth of the 'Five Human Relations' of Confucius," *Monumenta Serica* 29 (1970–1971): 27–37. There was nothing either natural or necessary about this conjuncture; however, it seems unlikely that this fortuitous quality could ever have been gleaned from a reading of Dong Zhongshu or Sima Qian.

5 See A. C. Graham, *Later Mohist Logic, Ethics, and Science* (Hong Kong: Chinese University Press, 1978), p. 6.

6 Ricci, *TZSY*, pp. 415–418. See also discussion in chapter 2.

7 For a discussion of the difficulty of establishing the real Kongzi, see Lionel M. Jensen, "Wise Man of the Wilds: Fatherlessness, Fertility, and the Mythic Exemplar, Kongzi," *Early China* 20 (1995): 407–437.

8 L. P. Hartley, *The Go-Between* (London: Hamish Hamilton, 1953), p. 1.

9   Clifford Geertz has recently pointed out that foreignness is not simply an inter-
    cultural phenomenon. And if one believes, as does Geertz, that meaning is so-
    cially constructed, then the difference between the present and the past in one
    culture may be as great as that between one culture and another. Inveighing
    against the narrowmindedness of Richard Rorty's endorsement of ethnocentrism
    as a response to cultural diversity, Geertz contends: "This view—that the puzzles
    raised by the fact of cultural diversity have more to do with our capacity to feel
    our way into alien sensibilities, modes of thought . . . we do not possess, and
    are not likely to, than they do with whether we can escape preferring our own
    preferences—has a number of implications which bode ill for a we-are-we and
    they-are-they approach to things cultural. The first of these, and possibly the
    most important, is that those puzzles arise not merely at the boundaries of our
    society, where we would expect them under such an approach, but, so to speak, at
    the boundaries of ourselves. *Foreignness does not start at the water's edge but at
    the skin's*" [emphasis added]. Clifford Geertz, "The Uses of Diversity," *Michigan
    Quarterly Review* (winter 1986): 112.

10 "Entering the horizon" is an allusion to Hans-Georg Gadamer, *Truth and Method*,
    trans. Garret Barden and William G. Doerpel (New York: Seabury Press, 1975),
    pp. 345–447.

11 The *Er ya*, probably the oldest Chinese etymology, contains no mention of *ru*. See
    Er ya, in *SSJZS*, vol. 12; *Guang ya shuzheng* (reprint; Beijing: Zhonghua Shuju,
    1983), *juan* 4.2, pp. 17a–b.; and Xu Shen, *Shuowen jiezi* (reprint; Beijing: Zhong-
    hua Shuju, 1963), p. 162.1.

12 See Zhang Binglin, "Yuan ru," in *Guogu lunheng* (reprint; Taibei: Guangwen
    Shuju, 1967), pp. 151–155 (hereafter cited as Zhang, "YR"); and Hu Shi, "Shuo ru,"
    in *Hu Shi wencun*, vol. 4 of 6 vols. (Taibei: Yuandong, 1953), pp. 1–82 (hereafter
    cited as Hu, "SR").

13 In fact the mainland Chinese scholar Zhou Gucheng suggested a few years ago
    that *ru* were probably the divinatory attendants of the hereditary ruling clan, Zi,
    of the Shang dynasty. See Zhou Gucheng, *Zhongguo tongshi*, vol. 1 of 2 vols.
    (Shanghai: Renmin Chubanshe, 1983), p. 103.

14 Zhang, "YR," pp. 154–155.

15 See Hu, "SR," pp. 6, 35–43.

16 The theoretical underpinnings of this analysis are derived from Mikhail Bakhtin,
    "Discourse in the Novel," in *The Dialogic Imagination: Four Essays by M. M.
    Bakhtin*, ed. Michael Holquist, trans. Caryl Emerson and Michael Holquist (Aus-
    tin: University of Texas Press, 1981), pp. 259–331.

17 The expression "figurative predication" is taken from James Fernandez. See
    James W. Fernandez, *Persuasions and Performances: The Play of Tropes in Cul-
    ture* (Bloomington: Indiana University Press, 1986), pp. 249–268, 288–292.

18 After recounting the many difficulties posed by the use of traditional dictionaries
    for historical phonology, Norman proposes an obvious, though often avoided,
    alternative: "Certainly another approach is possible: the reconstruction of the
    ancestor of the spoken (popular) forms of Chinese, working backward from the
    present spoken dialects. One important benefit of this approach would be to

establish a core of words which has evolved organically from the ancestral form of Chinese down to the present day." See Jerry Norman, *Chinese* (Cambridge: Cambridge University Press, 1988), p. 42.

19 This is my conclusion based on numerous discussions with both educated and semiliterate Chinese in Kunming, Yunnan, from February to July of 1991. When asked the meaning of *ru* they would say, with little deviation, that it referred to *chuantong zhengzhi zhidu* (the traditional political system), the chronology of which ranged from Han to Qing. Some respondents indicated that it represented "the emperor system" (*huangdi zhidu*) and thus signified a far-reaching network of control extending from center to periphery. Very few, and only those who were university professors, said that *ru* meant *xuezhe*, "scholars," and only one stated that it meant apostolic descent from Kongzi. In sum, *ru* for many contemporary Chinese should be understood as the handmaiden of autocracy if not autocracy itself. This definition, of course, is testament to the persistence of the collective memory of the *pi-Lin pi-Kong* campaigns of the Cultural Revolution of the 1970s.

20 For a survey of this tendency in the scholarship, see Joseph R. Levenson, *Confucian China and Its Modern Fate: A Trilogy* (Berkeley: University of California Press, 1968), vol. 1, pp. xxvii–xxxiii, vol. 2, pp. 3–73, vol. 3, pp. 61–82; Tu Weiming, *Confucian Thought: Selfhood as Creative Transformation* (Albany: State University of New York Press, 1985), pp. 7–18; and Wm. Theodore de Bary, *The Trouble with Confucianism* (Cambridge, Mass.: Harvard University Press, 1991).

21 This fact bears witness to the persistence of certain aspects of the May Fourth historical imagination, for it was here that the *ru* were considered an insidious collaborator of Manchu autocracy. See Vera Schwarcz, *The Chinese Enlightenment: Intellectuals and the Legacy of the May Fourth Movement of 1919* (Berkeley: University of California Press, 1986), pp. 23–93.

22 Derek Herforth, "From Annals via Homiletics to Analysis: Toward a Discourse-Based Typology of Early Chinese Historiography," paper presented at Seventh-fifth Meeting of the Speech Communication Association, San Francisco, Calif., November 19, 1989.

23 See Sima Qian, *Shiji*, 10 vols. (reprint; Beijing: Zhonghua Shuju, 1975), p. 3115.

24 Sima, *Shiji*, p. 3115.

25 Sima, *Shiji*, p. 3116. The *Zhuangzi*'s Robber Zhi, incidentally, makes much of this ill-fated alliance, parodying the absurd lengths to which the *ru* would go in service to a lord they considered honorable.

26 Sima, *Shiji*, p. 3116.

27 Sima, *Shiji*, p. 3117. Sima Qian quotes *Lunyu* 5.21 to convey that even in Kongzi's day the *ru* were well entrenched in Lu so that their persisting there, even until Liu's armies beckoned nearly four centuries later, hardly stretched credulity. For a phenomenology of the *da she* and *xiangyin* (seasonal [spring] rituals of some antiquity, which evolved into tributes to Zhou Gong and Kongzi in the former Han and which are described in detail in both the *Li ji* and the *Hou Hanshu*), see Marcel Granet, *Chinese Civilization*, trans. Kathleen E. Innes and Mabel Brailsford (Cleveland, Ohio: Meridian Books, 1958), pp. 152–193; and Derk Bodde, *Fes-*

tivals in Classical China: New Year and Other Annual Observances during the Han Dynasty, 206 B.C.–A.D. 220 (Princeton: Princeton University Press, 1975), pp. 356–361.

28 Zheng Xuan, *Zhengshi liji mulu,* as quoted in Duan Yucai, *Shuowen jiezi zhu* (reprint; Taibei: Hanjing wenhua shiye youxian gongsi, 1983), pp. 366.1, 366.2.

29 Recently the "Han" character of our understanding of Chinese antiquity and the "invested" historical construction of *ru* ascendancy by Sima Qian have been explored by Benjamin Wallacker. See Benjamin E. Wallacker, "Han Confucianism and Confucius in Han," in *Ancient China: Studies in Early Civilization,* ed. David T. Roy and Tsuen-hsuin Tsien (Hong Kong: Hong Kong University Press, 1978), pp. 215–228.

30 The "present emperor" of whom Sima Qian speaks is his own monarch, Wudi. *Shiji,* p. 3118.

31 I am alluding here to the lowly existence of Yan Hui, Kongzi's most loved disciple, as described in *Lunyu,* and to Tian Fen's elevation of numerous *ru,* as recounted by Sima Qian in *Shiji,* pp. 3117–3118. "Tian Fen [fl. 2d century B.C.E.] as prime minister demoted the words of Huang-Lao, and Xing-Ming of the hundred families [while] promoting many hundreds of classically literate *ru.* . . . [C]onsequently Gong Sunhong, because of his mastery of the *Chunqiu,* became third in rank to the Son of Heaven and was enfeoffed as Marquis of Pingjin."

32 See chapter 2.

33 The characterization is taken from the title of an essay by Homer Dubs that appears as an appendix to his translation of the *Han shu.* To his credit, Dubs argues for a long chronology of *ru* ascendance beginning with Han Gaodi (r. 202–195 B.C.E.) and ending with Han Yuandi (r. 48–33 B.C.E.). See Homer H. Dubs, trans., *The History of the Former Han Dynasty,* vol. 2 of 3 vols. (New York: American Council of Learned Societies, 1944), pp. 341–353. For the commonplace notion of *ru* "victory" coming with the reign of Han Wudi, see Herrlee G. Creel, *Confucius and the Chinese Way* (New York: Harper and Row, 1960), p. 234.

34 See *Liji zhengyi,* pt. 2, in *SSJZS,* vol. 6 (Shanghai: Guji Chubanshe, 1990), pp. 972–975.

35 See his "History, Anthropology, and Chinese Religion," in *Harvard Journal of Asiatic Studies* 40, no. 1 (June 1980): 201–248.

36 Michel Strickmann, "The Mao Shan Revelations: Taoism and the Aristocracy," in *T'oung Pao* 68 (1977): 1–64; and "On the Alchemy of T'ao Hung-ching," in *Facets of Taoism: Essays in Chinese Religion,* ed. Holmes Welch and Anna Seidel (New Haven: Yale University Press, 1979), pp. 123–192.

37 See Kristofer Schipper, "Vernacular and Classical Ritual in Taoism," in *Journal of Asian Studies* 45, no. 1 (Nov. 1985): 21–57.

38 See Ernest Fenollosa, *The Chinese Character as a Medium for Poetry* (1938; reprint; San Francisco: City Lights Books, n.d.), pp. 6–33; and Ezra Pound, *Confucius: The Unwobbling Pivot, The Great Digest, and The Analects* (New York: New Directions, 1969), pp. 20–23.

39 At least in the People's Republic it is also true that when people speak of language in an analytical way they are usually concerned with the written as opposed to

the spoken language. Thus, the tendency in Western scholarship not to mine the great depths of dialects for their "distinctive literatures and traditions" (justly lamented by Strickmann) and to rely on the *putong hua* administrative vernacular of the government in Beijing is perhaps more a consequence of cultural observation than political expediency. On the official and scholarly understanding of Chinese language as "written," see Susan D. Blum, "Han and the Chinese Other: The Language of Identity and Difference in Southwest China," Ph.D. diss., University of Michigan, 1994, chap. 3.

40 For a discussion of selected bronze inscriptions from the Zhou that contain charges also found in the *Shang shu* see W. A. C. H. Dobson, *Early Archaic Chinese, A Descriptive Grammar* (Toronto: University of Toronto Press, 1962), pp. 130–233; Jessica Rawson, *Ancient China: Art and Archaeology* (New York: Harper and Row, 1980), pp. 94–103; and Edward L. Shaughnessy, *Sources of Western Zhou History: Inscribed Bronzes* (Berkeley: University of California Press, 1991). An examination of two different indexed collections of oracle bone inscriptions yielded no evidence of *ru*, and this was also true of my examination of the *Jinwen gulin*. See Guo Moruo, ed., *Jiaguwen heji*, 13 vols. (Beijing: Zhonghua Shuju, 1978–1982); Shima Kunio, *Inkyo bokuji sorui*, 2d rev. ed. (Tokyo: Kyoku shoin, 1971); Zhou Fagao et al., eds., *Jinwen gulin* (Hong Kong: Chinese University Press, 1975); and Zhou Fagao, ed., *Jinwen gulin bu* (Taibei [Nangang]: Institute of History and Philology, Academia Sinica, 1983).

41 On the definitive heterogeneity of early Chinese texts, see the discussion in the epilogue, pages 268–79.

42 Ding Fubao, comp., *Shuowen jiezi gulin*, vol. 8 of 8 vols. (Shanghai: Yixue Shuju, 1931–1932), p. 3483.1.

43 We first see evidence of this intellectual/cultural phenomenon, in which the physical presence of the cultural other provokes genuine reflection on the meaning of the inherited cultural identity of the self, when northern China falls under Jurched rule in the twelfth century (1127). On intellectual reorientation and its concomitant reflection on the true meaning of *ru*, see Peter K. Bol, "Seeking Common Ground: Han Literati under Jurchen Rule," *Harvard Journal of Asiatic Studies* 47, no. 2 (Dec. 1987): 488–490, 504–508. A similar development occurs under the Mongols, especially among elites of the Zhedong region, and this has been analyzed in John Dardess, *Confucianism and Autocracy: Professional Elites in the Founding of the Ming Dynasty* (Berkeley: University of California Press, 1983), pp. 13–181, esp. 131–181.

44 See Dardess, *Confucianism and Autocracy*, pp. 14–19.

45 Wang Wei, "Yuan ru," in *Wang Zhong wenji*, in *SKQS*, vol. 1226, pp. 84.1–85.2.

46 Wang, "Yuan ru," p. 84.2.

47 See Song Lian, "Qiru jie," in *Song wenxian gong quanji*, *SBBY* edition (reprint; Taibei: Zhonghua Shuju, 1970), *juan* 36, pp. 4a–5a. The inspiration for Song's categorical analysis of *ru* may be found in bk. 9 of the *Xunzi jijie*, pp. 73–93; and Wang Chong, *Lunheng*, in *ZZJC*, vol. 7, pt. 5 (Beijing: Zhonghua Shuju, 1954), pp. 274–275. Two of the categories of *ru* enumerated by Song—*wenru* (literary *ru*) and *shiru* (gentlemanly *ru*)—are discussed by Wang Chong. For an explanation of

Song Lian's *ru* self-conception in the context of an emerging "Confucian professionalism" in the fourteenth century, see Dardess, *Confucianism and Autocracy*, pp. 156–173.

48 Song Lian, "Hetu shu," in *Song wenxian gong quanji, juan* 51, pp. 13b–15a.

49 Xu Shen, *Shuowen jiezi* (Beijing: Zhonghua Shuju, 1963). The work is believed to have been first presented in the form of a memorial to the emperor He (Liu Zhao, r. 88–106) in 100 C.E. Song Lian defines *ru* as *rouxu*, or "weak," using the rhyme of *xu* meaning "lesser wife," or concubine, to make his point. See "Hetu shu," p. 14b.

50 The emphasis on demeanor as a fundamental criterion of *ru* begins with Xunzi, who, with considerable detail, articulated a visible spectrum of *ru* practice. Wang Wei's explication of *ru*, particularly his castigation of *suru*, closely resembles Xunzi's earlier critique and shows plainly that while one could acknowledge a minimal historicity—i.e., the passage of antiquity—there was no concomitant sense of development. See Wang, "Yuan ru," pp. 85.1–85.2; and Song, "Qiru jie," pp. 4b–5a.

51 See Xu, *Shuowen jiezi*, p. 162.1; Zheng Xuan, "Liji mulu," in *Liji zhengyi, SSJZS*, vol. 7, pt. 1; and "Lunyu zhusu jiejing," in *Zhongguo zixue mingzhe jicheng*, vol. 2 (Taibei: 1968), pp. 169–170.

52 See Jiang Yong, *Xiangdang tukao* (Fusu tang, 1756), *juan* 1; and Cui Shu, "Lunyu yushuo," in *Cui Dongbi yishu*, ed. Gu Jiejang, vol. 5 (Shanghai: Yadong tushu guan, 1936).

53 On this textual shift see Pi Xirui, *Jingxue lishi* (Hong Kong: Zhonghua Shuju, 1961).

54 The *zhuzi* referred, of course, to Zhuangzi, Mozi, Xunzi, Han Feizi, Lü Buwei, Yanzi, Guanzi, Liezi, and Laozi, a diverse group of intellectual combatants who emerged, as did Kongzi, from the cultural detritus of the Warring States. *Zhuzi xue* was an eighteenth-century development within the broader *kaozheng* movement to reconstruct the authentic classics. Zhang Xuecheng has been recognized as an exemplar of this genre, yet it is important to note that Wang Zhong pursued a similar path. See Zhang Xuecheng, *Zhangshi yishu*, vol. 1 of 8 vols. (Shanghai: Shangwu, 1936), *juan* 2, pp. 2.2a–2.8b; and Wang Zhong, *Shuxue neipian* (reprint; Taibei: Guangwen Shuju, 1970).

55 Even today *yuanshi* as a description of *buluo* (tribes) or *minzu* (ethnic group) is commonly found in official scholarship on minorities in the People's Republic. On the official Communist Party stratigraphy of sociocultural development as derived from Lewis Henry Morgan and Joseph Stalin, see Blum, "Han and the Chinese Other," chap. 2. See also Frank Dikötter, *The Discourse of Race in Modern China* (London: Hurst, 1992), pp. 164–195.

56 Hu, "SR," p. 3.

57 Yan Fu was the first to translate Herbert Spencer for a Chinese audience in 1895, but three years later Zhang Binglin and Zeng Guangquan cotranslated an introduction to Spencer's thought in *Changyan bao*: Zhang Binglin, "Shibinsaier wenji," *Changyan bao*, no. 1 (May 1898), no. 2 (June 1898), no. 3 (July 1898), no. 4 (August 1898), no. 5 (August 16, 1898), no. 6 (August 26, 1898), no. 8 (September 1898). See also Martin Bernal, "Liu Shih-p'ei and National Essence," in *The Lim-*

its of Change: Essays on Conservative Alternatives in Republican China, ed. Charlotte Furth (Cambridge, Mass.: Harvard University Press, 1976), pp. 92–104; and Charlotte Furth, "Intellectual Change from the Reform Movement to the May Fourth Movement, 1895–1920," in *The Cambridge History of China,* ed. John K. Fairbank, vol. 12, pt. 1 (Cambridge: Cambridge University Press, 1983), pp. 354–364.

58 Hu Shi, "SR," p. 3. The last phrase of Hu's comment here is a paraphrase of a remark by Liu Xin from the "Yiwen zhi" read through Zhang's tripartite characterization. See Liu Xin, "Yiwen zhi," in *Han shu buzhu,* ed. Weng Xianquan, vol. 3 of 6 vols. (Taibei: Dingwen Shuju, 1974), p. 1728.

59 *Jinwen* is commonly taken in the sense of "new text," yet it could be rendered just as well as "new script," since it originated as an interpretive school (*jinwenjia*) on the basis of its study of texts written in the *lishu* script newly innovated in the Han. According to the received account, when the Qin burned the extant classic texts in 213 B.C.E., the *Shang shu*—composed of about one hundred chapters culled by Kongzi himself from the surviving records of the Xia, Shang, and Zhou— was completely destroyed. It is from this incendiary origin that the conditions of scholarly controversy emerged. There were no texts in old, pre-Qin script, only new script (*jinwen*) ones. The new script text of twenty-nine chapters of the *Shang shu* either was produced through the transcription of what the decrepit Fu Sheng (ca. 3d–2d century B.C.E.) was able to recite from memory or, by another legendary account, was found in the wall of Fu Sheng's house written in the new script. These events transpired under the reign of the Han emperor Wen (r. 179– 157 B.C.E.), but less than a century later under Emperor Wu fifty-eight chapters of another text was discovered bearing scribal forms from the era before the standardization of the script in the Qin.

It is alleged that this *guwen* (ancient script) text was discovered in one wall of Kongzi's home, exposed when some excavation of the premises was ordered by Emperor Wu. This work was transcribed in *lishu* with annotations by Kong Anguo (ca. 150–100 B.C.E. [who was believed to be a descendant of Kongzi]) and became known as the *guwen* version. The Han imperial bibliographers Liu Xiang (79–8 B.C.E.) and Liu Xin (46–23 B.C.E.) favored the *guwen* texts in their recensions, especially the *Zuo zhuan* commentary on the *Chunqiu*. For their tendentiousness in this regard—ignoring the more arcane commentaries on the *Chunqiu*, the *Guliang* and *Gongyang* that alone contained the true message of Kongzi—the Lius were charged by Kang Youwei and others with forgery and conspiracy to defraud subsequent generations. The best modern scholarly account of the legends of the combative *jinwen* and *guwen* texts and their authenticity remains that of Paul Pelliot, "Le Chou King en caractères anciens et le Chang Chou Che Wen," *Mémoires concernant l'Asie orientale* 2 (1916): 123–177. On the meaning of the textual controversy over new script and old script texts in the Former Han, see Jack L. Dull, "A Historical Introduction to the Apocryphal (Ch'an-Wei) Texts of the Han Dynasty," Ph.D. diss., University of Washington, 1966.

60 Chang Hao, *Liang Ch'i-ch'ao and Intellectual Transition in China, 1897–1907*

(Cambridge, Mass.: Harvard University Press, 1971); Lin Yü-sheng, *The Crisis of Chinese Consciousness: Radical Antitraditionalism in the May Fourth Era* (Madison: University of Wisconsin Press, 1979), pp. 3–55; and Schwarcz, *The Chinese Enlightenment*, pp. 12–54. I follow Schwarcz in identifying the differences between the iconoclastic generation of 1911 (Zhang Binglin, Liang Qichao, Liu Shipei) and that of 1919 (Chen Duxiu, Lu Xun, Qian Xuantong) as those separating *jiuguo* (saving the country) and *qimeng* (enlightenment). I believe that a generational perspective on the intellectual developments during the interval from 1898 to 1919, in which the two groups may be viewed as occupying two contiguous positions on a spectrum of cultural criticism and political engagement, does much to eliminate the misconception of a sui generis radical movement of "totalistic" iconoclasts. Furthermore, such an interpretation appears to mirror the way that many Chinese intellectuals today understand the relations between activists of 1898, 1911, and 1919, as shown by the 1988 television documentary *He shang*. See Chen Xiaolin and Su Xiaokang, *He shang* (reprint; Taibei: Jingeng Chubanshe, 1990).

61 Wolfgang Franke, *Reform and Abolition of the Traditional Chinese Examination System* (Cambridge, Mass.: Harvard University Press, 1960), pp. 48–71; and Sally Borthwick, *Education and Social Change in China: The Beginnings of the Modern Era* (Stanford: Hoover Institution Press, 1983), pp. 77–103.

62 On the quickening pace of substantive constitutional reform set by the Manchus following the constitutional missions of 1905–1906, see Meribeth E. Cameron, *The Reform Movement in China, 1898–1912* (Stanford: Stanford University Press, 1931), pp. 100–135; and E-tu Zen Sun, "The Chinese Constitutional Missions of 1905–1906," *Journal of Modern History* 24, no. 3 (September 1952): 251–268.

63 The interval from 1907 to 1908 was a very troubled one in the annals of Chinese republican radicalism. The reasons for the despair of radical activists are discussed in Martin Bernal, *Chinese Socialism to 1907* (Ithaca: Cornell University Press, 1976), pp. 198–226; and Michael Gasster, *Chinese Intellectuals and the Revolution of 1911: The Birth of Modern Chinese Radicalism* (Seattle: University of Washington Press, 1969), pp. 210–213.

64 The link between past and future was organic, ineluctable as Zhang himself made clear in his famous renunciation of Esperanto, *wanguo xinyu*. Speaking against those, like Wu Zhihui (1864–1954), who advocated universal adoption of Esperanto, he said: "They will say that our histories and biographies entomb the deeds of dead men, that our literature is empty verbiage, that it is of no practical benefit to the people, and that even to abandon it completely is permissible. They do not realize that the difference between man and the birds and beasts is precisely that he has the concept of what is past and what is yet to come. *If we say that the sense of the past may be erased, then that of the future may also be excised,* and man will know only this instant and nothing more" (emphasis added). Zhang Binglin, "Bo Zhongguo yong wanguo xinyu shuo," *Minbao*, no. 21 (June 10, 1908): 55.

65 An often unremarked irony in the conceptions of *guwen* and *jinwen* scholars is

that despite the vociferous protestations of the former against the latter's resurrection of the apocryphal texts on behalf of a new orthodoxy that enshrined the miraculous Kongzi as sage and savior, the distinction between the two discourses' view of Kongzi was negligible. Much as Sun Yat-sen is regarded as the *guofu* or national father of both the Republic of China and the People's Republic of China, Kongzi was the great cultural patriarch of both *jinwen* and *guwen* discourse. Recently another common link between these principal twentieth-century representatives of the *jinwen* and *guwen* traditions was put forward by Chang Hao who stressed the pivotal role of Buddhism in the respective intellectual syntheses of the two. According to Chang, both men were inspired by the bodhisattva ideal. See Chang Hao [Zhang Hao], *Chinese Intellectuals in Crisis: Search for Order and Meaning (1890–1911)* (Berkeley: University of California Press, 1987), pp. 24–31, 117–145.

66 The contributions of these scholars were offered in the spirit of clarification or criticism and, as much as they may have debated Zhang's or Hu's specific readings of classical texts, they never questioned the evolutionary frame on which the essays were built. See Feng Youlan, "Yuan ru mo," in *Zhongguo zhexue shi bu* (Shanghai, Shangwu, 1936); Guo Moruo, "Fu Shuoru," in Guo, *Qingtong shidai* (Beijing: Zhonghua Shuju, 1954); and Fu Sinian, "Zhan'guo zixia xulun," in *Zhongguo shanggu shilun wenxuan ji*, vol. 2 (1929).

67 I am alluding here to the late-nineteenth-century Western perception that China was "the sick man of Asia" (*Yazhou bingren*). For a memorable illustration of this contemptuous judgment of Chinese culture near the close of the Qing era, see Arthur H. Smith, *Chinese Characteristics* (New York: Fleming H. Revell, 1894), esp. pp. 16–97. It must be noted in this context that long before Lu Xun's "Medicine" or "The True Story of Ah Q," men like Zhang and Liang Qichao internalized this perception and in several publications early in the century referred to China as "sick."

68 Zhang Binglin, "Kedi kuangniu," in *Qiu shu* (1904 ed.; reprinted in *Zhongghua minguo gushi congliao*, ed. Luo Jialun, Taibei: Shijie Shuju, 1963), p. 2. Zhang's "double slave" has two senses. First, the people of China, the "Han minzu," were the slaves of their conquerors, the Manchus, and the slaves of the imperialist conqueror, the Western powers. In another sense, the Chinese people were enslaved by the Manchus who, in turn, were the slaves of the Western (European and American) capitalists. This piece appears first in the revised edition of *Qiu shu* and is intended as a correction of the errors in judgment that Zhang committed in his essay "Kedi," which constituted chap. 29 of the 1900 edition. Here he makes explicit his rejection of the few suggestions of *gongyang* theory that had crept into this earlier essay, including his identification of Kongzi and the traditional imperial families as the common lords (*gongzhu*) of Chinese culture. The double-slave characterization was echoed in the thoughts of both Yan Fu and Sun Yat-sen, the former calling China "the common slave of all powers," and the latter, in a novel formulation, deeming it a "hypocolony . . . subject to many powers and hence inferior to a colony." See also the discussion in Shimada Kenji, "Shingai kakumei ki no Kōshi mondai," in *Shingai Kakumei no kenkyū*, ed. Onagawa Hidemi and

Shimada Kenji (Tokyo: Chikuma shobō, 1978), pp. 15–18; and Shimada Kenji, *Pioneer of the Chinese Revolution: Zhang Binglin and Confucianism*, trans. Joshua A. Fogel (Stanford: Stanford University Press, 1990), pp. 113–114.

69 Joseph R. Levenson, "The Genesis of *Confucian China and Its Modern Fate*," in *The Historians Workshop: Original Essays by Sixteen Historians*, ed. L. P. Curtis Jr. (New York: Knopf, 1970), p. 286.

70 This of course would be confirmed again with the "May Fourth" appeal by Hu Shi and Lu Xun to "smash the shop of the Kong family" (*pohuai Kongjia dian*), where "the shop of the Kong family" (*Kongjia dian*) metonymically represented the entire classical heritage.

71 Liao Ping, *Huangdi jiangyu tu*, in *Liuyiguan congshu* (Chengdu: Cungu Shudian, 1925), p. 22. My translation, with several modifications, follows that of Derk Bodde in Fung Yu-lan, *A History of Chinese Philosophy*, vol. 2 of 2 vols. (Princeton: Princeton University Press, 1952), p. 712.

72 In the essay "Kedi" (Guest Emperor), written in 1899, which appeared in the first edition of *Qiu shu* in 1900, Zhang identified Kongzi and China's imperial families as the *gongzhu*, "the common lords" of its history. He says, "China's common lords from the Han dynasty forward have retained the same surname for over two thousand years. They are the descendants of Kongzi." See Zhang, *Qiu shu* (1900 edition; reprint; Shanghai: Guji Chubanshe, 1985), pp. 116–124. See also Tang Zhenchang, "Lun Zhang Taiyan," *Lishi yanjiu* (January 1978): 67–85, esp. 71, for the dates of the writing of "Kedi" and "Kedi kuangniu."

73 See Liang Qichao, "Hunan Shiwu xuetang chuji," in *Wuxu bianfa*, vol. 4 (Shanghai: Shanghai renmin Chubanshe, 1957), p. 505; and Shimada, "Shingai kakumei ki no Kōshi mondai," pp. 12–13.

74 See Paul Ricoeur, *Freud and Philosophy: An Essay on Interpretation* (New Haven: Yale University Press, 1971), p. 47.

75 Kang Youwei, *Kongzi gaizhi kao* (reprint; Beijing: Zhonghua Shuju, 1958), p. 164. See also Benjamin A. Elman, *From Philosophy to Philology: Intellectual and Social Aspects of Change in Late Imperial China* (Cambridge, Mass.: Council on East Asian Studies, Harvard University Press, 1984), p. 24, for a different translation. On the early elevation of Zhou gong above Kongzi, see John R. Shryock, *The Origin and Development of the State Cult of Confucius* (New York: Century, 1932), pp. 98–100, 131–142; and Léon Vandermeersch, "Aspects rituels de la popularisation du Confucianisme sous les Han," in *Thought and Law in Qin and Han China: Studies Dedicated to Anthony Hulsewé on the Occasion of his Eightieth Birthday*, ed. W. L. Idema and E. Zürcher (Leiden: E. J. Brill, 1990), pp. 89–107.

76 The *Shuowen jiezi* defines *yuan* as the "headwaters" of a spring *chuan*; hence, the received sense of origin or beginning. See Xu, *Shuowen jiezi*, p. 239.2.

77 As Michael Gasster has noted, one would have great difficulty determining what Zhang or Liu would object to in Kang's platform for the Baohuang Hui (Protect the Emperor Society): "To preserve intact the country's territory, its people and its tradition; to study matters relative to the preservation of the country, the race, and the tradition." See Gasster, *Chinese Intellectuals and the Revolution of 1911*, pp. 204–205.

78 Such cultural reification was explicit in the essentialist *ti/yong* (essence/function) dichotomy that provided the ideological justification for the initial phases of Chinese modernization. No scholar has better articulated this phenomenon of cultural abstraction under duress than Raymond Williams in *Culture and Society, 1780–1950* (New York: Harper Torchbooks, 1966), pp. xv–xvi. Where culture once meant a state or habit of the mind, or the body of intellectual and moral activities, it now refers to a whole way of life.

79 On the organization of the national heritage, *zhengli guogu*, see Irene Eber, "Hu Shih and Chinese History: The Problem of *cheng-li kuo-ku*," *Monumenta Serica* 27 (1968): 169–207; Shimada, "Shingai kakumei"; Charlotte Furth, "The Sage as Rebel: The Inner World of Chang Ping-lin," in *The Limits of Change*, ed. Furth, pp. 116–128; and Lawrence Schneider, "National Essence and the New Intelligentsia," in *The Limits of Change*, ed. Furth, pp. 69–74.

80 See Thomas S. Kuhn, *The Structure of Scientific Revolutions* (Chicago: University of Chicago Press, 1962).

81 Zhang, "YR," p. 154.

82 For a sampling of the scholarship inspired in some way by either Zhang's or Hu's essay, see Kitamura Sawakichi, *Jūgaku gairon* (Tokyo: Kan shoin, 1928), pp. 1–19; Hu, "SR," pp. 1–82; Feng Youlan, "Yuan ru mo"; Guo Moruo, "Fu Shuoru," pp. 103–128; Shigezawa Toshio, *Genshi jūka shisō to keigaku* (Tokyo: Iwanami shoten, 1949); Qian Mu, "Fu Hu Shi zhi Shuoru," *Journal of Oriental Studies* 1, no. 1 (January 1954): 123–128; Rao Zongyi, "Shi ru: Cong wenzi xunguxue shang lunru re yiyi," *Journal of Oriental Studies* 1, no. 1 (January 1954): 111–122; Gu Jiegang, *Qin-Han de fangshi yu rusheng* (Shanghai: Qunlian Chubanshe, 1955); Dai Junren, "Ru de laiyuan tuice," *Dalu zazhi* 37, no. 10 (1968): 1–5; Chen Zhengyan, "Ping jinren dui ru zhi qiyuan de tuice," *Shixue huikan*, no. 6 (1975): 111–117; Chow Tse-tsung, "Ancient Chinese Views on Literature, the *Tao*, and Their Relationship," *Chinese Literature: Essays, Articles, Reviews* 1, no. 1 (January 1979): 3–29; Diane Burdette Obenchain, "Ministers of the Moral Order: Innovations of the Early Chou Kings, the Duke of Chou, Chung-ni and Ju." Ph.D. diss., Harvard University, 1984, pp. 334–367; and Robert Eno, *The Confucian Creation of Heaven: Philosophy and the Defense of Ritual Mastery* (Albany: State University of New York Press, 1990), pp. 190–197, 289–292.

83 Gu Jiegang, *Gushi bian*, vol. 1 of 7 vols. (reprint; Hong Kong: Taiping Shuju, 1962), pp. 49–52. Gu's conclusions were only reinforced by the contemporaneous reconstructive labors of Henri Maspero and Marcel Granet, who said much the same of the legends of the culture heroes and even identified a recurring narrative pattern by which these tales were emplotted. See Henri Maspero, "Légendes mythologiques dans le *Chou King*," *Journal Asiatique* 204 (January 1924): 11–100; and Marcel Granet, *Danses et légendes de la Chine ancienne*, 2 vols. (Paris: Presses Universitaires de France, 1959).

84 Arthur W. Hummel, *Autobiography of a Chinese Historian* (Leiden: E. J. Brill, 1931), pp. 97–98; and Gu, *Gushi bian*, vol. 1, pp. 51–52.

85 Hummel, *Autobiography of a Chinese Historian*, p. 98; and Gu, *Gushi bian*, vol. 1, p. 52.

86 The "Yuan ru" edition cited by most authorities is that published in Zhang Bing-lin, *Guogu lunheng*, 2 vols. (National Heritage Evaluation of 1910) (reprint; Taibei: Guangwen Shudian, 1967). The *Guogu lunheng*, however, also appeared as one slip of the six-volume *Zhangshi congshu* (Collectanea of Mr. Zhang), published in 1919 in Hangzhou by the Zhejiang Library (Zhejiang tushuguan). A definitive date for the completion of the essay has not been established, yet on the basis of its inclusion in *Qiu shu* (the first edition of which, according to Martin Bernal, was written between 1899 and 1902) and its contents we may conclude that it was probably produced sometime during this same interval, shortly after Zhang's association with the *gujing jingshe* (Hall of Wondrous Remembrance of the Ancient Canon) on West Lake in Hangzhou. Owing to the high degree of consistency between the content and approach of this essay and those found in *Qiu shu*, I believe that portions of "Yuan ru" were completed before the turn of the century. The edition of "Yuan ru" I have used throughout is that found in *Guogu lunheng*, pp. 151–155, with commentary by Zhang himself. On the possible dates and circumstances of the essay's composition, see Zhang Yin, "Gujing jingshe zhi chugao," *Wenlan xuebao* 2, no. 1 (March 1936): 1–47; Shen Yanguo, *Ji Zhang Taiyan xiansheng* (Shanghai: Shangwu, 1946); Zhang Binglin, *Zhang Taiyan ziding nianpu* (Hong Kong: Longmen Shudian, 1965), pp. 4–11; and Martin Bernal, "Liu Shih-p'ei and National Essence," p. 372, n. 21.

87 This racialist distinction is explicit in "Kedi kuangniu," Zhang's revisionist preface to the second edition of *Qiu shu*. Among the familiar Chinese concepts borrowed from the vocabulary of Japanese nativism are *chuantong [dentō]* (tradition), *zizhi [jichi]* (autonomous, self-governing), *geming [kakumei]* (revolution), *minzu [minzoku]* (race), *guoxue [kokugaku]* (national studies), *guocui [kokutsui]* (national essence), and *guogu [kokuku]* (national past). As yet there is no scholarly work that identifies and analyzes the products of this cultural exchange.

88 From the inaugural issue to which Liu contributed "An Introduction to the Schools of Thought at the End of the Zhou," the *Guocui xuebao* was concerned with the resurrection of *zhuzi xue*. Much of the scholarly work published in the journal by Liu Shipei and Zhang Binglin was devoted to a revival of the philosophy of Chinese antiquity in its broadest form, wherein the intellectual pluralism of this formative epoch was understood as a sign of indigenous Chinese strength. Liu's piece on the early history of *ru* was consistent with this celebration of the vitality of ancient, prenormative Chinese culture. See *Guocui xuebao*, no. 1 (February 1905); and Bernal, "Liu Shih-p'ei and National Essence," p. 106.

89 Liu Xin, "Yiwen zhi," in *Hanshu buzhu*, vol. 3, p. 1738.

90 Liu Shipei, "Rujia chu yu situ zhi guan shuo," *Guocui xuebao*, no. 33 (August 20, 1908): 1b–2a. See also Obenchain, "Ministers of the Moral Order," p. 630, for a different translation of this passage. Liu divides the Zhou era into two moments, Western (1046–771 B.C.E.) and Eastern (771–256 B.C.E.). This has been the convention since the beginning of imperial time and has been followed religiously by sinologists. This distinction, which is based on the defeat of the Zhou in 771 B.C.E. and their removal to the east in Luoyi (near present-day Luoyang) does not

appear in texts of the era because the Zhou ceased to function as suzerains after this date. By the fourth century B.C.E., "Eastern Zhou" is in evidence and is certified two centuries later with the Han. I will use "post-Zhou" to refer to the period after 771 B.C.E. while retaining the traditional segregation of "Eastern" and "Western" when it appears in quoted works.

91 Liu Shipei, "Jindai Hanxue bianqian lun," *Guocui xuebao*, no. 31 (June 1908) and translated by R. Kent Guy in "The *National Essence Journal* and the Eighteenth Century," paper presented at the Association for Asian Studies meeting, San Francisco, April 1983.

92 Liu, "Rujia chu yu situ," pp. 1a–1b.

93 Liu, "Rujia chu yu situ," p. 1b.

94 Another, and intended, consequence of Liu Shipei's scholarship was his defense of Liu Xin, as noted in the text accompanying notes 89 and 90. The very title of the essay vindicated Liu Xin by reaffirming the legitimacy of his claim of *ru* descent from the *situ* (leader of the footsoldiers). While such support for the maligned Liu was not as dramatic as that of Zhang Binglin who carried a chop bearing the expression "Liu Zijun sishu dizi" (Self-trained disciple of Liu Zijun [Liu Xin]), it may have been more convincing, because Liu Shipei was able to link the "Yiwen zhi" (Imperial Bibliographic Catalogue) account with corroborating passages from the *Zhou li* (Rites of Zhou) and in turn assemble all the evidence in favor of a cultural history of *ru* from antiquity to the present. Insofar as this essay of Liu Shipei commanded assent, Liu Xin's definition of *ru* would be recognized as the first description of the genesis of China's traditional scholarly class. On Zhang's early obsession with Liu Xin, see Shimada Kenji, *Shō Heirin ni tsuite: Chūgoku dentō gakujutsu to kakumei*, p. 227.

95 The intellectual filiations between Liu and Zhang are well known and explicit in their first essay anthologies, *Rang shu* and *Qiu shu*. I am suggesting in this case that they were conscious of each other's labors on the question of *ru* and that this may account for the similarity in their interpretation of Kongzi and in the particular texts they selected in marshalling an authoritative erudition for their claims. On the mutual intellectual influence of the two men, see Bernal, "Liu Shih-p'ei and National Essence," p. 372, n. 21.

96 Zhang, *Qiu shu* (1904 edition), pp. 4–10. The term *jiuliu* was simply a Han literary conceit employed by Liu Xin to organize the rhetorical fellowships of the Zhan'guo era.

97 The studies were titled *Yuan xue* (The Genesis of "Learning"), *Yuan ren* (The Genesis of "Humaneness"), *Yuan bian* (The Genesis of "Change"), and *Yuan jiao* (The Genesis of "Teaching"). See Zhang, *Qiu shu*, chaps. 1, 16, 19, 47, 48. Wang Tao (1828–1897), the treaty-port compradore intellectual and reformer, anticipated Zhang in this endeavor, having written two essays with identical titles in the 1870s, *Yuan dao* and *Yuan ren*. I think Zhang's principal influence in these writings was Dai Zhen, especially his systematic redefinition of the conceptual staples of *ru* discourse in the introductory section of *Yuan shan*. See Wang Tao, *Taoyuan wenlu waipian* (Hong Kong, 1883), *juan* 1; and Dai Zhen, *Yuan shan* (Taibei: Shijie Shuju, 1974), pp. 3–8.

98 Furth, "The Sage as Rebel," p. 126. Such a construction of philological resemblance through a familial metaphor of origin and consanguinity was a popular, as well as persuasive, conceptual technology in the late nineteenth century among American and European scholars. See Thomas R. Trautmann, *Lewis Henry Morgan and the Invention of Kinship* (Berkeley: University of California Press, 1987), esp. pp. 59–83.

99 Zhang, "Bo Zhongguo yong wanguo xinyu shuo," p. 7.

100 In Zhang, *Qiu shu* (1904 edition).

101 Gu, *Gushi bian*, vol. 1, p. 24; Hummel, *The Autobiography of a Chinese Historian*, pp. 41–42; and Zhang Binglin, *Zhang Taiyan ziding nianpu*, pp. 14–18. My choice of the term "Confucianity" rather than "the religion of Confucius" for "Kongjiao" reflects the intentional imitative character of Kang Youwei's justification for his national religion. Convinced that it was the Christian religion that inspired Western cultures to their admirable achievements, Kang explicitly stated that Kongjiao was to operate as the Chinese equivalent—right down to the requirement of missionary service abroad!—of the Great Awakening Christianity with which he was so familiar.

102 Beginning with the founding of a national ministry of education (*xue bu*) in December 1905, the Qing government began to implement a domestic educational reform that, in effect, put into practice the Kongjiao advocacy of Kang Youwei under the guise of *guojiao*, the national religion. The "Imperial Educational Guidelines" set out the following year suggest that a genuine effort was made to establish a national religion centered around Kongzi, yet linked, not so subtly, to the reigning Manchu emperor. From that time on, each state-supported school was to have a room housing a wooden altar to Kongzi wherein students and faculty alike could "honor the national religion," *cun guojiao*, through daily worship of the sage. In another context, Martin Bernal has written that even the nativist exertions of the *guocui* (National Essence) coterie, in particular their agitation for societies of national studies that would effect a preservation of Chinese cultural essence, were by 1907 becoming a part of official discourse with Zhang Zhidong's founding of a "scholarly institute for the preservation of antiquity" (*cungu xuetang*). On the educational reforms undertaken in the wake of the abolition of the examination system, see Sally Borthwick, *Education and Social Change*, pp. 73–127. On the appropriation of a dissident national essence discourse by servants of the Qing state, see Bernal, "Liu Shih-p'ei and National Essence," pp. 107–108.

103 Zhang Binglin, "Kedi," in *Qiu shu* (1900 edition), pp. 116–124.

104 On the effect on his cultural critique of Zhang's "faith" in the theology of the Yogacara sect, see Chang, *Chinese Intellectuals in Crisis*, pp. 121–141. Despite his philosophical banishment of the *ru* tradition, Zhang paradoxically held to the *ru* legitimative conception of *daotong* (legacy of the way), believing that the transmission of *ru* tradition had been accomplished through an affinitive process of intellectual links despite a 1,200-year period between Mengzi and Cheng Yi when it was in abeyance. Gu Jiegang found this philosophical adherence to the discredited concept particularly galling and because of it withdrew his for-

mer enthusiastic support for Zhang's evidential studies. On this contradiction, see Gu, "Zixu," *Gushi bian*, vol. 1, pp. 26–27; and Hummel, *Autobiography of a Chinese Historian*, p. 46.

105 See Zhang Binglin, "Bo Kongjiao jianli yi," in *Zhang Taiyan quanji*, vol. 4 (Shanghai: Renmin Chubanshe, 1985), pp. 95–96.

106 Such defamiliarization, the reader will recall, was the method employed in the first chapters of this book in making Confucius an "object of renewed attentiveness." On *ostranie* as the method of formalism, see Fredric Jameson, *The Prison-House of Language: A Critical Account of Structuralism and Russian Formalism* (Princeton: Princeton University Press, 1972), pp. 50–91.

107 Zhang, "YR," p. 151. The essay is littered with other examples of this obscurantist tendency—like his use of the archaic *feng* rather than the common, contemporary *feng* (see glossary), meaning "bee"—one for which Zhang acquired considerable notoriety. Zhang Binglin's preference for the Chinese of the Song era rhyming dictionary, *Qieyun zhizhangtu*, was well known and the source of much good-natured criticism from both students and colleagues. I would suggest that this studied habit of Zhang's qualifies him as a "traditionalist" in Levenson's sense of his display of "a conscious will to narrow the vision." The arcane language of his style stood apart, not from his contemporaries alone, but from his idols as well. The prose of Zhang Xuecheng and Dai Zhen was never so difficult to parse out, and none of the modern Western scholars who have written on Zhang Binglin have neglected to mention the caution with which they have made translations of his work.

108 Although I have rendered *zhuzi* as "noncanonical masters," in the manner that has become conventional so as to assemble into a heterogenous but singly named mass all persuaders other than Kongzi, I prefer to place this designation within quotation marks. My reason for doing so is that the term *zhuzi* was first used to identify all the itinerant persuaders of the Warring States and their subsequent rhetorical traditions. Thus Kongzi and *ru* were still, even in the Former Han as the *guwen* texts were being canonized, *zhuzi*. As such the *rujia* (*ru* family) appears in the *zhuzi* section of the "Yiwen zhi." Also, the term *zi* does not necessarily mean "master" in the sense of a mentor, and consequently *zhuzi* may mean something like "assembled texts," referring to the sum total of extant texts collected by Han imperial bibliographers at the time of their inventory. It was not uncommon for a text or a collection of texts to be called *zi*, a sign of the student's devotion to a certain work and its elevation to the role of teacher. This, in fact, was how Zhu Xi understood what we have come to know as the Four Books, calling them, from the moment he completed the redaction, *Sizi* (The Four Masters). Over a century later, Wang Wei wrote an "Essay on the Four Masters," which confirms the persistence of this imaginative tendency even after the Yuan officialization of Zhu Xi's redactions in the form of the *Sishu*. In this light *zhuzi* do not resemble living teachers so much as inspirational figures who live through reiterative, pietistic constructions—the texts and commentaries of their followers. See *Hanshu buzhu*, vol. 3, pp. 1701–1784. On the personification of text as "master," see Wang Wei, "Sizi lun," in *SKQS*, vol. 1226, pp. 68.1–69.1.

109 The *Zhuzi bian* of Song Lian, which appeared in 1351, might be taken as the earliest attempt to evaluate the texts and doctrines of the pre-Qin schools in context. In eighteenth-century China the proper restoration of Kongzi to his context did not obtain the large following common to *kaozheng* (evidential research); instead this practice incited many conservative scholars, like Fang Dongshu (1772–1851), to attack the practice as blasphemous. Nevertheless, *zhuzi xue* experienced a revival in the nineteenth century, having adherents among both the Hanxue and *jinwen* coteries. Indeed, for the reform generation of the Guangxu era (1875–1908), *zhuzi xue* was an unquestioned feature of the interpretive toolkit, although for some reformers like Zhang Zhidong it remained subversive. See Song Lian, "Zhuzi bian," in *Song wenxian gong quanji* (reprint; Taibei: Zhonghua Shuju, 1970). For an example of eighteenth-century scholarly vilification of *zhuzi xue*, see Fang Dongshu, *Hanxue shangdui* (Taibei: Guangwen Shuju, 1963), *juan* 2, pt. 1, pp. 21b–24a. On the resurgence of *zhuzi xue*, especially as it was, like *jinwen*, a logical consequence of the Hanxue search for origins, see Yü Ying-shih [Yu Yingshi], *Zhongguo jindai sixiangshi shang de Hu Shi* (Taibei: Xuesheng Shuju, 1984), pp. 77–87; and Wang Fan-sen [Wang Fansen], *Zhang Taiyan de sixiang* (Taibei: Shibao, 1985), pp. 25–28.

110 See Zhang Binglin, "Jianlun," in *Zhang Taiyan quanji*, vol. 4 (Shanghai: Renmin Chubanshe, 1985), p. 473.

111 This was a choice made with evident self-consciousness by Zhang and Liu Shipei in the studies they prepared for the journal *Guocui xuebao*. "[T]he journal placed its own contributors," says Lawrence Schneider, "in a line of succession of critical scholarship carried on by scholars in a state of tension with politics (because of their disillusion with the government and/or the government's displeasure with them). . . . According to the journal it was precisely these kinds of scholars who transmitted the national essence each time it was threatened with obscurity." Lawrence Schneider, "National Essence and the New Intelligentsia," in *The Limits of Change*, ed. Furth, p. 64. On the growing perception of Hanxue (Han learning) as mere scholasticism, see Elman, *From Philosophy to Philology*, pp. 232–243.

112 As there was no particular tradition of textual interpretation through which *ru* was known, any attempt to reconstruct the term was necessarily innovative. Because Zhang was an outsider and lived at a time when the *ru* fellowship was socially disarticulated, his inquiry into *ru* was not preconstrained either in method or content as were, for example, the revised *daoxue* readings of works like the *Daxue* characteristic of the Tongzheng school. For Zhang the order, rank, and interpretation of Warring States works were not fixed, as was plainly evident in his disregard for the time-honored distinctions between the canonical and the noncanonical. In this respect, he betrayed the influence of his teacher Yu Yue, who had a special fondness for Mohism, as well as for the work of Wang Zhong. See Yu Yue, *Zhuzi pingyi* (Shanghai: Shangwu, 1935). See also Wang Zhong, *Shuxue neipian* (reprint; Taibei: Guangwen Shuju, 1970), sec. 3, pp. 1a–3a; and especially his *Mozi tonglun* of 1792.

113 Zhang, "YR," p. 151. The last of the three categories, *si*, I have chosen to trans-

late as "proper," as in *siming hao*, which according to Liang Shiqiu is the line that runs alongside words of a Chinese text to indicate a proper noun. "Private" or "personal" are adequate but not as appropriate. See Liang Shiqiu, *Zuixin shiyong Hanying cidian* (Taibei: Yuandong tushu Gongsi, 1971), p. 780.

114 *Mozi jiangu*, in *ZZJC*, vol. 4 (Beijing: Zhonghua Shuju, 1954), p. 211; and for another translation of this passage, see Graham, *Later Mohist Logic, Ethics, and Science*, pp. 324–325.

115 Wang Chong, *Lunheng*, pp. 243–244; and Alfred Forke, trans., *Lun-Heng: Miscellaneous Essays of Wang Ch'ung*, pt. 2 of 2 pts. (reprint; New York: Paragon Book Gallery, 1962), pp. 413–416.

116 Chad Hansen, *Language and Logic in Ancient China* (Ann Arbor: University of Michigan Press, 1983), pp. 82–83. See also Graham, *Later Mohist Logic, Ethics, and Science*, pp. 32–44.

117 Zhang, "YR," p. 151. The statement attributed here to Sima Xiangru recalls that of Chu Shaosun (105–30 B.C.E.) in chap. 127 of the *Shiji* who writes in describing the eremetic qualities of the worthy "from antiquity to the present worthies retired from the world. There are some who lived in jungles and marshes." See Sima, *Shiji*, p. 3221.

118 *Shuowen*, p. 162.1. Hu Shi was the first to travel this interpretive path, and many scholars in the last forty years have continued to follow his lead and the gloss from the *Shuowen*, believing *rou* (weakness) fundamental to their interpretations. See Hu, "SR," p. 2; and Rao Zongyi, "Shi ru: Zong wenzi xunguxue shang lunru de yiyi," pp. 111–122, esp. pp. 111–114. A good number of Western scholars have relied upon Xu Shen's gloss as well in constructing an image of ancient *ru* as weaklings. See Creel, *Confucius and the Chinese Way*, pp. 173–181; and Wolfram Eberhard, *The Local Cultures of South and East China* (Leiden: E. J. Brill, 1968), pp. 29–30.

119 For the original passage, see *Zhuangzi jijie*, in *ZZJC*, vol. 3, pt. 3, p. 203.

120 Zhang, "YR," p. 151. For the original text, see Huan Kuan, *Yantie lun*, in *ZZJC*, vol. 7, pt. 3, pp. 12–13.

121 And again, Zhang "refunctions" the significance of the passage from the received text. The story of the defection of *ru* from their lord, King Min of Qi, as retold (from the *Shiji*) in chap. 11 of *Yantie lun*, appears to serve two didactic purposes in the Han text. The first is to castigate *ru*, avowed experts in statecraft, for their repeated failure to preserve the state. Secondly, the tale provides an opportunity to bemoan the unfortunate consequences of the diaspora, that "within the country there were no good ministers." Zhang instead employs the narrative as evidence of the physical spread of *ru* doctrine in order to reinforce his claim for the former breadth of its significance. See Huan, *Yantie lun*, pp. 12–13; and Sima, *Shiji*, vol. 6, pp. 1895–1900.

122 These are the titles of chaps. 26, 24, 31, 32, and 51 of Wang Chong's *Lunheng*. See Wang, *Lunheng*, pp. 78–83, 67–74, 105–107, 107–114, 171–174.

123 Zhang, "YR," p. 151. All these legends predate Wang Chong and are collected in the four chapters cited by Zhang here. Couvreur offers two very probable readings of *ji* that have influenced my translation here. *Ji* is a local household regis-

try. It can also mean the registry of the birth order and relations of a noble household's males often placed above the mantle of a palace's entrance, which seems the most apt meaning here, where Zhang is emphasizing the inalienable nativeness of these story traditions and their commonality. *Gongzu* is an ambiguous compound that could be taken as a ducal (*gong*) clan or as "an undifferentiated or public clan," and I see no reason to choose between the two in this case, as both are consistent with the implications of Zhang's argument. See F. S. Couvreur, S.J., *Dictionnaire Classique de la Langue Chinoise* (reprint; Taibei: Book World Company, 1966), pp. 687–688.

124   This sorting out was more than simply the criticism of a skeptic. According to Henri Maspero, Wang and his contemporary Xu Shen "set themselves to composing works in which they highlighted the incoherence of the traditions and, still more, the contradictions among the very texts of the Classics." This disintegration of the received *ru* tradition, Maspero suggests, presaged the heroic commentarial labors of Ma Rong (79–166 C.E.) and Zheng Xuan. Xiao Gongquan offers an alternative view, seeing Wang Chong as a cynic whose unrestrained criticism of inherited traditions rendered history meaningless, thereby paving the intellectual path down which the eremetic "Neo-Daoists" of the Wei-Jin period would tread. See Henri Maspero, *Taoism and Chinese Religion*, trans. Frank A. Kierman Jr. (Amherst: University of Massachusetts Press, 1981), p. 65.

125   "Rujiazhe liu gai chu yu situ zhi guan." See *Hanshu buzhu*, vol. 3, p. 1728. The "Yiwen zhi" was an abridgment of Liu Xin's "Seven Summaries," or *Qilue*, which was probably submitted to Emperor Ai in 6 B.C.E., but is now lost.

126   There is an imaginative leap here of considerable proportions that abets Zhang's novel use of the *Yijing*. Clearly "xu" does not denote clouds above the sky; rather it is a scribal representation of clouds or rain over the conjunctive *er*.

127   *Zhuangzi jijie*, pp. 132–133. For an artist's depiction of the round caps (*yuanguan*) of the *ru* as well as the various jade ornaments worn at the belt, see Jiang, *Xiangdang tukao*, juan 1, pp. 19b–20a.

128   Zhang, "YR," pp. 151–152.

129   This unconventional interpretive tendency is very common among Japanese scholars of ancient China and is derived from the presumption that ancient graphs were pictures of the things they named. The preference for pictographic etymology, to the exclusion of phonological considerations, is displayed in the work of both Shirakawa Shizuka and Akatsuka Kiyoshi, to name two prominent exemplars. Shirakawa in fact repeats Zhang's graph hexagram equivalence of *xu* (wherein the meaning of the graph *xu* is presumed to be synonymous with the meaning of the hexagram *xu*) in his recension of the *Shuowen* and in a work on the tradition of Kongzi, justifying this method in the former case by appeal to Li Yangping (ca. 765–780 C.E.). See Shirakawa Shizuka, *Setsubun shingi*, vol. 8 of 16 vols. (Tokyo: Goten Shoin, 1972), p. 1605; and *Kōshi den* (Tokyo: Chu yo koronsha, 1972), pp. 70–72. See also Akatsuka Kiyoshi, *Chūgoku kodai no shūkyō to bunka—In ōchō no saishi* (Tokyo: Kadokawa shoten, 1977), pp. 349–353. Zhang's glossing of graphs by way of hexagrams is very curious indeed.

Names of hexagrams are assigned in an effort to represent the dominant image conveyed by the hexagram. Chinese graphs and hexagrams belong to two different semiotic systems, the former phonological in basis, the latter omenological. Thus to believe, as Zhang does, that the compound construction of hexagrams from trigrams mirrors the *huiyi* (joined) meanings construction of graphs is quixotic. Even if they both evolved from divinatory impulses in antiquity, they shared little else. Curiously though, the Mawangdui text of the *Yi* (excavated in 1973 in Hunan) would permit Zhang to forge a link between *xu* the hexagram and the connotations of wetness invariably associated with the graph *ru*. In this latter version of the *Yijing*, there is no fifth hexagram "to await." Instead, the text has an eighteenth hexagram *ru*, meaning short coat, the *guaci* of which reads: "Moistened (*ru*): There is a return; radiant receipt; determination is auspicious; beneficial to ford the great river." See Edward L. Shaughnessy, trans., *I Ching: The Classic of Changes* (New York: Ballantine Books, 1997), pp. 72–73.

130 Furthermore, as analysis of ancient script along with phonological reconstructions proceed, it has become evident that the number of graphs in the language derived from this hybrid construction is not as great as originally believed. See William Boltz, "Early Chinese Writing," *World Archaeology* 17, no. 3 (February 1986): 420–436; Norman, *Chinese*, pp. 58–74; and William Baxter, personal communication, 1987. By pointing out that Zhang's use of the hybrid composition hexagram *xu* to explain the meaning of the character *xu* was unconventional, I do not mean to evaluate the "truth" of his method or of his conclusions, simply to point out the manner in which he constructed an elaborate explanatory fiction out of a few evidentiary shards.

131 Xu, *Shuowen jiezi*, p. 242.1.

132 Zhang, "YR," pp. 151–153. In his work on the life of Kongzi, Shirakawa Shizuka makes an even more imaginative contribution to Zhang's theory in asserting that *xu* refers to the ritual exposure of the *wu* or shaman. The ancient graph for *xu* (see glossary), says Shirakawa, is an image of a shaman, shorn of all his body hair, performing a rain dance (*wu*). See his discussion in *Kōshi den*, pp. 73–74.

133 On paronomasia as a method for the elaboration of ancient Chinese sounds and the polysemousness to which such a process gives rise, see Boltz, "Early Chinese Writing," pp. 424–428; and Arthur Cooper, *The Creation of the Chinese Script*, Occasional Papers No. 20 (London: China Society, 1970), pp. 8–14.

134 *Hanshi waizhuan*, SBCK, *juan* 1, pp. 12a–b; Huang Kan, *Lunyu jijie yisu* (Taibei: Guangwen Shuju, 1968), *juan* 3, pp. 28b–29a; Wang Niansun, ed., *Guangya suzheng* (Beijing: Zhonghua Shuju, 1983), *juan* 4.2, pp. 17a–b. See also James Robert Hightower, trans., *Han Shih Wai Chuan [Hanshi waizhuan]: Han Ying's Illustrations of the Didactic Application of the "Classic of Songs"* (Cambridge, Mass.: Harvard University Press, 1952), p. 173.

135 Duan Yucai, *Shuowen jiezi zhu*, *juan* 8, pp. 3b–4a. "Wet" in this instance was taken by both Zheng and Duan as a metaphor for the thorough learning of the *ru*, as in "to immerse" or "to imbibe" the way of the *xianwang* (former kings), through study. The metaphor is amply attested in earlier literature, being used to convey the naturalness and ease with which learning was accomplished, as in Du

Yu's (Yuankai 222–284 C.E.) description of the proper way to appropriate the transmission of the classics, when he says that "appropriating the classics" is like being immersed in the rivers and the oceans and drenched from the marshes and the rains; doubts are then washed away so that principle is apprehended and [you] have obtained it." See Du Yu, "Xu," in *Chunqiu jingzhuan jijie, SBCK*, vol. 1 of 6 vols. (reprint; Shanghai: Shangwu, 1922), p. 2a. See also Xu, *Shuowen jiezi*, p. 228.1.

136 *Wu* (dance) traditionally has been associated with *Yubu* (the step of Yu)—a dance-like gait in which the right side of the body advances while the left foot is dragged as if vestigial. This pace was considered magical in that it was capable of producing trance and so governed the choreography of shamanic dance for the purposes of exorcism, imprecation, and conjuring absent spirits. The *Yubu* is described and its magical properties explained by Ge Hong (280–340 C.E.) in *Baopuzi, juan* 17 ("Deng She" [Ascending Mountains and Fording Streams]), where its links with water are obvious. Ge Hong, *Baopuzi*, in *ZZJC*, vol. 8, pt. 3, pp. 76–82, esp. 78–79. The dance is analyzed in Eberhard, *Local Cultures of South and East China*, pp. 72–77, where it is associated with the Yao culture. See also Marcel Granet, "Right and Left in China," in *Right and Left: Essays on Dual Symbolic Classification*, ed. Rodney Needham (Chicago: University of Chicago Press, 1971), pp. 53–56, and *Danses et légendes de la Chine ancienne*, vol. 2 of 2 vols. (Paris: Presses Universitaires de France, 1959), pp. 549–556.

137 Although he does not introduce this fragment as evidence corroborative of his interpretation of *ru*, Zhang may have remembered that Kongzi's disciple Zi Lu, a man of very humble status, wore a hat made of cock feathers. There is nothing I can find in the scriptural literature of *ru* that speaks of feathered caps, though there are very suggestive fragments from other pre-Qin texts that link wetness, feathers, and *ru*, albeit in a somewhat indirect way: in the new text (*jinben*) version of the *Zhushu jinian*, the "Bamboo Annals," under spring of the twenty-ninth year of the reign of Yao, there is a curious notation: "The elder of the *jiaoyao* descent group came to pay respects at court [offering as tribute] feathers immersed in water." Xu Wenqing, ed., *Zhushu jinian tongqian* (Taibei: Yiwen Shuju, 1966), p. 112. Zheng Xuan's commentary in this instance says that the Jiaoyao (see glossary) are a minority people of the southwest regions who grow to the diminutive height of three *chi* (less than three feet). The *ru* connection derives from Hao Yixing's claim in the *Shanhai jing jiansu* that indeed Jiaoyao is the name of a tribe of dwarfs or feeble persons from the Southwest, but this group is better known as *zhuru* or "dwarf dancers" (see glossary). It is a rhyming binome widely attested in the *Zuo zhuan, Shiji, Guo yu, Hanshi waizhuan*, and *Li ji*. See *Shanhai jing jiansu* (1809; reprint; Taibei: Guangwen Shuju, 1965), vol. 1, *juan* 6, pp. 5a–6a.

138 Zhang, "YR," pp. 151–152.

139 See *Zhuangzi yinde*, Ch'i Ssu-ho, comp., Harvard-Yenching Institute Sinological Index series no. 20 (Beijing, 1947), p. 33.

140 Dong Zhongshu, "Qiu yu," in *Chunqiu fanlu yizheng*, ed. Su Yu (Taibei: Hele tushu Chubanshe, 1975).

141   The received explanation concerning the synonymousness of Shang and Yin is that the latter was the name taken by the Shang themselves after the relocation of their capital by Pan Geng (ca. 1200 B.C.E.), though there is another interpretation that holds that the title Yin was assumed only after the defeat of the Shang in 1046 B.C.E. The former account is documented in the *Taiping yulan*, where the *Diwang shiji* (Chronology of the Lord Kings) is cited in chapter 83 as asserting that the capital was removed and from that time the Shang called themselves Yin. The vacillation between the two names in identifying this tribe (something evident in the writing of both Zhang Binglin and Hu Shi) reflects the tendency first evident in the *Shiji* to refer to the principal Shang settlement as either Yinxu or Shangxu. Yet, the distinction between Yin and Shang emphasized by Zhang derived its nativist power from analogy with the conquest of the Han by the Manchus. For a discussion of what the Shang may have called themselves and their identification as Yin by the Zhou even before the conquest, see Kwang-Chih Chang, "On the Character Shang in the Shang Dynasty," *Early China* 20 (1995): 69–77; and Kwang-Chih Chang, "Yin-hsü Tomb Number Five and the Question of the P'an Keng/Hsiao Hsin/Hsiao Yi Period in Yin-hsü Archaeology," in *Studies of Shang Archaeology: Selected Papers from the International Conference on Shang Civilization*, ed. K. C. Chang (New Haven: Yale University Press, 1986), pp. 72–79.

142   *Li ji zhengyi*, in *SSJZS*, vol. 6, pp. 129.2–130.1. See also James Legge, trans., *Li Chi, Book of Rites*, vol. 1 (New Hyde Park, N.Y.: University Books, 1967), pp. 138–139.

143   "When I was young I lived in Lu and wore the garment with large sleeves, [while] when I was older and lived in Song, I was capped with the *zhangfu* cap." *Li ji zhengyi*, in *SSJZS*, vol. 7, p. 972.1. See also Legge, trans., *Li Chi, Book of Rites*, vol. 2, p. 402.

144   For the hagiographic representation of Kongzi as descendant of the Shang see *Li ji zhengyi*, pp. 850.1–1033.1.

145   Considering that Zhang relies so heavily upon the common philological presumption of a changeless linguistic essence of the written form, it is curious that he did not have any interest in the oracle bones (*jiaguwen*). This lack of interest or rather incredulity about these epigraphic sources conveys something of his imaginative productivity. Apparently he considered the "dragon bones" discovered by Liu E in 1899 to be a hoax perpetrated by Liu and so he neglected a valuable source for the kind of reconstruction he undertook with "Yuan ru." A sense of the past could be pursued in a "scientific" manner yet it was through the received literary texts alone that this sense could be nurtured. Incidentally, Hu Shi, as well, doubted the authenticity of *jiaguwen*.

146   See *Shangshu zhengyi*, in *SSJZS*, vol. 2, p. 205.1.

147   Zhang, "YR," p. 152.

148   Ibid.

149   *Lunyu zhusu*, in *SSJZS*, vol. 11, p. 52.1.

150   Zhang, "YR," p. 153.

151   Zhang, "YR," p. 152. For the original passage, see *Hanshu buzhu*, vol. 3, p. 1728.

There is in this passage from *Qilue* an obvious admixture of the diverse intellectual currents of the early Han that reads to us today like an anachronism, as *yinyang* phrasing glosses the *Zhou li.*

152 Zhang, "YR," p. 153.

153 Ibid. "From Yanzi on down there were fifty-two families. All of them took an interest in shoddily illuminating virtue through government service and instruction, never attaining the Six Cultivations." Zhang excludes the texts of Yanzi (Master Yan) from his total, when according to Liu Xin there were fifty-three textual families. For that matter, at the time of the Liu clan's assembling of the imperial catalogue there were twelve different traditions of *Lunyu* study. See *Hanshu buzhu,* vol. 3, pp. 1716, 1727.

154 In this unconventional characterization of Kongzi as someone who recognized that the way to which he devoted himself was already eclipsed, Zhang has been recently joined by Stephen Owen. See his *Remembrances: The Experience of the Past in Classical Chinese Literature* (Cambridge, Mass.: Harvard University Press, 1986), pp. 13–22. The analysis here has been influenced by Owen's interpretation.

155 See Liu Xin, "Yiwen zhi." In an essay written, it seems, as a refutation of both Liu Shipei and Liu Xin, Hu Shi revealed the fictive quality, from the point of view of the compiler, of all the *zhuzi* official genealogies essayed by Liu Xin. See Hu Shi, "Zhuzi buchu yu wangguan lun," in *Zhongguo zhexue shi dagang* (Shanghai: Shangwu, 1929), pp. 1–10.

156 Zhang, "YR," pp. 152–153.

157 Gu Jiegang later came to much the same conclusion, as is evident in his *Qin-Han de fangshi yu rusheng* (Shanghai: Guji Chubanshe, 1982), pp. 70–105.

158 Zhang, "YR," p. 153.

159 A. C. Graham, *Chuang-tzu: The Inner Chapters* (London: George Allen and Unwin, 1981), pp. 139–140.

160 Zhang, "YR," p. 153.

161 Ibid.

162 Gasster, *Chinese Intellectuals and the Revolution of 1911,* p. 213.

163 Zhang, "YR," p. 154.

164 Ibid.

165 Ibid.

166 Guy, "The *National Essence Journal* and the Eighteenth Century," p. 3.

167 Zhang, "YR," p. 153.

168 The quotation is from Zhang Binglin, *Jianlun,* and is translated by James Polachek in "Gentry Hegemony: Soochow in the T'ung-chih Restoration," in *Conflict and Control in Late Imperial China,* ed. Frederic Wakeman Jr. and Carolyn Grant (Berkeley: University of California Press, 1975), p. 211. Of course there were distinct resonances in this *wei renmin fuwu* (serve the people) self-image of intellectual labor with the thought of Zhang Xuecheng, specifically his emphasis on "loving the people" (*qinmin*) by "renewing the people" (*xinmin*).

169 Nancy Streuver, "Fables of Power," *Representations* 4 (fall 1983): 108–127.

170 Kitamura, *Jūgaku gairon,* pp. 1–19.

171 Benjamin I. Schwartz, *Reflections on the May Fourth Movement: A Symposium* (Cambridge, Mass.: Harvard University Press, 1972), pp. 1–13.

172 Gu, *Gushi bian,* vol. 1, p. 13; and Hummel, *Autobiography of a Chinese Historian,* p. 20.

173 Wolfgang Franke, "Der Ursprung der Ju und ihre Beziehung zu Konfuzius und Lau-dsi" (The Origin of *Ru* and Their Relation to Confucius and Laozi), *Sinica* (special ed.) 1 (1935): 141–171; 2 (1936): pp. 1–42. The English abstract appeared in *China Institute Bulletin* 1 (1936): 1.

174 The expression is Hu Shi's and comes from the Haskell Lectures he delivered at the University of Chicago in the summer of 1933. See Hu Shi, *The Chinese Renaissance* (Chicago: University of Chicago Press, 1934), p. 77.

Chapter 4

1 Hu was actually born in Shanghai, the son of an imperial official, Hu Chuan (1841–1895), who was at the time of Hu's birth serving as a tariff collector in Shanghai. However, his ancestral residence was in Huizhou prefecture in the southeast of Anhui, near the Zhejiang border. Thus he was justified in claiming identification with the province's tradition of literary distinction, in particular the contribution to Dai Zhen, who had studied in Huizhou for a time, to this tradition. For the details of Hu Shi's early years see his recollections at age forty, *Sishi zishu* (Taibei: Yuandong Gongsi, 1974), pp. 1–57; and see Jerome Grieder's capsule biography in *Biographical Dictionary of Republican China,* ed. Howard L. Boorman and Richard C. Howard, vol. 2 of 4 vols. (New York: Columbia University Press, 1971).

2 See Liang Ch'i-Ch'ao, *Intellectual Trends in the Ch'ing Period,* trans. Immanuel C. Y. Hsü (Cambridge, Mass.: Harvard University Press, 1959), p. 26. In his account of intellectual genealogy in Anhui, Liang Qichao mistakenly identified Hu Shi as a descendant of the Hu clan of Jixi xian, thereby granting him an eighteenth-century scholarly pedigree.

3 See Hu Shi, "Xinxin yu fanxing," *Duli pinglun,* no. 103 (June 3, 1934): 4. On his years of study in the United States, the intellectual filiations cultivated there, and his return home to Shanghai, see Hu Shi, *Hu Shi liuxue riji,* vol. 1 of 4 vols. (Taibei: Shangwu, 1959), pp. 5–254.

4 See Wolfgang Bauer, *China and the Search for Happiness: Recurring Themes in Four Thousand Years of Chinese Cultural History,* trans. Michael Shaw (New York: Seabury Press, 1976), p. 15.

5 Guo Moruo, "Fu 'Shuo ru,'" in Guo, *Qingtong shidai* (Beijing: Zhonghua Shuju, 1954), p. 123.

6 Zhang Binglin's influence on a wider scholarship may have been less direct, but it was no less profound than that of Hu Shi. His numerous publications in the journals *Minbao* and *Guocui xuebao* were avidly read by a younger generation of revolutionaries and radical intellectuals drawn to Zhang in large part because of his passionate, uncompromising dedication to the establishment of a proud, independent China. The lectures he gave at the Guoxue Hui (National Studies So-

ciety) in Beijing (1913) on literature, etymology, and history were always well attended; members of the audience included Qian Xuantong, Mao Zishui, and Gu Jiegang, all of whom are known to us for their contributions to an understanding of Chinese historical methods, geography, and folklore. Counted among his students as well were the brothers Zhou—Zuoren and Shuren (Lu Xun)—both of whom admitted their intellectual debt to Zhang (the former by renunciation of him in 1926) and whose contributions to our knowledge of Chinese literature and of the experience of the twentieth-century Chinese intellectual must be acknowledged. Zhang's influences were those registered by affinitive transmission of ideas, and they were profound on that generation of Chinese intellectuals whose work helped to mold our apprehension not only of traditional but also of modern China. It could also be argued that the fiercely opinionated views on Chinese scholarship characteristic of the *Guocui xuebao*, particularly their elevation of *guwen* above the work of their Tongcheng and *jinwen* contemporaries, were decisively conveyed by Liang Qichao in his history of Qing thought, a work that has shaped the interpretive apparatus of Western intellectual historians of China.

Evidence of Hu Shi's influence is even more explicit. At the time he completed "Shuo ru," for example, Hu had already been three years in the academic post of dean of the College of Arts at Beijing University, of which in 1946 he would assume the chancellorship. Hu's international reputation as a spokesman for China and particularly for its intellectual revolution of May Fourth (1919) and his interaction with eminent Western intellectual figures like John Dewey and Bertrand Russell ensured that he would have a significant impact on students in China and students of China at a moment at which modern sinological studies were developing.

7   Jerome Grieder, *Hu Shih and the Chinese Renaissance: Liberalism in the Chinese Revolution, 1917–1937* (Cambridge, Mass.: Harvard University Press, 1970), p. 341.

8   Hou Wailu, *Zhongguo sixiang tongshi*, vol. 1 of 5 vols. (Beijing: Renmin Chubanshe), 1957, pp. 36–38; and Hsiao Kung-ch'üan [Xiao Gongquan], *Zhongguo zhengzhi sixiang shi*, vol. 1 of 6 vols. (Taibei: Zhonghua Shuju, 1954), pp. 53–55.

9   Feng Youlan, *Zhongguo zhexue shi* (Beijing: Taipingyang tushu Gongsi, 1968), pp. 1–14. On this effort to define Chinese thought with respect to the greater whole of philosophy, see John Ewell, "Reinventing the Way: Dai Zhen's Evidential Commentary on the *Mengzi Ziyi Shu Zheng*." Ph.D. diss., University of California, Berkeley, 1990, pp. 1–5.

10 Jacques Derrida, "Structure, Sign, and Play in the Discourse of the Human Sciences," in Derrida, *Writing and Difference*, trans. Alan Bass (Chicago: University of Chicago Press, 1978), pp. 278–293.

11 The bulk of my analysis of this essay is concentrated on its second, third, and fourth sections, as it is here that the body of argument is put forward and defended. Section 6, on the possibility that Laozi was a *ru*, is more of an immediate rejoinder to Zhang Binglin and does not add much to the larger interpretation of *ru* put forth in the rest of the essay. In these sections there is considerable redundancy of the kind common in the didactic prose style of the *Mozi*. Argumentative

conclusions are frequently reiterated in almost identical ways. The repetition of certain phrases does not always occur at predictable points and seems more like the work of someone genuinely excited by the conclusions to which his inquiry has brought him.

12 It appeared in the *Bulletin of the National Research Institute of History and Philology of the Academia Sinica (Guoli zhongyang yanjiuyuan lishi yuyan yanjiusuo jikan)* 4, no. 3. In 1935 it was included in an anthology of his recent essays published by the Commercial Press in Shanghai and called *Hu Shi lunxue jin zhu: Di yi ji*. The edition I have used is from *Hu Shi wencun* (The Collected Essays of Hu Shi), vol. 4, pp. 1–82, which is a slightly emended republication by the Yuandong Book Company of the *Hu Shi lunxue jin zhu* of 1953. This edition, now standard, has the advantage of including twenty-one additional pages of supplementary material on "Shuo ru" by Fu Sinian and Hu Shi.

13 Hu, "SR," p. 4.

14 The Chinese here is *jiaoshi*, the same word that is used for foreign missionaries. Hu's use of the term is not entirely consistent, as it is sometimes interchanged with its homophone, *jiaoshi* (see glossary). There is an intentional pun here, very effective in the context of Hu's analysis, as he describes *ru* as the hereditary instructors of ancient Yin religious rites and the missionaries as the purveyors of an understanding of these rites among the Zhou, who believed that successful assimilation of the Shang required their knowledge of such rites. Both words describe the profession of *ru* as religious functionaries of the Shang or as teachers of Yin religious practices to the Zhou. It is used mostly to refer to *ru* after the conquest of the Shang in their capacity as ritual instructors. But Hu was manipulating this term with full consciousness of its contemporary meaning of "Christian missionaries."

15 Throughout the essay Hu treats the Yin (also known as the Shang) and the Zhou as distinct and competitive ethnic groups, at one point speaking of a "Yin-Shang minzu de zhongxing," an ethnic revival/restoration of the Yin-Shang tribe. His understanding is vaguely racial, yet I think in this context the best way to identify his use of *minzu* is to employ the term "tribe" and not "race" or "ethnic minority." *Buluo* was the common term for "tribe" and was occasionally used by Hu; however, the term *minzu* is extremely common in Hu's descriptions of these peoples, their cultures, their religions, and even their geographies. I realize that I go against the grain by translating *minzu* as "tribe," but there is no better alternative in this context. *Minzu* is a very elusive term, so much so that Stevan Harrell has stated that it is untranslatable. Frank Dikötter insists that *minzu* means "nation" or "race" and that these terms convey the meaning it has had for indigenous understanding throughout this century. See Stevan Harrell, "Ethnicity, Local Interests and the State: Yi Communities in Southwest China," *Comparative Studies in Society and History* 32, no. 3 (July 1990): 515–548; Frank Dikötter, *The Discourse of Race in Modern China* (London: Hurst, 1992), pp. 97–111.

16 The term Hu uses is *rensheng guan* (view of life), a Chinese rendering of the German *Lebensphilosophie*, an expression that enjoyed wide currency in the 1920s. It was "translated" to China like a conceptual relic by Zhang Junmai

(Carson Chang) who studied briefly under Rudolph Eucken in Germany. Iron-ically, *rensheng guan* named the conceptual identity assumed by Hu Shi's oppo-nents, Zhang Junmai and Liang Qichao, in the "science versus view of life" de-bates that began in February 1923 and continued sporadically for nearly another decade when the same theoretical positions were defended *in alio esse* with the intellectual exchanges on "Cultural Construction on a Chinese Basis." See Char-lotte Furth, *Ting Wen-chiang: Science and China's New Culture* (Cambridge, Mass.: Harvard University Press, 1970), pp. 94–135; and Jerome Grieder, *Intellec-tuals and the State in Modern China* (New York: Free Press, 1981), pp. 255–269.

17 *Wangguo*—a nation vanquished, conquered, subjugated—is the term Hu employs to describe the Shang people, culture, and religion following the Zhou conquest. *Wangguo* was used by racially conscious revolutionaries in the early years of the twentieth century to describe China under the Manchus. In Tokyo in 1902, Zhang Binglin organized a political gathering that he called "Zhina wangguo erbai sishi'er nian jinian hui" (A Commemoration of the Two-Hundred and Forty-second Anniversary of the Conquest of China). One also finds it in Zou Rong's preface to *Geming jun*, which he dates with the notation, "Huang Han minzu wangguo hou zhi erbai liushi sui" (the two-hundred-sixtieth year after conquest of the nation of the august Han race). *Wangguo* may well have borne a contempo-rary significance also representing the perception of many Chinese intellectuals in the mid-1930s that China would soon be again a nation conquered by ethnic others—the Japanese. See Zou Rong, *Geming jun* (reprint; Beijing: Zhonghua Shuju, 1958), p. 1. On the prevalent sense among Chinese intellectuals at the time of Hu's writing of an imminent conquest of China by Japan, see Chou Min-chih, *Hu Shih and Intellectual Choice in Modern China* (Ann Arbor: University of Michigan Press, 1984), pp. 100–106.

18 Hu, *SR*, p. 1.

19 Hu, "SR," pp. 3–4.

20 Hu, "SR," p. 4.

21 Ibid.

22 Ibid. There is one final criticism, directed at an explicit inconsistency in Zhang's understanding of the genetic relationship of *dao* to *ru*. Of course in "Yuan ru" Zhang Binglin suggested that all the Warring States fraternities were known as *ru* insofar as *ru* was another name for *shushi*; but in another essay from the *Guogu lunheng*, "Yuan dao," he says, "the *ru* fellowship and the *fa* fellowship both came from *dao, dao* thus did not derive from *ru*." If *ru* is nothing more than a faction (*fenpai*) of the *dao*, reasons Hu, then *ru* cannot be a *leiming* (class name), much less a *daming* (generic name). This contradiction raises the question, then, of the historical relationship between the two fellowships, a question to which the last section of "Shuo ru" is devoted.

23 Hu, "SR," p. 5.

24 Ibid.

25 Philology (*xiaoxue*) is as much about style as it is about truth, perhaps even more so. And, having conventions and an established tradition of practice, it has more in common with Chinese artistic style than with science. This may be why

Joseph Levenson misunderstood *Hanxue* as a failed science in "The Abortiveness of Empiricism in Early Qing Thought," in Levenson, *Confucian China and Its Modern Fate: A Trilogy*, vol. 1 (Berkeley: University of California Press, 1968), pp. 3–14. My characterization of philology owes much to James Cahill's analysis of the perils of *xingsi* (representation; literally, "form-likeness") in the landscape painting of Zhang Hong (1577–1652?). See James Cahill, *The Compelling Image: Nature and Style in Seventeenth-Century Chinese Painting* (Cambridge, Mass.: Harvard University Press, 1982), pp. 1–35.

26 Xu Shen's glosses might be more accurately described as "archaistic," in that any definitions prepared after the Han standardization of the script cannot be taken as reliable phonological reconstructions or explications of the spoken customs of an earlier antiquity. We have known for some time, for example, that both the script and the text of the *Shi jing* were affected by later phonology, so that the text cannot be taken to reflect the phonology of the late Zhou, but, instead reflects a Zhou/Han hybrid phonology. As a result, the use of the *Shi jing* script to recover the phonology of ancient China (a practice not uncommon and followed by both Hu Shi and Zhang Binglin) cannot produce a genuine reconstruction of that language. So we return again to the necessity of faith. On the extreme difficulty of "authentic" reconstruction, see William Baxter, "The *Shijing*: A Zhou Text in Han Clothing," paper delivered at the Center for Chinese Studies, University of Michigan, Ann Arbor, Michigan, fall 1986.

27 Hu, "SR," p. 6. The *Guang ya* is a glossary purportedly compiled by Zhang Yi (fl. 230 C.E.?) in the third century C.E. The version Hu refers to here is probably the redacted *Guang ya suzheng* completed by Wang Niansun (1744–1832) in the early nineteenth century.

28 Hu, "SR," p. 6. It is obvious that Shizuka Shirakawa based his shamanistic reading of *ru/xu*—the image of a man shorn of all body hair—on Zheng Xuan's contention. This reading appears to be borne out in the oracle bone inscriptions, where the most ancient recorded evidence of the graph *xu* has a right-hand component of which the meaning is "knife" (see glossary). See Shirakawa, *Setsubun Shingi*, vol. 8 of 16 vols. (Tokyo: Goten Shoin, 1972), pp. 1603–1605.

29 *Xu* (sometimes pronounced "rou") is literally a lesser wife or concubine, and thus its resonance with "weak" comes from a consort's weaker status in a family.

30 Hu, "SR," p. 6.

31 Hu, "SR," p. 7.

32 Hu Shi describes the Shang in Kongzi's day as weak and resourceless, exhausted; it is the hybridization of these two cultures, which he will explain is exemplified in the teachings of Kongzi, that displays the brilliance of ancient Chinese culture. The characterization is reminiscent of Gu Jiegang, specifically his controversial thesis about barbarian invigoration of native culture. They are so similar that we might conclude that this conceptual model was a popular one in the 1920s and 1930s. This thesis, like Hu Shi's reading of relations between the Shang and Zhou, is a reflection of contemporary ethnic tensions. See Lawrence Schneider, *Ku Chieh-kang and China's New History: Nationalism and the Quest for Alternative Traditions* (Berkeley: University of California Press, 1971), pp. 209–272.

33 Hu, "SR," p. 11. Hu is referring to passages in the "Kang gao" and "Jiu gao" of the *Shang shu*. See James Legge, *The Chinese Classics*, vol. 3 of 5 vols: *The Shoo King* (reprint; Hong Kong: Hong Kong University Press, 1971), pp. 381–412.

34 On the equivalence of the names Yin and Shang, see n. 141, chap. 3.

35 Hu, "SR," p. 13.

36 As is common throughout this essay, Hu Shi has read the *Mozi* and *Zhuangzi* criticisms of *ru* poverty back upon an imagined condition of straitened circumstance following the defeat of the Shang. For remarks on the near-starvation and indigence of *ru*, see *Mozi jiangu*, pp. 178–182.

37 Hu, "SR," p. 57.

38 This concept, usually applied to the analysis of classes in "feudal" societies, is taken from Alexander Rüstow by way of Wolfram Eberhard and refers to a process of cultural layering that is concomitant with foreign conquest of a native culture. A succession of such assimilating conquests, then, yields a redundant stratification of cultures at the point of the first conquest, thus "*super*stratification." Ancient hierarchies of class, cult, and myth of the kind evident in the Zhou may also be explained in this manner. In fact, Eberhard, who believes that the feudal character of Chinese society appeared even before the Shang, sees the Zhou conquest as ethnic superstratification. Wolfram Eberhard, *Conquerors and Rulers: Social Forces in Medieval China*, 2d rev. ed. (Leiden: E. J. Brill, 1970), pp. 27–29.

39 See Benjamin I. Schwartz, *The World of Thought in Ancient China* (Cambridge, Mass.: Belknap Press of Harvard University Press, 1985), pp. 1–15; and Tu Weiming, *Confucian Thought: Selfhood as Creative Transformation* (Albany: State University of New York Press, 1985), pp. 1–18.

40 In another instance of the undisguised modernness of his essay, Hu uses the contemporary vernacular expression *zhishi fenzi* (intellectuals), just as he uses *minzu* (tribe) and *jieji* (class) as functional entities that can be applied unproblematically backward to antiquity.

41 Hu, "SR," p. 14.

42 These are some of the practices peculiar to the Shang, which were also found among the Zhou, according to Kwang-Chih Chang. Whether or not such practices were sui generis in the alluvial region just northeast of the intersection of the Wei, Huai, and Huang rivers, the Zhongyuan is a matter of some debate, however; William Watson claims that scapulimancy, bronze making, and shamanism are features endemic to the cultures of the Scytho-Siberian neolithic near Lake Baikal. See Kwang-Chih Chang, *Art, Myth, and Ritual: The Path to Political Authority in Ancient China* (Cambridge, Mass.: Harvard University Press, 1983), pp. 1–94; and William Watson, *Cultural Frontiers in Ancient East Asia* (Edinburgh: Edinburgh University Press, 1971), pp. 3–31.

43 Martin Bernal has pointed out that this interest in classical Western philosophy was consistent with an effort by the *guocui* coterie to fashion a renaissance identity for their age, one modeled on the sixteenth-century rebirth of European culture through the rediscovery of the classic texts of Hellenic thought. From the vantage of these men, Bernal writes: "The other pre-Ch'in [Qin] philosophers [the *zhuzi*] were seen as representatives of a period of Chinese vitality and spirit and as

the equivalents of their contemporaries, the classical Greek philosophers. The National Essence group wanted a revival of classical philosophy, a Chinese renaissance equivalent to that in the West, which they saw as having started with a refinement of classical culture that led to the creation of strong national states." Of course this renaissance should not, despite its apparent linguistic similarity, be confused with the Chinese renaissance advocated by Hu Shi during the 1930s. The *guocui* ideal of cultural rebirth through rediscovery of the "noncanonical" philosophers was a racialist one that they identified as *minzu guangfu* (the renaissance of the [Chinese] race). Hu's terminology, *Zhongguo fuxing* (the rebirth of China) was incompatible with that favored by Zhang. See Bernal, "Liu Shih-p'ei and National Essence," in *The Limits of Change*, ed. Charlotte Furth (Cambridge, Mass.: Harvard University Press, 1976), pp. 105–106.

44 It may be difficult to square this constant admiring reference to missionaries with Hu Shi's well-known agnosticism, or his profound dislike for Christian missionaries in the United States and China. Yet in 1915 just before he enrolled at Columbia University, he had a much more adulatory view of the missionary. Like the Jesuits centuries before him, who in a foreign country perceived themselves as identical with the "fathers" (*ru*) of the native religious tradition, Hu saw himself reflected in the very liminality of the missionary role: "The foreign missionary like a returned student from abroad, always carries with him a new point of view, a critical spirit, which is often lacking when a people have grown accustomed and indifferent to the existing order of things and which is absolutely necessary for any reform movement." And in this note from his diary we can glimpse more than his self-conception, the wording astonishingly similar to his characterization of the situation of the survivor *ru* at the moment of Kongzi's arrival. See Hu, *Hu Shi liuxue riji*, pp. 601–602.

45 There was certainly nothing speculative in this assertion. According to David Keightley, roughly 80 percent of the inscribed plastrons and scapulae unearthed to date (approximately 10 percent, it is estimated, of the entire corpus) have to do with ancestors. The remainder are devoted to weather, hunting, omens, and martial engagements. See Keightley, *Sources of Shang History: The Oracle Bone Inscriptions of Bronze Age China* (Berkeley: University of California Press, 1978), pp. 134–148.

46 Other than the several divining groups attached to the ruling Zi clan, the *be* seems the most appropriate comparison with the kind of "craft literate" minority Hu imagines the ancient *ru* to have been. On *be*, see John W. Hall, *Japan: From Prehistory to Modern Times* (New York: Dell, 1970), pp. 28–34; and Robert Reischauer, *Early Japanese History*, vol. 1 (Princeton: Princeton University Press, 1937).

47 Hu, "SR," pp. 14–15.

48 Hu exploits the near phonetic similarity between these two terms as a way of establishing a religious function for an office that, as it appears in Warring States texts, cannot be construed as religious, and furthermore, has nothing to do with funeral direction.

49 Allegedly authored by Zuo Qiuming who lived in the fifth century B.C.E., but the

chronicle is more likely to have been compiled no earlier than the fourth century B.C.E. Further, we cannot reliably ascertain who its compiler(s) was (were). For further discussion concerning the dating and the authenticity of the work, see Bernhard Karlgren, *On the Authenticity and Nature of the Tso Chuan* (Göteborg: Elandres Boktryckeri Aktiebolag, 1926).

50 My gloss of *xiang* as "ritual assistant" follows Jiang Yong, who believed *xiang* and *xiangli* meant "assistant at the rites." See Jiang Yong, *Xiangdang tukao* (Fusu tang, 1756), pp. 19b–20a.

51 Hu acknowledges that Kongzi assisted in mortuary rites, but offers the "Tan gong" chapter of the *Li ji* as the source for this information and never adduces evidence from the *Zuo zhuan* for his claim. For Kongzi's service to Ai Gong as *xiang*, see *Chunqiu Zuo zhuan zhu*, ed. Yang Bojun, vol. 4 (Beijing: Zhonghua Shuju, 1981), pp. 1578, 1718.

52 In the 1970s a cache of *meng* documents was discovered at Houma in Shanxi and analyzed by Chinese scholars. Hu, of course, with his appreciable skepticism toward archaeological evidence in the historical construction of antiquity, would not necessarily have known of this particular significance. It is not from this discovery alone, however, that the essential post-Zhou quality of the *meng* as a legal document can be established. A literary historical analysis such as was done by Dobson thirty years ago was certainly adequate to the task of interpreting *meng* and the culture out of which it arose. The *Zuo zhuan*, where I presume Hu acquired his understanding of the *xiangli*, contains a trove of passages from which one can collect a sense of the uniqueness of the *meng* as an institution and of the officers charged with seeing to its proper orchestration and completion. On the excavated *meng* texts of Houma, see Shanxisheng Wenwu Gongzuodui Weiyuanhui, eds., *Houma mengshu* (Shanghai: Wenwu Chubanshe, 1976). See also Susan Weld, "Covenant in Jin's Walled Cities: The Discoveries at Houma and Wenxian" (Ph.D. diss.: Harvard University, 1990), chap. 3.

53 See Roy A. Rappaport, "Sanctity and Lies in Evolution," in Rappaport, *Ecology, Meaning, and Religion* (Berkeley: North Atlantic Books, 1979), pp. 223–246.

54 *Chunqiu Zuo zhuan zhu*, vol. 4, pp. 1717–1718. In his translation of the passage, James Legge entirely misreads the circumstances surrounding the incident and so delivers a distorted rendering of the rhyme saying,

> How slow are they of Loo!
> They wake not though years go,
> And make us travel so,
> 'Tis their scholars with their books
> That thus trouble our two states.

See James Legge, *The Chinese Classics*, vol. 5: *The Ch'un Ts'ew with the Tso Chuen* (reprint; Hong Kong: Hong Kong University Press, 1970), p. 853.

55 *Chunqiu Zuo zhuan zhu*, p. 1578.

56 Ibid.

57 *Chunqiu Zuo zhuan zhu*, p. 1728.

58 Given Kongzi's unequivocal role in abrogating previous *meng* between Lu and Qi on ritual grounds, it is clear that to the people of Qi, his reservations were the

consequence of insistence on *rushu*. There is no Shang descent connection here, but still *ru* seems less elusive, identified as it is with Lu and a group of ritual choreographers. Additional anecdotal evidence from the "Luyu" chapter of the *Guo yu*, where one finds Kongzi oddly discoursing on the apotropaic properties of certain rhyming binomes, suggests that the connection between Lu and *ru* may have been one linking *ru* with Kongzi. See *Guo yu* (*SBBY* edition), p. 5.7a.

59 On the significance of the bearskin mask, or demon mask, and its function in the *nuo* rituals, see Derk Bodde, *Festivals in Classical China: New Year and Other Annual Observances during the Han Dynasty, 206 B.C.–A.D. 220* (Princeton: Princeton University Press, 1975), pp. 75–138.

60 *Hanshi waizhuan*, p. 9.9a. See also Édouard Chavannes, trans., *Les Mémoires historiques de Se-ma Ts'ien*, vol. 5 of 6 vols. (Paris: 1895–1907), p. 338–340, n. 6.

61 Over time this association has become even more jumbled, its meaning reinvented so that dogs in a house of mourning are removed and placed outside. The legend has now been drawn up into popular funerary rite and mourning in Taiwan. See Emily M. Ahern, *The Cult of the Dead in a Chinese Village* (Stanford: Stanford University Press, 1973), p. 198, where she reports: "Then, standing in the front of the hall, a lineage member dumps the rice and the chicken head on the ground while someone else calls a dog and directs him to the food. As soon as the dog has taken the chicken head in his mouth, he is beaten with a long, whiplike plant until he dashes away in a frenzy. It was explained to me that the dog represents a dead man, the chicken head the property of the family held first by the deceased . . . the wings and feet of the chicken the property held later by the descendants, and the bowl of rice one meal out of the usual three consumed in a day. . . . The dog, which stands for the dead man, is beaten, so that he will run far away and not return. He has enjoyed his share of the property so that he should not come back and bother the living."

62 See *Lunyu*, 3.4, 3.26, 7.9, and esp. 17.21. See also *Mengzi*, 1.1:3, 1.2:16, 7.1:39.

63 On p. 18 Hu says, "Some ten years ago, I had said that the 'three years of mourning' was something that the *ru* fellowship invented, and that it was most certainly not an ancient rite." It was the work of Fu Sinian on this topic that helped Hu to jettison this earlier conviction. Kongzi's comment in the *Lunyu* that "in mourning the father for three years, all beneath the sky (*tianxia*), mourn," convinced Hu of the "modernity" of this invention until he realized, at Fu's urging, that *tianxia* did not refer to the universe, but to the surviving Shang cultural remnants in the past-Zhou era states of Lu, Qi, Song, and Wei. In a critique, titled "Fu 'Shuo ru,' " of Hu's essay, Guo Moruo enthusiastically contested this claim of Shang pedigree and reminded Hu of his previous position. See Guo, "Fu 'Shuo ru,' " p. 123.

64 Hu, "SR," p. 21.

65 Hu, "SR," p. 17.

66 In this respect we should note that it was in the image of the Jesuits that Hu envisioned the missionaries of the term *jiaoshi*, and not the Protestant volunteers of the early twentieth century, toward whom he came to feel ungenerous.

67 The emphasis on nonresistance that Hu places on the teachings of Jesus and Kongzi was, I think, a genuine projection of his own temperament upon the

documents before him. Hu's philosophical and political predilections were well served by a posture he described in 1936 as "the pacifism of nonresistance," and that he gave up about this time. See Hu, "Zixu," in *Hu Shi liuxue riji*, p. 6.

68 See *Zhuangzi jijie*, pp. 203–204.

69 Many scholars since Hu Shi have emphasized this reading of *ru* as "weakling," most notably Herrlee Creel, who devoted an entire chapter of his *Confucius and the Chinese Way* to a discussion of "The Weaklings." In another, more philological vein, and independent of Hu Shi's observations, Peter Boodberg has established that *ru* were known to their contemporaries as weaklings or even sucklings. See Creel, *Confucius and the Chinese Way* (New York: Harper and Row, 1960), pp. 173–181; Boodberg, "The Semasiology of Some Primary Confucian Concepts," in *Selected Works of Peter A. Boodberg*, ed. Alvin P. Cohen (Berkeley: University of California Press, 1979), pp. 30–31, 36–37. See also Rao, "Shi ru," pp. 111–115.

70 Hu Shi, "Yibusheng zhuyi ("On Ibsenism"), in *Hu Shi wencun*, vol. 4, pp. 883–908. "On Ibsenism" was originally published in *Xin qingnian* 4, no. 6 (June 1918): 531–549. In this essay the image of the individual is that of a completely isolated, autarkic person and is reminiscent of Nietzsche's *Übermensch*. This is probably a consequence of Georg Brandes's work on Ibsen, which greatly influenced Hu at this time.

71 Hu Shi renounced Christianity just two years after his conversion in the summer of 1911 at the hands of the Chinese Christian Students' Association. Yet for roughly a year and a half following his conversion, Hu studied the Bible under the aegis of his Cornell University French professor, William Wistar Comfort. Comfort's instruction was intellectually rather than religiously formative, and its effects could be seen in Hu's writing throughout his career. The King James Version appeared to have provided Hu a cherished fund of ideas and quotations, and he often turned to it, or rather to the many passages of it he had committed to memory, in order to flesh out a point by comparison or simply to find *le mot juste*.

The best example of the persistence of the lessons of this religious training is his oft-cited response to Dean Acheson's Letter of Transmittal, which accompanied the *China White Paper*. Next to the passage "The ominous result of the civil war in China was beyond the control of the government of the United States. Nothing that this country did or could have done within the reasonable limits of its capabilities could have changed that result; nothing that was left undone by this country has contributed to it," Hu made the marginal notation "Matthew 27:24." The verse reads: "When Pilate saw that he could prevail nothing, but that rather a tumult was made, he took water, and washed his hands before the multitude, saying, I am innocent of the blood of this just person: see ye to it." A New Testament hermeneutic of the Bible, then, constituted an important strand in the fabric of Hu Shi's thought, and this is appreciably evident in "Shuo ru." On Hu's "conversion," see his own account in Hu Shi, *Hu Shi liuxue riji*, vol. 1, pp. 42–50. For his reaction to the *China White Paper*, see Hu's introduction to John Leighton Stuart, *Fifty Years in China: The Memoirs of John Leighton Stuart, Missionary and Ambassador* (New York: Random House, 1954), pp. xix–xx.

72 "But I say unto you, That ye resist not evil: but whosoever shall smite thee on thy right cheek, turn to him the other also. And if any man will sue thee at the law, and take away thy coat, let him have thy cloke also. And whosoever shall compel thee to go a mile, go with him twain." Matthew 5:39–41. In my interpretation of the sermon, I have been greatly influenced by an address given by Joseph Brodsky at Williams College in June 1984. Joseph A. Brodsky, "The Misquoted Verse: A Baccalaureate Sermon," *Williams Alumni Review* (summer 1984): 12–14.

73 Hu, "SR," pp. 17–18.

74 Hu Shi, "Da Sifu Kaoxin xiansheng," *Duli pinglun*, no. 180 (December 8, 1935): 5–8.

75 Hu Shi, *The Development of the Logical Method in Ancient China*, 2d ed. (New York: Paragon, 1963), p. 9.

76 Hu, "SR," p. 50. The quotation is from Isaiah 55:4.

77 Ibid. This quotation is from Isaiah 49:6.

78 Hu admits that "we have no way of knowing what the life of *ru* was like before Kongzi; however, I suspect that the *Zhou yi* hexagram *xu* may provide us a clue." And this is because "the earliest form of the character *ru* was *xu*, which later acquired the semantic classifier for 'person.'" See Hu, "SR," p. 22.

79 Hu, "SR," p. 25.

80 Hu, "SR," pp. 22–23. My translation follows Wilhelm with several modifications. See Richard Wilhelm, trans., *The I Ching; or, Book of Changes*, 3d ed., rendered into English by Cary F. Baynes (Princeton: Princeton University Press, 1967), pp. 24–27.

81 Hu, "SR," p. 23.

82 On this figurative parallel in the Christian imagination and the mechanics of its operation, see Eric Auerbach, *Mimesis: The Representation of Reality in Western Literature*, trans. Willard R. Trask (Princeton: Princeton University Press, 1953), pp. 73–74.

83 In the last pages of the essay Hu delivers himself of the opinion that Laozi, Kongzi, and Mozi were all *ru* and that they represented distinct, increasingly various tendencies within this tradition. See Hu, "SR," pp. 78–82.

84 For some choice examples of this charge of hypocrisy, one that would follow *ru* into the Han, see *Zhuangzi jijie* in *ZZJC*, vol. 3, pt. 3, pp. 132–134; *Mozi jiangu* in *ZZJC*, vol. 4, pt. 1, pp. 178–181; and *Yantie lun*, in *ZZJC*, vol. 7, pt. 3, p. 23.

85 See Liang Shuming, *Dong-Xi wenhua ji qi zhexue* (reprint; Taibei: Hongxiao Shudian, 1968), pp. 152–153, for a summary of the intellectual/emotional schism that Liang identifies as the fundamental distinction between Western and Chinese cultures. See also the insightful, quasi-Weberian analysis of Liang's momentous essay in Guy S. Alitto, *The Last Confucian: Liang Shu-ming and the Chinese Dilemma of Modernity* (Berkeley: University of California Press, 1979), pp. 82–125.

86 Hu Shi, "Religion and Philosophy in Chinese History," in *Symposium on Chinese Culture*, ed. Sophia H. Chen Zen (Shanghai: China Institute of Pacific Relations, 1931), p. 31.

87 Hu, "SR," p. 35.

88 Weber suggested that one way of conceiving of social evolution was in terms of "charisma," arguing that early societies were formed by an inspirational force embodied in a figure of pure charisma. Inevitably these associations, bound by ties to a charismatic leader—priest, prophet, chieftain, etc.—were routinized in the course of their institutional development. The critical institutional challenge for these ancient, ecstatic societies was succession. With the demise of the charismatic figure, how is the vitality of the society to endure? And, can a method be devised to stabilize this vitality? Weber reasoned that the twin genetic urges of society—charisma and institutionalization—dramatically displayed in the anxiety surrounding succession, were negotiated through a logic of contiguity. Whosoever was closest to the charismatic leader would inherit his charisma. Consequently, from that point on charisma would be passed by privileged, personal links of power, those that were most incontrovertible, those links in the chain of descent. The priest became a patriarch. Tradition, simple transmission by descent, Weber would point out, was the most appropriate and visible manifestation of this logic. See Max Weber, *The Protestant Ethic and the Spirit of Capitalism*, trans. Talcott Parsons (Boston: Scribners, 1958), pp. 153–188, *The Sociology of Religion*, trans. Ephraigm Fischoff (Boston: Beacon Press, 1963), pp. 20–31, 118–137, 207–222. This intellectual affinity may help to explain Western scholars' genial, uncritical acceptance of Hu Shi's interpretation. At the same time, the fact that Hu made a convincing case for the interwovenness of the separate processes of secularization in China and the West by way of his extended religious analogy reinforced the validity of his hypotheses.

89 See Hu Shi, "Du Liang Shuming xiansheng zhu de 'Dong-Xi wenhua ji qi zhexue,' " in *Hu Shi wencun*, vol. 2, pp. 172–175.

90 Hu, "SR," p. 42. The language of this epic, eschatological myth of the appearance of a sage every five centuries—"wubainian you shengren zhi xing"—is modified here by Hu Shi, because the expression in the *Mengzi* (bk. 2, pt. 2, chap. 13) is "wubainian bi you wangzhe xing" (after 500 years a king inevitably arrives). Reading the myth in this manner permitted Hu to reinforce his argument that the Shang, in their anxious anticipation of a just king, misapprehended Kongzi as a savior. Still, there is far more to this mythology than mere Shang revanchism, for David Pankenier has adduced a great weight of evidence that this belief was inspired by empirical Chinese observation of recurring preternatural astrological phenomena. A spectacular massing of the planets Jupiter, Mars, Mercury, Saturn, and Venus occurred in Aquarius/Pisces in 1953 B.C.E., and in Cancer in 1059 B.C.E. There was another gathering of four planets (Jupiter, Mars, Mercury, Saturn) in Scorpio/Sagittarius 1576 B.C.E. The five-century pattern of planetary massing (516.33 years to be exact) coincides with the chronology of the founding of each of the *sandai* (Three Eras)—Xia, Shang, and Zhou—as recorded in the Bamboo Annals. The movements of these bright objects against the background of the fixed stars, Pankenier maintains, were taken as sidereal hieroglyphs of the sky god, *tian*, signaling the bestowal of a mandate to rule the north China plain. See *Mengzi jizhu*, p. 259; and David W. Pankenier, "The Cosmo-political Background of Heaven's Mandate," *Early China* 20 (1995): 121–176, esp. 121–136.

91 Bauer, *China and the Search for Happiness*, pp. 15–16.

92 Hu distinguishes between the prophecy in its incipient form when the longing was for a cultural or tribal hero, and its subsequent manifestation as anticipation of a sage (*shengren*) or a savior (*jiushi de ren*). See Hu, "SR," pp. 37–42.

93 The antiquity of this ode (Mao 303) is well attested, as it appears in the Zhou Song section of the text, generally considered the oldest stratum of the *Shi jing* (ca. 1050–1000 B.C.E.). On the dating of the *Shi jing*, in particular that of the Zhou Song odes, see W. A. C. H. Dobson, "Linguistic Evidence in the Dating of *The Book of Songs*," in *T'oung Pao* 51 (1964): 322–334.

94 Hu, "SR," p. 39; and *Maoshi zhengyi*, in *SSJZS*, vol. 3 (reprint; Shanghai: Guji chubanshe, 1990), pp. 791.2–794.2. I follow James Legge's translation from *The Chinese Classics*, vol. 4, pp. 636–638.

95 The "Tian wen" of *Chuci* also mentions this association. Sima Qian recounts the tale of how Di Ku, the ancestress of the Shang, gave birth to these people through the magical intercession of a black bird (*xuanniao*). On this well-documented ornithological association, see Chen Mengjia, "Shangdai de shen-hua yu wushu." *Yanjing xuebao* 20 (1936): 485–576; and Sarah Allan, "Sons of Suns: Myth and Totemism in Early China," *Bulletin of the School of Oriental and African Studies* 44, pt. 2 (1981): 290–326. For the mythological links be-tween *xuanniao* and the birth of Kongzi, see Jensen, "Wise Man of the Wilds," pp. 424–430.

96 Keightley, "Legitimation in Shang China," unpublished manuscript (1975), and "The Religious Commitment: Shang Theology and the Genesis of Chinese Polit-ical Culture," *History of Religions*, vol. 17 (1978): 211–225; and Kwang-Chih Chang, *Shang Civilization* (New Haven: Yale University Press, 1980), pp. 158–194.

97 Karlgren, *Book of Odes*, p. 263.

98 This method of invoking or enticing spirits is very common in the odes of the *Shi jing*, its efficacy dependent on flattery of the spirit by encomium. For other examples of this invocational technique, see Odes 11, 51, 84, 86, 132.

99 Hu, "SR," p. 40.

100 Ibid. Meng Xizi wished for his sons to learn of the rites from Kong Qiu, claiming that "without rites one cannot stand." See *Zuo zhuan*, *SSJZS*, vol. 7, pp. 764.2–766.2. Du Yu's commentary, inspired by Meng's assertion that "Kong Qiu was a descendant of a sage who was slaughtered at Song," informs us that Kongzi was the sixth-generation descendant of Kong Fujia. Du's genealogical reconstruction is fully consistent with earlier identically emplotted anecdotal material from the *Zuo Zhuan* account of the third year of Duke Yin, where Mu Gong's final request is that his son become the ward of Kong Fujia. The young duke and foster parent are then killed by the tyrant Hua Du at Song in 710 B.C.E.

101 *Zuo zhuan*, *SSJZS*, vol. 7, pp. 764.2–766.2.

102 Hu explicitly defines Kongzi's historical significance as his being a "representa-tive of a magnificent historical trend extending over five to six hundred years." The trend he identifies is the transition from an otherworldly religious sanction to a humanistic social one. This makes Kongzi the representative of what Robert

Bellah has called "historic religion." See Robert N. Bellah, "Religious Evolution," in *Beyond Belief: Essays on Religion in a Post-Traditional World* (New York: Harper and Row, 1976), pp. 29–36.

103 Stephen Owen sees this distinction as a line that runs between two fundamentally different ways of interpreting experience, one mythopoeic, the other historical. See Owen, *Remembrances: The Experience of the Past in Classical Chinese Literature* (Cambridge, Mass.: Harvard University Press, 1986), pp. 8–14, 18–24.

104 Hu, *Hu Shi liuxue riji*, p. 46.

105 Hu, "SR," pp. 79–80.

106 See Karl Jaspers, *The Origin and Goal of History*, trans. Michael Bullock (New Haven: Yale University Press, 1953).

107 Hu seems to be convinced of more than just the common traits of Kongzi and Jesus as men and misappropriated messiahs. Near the end of the fourth section, he recounts the final moments of the Passion of Christ and his resurrection, emphasizing how the Jews believed him to be their king, though clearly from the point of view of the Romans such a notion was ludicrous. He proceeds to explain how Christ ascended into heaven and is now seated at the right hand of the Father. The retelling of this tale, astonishingly enough, is offered as an explanation of the Chinese tradition of calling Kongzi a *suwang* or uncrowned king, and the paragraph immediately following Hu's version of the Passion begins with: "The story of Kongzi is very much like this." In the end Kongzi and Christ resemble Jungian archetypes, symbols of universal processes. See Hu, "SR," pp. 50–51.

108 The holy book of the Jews is composed of three parts—Torah (literally, "Teaching," also known as the Pentateuch, the Five Books of Moses); Nevi'im (Prophets); and Kethuvim (Writings)—a letter from each makes up the whole of "Tanakh" (T + N + Kh).

109 If one were to judge from Paul's letters to the Romans and the Corinthians alone, the religion of the Patriarchs with its laws (Torah) was productive of all the evils enumerated here.

110 On religious genesis through subcult reaction see Daniel Lawrence O'Keefe, *Stolen Lightning: The Social Theory of Magic* (New York: Vintage Books, 1983), pp. 121–175.

111 Hu, *Hu Shi liuxue riji*, vol. 1, p. 456. The English is, of course, Hu's own.

112 Certeau, *The Writing of History*, p. 22.

113 See Tan Sitong, "Renxue," in *Tan Sitong quanji* (reprint; Beijing: Xinhua shudian, 1954), pp. 6–10.

114 For example, see Chen Duxiu, "Kongzi zhi dao yu xiandai shenghuo," *Xin qingnian* 2, no. 4 (December 1, 1916): 3–5; and "Rensheng zhenyi," in *Xin qingnian* 4, no. 2 (February 1, 1918): 90–93.

115 Joseph R. Levenson, "'History' and 'Value': Tensions of Intellectual Choice in Modern China," in *Studies in Chinese Thought*, ed. Arthur F. Wright (Chicago: University of Chicago Press, 1953), p. 165.

116 Hu Shi, "Shiping suowei Zhongguo benwei de wenhua jianshe,'" in *Hu Shi wencun*, vol. 4, p. 540.

117 For a truly exemplary essay in this emerging traditionalist genre, see the manifesto "Zhongguo benwei de wenhua jianshe xuanyan," in *Wenhua jianshe* 1, no. 4 (January 1935).

118 Hu Shi, "Shiping suowei Zhongguo benwei de wenhua jianshe,'" pp. 535–540, as quoted in *Sources of Chinese Tradition*, comp. Wm. Theodore de Bary, Wing-tsit Chan, and Chester Tan, vol. 2 (New York: Columbia University Press, 1964), pp. 194–195.

119 Tu Cheng-sheng, "Some Problems concerning the So-called Survivors of the Yin Dynasty," paper presented at the International Conference on Shang Civilization, East-West Center, University of Hawai'i at Manoa, Honolulu, September 7–11, 1982. On the basis of certain inscriptions from the Shang and Zhou, Tu argues that the "Yin survivors" of the conquest did not suffer the tragic fate described by Hu Shi. In fact, most survivors continued to hold land, kept servants, and in short, maintained both political power and social prestige. One last point worthy of note here is Tu's assertion that Hu's depiction of a vanquished, vestigially extant Yin culture was mistaken and that for fifty years scholars have presumed the characterization to have been accurate.

120 Ch'ien Mu, "A Historical Perspective on Chu Hsi's Learning," in *Chu Hsi and Neo-Confucianism*, ed. Wing-tsit Chan (Honolulu: University of Hawai'i Press, 1986), p. 40.

121 Hu, *The Development of the Logical Method in China*, pp. 6–7.

Epilogue

1 John U. Nef, *Cultural Foundations of Industrial Civilization* (Chicago: University of Chicago Press, 1958), pp. 128–133.

2 A. Eustace Haydon, foreword to Hu Shi, *The Chinese Renaissance* (Chicago: Chicago University Press, 1934), p. viii.

3 Hu, *The Chinese Renaissance*, p. 26.

4 E. J. Hobsbawm, *Nations and Nationalism since 1780: Programme, Myth, Reality*, 2d ed. (Cambridge: Cambridge University Press, 1992), p. 191.

5 On the distrust of metanarratives and the valorization of "petit récit" as cardinal features of postmodern culture see Jean-François Lyotard, *The Postmodern Condition: A Report on Knowledge*, trans. Geoff Bennington and Brian Massumi (Minneapolis: University of Minnesota Press, 1984); and David Harvey, *The Condition of Postmodernism* (Oxford: Basil Blackwell, 1989), pp. 42–65.

6 Maruyama Masao, *Nihon seiji shisōshi kenkyū* (Tokyo: Tokyo Daigaku shuppan, 1952), trans. Mikiso Hane as *Studies in the Intellectual History of Tokugawa Japan* (Princeton: Princeton University Press, 1974).

7 Harold Bloom, *The Anxiety of Influence: A Theory of Poetry* (New York: Oxford University Press, 1973); and "The Breaking of Form," in *Humanities in Review*, ed. Ronald Dworkin, Karl Miller, and Richard Sennett, vol. 1 (New York: New York University Press, 1982), pp. 127–156.

8 For his remarks on China as a "civilization developing outside of all logocentrism," see Jacques Derrida, *Of Grammatology*, trans. Gayatri Chakravorty

Spivak (Baltimore: Johns Hopkins University Press, 1976), pp. 74–93, esp. pp. 90–92.

9   Takeuchi Yoshio, *Rongo no kenkyū* (Tokyo: Iwanami, 1939), pp. 72–109. More recently and in a less speculative, more "scientific" manner, Kimura Eiichi has confirmed Takeuchi and has attempted to assign sections of the *Lunyu* to sentence groups by which it may be possible to identify the Lu and Qi contributions to the received text. See Kimura Eiichi, *Kōshi to Rongo* (Tokyo: Sobunsha, 1971), esp. pp. 211–230.

10 Even Paul de Man, who admitted that deconstruction is "the systematic undoing of understanding," was aware that the enterprise cleared ground for invention in the manner outlined by François Lyotard in his strategy of "petit récit": "The possibility now arises that the entire construction of drives, substitutions, repressions, and representations is the aberrant, metaphorical correlative of the absolute randomness of language, prior to any figuration of meaning." See Paul de Man, *Allegories of Reading: Figural Language in Rousseau, Nietzsche, Rilke, and Proust* (New Haven: Yale University Press, 1979); and Lyotard, *The Postmodern Condition.*

11 Richard Rorty, *Contingency, Irony, Solidarity* (Cambridge: Cambridge University Press, 1989); and *Consequences of Pragmatism* (Minneapolis: University of Minnesota Press, 1983).

12 *Mengzi zhushu*, in *SSJZS*, vol. 13, pp. 161.1–174.1.

13 *Mengzi zhushu*, pp. 164.1–169.1; *Han Feizi jijie*, in *ZZJC*, vol. 5, pt. 4, p. 299; and Lei Xueqi, ed., *Zhushu jinian yizheng* (Taibei: Yiwen Chubanshe, n.d.), pp. 38–39.

14 See *Zhuangzi jijie*, in *ZZJC*, vol. 3, pt. 3, p. 429. For an innovative structuralist reading of the wide divergence in Warring States understanding of legend, see Sarah Allan, *The Heir and the Sage: Dynastic Legend in Early China* (San Francisco: Chinese Materials Center, 1981), pp. 27–54.

15 See Benjamin I. Schwartz, "The Limits of 'Tradition Versus Modernity' as Categories of Explanation: The Case of Chinese Intellectuals," in *Intellectuals and Tradition*, ed. S. N. Eisenstadt and S. R. Graubard (New York: Humanities Press, 1973), p. 76.

16 Roxana Waterson, *The Living House: An Anthropology of Architecture in South-East Asia* (New York: Oxford University Press, 1990), p. 232.

17 Alasdair MacIntyre, *After Virtue: A Study on Moral Theory*, 2d ed. (Notre Dame, Ind.: University of Notre Dame Press, 1984), p. 207. Unfortunately, this understanding of the past as source of the present is, it seems, even less evident to contemporary Chinese intellectuals such as Gan Yang, who speaks of the *gujin zhi zheng* (conflict between past and present or tradition and modernity). On the persistence of this misunderstanding in recent "cultural discussion" (*wenhua taolun*), see Jing Wang, *High Culture Fever: Politics, Aesthetics, and Ideology in Deng's China* (Berkeley: University of California Press, 1996), pp. 86–91.

18 *Lunyu jizhu*, in Zhu Xi, *Sishu jizhu* (reprint; Taibei: Xuehai Chubanshe, 1984), p. 78. See Arthur Waley, trans., *The Analects of Confucius* (New York: Vintage Books, 1938), p. 100; and D. C. Lau, trans., *Confucius: The Analects* (reprint; New York: Penguin Classics, 1982), p. 71.

19 A. C. Graham, *Chuang Tzu: The Inner Chapters* (London: George, Allen and Unwin, 1981), pp. 192–193.

20 Stephen Owen, *Remembrances: The Experience of the Past in Classical Chinese Literature* (Cambridge, Mass.: Harvard University Press, 1986), pp. 16–23.

21 *Lunyu zhushu*, in *SSJZS*, vol. 12, pp. 26.2–27.1; Ezra Pound, *Confucius: The Unwobbling Pivot, The Great Digest and The Analects* (New York: New Directions, 1969), p. 203; and Waley, trans., *The Analects of Confucius*, p. 96.

22 *Lunyu zhushu*, p. 26.1; and Pound, *The Analects*, p. 202.

23 *Lunyu zhushu*, p. 25.1; Waley, trans., *The Analects of Confucius*, p. 94; and Pound, *The Unwobbling Pivot*, p. 201.

24 *Lunyu zhushu*, p. 15.1. For the complete text of "Jiong" (Stout, Mao 297), see *Maoshi zhengyi*, in *SSJZS*, vol. 3, pp. 762.1–762.2. The many interpretive renderings of the text of the *Shi jing* attributed to Kongzi are analyzed rather caustically by Donald Holzman in "Confucius and Ancient Chinese Literary Criticism," in *Chinese Approaches to Literature from Confucius to Liang Ch'i-ch'ao*, ed. Adele Austin Rickett (Princeton: Princeton University Press, 1978), pp. 21–41; and with less hostility by James J. Y. Liu in *Language—Paradox—Poetics: A Chinese Perspective* (Princeton: Princeton University Press, 1988), pp. 94–97.

25 See F. W. Mote, "The Arts and the 'Theorizing Mode' of the Civilization," in *Artists and Traditions: Uses of the Past in Chinese Culture*, ed. Christian Murck (Princeton: Princeton University Press, 1976), pp. 3–8.

26 This unflattering comparison is frequently found in social science terminology, particularly in the literature of modernization theory. On this conventional but unsound interpretive tendency, see Thomas Metzger, *Escape from Predicament: Neo-Confucianism and China's Evolving Political Culture* (New York: Columbia University Press, 1977), pp. 3–18, 191–235; Tetsuo Najita and Irwin Scheiner, eds., *Japanese Thought in the Tokugawa Period, 1600–1868: Methods and Metaphors* (Chicago: University of Chicago Press, 1978), pp. ix–xii; and Brian Stock, *Listening for the Text: On the Uses of the Past* (Baltimore: Johns Hopkins University Press, 1990), pp. 159–177.

27 The common epistemological distinction implied here is that which has been drawn between object (territory) and representation (map) by the philosopher Alfred Korzybski. The distinction, as interpreted by Gregory Bateson, underlies the argument of part 1. See Gregory Bateson, *Mind and Nature: A Necessary Unity* (New York: Bantam Books, 1980), pp. 32–33. Jonathan Z. Smith has employed this same dyad to convey incongruity, in particular the fruitful incongruity constitutive of symbolism, myth, tradition, and transcendence in native cultures. For me, as for Smith, the "map is not territory" problem is not limited to the observer who seeks to represent what she sees among others, paradigmatically represented by the ethnographer among the natives. The tension between the cognitive map one carries and the territory one walks is also indigenous to the observed culture. Natives, no less than anthropologists, find that they must regularly "adjust" their inherited conceptions in the face of experience that runs contrary to such conceptions. Myths and traditions are ideal, prescribed accounts, representations of what communities desire for themselves or their ancestors

under the best possible circumstances. The meaning of such constructs does not inhere in them but rather in the discrepancy between myth as a map organizing the paths of indigenous conception and the contingent territory of daily experience. See Jonathan Z. Smith, *Map Is Not Territory: Studies in the History of Religion* (Leiden: E. J. Brill, 1978), pp. 289–309. See also Marshall Sahlins, *Historical Metaphors and Mythical Realities: Structure in the Early History of the Sandwich Islands Kingdom* (Ann Arbor: University of Michigan Press, 1981), pp. 33–66, where this tension is insightfully articulated by means of another dyad, that of structure/practice.

28 The concept was first used by Heinrich Rickert to refer to an object that has historical significance for us as contemporary interpreters, with this significance being defined in terms of value relation. Weber formed his concept of the historical individual (later embodied in the "ideal-type") on the basis of Rickert's definition. See Max Weber, *The Methodology of the Social Sciences*, ed. and trans. Edward Shils and Henry A. Finch (New York: Free Press, 1949), pp. 50–112; and Wolfgang Schluchter, *The Rise of Western Rationalism: Max Weber's Developmental History* (Berkeley: University of California Press, 1981), pp. 13–24.

29 Stephen Toulmin, *Cosmopolis: The Hidden Agenda of Modernity* (Chicago: Chicago University Press, 1991), pp. 186–192; MacIntyre, *After Virtue*, pp. 190–209.

BIBLIOGRAPHY

Primary Sources

Alexandre, Noel. *Conformité des cérémonies chinoises avec l'idolatrie grècque et romaine.* Cologne: Les hautiers de C. L'Egmondt, 1700.

Bartoli, Daniello. *Dell'Istoria della Compagnia di Gésù: La Cina: Terza Parte dell' Asia.* 4 vols. Rome, 1663. Ancona: Giuseppe Aureli, 1843.

Boxer, C. R., ed. *A Propósitio dum livrinho xilográfico dos Jesuitás de Pequisu (Sécuo XVIII).* Macau: Imprensa Nacional, 1942.

——. *South China in the Sixteenth Century: Being the Narratives of Galeote Pereira, Fr. Gaspar da Cruz, O.P., Fr. Martin de Rada, E.A.S.A. (1550–1575).* London: Haklyut Society, 1953.

Chen Duxiu. "Kongzi zhi dao yu xiandai shenghuo" (The Way of Kongzi and Contemporary Life). *Xin qingnian* 2, no. 4 (December 1, 1916): 3–5.

——. "Rensheng zhenyi" (The Real Meaning of Life). *Xin qingnian* 4, no. 1 (February 1, 1918): 90–93.

Ch'ien Mu [Qian Mu]. "Fu Hu Shi zhi 'Shuo ru'" (A Refutation of Hu Shi's "Shuo ru"). *Journal of Oriental Studies* 1, no. 1 (January 1954): 123–128.

Chunqiu Zuo zhuan zhu (The Zuo Transmission of the Spring and Autumn Annals with Supplementary Commentary). 4 vols. Edited by Yang Bojun. Bejing: Zhonghua Shuju, 1981.

Coleridge, H. J., ed. *The Life and Letters of St. Francis Xavier.* 2 vols. London: Burns and Oates, 1902.

Couplet, Philippe, et al. *Confucius Sinarum Philosophus, sive Scientia Sinensis.* Paris: Horthemels, 1687.

Cordier, Henri. *Bibliotheca Sinica.* Paris, 1904–1924. Reprint, Taibei: Chengwen, 1966.

Cui Shu. "Lunyu yushuo" (Further Theories on the Lunyu). In *Cui Dongbi yishu* (The Surviving Works of Cui Dongbi). Edited by Gu Jiegang.

Di Ziji. *Kongzi biannian* (Annual Register of Kongzi). Zhejiang Shuju, 1887.

Ding Fubao. *Shuowen jiezi gulin* (Ancient Forest of the Explanation of Pattern and Elucidation of Graphs). 8 vols. Shanghai: Yixue Shuju, 1931–32.

Duan Yucai. *Shuowen jiezi zhu* (Annotations on Explanation of Pattern and Elucidation of Graphs). Reprint, Taibei: Hanjing wenhua shiye youxian gongsi, 1983.

Dong Zhongshu. "Qiu yu" (Seeking Rain). In *Chunqiu fanlu yizheng* (Evidential Meanings on the Luxuriant Dew of the Spring and Autumn). Edited by Su Yu. Taibei: Hele tushu Chubanshe, 1975.

Du Yu. *Chunqiu jingchuan jijie* (Spring and Autumn Classic and [Zuo] Tradition with Collected Commentaries). 3 vols. Reprint, Taibei: Zhonghua Shuju, 1965.

Erya zhushu (Literary Expositor, Annotations, and Commentaries). *SSJZS*, vol. 12. Reprint, Shanghai: Guji Chubanshe, 1990.

Guangya shuzheng (Extensive and Refined [Etymology] Annotations and Commentaries). Edited by Wang Niansun. Reprint, Beijing: Zhonghua Shuju, 1983.

Gu Jiegang, ed. *Ci Dongbi yishu* (The Surviving Works of Cui Dongbi). Taibei: Hele tushu Chubanshe, 1975.

Guo Moruo. "Fu 'Shuo ru'" (Refutation of "An Elaboration on *ru*"). In Guo, *Qingtong Shidai* (The Bronze Age). Beijing: Zhonghua Shuju, 1954.

Guo Moruo, ed. *Jiaguwen heji* (Collection of Oracle Bone Inscriptions). 13 vols. Beijing: Zhonghua Shuju, 1978–82.

Guoyu yijie (Commentaries on the Discourses of the States). *SBBY* edition.

——. *Gushi bian* (Critiques of Ancient History). 7 vols. Hong Kong: Taiping Shuju, 1962.

Guzman, Luis de. *Historia de las Missiones que han hecho los religiosos de la Compañia de Iesvs: para predicar el sancto evangelio en la India oriental, y en les reynos de la China y Japon*. Alcalá de Henares: Buida de I. Gracian, 1601.

Han Feizi jijie (Collected Commentaries on the Han Feizi). Edited by Wang Xianqian. In *ZZJC*, vol. 5, pt. 4.

Hanshu buzhu (Former Han History with Supplementary Commentaries). Compiled by Wang Xianqian. Reprint, Taibei: Dingwen Shuju, 1974.

Han Ying. *Hanshi waizhuan* (Han [Ying's] Illustrations of the Didactic Use of the Book of Odes). *SBCK* edition.

The Holy Bible. King James version. New York: Meridian Books, n.d.

Hu Shih [Hu Shi]. *The Chinese Renaissance*. Chicago: University of Chicago Press, 1934.

——. "The Chinese Renaissance." *Bulletin on Chinese Education* 2, no. 6 (1923): 1–36.

——. "Da Sifu Kaoxin xiansheng" (A Reply to Mr. Murobushi Kōshin). *Duli pinglun*, no. 180 (December 8, 1935): 5–8.

——. *The Development of the Logical Method in Ancient China*. 2d ed. New York: Paragon, 1963.

——. *Hu Shi liuxue riji* (Hu Shi's Diary of Study Abroad). 4 vols. Taibei: Shangwu, 1959.

——. *Hu Shi wencun* (The Literary Preserve of Hu Shi). 4 vols. Taibei: Yuandong, 1953.

——. "Religion and Philosophy in Chinese History." In *Symposium on Chinese Culture*, edited by Sophia H. Chen Zen, pp. 31–58. Shanghai: China Institute of Pacific Relations, 1931.

——. "Shiping suowei 'Zhongguo benwei de wenhua jianshe'" (A Critique of the So-called Chinese-Based Cultural Construction). In *Hu Shi wencun*. Vol. 4, pp. 535–540. Taibei: Yuandong, 1953.

——. *Sishi zishu* (Recollections at the Age of Forty). Taibei: Yuandong, 1974.

——. "Shuo ru" (An Elaboration on *ru*). In *Hu Shi wencun*. Vol. 4, pp. 1–82. Taibei: Yuandong, 1953.

——. "Xinxin yu fanxing" (Faith and Introspection). *Duli pinglun*, no. 103 (June 3, 1934).

——. "Yibusheng zhuyi" (On Ibsenism). *Xin qingnian* 4, no. 6 (June 1918): 531–549.

——. "Zhuzi buchu yu wangguan lun" (The Collected Masters did not Derive from the Heaven Office). In *Zhongguo zhexue shi dagang*, pp. 1–10.

——. *Zhongguo jexue shi dagang* (General Outline of the History of Chinese Philosophy). Shanghai: Shangwu, 1929.

Huainanzi (Book of [Prince] Huainan). Edited by Liu Wendian. In *ZZJC*, vol. 7, pt. 2. Reprint, Beijing: Zhonghua Shuju, 1990.

Huan Kuan, comp. *Yantie lun* (Discourses on Salt and Iron). In *ZZJC*, vol. 7, pt. 3. Reprint, Beijing: Zhonghua Shuju, 1990.

Huang Kan, ed. *Lunyu jijie yisu* (Collected Commentaries on the Lunyu with Subcommentary). 2 vols. Reprint, Taibei: Guangwen Shuju, 1968.

Huang Zongxi and Chuan Zuwang, comps. *Song-Yuan xue'an* (Scholarly Cases on Song and Yuan [*ru*]). 2 vols. Beijing: Zhongguo Shudian, 1990.

Huang Zongxi and Chuan Zuwang, comps. *Song-Yuan xue'an* (Scholarly Cases on Song and Yuan [*ru*]). 2 vols. Beijing: Zhongguo shudian, 1990.

Ikeda Suetoshi. *Inkyo shokei kohen shakubun ko* (Draft Annotations on "Inscriptions from the Wastes of Yinu: Latter Volume). Hiroshima: Hiroshima Daigaku Bungakubu Chūgoku Tetsugaku Kenkyūshitsu, 1964.

Illyricus, Matthias Flacius. *Clavis Scripturae Sacrae*. New edition, Jena: Johannis Ludovici Neuenhans, 1674.

Intorcetta, Prosper. *Sinarum Scientia Politico-Moralis*. In *Relations de divers voyages curieux*, by Melchisédec Thévenot, vol. 4. Paris, 1696.

Jao Tsung-i [Rao Zongyi]. "Shi ru: Cong wenzi xunguxue Shang lunru de yiyi" (An Explication of *ru*: From Explaining *ru* from the Angle of the Etymologies of the Graphs). *Journal of Oriental Studies* 1, no. 1 (January 1954): 111–122.

Jilin daxue lishixi, comp. *Yiqie fandongpai doushi zun Kongpai* (Every Reactionary Faction is a Revering Kongzi Faction). Beijing: Renmin Chubanshe, 1974.

Kong congzi (Kong Family Masters' Anthology). Reprint, Shanghai: Guji Chubanshe, 1990.

Kongzi jiayu (Family Sayings of Kongzi). Edited by Wang Su. Reprint, Shanghai: Guji Chubanshe, 1990.

Le Comte, P. Louis, S.J. *Nouveaux mémoires sur l'état présent de la Chine*. Paris: Jean Anisson, 1696.

Lei Xueji, ed. *Zhushu jinian yizheng* (Evidential Meanings on the Bamboo Annals). Taibei: Yiwen Chubanshe, n.d.

Li Madou [Matteo Ricci]. *Ershiwu yan* (Twenty-five Sayings). In *Tianxue chuhan*. Edited by Li Zhizao, vol. 1, pp. 331–349.

——. *Jiaoyou lun* (Treatise on Friendship). In *Tianxue chuhan*, vol. 1, pp. 299–320.

——. *Jihe yuanben* (The Elements of Euclid). In *Tianxue chuhan*, vol. 4, pp. 1921–2522.

——. *Jiren shipian* (Ten Discourses of a Strange Man). In *Tianxue chuhan*, vol. 1, pp. 117–281.

——. "Shuwen zeng Yubo Chengzi" (Transmission by Writing Bestowed upon Master Cheng Yubo [Cheng Dayue]). In *Sheyuan mocui* (The Wandering in the Garden Inkcake Collection). 2 vols. Edited by Tao Xiang. Beijing: n.p., 1929.

——. *Tianzhu shiyi* (The Real Significance of the Heavenly Master). In *Tianxue chuhan*, vol. 1, pp. 351–635.

Li Zhizao, ed. *Tianxue chuhan* (The Essentials of the Heavenly Learning). 6 vols. Reprint, Taibei: Xuesheng Shuju, 1965.

Liang Qichao. "Hunan Shiwu xuetang chuji" (First Collection from the Shiwu Academy of Hunan). In *Wuxu bianfa*, vol. 4. Edited by Qian Bozan et al. Shanghai: Shanghai renmin Chubanshe, 1957.

Liao Ping. "Huangdi jiangyu tu" (Geographic Charts for Sovereigns and Emperors). In *Liuyi guan congshu* (Collectanea of the Office of the Six Cultivations). Chengdu: Cungu Shudian, 1925.

Liu Shipei. "Jindai Hanxue bianqian lun." *Guocui xuebao*, no. 31 (June 20, 1908).

——. "Rujia chuyu situ zhi guan shuo" (On the Theory that the Ru Derived from the Office of the Leader of the Footsoldiers). *Guocui xuebao*, no. 33 (August 20, 1908): Xuepian, 1a–2b.

Liu Xin. "Yiwen zhi" (Record of Cultivations and Writings). In *Hanshu buzhu*, vol. 3. Edited by Wang Xianqian. Taibei: Dingwen Shuju, 1974.

Longobardo, Niccolò. *Traité sur quelques points de la religion des chinois*. Paris: J. Josse, 1701.

Lunyu zhushu (Lunyu with Annotation and Commentary). Edited by Ho Yan and Xing Ping. In *SSJZS*, vol. 11. Reprint, Shanghai: Guji Chubanshe, 1990.

Lüshi Chunqiu (Mr. Lu's Springs and Autumns). In *ZZJC*, vol. 6. pt. 4. Reprint, Beijing: Zhonghua Shuju, 1990.

Magaillans, Gabriel [Gabriel de Magalhaes]. *Nouvelle relation de la Chine, contenant la description des particularits les plus considerables de ce grand empire*. Translated by Benou. Paris: C. Barbin, 1688.

Mailla, J. M. A. de Moyriac de. *Histoire général de la Chine, ou annales de cet empire*. 13 vols. Paris: L'Abbé Grosier, 1777–1785.

Maoshi zhengyi (Corrected Interpretations of Mao's Edition of the Shi [jing]). In *SSJZS*, vol. 3. Reprint, Shanghai: Guji Chubanshe, 1990.

Mendoza, Juan González de. *Historia de las cosas mas notables, ritos y costumbres del gran reino de la China*. Valencia, 1596.

Mengzi zhushu (Mengzi with Annotation and Commentary). In *SSJZS*, vol. 13. Reprint, Shanghai: Guji Chubanshe, 1990.

The Morals of Confucius: A Chinese Philosopher. London: Randall, Taylor, 1691.

Mozi jiangu (Annotation of the Mozi). Edited by Sun Yirang. In *ZZJC*, vol. 4, pt. 1. Reprint, Beijing: Zhonghua Shuju, 1990.

Pantoja, Diego de. *Relacion de la entrada de algunos padres de la campagnia de Jesus en la China*. Valencia: Juan Chrysostomos Garris, 1606.

Pauthier, M. G. *Confucius et Mencius: Les Quatres Livres de philosophie morale et politique de la Chine*. Paris: Charpentier, 1841.

Pensées morales de Confucius. 2d ed. Paris: Victor Lecou, 1851.

Pfister, Louis. *Notices biographiques et bibliographiques sur les Jésuites de l'an-*

cienne mission de Chine, 1552–1773. 2 vols. Shanghai: Maison Catholique, 1932–1934.

Possevino, Antonio. *Bibliotecha selecta qua agitur de ratione studiorum in historia, in disciplinis, in salute omnium procuranda.* Rome, 1593.

Prémare, J. H. de. *Notitia Linguae Sinicae.* Malacca: Anglo-Chinese College, 1831.

Quintilian. *Institutio oratoria.* Vol. 3. Cambridge, Mass.: Loeb, 1959.

Ricci, Matteo. *Fonti Ricciane (Storia dell'Introduzione del Christianesimo in Cina).* 3 vols. Edited by Pasquale M. d'Elia, S.J. Rome: Libreria dello Stato, 1942–1949.

——. *Le Opere storiche del P. Matteo Ricci, S.J.* 2 vols. Edited by Pietro Tacchi Venturi. Macerata: F. Giorgetti, 1911–1913.

Sanz, Carlos, ed. *B. Escalante: Primera historia de China* [1577]. Reprint, Madrid: Libreria General Victoriano Suarez, 1958.

Schütte, Josef F., S.J. *Monumenta Historica Japoniae,* vol. 1. Rome: 1975.

Shanhai jing jianshu (Classic of Mountains and Seas with Commentary and Sub-Commentary). 1809. Commentary by Hao Yixing. Reprint, Taipei: Guangwen Shuju, 1965.

Shima Kunio. *Inkyo bokuji sorui* (Collected Inventory of the Oracle Texts from the Wastes of Yin). 2d rev. ed. Tokyo: Kyuko Shoin, 1971.

Shirakawa Shizuka. *Setsubun shingi* (New Meanings of Shuowen). 16 vols. Kyoto: Hakutsuru bijutsukan, 1970–1974.

Sima Qian. *Shiji.* 10 vols. Reprint, Beijing: Zhonghua Shuju, 1975.

Sommervogel, Carlos. *Bibliothèque de la Compagnie de Jèsus.* 12 vols. Brussels: O. Schepens, 1890–1932.

Song Lian. *Song wenxian gong quanji* (The Collected Works of Culture Eminent Song). *SBBY* edition. Reprint, Taibei: Zhonghua Shuju, 1970.

Tacchi Venturi, Pietro. *Opere storiche.* 2 vols. Macerata: Giorgetti, 1911–1913.

Tan Sitong. "Renxue" (*The Natural Science of Love*). In *Tan Sitong quanji* (Collected Works of Tan Sitong), compiled by Cai Shangsi and Fang Xing. Reprint, Beijing: Xinhua Shudian, 1954.

Thévenot, Melchisédec. *Relations de divers voyages curieux.* 4 vols. Paris, 1696.

Trigault, Nicolá, and Matteo Ricci. *De Christiana expeditione apud Sinas ab Societate Iesu Suscepta, es Matthaei Ricci commentarus libri.* Augsburg, 1615.

——. *Histoire de l'expédition chrétienne au royaume de la Chine.* Lille: Pierre de Hache, 1617.

——. *Histoire de l'expédition chrétienne au royaume de la Chine.* Paris: Desclée de Brouwer, 1978.

Voltaire, François. *Dictionnaire philosophique portatif.* Amsterdam: M. M. Rey, 1765.

——. *Essai sur les moeurs et l'esprit des nations et sur les principaux faits de l'histoire depuis Charlemagne jusqu'a Louis XIII.* Lausanne: J. H. Pott, 1780.

Wang Chong. *Lunheng* (Doctrines Evaluated). In *ZZJC,* vol. 6, pt. 5. Reprint, Beijing: Zhonghua Shuju, 1990.

Wang Wei. "Sizi lun" (On the Four Masters). In *Wang Zhong wenji. SKQS,* vol. 1226, pp. 68.1–69.1.

——. *Wang Zhong wenji* (Literary Collection of Wang Zhong). In *SKQS,* vol. 1226. Taibei: Shangwu, 1983, pp. 1–514.

——. "Yuan ru" (Origin of ru). In *Wang Zhong wenji. SKQS*, vol. 1226, pp. 84.1–85.2.

Wang Zhong. *Shuxue neipian* (Discourses on Learning, Inner Chapters). Reprint, Taibei: Guangwen Shuju, 1970.

Wicki, Josef, S.J., ed. *Documenta Indica*. Rome: Institutum Historicum S.J., 1970.

Xingli daquan shu (Great Compendium on the Nature and the Principle). Edited by Hu Guang. Reprint, Taibei: Shangwu, 1974.

Xu Changzhi, ed. *Shengchao Poxie ji* (The Sacred Dynasty's Collection Exposing Heresy). Reprint, Hong Kong: Jiandao Shenxue Yuan, 1996.

Xu Guangqi. *Xu Guangqi ji* (Collected Works of Xu Guangqi). Beijing: Zhonghua Shuju, 1963.

Xu Shen. *Shuowen jiezi* (Explanation of Pattern, Elucidation of Graphs). Reprint, Beijing: Zhonghua Shuju, 1963.

Xu Zongze. *Ming-Qing jian Yesu huishi zhu tiyao* (Essentials of the Interpretations of the Christian Scholars of the Ming-Qing Era). Taibei: 1958.

Xunzi jijie (Collected Commentaries on the Xunzi). Edited by Wang Xianqian. In *ZZJC*, vol. 2. Reprint, Beijing: Zhonghua Shuju, 1990.

Yang Chene. *Yang Qiyuan xiansheng nianpu* (The Chronological Biography of Mr. Yang Qiyuan). Shanghai: Shangwu, 1946.

Yuan shi (Yuan History). Reprint, Beijing: Zhonghua Shuju, 1976.

Zhang Binglin. "Bo Zhongguo yong wanguo xinyu shuo" (A Refutation of China's Use of Esperanto). *Minbao* 21 (June 10, 1908): 49–72.

——. "Bo jianli Kongjiao yi" (A Refutation of the Petition to Establish Confucianity). In *Zhang Taiyan quanji*, vol. 4. Shanghai: Renmin Chubanshe, 1985.

——. *Guogu lunheng* (Critical Evaluation of National Heritage). 1910; Reprint, Taibei: Guangwen Shudian, 1967.

——. "Jianlun" (Investigative Essays). In *Zhang Taiyan quanji*, vol. 4. Shanghai: Renmin Chubanshe, 1985.

——. *Qiu shu* (Peremptory Book). Shanghai, 1904. Reprinted in *Zhonghua minguo gushi congliao*, edited by Luo Jialun. Taibei Shijie Shuju, 1963.

——. *Qui shu*. Shanghai, 1900. Reprint, Shanghai: Guji Chubanshe, 1985.

——. "Shibinsaier wenji" (Spencer's Works). *Changyan bao*, no. 1 (May 1898), no. 2 (June 1898), no. 3 (July 1898), no. 4 (August 1898), no. 5 (August 16, 1898), no. 6 (August 26, 1898), no. 8 (September 1898).

——. "Yuan ru" (The Etiology of *ru*). In *Guogu lunheng*, pp. 151–155.

——. *Zhangshi congshu* (The Collectanea of Mr. Zhang). 6 vols. Hangzhou: Zhejiang Tushuguan, 1919.

——. *Zhang Taiyan quanji* (The Collected Works of Zhang Taiyan). 6 vols. Shanghai: Renmin Chubanshe, 1985.

——. *Zhang Taiyan ziding nianpu* (Zhang Taiyan's Chronological Autobiography). Hong Kong: Longmen Shudian, 1965.

Zhang Juzheng. *Sishu zhi jie* (Explanations on the Four Books). *SBBY* edition.

Zhu Xi. *Lunyu jizhu* (Collected Commentary on the Lunyu). In *Sishu jizhu*. Reprint, Taibei: Xuehai Chubanshe, 1984, pp. 55–193.

——. "*Lunyu* xu shuo" (Additional Explanations of the Lunyu). In *Sishu jizhu*. Reprint, Taibei: Xuehai Chubanshe, 1984, pp. 53–54.

——. *Mengzi jizhu* (Collected Commentary on the Mengzi). In *Jishu jizhu*, pp. 197–415.

——. "Renshuo" (Explanation of Humaneness). In *Zhuzi wenji*, vol. 7. Sibu congkan chubian jibu edition. Shanghai: Shangwu Chubanshe, n.d.

——. *Sishu jizhu* (Collected Commentary on the Four Books). Reprint, Taibei: Xuehai Chubanshe, 1984.

——. *Zhuzi yulei* (Classified Conversations of Master Zhu). Taibei: Shangwu, 1936. Reprint, Kyoto: Zhongwen Chubanshe, 1970.

——. *Zhuzi wenji* (Literary Collection of Master Zhu). Sibu congkan chubian jibu edition. Shanghai: Shangwu Chubanshe, n.d.

Zhuangzi jijie (Collected Commentaries on the Zhuangzi). Edited by Wang Xianqian. In *ZZJC*, vol. 3, pt. 3. Reprint, Beijing: Zhonghua Shuju, 1990.

Zhuangzi yinde (Concordance to Zhuangzi). Compiled by Ch'i Ssu-ho [Qi Sihou]. Harvard-Yenching edition, Sinological Index series no. 20. Beijing, 1947.

Secondary Sources and Translations

Adams, Robert M. *The Evolution of Urban Society*. Chicago: University of Chicago Press, 1966.

Ahern, Emily M. *Chinese Ritual and Politics*. Cambridge: Cambridge University Press, 1981.

——. *The Cult of the Dead in a Chinese Village*. Stanford: Stanford University Press, 1973.

Akatsuka Kiyoshi. *Chūgoku kodai no shūkyō to bunka—In ōchō no saishi* (China's Ancient Religion and Culture: The Sacrifices of the Yin Dynasty). Tokyo: Kadokawa shoten, 1977.

Alexander, Jeffrey. *Theoretical Logic in Sociology*. Vol. 3, *The Classical Attempt at Theoretical Synthesis: Max Weber*. Berkeley: University of California Press, 1983.

Alitto, Guy S. *The Last Confucian: Liang Shu-ming and the Chinese Dilemma of Modernity*. Berkeley: University of California Press, 1979.

Allan, Sarah. "Drought, Human Sacrifice, and the Mandate of Heaven in a Lost Text of the *Shang shu*." *Bulletin of the School of African and Oriental Studies* 47, pt. 3 (1984): 523–539.

——. *The Heir and the Sage: Dynastic Legend in Early China*. San Francisco: Chinese Materials Center, 1981.

——. "The Identities of Taigong Wang in Zhou and Han Literature." *Monumenta Serica* 30 (1972–73): 57–99.

——. "Shang Foundations of Modern Chinese Folk Religion." In *Legend, Lore, and Religion in China*, edited by Allan and Cohen, pp. 1–21.

——. *The Shape of the Turtle: Myth, Art, and Cosmos in Early China*. Albany: State University of New York Press, 1991.

——. "Sons of Suns: Myth and Totemism in Early China." *Bulletin of the School of African and Oriental Studies* 44, pt. 2 (1981): 290–326.

Allan, Sarah, and Alvin P. Cohen, eds. *Legend, Lore, and Religion in China*. San Francisco: Chinese Materials Center, 1979.

Anderson, Benedict. *Imagined Communities: Reflections on the Origin and Spread of Nationalism*. Rev. ed. London: Verso Editions, 1990.

Appleton, William W. *A Cycle of Cathay: The Chinese Vogue in England during the Seventeenth and Eighteenth Centuries*. New York: Columbia University Press, 1951.

Ariel, Yoan. *K'ung-ts'ung-tzu [Kongcongzi]: The K'ung [Kong] Family Masters' Anthology, A Study and Translation of Chapters 1–10, 12–14*. Princeton: Princeton University Press, 1989.

Atwell, William. "Notes on Silver, Foreign Trade, and the Late Ming Economy." *Ch'ing-shih wen-t'i (Qingshi wenti)* (December 1977): 1–33.

Auerbach, Erich. *Mimesis: The Representation of Reality in Western Literature*. Translated by Willard R. Trask. Princeton: Princeton University Press, 1953.

Ayers, William. *Chang Chih-tung [Zhang Zhidong] and Educational Reform in China*. Cambridge, Mass.: Harvard University Press, 1971.

Bakhtin, Mikhail. "Discourse in the Novel." In *The Dialogic Imagination*, edited by Michael Holquist, pp. 259–331.

——. [V. N. Volosinov]. *Marxism and the Philosophy of Language*. New York: Seminar Press, 1973.

——. *Problems of Dostoevsky's Poetics*. Ann Arbor, Mich.: Ardis, 1973.

——. *Rabelais and His World*. Translated by Hélène Iswolsky. Cambridge, Mass.: MIT Press, 1968.

Balazs, Étienne. *Chinese Civilization and Bureaucracy: Variations on a Theme*. Translated by H. M. Wright. New Haven: Yale University Press, 1964.

——. *Political Theory and Administrative Reality in Traditional China*. London: University of London, 1965.

Barnard, Noel. "The Nature of the Ch'in 'Reform of the Script' as Reflected in Archaeological Documents Excavated under Conditions of Control." In *Ancient China*, edited by Roy and Tsien, pp. 181–214.

Bate, W. Jackson. *The Burden of the Past and the English Poet*. Cambridge, Mass.: Harvard University Press, 1970.

Bates, Don, ed. *Knowledge and the Scholarly Medical Traditions*. Cambridge: Cambridge University Press, 1994.

Bateson, Gregory. *Mind and Nature: A Necessary Unity*. New York: Bantam Books, 1980.

Baudet, Henry. *Paradise on Earth: Some Thoughts on European Images of Non-European Man*. New Haven: Yale University Press, 1965.

Bauer, Wolfgang. *China and the Search for Happiness: Recurring Themes in Four Thousand Years of Chinese Cultural History*. Translated by Michael Shaw. New York: Seabury Press, 1976.

Baxter, William. *Handbook of Old Chinese Phonology*. The Hague: Mouton, 1992.

——. "Middle Chinese: A Study in Historical Phonology, A Review." *Harvard Journal of Asiatic Studies* 47 (December 1987): 635–656.

——. "The *Shijing*: A Zhou Text in Han Clothing." Unpublished paper, University of Michigan, Ann Arbor, 1986.

Baynes, Kenneth, James Bohman, and Thomas McCarthy, eds. *After Philosophy: End or Transformation?* Cambridge, Mass.: MIT Press, 1987.

Beasley, W. G., and E. G. Pulleyblank, eds. *Historians of China and Japan*. London: Oxford University Press, 1961.

Beck, B. J. Mansvelt. "The True Emperor of China." In *Leyden Studies in Sinology*, edited by Idema, pp. 23–33.

Bellah, Robert N. *Beyond Belief: Essays on Religion in a Post-Traditional World*. New York: Harper and Row, 1976.

——. "Religious Evolution." In Bellah, *Beyond Belief*, pp. 29–36.

Benjamin, Walter. *Illuminations*. Translated by Hannah Arendt. New York: Schocken Books, 1969.

——. *Reflections*. Translated by Harry Zohn. New York: Harcourt Brace and Jovanovich, 1979.

Bennett, Adrian Arthur. *John Fryer: The Introduction of Western Science and Technology into Nineteenth-Century China*. Cambridge, Mass.: Harvard University Press, 1967.

Bennett, Tony. *Formalism and Marxism*. London: Methuen, 1979.

Benveniste, Émile. *Problems in General Linguistics*. Translated by Mary Elizabeth Meek. Coral Gables, Fl.: University of Miami Press, 1971.

Berling, Judith. *The Syncretic Religion of Lin Chao-en [Lin Zhao'en]*. New York: Columbia University Press, 1980.

Bernal, Martin. *Chinese Socialism to 1907*. Ithaca: Cornell University Press, 1976.

——. "Liu Shih-p'ei [Liu Shipei] and National Essence." In *The Limits of Change*, edited by Furth, pp. 90–112.

——. "The Triumph of Anarchism over Marxism, 1906–1907." In *China in Revolution*, edited by Wright, pp. 96–142.

Bernard, Henri. *Le Père Mathieu Ricci et la société chinoise de son temps (1552–1610)*. 2 vols. Reprint, Tianjin: Hautes Études, 1937.

Bernstein, Richard. *Beyond Objectivism and Relativism*. Philadelphia: University of Pennsylvania Press, 1983.

Bettray, Johannes, S.V.D. *Die Akkommodationsmethode des P. Matteo Ricci S.I. in China*. Analecta Gregoriane, vol. LXXVI. Rome: Aedes Universitatis Gregorianae, 1955.

Blakeley, Barry. "Notes on the Reliability and Objectivity of the Tu Yü [Du Yu] Commentary on the Tso Chuan [Zuo zhuan]." *Journal of the American Oriental Society* 101 (1981): 207–212.

Bloom, Harold. *The Anxiety of Influence: A Theory of Poetry*. New York: Oxford University Press, 1973.

——. "The Breaking of Form." In *Humanities in Review*, edited by Dworkin et al., vol. 1, pp. 127–156.

——. *Ruin the Sacred Truths: Poetry and Belief from the Bible to the Present*. Cambridge, Mass.: Harvard University Press, 1989.

Bloom, Harold, and David Rosenberg. *The Book of J*. New York: Vintage Books, 1991.

Blum, Susan D. "Han and the Chinese Other: The Language of Identity and Difference in Southwest China." Ph.D. diss., University of Michigan, 1994.

——. "Of Motion and Metaphor: The Theme of Kinesis in *Chuang Tzu [Zhuangzi]*." Master's thesis, University of Michigan, 1986.

Blumenberg, Hans. *The Legitimacy of the Modern Age.* Translated by Robert C. Wallace. Cambridge, Mass.: MIT Press, 1983.
——. *Work on Myth.* Translated by Robert C. Wallace. Cambridge, Mass.: MIT Press, 1985.
Bodde, Derk. *Chinese Thought, Society, and Science: The Intellectual and Social Background of Science and Technology in Pre-Modern China.* Honolulu: University of Hawai'i Press, 1991.
——. *Essays on Chinese Civilization.* Edited by Charles LeBlanc and Dorothy Borei. Princeton: Princeton University Press, 1981.
——. *Festivals in Classical China: New Year and Other Annual Observances during the Han Dynasty, 206 B.C.–A.D. 220.* Princeton: Princeton University Press, 1975.
Bol, Peter Kees. "Seeking Common Ground: Han Literati under Jurchen Rule." *Harvard Journal of Asiatic Studies* 47, no. 2 (December 1987): 461–538.
——. *"This Culture of Ours": Intellectual Transitions in T'ang [Tang] and Sung [Song] China.* Stanford: Stanford University Press, 1992.
Boltz, William G. "Early Chinese Writing." *World Archaeology* 17, no. 3 (February 1986): 420–436.
——. "Kung Kung [Gong Gong] and the Flood: Reverse Euhemerism in the Yao Tien [Yao Dian]." *T'oung Pao* 67 (1981): 141–153.
Boodberg, Peter A. "The Semasiology of Some Primary Confucian Concepts." In *Selected Works of Peter A. Boodberg,* edited by Cohen.
Boorman, Howard, and Richard C. Howard, eds. *Biographical Dictionary of Republican China.* 4 vols. New York: Columbia University Press, 1967–71.
Borthwick, Sally. *Education and Social Change in China: The Beginnings of the Modern Era.* Stanford: Hoover Institution Press, 1983.
Bourdieu, Pierre. *The Logic of Practice.* Translated by Richard Nice. Stanford, Calif.: Stanford University Press, 1990.
——. *Outline of a Theory of Practice.* Translated by Richard Nice. Cambridge: Cambridge University Press, 1977.
Braga, J. M. "The Panegyric of Alexander Valignano, S.J." *Monumenta Nipponica* 5, no. 2 (1942): 523–535.
Braudel, Fernand. *The Mediterranean and the Mediterranean World in the Age of Phillip II.* Vol. 1. Translated by Sian Reynolds. New York: Harper and Row, 1972.
Brodsky, Joseph A. "The Misquoted Verse: A Baccalaureate Sermon." *Williams Alumni Review* (summer 1984): 12–14.
Brokaw, Cynthia. "Yüan Huang [Yuan Huang] (1533–1606) and the Ledgers of Merit and Demerit." *Harvard Journal of Asiatic Studies* 47, no. 1 (June 1987): 137–195.
Brooks, E. Bruce, and A. Taeko Brooks. *The Original Analects: Sayings of Confucius and His Successors, 0479–0249.* New York: Columbia University Press, 1997.
Brown, Peter. *The Cult of the Saints: Its Rise and Function in Late Christianity.* Chicago: University of Chicago Press, 1981.
——. *The Making of Late Antiquity.* Cambridge, Mass.: Harvard University Press, 1978.
——. *Religion and Society in the Age of St. Augustine.* London: Faber and Faber, 1972.
——. "The Saint as Exemplar in Late Antiquity." *Representations* 2 (spring 1983): 1–25.

——. *Society and the Holy in Late Antiquity*. Berkeley: University of California Press, 1982.

Burger, Thomas. *Max Weber's Theory of Concept Formation: History, Laws, and Ideal Types*. Durham, N.C.: Duke University Press, 1976.

Burke, Kenneth. *A Grammar of Motives*. Berkeley: University of California Press, 1969.

——. *The Rhetoric of Religion: Studies in Logology*. Berkeley: University of California Press, 1960.

Busch, Heinrich. "The Tung-lin Shu-yüan [Donglin shuyuan] and Its Political and Social Significance." *Monumenta Serica* 14 (1949–1955): 1–163.

Cahill, James. *The Compelling Image: Nature and Style in Seventeenth-Century Chinese Painting*. Cambridge, Mass.: Harvard University Press, 1982.

Calasso, Roberto. *The Marriage of Cadmus and Harmony*. Translated by Tim Parks. New York: Knopf, 1993.

Cameron, Meribeth E. *The Reform Movement in China, 1898–1912*. Stanford: Stanford University Press, 1931.

Cameron, Nigel. *Barbarians and Mandarins: Thirteen Centuries of Western Travelers in China*. New York: Weatherhill, 1970.

Certeau, Michel de. *The Writing of History*. Translated by Tom Conley. New York: Columbia University Press, 1988.

Cervantes, Fernando. *The Devil in the New World: The Impact of Diabolism in New Spain*. New Haven: Yale University Press, 1994.

Chan, Albert, S.J., "Michele Ruggieri, S.J. (1543–1607) and His Chinese Poems," *Monumenta Serica* 41 (1993): 129–176.

Chan, Hok-lam, and Wm. Theodore de Bary, eds. *Yüan [Yuan] Thought: Chinese Religion and Thought under the Mongols*. New York: Columbia University Press, 1982.

Chan, Wing-tsit. *Religious Trends in Modern China*. New York: Octagon Books, 1978.

——. *A Sourcebook in Chinese Philosophy*. Princeton: Princeton University Press, 1969.

——, ed. *Chu Hsi [Zhu Xi] and Neo-Confucianism*. Honolulu: University of Hawai'i Press, 1986.

Chang, Carsun [Zhang Junmai]. *The Development of Neo-Confucian Thought*. 2 vols. New York: Bookman Associates, 1957.

Chang Hao [Zhang Hao]. *Chinese Intellectuals in Crisis: Search for Order and Meaning (1890–1911)*. Berkeley: University of California Press, 1987.

——. *Liang Ch'i-Ch'ao [Liang Qichao] and Intellectual Transition in China, 1890–1907*. Cambridge, Mass.: Harvard University Press, 1971.

Chang, Kwang-Chih [Zhang Guangzhi]. *Art, Myth, and Ritual: The Path to Political Authority in Ancient China*. Cambridge, Mass.: Harvard University Press, 1983.

——. "On the Character *Shang* in the Shang Dynasty." *Early China* 20 (1995): 69–77.

——. *Shang Civilization*. New Haven: Yale University Press, 1980.

——. "Yin-hsü Tomb Number Five and the Question of the P'an Keng/Hsiao Hsin/Hsiao Yi Period in Yin-hsü Archaeology." In *Studies of Shang Archaeology*, edited by Chang, pp. 72–79.

——, ed. *Studies of Shang Archaeology: Selected Papers from the International Conference on Shang Civilization.* New Haven: Yale University Press, 1986.

Chang P'eng-yüan [Zhang Pengyuan]. "The Constitutionalists." In *China in Revolution,* edited by Wright, pp. 143–183.

Chaunu, Pierre. "Manille et Macao, face à la conjoncture des XVI et XVII siècles." *Annales: Économies, sociétés, civilisations* 17:555–580.

Chavannes, Édouard, trans. *Les Mémoires historiques de Se-ma Ts'ien.* 5 vols. Paris, 1895–1905. Reprinted in 6 vols., Paris: Librairie d'Amérique et d'Orient, 1967.

Chen, Edward K. Y. *Hypergrowth in Asian Economies: A Comparative Study of Hong Kong, Japan, Korea, Singapore, and Taiwan.* New York: Macmillan, 1979.

Chen Mengjia. "Shangdai de shenhua yu wushu" (Shang Era Spirits and Sorcery). *Yanjing xuebao* 20 (1936): 485–576.

Chen Shouyi. "Sanbainian qian de jianli Kongjiao lun" (Three Hundred Years before the Establishment of Confucianity). *Zhongyang yanjiuyuan lishi yuyan yanjiusuo jikan,* 6, no. 2 (1936): 136–162.

Chen Xiaolin and Su Xiaogang. *He shang* (Deathsong of a River). Reprint, Taibei: Jingeng Chubanshe, 1990.

Chen Zhengyan. "Ping jinren dui ru zhi qiyuan de tuice" (A Critical Assessment of Contemporary People's Theories on the Origin of *ru*). *Shixue huikan,* no. 6 (1975): 111–117.

Ch'en, Kenneth. "A Possible Source for Ricci's Notices on Regions near China." *T'oung Pao* 34 (1938): 179–190.

Cheng, Anne. *Étude sur le confucianisme Han: L'élaboration d'une tradition exégétique sur les classiques.* Paris: Institut des Hautes Études Chinoises, 1985.

Ch'ien, Edward. *Chiao Hung [Jiao Hong] and the Restructuring of Neo-Confucianism in the Late Ming.* New York: Columbia University Press, 1985.

Ch'ien Mu [Qian Mu]. "A Historical Perspective on Chu Hsi's [Zhu Xi's] Learning." In *Chu Hsi and Neo-Confucianism,* edited by Chan, pp. 32–42.

Chirgwin, A. M. "The Chinese Renaissance and Its Significance." *Contemporary Review* 125 (January 1924).

Chou Min-chih [Zhou Minzhi]. *Hu Shih [Hu Shi] and Intellectual Choice in Modern China.* Ann Arbor: University of Michigan Press, 1984.

Chow, Tse-tsung [Zhou Zezong]. "Ancient Chinese Views on Literature, the *Tao [Dao],* and Their Relationship." *Chinese Literature: Essays, Articles, Reviews* 1, no. 1 (January 1979): 3–29.

——. *The May 4th Movement: Intellectual Revolution in Modern China.* Stanford: Stanford University Press, 1960.

——, ed. *Wen-lin [Wenlin]: Studies in the Chinese Humanities.* Madison: University of Wisconsin Press, 1968.

Christian, William A., Jr. *Apparitions in Late Medieval and Renaissance Spain.* Princeton: Princeton University Press, 1981.

Clastres, Pierre. *Archeology of Violence.* Translated by Jeanine Herman. New York: Semiotext(e), 1994.

——. *Society against the State: Essays in Political Anthropology.* Translated by Robert Hurley. New York: Zone Books, 1987.

Clifford, James. "On Ethnographic Allegory." In *Writing Culture*, edited by Clifford and Marcus, pp. 98–121.

——. "On Ethnographic Authority." *Representations* 2 (spring 1983): 118–146.

——. "On Ethnographic Surrealism." *Comparative Studies in Society and History* 23 (1981): 539–564.

——. *The Predicament of Culture: Twentieth-Century Ethnography, Literature, and Art.* Cambridge, Mass.: Harvard University Press, 1988.

Clifford, James, and George E. Marcus, eds. *Writing Culture: The Poetics and Politics of Ethnography.* Berkeley: University of California Press, 1986.

Cohen, Alvin P., ed. *Selected Works of Peter A. Boodberg.* Berkeley: University of California Press, 1979.

Cohen, I. Bernard. *Revolution in Science.* Cambridge, Mass.: Belknap Press of Harvard University Press, 1985.

Cohen, Paul A. *Between Tradition and Modernity: Wang T'ao [Wang Tao] and Reform in Late Ch'ing [Qing] China.* Cambridge, Mass.: Harvard University Press, 1974.

——. *Discovering History in China: American Historical Writing on the Recent Chinese Past.* New York: Columbia University Press, 1984.

Cohen, Paul A., and John E. Schrecker, eds. *Reform in Nineteenth Century China.* Cambridge, Mass.: Harvard University Press, 1976.

Cooper, Arthur. "The Creation of the Chinese Script." *Occasional Papers of the China Society*, no. 20. London: China Society, 1978.

Coulanges, Fustel de. *The Ancient City: A Study on the Religion, Laws, and Institutions of Greece and Rome.* Translated by Willard Small. Boston: Lee and Shepard, 1901.

Couvreur, F. S. *Dictionnaire classique de la langue chinoise.* Paris, 1890. Reprint, Taibei: Book World, 1966.

Creel, Herrlee G. *Confucius and the Chinese Way.* New York: Harper and Row, 1960.

——. *Confucius, the Man and the Myth.* New York: John Day, 1949.

——. *Literary Chinese by the Inductive Method.* Vol. 2. Chicago: University of Chicago Press, 1939.

——. *The Origins of Statecraft in China.* Vol. 1. Chicago: University of Chicago Press, 1970.

——. *What Is Taoism? And Other Studies in Chinese Cultural History.* Chicago: University of Chicago Press, 1986.

Crump, James I. *Chan-kuo Ts'e [Zhan'guo ce].* London: Oxford University Press, 1970.

——. *Intrigues: Studies of the Chan-kuo Ts'e [Zhan'guo ce].* Ann Arbor: University of Michigan Press, 1964.

Dai Junren. "Ru de laiyuan tuice" (A Theory of the Origin of *ru*). *Dalu zazhi* 37, no. 10 (1968): 1–5.

Dai Zhen. *Mengzi ziyi shuzheng* (Evidential Commentary on Meanings of Terms in the Mengzi). Reprint, Taibei: Shijie Shuju, 1974.

——. *Dai Zhen wenji* (Literary Collection of Dai Zhen). Hong Kong: Zhonghua Shuju, 1974.

——. *Yuan shan* (The Origins of Goodness). Taibei: Shijie Shuju, 1974.

Dardess, John. *Confucianism and Autocracy: Professional Elites in the Founding of the Ming Dynasty.* Berkeley: University of California Press, 1983.

Davis, Edward L. "Arms and the Tao: Hero Cult and Empire in Traditional China." *Sodaishi kenkyūkai kenkyū hokoku* 2 (1985): 1–56.

——. "Society and the Supernatural in Sung [Song] China." Ph.D. diss., University of California, Berkeley, 1994.

Dawson, Raymond. *Confucius.* New York: Hill and Wang, 1982.

Dean, Kenneth. *Taoist Ritual and Popular Cults of Southeast China.* Princeton: Princeton University Press, 1993.

De Bary, Wm. Theodore. *East Asia: A Dialogue in Three Stages.* Cambridge, Mass.: Harvard University Press, 1986.

——. *Learning for One's Self: Essays on the Individual in Neo-Confucian Thought.* New York: Columbia University Press, 1991.

——. *The Liberal Tradition in China.* New York: Columbia University Press, 1983.

——. *The Message of the Mind in Neo-Confucianism.* New York: Columbia University Press, 1989.

——. *Neo-Confucian Orthodoxy and the Learning of the Mind-and-Heart.* New York: Columbia University Press, 1981.

——. "A Reappraisal of Neo-Confucianism." In *Studies in Chinese Thought,* edited by Wright, pp. 81–111.

——. *Self and Society in Ming Thought.* New York: Columbia University Press, 1970.

——. "Some Common Tendencies in Neo-Confucianism." In *Confucianism in Action,* edited by Nivison and Wright, pp. 25–49.

——. *The Trouble with Confucianism.* Cambridge, Mass.: Harvard University Press, 1991.

——. *The Unfolding of Neo-Confucianism.* New York: Columbia University Press, 1970.

De Bary, Wm. Theodore, and John W. Chaffee, eds. *Neo-Confucian Education: The Formative Stage.* Berkeley: University of California Press, 1989.

De Bary, Wm. Theodore, Chan Wing-tsit, and Chester Tan, eds. *Sources of Chinese Tradition.* 2 vols. New York: Columbia University Press, 1960.

Deeney, John J., ed. *Chinese-Western Comparative Literature: Theory and Strategy.* Hong Kong: Hong Kong University Press, 1980.

DeFrancis, John. *Visible Speech: The Diverse Oneness of Writing Systems.* Honolulu: University of Hawai'i Press, 1989.

D'Elia, Pasquale M., S.J. *Il Mappamondo Cinese del P. Matteo Ricci S.I. (Terza Edizione, Pechino, 1602) Conservato presso la Biblioteca Vaticana.* Rome: Vatican, 1938.

De Man, Paul. *Allegories of Reading: Figural Language in Rousseau, Nietzsche, Rilke, and Proust.* New Haven: Yale University Press, 1979.

Demiéville, Paul. "Chang Hsüeh-ch'eng [Zhang Xuecheng] and His Historiography." In *Historians of China and Japan,* edited by Beasley and Pulleyblank, pp. 167–185.

——. "La Pénétration du Bouddhisme dans la tradition philosophique chinoise." *Cahiers d'histoire mondiale* 3 (1956–1957).

Derrida, Jacques. *Of Grammatology.* Translated by Gayatri Chakravorty Spivak. Baltimore: Johns Hopkins University Press, 1976.

——. "Structure, Sign, and Play in the Discourse of the Human Sciences." In *Writing and Difference*, pp. 278–293.

——. *Writing and Difference.* Translated by Alan Bass. Chicago: University of Chicago Press, 1979.

DeWoskin, Kenneth J. *Doctors, Diviners, and Magicians of Ancient China: Biographies of Fang-shih [Fangshi].* New York: Columbia University Press, 1983.

——. "Music in the Han Court: The Challenge of Entertainment to Ideology." Unpublished manuscript.

Dikötter, Frank. *The Discourse of Race in Modern China.* London: Hurst, 1992.

Dobson, W. A. C. H. *Early Archaic Chinese.* Toronto: University of Toronto Press, 1962.

——. *The Language of the Book of Songs.* Toronto: University of Toronto Press, 1968.

——. *Late Archaic Chinese.* Toronto: University of Toronto Press, 1959.

——. "Linguistic Evidence and the Dating of the *Book of Songs*." *T'oung Pao* 51 (1964): 322–334.

——. "Some Legal Instruments of Ancient China: The *Ming* and the *Meng*." In *Wen-lin,* ed. Chow, pp. 269–282.

——, trans. *Mencius.* Toronto: University of Toronto Press, 1903.

Doré, Henri. *Recherches sur les superstitions en Chine.* 14 vols. Shanghai: Imprimerie de la Mission catholique, 1918.

Douglas, Mary. *Purity and Danger: An Analysis of the Concepts of Pollution and Taboo.* London: Routledge and Kegan Paul, 1966.

Duara, Prasenjit. *Rescuing History from the Nation: Questioning Narratives of Modern China* (Chicago: University of Chicago Press, 1995).

Dubs, Homer H. "An Ancient Chinese Mystery Cult." *Harvard Theological Review* 35 (October 1942): 221–240.

——. *Hsüntze [Xunzi], Moulder of Ancient Confucianism.* London: Arthur Probstbain, 1927.

——. "The Political Career of Confucius." *Journal of the American Oriental Society* 66: 273–282.

——. "The Victory of Han Confucianism." In *History of the Former Han Dynasty,* trans. Dubs, pp. 341–353.

——, trans. *The History of the Former Han Dynasty.* 3 vols. Baltimore: Waverly Press, 1938–1955.

Ducrot, Oswald, and Tzvetan Todorov. *Encyclopedic Dictionary of the Sciences of Language.* Translated by Catherine Porter. Baltimore: Johns Hopkins University Press, 1979.

Dull, Jack L. "A Historical Introduction to the Apocryphal (*ch'an-wei [chanwei]*) Texts of the Han Dynasty." Ph.D. diss., University of Washington, 1966.

——. "The Legitimation of Ch'in [Qin]." Paper presented at the Conference on Legitimation of Chinese Regimes. Asilomar, Monterey, Calif., June 15–24, 1975.

Dumont, Jean-Paul. *The Headman and I: Ambiguity and Ambivalence in the Field-working Experience.* Austin: University of Texas Press, 1978.

Dunne, George H., S.J. *Generation of Giants: The Story of the Jesuits in China in the Last Decades of the Ming Dynasty.* Notre Dame, Ind.: University of Notre Dame Press, 1966.

Durkheim, Émile. *Elementary Forms of the Religious Life.* Translated by Joseph Ward Swain. New York: Free Press, 1915.

Duyvendak, J. J. L. "Review of Pasquale d'Elia, *Le Origini Dell'Arte Christiana Cinese (1583–1640)."* *T'oung Pao* 35 (1940): 394–398.

Dworkin, Ronald, Karl Miller, and Richard Sennett, eds. *Humanities in Review.* Vol. 1. New York: Cambridge University Press, 1982.

Eagleton, Terry. *Walter Benjamin; or, Towards a Revolutionary Criticism.* London: Verso Editions, 1981.

Eastman, Arthur M., Alexander W. Allison, Herbert Barrows, Caesar R. Blake, Arthur J. Carr, and Hubert M. English, eds. *The Norton Anthology of Poetry.* New York: Norton, 1970.

Eastman, Lloyd. "Political Reformism in China before the Sino-Japanese War." *Journal of Asian Studies* 27, no. 4 (August 1968): 695–710.

Eber, Irene. "Hu Shih [Hu Shi] and Chinese History: The Problem of *cheng-li kuo-ku* [*zhengli guogu*]." *Monumenta Serica* 27 (1968): 169–207.

——. "Thoughts on Renaissance in Modern China: Problems of Definition." In *Studia Asiatica,* edited by Thompson, pp. 189–218.

——, ed. *Confucianism: The Dynamics of Tradition.* New York: Free Press, 1984.

Eberhard, Wolfram. *Conquerors and Rulers: Social Forces in Medieval China.* 2d rev. ed. Leiden: E. J. Brill, 1970.

——. *A Dictionary of Chinese Symbols.* London: Routledge and Kegan Paul, 1986.

——. *Local Cultures of South and East China.* Leiden: E. J. Brill, 1968.

——. "The Political Function of Astronomy and Astronomers in Han China." In *Chinese Thought and Institutions,* edited by Fairbank, pp. 33–70.

——. *Settlement and Social Change in Asia.* Hong Kong: Hong Kong University Press, 1967.

Ebrey, Patricia. "Women, Marriage, and the Family in Chinese History." In *Heritage of China,* edited by Ropp, pp. 197–223.

Ebrey, Patricia, and James L. Watson, eds. *Kinship Organization in Late Imperial China 1000–1940.* Berkeley: University of California Press, 1986.

Eco, Umberto. *The Search for the Perfect Language.* Translated by James Fentress. Oxford: Blackwell, 1995.

——. *A Theory of Semiotics.* Bloomington: University of Indiana Press, 1969.

Egan, Ronald C. "Narratives in *Tso Chuan* [*Zuo zhuan*]." *Harvard Journal of Asiatic Studies* 37 (1977): 323–352.

Eisenstadt, S. N., ed. *The Origins and Diversity of Axial Age Civilizations.* Albany: State University of New York Press, 1986.

Eisenstadt, S. N., and S. R. Graubard, eds. *Intellectuals and Tradition.* New York: Humanities Press, 1973.

Elman, Benjamin A. *Classicism, Politics, and Kinship: The Ch'ang-chou [Changzhou] School of New Text Confucianism in Late Imperial China.* Berkeley: University of California Press, 1990.

——. *From Philosophy to Philology: Intellectual and Social Aspects of Change in Late Imperial China.* Cambridge, Mass.: Council on East Asian Studies, Harvard University, 1984.

Elvin, Mark. "The Collapse of Scriptural Confucianism." *Papers on Far Eastern History* 41 (March 1990): 45–76.

——. *The Pattern of the Chinese Past.* Stanford: Stanford University Press, 1973.

Emmet, Dorothy, and Alasdair MacIntyre, eds. *Sociological Theory and Philosophical Analysis.* New York: Macmillan, 1970.

Eno, Robert. *The Confucian Creation of Heaven: Philosophy and the Defense of Ritual Mastery.* Albany: State University of New York Press, 1990.

Eoyang, Eugene. "The Maladjusted Messenger: *Rezeptionsästhetik* in Translation." *Chinese Literature: Essays, Articles, Reviews* 10 (1988): 61–75.

Etiemble. *Confucius (Maitre K'ong [Kong]).* Paris: Éditions Gallimard, 1986.

——. *Les Jesuites en Chine: La Querrelle des rites (1552–1773).* Paris: René Julliard, 1966.

Ewell, John. "Reinventing the Way: Dai Zhen's Evidential Commentary on the *Mengzi Ziyi Shu Zheng.*" Ph.D. diss., University of California, Berkeley, 1990.

Fabian, Johannes. *Time and the Other: How Anthropology Makes Its Object.* New York: Columbia University Press, 1983.

Fairbank, John King. *Chinabound: A Fifty-Year Memoir.* New York: Harper and Row, 1982.

——, ed. *Chinese Thought and Institutions.* Chicago: University of Chicago Press, 1957.

——, ed. *The Cambridge History of China.* Vols. 10, 12. Cambridge: Cambridge University Press, 1978, 1983.

Fairbank, John King, and Kwang-ching Liu, eds. *The Cambridge History of China.* Vol. 11. Cambridge: Cambridge University Press, 1980.

Falk, Marcia. *The Song of Songs: A New Translation and Interpretation.* San Francisco: Harper Collins, 1990.

Fang Shouchu. *Moxue yuanliu* (Origins of Mo Learning). Taibei: Zhonghua Shuju, 1957.

Febvre, Lucien. *The Problem of Unbelief in the Sixteenth Century: The Religion of Rabelais.* Translated by Beatrice Gottlieb, Cambridge, Mass.: Belknap Press of Harvard University Press, 1982.

Febvre, Lucien, and Henri-Jean Martin. *The Coming of the Book: The Impact of Printing, 1450–1800.* London: New Left Books, 1976.

Fehl, Noah. *Rites and Propriety in Literature and Life: A Perspective for a Cultural History of Ancient China.* Hong Kong: Hong Kong University Press, 1971.

Feigon, Lee. *Chen Duxiu: Founder of the Chinese Communist Party.* Princeton: Princeton University Press, 1983.

Feng Youlan. "Yuan Ru-Mo" (The Origins of *Ru* and *Mo*). In *Zhongguo zhexue shi bu.* Shanghai: Shangwu, 1936.

——. *Zhongguo zhexue shi* (A History of Chinese Philosophy). Beijing: Taipingyang Tushu Gongsi, 1968.

——. *Zhongguo zhexue shi bu* (A Revised History of Chinese Philosophy). Shanghai: Shangwu, 1936.

Fenollosa, Ernest. *The Chinese Character as a Medium for Poetry.* 1938. Reprint, San Francisco: City Lights Books, n.d.

Fernandez, James. *Persuasions and Performances: The Play of Tropes in Culture.* Bloomington: Indiana University Press, 1986.

Fingarette, Herbert. *Confucius: The Secular as Sacred.* New York: Harper Torchbooks, 1972.

———. "The Problem of the Self in the Analects." *Philosophy East and West* 29 (April 1979): 129–140.

Fogel, Joshua. *Politics and Sinology: The Case of Naitō Konan.* Cambridge, Mass.: Council on East Asian Studies, Harvard University, 1984.

Fogel, Joshua, and William T. Rowe, eds. *Perspectives on a Changing China: Essays in Honor of Professor C. Martin Wilbur on the Occasion of His Retirement.* Boulder, Colo.: Westview Press, 1979.

Forke, Alfred H., trans. *Lun Heng [Lunheng]: Miscellaneous Essays of Wang Ch'ung [Wang Chong].* 2 vols. Berlin, 1907–1911. Reprint, 2 vols. in 1. New York: Paragon Book Gallery, 1962.

Foucault, Michel. *The Archaeology of Knowledge.* New York: Colophon Books, Harper and Row, 1972.

———. "The Discourse on Language." In Foucault, *The Archaeology of Knowledge,* pp. 215–237.

———. "Nietzsche, Genealogy, History." In *The Foucault Reader,* edited by Rabinow, pp. 78–100.

———. *The Order of Things: Introduction to the Archeology of the Human Sciences.* New York: Vintage Books, 1970.

Franke, Wolfgang. "Der Ursprung der Ju [Ru] and Ihre Beziehung zu Konfuzius und Lau-dsi." *Sinica* (special edition) 1 (1935): 141–171; 2 (1936): 1–42.

———. *An Introduction to the Sources of Ming History.* Kuala Lumpur: University of Malaya Press, 1968.

———. *Reform and Abolition of the Traditional Chinese Examination System.* Cambridge, Mass.: Harvard University Press, 1960.

Frei, Hans W. *The Eclipse of Biblical Narrative: A Study in Eighteenth and Nineteenth Century Hermeneutics.* New Haven: Yale University Press, 1974.

Freud, Sigmund. "The Family Romance." In *The Freud Reader,* edited by Gay, pp. 297–300.

Fried, Morton. "Clans and Lineages: How to Tell Them Apart and Why—With Special Reference to Chinese Society." *Bulletin of the Institute of Ethnology, Academia Sinica* 29: 11–36.

Frye, Northrop. *The Great Code: The Bible and Literature.* San Diego: Harcourt Brace Jovanovich, 1983.

———. *The Stubborn Structure: Essays on Criticism and Society.* Ithaca: Cornell University Press, 1970.

Fu Sinian. "Zhan'guo zixia xulun" (Further Discussions on Warring States Knights-Errant). In *Zhongguo shanggu shilun wenxuan ji,* vol. 2, edited by Du Zhengsheng.

Fung Yu-lan [Feng Youlan]. *A History of Chinese Philosophy.* 2 vols. Translated by Derk Bodde. Princeton: Princeton University Press, 1952.

———. *The Spirit of Chinese Philosophy.* Translated by E. R. Hughes. London: Kegan Paul, French, Tubner, 1947.

Furth, Charlotte. "Intellectual Change from the Reform Movement to the May Fourth Movement, 1895–1920." In *The Cambridge History of China*, edited by Fairbank, vol. 12, pt. 1, pp. 354–364.

——. "The Sage as Rebel: The Inner World of Chang Ping-lin." In *The Limits of Change*, edited by Furth, pp. 113–150.

——. *Ting Wen-chiang [Ding Wenjiang]: Science and China's New Culture*. Cambridge, Mass.: Harvard University Press, 1970.

——, ed. *The Limits of Change: Essays on Conservative Alternatives in Republican China*. Cambridge, Mass.: Harvard University Press, 1976.

Gadamer, Hans-Georg. "Foreword to the Second German Edition of *Truth and Method*." In *After Philosophy*, edited by Baynes, pp. 339–350.

——. "Hermeneutics as Practical Philosophy." In *After Philosophy: End or Transformation?* edited by Baynes et al., pp. 324–338.

——. *Reason in the Age of Science*. Translated by Frederick G. Laurence. Cambridge, Mass.: MIT Press, 1981.

——. *Truth and Method*. Translated by Garret Barden and William G. Doerpel. New York: Seabury Press, 1975.

Gale, Esson M., trans. *Discourses on Salt and Iron: A Debate on State Control of Commerce and Industry in Ancient China*. Chaps. 1–19. Leiden: E. J. Brill, 1931.

Gale, Esson M., Peter A. Boodberg, and T. C. Lin, trans. *Discourses on Salt and Iron* (Yen T'ieh Lun: chaps. 20–28). *Journal of the North China Branch of the Royal Asiatic Society* 65 (1934): 73–110.

Gay, Peter, ed. *The Freud Reader*. New York: Norton, 1989.

Garrett, Mary. "Chinese Responses to the Jesuits' Argumentation during the late Ming–early Ch'ing [Qing]." Paper presented at the International Society for the History of Rhetoric, Göttingen, Germany, June 1989.

Gasster, Michael. *Chinese Intellectuals and the Revolution of 1911: The Birth of Modern Chinese Radicalism*. Seattle: University of Washington Press, 1969.

Geertz, Clifford. "Deep Play: Notes on the Balinese Cockfight." *Daedalus* 101 (1972): 1–37.

——. *The Interpretation of Cultures*. New York: Basic Books, 1973.

——. *Local Knowledge: Further Essays in Interpretive Anthropology*. New York: Basic Books, 1983.

——. *Negara: The Theatre State in Nineteenth-Century Bali*. Princeton: Princeton University Press, 1980.

——. "The Uses of Diversity." *Michigan Quarterly Review* (winter 1986): 105–123.

——. *Works and Lives: The Anthropologist as Author*. Stanford: Stanford University Press, 1988.

Gellner, Ernest. *Cause and Meaning in the Social Sciences*. London: Routledge and Kegan Paul, 1971.

——. *Plough, Sword, and Book: The Structure of Human History*. Chicago: University of Chicago Press, 1988.

Gernet, Jacques. *China and the Christian Impact*. Translated by Janet Lloyd. Cambridge: Cambridge University Press, 1985.

Giesey, Ralph E. *The Royal Funeral Ceremony in Renaissance France.* Geneva: E. Droz, 1960.

Gilbert, Rodney. *What's Wrong with China.* London: John Murray, 1926.

Giles, Herbert A. *Chinese Biographical Dictionary.* Shanghai: Kelly and Walsh, 1898.

——. *A Glossary of Reference on Subjects Connected with the Far East.* London: Curzon Books, 1878.

Goffman, Irving. *Frame Analysis.* New York: Harper and Row, 1974.

Goodrich, I. Carrington, and Chaoying Fang, eds. *Dictionary of Ming Biography, 1368–1644.* 2 vols. New York: Columbia University Press, 1976.

Graham, A. C. *Chuang-tzu [Zhuangzi]: The Inner Chapters.* London: George, Allen and Unwin, 1981.

——. *Disputers of the Tao [Dao]: Philosophical Argument in Ancient China.* LaSalle, Ill.: Open Court, 1989.

——. *Later Mohist Logic, Ethics, and Science.* Hong Kong: Chinese University Press, 1978.

——. "The *Nung-Chia [Nongjia]* 'School of the Tillers' and the Origins of Peasant Utopianism in China." *Bulletin of the School of Oriental and African Studies* 42, no. 1 (1979): 66–100.

Granet, Marcel. *Chinese Civilization.* Translated by Kathleen E. Innes and Mabel Brailsford. Cleveland, Ohio: Meridian Books, 1958.

——. *Danses et légendes de la Chine ancienne.* 2 vols. Paris: Presses Universitaires de France, 1959.

——. *Festivals and Songs of Ancient China.* Translated by E. D. Edwards. New York: E. P. Dutton, 1932.

——. *La Pensée chinoise.* Paris: Albin Michel, 1968.

——. *The Religion of the Chinese People.* Translated by Maurice Freedman. New York: Harper and Row, 1977.

——. "Right and Left in China." In *Right and Left,* edited by Needham, pp. 53–56.

Greenblatt, Stephen. *Marvelous Possessions: The Wonder of the New World.* Chicago: University of Chicago Press, 1991.

Grieder, Jerome. *Hu Shih [Hu Shi] and the Chinese Renaissance: Liberalism in the Chinese Revolution, 1917–1937.* Cambridge, Mass.: Harvard University Press, 1970.

——. *Intellectuals and the State in Modern China.* New York: Free Press, 1981.

Groot, J. J. M. de. *Sectarianism and Religious Persecution in China.* Reprint (2 vols. in 1), Taipei: Chengwen, 1970.

Guy, R. Kent. "The *National Essence Journal* and the Eighteenth Century." Paper presented at the Association of Asian Studies meeting, San Francisco, April 1983.

Hall, David L., and Roger T. Ames. *Thinking through Confucius.* Albany: State University of New York Press, 1987.

Hall, John W. *Japan: From Prehistory to Modern Times.* New York: Dell, 1970.

Hallyn, Fernand. *The Poetic Structure of the World: Copernicus and Kepler.* Translated by Donald M. Leslie. New York: Zone Books, 1990.

Hansen, Chad. *Language and Logic in Ancient China.* Ann Arbor: University of Michigan Press, 1983.

Hansen, Valerie. *Changing Gods in Medieval China, 1127–1276*. Princeton: Princeton University Press, 1990.

Harbsmeier, Christoph. "Confucius Ridens: Humor in the Analects." *Harvard Journal of Asiatic Studies* 50, no. 1 (June 1990): 131–162.

Harootunian, H. D. "The Consciousness of Archaic Form in the New Realism of Kokugaku." In *Japanese Thought in the Tokugawa Period*, edited by Najita and Scheiner, pp. 63–104.

——. *Things Seen and Unseen: Discourse and Ideology in Tokugawa Nativism*. Chicago: University of Chicago Press, 1988.

Harper, Donald. "A Chinese Demonography of the Third Century B.C." *Harvard Journal of Asiatic Studies* 45, no. 2 (Dec. 1985): 459–498.

——. "The *Wu Shih Erh Ping Fang [Wushi'er bingfang]*: Translation and Prolegomena." Ph.D. diss., University of California, Berkeley, 1982.

Harrell, Stevan. "Ethnicity, Local Interests and the State: Yi Communities in Southwest China." *Comparative Studies in Society and History* 32, no. 3 (July 1990): 515–548.

Hartley, L. P. *The Go-Between*. London: Hamish Hamilton, 1953.

Harvey, David. *The Condition of Postmodernism*. Oxford: Basil Blackwell, 1989.

Hatch, George C., Jr. "The Thought of Su Hsun (1009–1072): An Essay on the Social Meaning of Intellectual Pluralism in Northern Sung." Ph.D. diss., University of Washington, 1972.

——. "Virtue and Custom in Classical Antiquity." Paper presented at the Conference on Political Thought at the University of Toronto, Toronto, April 1–3, 1977.

Havelock, Eric A. *The Muse Learns to Write: Reflections on Orality and Literacy from Antiquity to the Present*. New Haven: Yale University Press, 1986.

Hawkes, David, trans. *The Songs of the South: An Anthology of Ancient Chinese Poems by Qu Yuan and Other Poets*. London: Penguin Books, 1985.

Haydon, A. Eustace. Foreword to *The Chinese Renaissance*, by Hu Shi.

Hegel, Robert E. *The Novel in Seventeenth-Century China*. New York: Columbia University Press, 1981.

Heller, Thomas C., Morton Sosna, and David Wellbrey, eds. *Reconstructing Individualism: Autonomy, Individuality, and the Self in Western Thought*. Stanford: Stanford University Press, 1986.

Henderson, John B. *The Development and Decline of Chinese Cosmology*. New York: Columbia University Press, 1984.

——. *Scripture, Canon, and Commentary: A Comparison of Confucian and Western Exegesis*. Princeton: Princeton University Press, 1991.

Henry, Eric. "The Motif of Recognition in Early China." *Harvard Journal of Asiatic Studies* 47, no. 1 (June 1987): 5–30.

Herbert, Edward. *A Confucian Notebook*. New York: Grove Press, 1960.

Herforth, Derek. "From Annals via Homiletics to Analysis: Toward a Discourse-Based Typology of Early Chinese Historiography." Paper presented at the Seventy-fifth Meeting of the Speech Communication Association, San Francisco, Calif., November 19, 1989.

Hevia, James L. *Cherishing Men from Afar: Qing Guest Ritual and the Macartney Embassy of 1793.* Durham, N.C.: Duke University Press, 1995.

———. "A Multitude of Lords: Qing Court Ritual and the Macartney Embassy of 1793." *Late Imperial China* 10, no. 2 (December 1989): 72–105.

Heyndrickx, Jerome, ed. *Philippe Couplet S. J. (1623–1693): The Man Who Brought China to Europe.* Monumenta Serica Monograph Series, vol. 22. Nettetal: Steyler, Verlag, 1990.

Hightower, James Robert, trans. *Han Shih Wai Chuan [Hanshi waizhuan]: Han Ying's Illustrations of the Didactic Application of the "Classic of Songs."* Cambridge, Mass.: Harvard University Press, 1952.

Hill, Christopher. *Some Intellectual Consequences of the English Revolution.* Madison: University of Wisconsin Press, 1980.

Hobsbawm, E. J. *Nations and Nationalism since 1780: Programme, Myth, Reality.* 2d ed. Cambridge: Cambridge University Press, 1992.

Hobsbawm, Eric, and Terrence Ranger, eds. *The Invention of Tradition.* Cambridge: Cambridge University Press, 1983.

Holquist, Michael, ed. *The Dialogic Imagination: Four Essays by M. M. Bakhtin.* Translated by Caryl Emerson and Michael Holquist. Austin: University of Texas Press, 1981.

Holzman, Donald. "Confucius and Ancient Chinese Literary Criticism." In *Chinese Approaches to Literature from Confucius to Liang Ch'i-ch'ao,* edited by Rickett, pp. 21–41.

———. "The Conversational Tradition in Chinese Philosophy. *Philosophy East and West* 6, no. 3 (1956–57): 223–230.

Homer and Jethro. *Homer and Jethro's "Cornfucius Say" Joke Book: A Collection of Corn-temporary Wit'n Wisdom.* Battle Creek, Mich.: Kellogg's Company, 1964.

Hou Wailu. *Zhongguo sixiang tongshi* (A Comprehensive History of Chinese Thought). 5 vols. Beijing: Renmin Chubanshe, 1957.

Howard, Roy J. *Three Faces of Hermeneutics: An Introduction to Current Theories of Understanding.* Berkeley: University of California Press, 1982.

Hsiao Kung-ch'üan [Xiao Gongquan]. *A Modern China and a New World: Kang Yu-Wei [Kang Youwei], Reformer and Utopian 1858–1927.* Seattle: University of Washington Press, 1975.

———. *Zhongguo zhengshi sixiang shi* (A History of Chinese Political Thought). 6 vols. Taibei: Zhonghua Shuju, 1954.

Hsü Cho-yun [Xu Zhuoyun]. *Ancient China in Transition: An Analysis of Social Mobility, 722–222 B.C.* Stanford: Stanford University Press, 1965.

Hsü Cho-yun [Xu Zhuoyun] and Katheryn M. Linduff. *Western Chou [Zhou] Civilization.* New Haven: Yale University Press, 1988.

Hsü Daulin [Xu Daolin]. "The Myth of the 'Five Human Relations' of Confucius." *Monumenta Serica* 29 (1970–71): 27–37.

Huang, Ray. *1587, A Year of No Significance: The Ming Dynasty in Decline.* New Haven: Yale University Press, 1981.

Hucker, Charles O. *A Dictionary of Official Titles in Imperial China.* Stanford: Stanford University Press, 1985.

Hughes, E. R. *The Invasion of China by the Western World*. London: Adam and Charles Black, 1937.

Hughes, Robert. *The Shock of the New*. New York: Knopf, 1981.

Hume, David. *The Natural History of Religion*. Stanford: Stanford University Press, 1957.

Hummel, Arthur W. *The Autobiography of a Chinese Historian*. Leiden: E. J. Brill, 1931.

——, ed. *Eminent Chinese of the Ch'ing [Qing] Period (1644–1912)*. 2 vols. Washington, D.C.: U.S. Government Printing Office, 1943–1944.

Huters, Theodore. "From Writing to Literature: The Development of Late Qing Theories of Prose." *Harvard Journal of Asiatic Studies* 47, no. 1 (June 1987): 51–96.

Hymes, Robert. "Lu Chiu-yüan [Lu Jiuyuan], Academies, and the Problem of Local Community." In *Neo-Confucian Education*, edited by de Bary and Chaffee, pp. 439–446.

——. *Statesmen and Gentlemen: The Elite of Fu-chou, Chiang-hsi [Fuzhou, Jiangxi], in Northern and Southern Sung [Song]*. Cambridge: Cambridge University Press, 1986.

Idema, W. L., ed. *Leyden Studies in Sinology*. Papers presented at the Conference held in Celebration of the Fiftieth Anniversary of the Sinological Institute of Leyden University, December 8–12, 1980. Leiden: E. J. Brill, 1981.

Idema, W. L., and E. Zürcher, eds. *Thought and Law in Qin and Han China: Studies Dedicated to Anthony Hulsewé on the Occasion of His Eightieth Birthday*. Leiden: E. J. Brill, 1990.

Jameson, Fredric. *Postmodernism, or, The Cultural Logic of Late Capitalism*. Durham, N.C.: Duke University Press, 1991.

——. *The Prison-House of Language: A Critical Account of Structuralism and Russian Formalism*. Princeton: Princeton University Press, 1972.

Jansen, Marius. "Japan and the Chinese Revolution of 1911." In *The Cambridge History of China*, edited by Fairbank, vol. 11, pp. 343–374.

Jaspers, Karl. *Vom Ursprung und Ziel der Geschichte*. Zurich: Artemis Verlag, 1949. Translated by Michael Bullock as *The Origin and Goal of History*, New Haven: Yale University Press, 1953.

Jensen, Lionel M. "The Genesis of *ru*: Ambiguity, Tradition, and Fellowship in Ancient China." Unpublished manuscript, 1987.

——. "The Invention of 'Confucius' and His Chinese Other, 'Kong Fuzi.' " In *positions: east asia cultures critique* 1, no. 2 (fall 1993): 414–449.

——. "Manufacturing 'Confucianism': Chinese and Western Imaginings in the Making of a Tradition." Ph.D. diss., University of California, Berkeley, 1992.

——. "Popular Cults and Confucian Paideia in Medieval China." Paper presented at the Symposium on Chinese Religion and Society (750–1300), University of Illinois, Champaign-Urbana, November 19, 1988.

——. "Wise Man of the Wilds: Fatherlessness, Fertility, and the Mythic Exemplar, Kongzi." *Early China* 20 (1995): 407–437.

——. "Zhu Xi's *daoxue* and the Rhetoric of Redemption." Paper prepared for "Topics in Chinese Rhetoric," a panel sponsored by the International Society for the History of Rhetoric, American Chapter, at the Seventy-fifth Meeting of the Speech Communication Association, San Francisco, November 19, 1989.

Jiang Yong. *Xiangdang tukao* (Evidential Chart of the Village Community). Fusu tang, 1756.

Johnson, Chalmers. *MITI and the Japanese Miracle: The Growth in Industrial Policy, 1925–1975*. Stanford: Stanford University Press, 1982.

Johnson, David. "The City-God Cults of T'ang and Sung China." *Harvard Journal of Asiatic Studies* 45, no. 2 (Dec. 1985): 363–457.

Johnson, David, Andrew J. Nathan, and Evelyn Rawski, eds. *Popular Culture in Late Imperial China*. Berkeley: University of California Press, 1984.

Jordan, David, and Daniel L. Overmyer. *The Flying Phoenix: Aspects of Chinese Sectarianism in Taiwan*. Princeton: Princeton University Press, 1986.

Kang Youwei. *Kongzi Gaizhi Kao* (Researches on Kongzi, the Reformer). Reprint, Beijing: Zhonghua Shuju, 1958.

Kangxi zidian (Kangxi Dictionary). Reprint, Hong Kong: Huachao cidian Chubanshe, n.d.

Kao, George. *The Translation of Things Past: Chinese History and Historiography*. Hong Kong: Chinese University Press, 1982.

Kapp, Robert A., ed. *Four Views of China*, Rice University Studies 59, no. 4 (1973).

Karlgren, Bernhard. *An Analytic Dictionary of Chinese and Sino-Japanese*. Paris: Paul Guenther, 1923.

——. "The Book of Documents." *Bulletin of the Museum of Far Eastern Antiquities* 22 (1950): 1–81.

——. *The Book of Odes*. Stockholm: Museum of Far Eastern Antiquities, 1950.

——. "The Early History of the *Chou Li* [*Zhou li*] and *Tso Chuan* [*Zho zhuan*] Texts." *Bulletin of the Museum of Far Eastern Antiquities* 3 (1931): 1–60.

——. *Grammata Serica Recensa*. Stockholm: Museum of Far Eastern Antiquities, 1972.

——. "Legends and Cults in Ancient China." *Bulletin of the Museum of Far Eastern Antiquities* 18 (1946): 199–365.

——. *On the Authenticity and Nature of the Tso Chuan [Zuo zhuan]*. Göteborg: Elandres Boktryckeri Aktiebolag, 1926.

——. *Philology and Ancient China*. Oslo, 1926. Reprint, Philadelphia: Porcupine Press, 1980.

Keeler, Ward. *Javanese Shadow Plays, Javanese Selves*. Princeton: Princeton University Press, 1987.

Keightley, David N. "Archaeology and Mentality: The Making of China." *Representations* 18 (spring 1987): 91–128.

——. "Dead but Not Gone: Cultural Implications of Mortuary Practice in Neolithic and Bronze Age China, ca. 8000 to 1000 B.C." Paper presented at the Conference on Ritual and Social Significance of Death in Chinese Society, Oracle, Arizona, January 1974.

——. "Early Civilization in China: Reflections on How It Became Chinese." In *Heritage of China*, edited by Ropp, pp. 15–54.

——. "Kingship and Kinship: The Royal Lineages of the Late Shang." Paper presented at the International Conference on Shang Civilization, East-West Center, University of Hawai'i at Manoa, Honolulu, September 7–11, 1982.

——. "Legitimation in Shang China." Unpublished manuscript. 1975.

——. "The Religious Commitment: Shang Theology and the Genesis of Chinese Political Culture." *History of Religions* 17 (1978): 211–235.

——. *Sources of Shang History: The Oracle Bone Inscriptions of Bronze Age China.* Berkeley: University of California Press, 1978.

——, ed. *The Origins of Chinese Civilization.* Berkeley: University of California Press, 1983.

Kelley, Donald R. *Foundations of Modern Historical Scholarship: Language, Law, and History in the French Renaissance.* New York: Columbia University Press, 1970.

Kemp, Anthony. *The Estrangement of the Past: A Study in the Origin of Modern Historical Consciousness.* New York: Oxford University Press, 1991.

Kierman, Frank A., Jr. *Ssu-ma Ch'ien's [Sima Qian's] Historiographical Attitude as Reflected in Four Late Warring States Biographies.* Wiesbaden: Otto Harrassowitz, 1962.

Kimura Eiichi. *Kōshi to Rongo* (Kongzi and the Lunyu). Tokyo: Sobunsha, 1971.

Kitamura Sawakichi. *Jūgaku gairon* (A General Outline of Ru Learning). Tokyo: Kan shoin, 1928.

Knoblock, John. *Xunzi: A Translation and Study of the Complete Works.* Vols. 1–3. Stanford: Stanford University Press, 1988–1992.

Knoespel, Kenneth J. "Milton and the Hermeneutics of Time: Seventeenth-Century Chronologies and the Science of History." *Studies in the Literary Imagination,* no. 22 (1989): 17–35.

Knowlton, Edgar C. "Words of Chinese, Japanese, and Korean Origin in the Romance Languages." Ph.D. diss., Stanford University, 1959.

Kong Dema and Ke Lan. *In the Mansion of Confucius' Descendants.* Beijing: New World Press, 1984.

Kramers, Robert Paul. *K'ung Tzu Chia Yü [Kongzi jiayu]: The School Sayings of Confucius.* Leiden: E. J. Brill, 1949.

Kuhn, Philip. "Local Self-Government under the Republic: Problems of Control, Autonomy, and Mobilization." In *Conflict and Control in Late Imperial China,* edited by Wakeman and Grant, pp. 270–273.

Kuhn, Thomas S. *The Structure of Scientific Revolutions.* Chicago: University of Chicago Press, 1962.

Kuper, Adam. *The Invention of Primitive Society: Transformations of an Illusion.* London: Routledge, 1988.

Kwok, Daniel. *Scientism in Chinese Thought, 1900–1950.* New Haven: Yale University Press, 1965.

Kwong, Luke S. K. *A Mosaic of the Hundred Days: Personalities, Politics, and Ideas of 1898.* Cambridge, Mass.: Harvard University Press, 1984.

Lach, Donald F. *Asia in the Making of Euope.* 2 vols. Chicago: University of Chicago Press, 1977.

Lach, Donald F., and Edwin J. Van Kley. *Asia in the Making of Europe.* Vol. 3, bks. 1–4. Chicago: University of Chicago Press, 1993.

Lancashire, Douglas, and Peter Hu Kuo-chen, trans. *The True Meaning of the Lord of Heaven.* St. Louis, Mo.: Institute of Jesuit Sources, 1985.

Lau, D. C., trans. *Confucius: The Analects.* Reprint, New York: Penguin Classics, 1982.

———, trans. *Mencius.* New York: Penguin Classics, 1970.

Le Blanc, Charles, and Susan Blader, eds. *Chinese Ideas about Nature and Society: Studies in Honor of Derk Bodde.* Hong Kong: Hong Kong University Press, 1987.

Lee, Thomas H. C., ed. *China and Europe: Images and Influences in the Sixteenth to Eighteenth Centuries.* Hong Kong: Chinese University Press, 1991.

Legge, James. *The Chinese Classics.* 5 vols. Reprint. Hong Kong: Hong Kong University Press, 1971.

———, trans. *Li Chi, Book of Rites.* 2 vols. New Hyde Park, N.Y.: University Press, 1967.

Leslie, Donald D. "Notes on the Analects." *T'oung Pao* 49 (1961–62): 1–27.

Leslie, Donald D., Colin Mackerras, and Wang Gungwu, eds. *Essays on the Sources for Chinese History.* Columbia: University of South Carolina Press, 1975.

Levenson, Joseph R. "The Abortiveness of Empiricism in Early Qing Thought." In *Confucian China and Its Modern Fate,* vol. 1, pp. 3–14.

———. *Confucian China and Its Modern Fate: A Trilogy.* 3 vols. Berkeley: University of California Press, 1968.

———. "The Genesis of *Confucian China and Its Modern Fate.*" In *The Historian's Workshop: Original Essays by Sixteen Historians,* edited by L. P. Curtis Jr., pp. 270–291. New York: Alfred A. Knopf, 1970.

———. " 'History' and 'Value': Tensions of Intellectual Choice in Modern China." In *Studies in Chinese Thought,* edited by Wright, pp. 146–194.

———. *Liang Ch'i-Ch'ao [Liang Qichao] and the Mind of Modern China.* Berkeley: University of California Press, 1967.

———. *Revolution and Cosmopolitanism: The Western Stage and the Chinese Stages.* Berkeley: University of California Press, 1971.

Lévi-Strauss, Claude. *The Savage Mind.* Chicago: University of Chicago Press, 1963.

Lewis, I. M. *Ecstatic Religion: Anthropological Study of Spirit-Possession and Shamanism.* Harmondsworth, England: Penguin, 1971.

Lewis, Mark Edward. *Sanctioned Violence in Early China.* Albany: State University of New York Press, 1990.

Leys, Simon, trans. *The Analects of Confucius.* New York: Norton, 1997.

Li Xueqin. *Eastern Zhou and Qin Civilizations.* New Haven: Yale University Press, 1985.

Li Zhi. *Xu Fenshu* (Another Book to Be Burned). Beijing: Zhonghua Shuju, 1975.

Liang Ch'i-ch'ao [Liang Qichao]. *Intellectual Trends in the Ch'ing [Qing] Period.* Translated by Immanuel C. Y. Hsü. Cambridge, Mass.: Harvard University Press, 1958.

Liang Jiamian, ed. *Xu Guangqi nianpu* (Chronological Biography of Xu Guangqi). Shanghai: Guji Chubanshe, 1981.

Liang Shiqiu. *Zuixin shiyong Han-Ying cidian* (A Contemporary Practical Chinese-English Dictionary). Taibei: Yuandong tushu gongsi, 1971.

Liang Shuming. *Dong-Xi wenhua ji qi zhexue* (Eastern and Western Cultures and Their Philosophies). Reprint, Taibei: Hongxiao Shudian, 1968.

Lin Mousheng. *Men and Ideas: An Informal History of Chinese Political Thought.* New York: John Day, 1942.

Lin Yü-Sheng [Lin Yusheng]. *The Crisis of Chinese Consciousness: Radical Antitraditionalism in the May Fourth Era.* Madison: University of Wisconsin Press, 1979.

Lindblom, Charles. *Politics and Markets.* New York: Basic Books, 1979.

Lindquist, Cecilia. *China: Empire of Living Symbols.* Translated by Joan Tate. Reading, Mass.: Addison Wesley, 1991.

Liu James J. Y. *Language—Paradox—Poetics: A Chinese Perspective.* Princeton: Princeton University Press, 1988.

Liu, Kwang-Ching, ed. *Orthodoxy in Late Imperial China.* Berkeley: University of California Press, 1990.

——. "Socioethics as Orthodoxy: A Perspective." In *Orthodoxy in Late Imperial China,* edited by Liu, pp. 53–100.

Liu Shu-hsien [Liu Shuxian]. *Zhuzi de lixue* (Master Zhu's Learning of Principle). Taibei: Xuesheng Shuju, 1985.

Liu Ts'un-yen [Liu Cunyan]. *Selected Papers from the Hall of Harmonious Wind.* Leiden: E. J. Brill, 1976.

Lo Guang [Stanislaus], ed. *Jinian Li Madou lai Hua sibai zhounian Zhong-Xi wenhua jiaoliu guoji xueshu hui yi lunwen ji* (International Symposium on Chinese-Western Cultural Interchange in Commemoration of the 400th Anniversary of the Arrival of Matteo Ricci S.J.) Taibei: Furen daxue Chubanshe, 1983.

Loewe, Michael. *Divination, Mythology, and Monarchy in Han China.* Cambridge: Cambridge University Press, 1994.

——. *Ways to Paradise: The Chinese Quest for Immortality.* London: George Allen and Unwin, 1979.

Louie, Kam. *Critiques of Confucius in Contemporary China.* New York: St. Martin's Press, 1980.

Lubac, Henri de. *La Rencontre du bouddhisme et de l'Occident.* Paris: Aubier, 1952.

Lundbaek, Knud. "The First Translation from a Confucian Classic in Europe." *China Mission Studies Bulletin* 1 (1979): 2–11.

——. "The Image of Neo-Confucianism in *Confucius Sinarum Philosophus.*" *Journal of the History of Ideas* 44 (1983): 19–30.

——. "Imaginary Ancient Chinese Characters." *China Mission Studies Bulletin* 5 (1983): 5–23.

——. "Notes sur l'image du néo-confucianisme dans la littérature européenne du XIIIe siècle." *Actes du IIIe colloque international de Sinologie de Chantilly.* Paris, 1983.

Lyotard, Jean François. *The Postmodern Condition: A Report on Knowledge.* Translated by Geoff Bennington and Brian Massumi. Minneapolis: University of Minnesota Press, 1984.

MacCormack, Sabine. *Religion in the Andes: Vision and Imagination in Early Colonial Peru.* Princeton: Princeton University Press, 1991.

McGrane, Bernard. *Beyond Anthropology: Society and the Other.* New York: Columbia University Press, 1989.

Macherey, Pierre. *Pour une théorie de la production littéraire.* Paris: Maspero, 1966.

Translated by Geoffrey Wall as *A Theory of Literary Production.* London: Routledge and Kegan Paul, 1978.

MacIntyre, Alasdair. *After Virtue: A Study in Moral Theory.* 2d ed. with postscript. Notre Dame, Ind.: University of Notre Dame Press, 1984.

Mackerras, Colin. *Western Images of China.* Oxford: Oxford University Press, 1989.

McMullen, David. *State and Scholars in T'ang China.* Cambridge: Cambridge University Press, 1988.

Mair, Victor. "Old Sinitic *MyAG, Old Persian MAGUS, and English 'Magician.'" *Early China* 15 (1990): 27–47.

——. *T'ang Transmission Texts.* Philadelphia: University of Pennsylvania Press, 1989.

——, trans. *Tao Te Ching: The Classic Book of Integrity and the Way.* New York: Bantam Books, 1990.

Markley, Robert. *Fallen Languages: Crises of Representation in Newtonian England, 1660–1740.* Ithaca: Cornell University Press, 1993.

Marty, Martin E., and R. Scott Appleby, eds. *Fundamentalisms Observed.* Chicago: University of Chicago Press, 1991.

Maruyama Masao. *Nihon seiji shisōshi kenkyū.* Tokyo: Tokyo Daigaku shuppan, 1952. Translated by Mikiso Hane as *Studies in the Intellectual History of Tokugawa Japan,* Princeton: Princeton University Press, 1974.

Maso, Mori. "The Gentry in the Ming—an Outline of the Relations between the *Shih-ta-fu [Shidafu]* and Local Society." *Acta Asiatica* 38:31–53.

Maspero, Henri. *China in Antiquity.* Translated by Frank A. Kierman Jr. Amherst: University of Massachusetts Press, 1978.

——. *La Chine antique.* Paris: Presses Universitaires de France, 1965.

——. "Légendes mythologiques dans le *Chou King* [Shu jing]." *Journal Asiatique* 204 (January 1924): 11–100.

——. *Taoism and Chinese Religion.* Translated by Frank A. Kierman Jr. Amherst: University of Massachusetts Press, 1981.

Mauss, Marcel. *A General Theory of Magic.* Translated by Robert Brain. New York: Norton, 1972.

——. *The Gift: Forms and Functions of Exchange in Archaic Societies.* Translated by Ian Cunnison. New York: Norton, 1967.

Mayer, Robert. *History and the Early English Novel: Matters of Fact from Bacon to Defoe.* Cambridge: Cambridge University Press, 1997.

Meissner, W. W. *Ignatius of Loyola: The Psychology of a Saint.* New Haven: Yale University Press, 1992.

Meskill, John. *Academies in Ming China: A Historical Essay.* Tucson: University of Arizona Press, 1982.

Metzger, Thomas A. *Escape from Predicament: Neo-Confucianism and China's Evolving Political Culture.* New York: Columbia University Press, 1977.

——. "Some Ancient Roots of Modern Chinese Thought: This-Worldliness, Epistemological Optimism, Doctrinality, and the Emergence of Reflexivity in the Eastern Chou [Zhou]." *Early China* 11: 60–117.

Milton, John. "On the Morning of Christ's Nativity." In *The Norton Anthology of Poetry,* edited by Eastman et al., pp. 299–304. New York: Norton, 1970.

Miyakawa Hisayuki. "An Outline of the Naitō Hypothesis and Its Effects on the Studies of China." *Far Eastern Quarterly* 14 (1955): 533–552.

Miyazaki Ichisada. *China's Examination Hell: The Civil Service Examinations of Imperial China.* Translated by Conrad Shirokauer. New Haven: Yale University Press, 1981.

Morohashi Tetsuji. *Daikanwa jiten* (Great Sino-Japanese Encyclopedic Dictionary). 12 vols. with index. Tokyo: Dai-shukan shoten, 1977.

Mote, F. W. "The Arts and the 'Theorizing Mode' of the Civilization." In *Artists and Traditions: Uses of the Past in Chinese Culture,* edited by Murck, pp. 3–8.

——. *Intellectual Foundations of China.* 2d rev. ed. New York: Knopf, 1987.

——. "A Millennium of Chinese Urban History: Form, Time and Space Concepts in Soochow [Suzhou]." In *Four Views of China,* edited by Kapp, pp. 35–65.

——, trans. *History of Chinese Political Thought.* Vol. 1, *From the Beginnings to the First Century A.D.* Princeton: Princeton University Press, 1979.

Moore, Sally F., and Barbara G. Myerhoff, eds. *Secular Ritual.* Amsterdam: Van Gorcum, 1977.

Mou Zongsan. *Cong Lu Xiangshan dao Liu Jishan* (From Lu Xiangshan to Liu Jishan). Taibei: Xuesheng Shuju, 1979.

——. *Xinti yu xingti* (The Substance of the Mind and the Substance of the Nature). 3 vols. Taibei: Xuesheng Shuju, 1981.

Mueller-Vollmer, Kurt, ed. *The Hermeneutics Reader.* New York: Continuum Books, 1988.

Mungello, David E. "Confucianism in the Enlightenment: Antagonism and Collaboration between the Jesuits and the Philosophes." In *China and Europe,* edited by Lee, pp. 99–127.

——. *Curious Land: Jesuit Accommodationism and the Origins of Sinology.* Honolulu: University of Hawai'i Press, 1989.

——. *The Forgotten Christians of Hangzhou.* Honolulu: University of Hawai'i Press, 1994.

——. "The Jesuits' Use of Chang Chü-cheng's [Zhang Juzheng's] Commentary in Their Translation of the Confucian Four Books (1687)." *China Mission Studies Bulletin* 3 (1981): 12–22.

——. *Leibniz and Confucianism: The Search for Accord.* Honolulu: University of Hawai'i Press, 1977.

——. "The Seventeenth-Century Jesuit Translation Project of the Confucian Four Books." In *East Meets West,* edited by Ronan and Oh, pp. 252–281.

——. "A Study of the Prefaces to Ph. Couplet's Tabula Chronologica Monarchiae Sinicae (1686)." In *Philippe Couplet, S.J. (1623–1693): The Man Who Brought China to Europe,* edited by Heyndrickx, pp. 183–199.

——, ed. *The Chinese Rites Controversy: Its History and Meaning.* Nettetal: Steyler Verlag, 1994.

Munro, Donald J. *The Concept of Man in Early China.* Stanford: Stanford University Press, 1969.

——. *Images of Human Nature: A Sung [Song] Portrait.* Princeton: Princeton University Press, 1988.

——, ed. *Individualism and Holism: Studies in Confucian and Taoist [Daoist] Values.* Ann Arbor: Center for Chinese Studies, University of Michigan, 1985.

Murck, Christian, ed. *Artists and Traditions: Uses of the Past in Chinese Culture.* Princeton: Princeton University Press, 1976.

Naitō Kenkichi. *Naitō Konan zenshu* (Collected Works of Naitō Konan). 14 vols. Tokyo: Chikuma shobō, 1972.

Naitō Torajiro. *Shinaron* (On China). In *Naitō Konan zenshu*, edited by Naitō Kenkichi, vol. 5.

Najita, Tetsuo, and Irwin Scheiner, eds. *Japanese Thought in the Tokugawa Period, 1600–1868: Methods and Metaphors.* Chicago: University of Chicago Press, 1978.

Needham, Joseph. *Science and Civilization in China.* 6 vols. to date. Cambridge: Cambridge University Press, 1955–.

Needham, Rodney, ed. *Right and Left: Essays on Dual Symbolic Classification.* Chicago: University of Chicago Press, 1971.

Nef, John U. *Cultural Foundations of Industrial Civilization.* Chicago: Chicago University Press, 1958.

Newman, Charles. *The Post-modern Aura: The Act of Fiction in an Age of Inflation.* Evanston, Ill.: Northwestern University Press, 1985.

Newman, Cardinal John Henry. *The Arians of the Fourth Century.* Westminster, Md.: Christian Classics, 1968.

Newton, Isaac. *The Chronology of the Ancient Kingdoms Amended.* London, 1728.

Nietzsche, Friedrich. *On the Genealogy of Morals.* Translated by Walter Kaufmann and R. J. Hollingdale. New York: Vintage Books, 1967.

Niranjana, Tejaswini. *Siting Translation: History, Post-Structuralism, and the Colonial Context.* Berkeley: University of California Press, 1992.

Nivison, David S. *The Life and Thought of Chang Hsüeh-ch'eng [Zhang Xuecheng] (1738–1801).* Stanford: Stanford University Press, 1966.

Nivison, David S. and Arthur F. Wright, eds. *Confucianism in Action.* Stanford: Stanford University Press, 1959.

Norman, Jerry. *Chinese.* Cambridge: Cambridge University Press, 1988.

Nussbaum, Martha C. *The Fragility of Goodness: Luck and Ethics in Greek Tragedy and Philosophy.* Cambridge: Cambridge University Press, 1986.

Obenchain, Diane Burdette. "Ministers of the Moral Order: Innovations of the Early Chou [Zhou] Kings, the Duke of Chou [Zhou], Chung-ni [Zhongni], and Ju [Ru]." Ph.D. diss., Harvard University, 1984.

O'Keefe, Daniel. *Stolen Lightning: The Social Theory of Magic.* New York: Vintage Books, 1982.

Onogawa Hidemi. "Liu Shih-p'ei [Liu Shipei] and Anarchism." *Acta Asiatica* 12 (1967): 70–99.

Onogawa Hidemi and Shimada Kenji, eds. *Shingai Kakumei no kenkyū* [Studies on the 1911 Revolution]. Tokyo: Chikuma shobō, 1978.

Ortner, Sherry. "On Key Symbols." *American Anthropologist* 75 (1973): 1338–1346.

Osborn, Carol. *How Would Confucius Ask for a Raise? 100 Enlightened Solutions for Tough Business Problems.* New York: Morrow, 1994.

Overmyer, Daniel L. *Folk Buddhist Religion: Dissenting Sects in Late Traditional China.* Cambridge, Mass.: Harvard University Press, 1976.

Owen, Stephen. *Remembrances: The Experience of the Past in Classical Chinese Literature.* Cambridge, Mass.: Harvard University Press, 1986.

——. *Traditional Chinese Poetry and Poetics: Omen of the World.* Madison: University of Wisconsin Press, 1985.

Palmer, Bryan D. *Descent into Discourse: The Reification of Language and the Writing of Social History.* Philadelphia: Temple University Press, 1990.

Palmer, Richard E. *Hermeneutics: Interpretation Theory in Schleiermacher, Dilthey, Heidegger, and Gadamer.* Evanston, Ill.: Northwestern University Press, 1969.

Pankenier, David W. "The Cosmo-political Background of Heaven's Mandate." In *Early China* 20 (1995): 121–176.

Paper, Jordan D. *The Fu-tzu [Fuzi]: A Post-Han Confucian Text.* Leiden: E. J. Brill, 1987.

Pauthier, M. G. *Confucius et Mencius: Les Quatres Livres de philosophie morale et politique de la Chine.* Paris: Charpentier, 1841.

Pelikan, Jaroslav. *The Vindication of Tradition.* New Haven: Yale University Press, 1984.

Pelliot, Paul. "Le Chou King [Shu jing] en caractères anciens et le Chang Chou Che Wen [Shang Zhou She Wen]." In Academie des inscriptions et belles-lettres, *Mémoires concernant l'Asie Orientale, Inde, Asie Centrale, Extreme-Orient.* Vol. 2 (1916), 123–177.

Pepper, Stephen C. *World Hypotheses: A Study in Evidence.* Berkeley: University of California Press, 1942.

Percy, Walker. *The Message in the Bottle.* New York: Farrar, Straus and Giroux, 1975.

Peterson, William J. "Why Did They Become Christians? Hsü Kuang-ch'i [Xu Guangqi], Li Chih-tsao [Li Zhizao] and Yang T'ing-yun [Yang Tingyun]." In *East Meets West*, edited by Ronan and Oh, pp. 129–152.

Pi Xirui. *Jingxue lishi* (History of Classical Studies). Hong Kong: Zhonghua Shuju, 1961.

Plaskow, Judith. *Standing Again at Sinai: Judaism from a Feminist Perspective.* New York: Harper and Row, 1990.

Pocock, J. G. A. *Politics, Language, and Time: Essays on Political Thought and History.* New York: Atheneum, 1973.

Polachek, James. "Gentry Hegemony: Soochow [Suzhou] in the T'ung-chih [Tongzhi] Restoration. "In *Conflict and Control in Late Imperial China*, edited by Wakeman and Grant, pp. 211–256.

Polo, Marco. *The Travels.* Translated by Ronald Latham. New York: Penguin Books, 1958.

Pound, Ezra, trans. *Confucius: The Unwobbling Pivot, The Great Digest, and The Analects.* New York: New Directions, 1969.

Pusey, James Reeve. *China and Charles Darwin.* Cambridge, Mass.: Harvard University Press, 1983.

Rabinow, Paul. *Reflections on Fieldwork in Morocco.* Berkeley: University of California Press, Quantum Editions, 1977.

———, ed. *The Foucault Reader*. New York: Pantheon, 1984.

Rabinow, Paul, and William M. Sullivan, eds. *Interpretive Social Science: A Reader.* Berkeley: University of California Press, 1978.

Rafael, Vicente L. *Contracting Colonialism: Translation and Christian Conversion in Tagalog Society under Early Spanish Rule.* Ithaca: Cornell University Press, 1988.

Rank, Otto. *The Myth of the Birth of the Hero and Other Writings.* Translated by F. Robbins and Smith Ely Jelliffe. New York: Vintage Books, 1964.

Rankin, Mary. *Early Chinese Revolutionaries: Radical Intellectuals in Shanghai and Chekiang, 1902–1911.* Cambridge, Mass.: Harvard University Press, 1971.

Rappaport, Roy A. "Sanctity and Lies in Evolution." In *Ecology, Meaning, and Religion*, pp. 223–246. Berkeley, Calif.: North Atlantic Books, 1979.

Rawlinson, John. *China's Struggle for Naval Development: 1839–1895.* Cambridge, Mass.: Harvard University Press, 1967.

Rawski, Evelyn Sakakida. *Education and Popular Literacy in Ch'ing [Qing] China.* Ann Arbor: University of Michigan Press, 1979.

Rawson, Jessica. *Ancient China: Art and Archaeology.* New York: Harper and Row, 1980.

Reischauer, Robert. *Early Japanese History*. Vol. 1. Princeton: Princeton University Press, 1937.

Rickett, Adele Austin, ed. *Chinese Approaches to Literature from Confucius to Liang Ch'i-Ch'ao [Liang Qichao].* Princeton: Princeton University Press, 1978.

Rickett, Allyn W. *Guanzi: Political, Economic, and Philosophical Essays from Early China.* Princeton: Princeton University Press, 1985.

Ricoeur, Paul. *Freud and Philosophy: An Essay on Interpretation.* New Haven: Yale University Press, 1971.

———. "The Model of the Text: Meaningful Action Considered as a Text." In *Interpretive Social Science: A Reader*, edited by Rabinow and Sullivan, pp. 73–101.

———. *Time and Narrative.* Vol. 1. Chicago: University of Chicago Press, 1984.

Riegel, Jeffrey. "The Four 'Tzu Ssu' [Zisi] Chapters of the *Li Chi* [*Li ji*]: An Analysis and Translation of the Fang Chi [Fang ji], Chung Yung [Zhong yong], Piao Chi [Biao ji], and Tzu I [Zi yi]." Ph.D. diss., Stanford University, 1978.

———. "Poetry and the Legend of Confucius's Exile." *Journal of the American Oriental Society* 106, no. 1 (1986): 13–22.

Rienstra, M. Howard, trans. *Jesuit Letters from China, 1583–1584.* Minneapolis: University of Minnesota Press, 1986.

Ronan, Charles E., S.J., and Bonnie B. C. Oh, eds. *East Meets West: The Jesuits in China, 1582–1773.* Chicago: Loyola University Press, 1988.

Ropp, Paul S., ed. *Heritage of China: Contemporary Perspectives on Chinese Civilization.* Berkeley: University of California Press, 1990.

Rorty, Richard. *Consequences of Pragmatism.* Minneapolis: University of Minnesota Press, 1983.

———. *Contingency, Irony, Solidarity.* Cambridge: Cambridge University Press, 1989.

———. *Philosophy and the Mirror of Nature.* Princeton: Princeton University Press, 1979.

Rouget, Gilbert. *Music and Trance: A Theory of the Relations between Music and Possession.* Chicago: University of Chicago Press, 1985.

Roy, David T., and Tsuen-hsuin Tsien, eds. *Ancient China: Studies in Early Civilization.* Hong Kong: Chinese University Press, 1978.

Ruan Yuan. *Chouren zhuan* (Biographies of Mathematical Astronomers). Shanghai: Shangwu, 1955.

Ruggieri, Michele. *Archivum Romanum Societatis Jesu.* Jap. Sin. 101, II.

Rule, Paul A. "The Confucian Interpretation of the Jesuits." *Papers on Far Eastern History* 6 (September 1972): 1–61.

———. *K'ung-tzu [Kongzi] or Confucius? The Jesuit Interpretation of Confucianism.* Sydney: Allen and Unwin Australia, 1986.

Ryckmans, Pierre, trans. *Les Entretiens de Confucius.* Paris: Gallimard, 1985.

Sahlins, Marshall. *Historical Metaphors and Mythical Realities: Structure in the Early History of the Sandwich Islands Kingdom.* Ann Arbor: University of Michigan Press, 1981.

———. *Islands of History.* Chicago: University of Chicago Press, 1985.

Said, Edward W. *Beginnings: Intention and Method.* Baltimore: Johns Hopkins University Press, 1975.

———. *Culture and Imperialism.* New York: Knopf, 1993.

———. *Orientalism.* New York: Pantheon Books, 1978.

Sardo, Eugenio Lo. "The Earliest European Atlas of Ming China: An Unpublished Work by Michele Ruggieri." *Actes du VIe colloque International de Sinologie.* Paris, 1994.

Sangren, P. Steven. *History and Magical Power in a Chinese Community.* Stanford: Stanford University Press, 1987.

Saussure, Ferdinand de. *Cours de linguistique générale.* Paris: Payot, 1972.

Savage, William. "In the Tradition of Kings: The Gentleman in the *Analects* of Confucius." Ph.D. diss., University of Michigan, 1984.

Schafer, Edward. *The Divine Woman: Dragon Ladies and Rain Maidens.* San Francisco: North Point Press, 1980.

———. "Ritual Exposure in Ancient China." *Harvard Journal of Asiatic Studies* 14 (1951): 130–184.

Schama, Simon. *Landscape and Memory.* New York: Knopf, 1995.

Schipper, Kristofer. "Vernacular and Classical Ritual in Taoism." *Journal of Asian Studies* 45, no. 1 (November 1985): 21–57.

Schluchter, Wolfgang. *The Rise of Western Rationalism: Max Weber's Developmental History.* Berkeley: University of California Press, 1981.

Schneider, Lawrence A. *Ku Chieh-kang [Gu Jiegang] and China's New History: Nationalism and the Quest for Alternative Traditions.* Berkeley: University of California Press, 1971.

———. *A Madman of Ch'u [Chu]: The Chinese Myth of Loyalty and Dissent.* Berkeley: University of California Press, 1980.

———. "National Essence and the New Intelligentsia." In *The Limits of Change,* edited by Furth, pp. 57–89.

Schopen, Gregory. "Filial Piety and the Monk in the Practice of Indian Buddhism: A Question of 'Sinicization' Viewed from the Other Side." *T'oung Pao* 70 (1984): 110–126.

Schuessler, Axel. *A Dictionary of Early Zhou Chinese.* Honolulu: University of Hawai'i Press, 1987.

Schwarcz, Vera. *The Chinese Enlightenment: Intellectuals and the Legacy of the May Fourth Movement of 1919.* Berkeley: University of California Press, 1986.

Schwartz, Benjamin I. *In Search of Wealth and Power: Yen Fu [Yan Fu] and the West.* Cambridge, Mass.: Harvard University Press, 1964.

——. "The Limits of 'Tradition Versus Modernity' as Categories of Explanation: The Case of Chinese Intellectuals." In *Intellectuals and Tradition,* edited by Eisenstadt and Graubard, p. 71–88.

——. *Reflections on the May Fourth Movement: A Symposium.* Cambridge, Mass.: Harvard University Press, 1972.

——. *The World of Thought in Ancient China.* Cambridge, Mass.: Harvard University Press, Belknap Press, 1985.

Searle, John. *Speech Acts: An Essay in the Philosophy of Language.* Cambridge: Cambridge University Press, 1969.

Shansisheng Wenwu Gongzuodui Weiyuanhui, eds. *Houma mengshu* (The Meng Texts of Houma). Shanghai: Wenwu Chubanshe, 1976.

Shapin, Steven. *A Social History of Truth: Civility and Science in Seventeenth-Century England.* Chicago: University of Chicago Press, 1994.

Sharf, Robert. "The Treasure-Store Treatise (Pao-ts'ang lun [Baocang lun]) and the Sinification of Buddhism in Eighth-Century China." Ph.D. diss., University of Michigan, 1991.

Shaughnessy, Edward L. "Recent Approaches to Oracle Bone Periodization: A Review." *Early China* 8 (1982–83): 1–13.

——. *Sources of Western Zhou History: Inscribed Bronzes.* Berkeley: University of California Press, 1991.

——, trans. *I Ching: The Classic of Changes.* New York: Ballantine Books, 1997.

Shen Yanguo. *Ji Zhang Taiyan xiansheng* (Remembering Mr. Zhang Taiyan). Shanghai: Shangwu, 1946.

Shigezawa Toshio. *Genshi jūka shisō to keigaku* (The Origins of *Ru* Thought and Classical Studies). Tokyo: Iwanami shoten, 1949.

Shimada Kenji. *Chūgoku kakumei no senkushatachi* (Forerunners of the Chinese Revolution). Tokyo: Chikuma shobō, 1970. Translated by Joshua A. Fogel as *Pioneer of the Chinese Revolution: Zhang Binglin and Confucianism.* Stanford: Stanford University Press, 1990.

——. "Shingai kakumei ki no Kōshi mondai" (The Kongzi Problem of the 1911 Revolution Era). In *Shingai kakumei no kenkyū,* edited by Onagawa Hidemi and Shimada Kenji, pp. 3–35. Tokyo: Chikuma shobō, 1978.

——. "Shō Heirin ni tsuite: Chūgoku dentō gakujutsu to kakumeie" (On Zhang Binglin: Traditional Chinese Scholar and Revolutionary). In *Chūgoku kakumei no senkushatachi,* pp. 167–271.

Shirakawa Shizuka. *Kōshi den* (Life of Kongzi). Tokyo: Chu yo koronsha, 1972.

Shryock, John R. *The Origin and Development of the State Cult of Confucius.* New York: Century, 1932.

Sivin, Nathan. "Copernicus in China." *Studia Copernicana* 6 (1973): 63–122.

——. "State, Cosmos, and Body in the Last Three Centuries B.C." *Harvard Journal of Asiatic Studies* (June 1995): 5–37.

——. "Text and Experience in Classical Chinese Medicine." In *Knowledge and the Scholarly Medical Traditions*, edited by Bates, pp. 177–204.

Smith, Arthur H., D.D. *Chinese Characteristics*. New York: Fleming H. Revell, 1894.

Smith, D. Howard. *Confucius and Confucianism*. London: Paladin Books, 1974.

Smith, Jonathan Z. *Imagining Religion: From Babylon to Jonestown*. Chicago: University of Chicago Press, 1982.

——. *Map Is Not Territory: Studies in the History of Religion*. Leiden: E. J. Brill, 1978.

Smith, Wilfred Cantwell. *The Meaning and End of Religion: A Revolutionary Approach to the Great Religious Traditions*. New York: Harper and Row, 1978.

Soothill, William Edward. *The Hall of Light: A Study of Early Chinese Kingship*. London: Lutterworth Press, 1951.

——, trans. *Analects of Confucius*. Yokohama, 1910. Reprint, London: Oxford University Press, 1951.

Spence, Jonathan D. "Claims and Counter-Claims: The Kangxi Emperor and the Europeans (1661–1722)." In *The Chinese Rites Controversy*, edited by Mungello, pp. 15–28.

——. *The Gate of Heavenly Peace: The Chinese and Their Revolution, 1895–1980*. New York: Viking Books, 1980.

——. *The Memory Palace of Matteo Ricci*. New York: Viking, 1984.

——. *The Question of Hu*. New York: Knopf, 1988.

——. *The Search for Modern China*. New York: Norton, 1990.

——. *To Change China: Western Advisers in China 1620–1960*. New York: Penguin Books, 1980.

Steiner, George. *After Babel: Aspects of Language and Translation*. New York: Oxford University Press, 1976.

Streuver, Nancy. "Fables of Power." *Representations* 4 (fall 1983): 108–127.

Stock, Brian. *The Implications of Literacy: Written Language and Models of Interpretation in the Eleventh and Twelfth Centuries*. Princeton: Princeton University Press, 1983.

——. *Listening for the Text: On the Uses of the Past*. Baltimore: Johns Hopkins University Press, 1990.

Strickmann, Michel. "The Mao Shan Revelations: Taoism and the Aristocracy." *T'oung Pao* 68 (1977): 1–64.

——. "On the Alchemy of T'ao Hung-ching [Tao Hongjing]." In *Facets of Taoism: Essays in Chinese Religion*. edited by Holmes Welch and Anna Seidel, pp. 123–192. New Haven: Yale University Press, 1979.

——. "History, Anthropology, and Chinese Religion." *Harvard Journal of Asiatic Studies* 40, no. 1 (June 1980): 201–248.

——, ed. *Tantric and Taoist Studies in Honour of R. A. Stein*. Vol. 2. Brussels: Institut Belge des Hautes Études Chinoises, 1983.

Stuart, John Leighton. *Fifty Years in China: The Memoirs of John Leighton Stuart, Missionary and Ambassador*. New York: Random House, 1954.

Sun, E-tu Zen. "The Chinese Constitutional Missions of 1905–1906." *Journal of Modern History* 24, no. 3 (September 1952): 251–268.

Tai Hung-chao, ed. *Confucianism and Economic Development: An Oriental Alternative*. Washington, D.C.: Washington Institute Press, 1989.

Takeuchi Yoshio. *Rongo no kenkyū* (Studies on the Lunyu). Tokyo: Iwanami, 1939.

Tambiah, Stanley J. *Culture, Thought, and Social Action: An Anthropological Perspective*. Cambridge, Mass.: Harvard University Press, 1985.

Tang Zhenchang. "Lun Zhang Taiyan" (On Zhang Taiyan). *Lishi yanjiu* (January 1978): 67–85.

Taussig, Michael. *Shamanism, Colonialism, and the Wild Man: A Study in Terror and Healing*. Chicago: University of Chicago Press, 1987.

Tedlock, Dennis. *The Spoken Word and the Work of Interpretation*. Philadelphia: University of Pennsylvania Press, 1983.

Teiser, Stephen F. *The Ghost Festival in Medieval China*. Princeton: Princeton University Press, 1988.

Thompson, Lawrence G. *Studia Asiatica: Essays in Asian Studies in Felicitation of the Seventy-fifth Anniversary of Professor Ch'en Shou-yi [Chen Shouyi]*. San Francisco: Chinese Materials Center, 1975.

Tillman, Hoyt C. *Confucian Discourse and Chu Hsi's [Zhu Xi's] Ascendancy*. Honolulu: University of Hawai'i Press, 1992.

——. "A New Direction in Confucian Scholarship: Approaches to Examining the Differences between Neo-Confucianism and Tao-hsüeh [Daoxue]." *Philosophy East and West* 42, no. 3 (July 1992): 455–474.

——. "The Uses of Neo-Confucianism Revisited: A Reply to Professor de Bary." *Philosophy, East and West* 44, no. 1 (January 1994): 135–142.

"Ting Li Zehou, Liu Shu-hsien [Liu Shuxian] tan 'He Shang'" (Listening to Li Zehou and Lin Shu-hsien Talk about Deathsong of a River). *Jiushi niandai*, no. 227 (December 1988): 88–91.

Todorov, Tzvetan. *The Conquest of America*. Translated by Richard Howard. New York: Harper and Row, 1984.

Torgovnick, Marianna. *Gone Primitive: Savage Intellects, Modern Lives*. Chicago: University of Chicago Press, 1990.

Trautmann, Thomas R. *Lewis Henry Morgan and the Invention of Kinship*. Berkeley: University of California Press, 1987.

Toulmin, Stephen. *Cosmopolis: The Hidden Agenda of Modernity*. Chicago: University of Chicago Press, 1991.

Treadgold, Donald W. *The West in Russia and China: Religious and Secular Thought in Modern Times*. Vol. 2, *China 1582–1949*. Cambridge: Cambridge University Press, 1973.

Trigault, Nicolá, and Matteo Ricci. *China in the Sixteenth Century: The Journals of Matthew Ricci, 1583–1610*. Translated by Louis J. Gallagher S.J. New York: Random House, 1953.

Tsou, Jung [Zou Rong]. *The Revolutionary Army: A Chinese Nationalist Tract of 1903*. Translated by John Lust. The Hague: Mouton, 1968.

Tsuda Sōkichi. *Suden no shi oshitaki kenkyū* (Studies on the Ideology of the Zuo Zhuan). Tokyo: Iwanami shoten, 1958.

Tu Cheng-sheng [Du Zhengsheng]. "Some Problems Concerning the So-Called Survivors of the Yin Dynasty." Paper presented at the International Conference on Shang Civilization, East-West Center, University of Hawai'i at Manoa, Honolulu, September 7–11, 1982.

Tu Wei-ming [Du Weiming]. *Confucian Ethics Today: The Singapore Challenge.* Singapore: Federal Publications, 1984.

——. "A Confucian Perspective on the Rise of Industrial East Asia." *Bulletin of the American Academy of Arts and Sciences* 42, no. 1 (October 1988): 32–50.

——. *Confucian Thought: Selfhood as Creative Transformation.* Albany: State University of New York Press, 1985.

——. "The Confucian Tradition in Chinese History." In *Heritage of China*, edited by Ropp, pp. 112–137.

——. "Cultural China: The Center as Periphery." *Daedalus* 120, no. 2 (spring 1991): 1–32.

——. "Hsiung Shih-li's [Xiong Shili's] Quest for Authentic Existence." In *Limits of Change*, edited by Furth, pp. 242–275.

——. *Humanity and Self-Cultivation: Essays in Confucian Thought.* Berkeley: Asian Humanities Press, 1979.

——. "The Rise of Industrial East Asia: The Role of Confucian Values." *Copenhagen Papers in East and Southeast Asian Studies* (April 1989): 81–97.

——. "The Search for Roots in East Asia: The Case of the Confucian Revival." In *Fundamentalisms Observed*, edited by Marty and Appleby, pp. 740–781.

——. "Toward a Third Epoch of Confucian Humanism: A Background Understanding." In *Confucianism*, edited by Eber, pp. 3–21.

——. "The 'Thought of Huang-Lao': A Reflection on the *Lao Tzu* [Laozi] and *Huang Ti* [Huangdi] Texts in the Silk Manuscripts of Ma-wang-tui [Mawangdui]." *Journal of Asian Studies* 39, no. 1 (November 1979): 95–110.

——. "'Wenhua Zhongguo' chutan" (Probing "Cultural China"). *Jiushi niandai*, no. 245 (June 1990): 60–61.

——, ed. *The Living Tree: The Changing Meaning of Being Chinese Today.* Stanford: Stanford University Press, 1994.

Twitchett, Denis. *Printing and Publishing in Medieval China.* New York: Frederic C. Beil, 1983.

Twitchett, Denis, and Michael Loewe, eds. *The Cambridge History of China.* Vol. 1. Cambridge: Cambridge University Press, 1986.

Tyler, Stephen A. "Post-modern Ethnography: From Document of the Occult to Occult Document." In *Writing Culture*, edited by Clifford and Marcus, pp. 122–140.

Übelhör, Monika. "The Community Compact (*Hsiang-yüeh* [*Xiangyue*]) of the Sung and Its Educational Significance." In *Neo-Confucian Education*, edited by de Bary and Chaffee, pp. 371–388.

Unger, Roberto Mangabeira. *Plasticity into Power: Variations on Themes of Politics, A Work in Constructive Social Theory.* Cambridge: Cambridge University Press, 1987.

Van Xuyet, Ngo. *Divination, magie, et politique dans la Chine ancienne.* Paris: Presses Universitaires de France, 1976.

Van der Loon, P. "The Ancient Chinese Chronicles and the Growth of Historical Ideals." In *Historians of China and Japan,* edited by Beasley and Pulleyblank, pp. 24–30.

——. "On the Transmission of the Kuan-Tzu [Guanzi]." *T'oung Pao* 41 (1952): 357–393.

Van Kley, Edwin J. "Europe's 'Discovery' of China and the Writing of World History." *American Historical Review* 76, no. 2 (1971): 358–385.

Vandermeersch, Leon. "Aspects rituels de la popularisation du Confucianisme sous les Han." In *Thought and Law in Qin and Han China,* edited by Idema and Zürcher, pp. 89–107.

——. *Wangdao ou la voie royale: Recherches sur l'esprit des institutions de la Chine archaïque.* Vols. 1–2. Paris: École Française d'Extrême-Orient, 1977–1980.

Vermeer, E. B., ed. *Development and Decline of Fukien Province in the Seventeenth and Eighteenth Centuries.* Leiden: E. J. Brill, 1990.

Vico, Giambattista. *On the Most Ancient Wisdom of the Italians Unearthed from the Origins of the Latin Language.* Translated by L. M. Palmer. Ithaca: Cornell University Press, 1988.

Vogel, Ezra. *The Four Dragons: The Spread of Industrialization in East Asia.* Cambridge, Mass.: Harvard University Press, 1992.

Wagner, Roy. *The Invention of Culture.* Revised and expanded edition. Chicago: University of Chicago Press, 1981.

Wakeman, Frederic, Jr. *The Great Enterprise: The Manchu Reconstruction of Imperial Order in Seventeenth-Century China.* 2 vols. Berkeley: University of California Press, 1985.

——. *History and Will: Philosophical Perspectives of Mao Tse-tung's [Mao Zedong's] Thought.* Berkeley: University of California Press, 1973.

——. "The Price of Autonomy: Intellectuals in Ming and Ch'ing [Qing] Politics." *Daedalus* 101, no. 2 (spring 1972): 35–70.

Wakeman, Frederic, Jr., and Carolyn Grant, eds. *Conflict and Control in Late Imperial China.* Berkeley: University of California Press, 1978.

Waldron, Arthur. *The Great Wall of China: From History to Myth.* Cambridge: Cambridge University Press, 1990.

Waley, Arthur, *Ballads and Stories from Tun-Huang [Dunhuang].* London: George Allen and Unwin, 1960.

——. *Three Ways of Thought in Ancient China.* New York: Doubleday Anchor, 1956.

——, trans. *The Analects of Confucius.* New York: Vintage Books, 1938.

——, trans. *The Book of Songs: The Ancient Chinese Classic of Poetry.* Edited with additional translations by Joseph R. Allen. New York: Grove Press, 1996.

——, trans. *The Nine Songs: A Study of Shamanism in Ancient China.* San Francisco: City Lights Books, 1973.

——, trans. *The Way and Its Power: A Study of the Tao Te Ching [Dao-de jing] and Its Place in Chinese Thought.* New York: Grove Press, 1958.

Wallacker, Benjamin E. "Han Confucianism and Confucius in Han." In *Ancient China,* edited by Roy and Tsien, pp. 215–228.

Walshe, W. Gilbert. "Some Chinese Funeral Customs." *Journal of the North China Branch of the Royal Asiatic Society* 35 (1903–1904): 26–64.

Wang Fen-sen [Wang Fansen]. *Zhang Taiyan de sixiang* (The Thought of Zhang Taiyan). Taibei: Shibao, 1985.

Wang Tao. *Tao yuan wenlu waipian* (Outer Chapters of the Literary Record of Wang Tao). Reprint. Shenyang: Liaoning renmin Chubanshe, 1994.

Wang, Jing. *High Culture Fever: Politics, Aesthetics, and Ideology in Deng's China.* Berkeley: University of California Press, 1996.

Wang, Y. C. *Chinese Intellectuals and the West, 1872–1949.* Chapel Hill: University of North Carolina Press, 1966.

Wang, Zhongshu. *Han Civilization.* Translated by K. C. Chang and collaborators. New Haven: Yale University Press, 1982.

Ware, James R., trans. *The Sayings of Confucius.* New York, 1955.

Waterson, Roxanna. *The Living House: An Anthropology of Architecture in South-East Asia.* New York: Oxford University Press, 1990.

Watson, Burton. *Ssu-ma Ch'ien [Sima Qian], Grand Historian of China.* New York: Columbia University Press, 1958.

——, trans. *The Complete Works of Chuang Tzu [Zhuangzi].* New York: Columbia University Press, 1968.

——, trans. *Courtier and Commoner in China: Selections from the History of the Former Han by Pan Ku [Ban Gu].* New York: Columbia University Press, 1974.

——, trans. *Records of the Grand Historian of China.* 2 vols. New York: Columbia University Press, 1961.

——, trans. *The Tso Chuan [Zuo zhuan].* New York: Columbia University Press, 1989.

Watson, James L. "The Structure of Chinese Funerary Rites: Elementary Forms, Ritual Sequence and the Primacy of Performance." In *Death Ritual in Late Imperial and Modern China,* edited by Watson and Rawski, pp. 3–19.

Watson, James L., and Evelyn S. Rawski, eds. *Death Ritual in Late Imperial and Modern China.* Berkeley: University of California Press, 1988.

Watson, William. *Cultural Frontiers in Ancient East Asia.* Edinburgh: Edinburgh University Press, 1971.

Weber, Max. *The Methodology of the Social Sciences.* Edited and translated by Edward Shils and Henry A. Finch. New York: Free Press, 1949.

——. *The Religion of China.* Translated by Hans H. Gerth. New York: Macmillan, 1964.

——. *The Protestant Ethic and the Spirit of Capitalism.* Translated by Talcott Parsons. New York: Scribners, 1958.

——. *The Sociology of Religion.* Translated by Ephraim Fischoff. Boston: Beacon Press, 1963.

Wechsler, Howard J. *Offerings of Jade and Silk: Ritual and Symbol in the Legitimation of the T'ang [Tang] Dynasty.* New Haven: Yale University Press, 1985.

Weld, Susan. "Covenant in Jin's Walled Cities: The Discoveries at Houma and Wenxian." Ph.D. diss., Harvard University, 1990.

Wesling, Donald. "Methodological Implications of the Philosophy of Jacques Derrida for Comparative Literature." In *Chinese-Western Comparative Literature: Theory and Strategy,* edited by Deeney, pp. 79–111.

White, Hayden. *Metahistory: The Historical Imagination in Nineteenth-Century Europe*. Baltimore: Johns Hopkins University Press, 1973.

——. "The Politics of Historical Interpretation: Discipline and De-Sublimation." *Critical Inquiry* 9 (September 1982): 113–137.

——. *Tropics of Discourse: Essays in Cultural Criticism*. Baltimore: Johns Hopkins University Press, 1978.

Wilhelm, Richard, trans. *The I Ching [Yijing]; or, Book of Changes*. 3d ed. Rendered into English by Cary F. Baynes. Princeton: Princeton University Press, 1967.

Williams, Raymond. *Culture and Society, 1780–1950*. New York: Harper Torchbooks, 1966.

——. *Keywords: A Vocabulary of Culture and Society*. Revised edition. New York: Oxford University Press, 1984.

——. *The Sociology of Culture*. New York: Schocken Books, 1982.

Wilson, Brian R., ed. *Rationality*. New York: Harper Torchbooks, 1970.

Wilson, Thomas A. *Genealogy of the Way: The Construction and Uses of the Confucian Tradition in Late Imperial China*. Stanford: Stanford University Press, 1995.

Winch, Peter. "Concepts and Actions." In *The Philosophy of History*, edited by Patrick Gardiner, pp. 41–50. Oxford: Oxford University Press, 1974.

Wolf, Arthur P., ed. *Studies in Chinese Society*. Stanford: Stanford University Press, 1978.

Wolf, Margery. *A Thrice-Told Tale: Feminism, Postmodernism, and Ethnographic Responsibility*. Stanford: Stanford University Press, 1992.

Wong Young-tsu. *Search for Modern Nationalism: Zhang Binglin and Revolutionary China*. New York: Oxford University Press, 1989.

Wright, Arthur. *Buddhism in Chinese History*. Stanford: Stanford University Press, 1958.

——, ed. *The Confucian Persuasion*. Stanford: Stanford University Press, 1960.

——, ed. *Studies in Chinese Thought*. Chicago: University of Chicago Press, 1953.

Wright, Arthur, and David S. Nivison, eds. *Confucianism in Action*. Stanford: Stanford University Press, 1959.

Wright, Arthur, and Denis Twitchett, eds. *Confucian Personalities*. Stanford: Stanford University Press, 1962.

Wright, Mary Claybaugh, ed. *China in Revolution: The First Phase, 1900–1913*. New Haven: Yale University Press, 1968.

Wu Hung. *The Wu Liang Shrine: The Ideology of Early Chinese Pictorial Art*. Stanford: Stanford University Press, 1989.

Wu Pei-yi. "Self-Examination and the Confession of Sins in Traditional China." *Harvard Journal of Asiatic Studies* 39, no. 1 (June 1979): 22–34.

Xu Wenqing, ed. *Zhushu jinian tongqian* (Comprehensive Commentaries on the Bamboo Annals). Taibei: Yiwen Shuju, 1966.

Xu Yuanhe. *Ruxue yu dongfang wenhua* (Ruism and Eastern Culture). Beijing: Renmin Chubanshe, 1994.

Yang Bojun. *Chunqiu Zuo zhuan cidian* (A Dictionary of the Zuo Commentary on the Spring and Autumn Annals). Beijing: Zhonghua Shuju, 1985.

Yang, C. K. "The Functional Relationship between Confucian Thought and Chinese Religion." In *Chinese Thought and Institutions*, edited by Fairbank, pp. 269–290.

———. *Religion in Chinese Society*. Berkeley: University of California Press, 1961.

Yang, Lien-sheng, ed. *Studies in Chinese Institutional History*. Cambridge, Mass.: Harvard University Press, 1961.

Yates, Robin D. S. "The City under Siege: Technology and Organization as Seen in the Reconstructed Text of the Military Chapters of *Mo Tzu [Mozi]*." Ph.D. diss., Harvard University, 1980.

———. "Social Status in the Ch'in [Qin]: Evidence from the Yün-men [Yunmen] Legal Documents. Part One: Commoners." *Harvard Journal of Asiatic Studies* 47, no. 1 (June 1987): 197–238.

Yeh, Wen-hsin [Ye Wenxin]. *The Alienated Academy: Culture and Politics in Republican China, 1919–1937*. Cambridge, Mass.: Harvard University Press, 1991.

Young, John D. *China and Christianity: The First Encounter*. Hong Kong: Chinese University Press, 1983.

Yü, Chün-fang [Yu Junfang]. *The Renewal of Buddhism in China: Chu-hung [Zhu Hong] and the Late Ming Synthesis*. New York: Columbia University Press, 1981.

Yu, Pauline. "Poems in Their Place: Collections and Canons in Early Chinese Literature." *Harvard Journal of Asiatic Studies* 50, no. 1 (June 1990): 163–196.

Yu Ronggen. "Studies on Confucius in Our Country in Recent Years." In *Confucius*, edited by Etiemble, pp. 285–291.

Yü Ying-shih [Yu Yingshi]. "O Soul, Come Back!—A Study of the Changing Conceptions of the Soul and Afterlife in Pre-Buddhist China." *Harvard Journal of Asiatic Studies* 47, no. 2 (December 1987): 363–397.

———. *Zhongguo jindai sixiang shi shang de Hu Shi* (Modern Chinese Thought to Hu Shi). Taibei: Xuesheng Shuju, 1984.

Yu Yue. *Zhuzi pingyi* (A Critical Discussion of the Collective Masters). Shanghai: Shangwu, 1935.

Zakaria, Fareed. "Culture Is Destiny: A Conversation with Lee Kuan Yew." *Foreign Affairs* 73, no. 2 (March/April 1994): 109–126.

Zen, Sophia H. Chen, ed. *Symposium on Chinese Culture*. Shanghai: China Institute of Pacific Relations, 1931.

Zhang Longxi. "The Myth of the Other: China in the Eyes of the West." *Critical Inquiry* 15 (autumn 1988): 108–131.

———. "The *Tao* and *Logos*: Notes on Derrida's Critique of Logocentrism." *Critical Inquiry* 11, no. 3 (spring 1985): 385–398.

———. *The Tao and the Logos: Literary Hermeneutics, East and West*. Durham, N.C.: Duke University Press, 1992.

Zhang Xincheng. *Weishu tongkao* (Collected Researches on Apocrypha). Vol. 1. Taibei: Dingwen Shuju, 1973.

Zhang Xuecheng. *Zhangshi yishu* (Surviving Works of Mr. Zhang). 8 vols. Shanghai: Shangwu, 1936.

Zhang Yin. "Gujing jingshe zhi chugao" (Preliminary Draft of a Gazetteer of the Refined Lodge for the Explication of the Classics). *Wenlan xuebao* 2 (March 1936): 1–47.

Zhongwen dacidian (Encyclopedic Dictionary of the Chinese Language). 10 vols. Taibei: Zhongguo wenhua daxue, 1977.

Zhou Fagao, ed. *Jinwen gulin bu* (Addition to the Ancient Forest of Bronze Inscriptions). Taibei (Nangang): Academia Sinica, Institute of History and Philology, 1983.

Zhou Fagao et al., eds. *Jinwen gulin* (Ancient Forest of Bronze Inscriptions). Hong Kong: Chinese University Press, 1975.

Zhou Gucheng. *Zhongguo tongshi* (A Comprehensive History of China). 2 vols. Shanghai: Renmin Chubanshe, 1983.

Zou Rong. *Geming jun* (Revolutionary Army). Reprint, Beijing: Zhonghua Shuju, 1958.

Zupanov, Ines. "Aristocratic Analogies and Demotic Descriptions in the Seventeenth-Century Madurai Mission." *Representations*, no. 41 (winter 1993): 123–148.

Zürcher, E. *The Buddhist Conquest of China: The Spread and Adaptation of Buddhism in Early Medieval China.* Leiden: E. J. Brill, 1959.

——. "Jesuit Accommodationism and the Chinese Cultural Imperative." In *The Chinese Rites Controversy: Its History and Meaning,* edited by Mungello, pp. 31–64.

——. "The Jesuit Mission in Fujian in Late Ming Times: Levels of Response." In *Development and Decline of Fukien Province in the Seventeenth and Eighteenth Centuries,* edited by Vermeer, pp. 417–457.

Zürcher, Erik, Nicolas Standaert, S.J., and Adrianus Dudink. *Bibliography of the Jesuit Mission in China (ca. 1580–ca. 1680).* Leiden: Centre of Non-Western Studies, Leiden University, 1991.

INDEX

Bartoli, Daniello: history of Jesuits in China, and identification of Chinese Christian converts with Donglin shuyuan, 52

Bauer, Wolfgang, 218, 221, 225

Beck, Cave: "universal character," 128. See also *characteristica universalis;* Chinese language: as ideographic or pictographic

Bellah, Robert: theory of religious evolution, 372n102

Benveniste, Émile: critical revision of Saussure, 337n14

Bernard, Henri: claims Ricci was first to use the term "Confucius," 88, 328n27; explains Jesuit antipathy for *fo* as a result of affiliation with Donglin shuyuan, 52

Bible, 59–60, 72; and Jesuits' chronology project, 126; limits of the Bible when considering natural theology, 94; use of the Bible to index ancient Chinese history, 242–44, 257

"Big Dipper of China": Zhang Binglin's complimentary reference to Kongzi, 186, 303

bonzes/bonsos [P] (Buddhist monks). *See* Jesuits as *fo*

boshi (gentlemen of broad learning), 204; a late-Han gloss of *ru*, 164–66, 204; normative interpretation of *ru* as, 159, 166–67. See also *ru* practitioners

Bouvet, Joachim: figurist belief that ancient Chinese texts prophesied revelation, 117

Boxer Indemnity Fund: scholarships for Chinese study abroad, 220

Boxers. See *Yihe quan*

Bo Yi, 19. *See also* culture heroes

Bronze Age (ca. 3000–1000 B.C.E.): rise of the general name (*daming*) *ru* during, 208. See also *ru* philology; Shang; Zhou

Brooks, E. Bruce, and A. Taeko Brooks: accretional theory of *Lunyu* composition and reconstruction of proper sequencing of *Lunyu* strata, 326n10

Burning of the Books (alleged), 164

canon: canonicity as a product of the interpretive closure of Han narrative, 189; disagreement among *jinwen* and *guwen* scholars regarding canon, 176; Jesuit/*ru* canon construction, 26, 59, 118. *See also* Sino-Jesuit textual community

cartography: function in Jesuit enculturation, 37–38. See also *mappamondo*

catechism, 36–39, 102, 312n13. See also *Tianzhu shiyi; Vera et brevis divinarum rerum expositio (Tianzhu shilu)*

Catholic Church: dupery of, 91–92; growing suspicion of Jesuit missionaries, 86; Inquisition, 65; and the *Padroado*, 41, 314n22; Reformation, 108, 332n90; Ricci's explicit frustration with ecclesiastical authorities, 322n94; Vatican authority, 46, 63, 67, 112, 119. *See also* Christianity; Jesuits

Chang, Kwang-Chih (K. C.), 145

changcheng (Great Wall): as idea rather than artifact, 287

Chao, Y. R., 220

characteristica universalis (universal system of characters), 123. *See also* Chinese language: as ideographic or pictographic

Chen Duxiu: advocacy of Chinese adoption of Christianity, 234

Cheng brothers (Chengzi): Cheng Mingdao, 86, 170; Cheng Yichuan, 86, 110, 170

Cheng/Zhu orthodoxy (*ru*), 101, 108

Chengzi. *See* Cheng brothers

Chen Houguang: opposition to *Tianzhu jiao*, 104–5, 332n81

Chen Jie: gloss on *ru*, 170. See also *ru* common glosses

Chen She: *ru*-supported leader of anti-Qin insurrection, 164; *Zhuangzi* commentary on *ru* alliance with him, 340n25

China: cultural traits of, equated to Confucian cultural traits, 142; equivalence of, to the West, 253; Jesuit elevation of, to world historical significance, 253;

reduced to the nexus of Confucius and Confucianism, 2, 5–11; reestablishing the ecumenical status of, 154; as a site of late-twentieth-century intellectual ecumenism, 222; and the West as "alleviative geometries," 262

China Mission, 7, 35, 119, 128. *See also* Jesuits; Sino-Jesuit textual company; Zhaoqing

Chinese Christian converts: assistance to Jesuit textual communities, 36–38, 72–73, 111–14; a mysterious man from Fujian, 72. *See also* Sino-Jesuit textual community

Chinese language: as "Confucian language," 129 (*see also* Confucian; Confucius); contemporary Chinese understandings of, 165, 341n39; contemporary revival of traditional characters, 11; elaboration of ancient Chinese through *jiajie* (phonetic borrowing), 195; first use of semantic classifiers (radicals), 195; hybrid constructions of graphs, 356n130; as ideographic or pictographic, 114, 168, 341n39, 355n129 (and hence "natural," 128–29); Jesuits' study of, 70 (*see also* Sino-Jesuit textual community; translation); and late-sixteenth-century European lexicon, 90–91; as the lost language of Adam, and indicative of God's presence, 115. *See also* literature; *ru* philology and links

Chineseness: as defined by seventeenth-century Chinese cultural elitists, 51; defined by the strict exclusion of *fo*, 51; Hu Shi's expansion of the referents of, 260–61; of Jesuit missionaries (*see* Jesuit nativeness; Jesuits as *fo*; Jesuits as *ru*); plural meanings of, 267; symbolized by *fo*, 44, 49; symbolized by *ru* and equated with Confucius, 49, 63–64, 79, 117, 130, 158, 163, 177 (see also *ru*); twentieth-century Chinese nationalists' culturalist definition of, 155

chinoiserie, 64, 129, 144, 248

Christiana expeditio (the Christian expedition), 7

Christianity: Chinese, obscured by time and heresy, 58; Chinese latent, 118–19; coherence of the world, when science and Christianity conjoin, 126–27; obscured by *fo*, 47, 316n40; proto-Christianity in the *Sishu* and *Liujing*, 56; *ru* and the fallacy of, 53, 124, 138, 147, 153–54 (*see also* figurism); and science, 126; similarity of Christian nonresistance with weak complacence of the Shang, 242; as a symbolic fund for historical reconstruction of Chinese antiquity, 244

chronology: biblical chronology, 126; Christian-Chinese chronological agreement contained in the *Confucius Sinarum Philosophus*, 121; chronology of the Septuagint, 126; and distinctions of true/false, 101; and "manufacture," 22; and *Tabula Chronologica Monarchiae Sinicae*, 126

chuanjiao (preaching the faith): of Jesuits (*see* Jesuit proselytism); Liang Qichao's *jinwen* guidelines for *chuanjiao*, 179

Chunqiu (Spring and Autumn Annals), 132, 177, 273

"Cin Nicò": neologizer of Tianzhu, 73–74, 324n109; dubious identity of, 324n108

City of God. See Augustine, Saint

Clavis Sinica, 51, 117, 318n58. *See also* real characters; universal language

Clavius (Christopher Clau), 60

colonialism, 80, 144–45, 280. *See also* hybrid community

commerce: of concepts and ideas, 9; of precious metals, 9. *See also* economy; global economy

Commonwealth: value of the symbol of Confucius for, 120

conceptual invention, 137–40, 157

Confucian: "Confucian language," 129; contemporary positivist reading, 140–41; as eponym, 129; as European reinvention, 34 (*see also* fetishization); first occurrence of the term, 121; gloss of China's antiquity influenced by Hu Shi and Zhang Binglin, 221; inadequacy and yet excessive application of

Cook, James, 32–33
cosmopolitanism: as antidote to nationalism, 264
Costa, Inácio da, 84, 114, 116. See also *Confucius Sinarum Philosophus; Sapientia Sinica*
Couplet, Philippe, 85, 122–27, 145–46; *Confucius Sinarum Philosophus,* 116; *Tabula Chronologica Monarchiae Sinicae,* 126. See also *Confucius Sinarum Philosophus*
Creel, Herrlee G., 142–43
crisis of representation, 118, 145
Cruz, Gaspar da, 87
Cui Shu, 24, 172
cultural construction on a Chinese basis. See "Zhongguo benwei de wenhua jianshe"
culture: cultural encounter, 139; cultural hegemony, 168; cultural imperialism, 144–45; culturalism, and twentieth-century nationalists' Chineseness debate, 155; cultural preservation, as disputed by *guwen* and *jinwen* scholars, 180; culture shock and textual productivity, 44, 315n29
culture heroes, 19, 58, 126; role in the constructed ancestry of *ru,* 203. *See also* Bo Yi; Fu Xi; Shun; Wen; Yao; Yi Yin; Yu
Cumfuceio [P], 80. *See also* Confucius; Kongzi
cuonhua [It] (*guanhua*), 288
custom: as transmission achieved through imitation, 171

Dai Zhen, 93, 100; esteemed by Zhang Binglin and Hu Shi, 220
daming (generic name; genus): earliest classification for *ru,* 191–94, 288
dao: Daoism, 122; Daoist canon, 167; and genesis of *ru,* 363n22; seventeenth-century European banishment of, 4; subordinated to *ru,* 139; viewed as a product of Satan, 95
Daoism. See *dao*
daotong (legacy of the way), 85; scholarly deployment as a *ru* trope, 162
daoxue (learning of the way), 170

daoyi (cultivations of the way): *ru* as peregrinating rural *daoyi* instructors, 184
Daxue (The Great Learning), 59, 114–16, 120–22, 132. See also *Sishu*
De arte cabalistica. See Reuchlin
de Bary, Wm. Theodore, 15–17
Decalogo (Ten Commandments), 38, 73
De Christiana expeditione apud Sinas (On the Christian Expedition among the Chinese, 1615): Trigault's Latin version of Ricci's *Storia,* 63, 66 figs, 321n85
deconstruction, 275, 375n10; and Enlightenment fetishization of China, 274
De Dao Jing. See Laozi
d'Elia, Pasquale: annotated translation of Ricci's mission history, 114; claims Ricci was first to Italianize Confucius, 88, 328n27; and Italian variants for Kongzi, 95–96
Delphic Oracle, 123–24
Deng Shi, 175
Derrida, Jacques: *le jeu* (play), 223, 273
Dewey, John: instructor of Hu Shi at Columbia, 220
Donglin shuyuan (Eastern Forest Academy), 51; and Jesuit anti-*foism,* 51–52, 102 (*see also* Fushe)
Dong Zhongshu: *Chunqiu fanlu,* 198; criticized by Zhang Binglin for confounding the generic, proper, and class names of *ru,* 205–6; imperial prominence of *ru* under his mentorship traced in the *Shiji,* 163–64
Dong Zuobin, 142
Duan Yucai, 172; *Shuowen jiezi zhu,* 197
Duke Ai. See Ai Gong; *Liji*
Duke Li. See Ricci, Matteo
Duke of Zhou. See Zhou Gong
Dunhuang, 21
Du Yu: commentary on the *Chunqiu,* 103

economy of delight, 267–70, 279, 285
economy: Asian economic "miracle," 4; economic hypergrowth, 11, 14, 308n18; industrial economy complemented by "the economy of delight,"

economy (*cont.*)
268; successes attributed to *ru*, 11. *See
also* commerce; global economy
ecumenism, 219, 221. *See* China: as a
site of ecumenism; *Confucius Sinarum Philosophus*
Elements. See Euclid
Epictetus: featured in the *Ershiwuyan*,
60
Ershiwuyan (Twenty-five sayings), 60
Er ya (early etymology), 159; non-
appearance of *ru* therein, 339n11
Escalante, Bernardino de, 87
Esperanto, 186; both advocacy and refutation of, 345n64
ethnic philosophy: defined, 71; ethnic
philosophers, 71, 73; Kongzi as ethnic
philosopher, 123; the *Sishu* as ethnic
philosophy, 59. *See also* Aristotle;
Plato
ethnology: and the Jesuit textual community, 116, 125, 138
etymology: as ideology, 209; and Western reception of "Yuan ru," 209
Euclid, 59–60
Europe: and contradictions between theology and science in the crisis of representation, 118–19; eager bandying of
"Confucius" and "Confucian" received
from Philippe Couplet and the second
generation of Jesuit missionaries, 138–
39; and fetishization of Kongzi, 91;
late-seventeenth-century philosophical debates between ancients and
moderns, 124; reception of Jesuit-
translated Chinese texts, 79, 86, 112–
13, 118–21; Renaissance, 209
evolution: early influence on both European and native Chinese imaginings of
China, 154; influence on twentieth-
century Chinese scholars' attempts to
trace the origins and development of
ru, 174; informing Hu Shi's "Shuo ru,"
222; informing Zhang Binglin's "Yuan
ru," 207–8; as metaphor for the pluralities of *ru*, 214; as parallel to the dissimilarity of past and present
meanings of *ru*, 160
expositio style. *See Tianzhu shilu*

fangshi (magician): early practitioners of
ru, 160
Fan Kuan: *Travelers among Streams and
Mountains* (painting), 157
feathers: in hats (see *yu; yuguan*); in ritual, 357n137
Feng Guifen: Tongzhi era reformer, 206–7
Feng Youlan, 176; inspired by Zhang
Binglin's "Yuan ru," 210; with Hu Shi,
attempts to make Chinese thought
more accessible to Westerners, 223
Fernandez, James W.: and figurative
predication, 161, 339n17
fetishization: of the concept "Confucius," 34, 91, 274; mutual, of China
and the West, 283–84. *See also* Confucian; Confucius; Larson, Gary
figurism: and revelation in the *Yijing*,
117. *See also* Christianity: Chinese latent; Christianity: obscured by *fo*;
Christianity: Chinese, obscured by
time and heresy
Five Classics. *See Wujing*
Five Masters of Northern Song, 170. *See
also* Cheng brothers; Shao Yong;
Zhang Zai; Zhou Dunyi
fo, 139; as product of Satan, 95; second-
and third-century translation
teams and *fo* terms, 114, 334n101;
seventeenth-century European banishment of, 4; sixteenth-century popularity in China influences Jesuits to
undertake the guise of, 42–48; superficial similarities to Christianity, 46–
47; and *yiduan*, 98. *See also* Jesuits as
fo; sanjiao; tre leggi diverse
Fonti Ricciane, 68. *See also* Ricci, Matteo
Foucquet, Jean-François, 117
Four Books. See *Sishu*
Four Little Dragons (Hong Kong, Singapore, South Korea, Taiwan), 15. *See
also* Confucianism: as foundation of
Asian industrialism
Franke, Wolfgang: *Der Ursprung der Ju
und ihre Beziehung zu Konfuzius und
Lau-dsi* (translation of Hu Shi's "Shuo
ru"), 3
Freud, Sigmund: concept of "family ro-
mance," 318n61

Guy, Kent, 206
Gu Yanwu, 100
guzhiru (*ru* of antiquity), 100, 290; of
    Zhang Binglin, 191. See also *ru*
Guzman, Luis de, 87, 328n26

habitus: defined, and descriptive of
    Jesuit community in China, 370n56
Hall, David. See *Thinking through
    Confucius*
Han Feizi, 86, 203
Hanlin Academy, 85
Hansen, Chad, 191
Han shu (first official history of the
    Han), 168, 195
Han Wudi, 155, 164
Hanxue (Han learning), 143; as coerced
    misdirection of Chinese scholarship,
    188, 353n111; and Jesuit denunciation
    of Neo-Confucianism, *dao,* and *fo,*
    143. See also *zhuzi xue*
Hartley, L. P.: *The Go-Between,* 156–57
Heavenly Master. See Tianzhu
Herdtrich, Christian: *Confucius Si-
    narum Philosophus,* 116
hermeneutics, 60; of belief, 62, 109; fig-
    urism as, 117; of *jinwen/guwen,* 178
heshang (native title), 41; emblematic of
    Chineseness, 143, 315n28; and Jesuits
    as *fo* (bonzes), 44–48. See also
    Chineseness
Hetu shu (Pivot of the River Chart): and
    tautological definition of *ru* as public
    practice of *ru,* 171–72
hexagrams, 333n99: as distinguished
    from Chinese graphs, 356n129; Euro-
    pean scholarly interest in, 333n99; as
    primitive language of Chinese or com-
    binatorial calculus, 333n99; used to
    gloss graphs, 195–96, 356nn129–30
    (see also *ru* philology). See also *Yijing*
He Xiu, 261
historicism: historicist style of Zhang
    Binglin and Hu Shi, 161; of Hu Shi's
    "Shuo ru," 223; and *ru,* 161
history: characterized as shards or traces
    (*guji*), 203, 277, 290; and national iden-
    tity debates, 176–77 (see also *guwen;
    jinwen*)

holy water, 105, 332n82
homes letrados [P]: invented indigenous
    tradition of the Jesuits, 56, 80, 159. *See
    also* Jesuits as *ru;* Sino-Jesuit textual
    community
Hong Xiuquan: Taiping Tianguo use of
    Shangdi for God, 324n109
houru: later *ru* of Song and Ming dynas-
    ties, 108, 110. See also *jinru*
Hou Wailu, 222
huangdi, 4; and *guwen* scholar Zhang
    Binglin's nativist *ru* chronology en-
    deavor, 182; inequivalence with em-
    peror as supreme lord, 316n48
Huang Kan, 85, 172; *Lunyu jijie yisu,*
    197
Huang Wendao: opposition to *tianzhu
    jiao,* 105–6
Huang Zhen, 105
Huaxia civilization, 195, 207; as scribal
    origins of *ru,* 209
Hu Chuan, 360n1
huiyi (joined meanings): as method of si-
    nograph construction, 195, 291. *See
    also* Chinese language
Hu Juren, 103
Hu Shi, 26–27, 173–74, 181; account of
    Shang messianism and the misap-
    propriation of Kongzi as "sage," 250–
    58; ambivalence toward Christian
    missionaries, 366n44; association of
    xiangli with *sannian zhi sang* (three-
    year rite of mourning), 240; belief that
    Laozi, Kongzi, and Mozi were *ru,*
    370n83; belief that *sannian zhi sang*
    was an archaistic invention of the *ru,*
    254–55; belief that *sannian zhi sang*
    was a Shang practice preserved by *ru*
    under the Zhou, 240–41, 248; "The
    Chinese Renaissance," 268–69; con-
    ception of *ru* as custodians of Shang
    memory, 231–34; conscious anachro-
    nism of, 365n40; conversion to Chris-
    tianity, 369n75; criticism of Zhang
    Binglin's "Yuan ru," 226–30; definition
    of *ru* as *xiangli,* 235–39; educational
    background, 220; expansion of the ref-
    erents of Chineseness, 260–61; in-
    spired by Judeo-Christian nonviolent

resistance, 242–44; interpretation of Kongzi and Christ as twin pillars of modern world civilization, 253–58; opposition to *Zhongguo benwei de wenhua jianshe* (Cultural Construction on a Chinese Basis), 261–62; philological approach to defining *ru* and "Shuo ru," 159–60; philosophical opposition to Liang Shuming, 247; reliance on the Bible as an anecdotal source, 259, 369n71; on *rufu* (*ru* garments) as signifying *rou* (weakness), 230; scholarly influence of, 360n6; Shang survivor prophecy of redemption, 250–51; his "Shuo ru" compared to Zhang Binglin's "Yuan ru," 222–27; similarities to the *ru* of Shang/Yin, 233; use of cosmopolitanism as antidote to nationalism, 264; use of *Yijing* hexagrams to gloss *ru*, 229, 245–46; vision of universal civilization, 259–64, 268–69; voted "The Greatest Living Chinese," 220; on *xu, ruan,* and *rou,* 228–29

hybrid canon, 59–60, 125. See also *Sapientia Sinica*

hybridity: of early-twentieth-century discourse of *ru*, 173; *ru*/Christian, of Sino-Jesuit community, 80, 114–15

Ignatius of Loyola, Saint, 60; compared to Confucius, 93

i letterati (the literati), 95; as neoteric interpreters, 122

il lume naturale (the light of nature), 55, 63, 104, 124; possessed by Kongzi, 74, 131

Illyricus, Matthias Flacius, 101

Il Milione (The Million; *Travels*). See Polo, Marco

imperial examination system: abolition of, 174

imperialism, 153–54; cultural imperialism, 144; and early-twentieth-century national identity debates, 176, 346n88

Inquisition. *See* Catholic Church

interpretation: interpretive consensus, 67–69; interpretive difference, 63; neoteric interpreters, 122; translations as

interpretive constructs, 141. See also *ru* interpretation; Sino-Jesuit textual community

In the Mansion of Confucius' Descendants. See Kongfu neizhai yishi— Kongzi houyi de huiyi

Intorcetta, Prosper, 84; *Confutii Vita,* 115; *Sapienta Sinica,* 114; *Sinarum Scientia Politico-Moralis,* 115

invention, 5, 118; "invent" as a working gloss for *zuo*, 23; invention of the indigenous tradition *homes letrados,* 80; joint invention, 73–75; mutually reinforcing Jesuit invention of Kong Fuzi and Confucius, 81–92; of *ru*/Jesuit conjoinment, 93; and *shuwen,* 110. *See also* manufacture; *zuo*

Isaacson: *Saturni Ephemerides: Tabula Historicochronologica,* 126

Italian language: and the orthography of Confucius, 88; renderings for *dao, fo,* and *ru*, 95–96 (see also *tre leggi diverse*)

i veri letterati (the true literati), 95, 122; compared to *i letterati,* 95

Jackson, Henry E.: correspondence with Hu Shi, 258

Jerome, Saint, 94

Jesuits: alignment with officials and elites, 105–6; appeasement of royal authority, 117–18; arrival in China, 3; as bearers and followers of *ru*, 34, 48–59, 70, 92–101, 316n47, 322n98; differing attitudes concerning native conversion, 320n73; early history of the Jesuit project, 311nn4–5; embedded in the conceptually familiar, Christianity, 139; European reception of Jesuit texts, 118–22; experience of daily life, 36–37 (*see also* letterbooks); favoring *ru* over *fo* and *dao*, 182; ideological character of Jesuit interpretation, 154; incognito as bonzes/*fo*, 39–48, 314n24; Jesuit nativeness and the invention of Kong Fuzi/Confucius, 86, 91, 96, 113, 223; Jesuit nativeness and *xianru*, 103; legacy for Western scholarship, 63; local reception of, 44–47; marginality of

Kongjiao ("Confucianity"; state religion of Kongzi), 175, 178, 292, 351n101; made official by the Manchus in 1907, 186, 351n102; Zhang Binglin's opposition to, 186

Kong Jie: elected *boshi* of Chen She, 164

Kongmiao (Kong temple): and *xianru* (first *ru*), *xianxian* (first worthies), and *xiansheng* (first sage) distinctions, 103

Kongmou (So-and-so Kong), 20–21

Kong Qiu, 33, 95, 155, 290. *See also* Confucius; Kongzi

Kong Yingda, 103

Kongzi, 5, 108, 139, 155; annual ceremonies honoring, 12, 64, 307n14; as author of *Xici juan*, 6; as bodhisattva, 22; characterized by Zhang Binglin as the "Big Dipper of China" (Zhina de daxiong xing) and outranker of culture heroes, 186–87; conceived as reformer by *jinwen* reformists, 178; contemporary symbolic capital of, 163; dubious historicity of, 156, 338n7; early-twentieth-century symbol of Chineseness, 177, 347n70; frequency of occurrence in *Lunyu*, 83, 325n9; Han mythology of him as *suwang*, 131, 373n107; and *jinwen* reformists, 175; modern Chinese restoration of, 11–14; orthographic variances of, 86–92; as patriarch of *guwen* and *jinwen* schools, 176, 199, 346n65; purported Shang descent of, 198–99, 252, 258, 372n100; as savior of Shang, 243–44; in *Shiji*, 64, 168; symbolic abduction of, 254; as symbol of Chinese civilization, 163; as symbol of Chineseness, 160; and twentieth-century nativism, 5; symbol of the rupture between ancient and modern meanings of *ru*, 202–3; as transmitter of an archaic *ru*, 156; underling of Zhou Gong, 179–80. *See also* Confucius

Kongzi and Jesus Christ: common humanitarianism, 221; as exemplars of historic religion, 253, 372n102; as mistaken messiahs, 220, 253, 373n107

Kongzi gaizhi kao (Researches on Kongzi as a Reformer; Kang Youwei, 1896), 179

Kongzi jiayu (Sayings of Kongzi), 21, 84

Kongzi's face: resembling that of a dog or the mask of an exorcist (*qi*), 239, 368n59; as dog in a house of mourning, 239, 368n61

Kong Shangtang (Confucius Restaurant), 13

Kongzi Yanjiusuo (Kongzi Research Institute), 12

Kuhn, Thomas, 181

Lach, Donald, 96

La Chaise, Père François de, 112

Lacouperie, Terrien de, 173

Laertius, Diogenes: *The Lives of the Philosophers*, 8

la legge de' letterati (the order of the literati; *ru*/Confucians), 39, 47, 62, 124, 138, 146, 253; as *Literatorum secta*, 69, 73, 313n15

Laozi, 170

Laozi, 86; as possible founder of *ru*, 226. See also *dao*

Larson, Gary: "Confucius at the Office," 6, 14, 18

Latin: and Chinese in the *Sapientia Sinica*, 114–15; declining linguistic hegemony and the orthography of Confucius, 90; magical efficacy of, 105

le Comte, Louis, 9, 117; *Nouveaux mémoires sur l'état présent de la Chine*, 117

legge (law; order), 50; compared to *secta*, 69. *See also* Jesuits; *ru*; Society of Jesus

Legge, James, 358nn142–43

legge degli Fatochei (*fojiao*), 95. See also *fo*

leggi di Sciechia (*shijia* [Shakyamuni]), 95

Leibniz, 112, 118 fig9, 123, 125; *characteristica universalis*, 123, 128; *Novissima Sinica*, 118. *See also* science and Christianity; theological ecumenism

leiming (class name; species): as second oldest category of *ru*'s meaning, 199–201, 292

letterati, 147

letterbooks, 46, 119

Macao, 22, 35–37, 40, 46, 70, 313n17
MacIntyre, Alasdair, 139, 277, 283
magicians. See *fangshi*
Magistratum Confucium ([under] the
    magistracy of Confucius), 123
man (barbarian), 106. See also *Shengchao
    Poxie ji*
Manchu, 26; as contemporary imagining
    of *ru*, 163, 340n21; Zhang Binglin's in-
    dictment of the Manchus, 188. *See
    also* conquest elites; Qing
mandarino, 50, 138; *mandarinum*, 49
manufacture, 18, 22–25. *See also* con-
    ceptual invention; *zuo*
Mao Zedong, 13, 22
mappamondo (world map of Matteo
    Ricci), 36–38, 38 fig4, 153; first edition
    (1584) purloined by Chinese, 37,
    312n12
map/territory: epistemology of, 376n27
Marian sodality (cult of the Virgin),
    116
Markley, Robert, 118
mathematics. *See* Newton; science
"matters of fact," 145, 338n17
May Fourth Movement (*Wusi yundong;*
    May 4, 1919), 24; and early-twentieth-
    century intellectual ecumenism, 222;
    historical imagination of, 340n21; ico-
    noclasm of, 345n60; interpretive hege-
    mony of, 340n21
McMullen, David, 21–22
Mencius. *See* Mengzi
Mendoza, Juan González de, 87, 328n25
meng (blood oath): Kongzi's role in abro-
    gation of, 238, 367–68n58; peculiar
    Warring States practice, 236–38,
    367n52; relationship to *xiangli*, 237–
    39, 367n52
Meng Xizi: death wish, 252–53
Mengzi (Mencius), 19, 109–10, 253, 276
Mengzi, 132; cited in Hu Shi's philologi-
    cal derivation of *ru* from *xu* as a source
    for the gloss "weak," 229
metaphorizations, 138
metaphysics. See *jinru; lixue*
metonymy, 65; of "Confucius" for things
    Chinese, 8, 117; of *ru*, 53
Minbao (Tongmeng Hui journal), 174

mingxin qiongxing (illumination of the
    mind and exhaustion of the nature),
    171. *See also* Wang Wei
minzu: as tribe, 362n15
missionary community, 7
Mission of the Indies, 36, 39, 67, 126
Missions Étrangères, 117, 122, 146
Modernii interpretes (modern inter-
    preters): upholders of *ru*, 122
modernization theory, 376n26
moderns, 124
Mo Di. *See* Mozi
Mongol taxation registry. See *ru hu*
monotheism: archaic, 119; Chinese, 112;
    Christian, 26; preached by Confutio,
    then destroyed in the alleged Burning
    of the Books, 94; preached by Kongzi,
    then forgotten, 33, 55; primordial, in
    Kongzi's texts, 62, 107; in *Tianzhu
    shiyi*, 61
Montesquieu, 9, 145, 306n7. *See also*
    Enlightenment
Mote, Frederick: influenced by Zhang
    Binglin and Hu Shi religious-to-
    secular evolutionary depiction of *ru*,
    218, 223
Mozi, 100
Mozi, 20–21, 155; Zhang Binglin's re-
    liance upon it, 187, 189–91
Müller, Andreas: and *Clavis Sinica*,
    318n58
Mungello, David E., 40, 60, 116, 313n16,
    314n21
mythic history. *See* culture heroes

national identity: concern with among
    Chinese intellectuals, 176–77
nationalism, 80, 147, 285; and cosmopol-
    itanism, 257–64; and racial biology,
    154; in *ru* debates, 155
nationhood, 121, 123, 124
native ground: the Jesuit/*ru* contest to
    claim, 102–7
naturae lumine, 74
natural language. *See* Chinese language;
    "real characters"
natural philosophers: and the semiotics
    of "real characters," 121
natural philosophy, 121; Confucius and

natural philosophy (*cont.*)
  Confucianism as late-seventeenth-century European evidentiary objects of, 145; and *Proëmialis Declaratio,* 121
natural theology, 56–58; as God-ly revelation, 94; as seed of true religion, 64, 124
Nef, John U.: *Cultural Foundations of Industrial Civilization* and "the economy of delight," 267–68
Neo-Confucianism, 15–17; and Hanxue revival, 143; truth/authenticity of, 17
Neoterici Interpretes (neoteric interpreters), 122
neoterics, 122; versus modern interpreters, 122
New Age philosophy, 4
New Testament, 59
New Text. See *jinwen;* Kang Youwei
Newton, 112, 121, 124, 126; calculus, 128; *Principia,* 121
Norman, Jerry, 162; and reconstruction of ancient Chinese, 339–40
normative interpretation, 167–68
nostri leggi (our order). *See* Jesuits; Society of Jesus
Nouveaux mémoires sur l'état présent de la Chine (Recent Memoirs on the Present State of China), 117
Novissima Sinica (Latest News from China), 118
nuo (timid): as gloss of *ru,* 170

Old Text. See *guwen;* Zhang Binglin
Opere Storiche. See Tacchi Venturi, Pietro
oracle bone inscriptions (*jiaguwen*), 195–96, 291; suspect authenticity of, 228, 358n145; typical content of, 366n45
oratio brevis, 122. See also *Confucius Sinarum Philosophus*
originary fable of *ru* (Zhang Binglin and Hu Shi), 158–59
osciani (Buddhist monks), 43. See also *fo*
Owen, Stephen: and *guji,* 203, 359n154, 373n103; interpretation of Kongzi and antiquity, 359n154

Padroado (patronage of King Sebastian), 41
Pankenier, David: planetary alignment and the mandate of heaven, 371n90. *See also* Shang
Pantoja, Diego de, 87, 328n26
Papebroch, Daniel, 125
Paper, Jordan, 143
paronomasia: method of ancient Chinese linguistic elaboration, 195; as practicable definition of *ru,* 170–72; as rhetorical style, 172
parousia, 273
Pasio, Francesco, 45
Paul, 56; Epistle to the Romans, 74
Pauthier, M. G., 81, 325n5
Peace of Westphalia, 113
Pelliot, Paul: account of *jinwen/guwen* rivalry, 344n59
perfect language, 154, 338n1
Petris, Francesco de, 116, 125
Pharisees and scribes, 256; as *ru* of the Jews, 256
Philip II of Spain (king), 3
philology: according to Zhang Binglin, 185–86; as method of historical reconstruction, 157, 168; relation to historical phonology, 364n26; as rhetorical style in West and in China, 363n25. See also *xiaoxue*
physicotheology: and epistemological crisis, 336nn127–28
Pi-Lin pi-Kong (criticize Lin Biao and Kongzi/Confucius) campaign, 11–12, 307n11, 340n19
Pirez, Francisco, 73
Planudes, 60
Plato, 59, 71; compared with Kongzi, 123, 335n117. *See also* ethnic philosophy
Polanyi, Karl, 153
Polo, Marco, 47
portugalization, 41. *See also* Goa; Macao
Portuguese language: as Jesuit missionary lingua franca, 91; and orthological confusion of Confucius, 90
positivism, 140–41
postage stamp of Kongzi, 14, 163
postmodernism, 269–71; and distrust of

Zhang Binglin's criticism of Dong Zhongshu for confounding the generic, proper, and class names of *ru*, 205

ru paronomastic glosses, 156; *ru rou ye* (*ru* means weak), 191, 228–29, 354n118, 356n135; *ru ru ye* (*ru* means wet), 172; *ruzhe ru ye* (the *ru* are wet), 172, 197

ru philology and links: another etymology of *ru*, 170; colloquial compounds of *rusheng, daru,* and *hongru,* 162–63; early referents, semantic ambiguity, and protean quality of *ru*, 155–56; etymological derivation from *xu*, fifth hexagram of the *Yijing,* 194–95; etymology of *ru* and its cognates, 161; graph, 160; linked with *wu*, 196; linked with *xu*, 194–96, 355n126; linked with *yu*, 195–96; links with *ruan*, 228–29; links with *xu*, 228–29; multiple referents of *ru*, 53; philological and phonological connections with *ru* (to sink), 196–98; possible origins, 168–69; semantic evolution of *ru*, 160–62; superseded by Confucianism, 162; in Zhang Binglin's etiology, "Yuan ru," 173, 181; Zhou bronze inscriptions consulted in the philological reconstruction of *ru*, 195

ru practitioners: as a clan of sorcerers, 195–96; displaced religious functionaries of Shang, 232; *fangshi* practitioners of *ru*, 160; as free-floating intelligentsia, clerks, etc., 159–60; Han definition of *ru* as *shi* (scholar), 159, 164; as members of *shi* (knight) class, 200, 232–33; as priests, 26, 160; as priests swathed in "weak" garments (*rufu*), 230–31; as purveyors of a philosophy of nonviolent resistance, 241–42; Qing definition of *ru* as *shi* (scholar; instructor), 203; as rainmakers, 197; as *shushi*, practitioners of magic and received scholarly techné, 174, 196, 226. *See also* Jesuits as *ru*; *zhuru*

ruxing (*ru* deportment), 198, 203

ruxue (*ru* learning), 5

Ruxue yu dongfang wenhua (Ruism and Eastern Culture). *See* Xu Yuanhe

ruzhe (the *ru*), 5

Sacerdos Christianus (Christian priest), 71, 74

Sacred Faith. See *Santa Fede*

sacrifice: animal sacrifice performed to Kongzi, 65–67, 68 fig6

Sahlins, Marshall, 32–33, 139

Sander, Reverend Nicholas: and manufacture as artifice, 310n39

sangli (Shang mortuary rites): preserved by Han, 235–36; decline of, 247

sanjiao (three teachings), 4, 49, 98; and interpretational difference, 63. See also *dao; fo; ru*

sannian zhi sang (three-year mourning rite): as mortuary rite of the Shang transmitted through *ru*, 240; as *ru* invention, 240, 368n63

Santa Fede (Sacred Faith), 40, 70. *See also* Jesuit proselytism

santo (saint), 94; Ricci's equation of *santo* with *shengren,* 330n49

Sapienta Sinica (Wisdom from China), 114–16, 115 fig8

sapientissimo (wise man), 94

Saturni Ephemerides: Tabula Historicochronologica. See Isaacson

Saussure, Ferdinand de, 144, 337n14

Scaliger, Joseph Justus, 126

scholae Confuciani (Confucian school), 159

scholar: popularity of and endurance as a gloss of *ru*, 159

scholasticism, 97; and Hanxue, 188

Sciechia, 47. See also *fo; leggi di Sciechia;* Ricci, Matteo

science: and Christianity, 57 (*see also* Christianity; evolution; figurism); epistemological observation as a source of narration, 338n17; and the Jesuit chronology project, 126–27; seventeenth-century science and the prize of local knowledge, 112–13. *See also* ethnology

Scientia Sinensis (Chinese Learning), 121, 146. See *Confucius Sinarum Philosophus*

scriptural texts: of *ru*, 159. See also
  Lunyu; Mengzi
Scripture, 59
secta, 69
sect of the literati, 64
secularization of *ru*, 160; Zhang Binglin
  and Hu Shi's consensus on, 222
Selected Sayings. See *Lunyu*
Septuagint: and Christian-Chinese chronology, 126
Sermon on the Mount: as inspiration for
  Hu Shi's depiction of *ru* weakness, 242
setta è di Laozu, 95
shamanic trance: associated with *Yubu*,
  357n136
Shang, 27; blackbird and foundational
  myth, 251–52, 372n95; conquered by
  Zhou and thenceforth known as Yin,
  231–32; and eschatological myth of
  sagely advent, 250, 371n90; and
  hybridization of Zhou culture, 230–
  33, 364n32, 365n42; identity with
  Jews, 221; identity with Yin, 198,
  358n141, 362n15; and Yin as eth-
  nonyms, 362n15
Shangdi ("One God"), 33, 121; and theological ecumenism, 123
Shang shu, 156, 177; figurist interpretation of, 117; and monotheism, 62; in
  the search for origins of *ru*, 168
Shao Yong, 170
Shaozhou mission, 48–49
Shengchao poxie ji (The Sacred Dynasty's Collection Exposing Heresy).
  See *Poxie ji*
Sheng Poxie ji. See *Poxie ji*
shengren ("man-god"), 33; Ricci's use of
  the term for both Kongzi and saints,
  69, 94; and *santo/sapientissimo* glossing conflict, 94
shi (scholar), 159, 166
Shi Huangdi (Qin emperor), 164
Shiji, 20, 64, 195; and first narration of
  ru, 163–68. See also Sima Qian
Shi jing (Book of Odes), 23, 109, 132, 156,
  161, 195, 273, 277–78; and monotheism, 62
shisan jing (Thirteen Classics): explained, 320n67

shiwen (contemporary prose), 101. See
  also *jinwen*
Shiwu xuehui, 179
shui (persuasion), 97; and disputation of
  Tianzhu shiyi, 97
Shun (culture hero), 106, 182, 297; subor-
  dinated to Kongzi, 187
"Shuo ru": early reception, 212–13; orga-
  nization and argument of, 225–33; rea-
  sons for enduring significance of, 222–
  24. See also Hu Shi
Shuowen. See *Shuowen jiezi*
Shuowen jiezi (Explanation of Pattern,
  Elucidation of Graphs; Han etymology, ca. 110 C.E.), 159, 169–71; common source for definition of *ru*, 171;
  Hu Shi's reliance upon, 228–29; Zhang
  Binglin's reliance upon, 191, 195–96.
  See also Xu Shen
Shuowen jiezi gulin, 170
Shuowen jiezi zhu (by Duan Yucai), 197
shushi (practitioners/scholars of magical
  and scholarly received techné), 174;
  role in Zhang Binglin's reconstruction
  of *ru*, 191, 193; as Warring States experts and *ru*, 191–92. See also *ru* glosses
shushi guan. See *yu* (turquoise
  kingfisher)
Shusun Tong (early Han *ru* official), 165
shuwen (transmission by writing), 109;
  as source of authority for claiming a legitimate defense of archaic *ru*, 108–9
shuwen texts: and apostolic tradition,
  110
shu yuan (private academies), 44, 64; as
  evidence of *ru*/Jesuit similitude, 93
signs: arbitrariness of, 337n14; and signifiers of, 144
silver: circulation of silver and other precious metals, 307n8
Sima Qian, 26, 64, 163–66: cited in
  Zhang Binglin's "Yuan ru," 189; depiction of *ru*, 165–66, 171; *Shiji*, 161
Sima Xiangru: on the immortals of *ru*,
  191
similitude, 94, 96
siming (proper name; type): last and
  most recent category of *ru*'s meaning,
  201–3, 297

Thévenot, Melchisedec: *Relations de divers voyages curieux*, 119, 334n111

Thinking through Confucius (Roger Ames and David Hall), 17–18, 25

tian ("heaven"), 121; as evidence of *ru*/Christian similitude, 93

tianshi dao (Way of the Celestial Master): as true official religion of China, 167

Tiantai sect: and God, 43

tianxia (the world; "below heaven"), 130

Tianzhu (Heavenly Master), 57, 60, 73, 105, 108, 324n108; conceptual reappropriation of Confusius and Tianshu, 73–75; as term of controversy, 117

tianzhu jiao, 105–6. *See also* Christianity

Tianzhu shilu (Veritable Record of the Heavenly Master, 1584): as doctrina, 38–39; Ricci and Ruggieri's catechism prepared for work among Chinese, 56, 70–74, 87, 92, 97, 114

Tianzhu shiyi (Real Significance of the Heavenly Master), 50, 73, 89, 108; Chinese reaction to, 104–6; formation of, 62; popularity of, 97; rhetorical strategy of, 97–102; Ricci's distinction between Kong Fuzi and Kongzi's indigenous names therein, 88; as textual portrait of accommodationism, 56–59

ti/yong (essence/function), 263, 298, 348n77

Tongcheng school, 208, 212, 298

Toulmin, Stephen, 283

tradition (*chuantong; dento*), 34, 281; defined, 270; as innovation, 277; as invention, 25, 276–78

"Transforming the Weak Ru into Tough and Aggressive Ru," 226. *See also* "Shuo ru"

translation, 7, 35, 72, 80, 125, 137, 139, 146; fidelity of, 80; of foreign concepts into the language of Chinese national identity, 154; and inchoate Christian monotheism, 7; waning fidelity of translation after the moment of cultural encounter, 139

transliteration: of *dao* and *fo* terms, 95

Travelers among Streams and Mountains. See Fan Kuan

Travels. See Polo, Marco

Treaty of Shimonoseki (1895), 174

tre leggi diverse (three different orders), 95, 122. *See also dao; fo; ru*

Trigault, Nicolá, 49, 63, 65 fig5, 69, 91, 123; with M. Ricci, the distinction of Confutio as *santo*, 94

Tu Cheng-sheng, 374n119

tuogu gaizhi ("pleading antiquity for reform" of Kang Youwei), 180

Tu Wei-ming: and postmodern (third wave) Confucianism, 15

unicorn (*qilin*): mythical fifth-century appearance near the end of Kongzi's life, 198

universal character, 128

universal civilization: imagined in Hu Shi's "Shuo ru," 221

universal language, 124. *See also Clavis Sinica*

universalism, 14–15; of Confucius, 7; of *ru* and Kongzi, 113

Valignano, Visitor Alessandro, 40, 112

value, 281; as constitutive force in history, 282

varie setta (various sects). *See dao; fo; ru; tre leggi diverse*

Vera et brevis divinarum rerum expositio (A True and Brief Exposition of Divine Things), 38–39, 70–75, 323n100

Verbiest, Ferdinand, 112

vernacular languages, 90; late-sixteenth-century independence of Italian and Portuguese from Latin, 90

Vico, Giambattista, 137

vitae sanctimonia: of Santo Kongzi, 95

Voltaire, 9, 58, 306n7

Wagner, Roy, 74

Waley, Arthur, 21

Wang Chong: cited in Zhang Binglin's "Yuan ru," 189–90; *Lunheng*, 171, 192–93, 354n123

wangguo (nativist term of self-deprecation), 298, 363n17

Wang Jingwei, 175

Wang Kaiyun: criticized by Zhang Bing-
lin, 186
Wang Pan: prefectural magistrate of
Zhaoqing, 39, 42, 44–45
Wang Qiyuan, 104
Wang Tao, 350n97
wanguo xinyu. See Esperanto
Wang Wei: defines *ru* as "learning of
sages and worthies," 170; "Yuan ru,"
170–71
Wang Zang. See *Rulin liezhuan*
Wang Zhong, 188
Wanli era: intellectual pluralism of,
108
Warring States (Zhan'guo shidai), 19; development of semantic classifiers (radicals), 195; intellectual pluralism of,
172; and *shui*, 97
Weber, Max, 14–15; *die Entzauberung
der Welt* and parallels with Hu Shi's
secularization thesis, 249–50, 371n88;
historical individualism, 281; ideal
type, 377n28; theory of routinization
of charisma, 249, 371n88; theory of the
accidental relation between capitalism
and Puritanism, 254. *See also* Heinrich
Rickert
Weishu (Apocryphal Texts), 177
Wen (culture hero), 203
Westphalia. *See* Peace of Westphalia
Wheelwright Bian (parable), 204
Wilhelm, Friedrich (Elector of Prussia),
112
Wilkins, John, 128; "real characters,"
128. *See also* Chinese language
William III of England, 123
Williams, Raymond, 155
woodblock technology, 70
world chronology, 124. *See also* Jesuit
Christian/*ru* chronology project
wu (an unbalanced right-footed shuffle;
dance): linked to *ru*, 197
wubai nian you shengren zhi xing:
Shang survivor prophecy of redemption, 250–51, 299
Wujing (Five Classics), 59, 112, 172
Wujing daquan (Great Compendium of
the Five Classics), 84
wulun, 318n61

Wuxu bianfa (Hundred Days Reforms),
179
wuyin (theory of five sounds): criticized
by Wang Chong, 190
Wu Zhihui: and Esperanto, 345n64

Xan ti [*Shangdi*], 123; etymological linking with Deus, Elohim, and Jehovah,
123. *See also Shangdi*
Xavier, St. Francis, 40–41, 112,
313nn17–19, 314n24
xiangli (assistants at the rites): identical with *ru*, 235–37; responsibility
for negotiation of *meng* (blood oaths),
236; as Shang religious functionaries,
235
xianru (first/former/archaic *ru*), 33, 100,
108, 154–58, 255; Jesuit use of the
term, 102
Xiang Yu, 164
xiansheng (first sage), 84–85; in contrast
to *primo santo*, 104
xianshi (first teacher), 84–85, 130
xianxian (former worthies), 103
Xiao Gongquan [Hsiao Kung-ch'uan],
222
xiaoxue (philology), 194, 300, 363n25
Xici zhuan: Kongzi's commentary of the
Yijing, 61, 132; Yang Xiong's commentary on, 109–10
xie (false; heresy; heterodox): in contrast
to *zheng*, 101
Xingli daquan (The Great Compendium
on Nature and Principle), 84–85; significance to Jesuit translation project,
85
xin ruxue (new Confucian learning), 15,
300
xinxue (a Ming construction of *ru*; learning of the heart), 16, 300
Xinxue weijing kao (A Study of the
Forged Classics of Xin Era, by Kang
Youwei), 179
xishi (Western scholar), 57; and
zhongshi, 61, 62, 98
xiucai (licentiate; cultivated talent), 46,
51, 106; disreputability of, 331n63;
Jesuits as, 99, 331n63; late-Ming uprisings, 331n63

xu (fifth hexagram of *Yijing*), 194, 300; symbolic of Shang tribal redemption, 245–46; used to gloss the graph *xu*, 195–96; and Zhang Binglin's graphemic analysis of *ru*, 194–99

xu (graph: "waiting" or "tarry"), 300; as etymonic nucleus of *ru*, 194–95

Xuan niao (Black Bird, ode 14303 of Shi jing), 251, 300; ornithological totem of Shang, 251–52

xue (learning): in Zhang Binglin's *Qiu shu*, 185

xuemai: and the dramatized late-Ming distinctions between native and foreign, 107, 301

Xu Guangqi ("doctor Paul"), 52, 60, 85, 102, 123–24; neologizer of celebrated phrase, "bu ru yi fo," 331n74; reputed baptism of, 323n98

Xunzi, 171

Xunzi, 86, 170

Xu Shen, 123, 170–72; *Shuowen jiezi* as a source for the definition of *ru*, 171, 343n49

Xu Yuanhe: *Ruxue yu dongfang wenhua*, 11

Yan Fu, 343n57

Yang (Sui emperor), 21

Yang Tingyun ("doctor Michael"), 52; reputed baptism of, 322n98

Yang Xiong: commentary on the *Xici zhuan*, 109–10

Yan Hui (disciple of Kongzi), 22, 103, 341n31

Yantie lun (Discourses on Salt and Iron), 192

Yanzi chunqiu, 20, 155

Yao (culture hero), 106, 122, 182, 301; subordinated to Kongzi, 187

Yazhou bingren, 301, 346n67

Yellow Emperor. See *huangdi*

yeman. See *man*

yiduan (heterodoxy), 98

Yihe quan (Righteous and Harmonious Fists, "Boxers"), 153

Yijing, 61, 79, 110, 112, 160, 240–46, 333n99; figurist reading of, 117; and monotheism, 62; source of proof for

Zhang Binglin and Hu Shi's etymological derivation of *ru* from *xu*, 229

Yin. *See* Shang

"Yiwen zhi" (Imperial Bibliographic Catalogue), 194, 301–2

Yi Yin (culture hero), 19

Yogacara Buddhism, 187

Yu (culture hero), 126, 182, 302

yu (rain): in Zhang Binglin's graphemic analysis of *ru*, 195–96

yu (turquoise kingfisher), 194–98; *yuguan* (turquoise kingfisher feather caps), 194, 198; *shushi guan* (turquoise kingfisher feather caps of *shushi*), 194, 197

yuan (etiology; primitive), 173

"Yuan ru" (authored by Wang Wei). *See* Wang Wei

"Yuan ru" (The Etiology of *Ru*; a chapter of Zhang Binglin's *Guogu lunheng*, 1910), 173–74, 188–94; as an alternative source of the meaning of *ru*, 182; and disavowal of legitimacy claims of Manchus and *jinwen* scholars, 207–8; and influence on American, European, Japanese, and Chinese scholarship, 182; scarcity of pre-Han textual citations, 189–90; scholarly reception and legacy of, 211–14; year of composition and publication, 182; Zhang Binglin's dependence on Han texts, 189; and *zhengli guogu*, 181. *See also* Zhang Binglin

yuanshi (primordial), 173, 343n55

Yuan Shikai, 206

Zeng Dian, 103

Zeng Shi, 104

Zengzi, 86

Zhang Binglin (Taiyan), 26; argument for ancient pluralism as a *guocui* defense against Manchu absolutism, 210; belief that different meanings reflect different conditions of the social aggregate, 209–10; characterizes Hanxue as coerced misdirection of Chinese scholarship, 188; and China as "double slave," 176, 346n68; denunciation of Esperanto, 186; disciple of Liu Shipei, 180,

Lionel M. Jensen is Assistant Professor of History and Director
of the Program in Chinese Studies at the University of Colorado,
Denver, and the editor of *Early China* 20 (1995).

Library of Congress Cataloging-in-Publication Data
Jensen, Lionel M.
Manufacturing Confucianism : Chinese traditions and
universal civilization / by Lionel M. Jensen.
Includes bibliographical references and index.
ISBN 0-8223-2034-7 (alk. paper). — ISBN 0-8223-2047-9 (pbk. : alk. paper)
1. Confucianism.   2. Confucianism—Relations—Christianity.
3. Jesuits—China.   4. Philosophy, Confucian.   5. China—
Civilization—Western influences.   I. Title.
BL 1852.J45   1997   181'.112—dc21   97-29986 CIP